NATURAL RESOURCES

NATURAL RESOURCES

Volume II
Genetic Diversity –
Platinum and the Platinum Group Metals

Editors

Mark S. Coyne
University of Kentucky

Craig W. Allin
Cornell College

Project Editor
McCrea Adams

Salem Press, Inc.
Pasadena, California   Englewood Cliffs, New Jersey

Managing Editor: Christina J. Moose   *Project Editor:* McCrea Adams
Research Supervisor: Jeffry Jensen   *Research Assistant:* Jun Ohnuki
Acquisitions Editor: Mark Rehn   *Production Editor:* Yasmine A. Cordoba
Photograph Editor: Karrie Hyatt   *Layout and Graphics:* James Hutson

Library of Congress Cataloging-in-Publication Data
Natural Resources / Editors: Mark S. Coyne, Craig W. Allin; project editor, McCrea Adams
    p. cm.
Includes bibliographical references and index.
ISBN 0-89356-912-7 (set : alk. paper). — ISBN 0-89356-914-3 (vol. 2 : alk. paper).
    1. Natural resources—United States—Encyclopedias. 2. Natural resources—Encyclopedias.
I. Coyne, Mark S., 1960-   . II. Allin, Craig W. (Craig Willard) III. Adams, McCrea, 1952-   .
    HC103.7.N278   1998
    333.7′03—dc21   97-43364
                                                                                      CIP

First Printing

PRINTED IN THE UNITED STATES OF AMERICA

Contents

Genetic diversity 323
Geochemical cycles 324
Geodes 327
Geological Survey, U.S. 327
Geology 328
Geothermal and hydrothermal
    energy 329
Germanium 335
Getty, J. Paul 336
Geysers and hot springs 336
Glaciation 339
Glass 340
Gneiss 343
Gold 344
Granite 349
Graphite 350
Grasslands 352
Green Revolution 354
Greenhouse gases and global climate
    change 356
Greenpeace 358
Groundwater 359
Guano 361
Gypsum 362

Haber-Bosch process 365
Hazardous waste disposal 365
Health, resource exploitation and 369
Helium 373
Herbicides 375
Horticulture 378
Hydroenergy 380
Hydrogen 385
Hydrology and the hydrologic
    cycle 386
Hydroponics 389
Hydrothermal solutions and
    mineralization 391

Ickes, Harold 393
Igneous processes, rocks, and mineral
    deposits 393
Incineration of wastes 399
Indium 401
Industrial Revolution and
    industrialization 402
Internal combustion engine 406

International Union for the
    Conservation of Nature and
    Natural Resources 408
Iodine 408
Iron 410
Irrigation 415
Isotopes, radioactive 417
Isotopes, stable 420
Izaak Walton League of America 421

Jackson, Wes 423

Kyanite 424

Lakes 426
Land Institute 430
Land management 431
Land-use planning 433
Land-use regulation and control 435
Landfills 436
Landsat satellites and satellite
    technologies 439
Law of the sea 443
Leaching 445
Lead 447
Leopold, Aldo 451
Lime 451
Limestone 454
Lithium 455
Lithosphere 456
Livestock and animal husbandry 457
Los Angeles Aqueduct 460

Magma crystallization 462
Magnesium 463
Magnetic materials 467
Manganese 468
Manhattan Project 470
Manufacturing, energy use in 471
Marble 474
Marine mining 476
Marine vents 479
Mercury 479
Metals and metallurgy 482
Metamictization 486
Metamorphic processes, rocks, and
    mineral deposits 486

Methane 492
Methanol 492
Mica 494
Mineral Leasing Act of 1920 495
Mineral resource ownership 496
Mineral resource use, early history of 499
Minerals, structure and physical
    properties of 504
Minerals Management Service 510
Mining safety and health issues 511
Mining wastes and mine reclamation 515
Mohs hardness scale 518
Molybdenum 519
Monoculture agriculture 522
Montreal Protocol 523
Muir, John 524
Multiple use approach 524

National Audubon Society 527
National Biological Service 527
National Environmental Policy Act 527
National Mining Association 528
National Oceanic and Atmospheric
    Administration 529
National Park Service and national
    parks 530
National Parks Act of 1930 532
National Wildlife Federation 534
Native elements 534
Natural Resources Conservation
    Service 535
Natural Resources Defense Council 537
Nature Conservancy 537
Nickel 538
Niobium 541
Nitrogen and ammonia 542
Nitrogen cycle 546
Nuclear energy 547
Nuclear Energy Institute 553
Nuclear Regulatory Commission 553
Nuclear waste and its disposal 554

Ocean current energy 558
Ocean thermal energy conversion 559
Ocean wave energy 561
Oceanography 563

Oceans 564
Oil and natural gas, chemistry of 571
Oil and natural gas, worldwide
    distribution of 573
Oil and natural gas drilling and wells 576
Oil and natural gas exploration 579
Oil and natural gas formation 581
Oil and natural gas reservoirs 583
Oil embargo and energy crises of 1973
    and 1979 586
Oil industry 589
Oil shale and tar sands 592
Oil spills 593
Olivine 595
Open-pit mining 596
Ophiolites 599
Organisation for Economic
    Co-operation and Development 600
Organization of Arab Petroleum
    Exporting Countries 601
Organization of Petroleum Exporting
    Countries 601
Orthosilicate minerals 602
Overgrazing 603
Oxides 605
Oxygen 606
Ozone layer and ozone hole debate 608

Paper 611
Paper, alternative sources of 616
Peat 617
Pegmatites 620
Perlite 621
Pesticides and pest control 622
Petrochemical products 624
Petroleum refining and processing 627
Phosphate 630
Phosphorus cycle 631
Pinchot, Gifford 632
Placer deposits 633
Plant domestication and breeding 636
Plant fibers 638
Plants as a medical resource 641
Plate tectonics 643
Platinum and the platinum group
    metals 646

NATURAL RESOURCES

Genetic diversity

Genetic diversity includes the inherited traits encoded in the deoxyribonucleic acid (DNA) of all living organisms and can be examined on four levels: among species, among populations, within populations, and within individuals. Populations with higher levels of diversity are better able to adapt to changes in the environment, are more resistant to the deleterious effects of inbreeding, and provide more opportunities for animal and plant breeders to cultivate types or varieties with qualities desired by humans.

GENETIC DIVERSITY IS the most fundamental level of biological diversity because genetic material is responsible for the variety of life. For new species to form, genetic material must change. Changes in the inherited properties of populations occur deterministically through gene flow (mating between individual organisms representing formerly separated populations) and through natural or artificial selection (which occurs when some types of individuals breed more successfully than others). Change can also occur randomly through mutations or genetic drift (when the relative proportions of genes change by chance in small populations). Populations with higher levels of diversity tend to do better—to have more survival options—as surroundings change than do populations (particularly smaller ones) with lower levels of genetic diversity.

Preservation Efforts. Conservation efforts directed at maintaining genetic diversity involve both germ plasm preservation (germ plasm kept in a steady state for periods of time) and germ plasm conservation (germ plasm kept in a natural, evolving state). The former usually involves *ex situ* laboratory techniques in which genetic resources are removed from their natural habitats. They include seminatural strategies such as botanical gardens, arboreta, nurseries, zoos, farms, aquaria, and captive fisheries, as well as completely artificial methods such as seed reserves or "banks," microbial cultures (preserving bacteria, fungi, viruses, and other microorganisms), tissue cultures of parts of plants and animals (including sperm storage), and gene libraries (involving storage and replication of partial segments of plant or animal DNA).

Conservation areas are the preferred *in situ* (at the natural or original place) means of protecting genetic resources. Ideally these include preserving the number and relative proportions of species and the genetic diversity they represent, the physical features of the habitat, and all ecosystem processes. It is not always enough, however, to maintain the ecosystem which the threatened species inhabits. It is sometimes necessary to take an active interventionist position in order to save a species. Controversial strategies can include reintroduction of captive species into the wild, sometimes after they have been genetically manipulated. Direct management of the ecosystem may also be attempted by either lessening human exploitation and interference or by reducing the number of natural predators or competitors. However, management of a specific conservation area varies in terms of what is valued and how preservation is accomplished.

Crop Diversity. One area of keen interest that illustrates the issues involved with the preservation of any kind of genetic diversity is how to preserve crop germ plasm. Largely conserved in gene banks, crop germ plasm was historically protected by farmers who selected for success in differing environments and other useful traits. Traditionally cultivated varieties (landraces) diversified as people spread into new areas. Colonial expansion produced new varieties as farmers adapted to new conditions and previously separated plant species interbred; other species were lost when some societies declined and disappeared.

By the early 1900's field botanists and agronomists were expressing concern about the rapidly escalating loss of traditionally cultivated varieties. This loss accelerated after the 1940's as high yielding hybrids of cereal and vegetable crops replaced local landraces. Wild relatives of these landraces are also disappearing as their habitats are destroyed through human activity. Gene banks preserve both kinds of plants because, as argued by Nikolai I. Vavilov in 1926, crop plant improvement can best be accomplished by taking advantage of these preserved genetic stocks. Vavilov also noted that genetic variation for most cultivated species was concentrated in specific regions, his "centers of diversity," most of which are regions where crop species originated.

The vulnerability to parasites and climate of an agriculture that relies on one or a few varieties of crops necessitates the maintenance of adequate reserves of genetic material for breeding. In addition to the preservation of species known to be useful, many people advocate preservation of wild species for aesthetic reasons as well as for their unknown future potential.

The Maintenance of Productivity. Farmers in developed nations change crop varieties every four to ten years in order to maintain consistent levels of food production. This necessitates an ongoing search for new breeds with higher yields and an ability to withstand several environmental challenges, including resistance to multiple pests and drought. Over time, older varieties either mutate, become less popular at the marketplace, or are unable to adapt to new conditions. However, farmers from poorer nations are not always able to take advantage of the new breeds or afford the expensive support systems, including chemical fertilizers. Moreover, not all types of crops have benefited equally from conservation efforts.

Another tension between the world's poor and rich nations concerns ownership of genetic diversity. The Convention on Biodiversity, signed by 167 nations in 1992, states that genetic materials are under the sovereign control of the countries in which they are found. This policy is particularly controversial regarding medicinal plants, because "biodiversity prospecting" for new drugs has economically benefited either individuals or corporations based in the developed countries.

FURTHER READING: Genetic diversity and conservation efforts are clearly described in Malcolm Hunter, Jr., *Fundamentals of Conservation Biology*, 1996, and discussed at a more sophisticated level in *The Preservation and Valuation of Biological Resources*, edited by Gordon H. Orians et al., 1990. For more on gene banks see Donald L. Plucknett et al., *Gene Banks and the World's Food*, 1987. For the history of crop diversity see John G. Hawkes, *The Diversity of Crop Plants*, 1983. For international efforts concerned

with protecting biodiversity see *Widening Perspectives on Biodiversity*, edited by Anatole F. Krattiger et al., 1994.

Joan C. Stevenson

SEE ALSO: Animal breeding; Biodiversity; Biological invasions; Biotechnology; Conservation; Conservation biology; Fisheries; Forest management; Monoculture agriculture; Plant domestication and breeding; Plants as a medical resource; Species loss.

Genetic engineering. *See* Animal breeding; Biotechnology; Plant domestication and breeding

Geochemical cycles

Geochemical cycles refer to the movement, or cycling, of elements through the biosphere and/or ecosystems. Both biotic (living) and abiotic (nonliving) components make up such systems.

GEOCHEMICAL CYCLES ARE generally considered to be those involving nutrient elements utilized by organisms in various ecosystems. Cycling involves both biological and chemical processes. While nearly all natural elements could be considered as being cycled through both abiotic and living systems, certain elements are most commonly described in such systems. These include carbon, nitrogen, phosphorus, and a variety of lesser elements (including iron, sulfur, and trace elements such as copper and mercury).

Although the cycling of elements is often thought of as occurring in a relatively rapid fashion, many of these elements spend long periods locked in abiotic systems. For example, carbon may be found in materials that require millions of years to cycle through ocean sediment back into the atmosphere. The fate of such elements depends on many factors, including their chemical properties and their ability to erode or return to the atmosphere. Some chemical elements, such as carbon, oxygen, and nitrogen, are incorporated into organisms from the atmosphere. Other elements, such as phosphorus, potassium, sulfur, and iron, are found mainly in rocks and sediments.

Carbon and Oxygen Cycles. The carbon and oxygen cycles are greatly dependent on each other.

Molecular oxygen, which represents approximately 20 percent of the atmosphere, is used by organisms through a metabolic process called respiration. In these reactions, the oxygen reacts

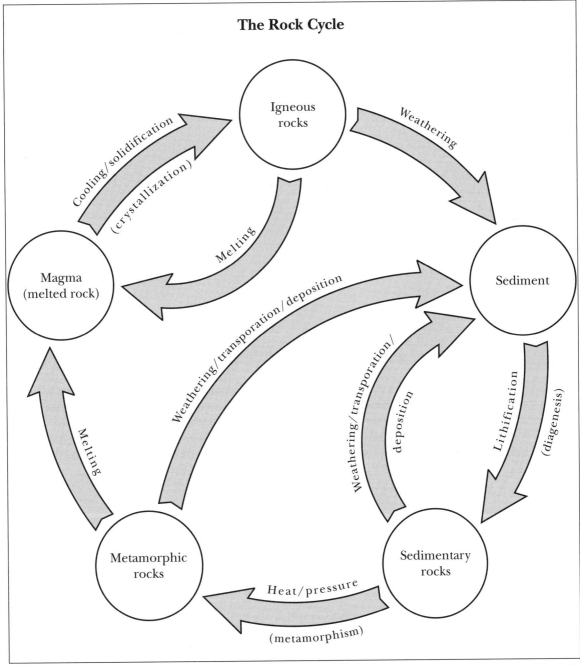

The Rock Cycle

The rock cycle, the basic geochemical cycle, operates on a time scale of hundreds of millions to billions of years. It includes subcycles such as the oceanic cycle and the biological cycle, which could be called parts of the "atmospheric-hydrologic-biological-sedimentary" cycle.

with reduced carbon compounds such as carbo-hydrates (sugars) and generates carbon dioxide (CO_2). Though carbon dioxide constitutes only a small proportion of the volume of the atmosphere (0.04 percent), it is in this form that it is used by primary producers such as plants. In the process of photosynthesis, utilizing sunlight as an energy source, plants and some microorganisms bind, or fix, the CO_2, converting the carbon again into carbohydrates, resulting in growth of the plant, or replication of the microorganism. The complex carbohydrates which are generated in photosynthesis serve as the food source for consumers—organisms such as animals (including humans) that eat the plants. The carbohydrates are then broken down, regenerating carbon dioxide. In a sense, the combinations of respiration and photosynthesis represent the cycle of life. Approximately 70 billion metric tons of carbon dioxide (10 percent of the total atmospheric CO_2) are fixed each year. The concentration of carbon dioxide in the atmosphere is a factor in regulating the temperature of Earth. Consequently, the release of large quantities of the gas into the atmosphere through the burning of fossil fuels could potentially alter the earth's climate.

Nitrogen Cycle. Nitrogen gas (N_2) represents 78 percent of the total volume of the atmosphere. However, because of the extreme stability of the bond between the two nitrogens in the gas, plants and animals are unable to use atmospheric nitrogen directly as a nutrient. Nitrogen-fixing bacteria in the soil and in the roots of leguminous plants (peas, clover) are able to convert the gaseous nitrogen into nitrites and nitrates, chemical forms that can be used by plants. Animals then obtain nitrogen by consuming the plants. The decomposition of nitrogen compounds results in the accumulation of ammonium (NH_4+) compounds in a process called ammonification. It is in this form that nitrogen is commonly found under conditions in which oxygen is limited. In this form, some of the nitrogen returns to the atmosphere. In the presence of oxygen, ammonium compounds are oxidized to nitrates (nitrification). Once the plant or animal has died, bacteria convert the nitrogen back into nitrogen gas, and it returns to the atmosphere.

Phosphorus Cycle. Unlike carbon and nitrogen, which are found in the atmosphere, most of the phosphorus required for biotic nutrition is found in mineral form. Phosphorus is relatively water insoluble in this form; it is only gradually dissolved in water. Available phosphorus is therefore often growth-limiting in soils (it is second only to nitrogen as the scarcest of the soil nutrients). Ocean sediments may bring the mineral to the surface through uplifting of land, as along coastal areas, or by means of marine animals. Enzymatic breakdown of organic phosphate by bacteria and the consumption of marine organisms by seabirds cycle the phosphorus into forms available for use by plants. Deposition of guano (bird feces) along the American Pacific coast has long provided a fertilizer rich in phosphorus.

Bacteria also play significant roles in the geochemical cycling of many other elements. Iron, despite its abundance in the earth's crust, is largely insoluble in water. Consequently, it is generally found in the form of precipitates of ferric (Fe^{+3}) compounds, seen as brown deposits in water. Acids are often formed as by-products in the formation of ferric compounds. The bacterial oxidation of pyrite (FeS_2) is a major factor in the leaching process of iron ores and in the formation of acid mine drainage. Likewise, much of the sulfur found in the earth's crust is in the form of pyrite and gypsum ($CaSO_4$). Weathering processes return much of the sulfur to water-soluble forms; in the absence of air, the bacterial reduction of sulfate (SO_4^{-2}) to forms such as hydrogen sulfide (H_2S) allows its return to the atmosphere. Since sulfide compounds are highly toxic to many organisms, bacterial reduction of sulfates is of major biogeochemical significance.

FURTHER READING: *Scientific American* (September, 1970) is a special issue consisting entirely of the discussion of various geochemical cycles. *Brock Biology of Microorganisms*, edited by Michael Madigan, John Martinko, and Jack Parker, 1996, contains excellent summaries of major geochemical cycles, with emphasis on the role of microorganisms. Karen Arms and Pamela Camp provide an excellent summary of biogeochemistry in *Biology*, 1995. Oceanography and the role of ocean-dwelling organisms is the focus of *An Introduction to Marine Biogeochemistry*, by

Susan Libes, 1992. Other texts that deal with specific subjects include *The Global Carbon Cycle*, by Martin Heimann, 1993, and *Biogeochemistry of Trace Metals*, by Domy Adriano, 1992.

Richard Adler

SEE ALSO: Biosphere; Carbon cycle; Carbonate minerals; Guano; Leaching; Nitrogen; Nitrogen cycle; Phosphorus cycle; Sulfur cycle.

Geodes

Geodes are roughly spherically-shaped bodies that are lined on the inside with inward-projecting small crystals surrounded by a layer of crystalline quartz. A host of different minerals may be found in the interior of some geodes, and when cut open a geode typically makes a beautiful display.

GEODES ARE MOST frequently found in limestone beds, but they may also occur in volcanic rocks and in some shales. Typically, a geode consists of a thin outer shell of dense chalcedonic silica (silicon dioxide) and an inner shell of crystals made of quartz or calcite. These crystals are often beautifully terminated, pointing toward the hollow interior. New crystal layers frequently grow on the terminations of old layers, sometimes nearly or even completely filling the geode. Many geodes are filled with water, while others that have been exposed at the surface for some time are dry.

Geodes typically range in size from less than five centimeters to more than thirty centimeters in diameter, but they can be much larger. Although the crystals are usually composed of quartz, they may also be composed of carbonate minerals, such as calcite, dolomite, and aragonite; of oxide minerals, such as hematite and magnetite; or of sulfide minerals, such as pyrite, calcopyrite, and sphalerite. In some geodes, there is an alternation of layers of silica and calcite, and almost all geodes show some kind of banding. When sulfide minerals are present, they are often the innermost crystals, whereas the carbonate minerals are typically next to the outermost layer of chalcedony (fine-grained, fibrous variety of quartz). Some geodes are partially filled by mounds of banded chalcedony in which successive layers differ markedly in color and translucency. These layers form a colorful agate when stained.

The origin of geodes is somewhat similar to the formation of large limestone caves. Groundwater dissolves some of the limestone and forms a cavity in the rock, and the cavity is usually left filled with salty water. Silica-bearing waters then coagulate into a gel that surrounds the salt solution. The geode grows by expansion due to osmotic pressure between the salty water trapped inside the silica gel shell and fresh water on the outside of the gel. These pressures cause the geode to expand until equilibrium is reached. Dehydration of the gel and subsequent crystallization occur, along with shrinkage and cracking of the geode wall, allowing mineral-bearing waters to percolate into the geode and deposit crystals on the cavity wall. Subsequent periods of water circulation and crystallization may follow, forming the characteristic layers of crystals.

Geodes are found in many parts of the world. One well-known type found in Uruguay is called hydrolite, or water stone, because it contains quartz crystals left when water containing silica in solution evaporated. Many highly prized geodes that are filled with beautiful crystals and curved-banded colors of agate can be found at various collecting sites in the United States, such as near Dugway, Utah, or Keokuk, Iowa.

Alvin K. Benson

SEE ALSO: Groundwater; Hydrothermal solutions and mineralization; Limestone; Quartz; Sedimentary processes, rocks, and mineral deposits; Silicates.

Geological Survey, U.S.

DATE ESTABLISHED: 1879

The United States Geological Survey is an agency of the Department of the Interior. Its directive involves topographical and geological mapping. It is also responsible for assessing the distribution and quality of mineral and water resources.

THE UNITED STATES Geological Survey (USGS) was formed as the result of a merger of separate surveys conducted under the authority of the Department of War and the Department of the Interior. These early surveys were the Geological Exploration of the 40th Parallel, the Geological and Geographical Survey of the Rocky Mountain Region, and the Geographical Survey West of the 100th Meridian. They were unified in 1879 by act of Congress. This new civilian agency was directed to conduct research in mining geology.

The first director of the USGS was Clarence King. He essentially organized the USGS into a bureau of mines and mining that primarily dealt with the western states. In 1881 John Wesley Powell became the director. Under his leadership the USGS extended its activities to include the eastern states, thus making it a national organization.

The present USGS consists of seven divisions. The first three are the Administrative, Publications, and Computer Center Divisions. It is their responsibility to support the other four divisions that do the actual research. These are the Topographic, Water Resources, Conservation, and Geologic Divisions.

The Topographic Division prepares and maintains the topographic maps of the United States and its possessions. It also prepares a national atlas and produces various special-purpose maps that provide an analysis of natural resources. The Water Resources Division is responsible for determining the location, amount, quality, and availability of all water, both surface water and groundwater. Flood control, pollution studies, and groundwater management are among the many activities of the Water Resources Division.

The Conservation Division deals with all operations involving prospecting for, developing, and extracting leasable minerals. These include coal, gas, oil, oil shale, phosphate, potash, and sodium compounds that are found on public lands. They also include resources on the continental shelf. The Conservation Division is also involved in the determination of the production potential of these resources. The Geological Division conducts research in four areas, conducting environmental, economic, experimental, and marine studies. Its activities provide detailed information on various minerals as well as information pertaining to land use and conservation of natural resources. Included within the activities of the Geological Division is basic research that is directed toward a better understanding of the earth as a whole.

The USGS is involved in many international projects that include providing assistance to developing countries and performing global research. The USGS also conducts research with the National Aeronautics and Space Administration (NASA) in lunar and planetary studies. It maintains special research centers such as the Hawaiian Volcano Observatory and the National Center for Earthquake Research in Menlo Park, California. The extent of future USGS activities depends upon how severely Congress cuts its budget. In the mid-1990's the USGS was suffering from staff cuts and limitations on funding for its research.

Paul P. Sipiera

SEE ALSO: Coast and Geodetic Survey, U.S.; Erosion and erosion control; Floods and flood control; Groundwater; Land management; Mining waste and mine reclamation; Oil and natural gas; Soil management; Strip mining.

Geology

Geology is the science that deals with the study of the earth. Among areas of geological study are the composition of the earth's materials and various geological processes in order to locate and exploit the earth's mineral resources.

GEOLOGY INVOLVES STUDYING how the earth was formed, what it is made of, how it works, how its component systems interact, how it affects humans, and how the activities of humans affect it. Geologists study the materials that constitute the earth, whether near the surface of the planet or buried deep within. They attempt to understand the processes that have modified those materials throughout geologic time. They examine the evidence of extinct life, of ancient chemical reactions, of physical changes as cataclysmic as asteroid impacts and as imperceptibly slow as the uplift of a mountain range. In the rocks, soils, and natural waters of the earth, geologists read and interpret history so old that the intellect cannot comfortably grasp its antiquity.

In the late twentieth century manned and unmanned space probes facilitated the study of the surfaces of several rocky bodies in the solar system and enabled scientists to study planets, satellites, asteroids, and comets in unprecedented ways. The investigation of the materials, processes, and histories of these bodies has become part of geological science and has modified and enhanced some of science's ideas about the earth.

Much of the knowledge gained by individual geologists and geologic teams—and subsequently shared within the scientific community—is ultimately synthesized to improve models of Earth processes that bear on the welfare of humanity. Such models aid in the discovery and recovery of natural resources, such as economically important minerals and fossil fuels, including gold, silver, oil, natural gas, and coal. The study of fossil fuels, metals, and other geologic materials useful to industry is called economic geology. Other models of the earth are used to predict soil and rock stability for the placement of major engineering structures, and still other models provide insight into the nature of geologic hazards, such as earthquakes, volcanoes, landslides, and floods. Some earth models also contribute to the detection and elimination of pollutants and other forms of environmental degradation in near-surface materials.

Outside academia, the geologic professions have historically been dominated by the energy and mineral industries, but since the mid-1980's there has been marked change as areas of specialization involving water supply and environmental concerns have claimed an increasing share of the employment market. This trend has paralleled the general increase in public awareness of environmental issues and the ideological shift from exploitation of natural resources to conservation. Although in the future many geologists will probably be involved with some facet of environmental geology, the more traditional fields of economic geology, energy resources and mineral acquisition, will continue to constitute important areas of research, development, and opportunity.

Alvin K. Benson

SEE ALSO: Earth's crust; Ecology; Igneous processes, rocks, and mineral deposits; Metamorphic processes, rocks, and mineral deposits; Minerals, structure and physical properties of; Oceanography; Sedimentary processes, rocks, and mineral deposits.

Geothermal and hydrothermal energy

Geothermal energy is the heat energy associated with the interior of the earth. The common usage of the term is to designate the thermal energy relatively near the surface of the earth that can be utilized by humans. Hydrothermal energy is the energy associated with hot water, whereas geothermal is a more general term. Geothermal energy has been exploited since early times. It is a source of energy with a low pollution potential that can be used for producing electricity as well as for heating and cooling and helping with a number of other needs.

A GEOTHERMAL SYSTEM comprises three elements: a heat source, a reservoir, and a fluid which transfers the heat. The heat source can be a magmatic intrusion or the earth's normal temperature, which increases with depth. The reservoir is a volume of hot permeable rock from which circulating fluids extract heat. Fluid convection transports the heat from the higher-temperature lower regions to the upper regions, where it can be accessed and used.

Causes of Geothermal Phenomena. While individuals in early mining operations may have noted the general increase in temperature with depth, it was not until the eighteenth century that subsurface temperature measurements were performed. The results often showed an increase in temperature with depth. The rate of increase varied from site to site. An average value that is often used today is a 2.5 to 3 degrees Celsius increase per 100 meters increase in depth from the surface. The geothermal gradient suggested that the source of the earth's heat was below the surface, but the exact cause of the heat was open to discussion for many years. It was not until the early part of the twentieth century that the decay of radioactive materials was identified as the primary cause of the heat. The thermal energy of the earth is very large; however, only a small portion is currently available for capture and utilization. The available thermal energy is primarily limited to areas where water or steam carries heat from the deep hot regions to, or near to, the surface. The water or steam is then available for capture and may be put to such uses as electricity generation and heating.

The interior of the earth is often considered to be divided into three major sections, called the crust, mantle, and core. The crust extends from the surface down to about 35 kilometers beneath the land and about 6 kilometers beneath the ocean. Below the crust, the mantle extends to a depth of roughly 2,900 kilometers. (Below, or inside, the mantle is the earth's core.) The crust is rich in radioactive materials, with a much lower density in the mantle and essentially none in the core. The radioactive decay of these materials produces heat. The earth is also cooling down, however. The volume of the mantle is roughly 40 times that of the crust. The combination of the heat generated from the decay of radioactive materials and the cooling of the earth results in the flow of heat to the earth's surface. The origin of the total heat flowing to the surface is roughly 20 percent from the crust and 80 percent from the mantle and core.

The outermost shell of the earth, made up of the crust and upper mantle, is known as the lithosphere. According to the concept of plate tectonics, the surface of the earth is composed of six large and several smaller lithospheric regions or plates. On some of the edges of these plates, hot molten material extends to the surface and causes the plates to spread apart. On other edges, one plate is driven beneath another. There are densely fractured zones in the crust around the plate edges. A great amount of seismic activity occurs in these regions, and they are where large numbers of volcanoes, geysers, and hot springs are located. High terrestrial heat flows occur near the edges of the plates, so the earth's most important geothermal regions are found around the plate margins. A concentration of geothermal resources is often found in regions with a normal or elevated geothermal gradient as well as around the plate margins.

History of Development. The ancient Romans used the water from hot springs for baths and for heating homes. China and Japan also used geothermal waters for bathing and washing. Similar uses are still found in various geothermal regions of the world. It was not until the early part of the nineteenth century that other uses of thermal waters were developed. An early example occurred in the Larderello area of Italy. In 1827 Francesco Larderel developed an evaporation process that used the heat from geothermal waters to evaporate the thermal waters found in the area, leaving boric acid. Heating the water by burning wood had been required in the past.

Also in the early nineteenth century, inventors began attempting to utilize the energy associated with geothermal steam for driving pumps and winches. By the early twentieth century, geothermal steam was being used to generate electricity in the Larderello region. Several other countries tried to utilize their own geothermal resources. Geothermal wells were drilled in Beppu, Japan, in 1919 and at The Geysers, California, in 1921. In the late 1920's Iceland began using geothermal waters for heating. Various locations in the western United States have used geothermal waters for heating homes and buildings in the twentieth century. Among these are Klamath Falls, Oregon, and Boise, Idaho.

After World War II many countries became interested in geothermal energy; geothermal resources of some type exist in most countries. It was viewed as an energy source that did not have to be imported and that could be competitive with other sources of electricity generation. In 1958 New Zealand began using geothermal energy for electric power production. One of the first power plants in the United States began operation at The Geysers, California, in 1960. Mexico began operating its first geothermal power plant at Cerro Prieto, near the California border, in 1973.

Leading countries in electric power production from geothermal resources in the later part of the twentieth century were the United States, the Philippines, Mexico, Italy, New Zealand, Japan, Indonesia, and El Salvador. In the Philippines and El Salvador the electric power produced from geothermal sources was nearly 13

The geothermal energy plant at The Geysers, California, is supplied by one of the largest dry-steam geothermal fields in the world. (Geothermal Resources Council)

percent of the total electric power produced in the country. Non-electric uses of geothermal energy occur in most countries. The leading non-electric users of geothermal energy for the same time period in terms of total usage were Japan, China, Hungary, the former Soviet Union, Iceland, the United States, Italy, France, Bulgaria, New Zealand, Romania, and Turkey.

Classification of Geothermal Resources. Geothermal resources are classified by the temperature of the water or steam that carries the heat from the depths to, or near, the surface. Geothermal resources are often divided into low temperature (less than 90 degrees Celsius or 194 degrees Fahrenheit), moderate temperature (90 to 150 degrees Celsius or 194 to 302 degrees Fahrenheit), and high temperature (greater than 150 degrees Celsius or 302 degrees Fahrenheit). There are still various opinions around the world on how best to divide and describe geothermal resources. The class or grouping characterizing the geothermal resource often dictates the use or uses that can be made of the resource.

A distinction that is often made in describing geothermal resources is whether there is wet or dry steam present. Wet steam has liquid water associated with it. Steam turbine electric generators can often use steam directly from dry steam wells, but separation is necessary for the use of steam from wet steam wells. In various applications the water needs to be removed from wet steam. This is achieved through the use of a separator, which separates the steam gas from liquid hot water. The hot water is then re-injected into the reservoir, used as input to other systems to recover some of its heat, or, if there are not appreciable levels of environmentally threatening chemicals present, discharged into the environment after suitable cooling.

Exploration. The search for geothermal resources is easier today than it was in the past because of the considerable amount of information and maps that have been assembled for many locations around the world and because of the availability of new instrumentation, techniques, and systems. The primary objectives in geothermal exploration are to identify geothermal phenomena, determine the size and type of the field, and identify the location of the productive zone. Further, researchers need to determine the heat content of the fluids that are to be discharged from the wells, determine the potential lifetime of the site, determine problems that may occur during operation of the site, and determine the environmental consequences of developing and operating the site.

Geological and hydrological studies help to define the geothermal resource. Geochemical surveys help to determine if the resource is vapor- or water-dominated as well as to estimate the minimum temperature expected at the resource's depth. Potential problems later in pipe scaling, corrosion, and environmental impact are also determined by this type of survey. Geophysical surveys help to define the shape, size, and depth of the resource. The drilling of exploration wells is the true test of the nature of the resource. Since drilling can be costly, use of previous surveys in selecting or siting each drill site is very important.

Use in Electricity Generation. The generation of electrical energy from geothermal energy primarily occurs through the use of conventional steam turbines and through the use of binary plants. Conventional steam turbines operate on fluid temperatures of at least 150 degrees Celsius. An atmospheric exhaust turbine is one from which the steam, after passing through the turbine, is exhausted to the atmosphere. Another form of turbine is one in which the exhaust steam is condensed. The steam consumption per kilowatt hour produced for an atmospheric exhaust unit is about twice that for a condensing unit. Atmospheric exhaust units are also simpler and cheaper.

The Geysers, California, has one of the largest dry-steam geothermal fields in the world. Steam rises from more than forty wells. Pipes feed steam to the turbogenerators at a temperature of 175 degrees Celsius. Some of the wells are drilled to depths as great as 9,000 feet. The geothermal field at Wairakei on North Island of New Zealand has been a source of electric power

for several decades. The hot water (near 300 degrees Celsius) rises from more than sixty deep wells. As the pressure falls, the hot water converts to steam. The flashing of hot water to steam is the major source of geothermal energy for electric power production.

Binary plants allow electricity to be generated from low- to medium-temperature geothermal resources as well as from the waste hot water coming from steam/water separators. Binary plants use a secondary working fluid. The geothermal fluid heats the secondary fluid, which is in a closed system. The working fluid is heated, vaporizes, drives a turbine, is cooled, condenses, and is ready to repeat the cycle. Binary plant technology is becoming the most cost-effective means to generate electricity from geothermal resources below 175 degrees Celsius.

In cascaded systems, the output water from one system is used as the input heat source to another system. Such systems allow some of the heat in waste water from higher temperature systems to be recovered and used. They are often used in conjunction with electric generation facilities to help recover some of the heat in the waste water or steam from a turbine.

Space Heating. Space heating by geothermal waters is one of the most common uses of geothermal resources. In some countries, such as Iceland, entire districts are heated using the resource. The nature of the geothermal water dictates whether that water is circulated directly in pipes to homes and other structures or (if the water is too corrosive) a heat exchanger is used to transfer the heat to a better fluid for circulation. Hot water in the range from 60 to 125 degrees Celsius has been used for space heating with hot water radiators. Water with as low a temperature as 35 to 40 degrees Celsius has been used effectively for heating by means of radiant heating, in which pipes are embedded in the floor or ceiling. Another way of using geothermal energy for heating is through the circulation of heated air from water-to-air heat exchangers. Heat pumps are also used with geothermal waters for both heating and cooling.

In district heating, the water to the customer is often in the 60 to 90 degrees Celsius range and is returned at 35 to 50 degrees Celsius. The distance of the customers from the geothermal resource is very important. Transmission lines of up to 60 kilometers have been used, but shorter distances are more common and desirable. When designing a district heating system, the selection of the area to be supplied, building density, characteristics of the heat source, the transmission system, heat loss in transmission, and heat consumption by customers are all important factors.

There are over 550 geothermal wells serving a variety of uses in Klamath Falls, Oregon. Utilization includes heating homes, schools, businesses, and swimming pools as well as snow-melting systems for sidewalks and a section of highway pavement. Most of the eastern side of the city is heated by geothermal energy. The principal heat extraction system is the closed-loop downhole heat exchanger utilizing city water in the heat exchangers. Hot water is delivered at approximately 82 degrees Celsius and returns at 60 degrees Celsius.

Hot water from springs is delivered through pipes to heat homes in Reykjavik, Iceland, and several outlying communities. This is the source of heating for roughly half of the homes in Iceland. The hot water is delivered to homes at 88 degrees Celsius. The geothermal water is also used for heating schools, swimming pools, and greenhouses, and is used for aquaculture.

Greenhouse Heating. Using geothermal resources to heat greenhouses is similar to using it to heat homes and other buildings. The objective in this case is to provide a thermal environment in the greenhouse so that vegetables, flowers, and fruits can be grown out of season. The greenhouse is supplied with heated water, and through the use of radiators, embedded pipes, aerial pipes, or surface pipes, the heat is transferred to the greenhouse environment. Forced air through heat exchangers is also used. The United States, Hungary, former Yugoslavia, China-Taiwan, Italy, and France all have considerable numbers of geothermal greenhouses.

Aquaculture. One of the major areas for the direct use of geothermal resources is in aquaculture. The main idea is to adjust the temperature of the water environment in a production pond so that freshwater or marine fish, shrimp, and plants have greater growth rates and thus reach harvest age more quickly. There are many schemes to regulate the temperature of the pond water. For supply wells where the geothermal water is near the required temperature, the water is introduced directly into the pond. For locations having a well-water temperature too high, the water is spread in a holding pool where evaporative cooling, radiation, and conductive heat loss to the ground can all be used to reduce the temperature to a level where it can be added to the main production pond.

Industrial Applications. The Tasman Pulp and Paper Company, located in Kawerau, New Zealand, is one of the largest industrial developments to utilize geothermal energy. Geothermal exploration started there in 1952; it was directed toward locating and developing a geothermal resource for a pulp and paper mill. In 1985 the company was using four wells to supply steam to the operations. The steam is used to operate log kickers directly, to dry timber, to generate clean steam, and to drive an electricity generator. Geothermal energy supplies about 30 percent of the total process steam and 4 percent of the electricity for the plant. Geothermal energy in the form of steam is used to dry diatomaceous earth in Nasmafjall, Iceland. The diatomaceous earth is dredged from the bottom of a lake and pumped 3 kilometers by pipeline to a plant where it is dried.

Numerous other industrial applications of geothermal resources exist in the world. These range from timber drying in Japan to salt production from evaporating seawater in the Philippines, vegetable drying in Nevada, alfalfa drying in New Zealand, and mushroom growing in Oregon.

Environmental Impact. The environmental impacts associated with the use or conversion of geothermal resources are typically much less than those associated with the use or conversion of other energy sources. The resource is often promoted as a clean technology without the potential radiation problems associated with nuclear energy facilities or the atmospheric emissions problems often associated with oil and coal electric plants. Nonetheless, although associated environmental problems are low, there are some present. In the exploration and development phases of large-scale geothermal developments, access roads and platforms for drill rigs must be built. The drilling of a well can result in possible mixing of drilling fluids with the aquifers intersected by the well if the well is not well cased. Blowouts can also pollute the groundwater. The drilling fluids need to be stored and handled as wastes.

Geothermal fluids often contain dissolved gases such as carbon dioxide, hydrogen sulfide, and methane. Other chemicals, such as sodium chloride, boron, arsenic, and mercury, may also be associated with the geothermal water. The presence of these gases and chemicals must be determined, and appropriate means must be selected to prevent their release into the environment. In some cases this problem is reduced by the reinjection of waste water into the geothermal reservoir.

The release of thermal water into a surface water body such as a stream, pond, or lake can cause severe ecosystem damage by changing the ambient water temperature, even if only by a few degrees. Any discharge of hot water from the geothermal site needs to involve a means of cooling the water to an acceptable level—one that will not cause environmental damage. This result is often achieved through the use of holding ponds or evaporative cooling. The removal of large volumes of geothermal fluid from the subsurface can cause land subsidence. This is irreversible and can cause major structural damage. Subsidence can be prevented by the reinjection of a volume of fluid equal to that removed.

Noise pollution is one of the potential problems with geothermal sites where electricity generation is conducted. Noise reduction can require costly measures. Since many geothermal electric generation sites are rural, however, this is often not a problem. The noise generated in direct heat applications is typically low.

Economics. The cost of a geothermal plant is usually higher than the cost of a similar plant run on conventional fuel. At the same time, the cost of the energy for operating a geothermal plant is much lower than the cost of conventional fuels. In order to be economically superior, the geothermal plant needs to operate long

enough to at least make up for this difference.

Cascaded systems can be used to optimize the recovery of heat from the geothermal water and steam and therefore to decrease the overall costs. Systems can be cascaded such that the waste water and heat from one is the input heat source to the next. An example is the cascading of systems used for electricity generation, fruit drying, and home heating. Finally, the distance between the geothermal source and the plant or user should be minimized, as there can be significant transmission losses in heat as well as high costs for pipe, pumps, valves, and maintenance.

Future Prospects. The competitive energy price against which geothermal energy competes in the United States decreased markedly between the early and late 1990's. It therefore became harder to justify the building of new geothermal plants. The main market for new geothermal power systems has shifted from the United States to Asia and Central America. Reservoir management, on the other hand, began to receive more visibility. Operators have begun to emphasize the critical importance of injection and the ability to locate new productive fractures for reservoir management. The sustainability of the geothermal reservoir is a major objective. The field at The Geysers in California has become an important test bed for managing the sustainability of geothermal production.

Geothermal heat pumps are economical, energy efficient, and available in most places. They provide space heating and cooling plus water heating. They have been shown to reduce energy consumption by 20 to 40 percent. There appears to be a continued growth in the use of these devices.

The current production of geothermal energy is third among renewable energy sources. The order of utilization is hydroelectric, biomass, geothermal, solar, and wind. The current level of geothermal utilization is very small relative to its potential.

In the United States the government has sponsored activities to bring the inventory of the nation's low- to moderate-temperature geothermal resources up to date. An important part of the project was to complete a collocation study associating these resources with communities and other potential users. A collocated community is defined as being within 8 kilometers of a geothermal resource with a temperature of at least 50 degrees Celsius. The activities in the western states involved identifying and encouraging those collocated communities to develop their geothermal resources.

FURTHER READING: Broad coverage of the entire field is given in *Geothermal Energy*, edited by Mary H. Dickson and Mario Fanelli, 1995. Another overview is presented in *Geothermal Energy: Its Past, Present, and Future Contributions to the Energy Needs of Man*, by Christopher H. Armstead, 2d ed. 1983. An excellent reference center is provided by the Geo-Heat Center at the Oregon Institute of Technology, which has a World Wide Web site at http://www.oit.edu/~geoheat. They have a library containing most publications dealing with geothermal energy and also have extensive holdings of articles, reports, and circulars. Current news and activities dealing with geothermal resources are discussed in the periodical publications *Geothermics* and *Geothermal Resources Council Bulletin*.

William O. Rasmussen

SEE ALSO: Geysers and hot springs; Hydrothermal solutions and mineralization; Plate tectonics; Seafloor spreading; Volcanoes.

Germanium

WHERE FOUND: Germanium is the thirty-sixth most abundant element in the earth's crust, with an average abundance of about 7 grams per metric ton. It occurs in small quantities in ores of silver, such as argyrodite, as well as in ores of copper and zinc, and is found most abundantly in Germany.

PRIMARY USES: Germanium is of central importance in the manufacture of semiconductor materials and devices, especially transistors. It is also used in a variety of optical devices.

DESCRIPTION: Germanium, symbol Ge, is located in Group IVA of the periodic table, having atomic number 32 and an atomic weight of 72.59. It is a hard, brittle, grayish-white metal.

Its melting point is 937.4 degrees Celsius, its boiling point is 2,830 degrees Celsius, and its specific gravity is 5.32.

GERMANIUM WAS DISCOVERED in 1886 by the German chemist Clemens Winkler and was named in honor of Germany. Germanium forms a diamondlike tetrahedral crystal lattice similar to that of silicon. On the Mohs hardness scale, its hardness is six (diamond is ten). Germanium exhibits valences of +2 and +4. The +2 state is both easily reduced to the element and also oxidized to +4 germanium. Finely divided germanium ignites in chlorine gas to form germanium tetrachloride, and germanium forms a tetrahydride with hydrogen, which is a gas under ordinary conditions.

Germanium is recovered by treating enriched wastes and residues from zinc sulfide ores, pyrometallic ores, and coal with hydrochloric acid to form a volatile liquid which is extracted with carbon tetrachloride and purified by distillation. The resulting germanium tetrachloride is treated with demineralized water to precipitate germanium dioxide, which is then reduced to germanium with hydrogen. The highly pure element, which contains impurities less than one part per million, is obtained by zone refining, a selective fusion-recrystallization process that concentrates impurities which can be removed from the melt.

Ultrapure germanium is an intrinsic semiconductor, which accounts for its major use in solid-state electronics. Furthermore, it can be produced in near-crystalline perfection more easily than any other semiconductor. Thus the electronic properties of germanium have been widely studied. The earliest research on semiconductors was done with germanium, and William Shockley used it to make the first transistor in 1948. At low temperatures, pure germanium is almost an insulator because its four valence electrons are localized in the bonds between neighboring atoms. At room temperature, sufficient electrons enter higher-energy levels, become mobile, and conduct a weak current. The conductivity of germanium can be improved by the addition (doping) of one part per million of a Group V element, such as arsenic, because it has one more electron than germanium, or by the addition of a Group III element, such as indium, which has one less valence electron than germanium.

The major use of germanium is in semiconductor devices, such as transistors, diodes, solar cells, and solar batteries. It is also used in infrared optical devices, such as lenses, prisms, and windows, and germanium dioxide is used to produce optical glasses of high refractive index. Magnesium germanate is used in phosphors, and an alloy of germanium and gold is used in dental materials.

Alvin K. Benson

SEE ALSO: Alloys; Arsenic; Copper; Indium; Silicon; Silver; Solar energy; Zinc.

Getty, J. Paul

BORN: December 15, 1892; Minneapolis, Minnesota

DIED: June 6, 1976; Sutton Place, Surrey, England

J. Paul Getty, oil entrepreneur, was an exception in the mid-twentieth century world of anonymous corporations.

J. PAUL GETTY's father, George F. Getty, an insurance lawyer, became wealthy during the Oklahoma oil boom. Young Getty began his oil career in 1914, also in Oklahoma, and within three years he was a millionaire. In the 1920's, father and son bought oil leases and drilled wells around southern California. His father died in 1930, and during the Great Depression, rather than drilling wells, Getty bought oil stock in other companies at depressed prices, particularly that of Tide Water Oil, the nation's ninth largest oil company. As stocks rose, Getty became a multimillionaire.

After World War II, Getty expanded into the Middle East, challenging the powerful existing oil interests, the so-called Seven Sisters. He discovered oil in the neutral zone between Saudi Arabia and Kuwait in 1953. By 1957 he was the richest person in America, his wealth exceeding one billion dollars. Getty's fortune was invested in many businesses, but he personally held the controlling interests, a rugged individualist in an

Oil magnate J. Paul Getty in 1962; at the time he was considered the richest man in the world. (Popperfoto/Archive Photos)

age of faceless corporations, a throwback to the likes of John D. Rockefeller and Andrew Carnegie. A trust fund had long been established for the Getty relatives. Getty's major bequest, $600,000,000, was to his museum in Malibu, California, making it the best endowed in the world, and after Getty Oil was sold to Texaco in 1984, the museum became Getty's lasting legacy.

Eugene Larson

SEE ALSO: Oil and natural gas exploration; Oil industry; Petroleum refining and processing; Rockefeller, John D.

Geysers and hot springs

Hot springs are natural pools or springs of hot water occurring where water heated within the earth reaches its surface. Geysers are essentially hot springs that erupt intermittently, throwing a stream of water, sometimes mixed with other materials, into the air.

THE HEAT THAT produces superheated water and the resulting geysers and hot springs originates in magma, molten rock beneath the earth's crust. Such heat travels to the surface most easily through underground faults and fissures. Many areas with geysers and other geothermal features are tectonically active, subject to earthquakes and volcanoes. The geyser fields of Iceland and of North Island, New Zealand, show this connection. Magma may also rise through the earth's crust and remain trapped and molten relatively near the earth's surface. The Yellowstone geyser basin in the western United States is believed to lie atop such a heat source. Heat can be carried upward through porous rock layers to reservoirs of underground water; this process may account for some hot springs in areas that show no other geothermal features. Geysers and hot springs often exist in proximity to related geothermal phenomena such as fumaroles (steam vents) and bubbling mud pots.

Geysers are relatively rare, because they require the right combination of water channels, water pool, and heat cycle as well as an opening through which the hot water is ejected. Major geyser fields are found in the Yellowstone basin, in Iceland, New Zealand, and Japan, and on the Kamchatka Peninsula in Asiatic Russia. Smaller groups or isolated geysers occur in a few other regions, including Oregon, Nevada, and California in the United States. In contrast, there are more than five thousand known hot springs. They exist in almost every country and have been used by humanity since the beginning of history, and probably before.

Geysers and Hot Springs as an Energy Resource. Hot springs water was diverted for warm baths by the Etruscans and then the Romans, and subsequently by most societies which prized cleanliness. In New Zealand, the Maoris used hot

The geyser fields of Yellowstone National Park contain more than half of the world's active geysers. In the 1990's scientists began "prospecting" for potentially valuable microorganisms in the park's geysers and hot springs. (McCrea Adams)

springs directly for cooking and laundry purposes as well as bathing. In present-day Iceland, hot springs supply hot-water heating to most of Reykjavik's houses. Such heating is also used for Iceland's greenhouses, enabling fruits and vegetables to be grown in a generally cold, inhospitable climate. Russia has several towns whose buildings are heated by geothermal wells. Similar heating systems have been developed in such diverse locations as Hungary, Japan, and Klamath Falls, Oregon. Hot springs water is also used in agriculture for soil warming, in fish hatcheries, and for egg incubators.

The promise of cheap and relatively nonpolluting energy from geothermal sources has been pursued since the early 1900's. An electrical plant using steam from steam vents to drive turbines was put into operation in Larderello, Italy, in 1913. Destroyed during World War II, it was later rebuilt as part of a larger power network. A large natural-steam plant was opened at The Geysers in northern California in 1960, but its output later slowed because of overdrilling. Other geothermal power plants were built from the late 1950's in various countries, including Mexico, Japan, New Zealand, and the former Soviet Union.

Large-scale exploitation of geyser fields, hot springs, and fumaroles to produce electricity presents two main problems. One is the threat of weakening the geothermal field through overuse. Geysers are fragile and complex. and many have already been destroyed through drilling or other human interference. The second is the necessity to shield equipment against damage from mineral deposits. This damage can be lessened by filtering the steam or by employing binary systems using natural hot water to turn low-boiling-point fluids such as isobutane into steam.

Social and Health Aspects. Hot springs have been prized by many societies for their actual and presumed health benefits. Hot-springs bathing is relaxing; the heat and buoyancy also ease the pain and immobility of arthritis and other joint and muscle ailments. Drinking water from hot springs may act as a purgative or offer other benefits because of its dissolved minerals. For example, Tunbridge Wells in Kent was considered a miracle spring in eighteenth and nine-

teenth century England; one reason was that its high iron content cured anemia.

Bottled water from various hot springs is sold commercially. Hot springs have been nuclei for resorts and spas since ancient times. Among the best known in North America are Warm Springs, Georgia (made famous by the patronage of President Franklin D. Roosevelt); Hot Springs, Arkansas; and White Sulphur Springs, West Virginia. The spectacular geyser fields of Yellowstone National Park, Wyoming, and to a lesser extent those of Rotorua, New Zealand, attract a large tourist trade.

Other Resources from Hot Springs and Geysers. Minerals extracted from hot springs water or taken from deposits at geyser sites include borax, sulfur, alum, and ammonium salts. Rivers that drain geothermally active areas pick up dissolved minerals that enrich soils or water supplies downstream. Neutral or alkaline hot springs support a variety of animal, plant, and bacterial life. During Yellowstone winters, elk and buffalo drink their water and browse the surrounding plant growth. A unique microbe from these springs is used in laboratory DNA replication, and others are being studied for use as biodegradable solvents and as possible survivals of very early life forms.

FURTHER READING: A basic source is John S. Rinehart, *Geysers and Geothermal Energy,* 1980. H. Christopher Armstead, *Geothermal Energy,* 2d ed. 1983, is primarily a text for geothermal engineers, but the opening chapters contain general information. "Energy from the Earth," part 1 of D. S. Halacy, Jr., *Earth, Water, Wind, and Sun: Our Energy Alternatives,* 1977, gives a worldwide perspective. "The Microbe Miners," *Audubon* 96, no. 6 (1994), describes Yellowstone's microbial resources and controversy over their ownership, and the "Summer" section of Seymour Fishbein's *Yellowstone Country: The Enduring Wonder,* 1989, contains striking photographs and much detail about the park's geysers and hot springs.

Emily Alward

SEE ALSO: Geothermal and hydrothermal energy; Hydrothermal solutions and mineralization; Marine vents; Plate tectonics; Steam and steam turbines.

Depositional Landforms Left by a Glacier

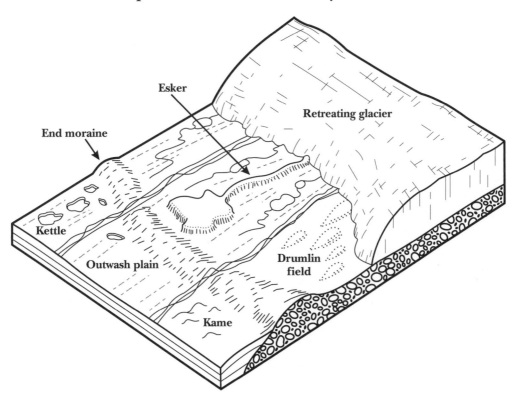

Glaciation

Glaciation is the effect of glaciers on the earth's surface, including erosion and the deposition of glaciated materials. Glaciers are related to a number of natural resources, helping to provide fresh water, rich soils, and deposits used for building materials.

THE AMERICAN GEOLOGICAL INSTITUTE'S *Dictionary of Geological Terms* defines glaciation as the "alteration of the earth's solid surface through erosion and deposition by glacier ice." As much as seventy-five percent of Earth's fresh water is tied up in the form of glaciers and ice caps. Glaciation has a profound effect on climate, and glaciation has important economic benefits. For example, water melted from glaciers is an important source of fresh water.

Glaciers begin above the snow line. Snow becomes compacted into granules, and as additional snow is added, weight and pressure lead to recrystalization in the form of dense glacial ice. Once the ice reaches sufficient thickness, the internal strength of the crystals is overcome by the weight of the ice, and the ice begins to flow in the form of a glacier. Glaciers can flow by internal deformation only, or by deformation in combination with basal sliding on a thin layer of melt water. As glaciers flow they erode the surface of the earth, scouring it and plucking up boulders large and small. Glaciated valleys are distinctly U-shaped, as contrasted with the typical V shape of river valleys.

Glacial scouring can create a number of land forms. These include small steep-sided valleys called cirques and sharp ridges called arêtes. Three or more cirque valleys can leave land in a recognizable horn shape, such as the famous Matterhorn in the Pennine Alps. Smaller glaciers feed larger glaciers much the same way that

The Hubbard glacier in Alaska "calving," or breaking apart, after reaching the ocean. (Photo Network)

small rivers feed larger ones. Since the depth of scour is proportional to the mass of the glacier, smaller tributaries can leave forms known as hanging valleys isolated hundreds of feet above a steep-sided main valley.

Rock and boulders pushed or carried along by a glacier form moraines, drumlins, and glacial till. As glaciers retreat, they leave their burden of rock behind. Erratics, boulders that have been carried great distances and then left behind as glaciers retreat, have been used since prehistoric times as construction material for homes and stone fences. Melt water from glaciers can sort transported sand and gravel, forming long sinuous eskers and land forms called kames. The finely graded sand and gravel is an important source of aggregate for the construction industry.

In some northern countries, melt water from glaciers is not only used as a source of fresh water but also—where there is sufficient height and volume—can be used to generate hydroelectric power. Glaciation has other important economic benefits. The scouring effect of glaciers creates a fine dust-sized material called loess. Wind eventually transports and deposits the mineral-rich loess, helping to create some of the richest agricultural soils in the world.

Ray Roberts

SEE ALSO: Agronomy; Climate and resources; Farmland; Hydroenergy; Hydrology and the hydrologic cycle; Sedimentary processes, rocks, and mineral deposits; Soil; Water.

Glass

RESOURCES USED: Silica (silicon dioxide, from sand), soda (sodium oxide), lime (calcium oxide), and small amounts of many other possible materials, including boron oxide, aluminum oxide, and magnesium oxide

"Glass" commonly describes materials rich in silicon dioxide that are produced by solidification from the molten state without crystallizing. Glass's many valu-

able qualities have made it one of the most widely used materials of the twentieth century, with applications ranging from windows to optical instruments to electronics.

GLASS, ALTHOUGH IT has been a commonplace material for centuries, is an exceptional substance: It is a solid that is technically considered a liquid. All other familiar solids are crystalline in structure. That is, they possess a definite, orderly internal geometric form that is a reflection of the arrangement of their constituent atoms. Their atoms are packed in repetitive forms called crystal networks or lattices. Liquids, in contrast, are termed amorphous in structure. They lack the rigid, repeating internal structure of solids. Glasses can be considered a borderline case between classic solids and liquids, and they have been called "amorphous solids."

Glasses are considered to be "supercooled" liquids—liquids chilled so rapidly that they never undergo the crystallization process of true solids. When a solid's molecules cool down from a molten state, the material undergoes a series of internal dynamic changes in response to the loss of heat. Molecules move in a more rigid fashion until reaching a point at which their patterns of movement and their interatomic bonds reach a state of discontinuity. This point of discontinuity is commonly called the freezing point of the solid; at this point it begins rapidly to lock into the pattern of crystallinity. Liquids, such as glasses, never actually reach this point of discontinuity and are considered to be in a "metastable" state. Glasses, besides possessing liquid-like structures, are typically also solutions; that is, they are composed of homogenous mixtures of substances possessing dissimilar molecular structures. The primary constituent of most common glass is silica, or silicon dioxide (SiO_2).

The properties of glass can be modified by industrial processes to suit various uses, but in general these properties include a generally excellent resistance to chemical corrosion; a high resistance to heat; an outstanding ability to insulate against electrical current, even at high voltages; high surface smoothness; good scratch resistance; a high ratio of weight to strength, coupled with a tendency toward brittleness; radiation absorbance and sensitivity; and a range of optical properties that include the ability to disperse, refract, or reflect light. All of the above properties have made various forms of glass a preferred material for numerous applications.

Ingredients and Manufacture. Silica—in the form of sand that is processed and cleaned before use—is the primary ingredient in almost all glass. In addition, the common glass that is generally used in such items as bottles, drinking glasses, lightbulbs, and window glass (sheet glass) contains soda (Na_2O), which makes the glass easier to work with in manufacturing, and lime (CaO), which overcomes weaknesses introduced by the soda. A wide range of other materials may be used in small amounts, among them aluminum oxide and magnesium oxide. The three most common types of glass are soda-lime glass, borosilicate glass, and lead glass. Lead glass, used in optics and "crystal" tableware, is soda-lime glass to which lead oxide is added to provide exceptional clarity and refractivity. Boron oxide is added in the production of borosilicate glass, used in kitchenware (such as Pyrex) and laboratory ware because it resists breakage during rapid temperature changes.

Both window glass (sheet glass) and plate glass are soda-lime glass, but their manufacturing processes are different. Window glass, for example, is cooled, flattened into shape by rollers, then finished and cut into standard sizes. The manufacture of plate glass is more complex; the glass is strengthened by annealing, then ground smooth and polished. Plate glass is stronger and has less distortion than window glass. Safety glass, or laminated glass, as used in automobile windshields, generally contains a layer of plastic between two layers of glass to keep the glass from shattering completely upon impact.

Historical Background. The production of synthetic glass has a very long history. Indeed, aside from metallurgy, glassmaking can be considered the oldest of industrial arts practiced by early civilizations. The use of natural high-silica minerals having glasslike properties, such as obsidian (produced by volcanic action and sometimes called volcanic glass), is even older. It can be traced many tens of thousands of years into prehistory back to the early Paleolithic era (the Old

Stone Age). Early humans and even proto-hominids made tools and weapons by "flintknapping": shaping obsidian and obsidian-like rocks and minerals by percussion and pressure flaking. These materials were artfully manipulated; prehistoric artisans took advantage of the natural tendency of glasses to be brittle and to break at the surface into chonchoidal fractures (arcuate shapes). Blades, chisels, awls, gouges, and other implements could be produced in this way.

The earliest artificial glass was produced at least three thousand years ago in Egypt for decorative purposes. Colored glazes were fired onto pottery or stone beads and other objects, originally in imitation of the surface colors and lusters of precious and semiprecious stones. Eventually experimentation led to the development of freestanding, three-dimensional glass objects such as vials and bottles. This development is believed to have occurred in Egypt around 1500 B.C.E. during the New Kingdom period. Eventu-

ally much higher transparency and ease of fabrication evolved with the discovery of the art of glassblowing, circa 50 B.C.E., in the area of Phoenicia (modern coastal Lebanon). Glassmaking and glassblowing spread rapidly throughout the Mediterranean world with the expansion of the Roman Empire but declined with the waning of the Roman civilization. Glassmaking centers survived in the Middle East and other areas. Eventually glassmaking experienced a resurgence in Europe beginning in the eleventh century, and new techniques and glass compositions were developed. Glass technology continued to improve gradually until the nineteenth century, when it experienced very rapid improvements due to the increasing needs of science and the new industries spawned by the Industrial Revolution. Experimenters such as Michael Faraday contributed greatly to the understanding of the physics and chemistry of glass during the nineteenth century. A glassblowing machine had been de-

Commercial architecture in the second half of the twentieth century has used glass extensively because of its appearance and smoothness, corrosion and heat resistance, and other valuable properties. Pictured is Detroit's Renaissance Center. (Jim West)

veloped by the 1890's, and in the early twentieth century automated machines were producing molded and blown glass items. The growing demands of science and industry in the twentieth century engendered the production of glasses of increasingly sophisticated composition and fabrication.

Uses of Glass. The earliest use of synthetic glass seems to have been in the form of decorative or artistic objects, including jewelry. Glass is still considered an artistic medium and an attractive material for decoration; it is used in sculpture, stained glass windows, vases, vials, jewelry, and mirrors. Particularly since the Industrial Revolution, however, glass has been much more extensively used in the form of utilitarian objects and devices. Plate glass, sheet glass, and wired glass are found in virtually every modern building and vehicle, whether automobile, boat, or aircraft. Countless glass bottles and jars are used in every country to store and transport liquids of all sorts. Lighting fixtures in the form of incandescent and fluorescent light bulbs and tubes are one of the most familiar of modern uses of glass, and they number in the billions. Hundreds of millions of glass cathode ray tubes (CRTs) are found worldwide in the form of television sets and video display terminals (VDTs) for personal computers. Military and civilian applications of optical-quality glass elements in the form of magnifying lenses for microscopes, telescopes, binoculars, periscopes, prisms, and other eyepieces also number in the millions and are in use on land, at sea, and in the air. Structural insulation in the form of glass fiber mats is a common manufactured good produced from fine, wool-like glass fibers.

Chemistry and physics laboratories use glass extensively in the form of piping, tubes, rods, storage vessels, vacuum flasks, and beakers. Some of the more sophisticated recent uses of glass are in the telecommunication industry. Optical fibers (or fiber optics) are very fine, flexible, high-quality glass strands designed to transmit signals in the form of light impulses.

FURTHER READING: An extremely thorough and informative treatment of all aspects of glass science, including history, uses, formation, structure, physics, chemistry, and inherent problems and limitations, can be found in *Glass Science*, by Robert H. Doremus, 2d ed. 1994. Another good source, of a less technical nature, that describes the details of composition and manufacture of the major types of glass is *How Glass Is Made*, by Alan J. Paterson, 1985. A succinct but informative book which describes the uses of many glass types and their respective manufacturing processes is *The Corning Glass Center*, by the staff of the Corning Glass Corp., 1958. This book features many illustrative examples. One of the most thorough and meticulous treatments of the history—and even the known prehistory—of glass, which also serves as a good introduction to the technical side of glass production, is *Glass and Archaeology*, by Susan Frank, 1982.

Frederick M. Surowiec

SEE ALSO: Aluminum; Boron; Ceramics; Crystals; Fiberglass; Oxides; Oxygen; Potash; Quartz; Sand and gravel; Silicates; Silicon.

Gneiss

WHERE FOUND: Gneiss is exposed in regions of uplift where erosion has stripped away surficial rocks (sediments and lower grade metamorphic rocks) to expose rocks that have been altered at depth. In North America, gneiss may be found in New England, in the central Atlantic states, the Rockies, the Cascades, and much of Canada.

PRIMARY USES: Gneiss, with mineralogy similar to that of granite, has similar uses except that it is generally restricted by the presence of a higher percentage of ferromagnesium minerals and micas which weather rapidly to weaken and discolor the finished stone. The major use is as riprap, aggregate, and dimension stone. Wavy foliation in polished slabs results in an especially decorative stone for monuments.

DESCRIPTION: The term "gneiss" (pronounced "nice") is loosely used to encompass many different mineral combinations and a variety of structures, and it includes a great many rocks of uncertain origins. In its narrowest meaning, gneiss is defined as a coarse-grained, feldspar-rich, metamorphic rock with a parallel structure (foliation) that assumes the form of streaks and bands.

GNEISS IS PRIMARILY identified by its structure rather than by its composition. It is a medium- to coarse-grained banded or coarsely foliated crystalline rock. The rock is characterized by a preferred orientation of platy grains such as biotite, muscovite, or hornblende, or the segregation of minerals into bands or stripes. Unlike schist, granular minerals are more common than platy minerals. Most gneisses are light to dark gray, pink, or red because of the high feldspar content. The most common gneisses are similar to granite in composition and resemble them except for the foliation. The predominant minerals are equidimensional grains of quartz and potassium feldspar, usually microcline. Sodium plagioclase may also be present. Biotite, muscovite, and hornblende, alone or in combination, are the most common minerals that define the foliation. Other minerals, almost exclusively metamorphic in origin, that may be present in minor quantities include almandine garnet, andalusite, staurolite, and sillimanite.

True gneiss is a high-grade metamorphic rock formed by recrystallization and chemical reaction within existing rocks in response to high temperature and pressure at great depths in the earth's crust. Often the precursor rock is a feldspar-rich sandstone, a clay-rich sediment such as shale, or granite. Gneissic fabric may be produced in some igneous rocks by flowage within a magma. Some gneisses are formed by intrusion of thin layers of granitic melt into adjacent schists which produces lit-par-lit structure or injection gneiss.

The rock name is often modified by the addition of a term to indicate overall composition, unique mineral, or structure. Thus, granitic gneiss or gabbroic gneiss may distinguish between gneisses composed predominantly of quartz and feldspars or those composed of calcium-rich feldspar and ferromagnesian minerals such as pyroxene. In like manner, garnet gneiss or sillimanite gneiss may be used to flag the appearance of an important metamorphic mineral. The term augen gneiss is used to describe those rocks which have prominent almond-shaped lenses of feldspar or feldspar and quartz, which are produced by shearing during the formation of the rock.

René A. De Hon

SEE ALSO: Feldspars; Metamorphic processes, rocks, and mineral deposits; Quarrying; Stone and rock.

Gold

WHERE FOUND: Although widely distributed in nature, gold is a rare element. It has been estimated that all of the earth's gold could be gathered into a single cube measuring only 60 feet on each side. Because of its rarity, gold is considered a precious metal. The largest deposits of gold have been found in the Republic of South Africa and the former Soviet Union (in the Urals and Siberia). Other large deposits have been found in the western United States of America and in Canada, Mexico, and Colombia.

PRIMARY USES: Gold is used in jewelry, decorations, electroplating, and dental materials. Other uses include medicinal compounds for the treatment of arthritis and the use of the [198]Au isotope, with a half-life of 2.7 days, for treating some cancers. Since gold is an excellent heat and electrical conductor, as well as remaining inert when exposed to air or moisture, it has also been used in precision scientific and electrical instruments. Specifically, gold has been used to coat space satellites, to transmit infrared signals, and to serve as the contact point for triggering the inflation of protective air bags in some automobiles. Few countries today use gold coinage systems; an exception is the Krugerrand coin of the Republic of South Africa. Most nations use gold symbolically as a standard of their monetary systems rather than as actual coinage. Similarly, international monetary exchanges remain based on the world market value of gold, but actual exchanges of gold are uncommon.

DESCRIPTION: Gold is represented by the chemical symbol Au, derived from the Latin word *aurum*, meaning "shining dawn." On the periodic table, gold (atomic number 79) is a member of Group IB of transition metals. This group, also known as the coinage metals, includes copper, silver, and gold. Chemically, gold behaves similarly to platinum, although the arrangement of its chemically reactive electrons is similar to that of copper and silver. Both gold and platinum are largely nonreactive metals. Elemental gold exists in eighteen isotopic forms in nature. The weighted mass average of these isotopes gives gold an atomic mass of 196.9665 atomic mass units. Pure gold is a soft, shiny, and ductile metal with a brilliant yellow luster. Changing from solid to liquid at 1,064 degrees Celsius, gold has a high melting point. To vaporize gold requires an even higher temperature (2,808 degrees Celsius). Highly purified gold has a specific gravity of 19.3 (at 20 degrees Celsius).

GOLD IS A RARE and precious metal. As such, pure gold has been highly valued and coveted by societies over millennia. Because of its nonreactive nature, elemental gold maintains its brilliant yellow luster. Because of this luster, gold is widely considered the most beautiful and unique of all the metals, which typically display colors of gray, red, or white-silver. Gold does not air-oxidize (tarnish) or corrode upon exposure to moisture. Similarly, it does not readily react to common acids or bases. Nonetheless, gold does dissolve in a reagent known as aqua regia, which is a mixture of nitric acid and hydrochloric acid; alone, neither acid acts upon gold. Aqua regia is a Latin term meaning the liquid (aqua) that dissolves the king (regia) of all metals. This reagent is used to separate gold from its ores.

Although predominantly inert, gold can be oxidized to form compounds. When it oxidizes, gold atoms may lose either one, two, or three outer electrons to generate a +1, +2, or +3 charged metal cation, respectively. The most common oxidation state of gold is the +3 form.

Gold is the softest of all metals; thus it is also the most ductile (capable of being drawn into thin wire) and most malleable (capable of being hammered into thin sheets, or foil). Gold can be hammered into foil sheets so thin that it would take 300,000 sheets, stacked on top of one another, to make a pile one inch high. It has been estimated that one gram of gold could be drawn into a wire that would span more than 1.5 miles.

Jewelry and coins are rarely made of pure gold because the very soft nature of pure gold makes these items susceptible to loss of gold mass as well as loss of the intended artistic form. To prevent this problem, gold is alloyed with metals such as copper (into materials called red, pink, or yellow gold), palladium, nickel, or zinc (called white gold), and silver or platinum. The extent to which gold is "diluted" by another metal in an alloy is expressed in carats. Pure gold is 24 carats, meaning that 24 out of 24 parts are made of gold. In 18-carat gold, 18 out of 24 parts of the alloy are gold, with the other 6 parts being some other metal. Similarly, 10-carat gold represents 10 of 24 parts being gold.

Historical Background. The Group IB metals, or coinage metals, were the first metals used in primitive cultures. It is believed that elemental

Gold in its native state. (U.S. Geological Survey)

metals were easy to find in nature because their bright lusters shone in natural light. Precious metals have been in use since at least seven thousand years ago by civilizations of the Middle East and Afghanistan. Wealthy members of these groups possessed decorative jewels fashioned from gold. The metalworkers of these ancient societies physically manipulated the gold using hammers or other tools to carve or cut the soft metal.

Exploration of the tomb of King Tutankhamen, from the fourteenth century B.C.E., revealed an entry guarded by gold funerary masks inlaid with colorful glass. A gold sarcophagus and gold panel behind the king's throne were also found. Between 4000 and 3500 B.C.E., the Egyptians and Sumerians learned to smelt silver and gold. They were able to generate fires in furnaces that could achieve the extreme temperatures required to melt metals, to cast molten metal into moulds, to forge metal, and to make alloys (by blending molten metals). The use of gold for dental fillings among wealthy Egyptians dates back to between 2680 and 2160 B.C.E.

In Mesopotamia, a region that is now part of Iraq, an ornate headdress of Queen Shub-ab, dated back to 2700 B.C.E., was fashioned with gold-carved leaves to adorn her face. Trading and business deals of Mesopotamia involved the exchange of precious metals, although there was no system of standardized coins. Archaeological studies have also shown that the Incan civilization of pre-Columbian South America possessed considerable goldworking skill and achieved mastery of soldering and welding techniques.

The alchemists of the medieval period believed that gold was one of the most important keys to immortality. They also believed that base metals, which were abundant and cheap, could be converted into gold, which was rare and expensive. It was assumed that by simple manipulation in the presence of a spiritual agent—such as the Philosopher's Stone—an elixir could be formed that possessed all the ingredients required for immortality. Because of its inert behavior and timeless beauty, gold was believed to impart some qualities required to achieve worldly immortality. During medieval times it was widely thought that the emperors and kings

who had the most gold would have the longest lives. If a king ruled for many years there could be long periods of economic stability, access to food, security of family, and safety from conquerors. Thus the pursuit of gold was very serious business, and the king's magician, who was usually an alchemist, was highly regarded in the king's court. As a final historical note, gold amalgams, mixtures of mercury and gold, were described in the year 27 B.C.E. by a Roman architect, Vitruvius. Mercury and gold amalgamation is still in use today as a means of collecting gold from sand deposits of riverbeds.

Distribution of Gold. Gold is widely distributed across the world's continents. Approximately two-thirds of the world's gold comes from South Africa, including the region near Johannesburg. Other major gold deposits have been found in regions of the Urals and Siberia (Russia), Canada, the western states of the United States, Mexico, and Colombia. Less significant deposits are found in Egypt, Australia, Asia, and Europe.

Two-thirds of all the gold produced in the United States originates in regions of South Dakota and Nevada. Locations of other important

Mine Production of Gold in U.S.
In Kilograms

State	1993	1994
Alaska	5,948	5,740
Arizona	2,710	1,980
California	35,800	30,100
Colorado	W	4,420
Montana	14,300	12,600
Nevada	211,000	214,000
New Mexico	995	W
South Dakota	19,200	W
Washington	7,110	7,410
Other states	37,300	50,100
Total	**331,000**	**326,000**

Source: U.S. Bureau of Mines, *Minerals Yearbook, 1994.* U.S. Government Printing Office, 1996.

Note: Alaska data is state data; other data is as reported to U.S. Bureau of Mines. W = withheld to avoid disclosing proprietary company data (amount included in "Other states" total). Data rounded to three significant digits.

U.S. gold finds include California, made famous by the California Gold Rush of 1849; Alaska, popularized by the Klondike Gold Rush of 1896; and Colorado, with a ski resort town named Telluride because the gold-containing ore telluride is found in the region.

Environmental Forms of Gold. Through geological activity, the genesis of elemental gold is favored by postmagmatic processes occurring in the presence of medium-intensity hydrothermal energy. Such activity upon gold-bearing lavas produces primary deposits of gold, in which elemental gold remains in the site where it was formed. Postmagmatic processes also favor the formation of quartz, copper and iron pyrites, and other minerals containing the metals copper, gold, cobalt, and silver. As could be expected, these minerals and metals often occur together. Because copper and iron pyrites have a golden luster, although it is less brilliant than that of gold, their presence in primary gold deposits posed problems for miners. These pyrites are responsible for the term "fool's gold," and many a miner was betrayed by partners, bankers, or himself when mistaking chunks of cheap copper and lead pyrites for real gold.

Gold can also be found in areas where mechanical processes acted upon sedimentary rock to yield secondary deposits of gold. Wind and water act to pulverize rock into sand and gravel. Through erosion, clastic and placer deposits of gold and platinum form. Since gold and platinum are inert, they remain unaltered by erosive forces. As rock erosion continues, the movement and accumulation of these metals along rivers occurs. Since these metals are seven times more dense than sand and gravel, they migrate downstream at a more sluggish rate. This sluggish movement, plus the heavy density of gold and platinum, encourages the metals to settle in riverbeds. Conglomerates, or large nuggets, of gold and platinum can be found only in placer deposits formed in this manner. Among the more famous nuggets found are a 93-kilogram nugget found in Hill End, Australia, and a 153-kilogram nugget found in Chile. The spectacular classic placer deposits found in the Klondike, in the Yukon (Canada), and near Sacramento, California, explain the subsequent gold bonanzas and

The Rabbit Creek open-pit gold mine in Nevada. Two-thirds of the gold mined in the United States comes from deposits in South Dakota and Nevada. (U.S. Geological Survey)

migration of prospectors, then settlers, into the American West. Secondary deposits have also yielded the abundant alluvial gold deposits found near Johannesburg, South Africa. By far, most gold is found in placers of sedimentary origin. In areas of recent erosion, gold is usually found in small, shapeless grains, in small sheets, or as flakes. When fine-grain gold is found in alluvial deposits, "panning for gold" is performed to separate the precious metal from the sand.

Formed in primary deposits, crystals of elemental gold may occur as veins or as dendritic (arborescent) aggregates in association with quartz crystals. Dendritic aggregates look as though the metallic crystal developed with a fernlike growth on large colorful and translucent quartz crystals. Gold veins are often natural alloys of gold and silver rather than pure gold. These naturally occurring gold-silver alloys are known as electrum, in which the silver content may range from 15 percent to 50 percent. Other natural alloys, as of gold and palladium (porpezite) or gold and rhodium (rhodite), are less frequently found. Gold also occurs in telluride ores, such as tetradymite, nagyagite, and sylvanite. These ores are primarily sulfide compounds of tellurium. In addition to tellurium (Te) and sulfur (S) atoms, tetradymite also contains gold and lead. Similarly, sylvanite and nagyagite (black tellurium) contain gold and silver, but in different arrangements and ratios. Elemental gold can be extracted from these minerals via chemical reactions.

Obtaining Gold. Gold is separated from rocks, minerals, and alluvial deposits by panning or sluicing methods. The extraction of gold from telluride ores (tetradymite, nagyagite, and sylvanite) requires chemical reactions. The use of cyanide compounds, formation of amalgams, or smelting gold may be necessary to extract the gold from ores. The extracted gold is frequently refined by electrolysis (the use of an electric current). Electrolysis is particularly useful in separating mercury-gold amalgams back into their separate and purified metallic state.

In telluride ores (minerals), gold is not in the free, elemental state; rather, it is in a cationic form. As a metallic cation, each atom of gold carries a positive charge of either +1 or +3. A chemical reaction involving the addition of potassium cyanide to the crushed rocks (covered with water) makes a new compound of gold that dissolves in the water. This layer of water can be collected off the crushed rock, and through electrolysis the gold cations can be converted into gold crystals.

Uses of Gold. As described previously, jewelry and decorative ornaments fashioned from gold are marketed using carats to describe the quantity of gold present. Compounds of gold are used for decorating china or glass items. Gold chloro compounds, containing gold cations having a +3 charge, are mixed with sulfurized terpenes or resins to form a mixture known as "liquid gold," which can be applied directly to glass or china.

Compounds of gold with +1 cations are used in rheumatology as an anti-inflammatory agent for the treatment of active, refractory forms of juvenile and adult rheumatoid arthritis. These biologically active compounds are sodium gold thiomalate and sodium gold (or auro) thioglucose; aurothioglucose seems to be less painful when injected into a muscle near the joint. The gold therapy must be started before permanent changes have occurred in the afflicted joints if it is to benefit the patient. Some of the side effects of these therapies include skin, liver, and kidney changes or damage. Approximately 20 percent of patients who try gold therapy have to discontinue treatment because of these adverse reactions. Fortunately, newer anti-inflammatory agents have limited the number of patients who need to try gold therapy for relief. Finally, gold is used in an abstract manner to represent currencies and monetary systems throughout the world. The origins of this ancient practice lie in Mesopotamian, Assyrian, and Lydian (western Turkey) societies.

Nutritional and Toxicity Aspects. Gold is not an essential element for life, although trace amounts are found in humans, and some plants concentrate the element. Trace amounts in humans may arise from ingestion of gold from certain alcoholic beverages, from gold dental amalgams, or from exposure to gold therapy for arthritis. Because gold is minimally absorbed by the digestive system, these trace amounts pose no toxic concern.

Environmental Impact in South America. Most of the world's gold deposits have been well exploited and are therefore nearly devoid of the precious metal. In the South American continent, which was the least mined of all continents up to the 1980's, the environment has begun to suffer from the hunt for gold. Past methods of obtaining gold have yielded to the more dangerous practice of using liquid mercury to form a mercury-gold amalgam in the panning process. To recover even the tiniest amount of gold, a large quantity of mercury must be used. In South American rivers, gold occurs in brown, iron-stained sand. Some deposits have been profitable even though only a few dollars worth of gold may be gathered per ton of sand panned and amalgamated. Whether or not gold is actually found, the leftover mercury is dumped directly into the rivers. Mercury, a neurotoxin, is lethal in high amounts. Reportedly, the dumping of untreated mercury has reduced populations of fishes, has caused high levels of mercury in fish eaten by people, and is likely to have health impacts on children, pregnant women, and future generations. Some researchers suspect that neurological symptoms that suggest mercury poisoning can already be seen in some South American population areas.

FURTHER READING: Colin A. Ronan traces the history of gold in *Science: History and Development Among the World's Cultures*, 1982. An excellent tabulation is presented in *The Timetables of Science*, by Alexander Hellemans and Bryan Bunch, 1988. An older, but enjoyable, historical account of gold and the human obsession with it can be found in *The Magic of Gold*, by Jennifer Marx, 1978. Finally, Timothy Green integrates stories of gold rushes and mining with historical accounts of the impact of gold on markets and economies in *The New World of Gold*, 1981. Beautiful photographic examples of naturally occurring gold can be found in Walter Schumann's field guide, *Handbook of Rocks, Minerals, and Gemstones*, 1993, and in a text in the Peterson Field Guide series, *Rocks and Minerals*, 1988. *Jewelry: 7000 Years*, edited by Hugh Tait, 1986, presents a photographic history of gold as depicted in jewels representing all the major phases in the history of humankind. See also Robert W. Boyle, *Gold: History and Genesis of Deposits*, 1987; Jeffrey St. John, *Noble Metals*, 1984; and Tom H. Watkins, *Gold and Silver in the West*, 1971.

Mary C. Fields

SEE ALSO: Alloys; Hydrothermal solutions and mineralization; Metals and metallurgy; Mineral resource use, early history of; Native elements; Placer deposits; Sedimentary processes, rocks, and mineral deposits.

Granite

WHERE FOUND: The continents are primarily granite, with a thin veneer of sedimentary rocks. Granite is found in the exposed core of linear mountain chains and regions of highly eroded continental shields associated with regional metamorphism. The Sierra Nevada mountain range consists of a composite granitic batholith that is 640 kilometers by 110 kilometers. Granites also form such notable sites as Mount Rushmore, South Dakota; Half Dome in Yosemite National Park, California; and Stone Mountain, Georgia.

PRIMARY USES: Granite is used extensively as building stone. It is strong and weather resistant. Cut and polished slabs are used for internal and external facing, and polished or horned blocks are used for ornamental stones as tombstones and monuments. Large blocks are used in sea walls and jetties. Smaller blocks and crushed stone are used as rip-rap.

DESCRIPTION: Granite is a medium- to coarse-grained igneous rock composed principally of interlocking grains of the light-colored silicate minerals—potassium feldspar, sodium-rich plagioclase, and quartz. The overall color may blend to reddish, pink, or white depending on which mineral predominates in the rock. Dark minerals may add a spotted appearance to the rock. Granite is an igneous rock formed at great depths in the earth's crust. The three essential minerals in granite are quartz, which makes up 20 to 40 percent of the rock, and feldspars in which potassium feldspar is more abundant than plagioclase. Five to 10 percent ferromagnesian minerals, usually biotite or hornblende, or muscovite are common as accessory minerals. Garnet, tourmaline, corundum, or even pyroxene may be present in some granites.

VARIATIONS IN TEXTURE and composition give rise to distinctive varieties of granite. Pegmatite is an extremely coarse-grained rock of granite composition formed in the late, fluid-rich stage of magma crystallization. Individual crystals may reach several inches or tens of feet in length. Aplite is a fine-grained granite with a sugary texture. Graphic granite is conspicuous by its intergrowth of quartz within orthoclase crystals, which gives a pattern similar to cuneiform writing. Alaskite is a granite with no dark minerals. Charnockite is granite containing hypersthene as its chief ferromagnesian silicate.

Granite magma is formed by melting continental crustal rocks and thick prisms of sediments that form along the margins of convergent plates. The melt migrates upward in the crust through overlying rocks by assimilation of surrounding rocks and by forcefully pushing rocks out of the way. As the magma moves upward, blocks of overlying rocks are incorporated into the melt. If the melt is hot enough, the included rocks may be melted. If the magma has cooled sufficiently, the blocks are preserved as xenoliths (foreign rocks) within the magma. Granite magmas cool to form large intrusive bodies known as batholiths (*bathos* for deep, and *lithos* meaning rock) and smaller intrusions such as dikes and sills. As batholiths are emplaced fairly deep in the crust, the surrounding materials are usually high grade metamorphic rocks such as schist and gneiss. Some granites may form by extreme metamorphism in which existing rocks are converted to granitic rock by recrystallization and chemical reaction with chemically active fluids.

René A. De Hon

SEE ALSO: Earth's crust; Feldspars; Igneous processes, rocks, and mineral deposits; Pegmatites; Plutonic rocks and mineral deposits; Quarrying; Stone and rock.

Graphite

WHERE FOUND: Natural graphite is distributed widely in the world. Major deposits are found in Ceylon, Sri Lanka, Korea, India, Austria, Germany, Norway, Canada, the former Soviet Union, the Adirondack region of New York in the United States, Mexico, China, Brazil, and Madagascar. The United States imports virtually all of the natural graphite it needs from the last four countries just listed. However, about 70 to 80 percent of the graphite used in the United States is synthesized from a wide variety of carbon-containing materials—for example, anthracite coal and petroleum coke. Synthetic graphite is denser, purer, and more expensive than the natural form.

PRIMARY USES: The most familiar use of graphite is in the manufacture of "lead" pencils, where it is mixed with clay and other materials and baked at high temperatures. The "Lead" increases in softness as the ratio of graphite to clay increases. Graphite has much more extensive use in the manufacture of lubricants and oilless bearings; electrodes in batteries and industrial electrolysis; high-temperature rocket casings, chemical process equipment, furnaces, and crucibles for holding molten metals; tanks for holding corrosive chemicals; and strong and lightweight composite materials that are used, for example, in airplanes and high-quality sports equipment such as tennis rackets and golf clubs. Graphite is also a component in the cores of some nuclear reactors as the moderator to slow down the neutrons, and it is the major raw material for synthetic diamonds.

DESCRIPTION: Graphite and diamond are the two predominant forms in which free carbon is found in nature. Graphite is a greasy, opaque, highly reflective black or gray solid. The density of synthetic graphite is 2.26 grams per cubic centimeter, but that of natural graphite is usually lower, varying from 2.23 to 1.48 grams per cubic centimeter, due to the presence of pore spaces and impurities. Graphite can be made to sublime directly to carbon vapor or to melt to liquid carbon at temperatures above approximately 3,500 degrees Celsius, depending on the pressure and other conditions. It can also be transformed into diamond at extremely high pressures and temperatures (for example, 100,000 atmospheres and 1,000-2,000 degrees Celsius). The rate of conversion of diamond back to graphite at atmospheric pressure is not significant below temperatures of about 4,000 degrees Celsius.

CARBON WAS KNOWN in prehistory in the forms of charcoal and soot, but it was not recognized as a chemical element until the second half of the eighteenth century. In 1779 graphite was shown to be carbon by Carl Wilhelm Scheele, a Swedish chemist, and in 1789 the name "graphite" was proposed by Abraham Gottlob Werner, a German geologist, and D. L. G. Harsten, from the Greek *graphein* (to write). Commercially, "lead" pencils were first manufactured in about

1564 in England during Queen Elizabeth's reign, using Cumberland graphite. In 1896 Edward Goodrich Acheson, an American chemist, was granted a patent for his process whereby graphite is made from coke, and within one or two years, production began on a large scale. Diamond was first synthesized from graphite between 1953 and 1955.

Distribution of Graphite. Although graphite can be found throughout the world, much of it is of little economic importance. Large crystals, called flake, occur in metamorphosed sedimentary silicate rocks such as quartz, schists, and gneisses and have an average crystal size of about four millimeters (ranging from fractions of a millimeter to about six millimeters). Deposits have also been found in the form of lenses up to 30 meters thick and stretching several kilometers, with average carbon content of 25 percent (reaching 60 percent in Madagascar). The graphite in these cases was probably formed from the carbon in organic materials. Deposits containing microcrystalline graphite (sometimes referred to as "amorphous carbon") can contain up to 95 percent carbon. In Mexico such amorphous carbon occurs in metamorphosed coal beds. The graphite deposit in New York occurs in a hydrothermal vein and was probably formed from carbon-bearing rocks during metamorphism in the region. Graphite occurs occasionally as an original constituent of igneous rocks (for example in India), and it has been observed in meteorites. The mining and purification process of natural graphite includes flotation followed by treatment with acids and then heating in a vacuum to temperatures on the order of 1,500 degrees Celsius.

Properties of Graphite. Graphite is composed of parallel planes of fused hexagonal rings of carbon atoms. It exists in two forms, alpha (also called hexagonal) and beta (also called rhombohedral), which have apparently identical physical properties but differ in their crystal structure. In the alpha form, the carbon atoms in alternate layers are directly above each other, while in the beta form, the carbons do not line up again until every fourth layer. In both forms, the distance between neighboring carbon atoms within the layers is 142 picometers, which is in-termediate between the length of typical single and double C—C bonds. The distance between the layers is 335 picometers. The larger distance between the layers reflects the weaker forces holding the planes together compared with the forces holding neighboring atoms together within the planes.

Because of its weak interplanar forces, the planes can readily slip past each other, causing graphite to cleave easily and preferentially parallel to its planes. This process accounts for its flaky appearance and excellent lubricating ability even when dry. The planar structure also causes several of its physical properties to be highly anisotropic (exhibiting different properties when measured in different directions). For example, its thermal conductivity is several hundred times larger, and its electrical conductivity is several thousand times larger, when measured parallel to the planes than perpendicular to them.

Graphite has the unusual property that it is very soft at room temperature (with a hardness between 0.5 and 1 on the Mohs scale, which is similar to talc) but has increasing strength at high temperatures. At about 2,000 degrees Celsius, its crushing strength is increased by 20 percent, and at about 3,000 degrees Celsius, its tensile strength is increased by 50 to 100 percent. Other important properties of graphite that are exploited in its many uses listed previously are its stability at high temperatures and in the presence of corrosive and reactive chemicals.

FURTHER READING: A comprehensive description of carbon, with a detailed treatment of graphite and diamond, is given in Norman Neill Greenwood and Alan Earnshaw, *Chemistry of the Elements*, 1984. Some of the data it contains, notably production data, and its lack of descriptions of forms of carbon discovered since 1984, are necessarily out of date. A primary resource is the United States Bureau of Mines's *Mineral Commodity Summaries 1988: An Up-to-Date Summary of Eighty-seven Nonfuel Mineral Commodities*, U.S. Government Printing Office, 1988. Most college-level freshman chemistry texts have an overview of the properties of graphite; for example see Ralph H. Petrucci and William S. Harwood, *General Chemistry, Principles and Applications*, 1993. Chris Pellant, *Rocks and Minerals*, 1992, contains a color photograph of natural graphite.

Leslie J. Schwartz

SEE ALSO: Crystals; Diamond; Metamorphic processes, rocks, and mineral deposits; Minerals, structure and physical properties of; Mohs hardness scale; Native elements; Gneiss; Talc.

Grasslands

Grassland ecosystems contain a great diversity of plant and animal life, and grasslands have supported human habitation for tens of thousands of years. Today grasslands are crucial in the growing of crops and the grazing of livestock.

ONE WAY THAT botanists and ecologists classify regions of the earth is according to their vegetation. Woodland, desert, tundra, and grassland are major classifications. All have their own types of climate, physical environment, soil, plants, and animals. Grasslands are so named because the dominant plant species are low plants, most notably various grass species. Throughout the world there are differing types of grasslands—some tropical, some temperate, some with a relatively moderate amount of rainfall, some with very little rainfall that are subject to harsh droughts. Grasslands have many regional names, including shrub steppe, the prairie of North America, and the pampa of South America. A savanna, or parkland, is typically a mixed zone, often considered a transitional region between grassland and forest. A grassland itself may be bordered by desert, parkland, or forest. Humans have lived in grassland environments for thousands of years, and in parts of the world it is impossible to determine which aspects of a grassland ecosystem are natural and which have been changed by countless generations of human activity related to agriculture and the grazing of domesticated animals.

Climate and Fire. The defining characteristics of grassland climates are a marked seasonal variation between the wet and dry seasons and a dry season or overall climate that is too dry for forests to develop. A major distinction can be drawn between temperate and tropical grass-lands, with tropical grasslands having higher temperatures and, generally, greater rainfall. In temperate grasslands annual rainfall is quite low, ranging from 10 to 30 inches (25 to 75 centimeters). In tropical and subtropical grasslands, rainfall is in the range of 25 to 60 inches (60 to 150 centimeters). With their distinct seasonal shifts, many grasslands are subject to monsoons in the rainy season and drought in the dry season. Drought periods may last from several weeks to several months.

Fire is a natural and prominent part of the grassland environment, and lightning fires are common. Fire can serve a number of purposes. As drought does, it can help maintain the grassland boundary, keeping forests from moving into the zone. Perhaps surprisingly, it also fosters the growth of grasses and grasslike plants by burning off old plant layers while leaving the growth zones of new plants, much of which are below the soil line, generally unharmed.

Soil, Plants, and Animals. Grassland and prairie soils are distinct from those of forest regions. Tropical grassland soils are often leached by periods of heavy rain and therefore tend to have relatively low nutrient levels. Temperate grassland soils retain many more of their nutrients and can be rich in humus (organic matter) as well, making them quite fertile. They therefore have long been used for crop production and grazing.

Both the plant and animal communities of grasslands are quite diverse, although grasses may compose up to 90 percent of grassland biomass. Grasses are well adapted to endure drought because of their root masses and because they can reproduce asexually if conditions make seed reproduction impossible. Some also go into a dormant state to survive the dry season. Perennial grasses and forbs are the most common plants, but there are also small shrubs, fungi, lichens, and mosses. In addition, some grasslands do have scattered trees, most often along stream channels. Small grassland animals include birds, reptiles, insects, worms, mice, and prairie dogs. Larger animals include large herbivores such as bison, elk, and wildebeest as well as the carnivores (wolves, the large cat species) that prey on them.

Grasslands and Humans. Humans have lived on, and relied on the resources of, grasslands for at least tens of thousands of years. Hunter-gatherers roamed grasslands and savannas, and the first agriculture was almost certainly practiced in grassland regions. Throughout the world, grasslands have extensively been converted from their natural state to areas used for grazing and crop production. A huge percentage of the world's commercial grains—notably corn, wheat, and soybeans—is grown in temperate grassland regions.

Many ecologists believe that human-induced changes to grasslands can have both positive and negative effects, in some cases stabilizing grassland regions, in others abusing them and unintentionally causing desertification. Humans have introduced non-native species of plants and animals, in some cases replacing native species. Cattle replaced the buffalo and elk that once roamed North America, for example. Grasslands can support a considerable amount of grazing activity, even by non-native animals, as long as overgrazing does not occur. Modern range management techniques are intended to ensure that animal numbers do not exceed a sustainable level. In order to protect their investments in livestock, humans have hunted, and in many areas virtually eliminated, the large grassland carnivores (wolves, bears, cats) that prey on grazing animals.

Human activities can also decrease or damage grassland habitats themselves; chief among these activities are suppressing the fires that are a natural part of grassland environment and draining prairie wetlands. Desertification is a significant problem. It is likely that some areas that have been inhabited by humans for thousands of years—such as lands around the Mediterranean Sea, as well as in Asia Minor, Iran, and India—that are now desertlike were once grasslands. In the twentieth century, desertification caused or exacerbated by human activity has been noted elsewhere—in central Africa, for example.

On the other hand, human activity can stabi-

Although grasses may compose up to 90 percent of grassland biomass, grassland plant and animal communities are diverse. (McCrea Adams)

lize and help maintain grasslands, and in many cases grasslands seem to adapt well to human habitation. One possible positive aspect of livestock grazing is that range managers can potentially control animal numbers and density far more than wild animals can be controlled, providing a stabilizing effect. Finally, there are now ongoing efforts to preserve some of the remaining small regions of relatively unaffected prairie in North America.

FURTHER READING: See Ruth C. Cushman and Stephen R. Jones, *The Shortgrass Prairie*, 1988; R. T. Coupland, ed., Grassland Ecosystems of the *World: Analysis of Grasslands and Their Uses*, 1979; and R. O. Whyte, *Grasslands of the Monsoon*, 1968. *Grasslands and Tundra*, 1985, in the Time-Life Planet Earth series, presents an easily understandable overview and has beautiful color photographs. Two older works that focus on North America are John E. Weaver, *North American Prairie*, 1954, and J. E. Weaver and F. W. Albertson, *Grasslands of the Great Plains*, 1956. M. S. Kipps, *The Production of Field Crops*, 6th ed. 1970, discusses the distribution of farmland, and Harold F. Heady and R. Dennis Child, *Rangeland Ecology and Management*, rev. ed. 1994, is an overview of range management. See also John D. Aber and Jerry M. Melillo, *Terrestrial Ecosystems*, 1991, and Robert H. Whitaker, *Communities and Ecosystems*, 2d ed. 1975.

McCrea Adams

SEE ALSO: Agriculture industry; Desertification; Dust Bowl of the 1930's; Farmland; Overgrazing; Rangeland; Soil management.

Gravel. *See* Sand and gravel

Green Revolution

DATE: Mid-1960's

Impending famine in the 1960's in the underdeveloped countries of Asia, Africa, and Latin America was averted by the Green Revolution, which was made possible by the introduction of hybrid "miracle grains" of wheat and rice.

FROM 1960 TO 1965 a number of poor countries in the world could not produce enough food for their growing populations. Population growth rates had almost doubled to 3.7 billion people in fifty years, with more than 900 million people not getting adequate nourishment to lead productive lives. Famine had been avoided during the post-World War II period of history only because production was high for American farmers and surplus grains were shipped overseas as food aid.

In 1966 and 1967 the Indo-Pakistan subcontinent suffered two consecutive crop failures due to monsoons. The United States shipped one-fifth of its wheat reserves to India and sustained sixty million persons in India for a two-year period on American food shipments. It became obvious as populations continued to grow that the United States would not be able to continue to supply enough food to feed the world's growing population adequately. In the mid-1960's American policy began to change from giving poor countries direct food aid to educating and helping them to increase their own food production.

The United States had, in the 1950's, responded to an ailing agricultural economy in Mexico by sending scientists from the Rockefeller Foundation to develop a new wheat that yielded twice as much grain as traditional varieties. The project was successful, and in 1962 the Rockefeller Foundation collaborated with the Ford Foundation to establish the International Rice Research Institute at Los Banos, in the Philippines. Two strains of rice, PETA from Indonesia and DGWG from China, were crossbred to produce a high-yield semi-dwarf variety of rice called IR-8.

Both the new rice and new wheat were developed to have shorter but stronger and stiffer stalks to support large heads of grain. Yields from the rice and wheat seeds were two to five times higher than traditional varieties as long as they were grown with large inputs of fertilizer, water, and pesticides.

Seeds were shipped to ailing countries. Asia expanded acreage planted in the new varieties from 200 acres to 34 million acres between 1965 and 1969. Pakistan's wheat harvest increased 60 percent between 1967 and 1969. India's production of wheat increased 50 percent, and the Philippines' production of rice was so successful that

The Green Revolution began with the development of high-yield varieties of rice. Pictured is mechanized rice harvesting in South Korea. (Jim West)

it stopped importing rice and became an exporter.

Positive Aspects. The new seeds were dependent on irrigation by tube wells (closed cylindrical shafts driven into the ground) and electrical pumps. Irrigation methods were installed in poor countries. This new availability of year-round water made it feasible for farmers to grow crops year round. The dry season, with its abundant sunlight, had previously been a time when crops could not be grown. With the advent of irrigation, the dry season became an especially productive growing season. Poor countries in tropical and subtropical regions were able to grow two, three, and sometimes four crops a year. Approximately 90 percent of the increase of the world's production of grain in the 1960's, 70 percent in the 1970's, and 80 percent in the 1980's is attributable to the Green Revolution.

The Green Revolution brought to politicians in less-developed countries the realization that

their countries could not depend permanently on food aid from other countries. Whereas leaders and politicians in these countries had previously concentrated on developing industrial projects, the extreme pressure of overpopulation on their limited food and land supplies caused them to address agricultural problems and give emphasis to programs to encourage production of food supplies. Countries that were affected by, and benefited from, the Green Revolution include India, Pakistan, Ceylon, the Philippines, Turkey, Burma, Malaysia, Indonesia, Vietnam, Kenya in East Africa, the Ivory Coast in West Africa, Tunisia, Morocco, Algeria, Libya, Brazil, and Paraguay.

Drawbacks and Environmental Impact. Large-scale pesticide application not only is costly but also can have an adverse effect on the environment. Only a small percentage of insecticides used on crops actually reach the target organism. The rest affects the environment by endangering groundwater, aquatic systems, pollinators, various soil-dwelling insects, microbes, birds, and other animals in the food chain. In addition, large water inputs are needed for proper irrigation of crops. Of the farmers who can afford to irrigate in poor countries, many do not do it properly, and thereby cause salinization, alkalization, and waterlogging of soils, rendering them useless for growing crops.

Large-scale application of fertilizers is costly and reaches a point where further applications do not produce the expected increase in yield and begin to cost far more than they are worth. Crop yields also decrease because of increased soil erosion, loss of soil fertility, aquifer depletion, desertification, and pollution of groundwater or surface waters.

The Green Revolution exemplifies monoculture agriculture, the planting of large areas with a single type of seed. This use of monotypes can create multiple environmental problems. In many cases, the widespread use of genetically homogeneous seed caused old varieties with great genetic variability to be abandoned. Crops consisting entirely of genetically homogeneous rice and wheat are more vulnerable to disease and insects, requiring inputs of agrochemicals which can be harmful to both the environment and human health. Planting vast acreages of monotypes has the potential to result in massive crop failure due to destructive fungi or chemical-resistant insects.

Moreover, Green Revolution techniques rely heavily on fossil fuel to run machinery, to produce and apply inorganic fertilizers and pesticides, and to pump water for irrigation. Gasoline is costly; it also has a history of being in short supply in many of the poor nations. Sociologically, the Green Revolution in poor countries favored wealthier farmers with the capital to pay for the considerable costs of irrigation, seeds, fertilizers, pesticides, and fossil fuels. This fact has accentuated the financial gap between the big and small farmers.

Outlook. The drawbacks of the Green Revolution have led farmers and scientists to seek safer and more diverse solutions to world food needs. Genetic engineers hope to be able to breed high-yield plant strains that have greater resistance to insects and disease, need less fertilizer, and are capable of making their own nitrogen fertilizer so as not to deplete the soil of nutrients. Proponents of integrated pest management (IPM) are investigating combinations of crop rotation, time of planting, field sanitation, and the use of predators and parasites as ways to control insects without the use of harmful chemicals. Regardless of developments in food production and technology, however, in the long term the most important aspect of addressing world food needs is to control population growth.

FURTHER READING: An excellent comprehensive study of the Green Revolution is found in *Seeds of Change*, by Lester R. Brown, 1970. The pros and cons of the Green Revolution are discussed in *Natural Resource Conservation*, by Oliver Owen, 3d ed. 1980, and *Environmental Science*, by Tyler Miller, 4th ed. 1993.

Dion C. Stewart

SEE ALSO: Fertilizers; Genetic diversity; Monoculture agriculture; Pesticides; Population growth; Rice; Wheat.

Greenhouse gases and global climate change

"Greenhouse gases" naturally heat the atmosphere by absorbing heat or infrared radiation from the earth's surface. They include carbon dioxide (CO_2), water vapor, chlorofluorocarbons (CFCs), hydrogenated chlorofluorocarbons (HCFCs), methane (CH_4), nitrous oxide (N_2O), and, to some extent, ozone (O_3). Increased concentrations of these gases since 1880 may be contributing to global climate change.

THE SMALL RISE in the surface air temperature of the earth since 1880 that has accompanied increased concentrations of greenhouse gases is sometimes called "global warming." Discussions of global warming processes have been confused by names that are imprecise and even inaccurate. For example, one commonly used term, the "greenhouse effect," refers to the absorption of terrestrial radiation by atmospheric gases. The gases have been presumed to trap heat the same way the glass of a greenhouse does. In actuality, however, the glass of a greenhouse inhibits heat loss by minimizing mixing with outside air. The greenhouse effect could be more accurately called the "atmospheric effect."

Without carbon dioxide and water vapor, the atmospheric temperature would be too cold to support life. The concern therefore is not with the "greenhouse [atmospheric] effect" itself, which in actuality is necessary for life on Earth. The cause for alarm is the apparent intensification or enhancement of the greenhouse effect, presumably caused by increases in the level of gases in the atmosphere resulting from human activities, especially industrialization. Thus the term "global warming" is a more precise description of this presumed phenomena.

The human activities suspected in global warming include removal of natural vegetation for urban and agricultural purposes, probably resulting in less carbon dioxide being removed and replaced by oxygen. Increased amounts of livestock have led to growing levels of methane. CFCs and HCFCs from aerosol sprays, coolants, and fire extinguishers have also increased.

Possible Effects of Global Warming. With more heat energy existing in the atmosphere, some scientists suspect that the atmosphere and oceans may begin to operate differently from the ways they have over the millennia. Any change in temperature would probably not be uniform over the globe. Since land heats up more quickly than water, the northern hemisphere, with its much larger land masses, would probably have greater temperature increases than the southern hemisphere. Areas that now are very productive agriculturally may no longer be so in the future. Melting of the polar ice caps from warmer temperatures could lead to widespread coastal flooding. Increased heat energy may lead to more intense atmospheric motion and to more severe weather. Higher temperatures might result in more drought, because warmer air usually leads to more evaporation. Similarly, ocean currents might change, both in their direction and in their temperature.

Problems of Prediction and Analysis. Analysis of these effects and predictions for the future are hampered by several factors, including lack of knowledge about all the components affecting

U.S. Greenhouse Gas Emissions
In Millions of Metric Tons

Type and Source	1988	1989	1990	1991	1992	1993	1994
Carbon dioxide (carbon content)	1,376.2	1,385.6	1,373.3	1,360.4	1,380.8	1,406.2	1,430.0
Methane gas	27.56	27.60	27.95	27.94	27.96	26.62	(NA)
Nitrous oxide	.416	.431	.438	.446	.444	.459	(NA)
Nitrogen oxide	21.05	21.08	21.02	20.83	20.84	21.22	(NA)
Nonmethane volatile organic compounds (VOCs)	22.64	21.52	22.01	21.32	20.88	21.14	(NA)
Chlorofluorocarbons (CFCs)	.278	.272	.231	.210	.187	.166	.133
Hydrochlorofluorocarbons (HCFCs)	.074	.076	.084	.091	.102	.112	.135

Source: U.S. Department of Commerce, *Statistical Abstract of the United States, 1996,* 1996.

atmospheric temperature. For example, as atmospheric temperature increases, the oceans would absorb much of that heat so that the atmosphere might not warm so quickly. But since the carbon dioxide absorption capacity of oceans declines as temperature increases, the oceans would be unable to absorb as much carbon dioxide as before (exactly how much is unknown). On the other hand, increased ocean temperatures might lead to more plant growth, including phytoplankton, and to a corresponding greater absorption of carbon dioxide. A warmer atmosphere could hold more water vapor, resulting in the potential for more clouds and more precipitation, thus resulting in lower air temperatures through reflection—or perhaps in higher temperatures through absorption of more infrared radiation. Another complication is that the concentration of water vapor has a much larger impact on the temperature of the atmosphere than does carbon dioxide. The level of water vapor has not yet been directly linked to industrialization.

Past Trends: Natural or Artificial? Whether a direct cause and effect relationship exists between greenhouse gases and surface temperature may be impossible to determine because the atmosphere's temperature has fluctuated widely over millions of years. Over the past 800,000 years, several long periods of very cold temperatures accompanied by glaciers have been interspersed with shorter warm periods. Since the most recent retreat of the glaciers, around 10,000 years ago, the earth has been relatively warm, most probably from natural processes. It should be kept in mind that so far the temperature increase of around 1.0 degree Fahrenheit that some scientists have attributed to greenhouse gases is within the range of normal (historic) trends. The level of atmospheric carbon dioxide remains very small, although it has risen from 0.028 percent of the volume of the atmosphere in 1860 to around 0.035 percent.

Warming has not been consistent since 1880, and for many years cooling occurred. However, the 1980's included some of the hottest years recorded for more than a century. In the early 1990's, temperatures did not keep climbing, perhaps because of ash and sulfur dioxide produced by large volcanoes. Later, temperatures appeared to rise again, indicating that products of volcanic eruptions may have masked the process of global warming.

FURTHER READING: Dean Edwin Abrahamson, ed., *The Challenge of Global Warming*, 1989, summarizes the scientific aspects of global warming and recommends policies to lessen possible consequences. Stephen Schneider, a leading climatologist, in *Global Warming: Are We Entering the Greenhouse Century?* 1989, describes climate mechanisms, makes predictions, and offers possible solutions and means of cooperation among business, government, and individuals. Matthew A. Kraljic, ed., *The Greenhouse Effect*, 1992, is a collection of articles defining the greenhouse effect, discussing the consequences of ignoring the potential problem, and analyzing solutions and policy considerations. John Firor, *The Changing Atmosphere*, 1990, uses climate warming as the center of a discussion of various atmospheric problems and tries to connect these with other economic and political issues. Ian Rowlands, *The Politics of Global Atmospheric Change*, 1995, discusses how political and economic factors influence reactions to proposed changes in carbon dioxide emissions.

Margaret F. Boorstein

SEE ALSO: Chemical Manufacturers Association; Earth Summit in Rio de Janeiro; Environmental law; United Nations Environment Programme.

Greenpeace

DATE FOUNDED: 1969

Greenpeace is an international environmental watchdog organization concerned with protecting the earth's natural resources.

GREENPEACE EVOLVED FROM activists' concerns about nuclear testing near Alaska in the late 1960's. Fearing catastrophic environmental damage, the organization's founders relied on confrontational tactics to draw attention to their cause. Notably, Greenpeace members sought to "bear witness": Simply being present where a

Greenpeace activists protesting the marketing of genetically engineered soybeans in October, 1996. (Reuters/Scott Olson/Archive Photos)

wrongdoing was committed symbolized one's objection to the act. This approach could entail such perilous and controversial tactics as sailing right up to a proposed nuclear test site and daring officials to set off devices with humans within the safety zone.

The idea of "bearing witness" expanded to include several other campaigns intended to protect the earth's natural resources and maintain biodiversity. Its activities on behalf of marine life, especially whales and seals, represented Greenpeace's fight to protect wildlife from human destruction. Through showdown-type encounters with whaling vessels and seal hunters, Greenpeace joined an international call for a decrease in—and ultimately the halting of—whale and seal hunting.

Other environmental issues soon moved the organization into new arenas. Campaigns emerged to arouse people's concern and educate the world to the environmental dangers associated with hazardous waste dumping, toxic chemical production, and global warming.

Greenpeace's techniques, although often controversial, brought international notice to its causes. The organization proved successful in raising public awareness of threats to the earth's natural resources and calling for action to protect them.

Jennifer Davis

SEE ALSO: Earth First!; Environmental ethics; Environmental movement; Friends of the Earth; Hazardous waste disposal; National Audubon Society; Nuclear energy; Sea Shepherd Conservation Society.

Groundwater

Groundwater is that portion of the earth's subsurface water that is contained within the zone of saturation.

It accounts for a much larger fraction of the total volume of water in storage on the earth than all of the combined fresh surface water.

GROUNDWATER IS ONE of the most valuable natural resources. In the United States, excluding hydropower generation and electric power plant cooling, it serves as the source of about 40 percent of the water used for all purposes. However, even though it is so widely used and so vital to the health and economy of all nations, the occurrence of groundwater is not only poorly understood but also subject to many misconceptions. For example, one common misconception is that groundwater flows in large underground rivers that resemble surface streams. Folklore has it that these streams can be detected by certain special individuals who practice "water dowsing." Such misconceptions have retarded the development and conservation of groundwater and have negatively affected the protection of water quality.

Infiltration. Groundwater is a major component of the hydrologic cycle, which is the constant movement of water above, on, and below the earth's surface. That fraction of precipitation that can infiltrate the earth's surface can become part of the subsurface component of the hydrologic cycle. Infiltration rates vary enormously, depending upon the intensity and duration of precipitation, land use, and the physical characteristics and moisture content of the soil. For example, the infiltration rates can range from a high of 25 millimeters per hour in mature forests on sandy soils to only a few millimeters per hour in clayey and silty soils to zero in paved areas.

The Unsaturated Zone. Subsurface water occurs in two distinct zones in the ground. The uppermost zone contains both water and air and is called the unsaturated zone. It is divided into three parts: a soil zone or soil-water belt, an intermediate zone, and the upper part of the capillary fringe. The soil-water belt extends from the top of the land surface to a maximum depth of about 1 to 2 meters. The porosity (the amount of openings in earth material) and the permeability (velocity of fluid flow within the earth material) are higher in the soil-water belt

than in the underlying intermediate zone. The capillary fringe is located in the lowest part of the unsaturated zone and results from the attraction between water and rocks. The thickness or depth of the unsaturated zone varies from zero in swamps to a few meters in humid regions to over 300 meters in deserts.

The Saturated Zone. The zone below the unsaturated zone has all interconnected openings filled with water and is called the saturated zone. The top of the saturated zone is marked by the water table, which is the level to which the hydraulic pressure is equal to atmospheric pressure. Water in the saturated zone is the only subsurface water that supplies wells, springs, and base flow to streams and is the only water which is properly called groundwater.

Groundwater Movement. In sharp contrast to surface water, groundwater moves very slowly. For example, surface water can move tens of kilometers per day, whereas groundwater flow ranges approximately from 1.5 meters per day to as low as 1.5 meters per year. This very slow movement means that any contaminant that gets into groundwater will be there for a long time.

As part of the hydrologic cycle, groundwater also furnishes the stream with base flow or dry-weather flow. This is why streams in humid areas have water flowing in the channel days after precipitation has occurred. Indeed, a large portion of stream flow is derived from base flow which is groundwater.

Groundwater Recharge. The source of groundwater is precipitation in the recharge area that has percolated through the unsaturated zone and reached the water table. Once there, groundwater flows down the hydraulic gradient to discharge areas along flood plains and streams. Average annual recharge rates in the United States range from zero in desert areas to as much as 600 millimeters per year in rural areas in Long Island, New York, and similar places along the Atlantic coastal plain that are underlain by permeable sands. These high recharge rates account for as much as 50 percent of average annual precipitation.

The rate of groundwater movement from recharge areas to discharge areas depends upon the permeability and porosity of the earth material. Shallow groundwater flow to discharge areas can be measured in days as compared with deep groundwater flow which can take decades, centuries or even millennia to reach a discharge area.

Groundwater Quality and Groundwater Pollution. Water is often referred to as the universal solvent because of its ability to dissolve at least small amounts of almost all substances that it contacts. Since groundwater moves very slowly, it has plenty of time to dissolve earth materials. Thus, groundwater usually contains large amounts of dissolved solids.

Groundwater pollution refers to any degradation of water quality that results from anthropogenic activities. In urban and suburban areas, these activities include disposal of industrial and municipal wastes in unlined landfills, leaking sewers, and application of lawn fertilizers, herbicides, and pesticides. Groundwater can be polluted in rural areas by septic tanks, animal feedlots, and application of crop fertilizers, herbicides, and pesticides. Other sources of groundwater pollution include leaking gasoline and home heating oil tanks, salt coming from unprotected stockpiles, and salt-water encroachment in coastal areas that have been overpumped. There have been numerous instances of groundwater pollution, such as municipal wells on Long Island, New York, being forced to close because of a pre-World War II application of fertilizers to potato fields, public supply wells being closed in Massachusetts because of excessive road salt applications, and well fields being contaminated by salt-water encroachment in Dade County, Florida, and Southern California (Manhattan Beach).

FURTHER READING: Excellent textbooks on groundwater include *Applied Hydrogeology*, by Charles W. Fetter, 1994; *Groundwater,* by R. Allan Freeze and John A. Cherry, 1979; and *Groundwater Hydrology*, by David K. Todd, 1980. A very well illustrated introduction to groundwater is *Basic Ground-Water Hydrology*, by Ralph C. Heath, 1983, U.S. Geological Survey Water-Supply Paper 2220. Groundwater quality problems are discussed by Charles W. Fetter in *Contaminant Hydrogeology*, 1993, and by Christopher M. Palmer in *Principles of Contaminant Hydrogeology*, 1992.

Robert M. Hordon

SEE ALSO: Aquifers; Glaciation; Hydrology and the hydrologic cycle; U.S. Geological Survey; Water; Water pollution and water pollution control; Water supply systems; Wetlands.

Guano

Accumulated bird excrement rich in nitrogen is known as guano. This renewable natural fertilizer is found in commercial quantities only on a few desert islands where millions of fish-eating sea birds roost undisturbed.

THERE IS ARCHAEOLOGICAL EVIDENCE that guano was collected and used by prehistoric Peruvian farmers, who called it *huano.* Nineteenth century application of guano to the exhausted soils of Europe was first advocated by the German agronomist Georg Leibig after its introduction in the 1830's by the noted scientist and South American explorer Baron Alexander von Humboldt. The dramatic increases it caused in wheat, corn, and cotton production created enormous demand for this product, which was soon being dug by hundreds of Chinese laborers forced to work on the Chinchas Islands south of Lima, Peru.

These rain-free guano islands are populated by millions of cormorants, gannets, and pelicans that fly out to sea daily to eat anchovies and sardines. The fish themselves feed on plankton they find in the cold, north-flowing Chile-Peru (Humboldt) Current. When this current is occasionally displaced by a warm (El Niño) countercurrent, the entire ecosystem collapses, and many sea birds begin to die of starvation.

A guano boom began in 1851, when the U.S. Congress passed legislation allowing any American citizen to declare uninhabited guano islands as territory of the United States. Under the provisions of this little-known act, several Caribbean and South Pacific islands were so claimed. One of them, Navassa, located midway between Cuba and Haiti, remains an undisputed U.S. territorial possession to this day under jurisdiction of the Coast Guard. Subfossil guano deposits found there are thought to be the excrement of a fish-eating bat.

Although the Peruvian government recognized guano as a strategic and highly valuable natural resource, little was done to protect the industry from foreign interests and political intrigue. In order to meet financial obligations and service debts, the government mortgaged its guano resources for quick cash loans from foreign business firms selling the increasingly valuable Chinchas guano.

Failure to protect the guano-producing birds, as well as ignorance of the complex ecology of their habitat, eventually resulted in the decline of the industry in the face of overwhelming competition from Chilean sodium nitrate deposits discovered in the 1870's. Not until the 1910's was any progress made in reviving the resource. Based on the advice of foreign ichthyologists and the American ornithologist Robert Cushman Murphy, good conservation practices were begun by Francisco Ballén, director of the newly created *Compañía Administradora del Guano.*

The impact of several disastrous El Niño events beginning in 1925, together with severe overfishing of anchovy stocks, has seriously retarded the buildup of new Peruvian guano deposits. Instead of hundreds of sailing clippers waiting to take on cargos, today only a single derelict hull is towed to the Chinchas periodically to harvest this "white gold." No longer exported, it is now used exclusively for the benefit of Peruvian agriculture.

Guano is also collected elsewhere in the world and used locally; farmers in Baja, California, and some regions of western Africa, for example, use it as fertilizer. Bat-guano deposits often occur in caves with sufficiently large bat populations. Seal excrement is also sometimes included in the definition of guano. Bird guano, however, has a higher concentration of fertilizing nutrients (notably nitrogen and phosphoric acid) than either bat or seal guano.

From the study of any deep undisturbed sequence of guano may come a valuable scientific record of environmental conditions that prevailed while it was accumulating. Identifying and dating ancient layers showing disturbed conditions can give statistical clues to hidden climatic cycles and the ability to predict future long-range changes in weather patterns.

Alan K. Craig

SEE ALSO: Fertilizers; Nitrogen and ammonia.

Gypsum

WHERE FOUND: Gypsum is the most common sulfate mineral. It is widely distributed in sedimentary rocks, frequently occurring with limestones and shales. It is commonly associated with minerals such as rock salt, anhydrite, dolomite, calcite, sulfur, pyrite, galena, and quartz. Gypsum is mined extensively in many parts of the world.

PRIMARY USES: Gypsum is used in the construction industry, especially for the manufacture of plasters, wallboard, and tiles; in cements; as a filler in paper and paints; and as a fertilizer and soil conditioner.

DESCRIPTION: Gypsum is a hydrated calcium sulfate ($CaSO_4 \bullet 2H_2O$). Its average molecular weight is 172.18, and its specific gravity is 2.32. This mineral forms white or colorless prismatic crystals; impurities may add a grayish, reddish, yellowish, bluish, or brownish tint. Its hardness on the Mohs scale is 1.5 to 2. Gypsum has a characteristic three-way cleavage; that is, it breaks along three different crystallographic planes. It is insoluble in water and soluble in acids. When heated to 190 to 200 degrees Celsius, gypsum loses three-quarters of its water of crystallization to become calcium sulfate hemihydrate ($2CaSO_4 \bullet H_2O$), also known as plaster of paris. Heating to over 600 degrees Celsius drives off all water to produce anhydrous or dead-burned gypsum.

GYPSUM, A WIDELY DISTRIBUTED sedimentary deposit, is a soft, colorless, or light-colored mineral that can be scratched with the fingernail. Its crystals often form arrowhead-shaped or swallowtail-shaped twins (two individual crystals joined along a plane). When heated to drive off much of its water of crystallization, gypsum is transformed into plaster of paris (so named because of the famous gypsum deposits of the Montmartre district of Paris, France). When reduced to a powder and mixed with water, plaster of paris forms a slurry that sets quickly and gradually reforms again as tiny interlocking crystals of gypsum. Its properties as a natural plaster make gypsum an important resource for construction and other industries. In 1994 the United States mined 17,200,000 metric tons of gypsum, and total world production was 101,000,000 metric tons.

Historical Background. The Chinese, Assyrians, and Greeks made decorative carvings from gypsum. The Greek philosopher Theophrastus (371-287 B.C.E.) wrote of burning gypsum to create plaster. Gypsum's properties as a plaster were also known to the early Egyptians, who used a crude gypsum plaster in such building projects as the pyramids. Gypsum gained widespread use as a soil conditioner in eighteenth century Europe. The development of a commercial method for retarding the setting of gypsum plaster in 1885 made it possible to use gypsum for more construction applications.

Gypsum forms white or colorless crystals; it typically has a three-way cleavage (breaks along three planes). (U.S. Geological Survey)

Distribution of Gypsum. Gypsum, the most common sulfate mineral, is widely distributed in sedimentary rocks. It forms thick, extensive evaporite beds, especially in rocks of Permian and Triassic age. In the United States, gypsum is present in rocks of every geologic era except the Cambrian. Because gypsum is normally deposited before anhydrite and salt during the evaporation of sea water, it often underlies beds of these minerals. Other minerals with which gypsum is frequently associated include dolomite, calcite, sulfur, pyrite, galena, quartz, and petroleum source rocks. Massive layers of gypsum frequently occur interbedded with limestones and shales, and lens-shaped bodies or scattered crystals are found in clays and shales. Gypsum is common in volcanic regions, particularly where limestones have been acted upon by sulfur vapors. It is also found in association with sulfide ore bodies. Extensive gypsum deposits are found in many localities throughout the world, including New York, Michigan, Iowa, Texas, Nevada, California, Great Britain, France, Spain, Germany, and Italy. In Arizona and New Mexico there are large deposits in the form of wind-blown sand.

Environmental Forms. Gypsum occurs in nature in five varieties: gypsum rock, a bedded aggregate consisting mostly of the mineral gypsum; gypsite, an impure, earthy variety that is found in association with gypsum-bearing strata in arid regions; alabaster, a massive, fine-grained form, white or delicately shaded and often translucent; satin spar, a white, translucent mineral with a fibrous structure and a silky luster; and selenite, a transparent, colorless, crystalline variety.

Gypsum is rarely found in its pure form. Deposits may contain quartz, sulfide minerals, carbonates, and clayey and bituminous materials. Gypsum dehydrates readily in nature to form anhydrite ($CaSO_4$), a mineral with which it is often associated; bassanite ($2CaSO_4 \cdot H_2O$) forms much more rarely. High-temperature and low-humidity environments favor the formation of anhydrite. Anhydrite can also hydrate to form gypsum. Gypsum deposits formed by the alteration of anhydrite may show folding due to the increased volume of the mineral in its hydrated state.

Obtaining and Using Gypsum. Gypsum is generally obtained through open-pit mining, although some underground mining is performed where the material is of a high quality or is close to the

Reflecting the widespread use of gypsum in the construction industry, the U.S. Gypsum Company refers to the location of its California mine as "Plaster City." (U.S. Geological Survey)

consuming market. Gypsum may be crushed and ground for use in dihydrate form, heated to produce plaster of paris, or completely dehydrated to form anhydrous gypsum.

Unaltered gypsum is commonly used to slow the rate of setting in portland cement. Other major uses include the manufacture of wallboard, gypsum lath, and artificial marble products. Its sulfate contents make it useful for agriculture, where it serves as a soil conditioner and fertilizer. Gypsum is used as a white pigment, filler, or glaze in paints, enamels, pharmaceuticals, and paper. It is also used in making crayons, chalk, and insulating coverings for pipes and boilers. Other uses are as a filtration agent and a nutrient in yeast growing.

Plaster of paris is used for builder's plaster and the manufacture of plaster building materials such as moldings and panels. In medicine, plaster of paris is used for surgical casts, bandages, and supports and for taking dental and other impressions. The anhydrous form of gypsum is used in cement formulations; in metallurgy; in the manufacture of tiles, plate glass, pottery, and paints; and as a paper filler. Because of its water-absorbing nature, it is also used as a drying agent.

Alabaster, a form of gypsum that can be carved and polished with ease because of its softness, is fashioned into ornamental vessels, figures, and statuary. Satin spar is used in jewelry and other ornaments.

FURTHER READING: Additional information can be found in Gordon T. Austin, "Gypsum," in the U.S. Bureau of Mines' *Minerals Yearbook, 1994* (vol. 1, *Metals and Minerals*), 1996; Jean W. Pressler, "Gypsum," in the Bureau of Mines' *Mineral Facts and Problems*, 1985; and Robert L. Bates, *Geology of the Industrial Rocks and Minerals*, 1969. An older but still useful reference is A. W. Groves, *Gypsum and Anhydrite*, 1958.

Karen N. Kähler

SEE ALSO: Cement and concrete; Evaporites; Fertilizers; Mohs hardness scale; Sedimentary processes, rocks, and mineral deposits.

Haber-Bosch process

A chemical process, developed in Germany in the early twentieth century, that enables nitrogen to be obtained from the atmosphere and transformed into ammonia, thus making it usable in products such as chemicals, pharmaceuticals, and fertilizers.

ALL LIVING THINGS need nitrogen. It is an essential component of compounds such as proteins and amino acids. Unfortunately, although plants and animals live in a world surrounded by nitrogen gas (78 percent of the atmosphere is nitrogen gas, a relatively inert compound), little of it is available to them. The stability of nitrogen gas, because of the strength of the triple bond in the molecule, means that of all nutrients in the biosphere, nitrogen is one of the least available nutrients for plant and animal growth. Only a few specialized bacteria, in a process called biological nitrogen fixation, are able to utilize the nitrogen gas surrounding them.

The Haber-Bosch process mimics biological nitrogen fixation on an industrial scale. One molecule of nitrogen gas (N_2) and three molecules of hydrogen gas (H_2) are combined to yield two molecules of ammonia (NH_3):

$$N_{2D} + 3H_2 \leftrightarrow 2NH_3$$

The reaction is reversible, and there is no tendency for ammonia to form unless an enzyme catalyst is used (as in biological nitrogen fixation) or the reaction is conducted at extremely high temperatures (450 degrees Celsius, or 842 degrees Fahrenheit) and extremely high pressures (200 atmospheres) in the presence of an iron catalyst.

The Haber-Bosch process, named for Fritz Haber (1868-1934) and Carl Bosch (1874-1940), two Nobel Prize-winning German chemists, was the first commercially successful process to overcome the chemical inertness of nitrogen gas and allow it to be transformed into ammonia, which can be utilized as a nitrogen fertilizer for plant growth. Fritz Haber developed the process in his laboratory at Karlsruhe, Germany. Carl Bosch made its industrial application possible by scaling up the laboratory process for his employers

at Badische Anilin und Soda Fabrik (BASF) in Ludwigshafen, Germany.

More than 80 million metric tons of nitrogen are produced by the Haber-Bosch process each year, almost half of what biological nitrogen fixation is thought to produce. Much is used directly for fertilizer. Most, however, is used for other processes, such as production of nitrogen-containing chemicals, pharmaceuticals, and explosives. The Haber-Bosch process, which became a commercial reality when the first plant began operating in 1913, allowed Germany to continue making armaments and explosives despite a blockade of its ports by England in World War I.

It is an energy-intensive reaction. The nitrogen in the Haber-Bosch process comes from air, but the hydrogen generally comes from the reaction of natural gas or methane with steam at high temperatures. Consequently, most of the cost associated with the process comes from the hydrocarbons used to heat the system and supply the hydrogen. As a result, the price of fertilizer nitrogen tends to fluctuate with the price of energy. The oil embargo instituted in 1973 by the Organization of Petroleum Exporting Countries (OPEC) had a trickle-down effect on agriculture, since it raised the cost of energy required for the Haber-Bosch process enormously. As a result, it had the unintended effect of stimulating research in biological nitrogen fixation as a cheaper alternative for improving the nitrogen fertility of soil.

Mark S. Coyne

SEE ALSO: Agriculture industry; Eutrophication; Fertilizers; Food shortages; Nitrogen and ammonia; Oil Embargo and energy crises of 1973 and 1979; Organization of Petroleum Exporting Countries; Soil management.

Halite. *See* Salt

Hazardous waste disposal

Hazardous waste disposal involves the care and remediation of solid or liquid wastes that have certain harmful effects on the environment or human health.

HAZARDOUS WASTES ARE largely the product of industrial society. Produced both by industry and by households, they pose hazards to human health and the environment. Remediation and cleanup of these wastes involves substantial economic cost. In the United States in the early 1990's, approximately 97 percent of all hazardous waste was produced by 2 percent of the waste generators. Beginning in the 1970's the United States and other Western democracies tried to regulate hazardous waste disposal. Hazardous waste disposal is also a serious problem in the countries of the former Soviet Union and in other Eastern European nations. Improper disposal of hazardous waste causes numerous environmental and health problems. For example, wastes placed in unlined landfills or lagoons may leach into surrounding soil and water supplies over time, while wastes placed in metal drums can corrode the drums and leak.

The Nature of Hazardous Waste. Hazardous waste disposal can release chemicals into the air, surface water, groundwater, and soil. High-risk wastes are those known to contain significant concentrations of constituents that are highly toxic, persistent, mobile, and bioaccumulative. Examples include dioxin-based wastes, polychlorinated biphenyls (PCBs), and cyanide wastes. Intermediate-risk wastes may include metal hydroxide sludges, while low-level wastes are generally high-volume low-hazard materials. Radioactive waste is a special category of hazardous waste, often presenting extremely high risk. Hazardous waste thus presents varying degrees of health and environmental hazard. When combined, two relatively low-risk materials may pose a high risk.

Factors that affect the health risk of hazardous waste for individuals include dosage received, age, gender, body weight, and weather conditions. The health effects posed by hazardous waste include carcinogenesis (the ability to cause cancer), genetic defects, reproductive abnormalities, and negative effects on the central nervous system. Environmental degradation resulting from hazardous waste can potentially render various natural resources, such as cropland or forests, useless. It may also harm animal life. Because the amount of waste in any period

is based on the amount of natural resources used up, the generation of both hazardous and nonhazardous waste poses a threat to the sustainability of the economy.

Means of Handling Hazardous Waste. In the past, because there were no standards for what constituted a hazardous waste, these materials were often buried or simply stored in unattended drums or other containers. This situation created a threat to the environment and human health when the original containers began to leak or the material leached into the water supply.

The technology for dealing with hazardous solid and liquid waste continues to evolve. By the 1990's there were two preferred solutions, and they both had a positive impact on reducing contamination of natural resources. The first approach is to reduce the volume of the waste material by generating less of it. The second is to recycle the hazardous material as much as possible. A third means of dealing with hazardous waste is to treat it so as to render it less harmful and often to reduce its volume. The least-preferred solution was to store the waste in a landfill.

Often hazardous waste is treated so as to reduce its toxicity. This can be accomplished by physical, chemical, or biological means. High-temperature incineration, for example, reduces such compounds as PCBs into safe products such as water and carbon dioxide. Incineration does not work for all liquids and solids, however, and it may produce highly toxic ash and sludge. Technologies such as the use of extremely high temperature (in the range of 10,000 degrees Celsius) plasma torches have the potential to reduce some hazardous wastes to harmless gases. Biotransformation is a process that simplifies a harmful compound into less harmful compounds; mineralization is a complete breakdown of organic materials into water, carbon dioxide, cellular mass, and inert inorganic residuals. Some hazardous solids that cannot be treated are stored in specially designed hazardous waste landfills.

The Statutory and Regulatory Framework. The basic statutory and regulatory framework for dealing with hazardous waste comes from the 1976

High-temperature treatment is one method of reducing waste toxicity. Here technicians control a toxic materials reactor in Fall River, Massachusetts, that immerses waste in extremely hot molten metal. (Reuters/Jim Bourg/Archive Photos)

amendments to the Solid Waste Disposal Act, which forms the basis for the Resource Conservation and Recovery Act (RCRA). RCRA was completely rewritten in 1984, and regulations resulting from it continued to be issued well into the 1990's. The Environmental Protection Agency (EPA) has published a list of more than five hundred chemical products and mixtures considered to be hazardous on *prima facie* grounds. EPA defines other substances to be hazardous based on four criteria: ignitability, corrosivity, reactivity, and toxicity. The EPA also established standards for responsibility and tracking of hazardous wastes, based on the principle that waste generators are responsible for their waste "from cradle to grave."

This principle has involved extensive record-keeping by waste generators and disposal sites as well as technical standards for disposal facilities including landfills, incinerators, and storage tanks. Landfills must have liners, have collection systems above the liners to trap liquid wastes that might leak out, and adhere to inspection and post-closure standards. Facilities that incinerate hazardous wastes must achieve a 99.99 percent reduction of the principal organic hazardous constituents. Emission and reduction standards were also set for other constituents. All surface storage tanks must have containment systems to minimize leaks and spills.

Congress' 1984 RCRA revisions involved a thorough overhaul of the legislation. Previously, sources that generated between 100 and 1,000 kilograms of hazardous waste per month were exempt from the provisions of RCRA. The 1984 provisions brought them under RCRA. Congress further tried to force the EPA to adopt a bias against landfilling of hazardous waste with the provision, "[N]o land disposal unless proven safe." Congress also added underground storage

Disposal of Hazardous Waste Products

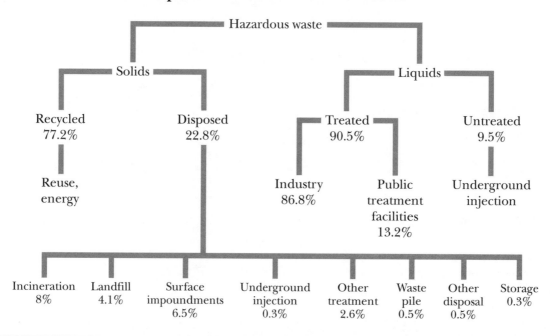

tanks for gasoline, petroleum, pesticides, and solvents to the list of facilities to be regulated and remediated.

RCRA was designed to deal with present and future hazardous wastes; it did not deal with material that had already been disposed of in some way. Congress passed the Comprehensive Environmental Response, Liability, and Compensation Act of 1980 (CERCLA), better known as Superfund, to deal with existing hazardous waste sites. Superfund was further amended in 1986 by the Superfund Amendments and Reauthorization Act (SARA). Superfund requires the EPA to regulate past hazardous waste disposal sites and to conduct the cleanup of such sites. EPA was required to devise a plan for the identification of these sites, select appropriate remedies, determine who will pay for the cleanup, and clean up the site. The resulting National Priority List identified more than twelve hundred priority hazardous waste sites. Superfund legislation did not specify the degree of restoration required, although the original standards required that sites be returned to conditions comparable to the standards established under existing envi-

ronmental legislation. Cleanup costs are often extremely high, yet full cleanup is often difficult, if not impossible, to obtain. Superfund also directed EPA to proceed with cleanup even while engaged in litigation against responsible parties ("shovels first"), a situation which has also increased the costs of implementation. The EPA has not been able to resolve the issue of how clean is clean enough for Superfund sites.

Compliance costs for RCRA and Superfund are substantial. By the early 1990's, yearly cost estimates for RCRA ranged from two to seven billion dollars. Some firms were already beginning to decrease their waste streams, however, so it continues to be difficult to estimate compliance costs. Estimates for cleaning up Superfund sites vary dramatically, depending on the degree of cleanup achieved. One set of figures is based on an average cost of thirty million dollars for each of two thousand Superfund sites, with a total of sixty billion dollars.

Not all hazardous waste falls under the RCRA rubric. When Congress drafted RCRA, several categories of waste were purposefully omitted: radioactive waste, mining waste, biomedical waste, military waste, and household waste. Superfund deals with all categories of dormant sites except for radioactive waste. Several other statutes (and ensuing EPA regulations) deal with these aspects of the hazardous waste problem.

Where Will Our Hazardous Waste Go? The costs for the cleanup and remediation of hazardous waste are substantial and are likely to continue to grow. This situation is particularly true in Eastern Europe and the former Soviet Union, where he magnitude of past dumping of hazardous materials is slowly becoming apparent. Less-industrialized nations are largely ignoring the hazardous waste issue in the mid-1990's, focusing instead on increasing productivity and the standard of living), but it will become an issue in the future.

The waste-minimization philosophy expressed in RCRA is a sound long-range strategy for dealing with hazardous waste. Some materials will have to continue to be deposited in landfills. Incineration offers a partial solution to reducing the volume of material, yet it poses an air-quality dilemma, as it can produce a highly toxic ash, often laden with heavy metals. As some firms have found, minimizing their waste stream affords them economic benefits as well as conserving natural resources. Household waste, which is not regulated by RCRA, often include minute quantities of hazardous materials, such as pesticides, and most of this waste was being landfilled in the mid-1990's. The cleanup of existing sites will continue to be a troubling problem, fraught with high cost and emotional controversies. The cleanup and disposal of radioactive civilian and military waste will be another major issue for the future.

FURTHER READING: Useful accounts of methods for dealing with hazardous waste are Michael D. LaGrega, Philip L. Buckingham, and Jeffrey C. Evans, *Hazardous Waste Management*, 1994, and Paul R. Portney, ed., *Public Policies for Environmental Protection*, 1990. Other helpful works include Joe Grisham, *Health Aspects of the Disposal of Waste Chemicals*, 1986, and Michael B. Gerrard, *Whose Backyard, Whose Risk*, 1994.

John M. Theilmann

SEE ALSO: Environmental Protection Agency; Incineration of wastes; Landfills; Mining wastes and mine reclamation; Nuclear waste and its disposal; Superfund legislation and cleanup activities.

Health, resource exploitation and

Pollution and other types of environmental degradation, unfortunate side-effects of resource exploitation, affect human health. Workers who mine or process resources are particularly susceptible to adverse effects because of repeated exposures or exposures at high concentrations. When the obtaining, processing, or consuming of resources disseminates pollutants throughout air, soil, or water, public health is affected as well.

HUMAN WELL-BEING IS inextricably linked to the earth's natural resources. These resources provide food, shelter, and warmth, as well as transportation, medicine, and a host of other improvements, conveniences, and luxuries that enhance the quality of life. Ironically, however, the act of exploiting resources can so affect the environment that human health is affected. Resources that are toxic (such as mercury and lead) or radioactive (such as uranium) become pollutants when mining, processing, or consumption releases them into the air, the water, and the food chain. Other wastes generated through resource exploitation are also discharged into the environment, compromising its ability to sustain life. Through overuse and misuse, human populations deplete and degrade soil and water, essential resources upon which their survival depends. Increasing population size makes it harder for ecosystems to withstand the stresses imposed upon them so that they cannot simultaneously meet human demands for materials, absorb wastes, and act as a life-support system. The growing population is also exhausting its frontiers: As pristine and productive areas disappear, so does the option of simply moving away from polluted or damaged ecosystems.

Modern societies recognize that resource exploitation involves tradeoffs. The needs and desires of the earth's huge human population cannot be met without some disruption of the environment or some risk to workers and public health. Risk-management efforts such as regulation and environmental cleanup are intended to minimize such adverse effects, notably where human exposure to chemicals is involved. Risk management relies heavily on risk assessments—science-based estimates that combine information on exposure levels and toxicity to assess the type and magnitude of human health risk a particular substance poses. Such estimates may be expressed as a probability (for instance, one additional case of cancer per thousand people) or a range of likely probabilities. Risk managers who determine acceptable exposure levels, impose restrictions on the use of toxic chemicals, and make other regulatory and policy decisions to protect human health base their decisions on risk-assessment results, economic considerations, legal constraints, and social concerns.

Laws, policies, and practices that pertain to resource exploitation and other activities that can degrade the environment have been influenced by an increasing public awareness of the associated health risks. Community opposition to the presence of dangerous or aesthetically offensive facilities in its vicinity—known as the "not in my back yard (NIMBY) syndrome"—often can keep an undesired operation out of a community. However, the NIMBY syndrome tends to push such facilities into minority and low-income communities that lack the financial and political clout to resist them. These areas generally experience more severe environmental contamination and are subjected to higher concentrations of harmful pollutants than their majority counterparts. Along the lower 85 miles of the Mississippi River, for instance, low-income residents share the area with over a hundred oil refineries and petrochemical plants; many experts attribute above-average incidences of cancers, massive tumors, and miscarriages among the residents to chemical pollution and have even dubbed the area "Cancer Alley."

The unequal societal distribution of environmental damage and health risk—known as "environmental injustice" or "environmental racism"—exists on a global scale as well. Developed nations often export environmentally controversial operations or products to developing countries. There, where unsafe water and inadequate sewage facilities are common, drinking and washing in water from tainted streams and wells can expose people to toxic pollutants. Economic considerations have led many mining and industrial operations to move from the United States to developing countries whose regulations pertaining to environmental protection, labor, and the like are often less restrictive. Similarly, manufacturers of dichloro-diphenyl-trichloroethane (DDT) and related pesticides—chemicals banned in the United States—continue to supply the pesticides to developing countries.

Occupational Health. Workers who obtain or process resources have the potential to be exposed to a set of harmful substances and conditions on a regular basis. Common workplace hazards include toxic chemicals, airborne dust, poor ventilation, noise, high humidity, and extremes of heat and cold. In the developed nations, efforts by labor organizations, management, and government to protect worker health have helped to track and control the incidence of work-related injuries and illnesses. Government agencies such as the United States' Occupational Safety and Health Administration (OSHA) and Mine Safety and Health Administration (MSHA) oversee and enforce regulations pertaining to such things as acceptable exposure levels, protective clothing, and health and safety training and notification of workers. Developing countries, however, often lack effective occupational health standards or enforcement. Workers there are also less likely to receive sufficient training or equipment to carry out their jobs safely.

In workers around the world, common occupational illnesses include hearing loss caused by excessive noise, skin disorders resulting from chemical exposures, lead poisoning, pesticide poisoning, and respiratory diseases resulting from particulate inhalation. Particulates are a problem in many industries: Wood, cotton, and mineral dusts, for instance, all can induce illness if inhaled. Particles measuring 0.5 to 5 micrometers in diameter settle in the lungs and, over time, can cause severe respiratory disease. The most well-publicized of the particulate-related illnesses are found among miners and mineral-processing workers. Coal miners are susceptible to black lung disease, a lung disorder caused by coal-dust inhalation. Silicosis, a fibrous lung disease brought on by silica dust, affects workers in quarries and limestone mines.

Perhaps the most notorious of the disease-causing particulates is asbestos. A useful fibrous mineral able to resist heat, friction, and chemical corrosion, asbestos was widely used through much of the twentieth century as an insulating and fireproofing material and as a strengthener in cement and plastics. Only after decades of use and dissemination throughout the urban environment was asbestos recognized as a health hazard. Inhaling asbestos fibers can cause asbestosis, a chronic lung inflammation whose symptoms may not appear until twenty to thirty years after exposure. More than 50 percent of asbestosis patients eventually die from lung cancer. Persons working directly with asbestos are most likely to be affected; however, extensive use of the mineral in public buildings, private residences, and consumer goods may place the general public at risk as well. (There has been considerable debate as to the seriousness of the asbestos danger to people not actively working with the material; some studies have indicated that the risk to the general population is actually quite small.)

In 1973, as part of the Clean Air Act, the United States Environmental Protection Agency (EPA) was charged with developing and enforcing regulations to protect the general public from asbestos exposure, notably during building demolition and renovation and asbestos-waste transport and disposal. In the 1980's, the EPA issued regulations controlling asbestos in schools and other public buildings. OSHA also promulgated standards that covered occupational exposures. While asbestos is still in use, its consumption has declined precipitously since the 1970's because of regulatory and economic factors and the increased use of alternative materials.

Effects of Air Pollution. Fuel consumption by motor vehicles is a major source of urban air pollution in many cities. Vehicles emit nitrogen oxides, which mix with water vapor to form acid precipitation. Nitrogen oxides may exacerbate some chronic lung ailments and reduce the body's natural immune response. In urban areas where leaded gasoline is still in use—notably in Latin America, Asia, and Eastern Europe—vehicle emissions are also a significant source of dispersed lead. Lead exposure is associated with neurological damage and motor-physical impairment in children. Blood-lead concentrations in the United States have decreased substantially since leaded fuels were phased out in the late 1970's.

Electric power plants that burn fossil fuels (oil, natural gas, and coal) are another source of nitrogen oxides. They also emit sulfur dioxide, particularly when high-sulfur coal is used. Like nitrogen oxide, sulfur dioxide produces acid precipitation. Normally, when inhaled, sulfur dioxide will react with moisture in the upper respiratory tract to produce sulfuric acid; however, if sulfur dioxide adheres to a respirable particle, it can travel deeper into the lungs and have a greater impact on health. The adsorption of sulfur dioxide onto coal particulates is believed to have been responsible for the severity of London's coal-smog disaster of 1952, which ultimately claimed around four thousand lives. In that year heavy use of coal-fired home heaters during a chilly December produced a thick smog that blanketed the city for four days and exacerbated existing respiratory illnesses, particularly in children and the elderly.

In the developing countries, smoky fuels (crop residues, wood, charcoal, and coal) used for cooking and heating in homes are a significant health hazard. Particulates from these fuels irritate the respiratory tract, contribute to chronic lung diseases such as bronchitis, emphysema, and asthma, and increase the risk of cancer. Women and children are most affected by smoky household fuels. In Beijing, the number of households using these fuels has been great enough that overall city air quality has been affected.

Effects of Water Pollution. The earth's streams, rivers, lakes, and oceans are multiple-use resources. They supply humankind with water and food, serve as a means for travel and transport, and provide recreation and scenic beauty. They also are widely employed for waste disposal, which frequently conflicts with their other uses. Industrial wastes introduce toxic organic chemicals and heavy metals into aquatic ecosystems, polluting the water and tainting the food chain. Industrial pollution of water was found to be responsible for an epidemic of organic mercury poisoning among the residents of Minamata, Japan, that was first identified during the 1950's. Mercury-containing wastes discharged into Minamata Bay by a plastics and petrochemical company contaminated fish and shellfish with methyl mercury. Residents who ate the seafood subsequently developed a profound central nervous system disorder. More than a thousand persons were ultimately identified as victims of Minamata disease.

Untreated or poorly treated human sewage is another hazardous pollutant of water. Aqueous discharge of this material introduces harmful bacteria and viruses that make waters unsafe for human consumption, washing, or recreation. In developing countries, where sewage is often released into open waterways, this practice can contribute to the spread of potentially fatal illnesses such as diarrheal disease and cholera.

Effects of Agrochemicals. Pesticides are used extensively in agriculture, as well as in forestry and rangeland management. Indiscriminate and excessive pesticide application has dire consequences for the environment and human health. Pesticides can enter the human body by being inhaled, by being ingested in drinking water or on food, and in some cases by being absorbed through the skin. Exposure at sufficiently high concentrations causes immediate pesticide poisoning. Where safety precautions are disregarded, the potential for overexposure is great. Exposure to lower concentrations has health implications as well. Environmentally persistent chemicals such as DDT, which do not readily break down after application, accumulate in body tissues and in the food chain. Many pesticides are immunotoxins, which even at low concentrations alter the human immune system and make a person more prone to contracting infectious disease. Children, the elderly, and persons whose health is already compromised are particularly susceptible. Pesticides may also weaken the immune system's ability to combat

certain cancers, such as Hodgkin's disease, melanoma, and leukemia.

Synthetic fertilizers are another type of agrochemical whose indiscriminate use poses a health risk. Nitrate that is not absorbed by crops can infiltrate into groundwater and thus contaminate drinking water. In infants, nitrate induces methemoglobinemia, or "blue baby syndrome," a serious and often fatal blood disease. The nitrate is converted in the infant's intestines to nitrite, which inhibits the blood's ability to carry oxygen. Brain damage or death by suffocation may result. In the United States, numerous cases of methemoglobinemia have been reported in California, Illinois, Missouri, Minnesota, and Wisconsin.

Effects of Radioactivity. Radioactive emissions occur when uranium is mined, milled, processed, and transported. Nuclear fission and breeder reactors also emit low levels of radiation; reprocessing plants that recover uranium-235 and plutonium from spent fuel rods emit more radiation than properly operating nuclear power plants. High-level radioactive wastes—which include spent fuel from reactors and radioactive water from nuclear power plants, reprocessing operations, and temporary spent-rod storage—require long-term storage in repositories capable of keeping the material safely isolated from the environment. While normal operations involve relatively low-level emissions, major accidents at nuclear power plants can introduce massive amounts of radioactivity into the environment.

Persons exposed to high radiation dosages (of 1000 rads or greater) die as a result of internal-organ damage and bone-marrow destruction. Humans may survive the symptoms of exposure to lower levels of radiation (100 to 1000 rads)—radiation burns, vomiting, diarrhea, fever, hair loss, and internal bleeding—but may experience subsequent genetic effects in the form of cancer and damage to sperm and ova. According to the National Academy of Sciences, a continuous exposure of 0.1 rem per year throughout a lifetime would be expected to produce 5.6 cancers per 1,000 people. The average person in the United States receives an annual radiation dosage of 0.3 rem from natural sources, 0.053 rem from medical sources, and less than 0.001 rem from nuclear power.

The 1986 explosion and reactor fire at the Chernobyl nuclear power plant in the former Soviet Union released approximately 185 million curies of radiation. Radiation spread across twenty countries, contaminating livestock and crops and exposing human populations as far away as West Germany, Sweden, and the United Kingdom. As of 1989, unsafe radiation levels (over 15 curies per square kilometer) were reportedly present in portions of Byelorussia (about 7,000 square kilometers), Russia (about 2,000 square kilometers), and Ukraine (about 1,500 square kilometers). It is unclear how many persons have died as a result of the Chernobyl disaster; reported deaths range all the way from 600 to 32,000. As of the mid-1990's, health effects attributed to the Chernobyl incident included a 10 to 15 percent increase in neuropsychological disorders in Ukraine and a tenfold increase in the rate of thyroid cancer among Ukrainian children.

Effects of Environmental Change. When resource exploitation imposes stresses on an ecosystem that cause it to change significantly, human health is frequently affected. Environmental change can deprive a community of food or fuel, make it more susceptible to diseases, or have other adverse effects. If environmental degradation is so severe as to force a community to evacuate or relocate, its people may be subjected to unhealthful conditions—such as crowding, poor sanitation, or psychological stress—that they did not experience previously.

Desertification, the transformation of once-productive land to a desertlike environment, is a side-effect of imprudent resource use. Poor agricultural, forestry, and rangeland management practices encourage soil erosion. In semiarid climates, extreme devegetation, soil nutrient depletion, and erosion lead to desertification. Human health is impaired through the loss of productive land. In sub-Saharan Africa, desertification has resulted largely from overgrazing and excessive harvesting of wood for fuel. The region's rapidly expanding population has exceeded the production capabilities of its agricultural land, and widespread malnourishment has resulted.

The consumption of fossil fuels, the burning of wood, deforestation, and other factors are contributing to a buildup of carbon dioxide in the atmosphere. Many scientists believe that the accumulation of carbon dioxide and other "greenhouse gases" is responsible for a global warming trend. Scientists considering the health implications of the "greenhouse effect" anticipate increased mortality due to heat stress, increased incidence of chronic and infectious respiratory diseases, more allergic reactions, and altered geographic ranges for insect-borne and parasitic diseases.

FURTHER READING: An excellent source is the World Resources Institute's *World Resources 1996-97*, 1996, part of an ongoing series published biennially. Lester B. Lave and Arthur C. Upton, eds., *Toxic Chemicals, Health, and the Environment*, 1987, includes chapters on how toxic chemicals enter the environment, how human exposure occurs, and how these substances affect the human body. Eric Skjei and M. Donald Whorton, *Of Mice and Molecules: Technology and Human Survival*, 1983, examines the health consequences of technological development. Henry M. Vyner, *Invisible Trauma: The Psychosocial Effects of the Invisible Environmental Contaminants*, 1988, considers the psychological and sociological impacts of environmental degradation. For more information on environmental justice, see Robert D. Bullard, ed., *Unequal Protection: Environmental Justice and Communities of Color*, 1994.

Karen N. Kähler

SEE ALSO: Air pollution and air pollution control; Asbestos; Environmental degradation, resource exploitation and; Greenhouse gases and global climate change; Mining safety and health issues; Nuclear waste and its disposal; Pesticides and pest control; Population growth and resource use; Water pollution and water pollution control.

Helium

WHERE FOUND: Helium is concentrated in some natural gas wells, particularly in Texas, Oklahoma, and Kansas. Helium is also found in the earth's atmosphere.

PRIMARY USES: The most important use of helium is as a cryogenic coolant, since it permits cooling to temperatures lower than any other substance. Helium is also used as a lifting gas for airships, as a replacement for nitrogen in the breathing gas for deep sea divers, and as an inert atmosphere for welding.

DESCRIPTION: Helium (abbreviated He), atomic number 2, belongs to the last column of the periodic table of the elements. It has two naturally occurring isotopes and an average molecular weight of 4.003. Helium is a gas, having a density of 0.1637 grams/liter at 25 degrees Celsius and 1 atmosphere of pressure. Helium boils at −268.9 degrees Celsius. It is the most chemically inert element in the periodic table.

HELIUM DOES NOT form any chemical compounds. It is the lightest of the noble gases, so light that it quickly escapes into space from the earth's atmosphere. Thus, much of the helium now found on the earth was produced by radioactive decay. In excess of 600 million cubic feet of helium is produced annually in the United States. A majority of this helium is used by government agencies, including the Department of Energy and the National Aeronautics and Space Administration (NASA).

Historical Background. Helium was discovered in 1868. A French astronomer, Pierre Janssen, observed the emission spectrum of the sun's chromosphere during the August 18 solar eclipse. He saw a yellow-orange emission line which did not correspond to that of any known element. Later that year, both Janssen and an English astronomer, Sir Norman Lockyer, observed this emission again. Lockyer named this new element helium, for the sun (*helios* in Greek).

In 1889 William Hildebrand, an American mineral chemist, extracted a gas from a uranium-bearing mineral, uranite. Sir William Ramsay, an English chemist, performed a similar extraction on cleveite, another uranium-bearing mineral. Ramsey sent the gas to Lockyer, who showed in 1895 that it had the same emission lines he previously observed in the sun, providing the first identification of helium on Earth.

Distribution of Helium. Small quantities of helium, pure helium-4, are produced by the radioactive decay of uranium or thorium in the earth. In locations where uranium or thorium concentrations are high, helium collects in the same cavities as natural gas. The largest concentrations of helium are found in some natural gas wells in New Mexico, Texas, Oklahoma, Utah, and Kansas in the United States, in Saskatchewan and Alberta, Canada, in the Republic of South Africa, and in Russia.

Helium is also present in the earth's atmosphere. Some of this helium was produced by radioactive decay in the earth and subsequently escaped into the air. However, high-energy cosmic rays hitting the earth's atmosphere also produce helium by spallation, a process in which a heavier nucleus breaks into two or more lighter nuclei when it is hit by a high-energy particle. Radioactive decay produces only helium-4, while spallation produces both helium-3 and helium-4. Thus, atmospheric helium has a much higher content of helium-3 than the helium obtained from natural gas wells.

Obtaining Helium. The United States Bureau of Mines, which established three experimental plants to extract helium from the Petrolia natural gas field in Clay County, Texas, had produced about 200,000 cubic feet of helium by 1920. Helium-bearing well gas, typically about 80 percent methane, is compressed and then treated to remove carbon dioxide, hydrogen sulfide, and water vapor. The remaining gas is cooled to a temperature of about −150 degrees Celsius, which liquifies almost all the hydrocarbons, leaving nitrogen and helium in the gas phase. This gas is compressed again, then cooled to −196 degrees Celsius, at which point the nitrogen liquifies, leaving almost pure helium in the gas phase.

Uses of Helium. Helium has a much lower density than air; thus a helium-filled balloon will rise. The first practical application of helium was as a lifting gas for lighter-than-air craft. Although hydrogen has an even lower density, making it a more efficient lifting gas than helium, the extreme flammability of hydrogen makes its use dangerous. The U.S. Navy experimented with rigid airships, called dirigibles, during the 1920's and 1930's. In the modern era, the Goodyear

Aircraft Corporation built a series of nonrigid airships, called blimps, which have been used as platforms for aerial photography. Helium-filled balloons are also used for scientific research in the upper atmosphere.

In 1908, Heike Kamerlingh-Onnes, a physicist at the University of Leiden, in Holland, liquified helium by compressing it to a high pressure, cooling it, then allowing the helium to expand through a small opening. Expansion causes a gas to cool, and some of the helium liquified.

Since the boiling point of helium under 1 atmosphere of pressure is −268.9 degrees Celsius, material brought into contact with liquid helium cools rapidly. In 1911, Kamerlingh-Onnes demonstrated that the electrical resistance of mercury vanishes at liquid helium temperature. He had discovered superconductivity.

Helium's most important use is as a cryogenic agent, but one of its most familiar uses is to fill balloons, making them lighter than air. (Yasmine Cordoba)

Helium is used to dilute oxygen in the breathing gas used by deep sea divers. Divers must breath an atmosphere at the same pressure as the surrounding water. At ocean depths the pressure is high, and both oxygen and nitrogen dissolve in body fluids. The oxygen is consumed, but the nitrogen remains in the fluids. If a diver returns suddenly to the surface, he can suffer the "bends," which results when the nitrogen expands rapidly. The substitution of helium, the least soluble gas known, for nitrogen allows divers to operate at depth and then return to the surface more quickly.

FURTHER READING: A good discussion of the sources and uses of helium is contained in Gerhard A. Cook, ed., *Argon, Helium, and the Rare Gases*, 1961. The history and extraction of helium are described in Charles H. Simpson, *Chemicals from the Atmosphere*, 1969. The production and uses of helium, particularly its use in cryogenics, are described in Isaac Asimov, *The Noble Gases*, 1966.

George J. Flynn

SEE ALSO: Atmosphere; Gases, inert or noble; Hydrogen; Oil and natural gas drilling and wells; Oil and natural gas reservoirs.

Herbicides

Herbicides are a class of pesticide used to kill or otherwise control unwanted vegetation. They are frequently employed in agriculture and forestry.

HERBICIDES ARE USED for the control of grasses, weeds, and other plant pests. These chemical compounds kill plants or inhibit their normal growth. In general, herbicides work by interfering with photosynthesis, so that a plant dies from lack of energy, or by a combination of defoliation (leaf removal) and systemic herbicidal action.

Herbicides are used to clear rights-of-way beneath power lines and along railways and roads. In agriculture and forest management, they are used to control weeds or to remove the leaves from some crop plants to facilitate harvesting. While herbicides may be employed in lieu of tillage, their use is more often in conjunction with tillage and other agronomic practices. During wartime, defoliants and other herbicides have been used to destroy plants that an enemy uses for cover during battle or for food.

Types of Herbicides. Herbicides may be selective or nonselective. Selective herbicides, such as amitrole, atrazine, monuron, pyridine, 2,4-dichlorophenoxyacetic acid (2,4-D), and 2,4,5-trichlorophenoxyacetic acid (2,4,5-T), target a particular plant pest, and will kill or stunt weeds among crop plants without injuring the crop. For example, 2,4-D targets soft-stemmed plants, while 2,4,5-T is effective against woody plants. Cereals are crops particularly suited for treatment with 2,4-D, since the compound does not harm narrow-leafed plants but kills broad-leaved weeds. Selective toxicity minimizes the environmental impact of an herbicide. Nonselective herbicides (also called broad-spectrum or general-usage herbicides) are toxic to all plants. Examples include dinoseb, diquat, paraquat, and arsenic trioxide. Nonselective compounds are best suited for areas where all plant growth is to be suppressed, such as along railroad rights-of-way.

Some compounds, known as contact herbicides, kill only those plant parts to which they are directly applied. Others, called systemic herbicides, are absorbed through the plant's foliage or roots and carried to other parts of the plant. When mixed with the soil, some herbicides kill germinating seeds and small seedlings.

Popular inorganic herbicides include ammonium sulfate, sodium chlorate, sulfuric acid solutions, and borate formulations. Among the organic herbicides are the organic arsenicals, substituted amides and ureas, nitrogen heterocyclic acids, and phenol derivatives. Phenoxy-aliphatic acids and their derivatives, a major group of organic herbicides, are selective poisons that readily travel from one part of a plant to another.

A California orange grove being sprayed with an herbicide. (U.S. Department of Agriculture)

History. Agricultural societies have used simple chemical herbicides such as ashes and common salts for centuries. In 1896 a fungicidal compound known as Bordeaux mixture (a combination of copper sulfate, lime, and water) was found also to be effective against some weeds. Subsequently, copper sulfate was employed as a selective weed killer in cereal crops. By the early 1900's sodium arsenate solutions and other selective inorganic herbicidal mixtures had been developed. In 1932 dinitrophenol compounds were introduced.

In the early 1940's a new generation of herbicidal compound emerged. In an attempt to mimic natural plant hormones, the defoliant 2,4-D was created. At low concentrations 2,4-D promotes retention of fruit and leaves; at higher concentrations, it overstimulates plant metabolism, causing the leaves to drop off. A related chemical, 2,4,5-T, came into general use in 1948. The years after World War II saw the first large-scale application of herbicides in agriculture and other areas. The new defoliants rapidly gained acceptance because of their effectiveness against broad-leaved weeds in corn, sorghum, small grains, and grass pastures.

A few years after their development, these defoliants were employed as chemical weapons. During its conflict with Communist guerrillas in Malaya during the late 1940's and early 1950's, Britain sprayed 2,4,5-T on crops and jungle foliage to deprive the guerrillas of food and cover. The United States conducted a similar antifood and antifoliage campaign in South Vietnam during the 1960's. In this campaign, dubbed "Operation Ranch Hand," massive quantities of herbicidal mixtures were sprayed from aircraft onto Vietcong food plantations, infiltration routes, staging areas, and bases. The quantity and frequency of the spraying greatly exceeded recommended levels; in addition, mechanical problems or military need often forced aircraft to dump their herbicide loads all at once, drenching the jungle below. Soldiers, civilians, and the environment were subjected to unusually high concentrations of defoliants. One of the herbicides used in this campaign was Agent Orange, a mixture that included 2,4-D and 2,4,5-T. Commercial preparations of 2,4,5-T contain varying amount of dioxin, a highly toxic contaminant. Agent Orange has been implicated in the increased incidence of still births and birth defects among the Vietnamese living in the areas sprayed, in the cancers and other illnesses suffered by American and Australian soldiers who were involved in the operation, and in birth defects among the children of these veterans. In 1970 the United States placed severe restrictions on domestic and agricultural use of 2,4,5-T, at about the same time the defoliation campaign was halted.

U.S. Regulation of Herbicides. In 1947 the Federal Insecticide, Fungicide, and Rodenticide Act (FIFRA) authorized the Department of Agriculture (USDA) to oversee registration of herbicides and other pesticides and to determine their safety and effectiveness. In December, 1970, the newly formed United States Environmental Protection Agency (EPA) assumed statutory authority from the USDA over pesticide regulations. Under the Federal Environmental Pesticide Control Act of 1972, an amendment to FIFRA, manufacturers must register all marketed pesticides with the EPA before the product is released. Before registration, the chemicals must undergo exhaustive trials to assess their potential impact on the environment and human health. The EPA's decision to grant registration is based on the determination that unreasonable adverse effects on human health or the environment are not anticipated within the constraints of approved usage. Since October, 1977, the EPA has classified all pesticides to which it has granted registration as either a restricted-usage (to be applied only by certified pest control operators) or unclassified (general-usage) pesticide.

FURTHER READING: For more information on herbicides and their composition, mode of action, and use, see Gary W. Hansen, Floyd E. Oliver, and N. E. Otto, *Herbicide Manual*, 1983; George W. Ware, *Complete Guide to Pest Control*, 1980, and his *Fundamentals of Pesticides*, 1986; and the chapter on herbicides in R. J. Cremlyn, *Agrochemicals*, 1991. Hugh D. Crone, *Chemicals and Society*, 1986, includes an extended discussion on herbicides, toxicity, public perception, and the use of Agent Orange. Rachel Carson, *Silent*

Spring, 1962, 1987, examines the environmental impact of indiscriminate use of herbicides and other pesticidal compounds.

Karen N. Kähler

SEE ALSO: Agriculture industry; Environmental Protection Agency; Food chain; Monoculture agriculture; Pesticides and pest control.

Horticulture

Horticulture is the branch of agriculture that is connected with the production of plants that are directly used by humans for food, medicine, and aesthetic purposes.

THE ABILITY TO PRODUCE crops, particularly those crops associated with food and fiber, is a major economic and natural resource. Horticulture, a $70 billion per year industry, is a multidisciplinary science that encompasses all aspects of production, for fun or profit, of intensively cultivated plants to be utilized by humans for food, medicinal purposes, or aesthetic satisfaction. Crop production is largely determined by a variety of environmental conditions, including soil, water, light, temperature, and atmosphere. Therefore, horticulture science is primarily concerned with the study of how to manipulate the plants or these environmental factors to achieve maximum yield. Since there is tremendous diversity in horticultural plants, the field is subdivided into pomology, the growth and production of fruit crops; olericulture, the growth and production of vegetable crops; landscape horticulture, the growth and production of trees and shrubs; and floriculture, the growth and production of flower and foliage plants. Each of these subdivisions is based on a fundamental knowledge of plant-soil interactions, soil science, plant physiology, and plant morphology.

Propagation. Horticulture science is concerned with all aspects of crop production, from the collection and germination of seed to the final marketing of the products. Plant propagation, protection, and harvesting are three areas of particular interest to horticulturists. Generally, propagation from seed is the most common and least expensive way of propagating plants. In order to prevent cross-pollination from undesirable varieties, plants to be used for seed production are grown in genetic isolation from other, similar plants. At maturity, the seed is collected and is usually stored at low temperatures and under 50 to 65 percent relative humidity to maintain full viability. The seed is often tested for viability prior to planting to determine the percentage of seed that should germinate. At the appropriate time, the seed is usually treated with a fungicide to ensure an adequate crop stand and planted under proper temperature, water, and light conditions. For most crops, the seed is germinated in small containers, and the seedlings are then transplanted to the field or greenhouse.

For many horticultural crops it is not feasible to produce plants from seed. For some, the growth from seed may require too much time to be economically practical. In other cases, the parent plants may produce too little or no viable seed, and in still others, there may be a desire to avoid hybridization in order to maintain a pure strain. For some plants, almost any part of the root, stem, or leaf can be vegetatively propagated, but chemical treatment of the detached portion to ensure regeneration of the missing tissue is often required.

For other plants, a variety of specific vegetative plant tissues, including the roots, bulbs, corms, rhizomes, tubers, and runners, must be used for propagation. Individual runners are used for propagation purposes, but a number of cuttings can be propagated from one rhizome. Tubers are propagated by slicing the organ into several pieces, each of which must contain an "eye" or bud. Corms and bulbs are propagated by planting the entire structure. A relatively new process of generating plants from cell cultures grown in the laboratory, called tissue culture, is a method often used to propagate pure lines of crops with a very high economic value. Grafting, a specialized form of vegetative propagation, is particularly useful in tree farming. The shoot from one plant with a particularly desirable fruit quality can be grafted onto the root stock of another, more vigorous plant with a less desirable fruit quality.

The growing of flowers is commonly called "horticulture"; specifically, however, flower production is "floriculture," only one branch of horticulture. (Yasmine Cordoba)

Pest Control. Since plants are besieged by a panoply of biological agents that utilize plant tissues as a food source, plant protection from pests is a major concern in the horticulture industry. Microbial organisms, nematodes, insects, and weeds are the major plant pests. Weeds are defined as unwanted plants and are considered to be pests because they compete with crop plants for water, sunlight, and nutrients. If left unchecked, weeds will drastically reduce crop yields because they tend to produce a large amount of seed and grow rapidly. Weed control is generally accomplished either by physically removing the weed or by use of a variety of herbicides that have been developed to chemically control weeds. Herbicides are selected on the basis of their ability to control weeds and, at the same time, cause little or no damage to the desired plant.

Plant protection from microbes, nematodes, and insects generally involves either preventing or restricting pest invasion of the plant, develop-ing plant varieties that will resist or at least tolerate the invasion, or a combination of both methods. The application of chemicals, utilization of biological agents, isolation of an infected crop by quarantine, and cultural practices that routinely remove infected plants or plant tissues are examples of the different types of control methods. A large number of different bactericides, fungicides, nematocides, and insecticides have been developed in recent years, and the use of these pesticides has been particularly useful in plant protection. Since many of these chemicals are harmful to other animals, including humans, the use of pesticides, and insecticides in particular, requires extreme caution. There is an increasing interest in the use of biological control methods because many of the chemical pesticides pose a threat to the environment. The development and use of pest-resistant crop varieties and the introduction of natural enemies that will not only reduce the pest population but also live harmoniously in the existing environment are two of the more promising biological measures being employed.

Harvest. A crop must be harvested once it has grown to maturity. Harvesting is one of the most expensive aspects of crop production because it is usually very labor intensive. For almost all crops, there is a narrow window between the time the plants are ready to harvest and the time when the plants are too ripe to be of economic value. Hence, the process requires considerable planning to ensure that the appropriate equipment and an adequate labor supply are available when the crop is ready to be harvested. Predicting the harvest date is of paramount importance in the planning process. The length of the harvest window, the length of the growing season that is necessary for a given plant to mature under normal environmental conditions at a given geographic location, and the influence of unexpected weather changes on the growing season all have to be considered in the planning process. Since nature is unpredictable, even the best planning schedules sometimes have to be readjusted in midseason.

Some crops are picked from the plant by hand and then mechanically conveyed from the field, while other crops are harvested entirely by hand. New mechanical harvesting equipment is continually being developed by agricultural engineers, and crops that lend themselves to mechanical harvesting are growing in importance as the manual labor force continues to shrink. After harvest, most crops are generally stored for varying lengths of time, from a few days to several months. Since postharvest storage can affect both the quality and appearance of the product, considerable care is given as to how the crop is stored. Sometimes storage improves the quality and appearance, while in other cases, it causes them to deteriorate. The ideal storage conditions are those that maintain the product as close to harvest condition as possible.

Future of the Resource. In order for horticulture to remain a viable resource in the future, advances in horticulture technology will have to continue to keep pace with the needs of an ever-increasing population. However, horticulturists will also have to be ever mindful of the fragile nature of the environment. New technologies must be developed with the environment in mind, and much of this new technology will center on advances in genetic engineering. New crop varieties that will both provide higher yields and reduce the dependency on chemical pesticides by exhibiting greater resistance to a variety of pests will have to be developed. The future development of higher-yielding crops that can be harvested mechanically and the production of new types of equipment to facilitate the harvesting process will also be important improvements in the horticulture industry.

FURTHER READING: *The Standard Cyclopedia of Horticulture*, by L. H. Bailey, 1947, has an excellent horticultural prospective and provides the general reader with a firm understanding of traditional horticulture, although it was published more than fifty years ago. One of the most valuable sources available on the practical aspects of plant propagation is *Plant Propagation: Principles and Practices*, by H. T. Hartmann and D. E. Kester, 4th ed. 1983. An authoritative presentation of numerous topics in food science, including the harvesting, preservation, and marketing of a variety of horticultural food crops, can be found in *Principles of Food Science*, by O. R. Fennema, 1976. *Horticulture Science*, by Jules Janick, 1986, contains sections on horticulture biology, environment, technology, and industry.

D. R. Gossett

SEE ALSO: Agricultural products; Agriculture industry; Biotechnology; Hydroponics; Monoculture agriculture; Plant domestication and breeding.

Hydroenergy

FIRST DEVELOPED OR USED: The first recorded uses of hydroenergy, or water power, occurred during the first century B.C.E. Water eventually drove mills for grinding grain, powered machine tools in factories, and, finally, in the twentieth century, became an important source of energy for generating electricity

ALTHOUGH DEVICES FOR moving water have existed since prehistoric times, apparently no one realized that water could be used to power mills or other equipment until approximately two thousand years ago. Farmers throughout the ancient Middle East used primitive water wheels, known as noria, to transfer water from one level to another, as from a flowing river to an irrigation canal. Similar devices, which consist of jars or buckets lashed to a wheel that is turned by the pressure of water flowing against it, can still be seen in use in Egypt and Iraq. Sometime around 100 B.C.E. an unknown inventor harnessed the power of the moving water to a mill for grinding grain.

The Roman Empire Through the Nineteenth Century. Following this innovation, the use of waterwheels for moving mill stones spread throughout the Roman Empire. The water-powered mill made possible a dramatic increase in the production of flour. Using manpower, which at that time was generally slave labor, sixteen to twenty man hours were required to grind sixty kilograms of grain. Even a very primitive water wheel, one with the equivalent of perhaps three horsepower in motive power, could produce two and one half times that amount in only one hour.

Waterwheels and milling techniques remained relatively unchanged until the Middle Ages. Between the years 800 C.E. and 1200 C.E., innovations in waterwheel technology exploded across Europe. Millwrights refined waterwheels for greater efficiency and adapted wheels for use in a wide variety of applications. In addition to milling grain, waterwheels drove fulling hammers for processing wool in manufacturing felt and softened hides at tanneries. Towns grew up around milling complexes in European cities. Millers constructed dams to regulate the flow of water, while land owners became wealthy through the lease fees collected for choice mill sites on rivers and streams. A narrow stream might be dammed to provide water for one wheel, while wider rivers, such as the Seine in France, were spanned by a series of waterwheels and mills all constructed side-by-side. Artisans devised varied types of waterwheels and gearing to use with different levels of available water, such as undershot, overshot, and breast wheels, and they built ingenious systems of stone dams and timber crib weirs to exploit every conceiv-

able source of moving water, from tidal flows to the smallest freshwater streams.

Waterwheels were also built in the Middle East, India, and China, but these never reached the level of complexity common in Europe even before the Renaissance. In the 1600's European colonists brought waterwheel technologies with them to the New World, and, not surprising, patterns of settlement followed streams and rivers inland from the ocean. Although the eighteenth century invention of the steam engine and its contribution to the Industrial Revolution changed patterns of industrial development in Europe and elsewhere, the steam engine did not eliminate the importance of water power to manufacturing. While steam engines quickly found applications in the mining industry, it took many years for steam power to displace water power elsewhere. Steam engines eventually allowed industry to develop factory sites lo-

European colonists brought waterwheel technology with them to the Americas in the 1600's. (Rich Olsen)

cated away from sources of moving water, but did not reduce the importance of water power to many factories already in place. In fact, the rapid expansion of the textile industry in the United States relied far more on water power than it did on steam, even though steam engines were commonplace by the 1820's.

Textile factories, such as those located in Lowell, Massachusetts, exploited water power by developing elaborate systems of drive belts that extended through factories which were several stories high and hundreds of feet long. Dams on the river above the town diverted water into multiple canals, allowing factory construction well back from the original banks of the river. The development of the water-powered Lowell sites began in the early years of the nineteenth century and continued for almost a hundred years. It was not until the twentieth century, following the invention of the electric motor and the widespread distribution of electrical power, that factories began to abandon water power as a motive source. Even then, only the presence of other factors, such as the buildup of silt in mill ponds and the movement of industry from the New England states to the South, may have pushed factory owners to implement changes in sources of motive power.

Twentieth Century Developments. At the beginning of the twentieth century, industry moved away from direct exploitation of hydroenergy through the use of waterwheels and began instead to use electricity generated from hydroelectric power plants. Hydroelectric power plants generate electricity by converting the motive power of the water into electrical current. The water enters the plant through a power tunnel or penstock that directs the water into a casing. The casing, which looks like a gigantic snail, narrows as it spirals in and directs the water toward the blades of a turbine that turns the shaft an electric generator. Early hydroelectric plants utilized designs that converted the force of the water striking the waterwheel directly into electrical energy, but engineers and scientists quickly developed more efficient turbines to take advantage of available water resources.

The amount of energy potential in a water power site depends on two factors. First is the effective head, or the height difference between the level of the water standing behind the dam (before the water enters the power tunnel) and where it will exit at the tailrace on the downstream side of the turbine. Second is the volume of water. A large volume of water can compensate for a low effective head, just as an extremely high head can compensate for a low volume of water. High head, low volume hydroelectric plants generally rely on impulse wheels. Water enters the casing around the wheel under tremendous pressure and strikes the wheel buckets with incredible force. As the wheel spins in response to the force of the water striking it, it turns the shaft of a generator to convert kinetic energy to electricity. Impulse wheels have a fairly low efficiency rating, but they are often the only practical turbines for use in situations where water is in short supply. These impulse wheels, also known as Pelton wheels, are vertical water wheels that to the observer share an obvious ancestry with the old-fashioned waterwheels seen in bucolic illustrations of gristmills and ponds. Impulse wheels were once widely used throughout the western United States, where effective heads of several hundred feet are common.

Most large modern hydroelectric plants use a different type of turbine, a reaction turbine, that exploits the pressure differential between the water entering the turbine casing and the tailrace below. Engineers such as James Francis turned the vertical waterwheel on its side. In the process Francis designed a turbine that create a partial vacuum in the space between the turbine and the tailrace. The Francis turbine and other reaction turbines work, in effect, by sucking the water through the turbine casing, causing the water to flow faster and to increase the overall efficiency of the system. Reaction turbines can be used in settings that have extremely low heads if a sufficient volume of water exists to create an effective pressure differential. Reaction turbines are especially well suited for applications in run-of-the-river power plants in which the dam diverting the water into the turbine may be only a few feet high.

The Early Promise of Hydroenergy. Noted conservationists of the early twentieth century, such as Gifford Pinchot, unabashedly pushed for the

The steep descent and high volume of water going over Niagara Falls, between Lake Erie and Lake Ontario, make it a tremendously effective source of electrical power. (Rich Olsen)

widespread exploitation of hydroelectric sites. Pinchot and others in the conservation movement encouraged the United States government to take a more active role in the development of hydroelectricity. The alternative to hydroelectricity was electricity generated by steam turbines, and steam required a fuel source such as coal or oil. Even before World War I first created shortages of fossil fuels, conservationists advocated greater use of renewable resources, such as hydroelectricity. Because hydroelectricity does not permanently remove water from a watershed—it merely diverts the flow to pass it through a powerhouse and then returns the water to the system—conservationists argued that hydroelectric sites should be exploited in order to conserve nonrenewable energy sources, such as coal. Conservationists devoted almost twenty years to lobbying for a water power bill, finally succeeding in 1920 with the passage of the Federal Water Power Act that created a Federal Power Commission.

Not surprisingly, the following decades witnessed an explosion of hydropower development. The size of early hydro development had been limited by the available technology, but engineers quickly solved problems that had restricted turbine and generator size. Construction journals and the popular press alike regularly reported on new dams and powerplants that would be the largest in the world, with each gigantic project being quickly supplanted by a newer, bigger project. In the United States this fascination with ever bigger hydroelectric projects became a physical reality with the construction of Hoover Dam on the Colorado River and the Bonneville Power Project along the Columbia. The arrival of the Great Depression in 1929 did not slow the construction boom. If anything, it may have accelerated it. In a time when millions of Americans were unemployed, massive construction projects such as Bonneville in the Pacific Northwest or the Tennessee Valley Authority dams in the South provided meaningful work.

Reassessing Hydro. By the 1950's the enthusiasm for large hydroelectric projects had abated. Conservationists who had once advocated hydroelectricity because it was clean and renewable began to realize that it nonetheless posed significant environmental problems. Construction of a high dam such as Ross Dam on Washington's Skagit River or Glen Canyon on the Colorado inevitably required that hundreds of square miles of land be permanently covered with water. Deserts, forests, farmland, and entire towns were all lost forever as reservoirs filled.

Nor were hydroelectric plants neutral in affecting aquatic life. The percentage of dissolved oxygen present in water changes as it passes through turbines, as does the water temperature. Water downstream from a hydroelectric plant may flow faster than before, vary widely in volume depending on power demands, and be warmer than it would be naturally. Some species of fish may disappear or be displaced by other species that find the changed conditions more favorable than the original native fish do. Upstream from the dam, the water on the surface of the reservoir will be both calmer and warmer than prior to construction, while the water at the bottom will be colder. Again, these changed conditions affect which fish will thrive and which fish will gradually disappear. Construction of a hydroelectric plant can change a stretch of a river from a trout stream into a bass lake.

The dam and power plant themselves present a physical barrier to spawning fish, a barrier that technical solutions such as fish ladders only partially solve. Fish may make it past the dam going upstream via a fish ladder, for example, but then be killed by pressure changes as they inadvertently pass through the turbines as they swim downstream.

In addition, twentieth century dam builders have had to relearn what the mill owners of the Middle Ages and the early Industrial Revolution knew: Dams stop sediment as well as water. Mill owners in past centuries had learned to drain mill ponds periodically to remove accumulated silt, but such a procedure is impractical for a mammoth hydroelectric power plant. The effective life of dams has also begun to be examined: If a 300-foot dam was designed and built in 1920 to last for fifty years, what happens when it is time to replace it? Although a number of small dams have been decommissioned or replaced, as of 1996 none of the truly high dams had yet been found unsafe.

The Promise of Hydroenergy. Despite the problems inherent in hydroelectricity, many environmentalists and advocates for sustainable development believe that the creation of small-scale hydroelectric power plants could significantly reduce reliance on nonrenewable fossil fuels. A typical small-scale hydroelectric plant might have a turbine rated at only 3,000 horsepower, as opposed to the 60,000 horsepower capacity of a large plant. On the other hand, where a large hydroelectric development, such as Glen Canyon, may cost millions of dollars, take many years to complete, and have a devastating environmental impact, small-scale hydro can be easily and cheaply implemented. Diversion dams for small-scale hydro need not even block the entire flow of a stream. That is, if a stream or river has a steady flow of water, a diversion dam to steer water into the power tunnel or penstock can be constructed that extends only partway across the stream bed, allowing the water and aquatic life to continue their normal passage almost free from restriction. Such small dams can utilize indigenous materials, such as timber or rocks available on the site, making construction in underdeveloped regions easy and affordable.

In the United States, development of small-scale hydroelectric power plants is being explored by independent power producers. Changes in federal energy regulations require public utilities to purchase electricity produced by independent power producers, which can be companies that generate excess electricity as part of their normal manufacturing process, as well as firms that have chosen to develop alternative energy sources rather than using fossil fuels. Small hydroelectric plants once existed in many small towns throughout the nation but were abandoned as economies of scale pushed public utilities to invest in larger plants or steam turbines. Exploiting these sites suited for small-scale run-of-the-river hydroelectric power is both possible and desirable. Hydroenergy harnessed by a 600-foot-high dam can be an environmental disaster, but hydroenergy behind a 6-foot dam has few negative side effects.

FURTHER READING: In *Stronger than a Hundred Men: A History of the Vertical Water Wheel*, 1983, Terry Reynolds provides a detailed history of the uses of water power from ancient times to the twentieth century. Jean Gimpel's *The Medieval Machine: The Industrial Revolution of the Middle Ages*, 1976, discusses the role of water power in the growth of industry and trade in the Middle Ages. Readers interested in the more recent history of water power will also enjoy *The Texture of Industry: An Archeological View of the Industrialization of North America*, by Robert B. Gordon and Patrick M. Malone, 1994, which is lavishly illustrated with photographs and drawings. A variety of perspectives on hydroenergy development in the late twentieth century can be found in three works: *Hydropower 2002: Reclamation's Energy Initiative*, a report prepared by the U.S. Bureau of Reclamation and published by the Department of the Interior, 1991; John S. Gladwell and Calvin C. Warnick's *Low-Head Small Hydroelectric Projects for Rural Development*, 1978; and *Hydro: An Examination of an Alternative Energy Source*, edited by Louis J. Goodman, John N. Hawkins, and Ralph N. Loveby, 1981. Finally, John S. Gulliver and Roger E. A. Arndt include a comprehensive discussion on the ecological effects of hydroelectric development in *Hydropower Engineering Handbook*, 1991.

Nancy Farm Mannikko

SEE ALSO: Dams; Electrical power; Energy storage; Federal Energy Regulatory Commission; Streams and rivers; Tidal energy; Water rights.

Hydrogen

WHERE FOUND: Hydrogen is the most abundant substance in the universe and is the principal constituent of stars such as the sun. Because of its low molecular weight, gaseous hydrogen is not retained in the earth's atmosphere, and it must be produced by the decomposition of its chemical compounds. The principal source of hydrogen is water, from which the hydrogen must be extracted by chemical reaction or electrolysis.

PRIMARY USES: Hydrogen is useful both as a chemical reactant and as a source of energy. Hydrogen is used in the commercially important Haber-Bosch process for the production of ammonia. It is added to oils and fats to raise their melting points. It is also used as a fuel in certain engines and in fuel cells. The production of energy by the controlled fusion of hydrogen nuclei is being explored as an alternative to fossil and nuclear (fission) energy sources.

DESCRIPTION: Hydrogen (chemical symbol H), atomic number 1, is the simplest chemical element, existing under normal conditions as a diatomic gas or in chemical combination with other elements. It has three isotopes. The lightest isotope, atomic mass 1.00797, is sometimes referred to as protium to distinguish it from the much rarer deuterium, or heavy hydrogen, with atomic mass 2.014. The third isotope, tritium, with atomic mass 3.016 and a half-life of 12.26 years, is produced in trace amounts by cosmic rays bombarding the atmosphere. Hydrogen has a melting point of −259.14 degrees Celsius and a boiling point of −252.87 degrees Celsius.

NEARLY ALL THE HYDROGEN that exists on earth is found in chemical combination with other elements. Hydrogen gas may be produced by the action of an acid on a reactive metal, by the electrolysis of water, or by the reaction of water with carbon or hydrocarbons at high temperature. Since the vast majority of chemical compounds involve hydrogen, there is little point in trying to identify a separate chemistry of hydrogen. As the supply of hydrogen available is inexhaustible for all practical purposes, the main reason for including it in a discussion of natural resources is the effect of hydrogen-based technologies on the use of more limited resources.

Historical Background. Credit for the discovery of hydrogen is generally awarded to the English scientist Henry Cavendish, who collected the flammable gas released when iron and other metals reacted with acid and reported its properties in 1766. Later, English surgeon Anthony

Carlisle and English chemist William Nicholson made use of the newly developed voltaic pile to produce hydrogen through the electrolysis of water. Because of its inherently low density, hydrogen was used to provide buoyancy for balloons and other lighter-than-air craft, a practice that ended with the destruction by fire of the zeppelin Hindenburg in 1937. Helium replaced hydrogen for buoyancy applications.

Hydrogen Combustion. Hydrogen is a very dense energy source in the sense that the combustion of a few grams of hydrogen in air releases a great deal of heat energy. The usefulness of hydrogen as a fuel is somewhat limited by its very low boiling point and the fact that it readily forms an explosive mixture with oxygen from the air. Hydrogen tends to be used as a fuel only in situations where weight is an overriding concern. Thus it is used to provide electrical power in spacecraft. There is some interest in using hydrogen as a fuel for motor vehicles, because the only combustion product is the environmentally acceptable water. Use of hydrogen in the load leveling of power generating systems has also been proposed. In this case it would be produced by electrolysis when demand for electrical energy is low and used to power fuel cells during peak demand periods. Hydrogen can be produced from solar energy either by using photovoltaic cells to electrolyze water or directly by a photogalvanic process in which light energy absorbed by a semiconducting material is used directly to split the hydrogen-oxygen bond in water. Steam reacts with coal to form synthesis gas, a mixture of hydrogen, carbon monoxide, carbon dioxide, and methane that can be burned as a fuel or exposed to a catalyst to form further hydrocarbons.

Hydrogen in Metals. Because of its small size, hydrogen can enter the lattice structure of many metallic elements. This creates a problem in steels, particularly in oil drilling equipment, in which hydrogen embrittlement can cause mechanical failure. On the other hand, a number of transition metals, notably palladium, can absorb large quantities—up to one hydrogen atom per metal atom—of hydrogen and release it under controlled conditions, thus offering the potential for safe and compact storage of this high-energy fuel.

Hydrogen Fusion. Much research in the later third of the twentieth century was directed toward achieving hydrogen fusion under controlled conditions on earth. The principal engineering challenge has been the containment of the extremely hot plasma necessary for sustained nuclear fusion, but at least partial success has been obtained with the tokamak, a device which uses strong magnetic fields to confine the plasma. Considerable excitement was generated within the scientific community in 1989 when two electrochemists at the University of Utah announced that they had achieved deuterium fusion by electrochemical means in a table-top apparatus. Numerous attempts were made to repeat their experiment, with disappointing results. Within a few years most scientists had come to consider the evidence for "cold fusion" to be inconclusive at best.

FURTHER READING: The chemistry of hydrogen is discussed in all chemistry texts. A modern one with an environmental emphasis is *Chemistry in Context*, by A. Truman Schwartz et al., 1994. Discussion of applications of hydrogen in the future energy economy of advanced nations can be found in T. B. Johansson et al., *Renewable Energy: Sources for the Future*, 1993. The *International Journal of Hydrogen Energy* publishes technical articles on applications of hydrogen to energy generation.

Donald R. Franceschetti

SEE ALSO: Coal gasification and coal liquefaction; Fuel cells; Haber-Bosch process; Nuclear energy; Solar energy.

Hydrology and the hydrologic cycle

Hydrology is the study of the earth's water. It involves a number of scientific disciplines related to its acquisition, planning, and management. The hydrologic cycle is the cycle that water passes through as it is transformed from seawater to atmospheric moisture to precipitation on land surfaces and its eventual return to water vapor or the sea.

UNLIKE ANY OTHER PLANET in our solar system, the earth has a vast abundance of water. More than 70 percent of the earth's surface is covered by water. Therefore, the life that has evolved on the earth is extremely dependent on water for continued survival. The American Geologic Institute's *Dictionary of Geological Terms* defines Hydrology as "the science that relates to the water of the earth." It can also be described as the study of the earth's water in all its forms and areas of occurrence. This study includes an array of scientific disciplines including civil engineering, geology, oceanography, chemistry, geography, and ecology, to name only a few.

Importance of Water as a Resource. On a casual appraisal, the abundance of water on earth would seem to make it unlikely that it would be considered an important natural resource. However, as Benjamin Franklin observed, "When the well's dry, we know the worth of water." Despite the vast volumes of water on our planet, fresh water is in fact one of our most important natural resources. Without it, much terrestrial life, including humans, could not exist. Water fit for human consumption is an absolute necessity, and much of the earth's water is too salty to be consumable by humans. Although desalinization is possible, it is not currently economically feasible on a large scale. Although not readily consumable by humans, the water in the oceans is of unquestionable importance as a resource. It supports the biodiversity of the oceans, and all creatures of the earth are either directly or indirectly dependent on it for survival. Water of acceptable quality is necessary for irrigation and livestock operations. Huge quantities of water are necessary for certain industrial processes and as a coolant for various industrial processes.

Occurrence. Although estimates vary, as much as 97.2 percent of the earth's water exists in the form of the seawater found in the oceans. Of the remaining percentage, much is tied up in ice caps, glaciers, saline lakes, and soil moisture. Freshwater lakes, rivers, and streams account for a surprisingly small percent of the total of the earth's water, perhaps as little as 0.009 percent.

Fresh groundwater accounts for roughly 0.61 percent of the overall total. It can be seen by this comparison that fresh groundwater sources far outweigh surface water sources. In reality, only a small portion of the earth's water is readily available in the form of fresh water. Although the amounts are comparatively small, much of the study of hydrology involves fresh groundwater and surface water because of its crucial importance. The search for new sources of groundwater is primarily accomplished by exploratory drilling coupled with a knowledge of hydrologic and geologic processes. Artificial lakes and reservoirs increase the supply of water by lengthening the residence time of surface water.

Importance of Water. Since World War II, agricultural, residential, and industrial demands on water supplies have increased dramatically. In areas such as California and Idaho, where groundwater is extensively used for irrigation, some sources of fresh water appear to be dwindling rapidly. Although its full extent is not known, human pollution of water resources is also a major concern. The *EPA Journal* reported in 1994 that data provided by the states indicated that roughly 40 percent of assessed rivers and lakes and more than 30 percent of assessed estuaries were not suitable for fishing, swimming, or other uses. Civil engineers, geologists, chemists and others work in concert with cities and other governmental agencies to expand water supplies, to provide better planning for future water use, and to protect remaining sources of water.

The Hydrologic Cycle. Although there is no true beginning or end to the hydrologic cycle, descriptions often begin with the oceans. Solar radiation provides the energy for the cycle. Solar radiation not only transforms some of the earth's liquid waters to water vapor but also leads to a planetary heat imbalance. In general the northern hemisphere has a net heat loss to space, and equatorial areas have a net heat gain. To counteract this imbalance, heat is transferred in the form of ocean currents and atmospheric currents.

As water evaporates from the oceans, it leaves behind many of its impurities, including salts. As water vapor collects in clouds it is carried along by atmospheric currents. When conditions are right, atmospheric water vapor precipitates as rain, snow, sleet, and so on. Some of this precipitation falls back on the oceans to begin the cycle again, but some falls on land surfaces.

Of the precipitation that falls on land sur-

The Hydrologic Cycle

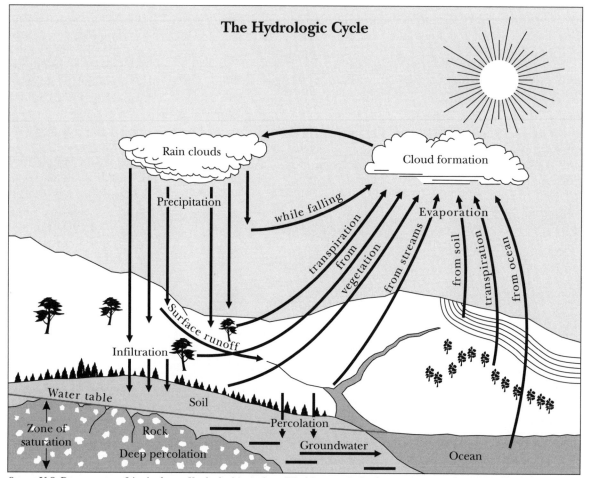

Source: U.S. Department of Agriculture, *Yearbook of Agriculture* (Washington, D.C.: Government Printing Office, 1955).

faces, much becomes locked up in ice caps and glaciers, but some falls in the form of rain (or snow that melts when temperatures rise). The majority of the precipitation that falls on land surfaces runs off in the form of surface flow, referred to as overland flow. This flow is observed in the complex surface drainage systems of streams, creeks, rivers, and lakes. The residence time of surface water can be as short as a few days or weeks. Surface water is a major area of study. Evaporation from surface water adds to atmospheric moisture, as does water vapor that transpires from the leaves of trees and other plants.

Although the majority of precipitation takes the form of overland flow, in areas where surface soil or rock is porous and permeable, water can move downward into the ground by the process of infiltration. This water of infiltration becomes groundwater. Groundwater flows through void spaces in soil or rock; therefore its flow is restricted by the porosity and permeability of the material it enters. The residence time of groundwater can be on the order of months, centuries, or even thousands of years. In essence the water is stored for a time. The soil zone or rock strata in which the water is stored is called an aquifer. Aquifers are further categorized as major and minor, and as confined or unconfined. An unconfined aquifer, also called a water table aquifer, is said to have a water table. A confined aquifer has a potentiometric surface, or level to which water will rise rather than a water table.

Since precipitation and infiltration have seasonal variability, the height of the water table in an unconfined aquifer also has seasonal variability. There is complex interaction between groundwater and surface water, based on gravity and the height of the water column, expressed as hydrostatic head. An axiom is that water moves from high head to low head. Another way to view this is by picturing a lake. Water tries to move from high elevation to low elevation; the ultimate level is sea level. The same is true for groundwater.

In the absence of geologic complexity, the water table in an unconfined aquifer tends roughly to follow the topographic surface. This creates areas of higher hydrostatic head and areas of lower hydrostatic head, providing a gravitation impetus for groundwater flow, expressed numerically as the gradient. As groundwater flows from higher elevations to lower elevations, it encounters incised stream beds that may have a base level lower than the level of the water table. In this instance, groundwater will discharge to the stream bed, creating the base flow of the stream. In this situation, the stream is considered a gaining stream. If the incised bed of the stream has a higher elevation than the groundwater, the stream can lose surface water to groundwater by the process of infiltration; in this instance the stream would be considered a losing stream. Because of the seasonal variation in the water table, streams can seasonally change from gaining to losing and vice versa.

Because of geologic processes, many beds of rock, or strata, are not flat. As the strata composing an aquifer dip away, groundwater can become confined under a less permeable layer such as a shale. In this type of aquifer the recharge area of the strata exposed at the surface is at a higher elevation than down-dip portions of the strata under the confining bed. The water table at higher elevations exerts hydrostatic pressure on the confined portion of the aquifer at lower elevations. A well penetrating the confined portion of an aquifer is said to be artesian because the hydrostatic pressure causes the water column in the well to rise above the confining layer, and in many cases water from confined aquifers will flow to the surface.

FURTHER READING: A significant work on the subject of hydrology is contained in *Applied Hydrogeology*, by C. W. Fetter, 1980. A highly recog-

nized text regarding groundwater as it relates to hydrology is *Groundwater*, by R. Allen Freeze and John A. Cherry, 1979. Updates on water quality and other subjects can be found in the *EPA Journal*, published by the U.S. Environmental Protection Agency. A very good presentation on the overall subject of water can be found in *Water*, National Geographic Society Special Edition, 1993.

Ray Roberts

SEE ALSO: Aquifers; Atmosphere; Biodiversity; Geochemical cycles; Glaciation; Groundwater; Lakes; Oceans; Streams and rivers; Water pollution and water pollution control; Water rights.

Hydroponics

The term "hydroponics" literally means water culture and originally referred to the growth of plants in a liquid media. It now applies to all systems used to grow plants in nutrient solutions with or without the addition of inert material (synthetic soil) for mechanical support.

THE ABILITY TO produce food and fiber for an ever growing population is the most fundamental of all resources, and hydroponics has become an important method of crop production. The increase in the number of commercial greenhouse operations has resulted in a tremendous increase in the use of hydroponic systems. Greenhouses are now utilized in the production of a wide array of bedding plants, flowers, trees, and shrubs for commercial as well as for home and garden use. Cash receipts from greenhouse and nursery crops total more than $4 billion annually. In some arid regions, the vast majority of vegetable crops are produced in greenhouses.

Types of Hydroponic Systems. The four most commonly used hydroponic systems are sand-culture systems, aggregate systems, nutrient film techniques, and floating systems. While these systems are similar in their use of nutrient solutions, they vary in both the presence and type of supporting medium and in the frequency of nutrient application. In sand culture, coarse sand is used in containers or spread over an entire greenhouse floor or bed on top of a recirculating drain system. A drip irrigation system is used to apply nutrient solution periodically, and a drainage system is used to collect the excess solution as it drains through the sand. In an aggregate open system, plants are transplanted into plastic troughs filled with an inert supporting material, and nutrient solution is supplied via drip irrigation. The aggregate system, as well as the sand culture, are open systems because the nutrient solution is not recycled. In the nutrient film technique, there is an absence of supporting material. Seedlings are transplanted into troughs through which the nutrient solution is channeled, and the plants are in direct contact with the nutrient solution. In this closed system, the nutrient solution is channeled past the plant, collected, and reused. The floating hydroponic system involves the floating of plants over a pool of nutrient solution, but in the mid-1990's this system was only in the experimental stages.

While the nutrient film technique and floating hydroponic systems are primarily used in research applications, the sand culture and aggregate systems are commonly used in commercial plant production. These two systems require the use of a nutrient solution and synthetic soil for mechanical support. Although a variety of nutrient solutions have been formulated, one of the earliest was developed in 1950, and this solution and slight modifications of it are still very popular. Since 1950 other nutrient solutions with different concentrations of chemical salts have been developed, but the elemental ratios are very similar to the original solution.

Materials Used for Mechanical Support. A large variety of both organic and inorganic materials have been used to formulate the synthetic soils used for mechanical support in hydroponic systems. Commonly used organic materials include sphagnum moss, peat, manures, wood, and other plant residues. Sphagnum moss, the shredded, dehydrated remains of several species of moss in the genus *Sphagnum*, is specifically harvested for the purpose of producing synthetic soil. "Peat" is a term normally used to describe partially decomposed remains of wetlands vegetation that has been preserved under water. Moss peat is the only type of peat suitable for synthetic soil mixes. Moss peat is harvested from peat bogs, dried,

compressed into bales, and sold. Animal manures are almost never used in commercial synthetic soil mixtures because they require costly handling and sterilization procedures. Wood residues such as tree bark, wood chips, shavings, and sawdust are generally produced as by-products of the timber industry. A variety of other plant residues, including corn cobs, sugarcane stems, straw, peanut hulls, and rice hulls have been substituted for peat in synthetic soil mixtures in localities where there is sufficient supply of these materials.

Commonly used inorganic materials include vermiculite, sand, pumice, perlite, cinders, and calcined clay. Vermiculite is a very lightweight material produced by heating mica to temperatures above 1,090 degrees Celsius. Sand is one of the most preferred materials for formulating synthetic soils because it is both inert and inexpensive, but it is very heavy compared to other commonly used materials. Pumice, a natural glasslike material produced by volcanic action, provides a good inert supporting material when ground into small particles. Perlite, a porous material that will hold three to four times its weight in water, is produced by heating lava at temperatures above 760 degrees Celsius. Cinders are derived from coal residues that have been thoroughly rinsed to remove harmful sulfates. Calcined clay is derived from the mineral montmorillonite baked at temperatures above 100 degrees Celsius.

Future Use of Hydroponics. The use of hydroponics will increase in the future as the population continues to grow and as more and more farmland is converted to urban use. Modern greenhouses can be constructed almost anywhere—on land that is unsuitable for agriculture and wildlife and on the tops of buildings in metropolitan areas. Improved technology will result in the development of better hydroponic systems as well as an increase in the economic feasibility of greenhouse production.

FURTHER READING: An excellent review with much of interest on hydroponic technology is M. H. Jensen and W. L. Collins, "Hydroponic Vegetable Production," *Horticultural Reviews* 7 (1985). A treatise on the use of liquid culture to grow plants, along with discussions of hydroponic culture techniques, is presented in *A Guide for the Hydroponic and Soilless Culture Grower*, by J. B. Jones, Jr., 1983. *Horticulture Science*, by Jules Janick, 1986, contains a section on hydroponics and synthetic soils and their use in horticulture. *The Nature and Properties of Soil*, by N. C. Brady, 1974, is an excellent book dealing with a wide range of soil characteristics; it is often used as a textbook for introductory soil classes.

D. R. Gossett

SEE ALSO: Horticulture; Monoculture agriculture; Plant domestication and breeding; Soil.

Hydrothermal solutions and mineralization

Hydrothermal solutions are "hot-water" solutions rich in base metals and other ions that create deposits of minerals. Most hydrothermal solutions are exhalations from magmas, but some hydrothermal deposits have no identifiable magma source. Hydrothermal processes are responsible for the major part of the world's base metals upon which modern society is so dependent. They have given rise to many of the great mining districts of the world.

ESSENTIAL CONDITIONS FOR the formation of hydrothermal mineral deposits include metal-bearing mineralizing solutions, openings in rocks through which the solutions are channeled, sites for deposition, and chemical reaction resulting in deposition. The term "ore" is used for any assemblage of minerals that can be mined for a profit. "Gangue" is the nonvaluable mineral that occurs with the ore.

During the crystallization of igneous rocks, water and other volatile fluids concentrate in the upper part of the magma. These volatiles carry with them varying amounts of the ions from the melt, including high concentrations of ions that are not readily incorporated into silicate rock-forming minerals. If the vapor pressure in the magma exceeds the confining pressure of the enclosing rocks, the fluids are expelled to migrate though surrounding country rock. These solutions travel along natural pathways in the rock such as faults, fissures, or bedding planes in stratified rocks. As the solutions migrate away from their source region, they lose their mineral content through deposition in natural openings in the host rock (forming open space-filling deposits) or by chemical reaction with the host rock (forming metasomatic replacement deposits). A part of these solutions may make it to the surface to form fumaroles (gas emanations) or hot springs. In addition, some hydrothermal solutions may be derived from water trapped in ancient sediments or by dehydration of water-bearing minerals during metamorphism.

The observed volatiles from magmas, as seen during volcanic eruptions and at fumaroles, are 80 percent water. Carbon dioxide, hydrogen sulfide, sulfur, and sulfur dioxide are also abundant. Nitrogen, chlorine, fluorine, boron, and other elements are present in smaller amounts. In addition, metal ions are carried in this residual fluid. Especially abundant are the base metals—iron, tungsten, copper, lead, zinc, molybdenum, silver, and gold. Quartz is the most common non-ore or gangue mineral deposited. Calcite, fluorite, and barite are also common as gangue minerals. Base metals combined with sulfur as sulfide minerals, with arsenic as arsenides, or with tellurium as tellurides form the most common ore minerals. Gold often occurs as a native mineral.

Nature of Open Spaces. Hydrothermal solutions find ready-made escape routes through the surrounding country rock in the form of faults and fissures. Ore and gangue minerals of cavity-filling deposits are found in faults or fissures (veins), in open spaces in fault breccias, in solution openings of soluble rocks, in pore spaces between the grain of sedimentary rocks, in vesicles of buried lava flows, and along permeable bedding planes of sedimentary strata. The shape of the mineral deposit is controlled by the configuration of structures controlling porosity and permeability. Fracture patterns, and therefore veins, may take on a wide variety of geometric patterns, ranging from tabular to rod-shaped or blanketlike deposits.

Some deposits are characterized by ore minerals that are widely disseminated in small amounts throughout a large body of rock such as an igneous stock. These igneous bodies undergo intense fracturing during the late stage of consolidation, and residual fluids permeate the fractured rock to produce massive deposits of low-grade ores. In such deposits, the entire rock is extracted in mining operations. The famous porphyry copper deposits of the southwestern United States, including those of Santa Rita, New Mexico; Morence, Arizona; and Bingham, Utah, are of this type, as are the molybdenum deposits of Climax, Colorado.

Metasomatic Replacement. Some hydrothermal deposits are emplaced by reaction of the fluids with chemically susceptible rocks such as limestone or dolostone. Metasomatic replacement is defined as simultaneous capillary solution and deposition by which the host is replaced by ore and gangue minerals. These massive deposits or lodes take on the shape and the original textures of the host. Replacement is especially important in deep-seated deposits where open spaces are scarce. Replacement deposits of lead-zinc are common in limestones surrounding the porphyry copper of Santa Rita, New Mexico, and at Pioche, Nevada.

Classification by Temperature and Depth. Veins are zoned, with higher-temperature minerals deposited near the source and lower-temperature minerals farther away. Hypothermal or high-temperature and high-pressure mineral assemblages include the minerals cassiterite (tin), scheelite and wolframite (tungsten), millerite (nickel), and molybdenite (molybdenum), associated with gangue minerals quartz, tourmaline, topaz, and other silicates. The mineral deposits of Broken Hill, Australia, the tin deposits of Cornwall, England, and Potosi, Bolivia, and the gold of the Homestake Mine, South Dakota, are hypothermal. Mesothermal, or moderate-temperature and moderate-pressure deposits consist of pyrite (iron sulfide), bornite, chalocite, chalcopyrite and enargite (copper), galena

(lead), sphalerite (zinc), and cobaltite or smaltite (cobalt). Gangue minerals include calcite, quartz, siderite, and rhodochrosite. The zinc-lead-silver replacement deposits of Leadville, Park City, and Aspen, Colorado, and the Coeur d'Alene, Idaho, lead veins are mesothermal. Epithermal or low-temperature, near-surface deposits are often associated with regions of recent volcanism. The ore is characterized by stibnite (antimony), cinnabar (mercury), native silver and silver sulfides, gold telluride, native gold, sphalerite, and galena. Gangue minerals include barite, fluorite, chalcedony, opal, calcite, and aragonite. The extensive silver-gold mineralization of the San Juan Mountains of Colorado, including Cripple Creek, Ouray, and Creede, are epithermal deposits. Telethermal deposits are formed by hydrothermal solutions that have cooled to approximately the same temperature as the near-surface rocks. These solutions may originate as mobilized connate and deeply circulating meteoric waters rather than fluids expelled from magma. The principal ore minerals are sphalerite and galena, with gangue minerals marcasite, fluorite, calcite, and chalcopyrite. The "Mississippi Valley-type" deposits of the tri-state district of Missouri, Kansas, and Oklahoma exemplify this low-temperature mineralization.

FURTHER READING: Waldemar Lingren's *Mineral Deposits*, 1933, is a classic text. A more recent book with comprehensive coverage is *The Geology of Ore Deposits*, by John M. Guilbert and Charles F. Park, Jr., 1986. *Geochemistry of Hydrothermal Ore Deposits*, edited by H. L. Barnes, 1979, includes papers by different authors on various aspects of ore formation.

René A. De Hon

SEE ALSO: Magma crystallization; Open-pit mining; Pegmatites; Secondary enrichment of mineral deposits; Underground mining.

Ickes, Harold

BORN: March 15, 1874; Frankstown Township, Pennsylvania
DIED: February 3, 1952; Washington, D.C.

Ickes, U.S. secretary of the interior from 1933 to 1946, expanded the responsibilities and powers of the Department of the Interior in the areas of conservation and preserving the nation's natural resources.

HAROLD L. ICKES was a lawyer, journalist, and municipal reformer in Chicago before his appointment as secretary of the interior. His selection was political; Franklin D. Roosevelt, a Democrat, was eager to gain the support of progressive Republicans and chose Ickes, who quickly became one of the most powerful figures in the nation. Always contentious and ready to battle for his beliefs, Ickes' enemies and admirers were legion.

As interior secretary, Ickes administered the

Harold Ickes was a powerful figure as U.S. secretary of the interior from 1933 to 1946 during Franklin D. Roosevelt's administration. (Archive Photos)

Biological Survey, the Bureau of Fisheries, and the Grazing Division. Particularly committed to the wilderness ideal, he added several parks and monuments to the National Park System and opposed their over-development. He fought to have the Forest Service transferred to the Department of the Interior but lost; he also failed to obtain his ultimate dream: to turn the Department of the Interior into the Department of Conservation.

In the enduring struggle within the conservation movement between preservationists and utilitarian conservationists, Ickes personified both strains but leaned toward the former. Nevertheless, as head of the Works Progress Administration (the WPA, one of the New Deal agencies), he supported the building of dams and other massive public works projects that remade the land and provided jobs during the Depression. Still, like few others in American government, Ickes exemplified the importance of the wilderness to the human spirit.

Eugene Larson

SEE ALSO: Conservation; Department of the Interior, U.S.; National Park Service and national parks; Roosevelt, Franklin D.; Roosevelt, Theodore; Taylor Grazing Act.

Igneous processes, rocks, and mineral deposits

Igneous rocks and mineral deposits, created by the crystallization and solidification of magma, are found all over the world. Many of the world's most economically important mineral deposits result, directly or indirectly, from igneous activity.

IGNEOUS ROCKS ARE created by the crystallization and solidification of hot, molten silicate magma. Magma consists of silicate liquid (the major component is the silica molecule SiO_4^{-4}), solid crystals, rock fragments, dissolved gases such as carbon dioxide, water, and various sulfurous oxides. Familiar examples of igneous rocks are granite (an "intrusive" or "plutonic" rock that is crystallized at depth) and basalt (as in dark "extrusive" lava flows, such as those in Hawaii). Igneous rocks are found worldwide on all continents, on oceanic islands, and on the ocean floors. They are particularly common in mountain ranges or other areas where the earth has undergone tectonic activity. Oceanic islands, such as Hawaii and Iceland, are nearly exclusively igneous in origin, and the world's oceans are floored by basalt lava flows.

Metallic ores produced by igneous activity may be mined directly from the igneous rocks or obtained through the injection of hydrothermal (hot water) veins into adjacent rocks. Some of the most important commodities obtained from igneous sources include copper, nickel, gold, silver, platinum, iron, titanium, tungsten, and tin. Nonmetallic products include crushed stone, construction stones for buildings and monuments, and some precious and semiprecious gemstones.

Igneous (from the Latin word *ignis*, meaning fire) rocks form by the crystallization of hot, molten magma produced by the heat of the earth's interior. Surface exposures of igneous rock bodies are widespread throughout the globe. On continents they mostly occur in mountainous areas or ancient "Precambrian shield" areas where billions of years of erosion reveal the roots of old mountain ranges. In the oceans igneous rocks cover the floors of ocean basins below a thin layer of sediment. Most oceanic islands owe their very existence to ocean floor volcanic eruptions that produce volcanoes of sufficient stature to project above the waves. Familiar examples are the Hawaiian chain, the Galápagos Islands, and Iceland.

Types of Igneous Rocks. Igneous rocks are divided into two major categories defined by their mode of emplacement in or on the earth's crust. If molten magma cools and solidifies below the surface, the rocks are called "intrusive" or "plutonic." Because these rocks generally take a long time to cool and solidify (a process called "crystallization"), their component minerals grow large enough to see with the naked eye (coarse-grained rocks). On the other hand, if magma flows out onto the earth's surface, it forms "extrusive" or "volcanic" rock. These rocks lose heat rapidly to air or water, and the resulting rapid crystallization produces tiny, nearly invisible crystals (fine-grained rocks). Some volcanic

rocks cool so quickly that few crystals have time to form; these are glassy rocks such as obsidian. Two kinds of volcanic rock exist: lava flows and "pyroclastic" deposits formed by explosive volcanism. Pyroclastic materials (volcanic ash) are deposited as layers of particles that have been violently ejected into the air.

Igneous rocks are also classified according to chemical composition. At one extreme are the light-colored "felsic" rocks that contain high concentrations of silica (up to about 75 percent silicon dioxide, SiO_2) and relatively little iron, magnesium, and calcium. Examples of felsic rocks are granite, a plutonic rock, and its volcanic equivalent, rhyolite (obsidian glass is rapidly cooled rhyolite).

At the other extreme are the dark "mafic" rocks with relatively low silica (as low as about 46 percent SiO_2) but with higher concentrations of iron, magnesium, and calcium. Examples of mafic rocks are gabbro (plutonic) and its volcanic equivalent, basalt. Rocks of intermediate composition also exist, for example plutonic diorite and its volcanic equivalent, andesite. It is andesite (and a more silicic variety called "dacite") that is expelled from the potentially explosive volcanoes of the Cascade Range in the American Pacific Northwest (Mount St. Helens, Mount Rainier, Mount Hood, and others).

Intrusive (Plutonic) Structures. Intrusive igneous rock bodies come in many shapes and sizes. The term "pluton" applies to all intrusive bodies but mainly to granitic rocks (granites, diorites, and related rocks). Specific terms applied to plutons mostly describe the size of the body. "Stocks" are exposed over areas less than 100 square kilometers, whereas "batholiths" are giant, commonly lens-shaped, bodies that exceed 100 square kilometers in exposed area. The Sierra Nevada range in eastern California is a good example of a batholith.

Some specialized pluton varieties are "laccoliths," commonly mountainous areas (for example, the Henry and La Salle mountains in Utah) in which intrusive granitic magma has invaded horizontal sedimentary layers and has bowed them up into a broad arch. A "phacolith" is similar to a laccolith only the magma has invaded folded sedimentary rocks so that the plu-

Simple Classification of Igneous Rocks

	Felsic	*Intermediate*	*Mafic*	*Ultramafic*
Extrusive (volcanic)	rhyolite	dacite/andesite	basalt	
Intrusive (plutonic)	granite	tonalite/diorite	gabbro	peridotite

← increasing silica

increasing iron and magnesium →

ton itself appears to have been folded.

Minor intrusive bodies include "sills," tabular bodies intruded parallel to rock layers (a laccolith can be considered a "fat sill"), and "dikes," tabular bodies that cut across rock layers. Sills and dikes are common features around the margins of plutons where they contact "country rock" (older, pre-intrusion materials).

Another intrusive body, mostly produced by mafic (gabbroic) magmas, is the "lopolith." Lopoliths are relatively large funnel-shaped bodies (on the order of large stocks or small batholiths) in some cases created where magma fills the down-warped part (syncline) of a fold structure. An excellent example is the Muskox intrusion of northern Canada; another possible one (one limb is unexposed under Lake Superior) is the Duluth gabbro intrusion of northeastern Minnesota.

Extrusive (Volcanic) Structures. The nature of volcanoes and volcanic rock deposits in general are greatly influenced by the composition of their parent magmas. Basalt magma is a low viscosity liquid (it is thin and flows easily) and thus produces topographically low, broad volcanic features. Typical of these are the "fissure flows" (also known as plateau basalts) in which basalt lava issues from fractures in the earth and spreads out almost like water in all directions. Examples are the Columbia River basalt plateau in Oregon and Washington, the Deccan Plateau in India, and the Pirana basalt plateau in Brazil. The basalt flows that floor the oceans are underwater versions of fissure flows.

Basaltic volcanoes tend to have low profiles but laterally extensive bases typified by the "shield" volcanoes of Hawaii and other areas. These volcanoes resemble giant ancient shields lying on the ground. Pyroclastic eruptions of basalt, powered mostly by the violent release of dissolved carbon dioxide, produce cinder-cone volcanoes, otherwise known as "Strombolian" volcanoes, after the Italian volcano Stromboli.

In contrast to mafic magmas, the more silica-rich felsic and intermediate magmas are more viscous, thus flow less readily. This magma tends to pile up in one place producing towering volcanoes of mountainous proportions. Because felsic-intermediate magmas also tend to contain significant dissolved water, steam trapped during eruption may explode violently, producing thick blankets of volcanic ash near the volcano. The best North American example of these potentially violent volcanoes, called "stratovolcanoes" or "composite" volcanoes, is the Cascade Range in the Pacific Northwest. The terms for these volcanoes reflect their tendency to have layers of mud and lava flows (generally andesite or dacite) that alternate with pyroclastic ash deposits. Stratovolcanoes occur worldwide, particularly at continental margins and in the oceans near continents where "lithospheric plates" (thick horizontal slabs of crust and upper mantle) collide, with one plate moving under the other (subduction zones). Volcanism associated with subduction zones has produced the Andes of South America as well as islands such as Japan, the Philippines, New Zealand, the Aleutian islands of Alaska, and the islands of Indonesia.

Another important volcanic feature is the

"rhyolite complex," or "caldera complex," exemplified by Yellowstone National Park in Wyoming and the Valles Caldera (Jemez Mountains), New Mexico. When fully active, these areas produce violently explosive volcanism and rhyolite lava flows that blanket many square kilometers. The most violent activity occurs when the roof of a large underground magma chamber collapses into the shallow void created by expulsion of magma during previous eruptions. The crater formed during this process is called a caldera. Roof collapse during caldera formation has the effect of ramming a large piston into the heart of the magma body violently expelling gas-charged, sticky rhyolite into the atmosphere, from which it may cascade along the surface as a *nuée ardente* (French for "glowing cloud"). These roiling infernos of hot noxious gases, bubbling lava fragments, and mineral crystals are capable of speeds in excess of 300 kilometers per hour and temperatures in excess of 400 degrees Celsius. They deposit ash blankets (welded ashflow tuffs) over wide regions, as in the case of Yellowstone. Stratovolcanoes (described above) can also form calderas and ashflow deposits, as exemplified at Crater Lake, Oregon.

Ore Deposits of Felsic-intermediate Rocks. Granite and related rocks are the source of many metals and other products that are the foundation of an industrial society. Quartz veins intruding granite may contain gold and other precious metals, as in the "mother lode" areas of the Sierra Nevada Range in California. These veins originate as hydrothermal deposits, minerals precipitated from hot-water fluids flowing through fractures in cooling granitic bodies. Felsic and intermediate composition igneous rocks contain significant dissolved water in their magmas (called "juvenile" water), which is finally expelled as hydrothermal fluids in the late stages of plutonic crystallization. Hydrothermal veins occur in the parent granite itself or are injected into the surrounding rocks. Many important metallic ore bodies formed as hydrothermal deposits.

So-called "porphyry copper" deposits such as those of the American southwest (Arizona, New Mexico, Colorado, and Utah) are low-grade deposits of widely scattered small grains of chalcopyrite ($CuFeS_2$) and other copper minerals in felsic plutonic and volcanic rocks, mostly residing in a multitude of very thin hydrothermal veins. Some porphyry copper deposits also have considerable deposits of molybdenite (in the sulfide molybdenite, used in high-temperature alloys), especially at the Questa mine in New Mexico and at Climax, Colorado.

By far the greatest concentration of valuable minerals associated with granitic rocks come from pegmatite deposits. Like hydrothermal deposits, pegmatites form in the late stages of granite crystallization after most of the other rock-forming minerals have already crystallized. Another similarity to hydrothermal fluids is their high volatile content—materials that tend to melt or form gases at relatively low temperatures, such as water, carbon dioxide, and the halogens fluorine and chlorine. Elements with large atomic sizes (ionic radii) and valence charges also tend to concentrate in pegmatitic fluids because the majority of minerals in granites (mostly quartz and feldspars) cannot accommodate these giant atoms in their mineral structures. Thus, pegmatite deposits may contain relatively high concentrations of uranium, thorium, lithium, beryllium, boron, niobium, tin, tantalum, and other rare metals. The high water content of pegmatite fluids, some of it occurring as vapor, allows minerals such as quartz, feldspar, and mica to grow to enormous sizes, the largest being on the order of railway boxcars. Pegmatites are generally fairly small bodies, some deposits being no larger than a small house; they may also occur as veins or dikes. Excellent North American examples containing rare and exotic minerals are located in the Black Hills of South Dakota, Maine, New Hampshire, North Carolina, the Adirondacks of New York state, Pala and Ramona in California, and Bancroft and Wiberforce, Canada. Notable international occurrences are in Brazil (Minas Gerais), Russia (the Urals and Siberia), Greenland, Italy, Australia, Germany (Saxony), the Malagasy Republic, and Sri Lanka.

Ore Deposits in Mafic and Related Rocks. Owing to their low viscosity, mafic magmas produce some unique mineral deposits compared with thicker felsic magmas. In plutonic settings formed early, heavy mineral crystals can easily

Typical Ore Minerals Associated with Igneous Rocks

Rock Type	Mineral	Metal or Other Commodity Obtained
Felsic—Intermediate		
Granite	Feldspar	Porcelain, scouring powder
	Native gold	Gold
Pegmatite	Cassiterite	Tin
	Beryl	Beryllium, gemstones (emerald; aquamarine)
	Tourmaline	Gemstone
	Spodumene	Lithium
	Lepidolite	Lithium
	Scheelite	Tungsten
	Rutile	Titanium
	Apatite	Phosphorus
	Samarskite	Uranium, niobium, tantalium, rare-earth elements
	Columbite, Tantalite	Niobium, tantalium, used in electronics
	Thorianite	Uranium, thorium
	Uraninite	Uranium
	Amazonite (microcline feldspar)	Gemstone
	Rose quartz	Gemstone
	Topaz	Gemstone
	Sphene (titanite)	Titanium, gemstone
	Muscovite mica	Electrical insulation
	Zircon	Zirconium
Rhyolite	Chalcopyrite	Cooper
	Molybdenite	Molybdenum
Mafic—Ultramafic		
Gabbro and Anorthosite	Ilmenite	Titanium
	Labradorite (plagioclase feldspar)	Gemstone
	Chalcopyrite	Copper
	Bornite	Copper
	Pentlandite	Nickel
Peridotite	Chromite	Chromium
	Native platinum	Platinum
	Sperrylite	Platinum
	Serpentine	Nickel (from weathered soils)

sink through the magma to form crystal-rich layers on the bottom of the magma chamber. These gravitationally deposited layers are called "cumulates" (from the word accumulate) and, depending on their mineralogical makeup, may constitute important ore bodies. Because cumulates are generally enriched in iron and depleted in silica compared with their mafic parent magma, they are termed "ultramafic," the common rock type being "peridotite," a rock rich in olivine $[(Fe,Mg)_2SiO_4]$. Most of the world's chromium that is used in high-temperature, corrosion-resistant alloys comes from cumulate layers of the mineral chromite $(FeCr_2O_4)$, mostly mined in South Africa. The other major commodity recovered from cumulates are the precious metals platinum and palladium, mined in South Africa and Russia.

Intrusive mafic magmas may also form layers of sulfide-rich minerals called "late-stage immiscible segregations" that constitute some of the richest copper and nickel ore bodies in the world. As some mafic magmas cool and change chemically, sulfur and metal-rich fluids may separate from the silicate liquid, just as oil would from water. These "immiscible" (incapable of mixing) sulfide droplets then sink through the lower density silicate magma to form thick layers of "massive sulfide" deposits on the magma chamber floor. The major minerals in massive sulfide copper-nickel mines are chalcopyrite, bornite (Cu_5FeS_4), pyrrhotite $(Fe_{1-x}S)$, and pentlandite $[(Fe,Ni)_9S_8]$. Platinum, gold, and silver, among minerals, are commonly recovered as by-products. Major magmatic segregation sulfide mines are located in South Africa (Messina and Bushveld districts, Transvaal) and Norway, and at Sudbury, Ontario, Canada, which has ore rich in nickel.

Titanium and iron ores may also form as magmatic segregations. Massive titanium ores, mostly the oxide ilmenite $(FeTiO_3)$, are mined from anorthosite rock, a plagioclase $[(Ca,Na)AlSi_3O_8]$ feldspar-rich variation of gabbro. Typical examples of these deposits occur in the titanium mines in the Adirondacks of New York state and at Allard Lake, Quebec. Iron deposits of this type, mostly the mineral magnetite (Fe3O4), are located at Kiruna, Sweden, the Ozarks of Missouri, Durango, Mexico, and Algarrobo, Chile.

Other Important Igneous Commodities. Some valuable mineral commodities are recovered from igneous rocks that do not lend themselves to simple classification. For example, diamonds occur in deposits called "kimberlites," a type of general deposit called "diatremes," explosively injected mixtures of mantle (mostly serpentine) and crustal materials that in rare localities contain diamonds. The diamonds form deep in the upper mantle, where pressures are sufficiently high to produce them by the reduction (removal of oxygen) of carbon dioxide. They are then injected into more shallow crustal levels upon the carbon dioxide-powered eruption of kimberlite. Diamonds are mostly mined in South Africa, Ghana, Congo (formerly Zaire), Russia, Brazil, India, and the United States (Murfreesboro, Arkansas).

Two other deposits with chemical affinities to kimberlites are "nepheline syenites" and "carbonatites." Like kimberlites, these bodies are rare, and their magmas probably originate deep in the earth's mantle. Nepheline syenites contain mostly the mineral nepheline $(NaAlSiO_4)$ and are sources of apatite (phosphate mineral) and corundum (Al_2O_3), used as an abrasive. Nepheline itself is used to make ceramics. Carbonatites are very unusual igneous deposits in that they are composed mostly of the carbonate mineral calcite $(CaCO_3)$. They have become increasingly important as sources of the rare elements niobium and tantalum, used in the electronics industry.

FURTHER READING: A concise and well-illustrated treatment of igneous rocks and processes can be found in *Petrology: Igneous, Sedimentary, and Metamorphic*, by Ernest G. Ehlers and Harvey Blatt, 1982. For a more advanced treatment, try *Igneous and Metamorphic Petrology*, by Myron G. Best, 1982. Another excellent source is *Igneous Petrology*, by Loren A. Raymond, 1995. To explore economic minerals provided by igneous rocks, see *Economic Mineral Deposits*, by Mead L. Jensen and Alan M. Bateman, 3d ed. 1981. An excellent book for researching the tectonic settings (mountains, rift valleys, and other environments) of mineral deposits, including those of batholiths, porphyry copper deposits, oceanic mineral deposits, and many others, is *Economic Deposits and Their Tectonic Setting*, by Charles S. Hutchinson, 1983. This book has a useful appendix in which mineral commodities are listed alphabetically along with production statistics, uses, and principal ore minerals.

John L. Berkley

SEE ALSO: Beryllium; Boron; Chromium; Copper; Feldspars; Geology; Gold; Granite; Lithium; Magma crystallization; Molybdenum; Nickel; Pegmatites; Plate tectonics; Plutonic rocks and mineral deposits; Pumice; Quartz; Tantalum; Tin; Titanium; Tungsten; Uranium; Volcanoes; Zirconium.

Incineration of wastes

The incineration of wastes provides a means for reducing the volume of various sorts of waste by destroying the organic components of waste.

THE INCINERATION OF household and hazardous waste material can help to reduce its volume and can provide the potential for electric power generation. The incineration of waste material is not a preferred strategy, however, because it does not stop the depletion of natural resources, and it may cause further environmental problems such as air pollution.

Thermal methods have been developed for dealing with solid, liquid, and the in-between slurry types of waste. Household trash has long been incinerated, often in backyard settings, but many governments now regulate this method except in rural areas. Some cities have built large incinerators for burning solid household waste; these are designed to reduce the waste stream as well as to provide for energy generation. Several types of incinerators have also been developed to deal with hazardous liquid and solid wastes in carefully regulated circumstances. By the mid-1990's some of these incinerators were also being used for energy production, although not on a large scale.

Household Waste and "Trash-to-Energy" Programs. The large volume of household waste is becoming an increasing problem for many localities in the United States. Landfill space is at a premium in some areas, and incineration offers a means of reducing the waste stream through the destruction of organic material. Open burning is prohibited by the Clean Air Act as well as by many municipal ordinances. However, incineration in grate type furnaces or kilns can reduce toxic releases to the air, and well-designed facilities can capture the ash for landfilling. This approach involves extensive sorting so that primarily organic material will be incinerated.

Because waste incineration requires high temperatures, a possibility exists for the generation of electrical energy as a by-product of the process. In the late 1970's and early 1980's "trash-to-energy" processes appeared to have a promising future in several U.S. metropolitan areas. Several local governments intended to use incinerators to generate electrical energy, either on their own or in tandem with an electric utility. However, a number of factors hampered the adoption of this approach. There were significant costs involved in sorting waste, and there was public reluctance to accept waste incineration. Landfill fees proved to be cheaper than incineration, and low-cost electric power continued to be available from other sources. Charlotte, North Carolina, for example, adopted a trash-to-energy program in the 1980's but abandoned it in the early 1990's as energy costs remained low and the costs of operating the incineration facility continued to increase. When and if energy prices increase sufficiently, a trash-to-energy program may become economically viable if public suspicion can be overcome.

Hazardous Waste Incineration. Thermal methods have been a commercial success in dealing with many types of hazardous industrial wastes as well as in cleaning contaminated Superfund sites. The Resource Conservation and Recovery Act regulates the incineration of both liquid and solid hazardous wastes in the United States. Although some municipal incinerators were intended to provide electrical energy as well as reduce the volume of waste, hazardous waste incineration is intended primarily to reduce the waste stream. In only a few cases is energy generation a product of the process, and they usually involve specialized thermal methods such as

Trash collected and dumped before incineration at a trash-to-energy incinerator facility in Detroit, Michigan. (Jim West)

firing cement kilns with certain types of liquid hazardous waste.

Liquid injection incinerators are the most common type of thermal method for dealing with hazardous waste. As the name implies, this method deals almost exclusively with pumpable liquid wastes. The waste material is injected into the burner or combustion zone of an incinerator through atomizing nozzles. When low heating value waste, such as aqueous-organic material, is being incinerated, it is necessary to use secondary burners. These incinerators operate at temperature levels from 1,000 degrees to 1,700 degrees Celsius. Residence time for the combustion products ranges from milliseconds to 2.5 seconds. Liquid injection incinerators are carefully regulated as to the type of waste they can burn, the release of gaseous products, and the disposition of the ash.

Three major types of solid waste incinerators exist: grate type incinerators, hearth type incinerators, and fluidized bed incinerators. Grate type incinerators are generally not suitable for hazardous waste incineration because the high temperatures necessary for the decomposition of many hazardous compounds can destroy the grates. There are several types of hearth type incinerators, the most common being rotary kilns, controlled air (two chamber fixed hearth) systems, and multiple hearth incinerators. The nonslagging type of rotary kiln, often used in the United States, does not require close monitoring, but it also does not have the feed flexibility that a slagging system does. Both types are viable and produce significant energy that can be used to burn additional waste. Multiple hearth systems were originally designed to handle sewage sludge, but they have been adapted to other circumstances. Fluidized bed technology utilizes a sand or alumina bed sitting on a porous surface. An air flow from below with a carefully controlled velocity places the bed of sand in suspension. Some rotary kilns and fluidized bed systems are portable and have been used to incinerate contaminated soil at Superfund sites and soil contaminated by underground fuel tanks.

Issues of Concern. In the United States there is a high level of suspicion regarding thermal methods for handling waste materials. This suspicion applies particularly to hazardous waste incinerators, but municipal incinerators are often opposed as well. The public's worries about safety have helped to curtail the adoption of municipal trash-to-energy facilities in the United States. They have also led to citizen protests regarding local hazardous waste incinerators. Yet the incineration of liquid and solid hazardous organic materials can reduce substantially the amount of hazardous material that needs to be landfilled. Before trash-to-energy incinerators can become fully viable, citizen opposition needs to be reduced, and the costs of operation need to be controlled. Hazardous waste incineration does produce highly toxic ash that requires careful handling, often in specially designed landfills. It is thus not a panacea for curtailing the use of natural resources; rather, it is simply a means of reducing the volume of waste.

FURTHER READING: A helpful introduction to hazardous waste incineration can be found in Michael D. LaGrega, Phillip L. Buckingham, and Jeffrey C. Evans, *Hazardous Waste Management*, 1994. See also Louis Blumberg and Robert Gottlieb, *War on Waste*, 1989, and Homer A. Neal and J. R. Schubel, *Solid Waste Management and the Environment*, 1987.

John M. Theilmann

SEE ALSO: Air pollution and air pollution control; Landfills; Superfund legislation and cleanup activities; Waste management and sewage disposal.

Indium

WHERE FOUND: Indium is widely distributed in the earth's crust in small amounts. It is fairly rare, being about as common as silver. Indium is never found as a free metal but only in combination with other elements. It is found as a trace component in many minerals, particularly in ores of zinc, copper, lead, and tin. The richest concentrations of indium are found in Colorado, Argentina, the United Kingdom, and Canada.

PRIMARY USES: Indium is used for a variety of purposes in the electronics industry, including liquid-crystal displays and transistors. It is also used in batteries, solders, coatings for glass, sealants, and alloys that melt at low temperatures.

DESCRIPTION: Indium (abbreviated In), atomic number 49, belongs to Group IIIA of the periodic table of the elements and resembles aluminum in its chemical and physical properties. It has two naturally occurring isotopes and an average atomic weight of 114.82. Pure indium is a soft, white metal. Its density is 7.31 grams per cubic centimeter; it has a melting point of 156.61 degrees Celsius and a boiling point of 2,080 degrees Celsius.

INDIUM, A FAIRLY uncommon element, occurs in the earth's crust with an average concentration of about one part in ten million. It is most commonly found in ores that are rich in zinc, particularly those which contain sphalerite (zinc sulfide). It is also found in ores of copper, lead, and tin.

Indium was discovered in 1863 by Ferdinand Reich and Theodor Richter. It was not produced in large amounts until 1940. Its first major industrial use was in the production of automobile and aircraft engine bearings, where it added strength, hardness, resistance to corrosion, and ability to retain a coating of oil. In the 1960's it was first used in transistors.

Indium is usually obtained as a by-product of zinc production. A variety of methods exists for obtaining indium from the residue left over after most of the zinc is removed from the ore. One method involves treating the residue with dilute sulfuric acid to dissolve the remaining zinc. The undissolved material left behind is then treated with stronger acid to dissolve the indium. The indium is treated with zinc oxide to obtain indium hydroxide or with sodium sulfite or sodium bisulfite to obtain indium sulfite. Pure indium metal is then obtaining by subjecting these compounds to electrolysis.

Indium is often combined with other metals such as bismuth, cadmium, lead, and tin to form alloys with a low melting point. These are used in fuses and heat-detecting sprinkler systems. It has also been mixed with lead to form solders that remain flexible over a wide range of temperatures. Molten indium has the unusual property of clinging to glass and other smooth surfaces and is often used to form seals and coatings. High-purity indium is used in combination with germanium to form transistors. The electronics industry also uses indium in liquid-crystal displays, infrared detectors, and solar cells.

Rose Secrest

SEE ALSO: Alloys; Aluminum; Metals and metallurgy; Zinc.

Industrial Revolution and industrialization

The term "Industrial Revolution" describes that historical period in which the exploitation of new energy technologies led to industrialization—the centralization of production with a reorganization of human living patterns and increased consumption of a broad range of natural resources.

THE INDUSTRIAL REVOLUTION is generally considered to have begun in England in the eighteenth century and to have spread to North America, northern Europe, and then further throughout the world. It is still underway in emerging nations of Asia, Africa, and Latin America. Industrialization is characterized by increased consumption of energy and material resources, centralization of production, the growth of urban populations, and the evolution of extensive transportation and energy distribution infrastructures.

The production of nonagricultural goods has followed a common historical pattern in many parts of the world. At first, families (or somewhat larger tribal units) make enough for their own needs. Then a type of trade develops in which individuals specialize in the production of a limited number of goods, and a market economy—allowing the accumulation of money or capital—

is established. The buying and selling then increasingly comes under the control of merchants who buy from the producers and arrange transport to the buyers. At first domestic manufacture prevails; in other words, production occurs within or near the home. Eventually an industrial stage is achieved: Labor is centralized so that investment can be made in the means of production and economies of scale can be realized.

Preconditions. In order for factory production to supplant domestic production in a nation or region, there must be adequate supplies of human power, mechanical energy, and capital. A transportation infrastructure must be in place. Further, some rudimentary knowledge of science and engineering is required, as are adequate materials with which to build machinery. Cultural assumptions are also important. Industrialization will not occur unless improvements in material wealth are considered both possible and desirable by those in positions of political and economic power.

The Industrial Revolution could not have occurred before an agricultural revolution made it possible for a smaller proportion of the population to be directly involved in food production, thereby freeing individuals to move to cities. Historians view the agricultural revolution as beginning with the transition in western Europe, about the year 1600, from open fields to enclosed individual farms and the subsequent introduction of new crops (particularly feed for livestock), new tools for plowing and planting, and improvements in livestock. With the increased availability of animal muscle power and fertilizer from animal waste, farms became more productive, but they were also more expensive to run. Rural populations stratified into farm owners, tenants, and paid workers. The latter, having no direct tie to the land, were free to move to the city in search of work, and they formed the first pool of industrial workers.

Because building a factory requires capital and entrepreneurs who can afford to wait a period of time to realize a return on their investment, the Industrial Revolution also had to await the accumulation of wealth by merchants and the founding of banks with sufficient funds to finance industrial construction. Further, the centralization of production could only be effective with the availability of dependable transport of raw materials to, and finished goods from, the factories. Perhaps the most characteristically "industrial" feature of the revolution, and certainly the one with the greatest direct impact on natural resources, was the development of easily controlled mechanical power, essential to both production and the infrastructure upon which mechanized production depends.

The Steam Engine. Prior to the eighteenth century the only available sources of mechanical energy were muscle, wind, and flowing or falling water. The latter had been widely exploited in milling and other industries. The development of the steam engine appears to have been a by-product of the metal and coal mining industries. A major problem in mining was water that seeped into mine shafts, and in 1698 English inventor Thomas Savery introduced a water-lifting device based on steam pressure.

By 1713 an English craftsman named Thomas Newcomen had produced the first steam engine that could function at atmospheric pressure. The basic Newcomen design was improved by James Watt, a Scottish instrument maker, in the period between 1765 and 1790. By 1820 some sixty steam engines were at work in Birmingham, England, generating a total of about 1,000 horsepower. A scant eighteen years later there were slightly more than three thousand steam engines in the United States—on steamboats, in railroad locomotives, and in manufacturing use.

The steam engine converts heat energy into mechanical energy. Its development meant that mechanical power could be available wherever there was an adequate supply of fuel. The burning of coal, which had already begun to replace wood for home heating, became the principal source of power for the Industrial Revolution, with the early steam engines providing a means both of pumping water from mine shafts and of cutting the coal from deposits. With the extensive use of coal came the first industrial air pollution, with soot and sulfur oxides being released into the air.

Industrialization of the Textile Industry. The production of fiber and cloth was the first manufac-turing process to be industrialized, and cotton proved to be the fiber most amenable to the mechanized processing. Cotton is converted into cloth by the processes of carding, spinning, and weaving, in which the fibers are separated from one another, wound into thread or yarn, and then woven into fabric. The first spinning machine was put into production in London in 1740, with a carding machine developed about a decade later. Improvements in both these technologies were achieved by the English inventor James Hargreaves, who patented the "spinning jenny" in 1770 and a carding engine in 1775. The power loom was introduced by Edmund Cartwright, an English clergyman turned industrialist, in 1785. The number of power looms in England and Scotland grew from about fourteen thousand in 1820 to a hundred thousand in 1833.

The explosive growth of the textile industry had important implications for land use and for

Textile manufacturing in mid-nineteenth century New England. (Archive Photos)

world politics. The British government sought to prevent the designs for textile machinery from leaving England so as to maintain a monopoly on textile production. The American textile industry began in 1790 when an English immigrant named Samuel Slater built successful water-powered spinning machines in Pawtucket, Rhode Island. Following the invention of the cotton gin (which separates cotton fiber from the seed) by the American Eli Whitney in 1793, cotton became a principal crop in the southern United States. Following the industrialization of the American textile industry, the need for sources of raw cotton and markets for finished textiles became a major determinant of British colonial policy in the middle East and India.

Transportation. With industrialization came the need for more efficient transportation of raw materials to manufacturing centers and of finished goods to consumers. The first steamboat, in which a steam engine produced the motive power for a paddlewheel, was demonstrated in 1787 by John Fitch, an American inventor. Regular steamboat service was not established until twenty years later, when American engineer Robert Fulton introduced regular service on New York's Hudson River. The first propeller-driven steamships were introduced in 1836, and in 1845 a propeller-driven ship crossed the Atlantic, inaugurating a new era in world-wide shipping.

The second major vehicle for the transport of goods and services was the railroad. The first designs that were called "railroads" consisted of short lengths of wooden rail on which horses moved coal for short distances. In 1804 an English inventor named Richard Trevithick mounted a steam engine on a four-wheeled carriage and used his invention to pull a 9-ton load of coal over 9 miles of track. The first public railroad began operation in England in 1825. By that time railroad-building had already spread to the United States. With government support, the railroads rapidly expanded across North America, fueling the westward migration of farmers and cattlemen and resulting in the conversion of vast areas of wilderness to agricultural use.

The Chemical Industry. The chemical industry is somewhat unusual in that most of its products are meant for use in other industries. It also is probably the industry with the greatest impact on natural resources other than energy resources. Sulfuric acid, used in the bleaching of textiles and the cleaning of metals, was perhaps the first major "chemical" to be used. At the end of the eighteenth century, new sources of alkali were being sought to meet the demands of glassmaking and soapmaking. The depletion of the forests of Europe to produce charcoal had led to a scarcity of potash (potassium carbonate), traditionally obtained from wood ash. In 1780 Nicolas Leblanc developed a process whereby soda ash (sodium carbonate) could be produced from salt, chalk, and sulfuric acid. The modern chemical industry began about 1840 when chemists discovered that numerous organic chemicals could be extracted from coal tar, a by-product of the use of coke in blast furnaces. In addition to aromatic hydrocarbons such as benzene and toluene, then thought of mainly as solvents, the nitrogen-containing compound aniline and an entire family of aniline dyes were obtained. A great number of new chemical compounds and industrial by-products were thus released into industrial wastewater.

The Internal Combustion Engine. While the steam engine was the original workhorse of the Industrial Revolution, it had many inefficient features. Heat energy, provided by burning wood or coal, was used to heat water, creating the steam that provided the moving force for a piston, which in turn produced the actual mechanical motion. Much of the generated heat energy escaped in the process. The strategy of using the fuel as the working material—thereby eliminating the middle steps in the production of motion—was realized in the internal combustion engine, developed in the years 1863 to 1866 by a German traveling salesman, Nikolaus August Otto.

The compactness of the internal combustion engine made it an extremely attractive power source for self-powered vehicles, including the automobile and the truck. The automobile became a major product of industry in the United States. The motor truck provided the capability to deliver goods wherever there was a road. Possibly no single aspect of industrialized society has had as much effect on land use and air quality as the automobile. In 1908 Henry Ford introduced the Model T, the first automobile to be affordable by many Americans. Within twenty years more than half of all American families owned motorcars. Petroleum refining and road construction became major industries. Unfortunately, the combustion of gasoline in the automobile engine was not complete, so carbon monoxide and volatile hydrocarbons were released into the air. To keep the engines running smoothly, tetraethyl lead was added to gasoline, resulting in the release of lead in automobile exhausts. Eventually improvements in engine design and the introduction of the catalytic converter were able to reduce the amount of polluting material released per mile traveled.

Electricity. Italian physicist Alessandro Volta invented the electric battery in 1800, opening a new energy source to development. After the invention of the electromagnet by William Sturgeon in 1825, a number of inventors strove to perfect the electromagnetic telegraph, by which messages could be sent over wires almost instantaneously. Exploitation of the telegraph required the stringing of telegraph lines between major cities. Much of the development of electrical technology was driven by the potential for long-distance communication. The discovery of the electric motor and generator marked a new freedom in the generation of mechanical energy. Electrical energy could be produced wherever convenient and transmitted at low cost to wherever it might be needed. In particular, electricity could be generated by the energy of falling water, either at a natural waterfall, such as at Niagara Falls, or by damming the flow of rivers.

An explosion in energy consumption was heralded by Thomas Edison's invention of the incandescent electric light in the late nineteenth century. In order for profits to be generated by this innovation it was necessary to establish networks of generators, transmission lines, and transformers for the distribution of electrical energy. These networks could be powered by falling water (hydroenergy), by the burning of coal, oil, or natural gas, or, following World War II, by the energy released by nuclear fission. Each of these sources carried its own environmental price. The burning of fossil fuels produced air pollution, and nuclear energy plants produced nuclear waste as well as excessive quantities of heat, leading to the thermal pollution of streams and lakes. Even hydroelectric power, widely considered a "clean" and renewable energy source, alters local ecosystems and interferes with scenery; moreover, dams have a limited life cycle because they are eventually filled in with sediment.

Impact on Natural Resources. The course of industrialization in western Europe and the United States demonstrates dramatically the interconnections between technological change, social and economic conditions, and the utilization of natural resources. Overall, industrialization is accompanied by an increased use of natural resources, punctuated by innovations and discoveries that may shift consumption from one resource to another. While industrialization has historically resulted in varying degrees of environmental degradation—ranging from deforestation to damage from huge strip mines to air and water pollution—advances in technology frequently allow a more efficient use of resources, moderating the demand for individual scarce resources and limiting environmental impact. The evolution of automobiles over the last forty years of the twentieth century, for instance, saw a reduction in metal usage, greatly increased fuel economy, the elimination of lead release to the environment, and a reduction in other pollutants.

There has been considerable debate over the question of whether continuing worldwide industrialization, coupled with population growth, will deplete crucial resources such as oil and certain mineral resources in the near future. On the one hand, reserves of materials such as oil are finite. On the other hand, a number of factors seem to be mitigating the problem. Automation and computers are being employed in industry to use resources more efficiently and minimize waste, reducing the drain on resources. Improvements in renewable energy resources such as solar and wind power, together with recycling technologies for key materials, offer at least the possibility of continued industrialization without the exhaustion of essential resources in the foreseeable future.

FURTHER READING: The role of the Industrial Revolution in determining the character of modern society is examined by Jacob Bronowski in *The Ascent of Man*, 1973. More scholarly treatments, with discussions of the impact on natural resources, can be found in *Technology and Western Civilization*, edited by Melvin Kranzberg and Carrol W. Pursell, Jr., 1967, and in even greater depth in *The Industrial Revolution*, vol. 4 in the multivolume *A History of Technology*, edited by Charles Singer et al., 1958. A good overview of industrialization in the United States can be found in *Technology in America*, edited by Carrol W. Pursell, Jr., 1990.

Donald R. Franceschetti

SEE ALSO: Air pollution and air pollution control; Capitalism and resource exploitation; Coal; Developing countries, resource use by; Environmental degradation, resource exploitation and; Internal combustion engine; Iron; Manufacturing, energy use in; Oil industry; Steam engine; Steel industry; Transportation, energy use in; Watt, James.

Internal combustion engine

Along with the electric motor, the internal combustion engine became the most widely used source of motive power in twentieth century technology. Its advantages of speed and intermittent operation made it a popular power source for transportation. Widespread use depended on a steady source of liquid fuel, so a huge demand for petroleum products was created.

THE INTERNAL COMBUSTION ENGINE uses the principle that an explosive mixture of air and fuel contained in a space will expand when ignited. Three basic types of engines developed from that principle: atmospheric, which used the pressure of the atmosphere to move a piston after an explosion created a vacuum; noncompression, which exploded a mixture of air and fuel in a chamber; and precompression, which compressed a mixture of air and fuel before ignition. Designers used either a reciprocal or turbine action as the basic motion in the devices.

Historical Background. As early as the seventeenth century, gunpowder-fueled cannons demonstrated the power generated by internal combustion. This knowledge led Christian Huygens to produce the first such gunpowder-powered device in 1673; it had little practical success. Although several people experimented with internal combustion designs for more than a century and a half after Huygens' pioneering efforts, no successful efforts emerged until William Murdoch produced a reliable source of coal gas as fuel for these engines in 1790. From that date until the 1850's, several inventors experimented with a variety of devices used to produce motive or stationary power. None was practical, and none saw commercial success, yet these efforts were important in the development stage of internal combustion power.

Jean-Joseph-Étienne Lenoir produced the first commercially viable internal combustion engine in 1859; it used town coal gas for fuel. Lenoir's noncompression engine generated as much as three horsepower and sold widely in the 1860's. However, its high fuel consumption, size, rough operation, and extensive maintenance demands kept it from developing into a major power source. The creation of a practical engine depended on the ingenuity of German engineers and on the ready availability of petroleum-based fuels.

Nineteenth century German inventor Nikolaus August Otto sensed that the Lenoir engine would have a greater potential if powered by a portable liquid fuel. That awareness motivated Otto to begin a long process of improving the Lenoir engine and creating his own design, which became the standard for decades. This process was typical of much innovation in technology: An inventor and a developer/financier formed a team to improve an existing design. In Otto's case, he was fortunate to work with Eugen Langen, who provided both technical and financial assistance in the development of an atmospheric engine.

By 1876 Otto had learned the importance of precompression and devised his famous "silent Otto engine": a four-stroke cycle engine using intake of fuel, compression, ignition, and expansion and exhaust phases. Using this Otto method of power generation in a four-cylinder engine, Gottlieb Daimler in 1885 used an early

Standard Four-Stroke Internal Combustion Engine

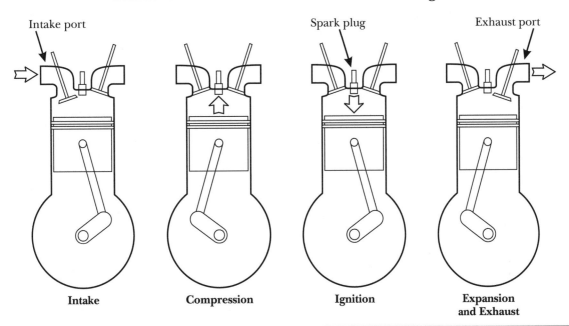

Intake port Spark plug Exhaust port

Intake **Compression** **Ignition** **Expansion and Exhaust**

A generalized depiction of the four-stroke internal combustion engine. Intake: Air enters the cylinder and mixes with gasoline vapor. Compression: The cylinder is sealed, and the piston moves upward to compress the air-fuel mixture. Ignition: The spark plug ignites the mixture, creating pressure that drives the piston downward. Expansion (exhaust): The burned gases exit the cylinder.

form of gasoline to power the engine and created the prototype for the widely used automobile engines of the twentieth century. The use of petroleum fuel increased the mobility and convenience of the automobile and created a growing demand for both gasoline and the Otto-type engine. The practical motorcar also depended on further improvements to the Otto engine, such as Wilhelm Maybach's carburetor (1892) and an electric spark ignition system that was developed by 1900. These features made the car powered by an internal combustion engine a new and popular transportation device in the early years of the twentieth century.

Applications. The internal combustion engine also powered airplanes, marine vehicles, trucks, and factory machines. By the early 1900's, Rudolf Diesel's self-ignition engines, relying on fuel oil, saw use in heavy-duty applications. Frank Whittle's development work in Britain on a gasoline-powered turbine engine in the 1920's and 1930's led to jet aircraft toward the end of

World War II. These became widespread in aviation in the postwar era and added to the demand for petroleum fuels. These diverse uses of the internal combustion engine and its dependability made this design a favorite in the marketplace for over a century despite its inefficiency and the fact that it polluted the environment.

Resource Use. The demand and consumption of petroleum as a fuel grew with the increased uses of the internal combustion engine in the twentieth century. For example, in the United States gasoline use increased more than tenfold from 1910 to 1950 as Americans embraced the car culture, and it tripled between 1950 and 1990, an era of suburban growth and multiple-car families. Gasoline consumption far outpaced domestic petroleum production, and the United States tripled the amount of oil it imported in the short time period from 1967 to 1973. In the 1990's, the United States continued to import more than half of the petroleum it consumed each year. Although the internal combustion engine was the preeminent mobile power source of the late twentieth century, its use of nonrenewable energy resources and the pollutants it released generated a growing interest in finding alternative sources of reliable mobile power.

FURTHER READING: C. Lyle Cummins, Jr.'s *Internal Fire*, 1976, is a comprehensive history of the internal combustion engine with a wealth of material on many contributors to the development of such engines. M. G. Lay's *Ways of the World: A History of the World's Roads and of the Vehicles That Used Them*, 1992, contains straightforward and thorough treatments of internal combustion and the development of the automobile. Rudy Volti's "Why Internal Combustion?" *American Heritage of Invention and Technology* 6 (Fall, 1990), presents the reasons the internal combustion engine won the competition from steam and electricity to become the dominant power source for the automobile. The annual *Statistical Abstract of the United States* for individual years and *Historical Statistics of the United States, Colonial Times to 1970*, 1975, both from the U.S. Government Printing Office, are excellent sources of information regarding resource use in the United States.

H. J. Eisenman

SEE ALSO: Air pollution and air pollution control; Clean Air Act; Gasoline and other petroleum fuels; Oil and natural gas, worldwide distribution of; Oil embargo and energy crises of 1973 and 1979; Oil industry; Petroleum refining and processing; Transportation, energy use and.

International Union for the Conservation of Nature and Natural Resources

DATE ESTABLISHED: 1948

The IUCN, also known as the World Conservation Union, plays a major role in developing and implementing conservation treaties, conventions, and agreements.

THE FOUNDING OF this nongovernmental organization was an integral aspect of the postwar evolution of international environmental politics. It was established as the International Union for the Protection of Nature (IUPN). Its intended focus was the preservation of wildlife and the natural environment, education, scientific research, legislation, and the collection, analysis, and dissemination of data and information. Over several years, the IUPN's agenda broadened from a focus on wildlife protection to include the protection of renewable resources. This larger scope was reflected in its 1956 name change to the International Union for Conservation of Nature and Natural Resources (IUCN). Regardless of either of these names, the organization is popularly known as the World Conservation Union.

The IUCN has a federative structure with four categories of membership: states, governmental agencies, and national and international nongovernmental organizations. There are also nonvoting affiliates as well as nonvoting individual and organizational supporters. The IUCN does its work through a number of specialized commissions and committees. The union is headquartered in Gland, Switzerland, with an environmental law center in Bonn, Germany, and conservation monitoring centers at Cambridge and at Kew in the United Kingdom. In addition, the IUCN has regional offices in Africa, Central American, and Asia. It reports on its activities in the *IUCN Bulletin*, and it publishes reports and books on conservation issues.

Marian A. L. Miller

see also: Conservation; Environmental movement; Natural Resource Defense Council; Renewable and nonrenewable resources; United Nations Environment Programme; Wildlife.

Iodine

WHERE FOUND: Iodine is widely distributed at a low concentration; only in brines and caliche ores is the concentration sufficient to make separation practical.

PRIMARY USES: Iodine is used primarily in animal feed supplements, catalysts, inks, colorants, photographic equipment, and disinfectants. An important use is in iodized salt, which prevents goiter.

DESCRIPTION: Iodine (abbreviated I), atomic number 53, belongs to Group VII (the halogens) of the periodic table of the elements and resembles chlorine in its chemical properties. One stable isotope exists with an atomic weight of 126.9045. At room temperature, iodine is a purple-black color with a metallic sheen. Its elemental form is diatomic (two atoms of iodine bonded together). The solid has a density of 4.942 grams per cubic centimeter and sublimes easily. The melting point of iodine is 113.7 degrees Celsius, and the boiling point is 184.5 degrees Celsius.

THE SON OF a saltpeter manufacturer, Bernard Courtois, first noticed iodine in 1811 while extracting compounds from the ash of algae gathered along the seashore. He observed a cloud of violet vapor and an irritating odor. Courtois tested the dark crystals that formed on cold objects as well as he could in his simple laboratory. Because he suspected that this was a new element, he provided samples to two of his friends, Charles-Bernard Desormers and Nicolas Clement at the Conservatoire des arts et des métiers. With better equipment, they continued the investigation of this new substance and in 1813 announced the discovery of iodine. The name comes from the Greek word *iodes*, for "violet-like." The first iodine-containing mineral was found in Mexico in 1825. The discovery of iodate as a contaminant of the Chile saltpeter beds was an even more important discovery.

Iodine is the sixtieth element in order of abundance, at 0.46 parts per million in the earth's crust. Commercial deposits are usually iodates such as lautarite $Ca(IO_3)_2$ and dietzeite $7Ca(IO_3)_2 \bullet 8CaCrO_4$. Some brines in Louisiana, California, and Michigan contain 30 to 40 parts per million iodide ion, while some Japanese brines contain 100 parts per million. Iodine is only 0.05 parts per million in seawater, but some sea plants concentrate iodine up to 0.45 percent (4,500 parts per million) of their dry weight.

Obtaining Iodine. The method of iodine production depends on the source of the iodine. From the Chilean saltpeter beds, the sodium iodate is dissolved by an alkaline solution, converted to iodide ion by reaction with sodium hydrogen sulfite, and iodine is then precipitated by adding iodate solution. From brines, the iodide ion is converted to iodine by reaction with chlorine. Air blowing through the solution collects the iodine, which then precipitates. Purification is by resublimation. In an alternate method the iodide ion is precipitated with silver ion, reacted with iron to make iron iodide, and reacted with chlorine to produce iodine. The newest method uses an ion-exchange resin to collect the iodine after it has reacted with chlorine. The annual production of iodine is about 17 million kilograms.

Uses of Iodine. Iodine has a multitude of small-percent usages. It is used in catalysts for synthetic rubber manufacture, stabilizers, dyestuffs, pigments, sanitizers, photographic chemicals for high-speed negatives, pharmaceuticals, lithium-iodine batteries, high-purity metals, motor fuels, and lubricants. An alcohol solution of iodine called tincture of iodine is a well-known antiseptic. A new use may be in trifluoromethyl iodide (CF_3I) as a replacement for chlorofluorocarbons as refrigerants. The trifluoromethyl iodide does not cause the damage to the ozone layer that the chlorofluorocarbons do. Radioactive iodine, either I-123 or I-131, can be used to treat thyroid disease, including cancer, or to generate an image of the thyroid. Iodine can also be used as a contrast agent in producing X rays of soft tissue such as the gall bladder. Uses of iodine will continue to develop, as it is a reactive element which forms compounds with every group of elements except the noble gases.

Nutritional Aspects. Iodine is a necessary trace element in animals. An iodine deficiency may cause a range of problems, including goiter, mental retardation, increased stillbirths and miscarriages, and the severe mental and physical handicaps of cretinism. Common table salt ("iodized" salt) contains iodine at a 0.01-percent level, which is enough to safely prevent the above ailments. Iodine is used in the body to produce the growth-regulating hormone thyroxine. An excess of iodine may lead to thyroid cancer or interfere with hormone production. Although throughout history, iodine shortage has normally been the problem, the use of iodine in animal feed, sanitizers, and food processing causes Americans to consume many times the recommended daily allowance of iodine. The effects of this are not truly known, but it may prove to be unhealthy. Iodine is highly toxic to plants and does not appear to be necessary for plant life.

FURTHER READING: More detail on the discovery of iodine is in *Discovery of the Elements*, by Mary Elvira Weeks, 1960. The annual *Minerals Yearbook* (vol. 1, *Metals and Minerals*), from the U.S. Bureau of Mines (after 1996, published by the U.S. Geological Survey), has considerable information on the production, uses, and availability of iodine. Two books that provide a nice summary of iodine reactions are *Chemistry of the Elements*, by N. N. Greenwood and A. Earnshaw, 1984, and *Chemical Periodicity*, by R. J. Sanderson, 1960. The nutritional aspects of iodine are treated in *Trace Elements in Human and Animal Nutrition*, by E. J. Underwood, 1962. *A Simple Matter of Salt*, by Renate L. Fernandez, 1990, is a study of iodine deficiency in Spain. The *FDA Consumer* has had several articles on iodine, including vol. 15, no. 3 (1981); vol. 26, no. 10 (1992); and vol. 16, no. 8 (1982). Another useful article is *Element Concentrations Toxic to Plants, Animals, and Man*, U.S. Geological Survey Bulletin 1466, 1979.

C. Alton Hassell

SEE ALSO: Agricultural products; Lithium; Ozone layer and ozone hole debate; Synthetic rubber.

Iron

WHERE FOUND: Iron is one of the most abundant metals in the world, constituting 35 percent of the entire earth and 5 percent of the earth's crust. It combines with other elements in hundreds of minerals, the most important of which are hematite and magnetite. The former Soviet Union, Brazil, Australia, China, and the United States are the five top iron ore mining areas.

PRIMARY USES: Iron and its principal alloy, steel, are widely used in tools, machines, and structures. Historically, discoveries and inventions involving the many uses of iron have been crucially important. Iron is also essential to biological life.

DESCRIPTION: Iron is a chemical element (symbol Fe, from the Latin *ferrum*) and a metal of the transition Group VIII on the periodic table. Its atomic number is 26 and its atomic weight 55.487. Iron's melting point is 1,535 degrees Celsius, its boiling point 3,000 degrees Celsius, and its density 7.86 grams per cubic centimeter.

IRON IS THE cheapest and most widely used metal in the world. It is used in three main products: wrought iron, steel, and cast iron. Although each is approximately 95 percent iron and is produced with the same fuel, they have vastly different properties, arising from different production methods. Wrought iron, containing negligible amounts of carbon, has a melting point so high that it was not achieved by humans until the nineteenth century. When hot, wrought iron can be forged and welded, and even when it is cold it is ductile—capable of being shaped and hammered. Steel contains 0.25 to 1.25 percent carbon, with a lower melting point than wrought iron. It can be forged when hot and is extremely hard when quenched (cooled quickly by plunging into water or another cooling medium). Cast iron, with approximately 2 to 4.5 percent carbon, is easily melted and poured into molds. When cool it is soft and easily machined, but it is brittle and does not withstand tension forces well.

Historical Background. Iron was probably discovered accidentally in the late Bronze Age when it was found in the ashes of fires that had been built on top of red iron ore. Artifacts of iron weapons and tools have been found in Egypt (including the Great Pyramid of Giza) dating to 2900 B.C.E. It has probably been made on a regular basis since at least 1000 B.C.E. The Chinese had independently developed their own furnaces and techniques for producing cast iron by the sixth century B.C.E. The Romans acquired ironworking technology from the Greeks and spread it throughout northern Europe. Because iron ore was readily available throughout the Near East and Europe, iron was less expensive than copper and bronze, the "metals of aristocracy." As a result, it was used to make many everyday tools and utensils, earning its later nickname, "the democratic metal."

Historical Production Methods. Through the Middle Ages, the common method of producing iron was the bloomery method. A bloomery may have been as simple as a circular hollow in the ground, several feet deep and several feet across. The iron ore was heated in a bed of burning charcoal within this hollow, often with the use of bellows to increase the fire's temperature. As it was heated to about 800 degrees Celsius (normally the highest temperature attainable in early bloomeries), the oxygen in the ore separated from the iron and combined with carbon to form slag. The iron changed to a pasty mass called the "bloom." The operator removed the bloom when he judged it was ready and alternately hammered and reheated it to remove the slag and to consolidate the iron. The final product was wrought iron, produced at temperatures below iron's melting point, a process referred to as the "direct" method. Sometimes the iron would accidentally melt in the bloomery; this was undesirable, because prolonged exposure allowed the iron to absorb carbon from the charcoal, creating cast iron. Because of its lack of ductility and low resistance to abrasion, cast iron was unsuitable for working into tools and weapons and was therefore considered worthless.

The Blast Furnace. The major limitation of the bloomery was its low volume of output per unit of labor. Even when bloomery technology had fully matured, a large bloom might weigh only two hundred pounds, and the annual output of that bloomery would probably have been less than twenty tons of wrought iron. In an effort to increase output, the blast furnace was developed (by building up the walls of the bloomery, according to some sources). This new technology was so successful that by the middle of the sixteenth century the blast furnace had replaced the bloomery as the prevalent method of iron production.

Early blast furnaces stood about 15 feet high, later reaching 35 feet or more. (The use of coke—made by heating coal in an airtight container to drive out gases and tar—as a fuel, beginning in the early 1700's, allowed taller furnaces, since it did not crush as easily as charcoal and could be stacked higher.) The interior cavity widened as it descended from the top opening for about two-thirds of the furnace's height. At that point the cavity began to narrow, culminating in a chamber at the very bottom of the furnace, called the crucible.

The structure of the furnace created a chimney effect, drafting air through it to accelerate combustion; waterwheel-powered bellows usually supplemented the draft. The ore, charcoal, and limestone (a flux) were dumped into the blast furnace from above. As the ore melted and the level of raw materials dropped, more would be added on top of them. In this way, it was possible to keep a furnace in continuous operation for months at a time. As the ore slowly worked its way toward the crucible, it was exposed for a prolonged period to heat, which melted it (at about 1,400 degrees Celsius), and carbon, which it absorbed. The molten iron collected in the crucible, and the slag, floating on top of the iron, was pulled off through side openings. The end product was a large volume of molten iron with a high carbon content—cast iron.

The molten iron could be tapped directly from the crucible. Some of it would be poured into oblong molds pressed into damp sand. These molds were usually laid out with several smaller molds attached at right angles to the largest mold, reminding the ironworkers of a sow and suckling pigs—hence the term "pig iron." The pig iron would later be converted to wrought iron at a forge. The molten iron might also have been cast directly into molds for stove and fireplace parts, pots and pans, cannons, cannon balls, and many other products. In the nineteenth century cast iron was also used for machine parts, railroad tracks, and structural elements. By that time cast iron had found many uses, and the demand for iron products increased dramatically.

A blast furnace could produce, typically, 200 tons of iron per year—a tenfold increase over the bloomeries. In producing a larger output for less labor, however, a tradeoff was necessary: the addition of another step in the process. To create wrought iron—the most desirable iron product until the late nineteenth century—from the cast iron coming from the blast furnace, the carbon had to be removed. This was done in a refinery hearth in which the bloom was heated indirectly without coming in contact with the fuel. In this way, the carbon already present burned off, and no additional carbon was absorbed from the fuel. Despite this added step, the blast furnace produced a much larger volume of iron, and for less labor, than previous methods had. As a result, the development of the blast furnace was the key to making iron products much more common beginning in the fifteenth century.

Even with the blast furnace, the production of good wrought iron was limited by the use of coke. Coke introduced more impurities to the cast iron than charcoal had, making it more difficult to produce high-quality wrought iron. In 1784 an Englishman, Henry Cort, devised a new process to address this problem. Known as the "puddling process," it began by heating the pig iron in a coke-fired reverberatory furnace (one in which the heat was reflected off the roof of the furnace in order to keep the iron from coming in contact with the coke). Workers stirred the molten metal to expose more of it to the air, thus burning off carbon. As the carbon content decreased, the melting temperature increased, and the metal gradually stiffened, separating it from the more liquid slag. When the process was complete, workers gathered the low-carbon iron

U.S. and World Iron and Raw Steel Production, 1994

United States production

Pig iron	49,400,000
Direct-reduced iron	480,000
Raw steel	91,200,000

World production

Pig iron	512,000,000
Direct-reduced iron	27,800,000
Raw steel	726,000,000

Source: U.S. Bureau of Mines, *Minerals Yearbook, 1994.* U.S. Government Printing Office, 1996.
Note: Figures are in metric tons.

in a "puddle ball" and shaped it in a rolling mill. Thanks to Cort's puddling process, wrought iron became an important factor in the Industrial Revolution. Its dominance of the iron market lasted until the 1860's, when steel production began on a large scale via the Bessemer process.

Iron Ores. The principal iron ores are hematite, magnetite, limonite, pyrite, siderite, and taconite. Hematite and magnetite are the richest and most common ores. They are known as iron oxides because they are compounds of iron and oxygen.

Hematite (Fe_2O_3) can contain as much as 70 percent iron but usually contains closer to 25 percent. Significant deposits are found near Lake Superior, and in Alabama, Australia, Belgium, and Sweden. It may appear in colors ranging from black to dark red and may occur as shiny crystals, grains of rock, or loose particles. Magnetite (Fe_3O_4) is a black magnetic material often called black sand. Limonite ($2Fe2O33H2O$), or brown hematite, is a hydrated variety of hematite; it is also called bog-iron ore. It can contain as much as 60 percent iron ore and is yellowish to brown in color. It is found in Australia, France, Germany, the former Soviet Union, Spain, and the United States.

Pyrite (FeS_2), also called fool's gold because of its shiny yellowish surface, is about half sulfur. Siderite ($FeCO_3$) is a gray-brown carbonate ore that was once found in large deposits in Great Britain and Germany. Taconite is a hard rock that contains specks or bands of either hematite or magnetite.

Obtaining Iron Ore. An ore's quality for commercial purposes depends on several factors. While a pure ore may contain as much as 70 percent iron, ores are seldom found in their pure state. It is more realistic to expect a 50 to 60 percent iron content. At less than 30 percent, an ore is probably uneconomical. Other factors in determining an ore's quality include the amount of constituents such as silicon and phosphorus in the ore, the geographical location of the ore, and the ease with which it can be extracted and processed.

In prehistoric times iron ore was probably gathered from meteorites, high-grade outcroppings, and other sources that required little or no work to extract. As the demand increased and those sources were exhausted, mining techniques had to be developed to extract iron ore from the earth.

Most iron ore is obtained either by the open-pit mining process or by hard-rock shaft mining. Open-pit mining is employed when the ore is lying near the surface. Large machinery removes the overlying soil and rocks (called overburden) to expose the ore. It is then broken up with explosives and loaded onto a transportation system (usually large earth-moving trucks) by huge power shovels. As the process continues, the equipment digs deep into the earth, creating a large pit often several square miles in area and 500 feet or more deep. Most of the world's iron ore is mined in this way.

Ore that lies deep below the surface is removed via the more traditional hard-rock shaft mining. A shaft is sunk near the deposit from which tunnels and additional shafts branch out into the deposit. Shaft mining is much more expensive and dangerous than open-pit mining and is normally used only for very high-grade ore that cannot be reached in any other way.

Processing Iron Ore. All ores must be processed before being sent to the blast furnace; the ore's quality and iron content determine the degree and type of processing needed. At a minimum, ore must be crushed, screened, and washed prior to reducing in a blast furnace.

In the screening process, ore is separated into lumps that are large enough to be put into the blast furnace (7 to 25 millimeters across) and smaller particles called fines. Fines are not suitable for use in a blast furnace because the particles will pack together and hinder the efficient flow of hot gases. To correct this, a process called sintering is used to make larger particles out of the fines. Sintering begins by moistening the fines to make particles stick together. Coke is then added to the mixture. After passing under burners, the coke ignites, heating the fines until they fuse into larger particles suitable for use in the blast furnace.

As the best ore deposits become exhausted (or become uneconomical to mine because of their inaccessibility), methods of upgrading low-quality ore become necessary. Collectively, these processes are known as beneficiation. The first step in beneficiation is to concentrate the ore by one of several techniques. The general objective is to concentrate the iron and remove the silica. Most techniques rely on the difference between the density of iron and that of the surrounding rock to separate the two materials. Ore might be leached and dried, pulverized and floated in a mixture of oil, agglomerated into larger particles, or separated magnetically. Concentrating the ore by these techniques reduces both the shipping costs and the amount of waste at the blast furnace plant.

After beneficiation, the concentrated ore is a very fine powder that would not work properly in a blast furnace. Since the concentrate is too small even for sintering, the pelletizing process is used. In pelletizing, the concentrate is moistened and tumbled in a drum or on an inclined disk, and the resulting balls of ore are fired to a temperature of about 1,300 degrees Celsius to dry and harden them. These pellets are usually about 10 to 15 millimeters across and are then ready for the blast furnace.

Modern Iron Making. Although the exact chemical processes have been fully understood only during the twentieth century, the goal of iron making has always been to release oxygen from its chemical bond with iron. The blast furnace is the most efficient and common way to do this. Modern blast furnaces work on the same principles as those developed in the fifteenth century, but they are larger and have benefited from centuries of refinement to the design, materials, and process. A modern blast furnace may be as much as 30 meters tall and 10 meters in diameter. Because of improvements in materials, a blast furnace may stay in continuous operation for two years, requiring maintenance only when its brick lining wears out. Some of the most important advances involve the use of mathematical modeling and supercomputers to provide more accurate and timely control over the process. The output of a modern furnace may exceed 10 million kilograms per day.

A twentieth century blast furnace has five readily identifiable sections; from the top down they are: throat, stack, barrel, bosh, and hearth (or crucible). The ore, coke, and limestone (col-

U.S. Consumption of Iron Ore and Agglomerates, 1994
In Thousands of Metric Tons

| | *Integrated Iron and Steel Plants* | | | | *Other* | |
Year	Blast Furnaces	Steel Furnaces	Sintering Plants	Miscellaneous	Direct-reduced Iron for Steelmaking	Nonsteel End Uses
1993	63,900	76	5,790	86	441	1,130
1994	65,500	80	5,770	103	716	958

Source: U.S. Bureau of Mines, *Minerals Yearbook, 1994.* U.S. Government Printing Office, 1996.

lectively called the charge) enter the furnace through the throat. The distribution and timing of the charge is carefully monitored at all times to ensure proper operation. The throat opens onto the stack, which resembles a cone with the top cut off. The stack widens as it descends because the temperature of the charge increases as it works its way down the furnace, causing the charge to expand. The next section, the barrel, is a short, straight section that connects the stack to the bosh, a shorter, upside-down version of the stack. The bosh narrows as it descends because the iron is beginning to liquefy and compact by the time the charge reaches the bosh. At the bottom of the bosh are nozzles called tuyeres through which blast air is blown into the furnace. The air coming through the tuyeres has been preheated to about 1,000 degrees Celsius or higher, and oxygen is sometimes added to it. This hot air causes the coke in the charge to burn. The oxygen in the air combines with carbon from the coke to create carbon monoxide gas, which in turn removes the oxygen from the ore. The burning coke also produces temperatures up to 3,000 degrees Celsius to melt the iron. The liquid metal collects in the bottom section, called the hearth or crucible. Just as in earlier furnaces, the slag floats on the molten iron, and workers periodically pull it off through openings in the side of the furnace.

Several direct reduction processes (in which the temperature never exceeds iron's melting point) have been developed in the twentieth century but are used only in special circumstances. The basic process relies on hot gases to reduce the iron ore in a way roughly analogous to the process of the earlier bloomeries. Since the iron is never completely melted, slag never forms, and the final product contains impurities that must be removed during the steelmaking process. Direct reduction furnaces can be built more quickly and cheaply than blast furnaces, and they produce less pollution. The disadvantages are that they require a supply of cheap natural gas and the iron ore must be processed to a very high grade.

Modern Iron Products. The vast majority of iron produced in blast furnaces is converted to steel. The remainder is cast as pig iron and later converted to either cast iron or wrought iron. At a foundry, the pig iron is melted to a liquid state in a cupola (a small version of a blast furnace) and then cast in molds (some of them are still made with damp sand) to make machine parts, pipes, engine blocks, and thousands of other items. Wrought iron is made in limited quantities in the twentieth century. Its production begins by melting pig iron and removing impurities. The molten iron is then poured over a silicate slag and formed into blooms which can then be shaped into products.

Iron Alloys. Iron is used in a vast range of special-purpose alloys developed for commercial applications. The major classifications of these alloys are discussed below only in broad outline; within each grouping there remains an enormous variety because of the wide range of special needs.

Magnetic alloys are either retentive (hard) or nonretentive (soft) of magnetism. The hard alloys remain magnetized after the application of a magnetic field, thus creating a permanent

magnet. One family of hard alloys contains cobalt and molybdenum (less than 20 percent of
each), while another contains aluminum, nickel,
cobalt, copper, and titanium. Once magnetized
they are used in such applications as speaker
magnets, electrical meters, and switchboard instruments due to the constancy of their magnetic field and their resistance to demagnetiza-
tion. The soft alloys also fall into two families:
those with nickel and those with aluminum. The
nickel alloys are used in communications and
electric power equipment, while those containing aluminum are used to carry alternating current.

High-temperature alloys, used in high-temperature environments such as turbine blades in
gas turbines and superchargers, are generally referred to as either iron-based, cobalt-based, or
nickel-based. They are formulated to retain their
chemical identity, physical identity, and the
strength required to perform their intended
function, all at extreme high temperatures.

The most common electrical-resistance alloys
are best known as heating elements in toasters,
radiant heaters, water heaters, and so on. They
usually contain nickel (as much as 60 percent),
chromium (approximately 20 percent), and
sometimes aluminum (approximately 5 percent). Alloys without the nickel have higher re-
sistivity and lower density and are used in poten-
tiometers, rheostats, and similar applications.

Corrosion-resistant alloys are designed to resist corrosion from liquids and gases other than
air or oxygen and usually contain varying
amounts of nickel and chromium along with
combinations of molybdenum, copper, cobalt,
tungsten, and silicon. No one alloy is capable of
resisting the effects of all corrosive agents, so
each is tailored to its intended purpose.

The powdered iron technique employs iron
which has been finely ground and mixed with
metals or nonmetals to form the desired alloys.
After a binder is added, the mixture is pressed to
the desired shape in a mold. This process has
the advantages of very precise control over the
makeup of the alloy and the ability to form iron
pieces to precise dimensions with little or no
working required afterward.

Biological Iron. Iron is important to almost

every organism and is used in a variety of ways. It
is involved in oxygen transport, electron transfer, oxidation reactions, and reduction reactions. Iron is a constituent of human blood.
Some iron compounds have medical uses, such
as stimulating the appetite, treating anemia, co-
agulating blood, and stimulating healing.

FURTHER READING: For the general reader,
the available textbooks and monographs on the
subjects of obtaining and processing iron are
very narrow in their scope and highly technical
in their treatment. An exception is *Foundations of
Iron and Steel Metallurgy*, by W. H. Dennis, 1967.
For a discussion of the latest technologies, the
reader is advised to consult a recent edition of a
technically oriented encyclopedia. The following
works provide the lay reader with a clear explanation of iron-making technology within its historical and economic context. *Sloss Furnaces and
the Rise of the Birmingham District*, by W. David
Lewis, 1994, focuses on iron making in Alabama
but provides ample explanations of general iron-
making processes with good, well-placed illustrations. *The British Iron Industry: 1700-1850*, by J. R.
Harris, 1988, deals with iron as a factor in the
Industrial Revolution in England. For a broader
American account of iron-making, see *American
Iron: 1607-1900*, by Robert B. Gordon, 1996.

Brian J. Nichelson

SEE ALSO: Alloys; Bessemer process; Coal; Industrial Revolution and industrialization; Metals
and metallurgy; Mineral resource use, early history of; Open-pit mining; Steel; Steel industry;
United States, resources and resource use in.

Irrigation

*Because agriculture is basic to human existence, irriga-
tion has been practiced since prehistoric times. Essentially irrigation is the application of water to soil to
overcome soil moisture deficiency so that crops can have
adequate water supply for optimal food production.
Irrigation is essential to sustained large-scale food production.*

IRRIGATION SYSTEMS WERE important to many
ancient civilizations. They were the basis of life
in the ancient civilizations of Egypt, India,

China, and Mesopotamia (modern day Iraq). Some irrigation works in the Nile Valley that date back to around 3000 B.C.E. still play an important role in Egyptian agriculture. In the United States the first irrigation systems were developed by American Indians, and traces of ancient water distribution systems, made up of canals, were still visible in 1989.

Scope and Land Requirements. In 1977 the Food and Agriculture Organization (FAO) of the United Nations estimated that the total global land area under irrigation was 223 million hectares. It is projected that by the year 2000 about 271 million hectares will be irrigated. In the United States 24 million hectares were irrigated for crop production in 1986. Some form of irrigation is practiced in every country in the world. Although irrigation results in increased food production, it is extremely water intensive. For example, to grow 1 metric ton (approximately 2,200 pounds) of grain (adequate for 50 percent of an average person's supply for five years and six months) requires as much as 1,700 cubic kilometers of water per person per year. In the United States 41 percent of total freshwater withdrawals is for irrigation. The value of irrigation is that it greatly increases agricultural productivity. For example, in 1979 the FAO reported that although irrigated agriculture represented only about 13 percent of global arable land (agricultural land that, when properly prepared for agriculture, will produce enough crops to be economically efficient), the value of crop production from irrigated land was 34 percent of the global total production.

For irrigation to be economically viable, the land in consideration must be able to produce enough crops to justify the investment in irrigation works. The land must be arable and irrigable; that is, sufficient water for irrigation must exist. Soil suitable for irrigation farming has the following attributes. The soil must have a reasonably high water holding capacity and be readily penetrable by water; the rate of infiltration (percolation) should be low enough to avoid excessive loss of water through deep percolation beyond the root zone of the crops. The soil must also be deep enough to allow root development and permit drainage of the soil, and it must be free of harmful (toxic) salts and chemicals—especially those that tend to bond to soil and reach dangerously high concentrations. Finally, it must have an adequate supply of plant nutrients.

Land slopes should permit irrigation without excessive runoff accompanied by high erosion rates. The land should be located in an area where irrigation is feasible without excessive pumping or conveyance costs. Generally the land should permit the planting of more than one type of crop so that the investment in irrigation works can be utilized year-round, and ideally should allow the flexibility of planting more economically viable crop types should economic conditions dictate such changes.

Types of Irrigation Systems. Generally, irrigation systems can be classified as nonpressurized (also known as gravity or surface systems) and pressurized systems. Historically, nonpressurized systems in which water was flooded onto the soil surface via open channels were the first to be constructed. In fact, nonpressurized systems preceded pressurized ones by thousands of years. Nonpressurized systems include canals, open channels, and pipes that are not flowing full. Pressurized systems include all types of sprinkler systems and low-pressure nozzle systems.

There are five basic methods of implementing irrigation systems: flooding, furrow irrigation, subirrigation, trickle irrigation, and sprinkling. Several subcategories exist within these five basic categories. Flooding systems include wild flooding, controlled flooding, check flooding, and basin flooding applications. In all cases the irrigated area is flooded with water. The degree to which that flooding is controlled or administered differentiates the types of flooding. For example, in wild flooding there is not much control or preparation of the land being irrigated. In contrast, check flooding is accomplished by admitting water into relatively level plots surrounded by levees. In check flooding the check (area surrounded by levees) is filled with water at a fairly rapid rate and the water is allowed to infiltrate into the soil.

Furrow irrigation is used for row crops—hence the name (a furrow is a narrow ditch between rows of plants). In this method evapora-

Sprinkler irrigation in California's Salinas Valley. (Ben Klaffke)

tion losses are minimized and only about 20 to 50 percent of the area is wetted during irrigation, in contrast to flooding irrigation. In sprinkler application water is sprinkled on the irrigated land. The sprinkling is possible because the water is delivered under pressure. Sprinkler systems provide a means for irrigation in areas where the topography does not permit irrigation by surface methods.

Subirrigation methods are useful in areas where there is permeable soil in the root zone and a high water table. In this method irrigation water is applied below the ground surface to keep the water table high enough so that water from the capillary fringe is available to crops. Subirrigation has the advantages of minimizing evaporation loss and requiring minimal field preparation. In trickle (or drip) irrigation a plastic pipe with perforations is laid along the ground at the base of a row of crops. The water issuing from the perforations is designed to trickle. Excellent control is achieved, and evaporation and deep percolation are minimized.

FURTHER READING: Irrigation systems are discussed in detail in *Water Resources Engineering*, by Linsley et al., 1992; *Irrigation System Design: An Engineering Approach*, by Richard H. Cuenca, 1989; and *Irrigation*, by Josef D. Zimmerman, 1966. Detailed data on world resources with respect to irrigation and water supply are published by the World Resources Institute in *1990-1991 World Resources*, 1990.

Emmanuel U. Nzewi

SEE ALSO: Dams; Hydrology and hydrologic cycle; Streams and rivers; Water; Water rights; Water supply systems.

Isotopes, radioactive

WHERE FOUND: Because all the known elements have at least one radioactive isotope, either natural or artificially produced, the radionuclides are found in the earth's crust, in its surface waters, and in the atmosphere.

PRIMARY USES: Radioisotopes are used in many areas of science and industry as tracers or as radiation sources. They provide fuel for the nuclear generation of electricity and have found both diagnostic and therapeutic uses in medicine.

DESCRIPTION: Radioactive isotopes are unstable nuclides that decay ultimately to stable nuclides by emission of alpha, beta, gamma, or proton radiation, by K capture, or by nuclear fission.

THE STORY OF RADIOACTIVITY begins with Wilhelm Roentgen's work with cathode ray tubes. Roentgen allowed cathode rays to impinge on various metal surfaces and observed that highly penetrating radiations, which he called X rays, were produced. He noted similarities between the X rays and sunlight in that both could expose a photographic plate and could cause certain metals and salts to fluoresce.

This fluorescence was of interest to Henri Becquerel, who discovered by accident that crystals of uranium salt left on a photographic plate in a drawer produced an intense silhouette of the crystals. Although his understanding of the phenomenon was very limited at the time, what Becquerel had observed was the effect of uranium radioactivity.

Marie and Pierre Curie pursued the study of this phenomenon with other minerals. They worked to isolate and characterize the substances responsible and were able to isolate and purify samples of polonium and radium. Other scientists worked at the same time to characterize the radiations emitted. In 1903 Ernest Rutherford and Frederick Soddy proposed that the radiations were associated with the chemical changes that radiation produced, and they characterized three types of radiation: alpha (α), beta (β), and gamma (γ) rays. Since 1901 twenty-one Nobel Prizes have been awarded for work related to various radioactive phenomena.

Radioactivity. Alpha, beta, and gamma radiation are the three types of naturally occurring radioactivity; they result in the transmutation of one chemical nucleus to another.

Alpha decay is the ejection from the nucleus of a particle equivalent in size to a helium nu-

cleus. The daughter nucleus has an atomic number (Z) two less than that of the parent and a mass number (A) four less than the parent. The equation below represents the emission of an alpha particle from a polonium nucleus to produce an isotope of lead.

$$^{210}_{84}\text{Po} \rightarrow {}^{206}_{82}\text{Pb} + {}^{4}_{2}\text{He} + \gamma$$

Beta decay results from the change within the nucleus of a neutron into a proton. Z increases by one, while A is unchanged. The equation below illustrates beta emission by phosphorus to become sulfur.

$$^{32}_{15}\text{P} \rightarrow \beta^{-} + {}^{32}_{16}\text{S}$$

In gamma decay, electromagnetic radiation is emitted as a nucleus drops to lower states from excited states. It is the nuclear equivalent of atomic line spectra that show wavelengths of visible light emitted by atoms when electrons drop from higher to lower energy levels. Nuclear fission is an extremely important process by which isotopes of the heavy elements such as uranium-235 capture a neutron and then split into fragments.

$$^{235}_{92}\text{U} + {}^{1}\text{n} \rightarrow {}^{140}_{56}\text{Ba} + {}^{94}_{36}\text{Kr} + 2 \text{ neutrons}$$

The neutrons produced are captured by other nuclei, which in turn fission, producing a chain reaction. This is the process that resulted in the first atomic bomb and is now used in nuclear plants to produce electric power.

The Production of Energy. The use of nuclear fission to produce energy is based on a principle formulated by Albert Einstein, $E = mc^2$. E is energy, m refers to mass, and c is a constant equal to 3.0×10^8 m/c. The complete conversion of one gram of matter per second would produce energy at the rate of nine trillion watts.

The main particles contained in the nucleus of an atom are protons and neutrons. The mass of a given nucleus is less than the sum of the masses of the constituent protons and neutrons. This mass defect has been converted, according to the equation above, to energy (binding energy) in the process of forming the nucleus. The separation of the nucleus into its constituent particles would require replacement of this energy. The binding energy per nucleon is a measure of the stability of a particular nucleus. Those nuclei having mass numbers between 60 and 80 have the highest binding energy per nucleon and are therefore the most stable. A large nucleus such as uranium can split into fragments whose size are in the 60 to 80 mass range. When this happens, the excess binding energy is released.

Radioisotopes in Research. There are a number of ways in which radioisotopes are used in the fields of chemistry and biology. Radioimmunoassay (RIA) is a type of isotopic dilution study in which labeled and unlabeled analyte compete for limited amounts of a molecule that binds the analyte very specifically. RIA is used worldwide in the determination of hormones, drugs, and viruses. The technique is so specific that concentrations in the picomolar region can be measured. Another major use of radioisotopes is as tracers that determine metabolic pathways, transport processes, and reaction mechanisms. A compound labeled with a radioactive isotope is introduced into the process, and the radioactivity allows the compound to be followed through the mechanism.

Pharmacokinetics is the study of the rates of movement and biotransformation of a drug and its metabolites in the body. Many kinetic parameters, such as a drug's half-life in the body, can be determined by using radiolabeled drugs and measuring radioactivity after some type of chromatographic separation of the parent drug from its metabolites.

Radiopharmaceuticals are substances labeled with radionuclides that are used in the visualization of organs, the location of tumors, and the imaging of biochemical processes. This usage is based on the fact that a substance that is found in a healthy cell at a certain concentration has a different concentration in damaged cells. The particular isotope used depends on the organ or biochemical process under study.

Radioisotopes in Industry. Radioisotopes are used in many ways in industry. Gamma rays from cobalt-60 are used to examine objects for cracks and other defects. Radioisotopes can be used to measure thickness of all types of rolled materials and as tracers in locating leaks in pipes carrying liquids or gases. The fill level of closed containers is monitored by absorption or scattering of radiation.

In the chemical industry radioisotopes are used to indicate the completeness of a precipitation reaction. A radioisotope of the element to be precipitated is added to the solution to be precipitated. When the filtrate is free of radioactivity, precipitation is complete.

Other Uses. Radioisotopes are used in dating ancient rocks and fossils. Carbon is used in dating fossils. All living organisms are assumed to be in equilibrium with their environment, taking in carbon in food and expelling it through respiration and other processes. A living organism is assumed, when it dies, to have a certain percentage of carbon-14, radioactive carbon. As the fossil ages the carbon-14 decays by beta emission, and its percentage is reduced. Since the decay rate is known, a reasonable age estimate can be obtained by measuring the rate of radioactive emission (proportional to percentage carbon-14) from the fossil. Uranium is used in a similar way to date rock samples that contain a mixture of uranium and lead which is at the end of its decay chain.

FURTHER READING: *Radioisotopes,* by D. Billington, G. G. Jayson, and P. J. Maltby, 1992, gives a good description of the modes of radioactive decay, the production and measurement of radioactivity, and its uses in the fields of biology and medicine. C. C. Thornburn's *Isotopes and Radiation in Biology,* 1972, treats similar topics. *Radiochemistry and Nuclear Methods of Analysis,* by W. Ehmann and D. Vance, 1991, gives a broad treatment of the phenomenon of radioactivity and of the many ways that radioactivity can be used as an analytical tool. *General Chemistry,* by J. Umland, 1993, contains a chapter on nuclear chemistry, and *College Physics,* by R. Serway and J. Faughn, 1992, gives a basic introduction to the topic in two chapters on nuclear physics and its applications. Radiation and Radioactivity on *Earth and Beyond,* by I. Draganić, Z. Draganić, and J. Adloff, 1990, contains interesting chapters on radioisotopes in space and on both contemporary and ancient Earth.

Grace A. Banks

SEE ALSO: Atomic Energy Commission; Isotopes, stable; Manhattan Project; Nuclear energy; Nuclear Regulatory Commission; Plutonium; Radium; Thorium; Uranium.

Isotopes, stable

WHERE FOUND: Stable isotopes comprise the bulk of the material universe. Some elements are found in only a single form, while others have several isotopes. For study and application, it is necessary to separate the various isotopes from one another. A number of methods have been developed to accomplish isotope separation.

PRIMARY USES: Analysis of stable isotopes and isotopic composition is used extensively in a wide variety of fields, including soil and water analysis, plant tissue analysis, determination of metabolic pathways in plants and animals, including humans, archaeology, forensics, the geosciences, and medicine.

DESCRIPTION: An isotope is one of two or more species of atom that have the same atomic number (number of protons) but different mass numbers (number of protons plus neutrons). Stable isotopes are those which are not radioactive. Because the chemical properties of an element are almost exclusively determined by atomic number, different isotopes of the same element will exhibit nearly identical behavior in chemical reactions. Subtle differences in the physical properties of isotopes are attributable to their differing masses.

THERE ARE APPROXIMATELY 260 stable isotopes. While most of the eighty-one stable elements that occur in nature consist of a mixture of two or more isotopes, twenty occur in only a single form. Among these are sodium, aluminum, phosphorus, and gold. At the other extreme, the element tin exhibits ten isotopic forms. Two elements with atomic numbers less than 84, technetium and promethium, have no stable isotopes. The atomic weight of an element is the weighted average of its isotope masses as found in their natural distribution. For example, boron has two stable isotopes: boron-10 (isotope with mass number 10), which accounts for 20 percent of naturally occurring boron, and boron-11, which accounts for 80 percent. The atomic weight of boron is therefore $(0.2)\times(10) + (0.8)\times(11) = 10.8$. In those elements which have naturally occurring isotopes, the relative abundance of the various isotopes is found to be remarkably constant, independent of the source of the material. There are cases in which the abundances are found to vary, and these are of practical interest.

Discovery of Stable Isotopes. In the early part of the twentieth century the discovery of radioactivity, radioactive elements, and the many distinctly different products of radioactive decays, showed that there were far more atomic species than could be fit into the periodic table. Although possessing different physical properties, many of these species were chemically indistinguishable.

In 1912 Joseph J. Thomson, discoverer of the electron, found that when a beam of ionized neon gas was passed through a properly configured electromagnetic field and allowed to fall on a photographic plate, two spots of unequal size were exposed. The size and location of the spots were those which would be expected if the original neon consisted of two components—about 90 percent neon-20 and 10 percent neon-22. Later Francis Aston improved the experimental apparatus so that each isotope was focused to a point rather than smeared out. The device he developed, known as a mass spectrograph, allows much greater precision in the determination of isotope mass and abundance.

Separation of Isotopes. All methods for separating stable isotopes are based on mass difference or on some isotopic property which derives from it. The difficulty of isotope separation depends inversely upon the relative mass difference between the isotopes. For example, the two most abundant isotopes of hydrogen are ordinary hydrogen (hydrogen-1) and deuterium (hydrogen-2). These isotopes have a relative mass difference of $(2-1)/1=1$, or 100 percent. The mass difference between chlorine-35 and chlorine-37, by contrast, is only $(37-35)/35=0.057$, or 5.7 percent.

There are two types of separation methods. The only single-step method is electromagnetic separation, which operates on the principle that the curvature of the path of a charged particle in a magnetic field is dependent on the particle mass. This is the same principle on which the mass spectrograph is based. Though it is a single-step technique, the amount of material which can be separated in this way is very small. All other processes result in a separation of the original material into two fractions, one slightly enriched in the heavier isotope. To obtain significant enrichment the process must be repeated a number of times by cascading identical stages. Such multistage methods include gaseous centrifugation, aerodynamic separation nozzles, fractional distillation, thermal diffusion, gaseous diffusion, electrolysis, and laser photochemical separation. For example, in centrifugation a vapor of the material to be separated flows downward in the outer part of a rotating cylinder and upward in the center. Because of the mass difference, the heavier isotope will be concentrated in the outer region and can be removed to be enriched again in the next stage.

Use of Stable Isotopes. Most stable isotope applications are based on two facts. First, isotopes of a given element behave nearly identically in chemical reactions. Second, the relative abundances of isotopes for a given element are very nearly constant. The three principal types of applications are those in which deviations from the standard abundances are used to infer something about the environment and/or history of the sample, those in which the isotopic ratio of a substance is altered so that the substance may be traced through a system or process, and those in which small differences in the physical properties of isotopes are used to understand process dynamics.

As an example of the first type of application, consider that the precise isotopic composition of water varies with place and time as it makes its way through the earth's complex hydrologic cycle. Knowledge of this variation allows for the study of storm behavior, identification of changes in global climatic patterns, and investigation of past climatic conditions through the study of water locked in glaciers, tree rings, and pack ice. The cycling of nitrogen in crop plants provides an example of stable isotope tracer methods. Fertilizer tagged by enriching (or de-

pleting) with nitrogen-15 is applied to a crop planting. Subsequent analysis makes it possible to trace the quantities of fertilizer taken up by the plants, remaining in the soil, lost to the atmosphere by denitrification, and leached into runoff water.

FURTHER READING: For a good general description of isotopes see Isaac Asimov, *The History of Physics*, 1984. A detailed description of stable isotope application is found in Michael DeNiro, "Stable Isotopy and Archaeology," *American Scientist* 75 (March/April, 1987). Several excellent, if somewhat technical, articles are found in *Stable Isotopes in Ecological Research*, edited by P. Rundel, J. Ehleringer, and K. Nagy, 1989. For examples of applications, see *Separated Isotopes: Vital Tools for Science and Medicine*, prepared by the National Research Council, 1982.

Michael K. Rulison

SEE ALSO: Biotechnology; Hydrology and the hydrologic cycle; Isotopes, radioactive; Nitrogen cycle: Nuclear energy; Soil testing and analysis.

Izaak Walton League of America

DATE ESTABLISHED: 1922

Members of the Izaak Walton League of America pledge to strive for the purity of water, the clarity of air, and the wise stewardship of the land and its resources. They seek to understand nature and the value of wildlife, woodlands, and open space.

FOUNDED IN CHICAGO by fifty-four fishermen to protect fish habitat, the Izaak Walton League of America (IWLA) has grown into a national organization of more than fifty thousand members encompassing all conservation activities. With a diverse membership of fishers, hunters, urban environmentalists, and conservationists in general, the IWLA is a respected voice of commitment and moderation throughout the environmental community. The league is organized as a bottom-up democracy. All policies are developed by local chapters and, after passing through state divisions, become official policy after action by a national convention of delegates from each chapter.

The IWLA has been instrumental in obtaining wilderness status for parts of the Boundary Waters Canoe Area in Minnesota, establishing the National Elk Refuge in Wyoming, cleaning up Chesapeake Bay, and maintaining a strong conservation reserve program in farm bill authorizations. Permanent projects include the league's well respected, and often copied, Save-Our-Streams Program, in which local chapters and other groups "adopt" a stream. Using techniques developed by national staff, members monitor stream quality, identify pollution sources, and work to clean up problems. A Midwest Office of the IWLA is an important watchdog that observes the power industry, monitoring environmental degradation of the Mississippi River basin and supporting alternative energy sources.

John R. Dickel

SEE ALSO: Conservation; Environmental movement; Streams and rivers; Water pollution and water pollution control; Wilderness; wildlife.

Jackson, Wes

BORN: June 15, 1936; near Topeka, Kansas

Jackson, a plant geneticist by training, is one of the leading critics of modern industrialized agriculture. Cofounder of the Land Institute, he has envisioned a radically different approach to farming based on ecological models and on "polycultures" rather than monocultures.

WES JACKSON, president of the Land Institute at Salina, Kansas, was born in 1936 near Topeka, Kansas, where he grew up on a forty-acre farm. His formal education includes a B.A. in biology at Kansas Wesleyan University in 1958, an M.S. at the University of Kansas in 1967, and a Ph.D. in plant genetics at North Carolina State University in 1967. He taught at Kansas Wesleyan and at California State University, Sacramento, where he established an environmental studies program. Becoming involved in the growing environmental movement, he and his wife Dana left California to found the Land Institute in 1976. Jackson is recognized for the development of strategies for using nature as the model for achieving a more sustainable approach to agriculture.

Jackson is one of a number of people who have criticized mainstream American agriculture; others include Wendell Berry, Gary Paul Nabham, and Robert Rodale. Jackson has characterized this type of agriculture as "extractive" in that it uses, or extracts, considerable amounts of resources—including soil, water, and petroleum—to grow food; furthermore, it is capital-intensive, and its chemicals pollute streams and groundwater. Jackson and the Land Institute have come in for their share of criticism, with some calling their efforts impractical and doomed to failure. Nonetheless, they also have staunch supporters and have been very influential in expanding modern views of agriculture. One example is the examination of the sociocultural aspects of how a society decides to produce its food; another is the growth of new interdisciplinary approaches such as agroecology.

The author of several books, including *New Roots for Agriculture* (1980) and *Altars of Unhewn Stone: Science and the Earth* (1987), and numerous articles, Jackson was honored by being named a Pew Scholar in 1990 and a MacArthur Fellow in 1992. He was named by *Life* magazine as one of the eighteen individuals they predict will be among one hundred of the "important Americans of the twentieth century" and designated by the *Utne Reader* as one of a hundred "visionaries who could change your life."

Thomas A. Eddy

SEE ALSO: Agriculture industry; Agronomy; Erosion and erosion control; Land Institute; Monoculture agriculture; Soil management.

Kyanite

WHERE FOUND: Kyanite-group minerals occur most commonly in metamorphosed high-alumina shales. Relatively high pressures and temperatures produce kyanite, intermediate pressures and high temperatures produce sillimanite, and low temperatures and pressures produce andalusite. Because metamorphosed high-alumina shales are common in the mountain belts of the world, kyanite group minerals are widely distributed. However, concentrations of the minerals in reasonably large crystal size are required for economic production. Major kyanite ore reserves are found in the southern Appalachian Piedmont and in India. Sillimanite has been mined in India, Australia, and South Africa. Large deposits of commercial-grade andalusite occur in France, South Africa, and North Carolina.

PRIMARY USES: Kyanite minerals are used in high-temperature metallurgical processes and in high-strength porcelain manufacture.

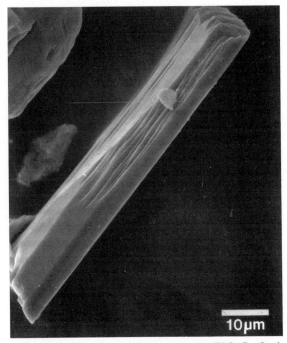

Photomicrograph of silt-sized kyanite grain. (U.S. Geological Survey)

DESCRIPTION: Kyanite is an aluminum silicate mineral, Al_2SiO_5, also written $Al_2O_3 \bullet SiO_2$. Two other minerals, sillimanite and andalusite, have identical composition but crystallize in different forms determined by the temperature and pressure at the time of crystallization. The three minerals are polymorphs (different forms) of Al_2SiO_5 and constitute the kyanite, or sillimanite, group of minerals. Kyanite crystallizes as blade-shaped crystals with vitreous luster and white to blue color. Sillimanite is most commonly finely fibrous and brown in color. Andalusite occurs as elongate, cigar-shaped crystals in a variety of colors.

KYANITE MINERALS REQUIRE varying amounts of preparation before use. Massive aggregates of kyanite and sillimanite that occur in India have been sawed or carved to desired shapes, but kyanite group mineral resources in Europe and North America normally require separation of the minerals from associated quartz, micas, and other minerals, resulting in a granular product. The granules, which do not adhere to one another, are mixed with various materials, usually including fireclay and water, to produce a moldable product that can be used as mortar between refractory bricks or molded into bricks or other useful shapes.

As a high-temperature furnace lined with "green" (unfired) superduty refractory bricks is heated, the kyanite group minerals in the green brick and mortar convert to mullite. Uniquely, the volume of mullite and silica glass resulting from the conversion of kyanite to mullite is about 18 percent greater than the original volume of kyanite. The volume increase occurs at about the same temperature that other materials are shrinking in volume, and this phenomenon tends to mechanically stabilize the furnace lining. Therefore, there is a significant advantage to including raw kyanite in the green products.

The kyanite group minerals are used as superduty refractories in high-temperature metallurgical processes, especially steel production, and in high-strength porcelain products, typically automobile spark plug insulators. On heating to about 1,400 degrees Celsius, the kyanite group minerals alter to mullite ($3Al_2O_3 \bullet 2SiO_2$) plus silica glass. Mullite remains stable and strong to 1,810 degrees Celsius. The kyanite group minerals are therefore very desirable as refractories in steel and glass furnace linings and as materials for kiln furniture (product supports) in high-temperature ceramic manufacture.

Kyanite group minerals compete economically with synthetic mullite refractories. Synthetic mullite is produced by heating or fusing an appropriate mixture of high alumina and sili-ceous materials. Near Americus, Georgia, naturally occurring mixtures of bauxite and kaolin—and at Niagara, New York, alumina and glass-grade silica sand—are used to produce synthetic mullite.

Robert E. Carver

SEE ALSO: Metamorphic processes, rocks, and mineral deposits; Minerals, structure and physical properties of; Orthosilicate minerals; Ceramics; Clays.

Lakes

Lakes are inland bodies of water that fill depressions in the earth's surface. They are generally too deep to allow vegetation to cover the entire surface and may be fresh or saline.

LAKES ARE STANDING BODIES of water that occupy hollows or depressions on the surface of the earth. Small, shallow lakes are usually called ponds, but there is no specific size and depth that is used to distinguish ponds from lakes. The scientific study of the physical, chemical, climatological, biological, and ecological aspects of lakes is known as limnology.

Precipitation is the primary source of water for lakes, either in the form of direct runoff by streams that drain into the depression or groundwater that slowly seeps into the lake by passing through subsurface earth materials. Although lakes are generally thought of as freshwater bodies, many lakes in arid regions become very salty because of the high evaporation rate, which concentrates inflowing salts. The Caspian Sea, the Great Salt Lake, and the Dead Sea are classic examples of saline lakes.

Freshwater and saline lakes account for 0.009 and 0.008 percent of the total amount of water in the world, respectively. Although this is a minute fraction of the world's water—almost all of it is in the oceans and in glaciers—lakes are an extremely valuable resource. In terms of ecosystems, lakes are divided into a pelagial (open-water) zone and a littoral (shore) zone where macrovegetation grows. Sediments free of vegetation that occur below the pelagial zone are in the profundal zone.

The renewal times for freshwater and saline lakes range from 1 to 100 years and 10 to 1,000 years, respectively. The length of time varies directly with lake volume and average depth, and indirectly with a lake's rate of discharge. The rate of renewal, or turnover time, for lakes is much less than that of oceans and glacial ice, which is measured in thousands of years.

Lake size varies enormously. Lake sizes range from small depressions of a hectare or less to the Caspian Sea, which covers 371,000 square kilometers and is the largest in the world. This one

body of saline water is larger than all of Germany. The Great Lakes of North America (Lakes Superior, Huron, Michigan, Erie, and Ontario) make up the greatest continuous mass of fresh water on the planet, with a combined area of over 245,000 square kilometers—larger than the total area of Great Britain. The largest single freshwater lake in the world is Lake Superior, with a surface area of more than 82,000 square kilometers—nearly the size of Ireland. Other major freshwater lakes include Lake Victoria in Africa, Lake Huron, and Lake Michigan, with approximate areas of 69,000, 60,000, and 58,000 square kilometers, respectively.

Lake Baikal (or Baykal) in Russia not only is the deepest lake in the world (1,620 meters) but also contains the largest amount of fresh water (23,000 cubic kilometers). This one lake alone contains approximately 20 percent of all of the fresh water in the world. The combined volume of all of the five Great Lakes is larger, with 24,620 cubic kilometers. Thus, Lake Baikal and the Great Lakes account for over 40 percent of the total amount of fresh water in the world. The second and third largest freshwater lakes in the world in terms of volume are Lake Tanganyika in Africa and Lake Superior, with 18,900 and 11,600 cubic kilometers, respectively. Lake Tanganyika is also the second deepest lake in the world (1,433 meters). Lake Titicaca in the Andes Mountains of Peru and Bolivia is the highest lake in the world at 3,800 meters elevation, while the Dead Sea in Israel and Jordan is the lowest, at an elevation of 394 meters below sea level.

Origins of Lakes. Lakes are unevenly distributed on the earth's surface. Nearly half of the world's lakes are in Canada, and Minnesota is proud of its reputed count of ten thousand lakes. Both Canada and Minnesota were deeply affected by continental glaciation during the various stages of the Pleistocene epoch, or Ice Age, which lasted for approximately two million years. Indeed, most of the world's lakes were formed as a consequence of the movement of continental ice sheets during the Pleistocene. For example, the Great Lakes were formed by advancing ice sheets that carved out large basins in the bedrock. In many other instances, existing valleys were eroded and deepened by glacial ad-

One of Minnesota's thousands of lakes, formed by glaciation during the Pleistocene epoch. (Jim West)

vance, resulting in the formation of large lakes such as Great Bear Lake and Great Slave Lake in central Canada (30,200 and 27,200 square kilometers, respectively). In some instances, long, narrow valleys were oriented parallel to the movement of the ice sheet. When the ends of these valleys became blocked by glacial debris, the basins filled up with water to form long, narrow lakes. The Finger Lakes of western New York State provide an excellent example of this process. Numerous small lakes and ponds were formed in kettles, which are small depressions found in glacial deposits called moraines. Blocks of stagnant ice that became trapped in the morainal deposits melted and formed kettle lakes. Minnesota and many other areas in the upper Midwest and central Canada have numerous kettle lakes with this type of origin.

Tectonic activity in the crust of the earth formed lake basins in a number of ways. For example, faulting results in rift valleys that can fill with water. The downfaulted block is referred to as a graben and accounts for the deepest lakes in the world, Lakes Baikal and Tanganyika. These lakes are also unusual in that they contain a large number of relict endemic species of plants and animals. Indeed, over 80 percent of the plant and animal species in Lake Baikal are endemic only to this lake. Examples of graben lakes in the United States include Lake Tahoe, in the Sierra Mountains of California and Nevada, and Pyramid Lake, north of Reno in Nevada. The Truckee River flows from Lake Tahoe into Pyramid Lake.

Several large, isolated lake basins have resulted from tectonic movements that caused moderate uplift of the marine sea bed. The Caspian Sea and the Aral Sea in central Asia were separated by uplifted mountain ranges in the Miocene epoch (from 5 to 24 million years ago). Lake Okeechobee in central Florida, which is the second largest freshwater lake in the coterminous United States, with an area of 1,880 square kilometers (Lake Michigan is the larg-

Lake Tahoe, on the California-Nevada border, is a graben lake. These deep lakes form when a rift valley, caused by faulting, fills with water. (R. Kent Rasmussen)

est), was a shallow depression in the seafloor when it was uplifted during the Pliocene Epoch some 2 to 5 million years ago as part of the formation of the Floridian peninsula.

The third major natural cause of lakes is volcanic activity. Lava flows can block stream valleys and form lake basins, and collapsing volcanic craters form large basins called calderas. Crater Lake in Oregon, with an area of 64 square kilometers and a depth of 608 meters (making it the seventh deepest in the world) is a well-known example of a caldera lake. The fourth type of natural origin occurs in humid regions underlain by limestone. This type of rock is very susceptible to being dissolved by percolating water. In time, the limestone goes into solution, and the result is a conical and circular sinkhole. These sinkhole lakes are very common in limestone areas of the Balkans and the midwestern United States, and in central Florida. Oxbow

lakes develop in meandering stream channels of gently sloping alluvial floodplains that have been abandoned by lateral shifts of the river. These are very common in the floodplain of the lower Mississippi River.

Lakes, whatever the nature of their origin, are ephemeral features on the earth's surface. In contrast to many other landforms on the earth, such as mountains and valleys, lakes are very transient. Drier climatic conditions, erosion of an outlet, natural and human-induced sedimentation, water diversion, and nutrient inflow inexorably result in a short life span of hundreds to thousands of years. On a geological time scale, this longevity is extremely short.

Lake Stratification. Solar heating of a lake results in thermal stratification, which is a major factor in lake structure. This process is the most important physical event in the annual cycle of a lake. Thermal stratification is common in many midlatitude lakes that are deeper than approximately 10 meters. During the high sun or summer months, an epilimnion—a warm, lighter, circulating, and relatively turbulent layer—develops in the surface waters; it has a range of thickness of about 2 to 20 meters. A lower level of denser, cooler, and relatively quiet water develops below the epilimnion. The vertical extent of this hypolimnion level can be large or small, depending on the depth of the lake. The thermocline, or metalimnion, forms a zone of transition between the two layers where the temperature changes abruptly. It is generally several meters in thickness. The stratification is not caused by the temperature change but rather by the difference in the densities of the water in the epilimnion (lighter) and the hypolimnion (heavier). As the fall season approaches, heat loss from the surface exceeds heat inputs, and the epilimnion cools, becomes denser, and mixes with the deeper layers. Eventually, all of the water in the lake is included in the circulation as the fall turnover begins. Most lakes experience a seasonal cycle of stratification and mixing that is a key component of their ecology.

Reservoirs. Reservoirs are artificial lakes; they range from small farm or fish ponds of less than a hectare in size to massive impoundments. The three largest reservoirs in terms of capacity are Bratsk on the Angara River in Siberia, Lake Nasser on the Nile in Egypt, and Lake Kariba on the Zambezi River, which forms the boundary between Zimbabwe and Zambia in Africa. The largest reservoirs in the United States are Lake Mead and Lake Powell on the Colorado River. Reservoirs are built for hydropower, flood control, navigation, water supply, low flow maintenance for water quality purposes, recreation, or any combination thereof. Reservoir management is a specialized field, since water releases and storage requirements must fit in with the operating schedule for each system and watershed.

Although dams and reservoirs have brought many benefits to society, they are associated with several environmental problems. For example, the dams on the Columbia River in the Pacific Northwest make it much more difficult for salmon to return upstream where they spawn. Fish ladders have provided only a partial solution to this problem. Large impoundments such as Lake Mead (behind Hoover Dam on the Colorado River) can store so much water that the additional weight on the earth's crust has been linked to small to moderate earthquakes in parts of Nevada hundreds of kilometers away. Reservoirs, by design, regulate the flow of water downstream. In the process of doing so, they deny the river its normal seasonal flush of water in the spring, which is necessary for a healthy aquatic ecosystem. As a means of addressing this flushing problem on the Grand Canyon portion of the Colorado River, a large amount of water was released from Lake Powell, which is upstream from the Grand Canyon, in a short period of time so as to replicate the spring flood. Considerable hydropower revenues were lost in this experiment, but there were many benefits to the ecology of the river.

Eutrophication. The aging of a lake by biological enrichment is known as eutrophication. The water in young lakes is cold and clear, with minimal amounts of plant and animal life. The lake is then in the oligotrophic state. As time goes on, streams that flow into the lake bring in nutrients such as nitrates and phosphates, which encourage aquatic plant growth. As the fertility in the lake increases, the plant and animal life increases, and organic remains start accumulating on the bottom. The lake is now becoming eutrophic. Silt and organic debris continue to accumulate over time, slowly making the lake shallower. Marsh plants that thrive in shallow water start expanding and gradually fill in the original lake basin. Eventually the lake becomes a bog and then dry land.

This natural aging of a lake can take thousands of years, depending upon the size of the lake, the local climate, and other factors. However, human activities can substantially accelerate the eutrophication process. Among the problems caused by humans are the pollution of lakes by nutrients from agricultural runoff and poorly treated wastewater from municipalities and industries. The nutrients encourage algal growth, which clogs the lake and removes dissolved oxygen from the water. The oxygen is needed for other forms of aquatic life. The lake has now entered a hypereutrophic state as declining levels of dissolved oxygen result in incomplete oxidation of plant remains, a situation that eventually causes the death of the lake as a functioning aquatic ecosystem. In a real sense, the lake chokes itself to death.

Climatic Effects. Lakes moderate local climates. Since the specific heat of water is five times that of dry land, lakes ameliorate cold-air-mass intrusions in midlatitude regions. The resultant extension of the frost-free period can be very beneficial to agriculture. The successful vineyards on the shores of the Finger Lakes in New York and the fruit tree belts in upper New York just south of Lake Ontario are a well-known example of this benefit. Even in Florida, the presence of Lake Okeechobee helps the agricultural areas on the southern and southeastern shores; cold air from the northwest is warmed as it passes over the lake.

The Great Lakes are associated with a "lake effect" that results in additional snow falling in those areas where cold Canadian air masses pass over the lakes from the northwest in the winter, pick up moisture from the relatively warmer water, and then precipitate the snow on the southern and eastern shores of the lakes. The amounts of snow deposited during these routine occurrences can be quite substantial.

FURTHER READING: One of the most widely cited reference works on lakes is *Limnology*, by Robert G. Wetzel, 1983. Other standard textbooks include *Textbook on Limnology*, by Gerald A. Cole, 1983, and *Limnology*, by Charles R. Goldman and Alexander J. Horne, 1983. Mary J. Burgis and Pat Morris have written a very readable account of the flora and fauna associated with the wide variety of lakes found on the earth in *The Natural History of Lakes*, 1987. *Reservoir Limnology: Ecological Perspectives*, edited by Kent W. Thornton, Bruce L. Kimmel, and Forrest E. Payne, 1990, is a study of artificial lakes (reservoirs). A variety of technical studies of different types of lakes is available in *Limnology Now: A Paradigm of Planetary Problems*, edited by Ramon Margalef, 1994. The details of measuring lakes are covered in *A Manual of Lake Morphometry*, by Lars Hakanson, 1981. A short but very informative tabulation of water quality in selected lakes in the world is available in *Water Quality of World*

River Basins, by Andrew S. Fraser, Michael Meybeck, and Edwin D. Ongley, 1995. Details on sediment processes in lakes can be found in *Principles of Lake Sedimentology*, by Lars Hakanson and Mats Jannson, 1983.

Robert M. Hordon

SEE ALSO: Dams; Ecosystems; Eutrophication; Glaciation; Groundwater; Hydrology and the hydrologic cycle; Streams and rivers; Water supply systems; Wetlands.

Land Institute

DATE ESTABLISHED: 1976

Founded in September, 1976, by Wes Jackson, the Land Institute's 275-acre research and education facility has five programs that seek to develop a sustainable agriculture and prosperous, enduring human communities.

PLANT GENETICIST WES JACKSON and his wife, Dana Jackson, founded the Land Institute to perform agricultural research and development. Extremely critical of industrialized agriculture, Jackson sought to explore the possibilities of "perennial polyculture" as an alternative to the growing and harvesting of annual grains. One of his primary concerns was to halt the soil erosion that he believed was exacerbated by current monoculture agriculture techniques and that he believed would eventually lead to a crisis in American agriculture. The Jacksons established the Land Institute in Salina, Kansas, on a minimal budget, constructing the institute's building themselves.

The institute has a greenhouse and uses surrounding prairie acreage for research and ecological observation; it has a small number of students in its program each year. Wes Jackson became the institute's primary theorist, and Dana was its administrator. Through the institute, Jackson has sought to develop what he referred to as an ecological agriculture. This would be based on growing mixtures of plants rather than monocultures and on perennials rather than annuals. Significant challenges include breeding perennials with increased seed yields and with heads of grain that resist shattering (wild grains typically release their seeds if knocked). The Land Institute is engaged in a long-term project; Jackson himself has said it could be a hundred years before results are achieved.

The Land Institute has five major programs. The Natural Systems Agriculture Program envisions an agricultural system that is sun powered and free of soil erosion, uses no alien chemicals or fossil fuels, is genetically diverse, and is able to meet human needs, especially food needs. These goals are to be accomplished by modeling agricultural systems on natural ecosystems. The Sunshine Farm Research Program is a farm-scale operation using crops, animals, and equipment in a self-sustaining system without the use of conventional farm chemicals or fossil fuels.

The Matfield Green Project proposes ecology as an organizing principle for human communities in order to minimize dependence on nonrenewable resources and foster cultural innovations and adaptations. The Intern Program at Salina gives selected postgraduate students a forty-three-week experience in research, classroom discussion, lectures, and farm labor. These students develop into informed multidisciplinary leaders who are dedicated to building a sustainable agriculture and integrating it into a sustainable society.

Finally, the Education and Public Policy Program promotes the Land Institute's "nature as measure" paradigm. The organization's Land Report and numerous other educational outreach projects demonstrate the resilience and sustainability of natural systems and explain how they apply to agriculture and human communities.

Thomas A. Eddy

SEE ALSO: Agriculture industry; Agronomy; Erosion and erosion control; Jackson, Wes; Land management; Monoculture agriculture; Soil management.

Land management

Efforts put toward using land to its best advantage are collectively called land management. Land management decisions affect both public and private lands, and they entail such issues as what use or uses—agriculture, forestry, mining, industry, residential development, and ecological preservation—should be encouraged or discouraged in a given area. Appropriate land management has become increasingly important as concerns about pollution and the environment have grown.

LAND MANAGEMENT IS a term that describes decisions and practices regarding the uses of land. Land management may emphasize any one of a variety of different land uses. Farmers, for example, may manage their acreage to obtain the most efficient crop production, while city planners seek to ensure that land within their boundaries is used to benefit the community as a whole. The land that comprises the fifty United States covers about 3.5 million square miles, and to some extent laws govern the management of every inch, public or private. The intent of much of this legislation is to prevent practices that pollute or harm the environment in other ways. Whether landowners wish to harvest timber, graze livestock, or operate ski areas, legislation sets clean air and water requirements. Permits are also required for any activity that disturbs stream beds or changes the channel of a water course.

As population increases, public land administrators are under greater pressure to resolve conflicts over land use while protecting the land from abuse. Myriad questions may be raised. How much timberland should be cut for forest products, and how much preserved for watershed and wildlife? Should New York City restrict economic development in the Hudson River watershed to reduce pollution caused by stormwater runoff?

Public Land Management: Multiple Use and Dominant Use. In 1960 Congress passed the Multiple Use-Sustained Yield Act. In many respects it simply codified practices (particularly regarding forest management) that had been followed informally since the early twentieth century. Under a multiple use approach, land is managed so as to support more than one use (such as forestry and recreation) simultaneously. Sustained yield refers to management (again, particularly forest management) that fosters continuous production without depleting the resource.

A few years later, in 1964, the Public Land Law Review Commission was chartered to study federal land policies. Its report, released in 1970, was criticized for its recommendation that there be designated areas on public lands that would produce income for private companies, such as mining and ranching interests. Termed "dominant use," the concept was not new. In 1878 John Wesley Powell, an explorer and member of a commission to study public lands, had proposed that public lands be classified according to whether the land's most appropriate use was irrigated farming, livestock grazing, timber harvesting, or other uses. Critics of dominant use argued that a variety of activities should be allowed in any given area of public land.

Congress formed separate management systems requiring different management approaches for national forests, parks, wildlife refuges, and grasslands. In 1964 the Wilderness Act created another form of land management, one that recognized and emphasized recreation. The result was more hiking and biking trails, ski areas, and campgrounds, as well as improved access to these recreational opportunities. In areas where primary uses overlap, such as a forest-covered mountain, a multiple use approach permits different activities on or near the same site, such as logging alongside a ski area boundary.

A flurry of legislation in the 1970's, including the Federal Land Policy and Management Act and the National Forest Management Act, both enacted in 1976, had important consequences for public lands. For the first time, public comment was invited, and input from many diverse groups made it nearly impossible to set common goals for public land management. Gridlock developed among those with various private rights to public lands (such as ranchers with grazing rights, outfitters and guides with hunting rights, and forest products companies with timber-cutting rights) and wilderness supporters with recreational use rights.

Water, Mining, Rights-of-Way, and Wildlife. Water rights are extremely important in the arid West. Land managers may register water rights and can then withdraw water if it is available.

When allocation is restricted, those with the earliest dates of water use receive their allocations first. Such is not the case in the East, where water rights are not an issue. City dwellers can expect a rush of water when they turn a faucet and are not faced with negotiating their individual water rights. The greatest source of income from U.S. public lands is royalties from oil, gas, and coal. Ninety percent of federal lands were once open to mining, but with passage of the Wilderness Act (1964), many public lands became off-limits to mining. A variety of legislation covers mining on federal land, the central act being the General Mining Law of 1872. It has provisions allowing citizens to lay claim to a specific tract of federal land for an annual fee. The claimant then has mining and surface rights. This law is still in effect but has been limited through the years. In 1920 oil and coal were removed from coverage under the act and covered by separate legislation; in 1955 common rocks and minerals were withdrawn, and in 1976 all national parks were withdrawn.

Both public and private land managers routinely exchange right-of-way agreements to allow passage of livestock or access to timber sales. Private landowners of vast tracts of forest or rangeland often permit public access for recreational use. Wildlife on public and private land is subject to state and federal regulations, and game harvests are regulated. In many states private landowners with farmland damaged by game animals can apply for a depredation hunt, but they cannot legally trap or harvest the animals without state permission. Similarly, hunting seasons for waterfowl and migratory game birds are set by the federal government, and these seasons must be followed by all land managers, public and private.

Federal, State, and Private Management. There has been considerable debate concerning the effectiveness of private versus public management, and of federal versus state or local management. Private landowners have a strong financial incentive to take care of their land and use it wisely, or at least profitably. Public managers do not have the same motivation. Some advocates propose returning federal public lands to state and local ownership or control, thereby letting those people paying the bills—the local taxpayers—see that the lands are managed wisely. Opponents of this proposal argue that state managers could not manage the land as effectively as federal managers and fear that eventually the land would be acquired by private owners. There are existing state public lands; most are small and scattered parcels, many of which were gained from education land grants. Although land exchanges have consolidated some tracts, these small parcels are difficult to manage effectively. Proponents of the transfer of federal lands to state control claim that bigger parcels would result in improved land management by state administrators.

FURTHER READING: *Public Lands and Private Rights: The Failure of Scientific Management,* by Robert H. Nelson, 1995, analyzes public policy. *Federal Land, Western Anger: The Sagebrush Rebellion and Environmental Politics,* by R. McGreggor Cawley, 1993, explores the interplay between resource exploitation and economic, social, and political experiences.

J. A. Cooper

SEE ALSO: Bureau of Land Management, U.S.; Forest management; General Mining Law of 1872; Land-use planning; Land-use regulation and control; Multiple use approach; Public lands; Sagebrush Rebellion.

Land-use planning

Land-use planning is a management technique used to protect the environment while fostering responsible and compatible economic development. The basic philosophy of land-use planning is to mediate and avoid conflicts between land uses and users, avoid hazards, conserve natural resources, and generally protect the environment through the use of sound ecological and economic principles.

SOME FORM OF planning is involved in most decisions about land use, but the term land-use planning usually refers to a scale of decision making greater than that of an individual land unit. Land-use planning usually involves government at one level or another in the decision-making process and is usually concerned with reconcil-ing the goals and objectives of individuals and groups that may be in conflict concerning prospective land uses.

The purpose of land-use planning is to make the most sensible, practical, safe, and efficient use of parcels of land. Much of the motivation for land-use planning arises from the current reality that a large and growing population occupies a fixed expanse of real estate and that some land is unstable and unsuitable for certain types of usage. Because land-use decisions are based, in part, on scientific and engineering considerations, land-use planning involves a great deal of interdisciplinary team work. Planners must weigh and consider decisions about the potential economic or practical benefits from a given use of the land and the possible negative environmental or aesthetic impacts. As a result, land-use planning often takes the form of assessing the suitability of a particular parcel of land for a particular purpose and proceeds somewhat like an environmental impact assessment.

Conflicting Values and Objectives. Land-use planning is conducted to reflect differences in goals between individual land users and the public as a whole or among broad interest groups within the general population. Individual land users may be concerned with selling or utilizing land to maximize its profitability, while government or concerned portions of the public may perceive greater utility in retaining the land as is, or for an alternate purpose. Similarly, individual land users may be content to manage their land in a fashion that does not maximize output, while the government may seek to use the land in such a way as to increase the resource's output. It is the goal of land-use planning to aid in resolving these conflicting societal values concerning land resources.

At one level, land-use planning is concerned with reconciling conflicting objectives. At another level, planning seeks to mediate or adjudicate between the objectives of interest groups and work to establish compromise in goal setting for the management of public lands so as to balance broad policies among land-exploiting sectors of the population. As a result, few environmental topics are as controversial as land-use planning. The controversy envolves several fac-

The Land-Use Planning Process

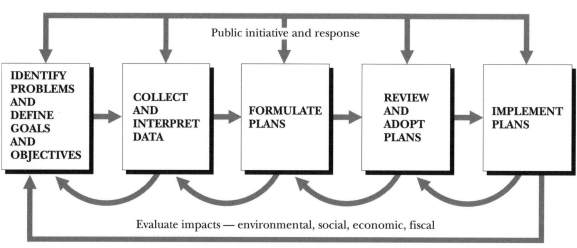

Public initiative and response

| IDENTIFY PROBLEMS AND DEFINE GOALS AND OBJECTIVES | COLLECT AND INTERPRET DATA | FORMULATE PLANS | REVIEW AND ADOPT PLANS | IMPLEMENT PLANS |

Evaluate impacts — environmental, social, economic, fiscal

COLLECT DATA

Earth science and other
   information
Background studies
   Existing land use
   Transportation
   Economic
   Political
   Social
Land capability studies

FORMULATE PLANS

Land use
Watershed
Natural resources
Hazard mitigation
Open space
Waste management
Public facilities

IMPLEMENT PLANS

Zoning and subdivision regulations
Erosion and sedimentation control
   ordinances
Building and housing codes
Environmental impact statements
Capital improvement programs
Health and information codes

tors. First, unlike concerns over environmental pollution, which can be measured, evaluated, and possibly corrected, it is difficult to determine the "best use" of the natural environment as opposed to the "most profitable use." Second, landowners often fear that planning will take away their right to decide what to do with their property. A frequent problem in land-use planning is that individual judgments about the relative importance or value of different land considerations are involved, and these judgments often differ sharply. For example, an old-growth forest may appeal to a lumber company as a source of valuable timber, whereas campers may prefer it to remain pristine and unlogged. As a result, land-use planning has become an important political and environmental issue.

Politics and the Planning Process. In the end, sound land-use planning depends on how political power is distributed and exercised. Land-use planning is not value free. Professional planners contribute the means of planning, but the ends and objectives are highly subjective and political in nature. They depend on how land is perceived by society, on whether land use should be dictated by market forces and the pursuit of profit by its owner, or whether land should be regarded as a common-property resource like air or water, and on whether land is seen as an inheritance to which an obligation of stewardship is owed to future generations.

Land-use planners, like land users, often have multiple goals, and the methods and techniques of planning are highly diverse and usually include a variety of steps. In any land-use planning project the first and most essential step is to identify and define issues, goals, and objectives concerning the lands in question. This step is usually accomplished through a combination of public input and scientifically based research and assessment. Data on the lands, including a complete inventory of resources and hazards, must be collected, analyzed, and interpreted. Based on the collected data a series of land-use alternatives can be developed and tested; the results of this process can be used to formulate a potential land-use plan. After review, the plan can be adopted or revised prior to implementation. The key to the entire planning process is to match the natural capability of a land unit to specific potential uses.

FURTHER READING: A good primary treatment of land-use planning can be found in *Land-Use Planning: From Global to Local Challenge*, by Julius Fabos, 1985. An interesting book presenting a comprehensive planning model treating people and their environment as a whole is Allan Savory, *Holistic Resource Management*, 1988. A clearly written and richly illustrated book dealing with creating a harmonious interplay between cultural and natural values is *Landscape Ecology Principles in Landscape Architecture and Land-Use Planning*, by W. E. Dramstad et al., 1996. *Changes in Land-Use and Land Cover: A Global Perspective*, edited by W. B. Meyer and B. L. Turner, 1991, deals with the relationship between human activities and land use.

Randall L. Milstein

SEE ALSO: Bureau of Land Management, U.S.; Land management; Multiple use approach; Population growth and resource use; Public lands; Mineral resource ownership; Soil management.

Land-use regulation and control

Government regulation and control of land use represents the point at which land management and land-use planning considerations become official policy that is enforced by law. Such government regulation is frequently controversial.

LAND-USE REGULATION and control represent the sets of rules established by governing entities in a particular area that permit or prohibit certain activities on a parcel of land. Numerous activities can have significant impacts on land, so a specific set of guidelines must be in place regarding the land uses that are considered to be of greatest importance. Subdivision controls were originally designed to obtain accurate land records as land was described, sold, and legally recorded. Later these controls were better described as development controls, because subdivision laws resulted in standards for design and construction work. Zoning is the most well-known means of land-use control used by local governing bodies: A geographic area is divided into sectors or zones based on the specific land-use controls established for these areas. The most general land-use classes include agricultural, commercial, industrial, and residential, since these classes occur even in small towns and may occur in larger urban areas. Zoning ordinances contain a map which indicates the zones for the regulated areas and a text or narrative which explains the legal or allowed activities that may occur in each zone.

Types of Regulation and Control. Various levels of government use specific types of land-use controls to allow, encourage, discourage, or forbid resource exploitation in given areas. One example is regulations concerning the development of floodplains or other potentially high-risk areas. A floodplain can be an excellent site for development as long as a carefully designed land-use plan incorporates a detailed cost-versus-benefit analysis of the advantages and disadvantages of building in this ecologically sensitive zone. Attempts to determine the true cost of developing the floodplain must consider the benefits of floodwater storage, aesthetic beauty, linear parkland, and opportunities for viewing animal or plant communities. Decisions on these kinds of complex and controversial development proposals should consider the full range of environmental, social, political, and legal issues that will affect the area. Scenic areas are valuable because of their aesthetic beauty: however, they are also attractive building sites because of that beauty.

Government entities have used land-use controls to foster conservation and preservation efforts in areas that are recognized as environmentally significant. Determination of environmental significance may be based on the limited acreage of the resource or on the presence of endangered or threatened species within the boundary area. A growing emphasis on ecosystem-level (large-scale) approaches to conservation and management of terrestrial and aquatic areas has caused local governments to reconsider some of the adverse affects of their localized, community-based development plans. Since ecosystems can encompass a regional area, a wider view must be taken by the regional planning organization to mesh environmental preservation issues with environmental planning goals. Land-use regulation must be based on an understanding of the balance between environmental science and the discipline of urban planning.

Land Management and Land-Use Planning. The regulation of land use is based on, and linked to, the processes of land management and land-use planning. Land management focuses on the proper maintenance of the land's condition and quality to maintain the property in the most efficient manner. Management should consider the land as a natural resource to be preserved and maintained as a valuable commodity. Land management can be regulated and controlled by governing entities through the use of subdivision and zoning laws. In rural areas, regional planning organizations can exert a strong influence on major land-management decisions if a proactive view has already focused on mid- to long-term development issues. Regional organizations generally have less policy enforcement strength than the local governing board. A properly conducted management plan comprises a number of steps that focus on the various parts of the selected environment; these must be accurately inventoried before a land-management plan is implemented.

Land-use planning focuses on the systematic definition and thoughtful design of the methods to be used to effect the present and future uses of land. The plan must be developed through intensive examination of the site conditions and project alternatives that may affect the implementation of the project. The site conditions inventory must include data collected from the soils, vegetation (plant cover), hydrology, and climatic conditions, which will be analyzed and reported as part of a summary of the plan. In addition, data acquired by remote sensing may be incorporated into the overall plan, because such data is significant on a large scale.

Trends in Planning and Control. Trends in land-use planning and control include increased public and institutional interest and participation, development of new land-use planning tools, and a larger role for environmental considerations. "New" land-use planning tools may be better thought of as creative combinations of older methods to achieve the desired outcome. Environmental and natural resource issues have caused citizens and planning organizations to consider further the benefits of including surrounding natural habitats as an enhanced part of the overall plan. Land-use regulation has begun to focus more intensely on the education of the public, because this is often the group that will make the final decision about whether a plan is accepted or doomed to failure.

FURTHER READING: An excellent overview of various aspects of land-use planning is contained in *The Practice of Local Government Planning*, edited by Frank S. So and Judith Getzels, 1988. An additional thorough reference is *Contemporary Urban Planning*, by John M. Levy, 1994. A broad overview of rural and urban land management issues is contained in *Planning the Uses and Management of Land*, edited by M. T. Beatty, G. W. Petersen, and L. D. Swindale, 1979.

Richard Wayne Griffin

SEE ALSO: Land management; Land-use planning; Public lands; Rangelands; Sagebrush Rebellion.

Landfills

Landfills, repositories for general municipal waste, have the potential for contaminating resources, most notably water resources.

LANDFILLS ARE NATURALLY occurring depressions or artificial excavations that serve as repositories for municipal waste or general refuse. The waste is usually buried under successive layers of clay or other earth materials as the debris gradually accumulates. Generally, municipal wastes consist mostly of paper products (greater than 50 percent), with significant foodstuffs, glass, metals, minor garden and lawn debris, plastics, and wood scrap. Some special facilities are authorized to receive toxic waste such as industrial chemicals and contaminated soil. Carla W. Montgomery, in *Environmental Geology* (3d ed. 1992), states that a municipal sanitary landfill requires a land commitment of 1 acre per year for each 10,000 people if the facility is filled to a depth of about 3 meters.

Types and Site Selection. There are two types of repositories: area landfills and depression landfills. Area landfills are large open areas generally situated on low-lying, relatively flat terrain. Extensive excavation is involved, and the excavation is generally filled in sections. Depression landfills, characterized by individual cells, are usually located in places with irregular topography. The cells are long rectangular cuts that usually range from 100 meters to 150 meters long, up to 50 meters wide, and from 8 to 10 meters deep.

The location of a sanitary landfill is usually based on the following criteria. The primary consideration is the presence of a suitable host rock such as shale or marl with a minimum site thickness of 15 meters. If not structurally disturbed, these argillaceous rocks provide a nearly impervious container for long-term storage of waste material. The facility should also be sited in an area of low to moderate-relief where the base of the landfill will be well above the groundwater table during all seasons of the year. The site should be within a moderate haul distance from the communities served and have an all-weather road network available. Geologic faults, both small and large, should be avoided. If present, these features could provide avenues for the downward or lateral migration of mineralized fluids generated in the landfill. The site should also not be near an airport because of the possibility of birds attracted to the site encountering aircraft in flight.

Design and Procedure. Most landfills employ a multiple-barrier approach to contain the materials placed at the site. The base and sides of the excavation are generally covered by an impervious synthetic (plastic) sheet and/or a compacted clay liner. The landfill is topped by a clay cap that is more than a meter thick. A clay dike

Schematic of a Municipal Landfill

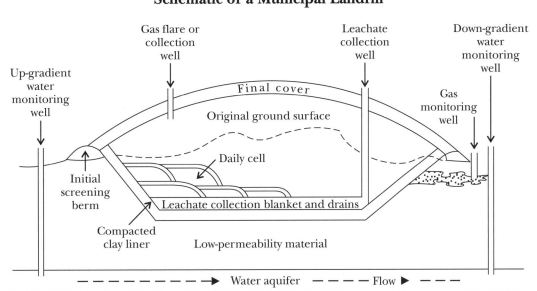

Note: Not to scale.

is sometimes constructed within the earthen cavity to separate the main trash collection area from a leachate collection basin. Dry wells surrounding the landfill monitor the vadose zone. This zone is a band above the water table where some water droplets suspended within the layer migrate downward toward the water table or move laterally to a discharge point. Deep wells on the fringe of the site penetrate the water table and monitor the quality of water stored there.

Potential Hazards and Problems. There are numerous potential health-related problems associated with the storage of municipal waste. Joel B. Goldsteen, in *Danger All Around* (1993), points out some of the major concerns about waste storage on the Texas and Louisiana Gulf Coast. Among the possible hazards are fluid (leachate) generation, gas generation, air and noise pollution, flooding, land subsidence, and fire.

Leachate is an undesirable fluid produced in most landfills as solid waste comes in contact with downward-percolating water within the vadose zone or migrating groundwater. Generally the fluid is acidic, with a high iron concentration (up to 5,000 parts per million). In rare cases the leachate produces a "bathtub effect" and overflows the confines of the landfill. This overflow may lead to contamination of surface waters. The leachate can also "burn" through the synthetic liner and escape through porous and permeable strata. The leachate may dissolve channelways in carbonate bedrock and result in groundwater pollution.

Anaerobic decomposition of compacted organic matter initially produces CO_2 and SO_2 that yields such gases as methane (CH_4) and hydrogen sulfide (H_2S). The methane that is generated may be sold locally, used in the landfill operation, or flared. However, the sulfurous gases are generally not recovered and may produce a strong, undesirable odor similar to rotten eggs. Brooks Ellwood and Burke Burkart, in *The

Landfills pose a number of potential resource contamination problems, especially if they are not properly constructed and monitored. (Jim West)

Sanitary Landfill as a Laboratory (1996), note that upward-fluxing methane gas can produce authigenic magnetic minerals (primarily maghemite) in the capping soils of some landfills.

Small-size particle matter and noise from trucks traveling to and from the landfill site can disturb residents in the area. This is particularly a problem if the truck route passes near residences or schools. Liquid hazardous chemicals placed in the landfill may crystallize and form airborne particles that can be inhaled by local residents or settle in the surrounding area.

If the landfill is poorly located, such as on or near the floodplain of a drainage course, there is the potential for flooding. Floodwaters could erode the landfill and release hazardous fluids from the site. More than five thousand cities and small communities in the United States are located totally or in part on floodplains.

During operation of the landfill and after abandonment of the facility, materials within the landfill continue to adjust to changing physical conditions within the accumulation. These adjustments usually result in surface cracking and settlement.

Spontaneous combustion of flammable materials in a landfill can result in localized fires. Shredded rubber tire chips are sometimes placed at the base of the clay-lined landfills to help funnel fluids generated in the landfill to a collecting basin; it is a particular problem if these begin to burn. These fires are difficult to extinguish and may burn for days. The plume of smoke from the fires is usually considered dangerous because of substances added to the rubber during manufacturing.

Other problems include aesthetic considerations. Erosion sometimes produces short, narrow gullies that expose layered trash in the landfill. These areas are eyesores characterized by the exposed garbage, blowing trash, and circling birds. Vermin (rabbits, mice, rats) as well as various insects (ants, beetles, flies, and roaches) are common residents or visitors.

Monitoring and Legislation. Landfills are usually monitored by visual inspection and through the use of recorded data from test wells that measure water quality within and around the site. Deep wells are bored below the undisturbed bedrock surface and sealed with a primary casing that is cemented in place. The casing minimizes infiltration from fluids within the landfill.

Legislative requirements usually restrict landfills from certain areas such as airports, active fault zones, floodplains, wetlands, and unstable land. The design of landfills must include liners and a leachate collection system. Operators of landfills are required to monitor groundwater for specific toxic chemicals; they must also provide financial assurance criteria (usually bonds) to ensure that monitoring of the facility will continue for at least thirty years after closing.

FURTHER READING: Edward Keller, *Environmental Geology*, 1996, has additional coverage on secure sanitary landfills and waste management. Another secure landfill designed for hazardous chemical waste is shown in a diagram in Ronald Tank, *Environmental Geology*, 1983. Nicholas Coch, *Geohazards: Natural and Human*, 1995, has an excellent discussion of leachate chemical composition and a diagram showing the design of a sanitary landfill that eliminates leachate production and migration. Lawrence Lundgren, *Environmental Geology*, 1986, also discusses control of leachate production and migration of the fluid under acceptable conditions. The methods of sanitary landfill operation are summarized diagrammatically in Christopher C. Mathewson, *Engineering Geology*, 1981.

Donald F. Reaser

SEE ALSO: Air pollution and air pollution control; Groundwater; Hazardous waste disposal; Superfund legislation and cleanup activities; Waste management and sewage control; Water pollution and water pollution control.

Landsat satellites and satellite technologies

Since 1972 a series of earth resources satellites have collected images of the earth. They gather information about various surface or near-surface phenomena, including weather, landforms, and land-use patterns. Satellites are used for crop forecasting, mineral and energy resource exploration, navigation and survey applications, and the compilation of resource inventories.

LANDSAT SATELLITES and similar satellite technologies designed for collecting information about the earth use a process known as remote sensing. Remote sensing is the collection of data about an object or area without being near or in physical contact with it. Satellites occupy various orbits above the earth. Some orbit from pole to pole, some circle around the equator, and others remain fixed above a specific geography.

The first remotely sensed images may have been acquired in 1858 by Gaspard Tournachon, who mounted a camera to a balloon and raised it 80 meters above Bievre, France, thereby taking the first aerial photograph. The first attempt at remote sensing from rockets was made by Ludwig Rahrmann, who was granted a patent in 1891 for "obtaining bird's eye photographic views." Rahrmann's rocket-launched camera, recovered by parachute, rarely exceeded 400 meters in height. The first cameras carried by modern rockets were mounted on captured German V-2 rockets launched by the U.S. Army over White Sands, New Mexico, shortly after World War II.

Comprehensive imaging of the earth's surface from a platform in space began with the development of a series of meteorological satellites in 1960. These first efforts, crude by later standards, were exciting at the time. However, scientists wanted to see more than cloud patterns. Later, during the manned space program, Gemini 4 took a series of photographs of northern Mexico and the American Southwest that guided geologists to new discoveries. The success of these and other attempts at space photography led to a program to develop satellites that could provide systematic repetitive coverage of any spot on the earth.

The Landsat Series. In 1967 the National Aeronautics and Space Administration (NASA) began to plan a series of Earth Resources Technology Satellites (ERTS). The first, ERTS-1, was launched on July 23, 1972. It was the first satellite dedicated to systematic remote sensing of the earth; it used a variety of medium-resolution scanners. Perhaps most important, all images collected were treated according to an "open skies" policy; that is, the images were accessible to anyone. This policy created some concern in the government because of the Cold War tensions of the time. However, scientists realized that the advantages of worldwide use and evaluation of remotely sensed data far outweighed any concerns of disclosure. The project was judged to be a tremendous success by researchers worldwide.

A second ERTS satellite was launched on January 22, 1975, and named Landsat, for "land imaging satellite," to distinguish it from Seasat, an oceanographic satellite mission. Therefore, ERTS-1 was retrospectively renamed Landsat 1, and subsequent satellites were identified as Landsat 2 (1975), 3 (1978), 4 (1982), and 5 (1984). Landsat 6, launched in 1993, failed; it did not achieve orbit. As of 1997, Landsat 7 was scheduled for a 1998 launch.

The Landsat satellites orbit the earth, north to south, about every 103 minutes. The first three Landsats orbited at an altitude of approximately 900 kilometers; Landsats 4 and 5 have somewhat lower orbits. Orbiting in sun-synchronous orbits, they cross each latitude at the same time each day. This renders every image with the same sun angle (shadows) as recorded in previous orbits. The onboard scanners record a track 185 kilometers wide and return to an adjacent western track twenty-four hours later. For example, if the satellite's target was the state of Iowa, eastern Iowa would be scanned on Monday, central Iowa on Tuesday, and the western part of the state on Wednesday. This cycle of images could then be repeated every eighteen days, or about twenty times per year.

The Landsat satellites have carried a variety of imaging systems, designed to record different parts of the electromagnetic spectrum. The images are transmitted back to Earth in a manner similar to television transmission. The early Landsat satellites had a return beam vidicom (RBV) system and a multispectral scanner system (MSS). Later missions replaced the RBV (which experienced a number of technical problems) with the more sophisticated thematic mapper (TM). The RBV system was a series of three television-type cameras aimed at the same ground area. Each camera recorded its image in a different frequency of light. After being received at an earth station, the images could be viewed individually or combined (either electronically or optically) to form a single image. The MSS is a collection of scanning sensors, each of which collects data from a different portion of the spectrum. Two cameras collect images in the visible spectrum: green light and red light; the other two collect in the near infrared.

Each MSS image covers an area of about 185 by 185 kilometers. This renders a scale of 1:1,000,000 and an area of 34,000 square kilometers per frame. The resolution of the scanners is largely dependent on the atmospheric conditions and the contrast of the target, but under ideal conditions they can resolve an area about 80 meters square. Therefore, any objects seen by the scanner must be the size of a football field or larger. In the early to mid-1970's this was considered medium resolution capability. It is sufficient to resolve various natural phenomena but not detailed enough to adequately describe areas sensitive to national security.

Once transmitted to Earth, the images are retained in digital format and/or scanned onto photographic film. As film, they become black-and-white images and can be optically registered to create a single image. Then a color image can be created by passing red, blue, and green light through each negative. This color is not intended to re-create the natural scene but rather to enhance the contrast between various features recorded in different wavelengths. It is this ability to contrast target phenomena to the background or "noise" that makes this research tool so powerful. Once the target has been so delineated, a computer can inventory and/or map the target phenomena. The usefulness of Landsat MSS images has been demonstrated in many fields, among them agriculture and forestry, geology and geography, and land-use planning. The World Bank uses these images for economic geography studies. A distinct advantage of this database is the "big picture" perspective afforded by the format: A single MSS Landsat image can replace over sixteen hundred aerial photographs of 1:20,000 scale. However, with the increase of aerial coverage comes a decrease in resolution. Therefore, these images may best be used as a complementary or confirming database to be used with other aerial imagery and

ground surveys. Identifying the appropriate season for viewing a phenomenon or target is critical. For geographic features, the low sun angle and "leaf-down" conditions of winter are an advantage. For biological phenomena, wet-dry seasons and time of year are critical. A riverbed or lake can disappear in dry conditions or be misinterpreted as a pasture if covered with green moss or algae. Therefore, matching the target to time of year and seasonal conditions must be a consideration when selecting a time window for observation.

Uses and Benefits. The power of this perspective is revealed when satellite images are used to examine regional or area formations, structures, and trends. The extent of many geologic structures has been delineated with satellite imagery. For example, Landsat imagery has clearly identified impact craters, such as the Manicougan ring in east-central Quebec, Canada, and fault systems, such as those of California's San Andreas fault and Georgia's Brevard fault zone. These systems extend hundreds of miles and are difficult, if not impossible, to perceive from the ground.

Additionally, satellite imagery has suggested areas for new fossil fuel and mineral exploration by decoding rock structure, potential oil and gas traps, and fault lines. Many of the areas involved are relatively inaccessible, and remote sensing has provided a map base and assisted in decoding the structures. Examples include the complex sedimentary structures on the east side of the Andes, ranging from Brazil to Argentina, and a number of structures in countries of the former Soviet Union: the Caspian Sea states of Azerbaijan, Kazakhstan, and Turkmenistan, northern Russia's tundra, the Timan-Pechora region near the Barents Sea, and western Siberia's Priobskoye region. Remote sensing is assisting the exploration of these remote areas, for which reliable topographic and geologic maps are scarce or nonexistent.

The usefulness of satellite images is by no means restricted to energy exploration. The imagery has been used to inventory agriculture crop acreage and yields and to monitor irrigation and treatment programs. Therefore it aids in commodities analysis. It also aids in environmental monitoring. Different plants reflect different spectral energies, and sensors can differentiate these wavelengths. In this way the distribution and health of forests and wetlands can be mapped. Extreme environmental impacts can be assessed as well: The effects of disasters such as the Mount Saint Helens volcanic eruption, oil spills, droughts, forest fires, floods, and hurricanes can be mapped and inventoried via the satellite platform.

Generally TM images can be used for a wider range of applications than MSS images can. The reason is that the TM records through more spectral bands with a greater spacial resolution (30 × 30 meters, compared with the MSS 79 × 79 meters). The MSS images are most useful describing and delineating large-scale phenomena such as geologic structures and land cover. The TM is perhaps more beneficial for land-use description and planning.

Other Satellite Programs. In 1986 the French government, with Sweden and Belgium as partners, launched the first of a series of "Système Probatoire d'Observation de la Terre" (SPOT)

Remote Sensing Measurement of Plume from Mount St. Helens, 1980

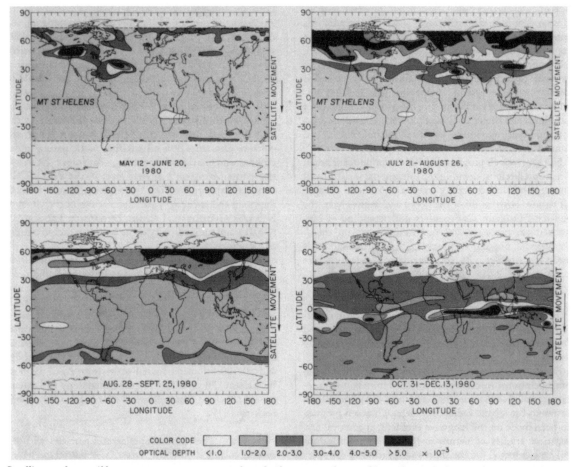

Satellites make possible numerous measurements of earth phenomena that could not be tracked any other way, such as the spreading volcanic plume from the 1980 eruption of Mount St. Helens in Washington.

Source: National Oceanic and Atmospheric Administration, U.S. Department of Commerce, and National Aeronautics and Space Administration. *Space-Based Remote Sensing of the Earth and Its Atmosphere: A Report to Congress.* Washington, D.C.: U.S. Government Printing Office, 1986.

satellites. This commercial system was designed to compete with the American Landsat program. The resolution on this satellite is 10 meters for the black-and-white imagery and 20 meters for color imagery. SPOT has the further advantage of being able to create stereoscopic images.

Other satellite systems are also scanning the surface of the earth. For example, there are meteorological satellites serving the needs of the United States' National Oceanographic and Atmospheric Administration (NOAA). Another large-scale satellite endeavor is the Geostationary Operational Environmental Satellite (GOES) series. A "geostationary" satellite can remain stationary over a specific point above the earth and observe it twenty-four hours a day. A third class of meteorological satellite is the U.S. Defense Meteorological Satellite Program (DMPS). All these carry relatively coarse-resolution sensors (measured in kilometers) in order to cover the widest area in their frame-by-frame coverage. Another class of satellites, the Seasat satellites, monitors the oceans. They scan in the microwave wavelengths and have proven themselves to be reliable in mapping temperatures and detecting chlorophyll and suspended solids.

While not revealing any information about the earth itself, a class of navigation satellite known as the Navstar Global Positioning System (GPS) assists in resource development in a different way. This system began in March of 1994 and is funded by and controlled by the U.S. Department of Defense, although there are many civilian users worldwide. The GPS system consists of twenty-four satellites spaced so that between five and eight are visible from any point on Earth. By triangulation of a radio signal broadcast from each, users may accurately locate their position on the ground. Anyone with the necessary equipment can receive these signals. The military intentionally degrades the signal so that civilian users can be accurate to only 100 meters or so, while military users can locate a position to within 20 meters. GPS is a valuable tool for people working in areas where maps are of poor scale or are nonexistent.

Remote sensing from near space orbital platforms has revolutionized how we see the earth and contributed greatly to the disciplines of agri-

culture, cartography, environmental monitoring, forestry, geology and geography, land-use planning, meteorology, and oceanography. Its impact has been not only scientific but also political. As other countries launch satellites, information concerning the earth becomes more democratic, and political boundaries become more artificial. Remote sensing has established itself as an invaluable tool for scientific investigation, but its data must be used and interpreted appropriately and in conjunction with other research tools and databases.

FURTHER READING: Among the good sources for further study are F. J. Doyle, *Status of Satellite Remote Sensing Programs*, Report 82-237 of the United States Geological Survey, 1992; P. Francis and P. Jones, *Images of Earth*, 1984; C. Scheffield, *Earthwatch: A Survey of the World from Space*, 1981; and B. F. Richardson, Jr., ed., *Introduction to Remote Sensing of the Environment*, 1978. P. Strain and F. Engle, *Looking at Earth*, 1992, contains many satellite images, providing a continent-by-continent look at the earth. See also R. P. Gupta, *Remote Sensing Geology*, 1991; David Wells, ed., *Guide to GPS Positioning*, 1989; and the NASA publications *Landsat Data Users Handbook*, doc. no. 76SDS4258, 1976, 1979, and 1984, and *Third Earth Resources Technology Satellite Symposium*, NASA SP-356, 1974.

Richard C. Jones

SEE ALSO: National Oceanic and Atmospheric Administration; Oil and natural gas exploration; U.S. Geological Survey.

Law of the sea

DATE: Law of the Sea Treaty signed December 10, 1982; took effect November 24, 1994

The Law of the Sea Treaty of 1982 was designed to help ensure and maintain the peaceful use of the seas for all nations; its signatories hoped to accomplish this goal by standardizing and regulating areas of potential conflict between nations. Some important areas covered by this treaty include ship safety, mineral exploration and exploitation, and environmental protection.

THE PHRASE "law of the sea" implies that activities at sea, like those on land, are subject to the rule of law and that compliance with the law is mandatory and enforced. In fact, the "law of the sea" is not a law but an agreement among nations. This agreement sets standards and regulations on all activities at sea and establishes clear lines of national jurisdiction. Compliance is voluntary, and there is no provision in the 1982 agreement for its enforcement. Despite the apparent weaknesses of such an agreement, compliance on most points has been excellent. The reason is that the "law of the sea" is based on a fundamental principle on which all nations can agree: the freedom of the seas.

Early Concepts. As long as there have been ships, there has been some concept of freedom of the seas. While there were no written rules, a spirit of cooperation among mariners existed during times of peace. By the seventeenth century the Dutch had begun global maritime trade, and their economy was very much dependent on free access to the seas. In 1609 Hugo Grotius, a Dutch lawyer, was asked to codify the concept of freedom of the seas. Grotius produced a large treatise on the law of the seas entitled *Mare Liberum* (1609). This work established the "freedom of the seas" as a concept based on law. The conclusion of Grotius was that all nations could use the oceans provided they did not interfere with one another's use. This first attempt at a law of the sea recognized three divisions of the seas: internal waters, territorial seas, and the high seas. Grotius maintained that a nation had sovereignty over internal and territorial seas but that the high seas were open to all. This concept of the law of the sea survived into the twentieth century.

The Truman Proclamation. In 1947 President Harry S Truman of the United States was advised by geologists of the potential of large oil reserves on the continental shelf. To protect these resources, Truman declared that all resources of the continental shelf belonged exclusively to the United States. This became known as the Truman Proclamation. It had broad international implications, with many nations issuing similar decrees regarding the continental shelf.

The Geneva Conferences. Because of increased economic and military activity at sea, it became apparent that some formal agreement regarding the use of the oceans was needed to ensure peace. In 1958 and again in 1960, conferences on the law of the sea were convened in Geneva. A treaty was drafted and ratified; it included many basic issues on which there was wide agreement. Two points included in the treaty were particularly important. The depth limit of the continental shelf was limited by treaty to 200 meters. This depth limit included an "exploitability clause," however, whereby a nation could exploit ocean resources below 200 meters on adjacent seafloor if it had the technology to do so. Such a concept was favorable to the industrial nations and placed less-developed nations at a disadvantage.

After 1960 many formerly colonial countries received independence; these were primarily nonindustrial states. They feared that the ocean's resources would be exploited by the industrial nations. So great was the fear that in 1967 the nation of Malta proposed to the United Nations that a treaty be developed that would reserve the economic resources of the seafloor. The Maltese ambassador, Arvid Pardo, further declared that the ocean floor should be reserved for peaceful uses alone and that the ocean resources were the "common heritage of all mankind."

The Third Law of the Sea Conference. The Third Law of the Sea Conference was begun in 1973 and continued meeting until 1982. The major result of this conference was the Law of the Sea Treaty dealing with boundary issues, economic rights of nations, rights of passage through straits, the freedom of scientific research, and the exploitation of ocean-floor resources.

The Law of the Sea Treaty established the width of the territorial sea at 12 nautical miles. This could be modified to allow passage of ships through narrow straits critical to international commerce. The territorial sea is under the direct jurisdiction of the adjacent nation, and that nation may enforce its laws and regulate the passage of ships through it. Beyond the territorial limit, a coastal nation or any inhabitable land can also declare an exclusive economic zone (EEZ) of 200 nautical miles. The EEZ is open to ships of all nations, but the resources within it can be exploited only by the nation declaring the EEZ.

The Law of the Sea Treaty established regulations on scientific research in the oceans. While the freedom of scientific research in the open ocean is universally recognized, investigations in a nation's territorial seas and EEZ require the permission of that nation. The treaty also governs the mining of deep sea mineral resources. In certain locations on the deep seafloor, there are nodules of manganese, cobalt, nickel, and copper. Exploitation of these resources requires a highly advanced and expensive technology. Such requirements place less-developed nations at a disadvantage. The Law of the Sea Treaty attempts to address this problem. Any group wishing to mine the deep seafloor must declare its intent to do so and state the geographic location of the mining operation. An international authority will grant permission to mine. All revenues from a successful mining operation on the deep seafloor must be shared among the nations of the world. Further, the technology used to mine the deep seafloor must be shared with all nations.

The Law of the Sea Treaty leaves many issues unresolved and others open to multiple interpretations. Despite areas of disagreement, however, most maritime nations adhere to the majority of the provisions of the Law of the Sea Treaty.

FURTHER READING: A good basic reference on the Law of the Sea Treaty and its effects on the United States is presented in E. M. Borgese, "The Law of the Sea," *Scientific American* 247, no. 3 (1982). An excellent reference on the historical development of the law of the sea and on the Law of the Sea Treaty is included in *Introduction to Oceanography*, by David A. Ross, 1988. The impact of the Law of the Sea Treaty on scientific research is examined by D. A. Ross and J. A. Knauss, "How the Law of the Sea Treaty Will Affect U.S. Marine Science," *Science* 217 (September 10, 1982). Fears and questions regarding the Law of the Sea Treaty are discussed in B. Zuleta, "The Law of the Sea: Myths and Realities," *Oceanus* 25, no. 3 (1982).

Richard H. Fluegeman, Jr.

SEE ALSO: Exclusive economic zones; Fisheries; Manganese; Marine mining; Oceanography; Oceans.

Leaching

Leaching is the removal of insoluble minerals or metals found in various ores, generally by means of microbial solubilization. Leaching is significant as an artificial process for recovering certain minerals, as an environmental hazard, notably as a result of acid mine drainage, and as a natural geochemical process.

LEACHING IS AMONG the processes that concentrate or disperse minerals among layers of soil. Leaching is a natural phenomenon, but it has been adapted and applied to industrial processes for obtaining certain minerals. The recovery of important resource metals such as copper, uranium, and gold is of significant economic benefit. However, if the metal is insoluble or is present in low concentration, recovery through conventional chemical methods may be too costly to warrant the necessary investment. Bioassisted leaching, often referred to as microbial leaching or simply bioleaching, is often practiced under such circumstances. The principle behind such biotechnology is the ability of certain microorganisms to render the metal into a water-soluble form.

Bioleaching of Copper Ore. The production of copper ore is particularly illustrative of the leaching process. Low-grade ore containing relatively small concentrations of the metal is put into a leach dump, a large pile of ore intermixed with bacteria such as *Thiobacillus ferrooxidans*. Such bacteria are able to oxidize the copper ore rapidly under acidic conditions, rendering it water soluble. Pipes are used to distribute a dilute sulfuric acid solution over the surface of the dump. As the acid percolates through the pile, the copper is solubilized in the solution and is collected in an effluent at the bottom of the pile. Two forms of the copper are generally found in the crude ore: chalcocite, Cu_2S, in which the copper is largely insoluble, and covellite, CuS, in which the copper is in a more soluble form. The primary function of the *Thiobacillus* lies in the ability of the bacteria to oxidize the copper in chalcocite to the more soluble form.

A variation of this method utilizes the ability of ferric iron, Fe^{+3}, to oxidize copper ore. Reduced iron (Fe^{+2}) in the form of pyrite (FeS_2) is already present in most copper ore. In the presence of oxygen and sulfuric acid from the leaching process, the *Thiobacillus* will oxidize the ferrous iron to the ferric form. The ferric form oxidizes the copper ore, rendering it water soluble, but becomes reduced in the process. The process is maintained through continued reoxidation of the iron by the bacteria. Since the process requires oxygen, the size of the leach dump may prove inhibitory to the process. For this reason, large quantities of scrap iron containing ferric iron are generally added to the leach solution. In this manner, sufficient oxidizing power is maintained.

Generally speaking, those minerals that readily undergo oxidation can more easily be mined with the aid of microbial leaching. As illustrated in the above examples, both iron and copper ores lend themselves readily to such a process. Other minerals, such as lead and molybdenum, are not as readily oxidized and are consequently less easily adapted to the process of microbial leaching.

Leaching of Gold. The extraction of gold from crude ore has historically involved a cyanide leaching process in which the gold is rendered soluble through mixing with a cyanide solution. However, the process is both expensive and environmentally unsound, owing to the highly toxic nature of the cyanide. In an alternative approach that uses bioleaching as a first stage, crushed gold ore is mixed with bacteria in a large holding tank. Oxidation by the bacteria produces a partially pure gold ore; the gold can then be more easily recovered by a smaller scale cyanide leaching. The process was first applied on a large scale in Nevada; a single plant there can produce 50,000 troy ounces of gold each year.

Acid Mine Drainage. The spontaneous oxidation of pyrite in the air contributes to a major environmental problem associated with some mining operations: acid mine drainage. When pyrite is exposed to the air and water, large amounts of sulfuric acid are produced. Drainage of the acid can kill aquatic life and render water undrinkable. Some of the iron itself also leaches away into both groundwater and nearby streams.

Natural Leaching and Geochemical Cycling. The leaching of soluble minerals from soil contributes to geochemical cycling. Elements such as nitrogen, phosphorus, and calcium are all found in mineral form at some stages of the geochemical cycles that are constantly operating on the earth. Many of these minerals are necessary for plant (and ultimately, human) growth. For example, proper concentrations of calcium and phosphorus are critical for cell maintenance. When decomposition of dead material occurs, these minerals enter into a soluble "pool" within the soil. Loss of these minerals through leaching occurs when soil water and runoff remove them from the pool. Both calcium and phosphorus end up in reservoirs such as those in deep ocean sediments, where they may remain for extended periods of time.

Percolation of water downward through soil may also result in the leaching of soluble nitrogen ions. Both nitrites (NO_2^-) and nitrates (NO_3^-) are intermediates in the nitrogen cycle, converted into such forms usable by plants by the action of bacteria on ammonium compounds. Nitrate ions in particular are readily absorbed by the roots of plants. The leaching of nitrites and nitrates through movement of soil water may result in depletion of nitrogen.

In addition to the loss of nitrogen for plants, leaching can lead to significant environmental damage. Since both nitrite and nitrate ions are negatively charged, they are repelled by the negatively charged clay particles in soil, particularly lending themselves to leaching as water percolates through soil. High concentrations of nitrates in groundwater may contaminate drinking water, posing a threat to human health.

FURTHER READING: A general discussion of mineral development and leaching of soils is found in *Environmental Geology*, by Edward Keller, 1992. More thorough treatments of the role played by microorganisms in bioleaching are found in *Brock Biology of Microorganisms*, by Michael Madigan, John Martinko, and Jack Parker, 1996, and *Microbial Ecology*, by Ronald Atlas and Richard Bartha, 1993. The effects of the leaching of minerals into groundwater are described in *Soil Ecology*, by Ken Killham, 1994.

Richard Adler

SEE ALSO: Biotechnology; Igneous processes, rocks, and mineral deposits; Mining wastes and mine reclamation; Secondary enrichment of mineral deposits; Sedimentary processes, rocks, and mineral deposits; Soil degradation.

Lead

WHERE FOUND: Lead is widely distributed in the earth's crust; it has a clarke, or estimated percentage of the crustal weight, of 0.0013, making it more common than silver or gold but less common then copper or zinc; these are the four minerals with which lead is most commonly found in ore deposits. All five may occur together in a deposit, or only two or three may occur in concentrations sufficiently rich to be economically attractive to miners.

PRIMARY USES: The major use of lead in the United States is in the lead-acid batteries used in automotive vehicles. Because lead is so toxic, a fact that has been known since ancient times, many of its former uses have been curtailed or discontinued. While it is still used in cables, ammunition, solders, shielding of radiation, and electrical parts, two of its major uses—in paints and as an anti-knock additive in gasoline—were phased out during the 1970's and 1980's. Nevertheless, lead production has been maintained at about the same level as before the phase out. Should a suitable substitute ever be developed for lead-acid batteries, the use of lead will decline to very low levels.

DESCRIPTION: Lead (abbreviated Pb), atomic number 82, belongs to Group IV of the periodic table of the elements. It is a mixture of four stable isotopes and has twenty-seven other isotopes, all radioactive, as a result of lead being the end product of three series of radioactive elements: the uranium series, actinium series, and thorium series. It has an average atomic weight of 207.2 and a density of 11.35 grams per cubic centimeter; it has a melting point of 327.5 degrees Celsius and a boiling point of 1,740 degrees Celsius.

LEAD IS SOFT, malleable, and ductile, and is second only to tin in possessing the lowest melting point among the common metals. It may well have been the first metal smelted by humans, although it was probably not the first metal used—an honor claimed by either gold, silver, or copper, which occur naturally in their metallic states. The fact that the principal ore of lead, galena (lead sulfide), frequently resembles the metal itself in its gray-black metallic color probably encouraged early humans to experiment with crude smelting. Inorganic lead also occurs as a carbonate (cerrusite), sulfate (anglesite), and oxides. Organic compounds of lead exist; these were used for many years in automobile gasoline as anti-knock additives (tetraethyl and tetramethyl lead). Lead is widely distributed in the environment, but except in bedrock, concentrations are largely a consequence of human activity. Clair Patterson demonstrated that dramatic human-related increases in lead concentrations exist in the oceans, in polar ice sheets, and in the atmosphere. Before the human use of lead, the global flux into the oceans was only one-tenth to one-hundredth what it is today; lead in the atmosphere has increased a hundredfold globally and a thousandfold in urban areas.

Historical Background. While lead apparently was not the first or second metal to attract early humans, because it did not occur in a metallic state, it was exploited relatively early and may have been smelted in Anatolia as early as 7000-6500 B.C.E.. The softness and malleability of lead proved to be both attractive and undesirable to people in antiquity. Most early lead mining was carried on to recover the associated silver, the lead remaining from the process being piled in waste heaps. Lead may be strengthened by alloying with other metals, but this process was carried out only to a limited degree in lead's earliest usage.

While lead may not have proved attractive for uses requiring strength and hardness, its malleability caused the Romans, in particular, to put it to widespread use in piping, roofing, and vessels. In addition, lead compounds were used in paints, cosmetics, and as additives to wine and food. Lead poisoning was therefore widespread. The problem was recognized possibly as early as 370 B.C.E. by Hippocrates and certainly was known by Nikander in the second century B.C.E.

The Romans nevertheless continued to press lead into a variety of services until the fall of their empire. Some authorities believe that lead poisoning was central to this fall, and many more believe that it at least contributed (especially to the disorganization of Roman leaders). Others maintain that the critical lead-related factor in the decline of Rome was the exhaustion of the richer silver-bearing ores. Exhaustion of mines or ores at any period in history is usually a function of the technology and economics of the time; many of these ores were particularly rich by modern standards. Silver was critical to maintenance of the Roman financial system, and the decline in its availability brought economic chaos.

Medieval production of lead declined dramatically in Europe following the fall of the Roman Empire, although recurring cases of lead poisoning during this period serve as a reminder that lead was still utilized widely in storage vessels. The Industrial Revolution, beginning with its earliest stages, revived the production level of lead, both for itself and as a by-product of silver mining. The expansion of European exploration into the Western Hemisphere and of European colonization worldwide from the fifteenth century onward undoubtedly contributed to the rise in lead production. Gold and silver were sought avidly in these expansions of domain, and lead mining frequently serves as the final use or "mop-up" stage in the life history of a mining district. Also, industrial uses and mining technology became increasingly sophisticated, leading to a new demand for lead and zinc, its frequent associate, especially beginning in the nineteenth century. The production curve of lead and zinc goes exponentially upward through history, with far greater production today than in earlier centuries.

Distribution of Lead. Considering that only an estimated 0.0013 percent of the earth's crust is lead, it is surprisingly widely distributed in the environment. Lead is found in both crystalline (igneous and metamorphic) and sedimentary rocks. Because it is the stable end product of radioactive disintegration of minerals that form in igneous rocks (indeed, it is the rate of this disintegration that is employed to determine the age of the rock), virtually all older crystalline rocks contain at least tiny amounts of lead. As sedimentary rocks are derived from the weathering, erosion, and sedimentation of fragments from existing rocks, it follows that lead compounds will be among those that are sedimented. The higher concentrations of lead—those that pose toxicity problems or are valuable to miners—depend upon quite different processes. Some toxic concentrations of lead are transported by water and then sedimented or absorbed by rock particles, depending on the salinity or acidity levels of the solution. Most toxic concentrations of lead, however, are transported as dust by the atmosphere.

Deposits of lead ore exist at far higher concentrations than those levels that pose problems in water, dust, or soil. They are the result of natural geologic processes, including igneous intrusions, mountain building, and the flow of hot and cold solutions through bedrock over millions of years. The richest lead ores may contain 20 to 25 percent lead, usually with substantial fractions of zinc and minor quantities of silver. Copper and gold are also frequently associated with lead deposits, or vice versa (minor amounts of lead are usually found in copper ore).

Obtaining Lead. The largest lead deposits in the United States and Europe are of the Mississippi Valley type: lead sulfide (galena) deposits of uncertain origin in limestone or dolomite rocks. Many large mines throughout the world are found in crystalline rocks, where they are usually associated with igneous intrusions. Some lead is recovered as a by-product of the mining of copper or other associated minerals from large open-pit mines developed in low-grade ores, called porphyries. This type of recovery is a triumph of twentieth century technology and engineering, because the ores frequently contain less than 0.5 percent copper, with even smaller fractions of lead. Most lead is recovered from underground mines that are exploiting much smaller concentrations in veins or disseminated beds of lead-zinc, zinc-lead, or lead-silver ores.

United States primary lead production (lead from mines) is about 350,000 to 400,000 metric tons each year, while secondary lead (recycled from scrap, chiefly automotive batteries) is

Leading Lead-Producing Countries, 1994
Mine Production of Lead in Concentrates

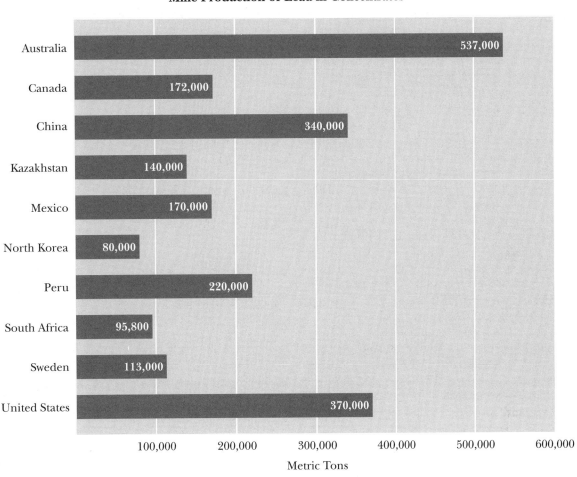

Source: U.S. Bureau of Mines, *Minerals Yearbook, 1994.* U.S. Government Printing Office, 1996.
Note: World 1994 production of lead in concentrates was approximately 2.8 million metric tons.

about 900,000 metric tons each year. World mine production is somewhat greater than lead from secondary sources: about 2.8 million metric tons from mines, 2.4 million metric tons from secondary sources. Recycling should prove even more important in the future as the very richest deposits—those in which the lead content of the ore ranges between 5 and 10 percent—are depleted. This type of "exhaustion" of a deposit is a function of the prevailing technology and economics. In the first half of the twentieth century, the tri-state lead-zinc mining district of Missouri, Oklahoma, and Kansas was the world's greatest.

Production there essentially ceased in the 1950's, not because the lead and zinc were literally exhausted but because the concentrations available dropped below the level at which mining could be done profitably. Technology is continuously improving, however, and the history of mining is filled with examples (particularly concerning the five associated metals gold, silver, copper, lead, and zinc) where improvements in technology, combined with changing economic conditions, have made it possible to reopen or rework older and less attractive deposits. Some mine tailings or waste dumps have been reworked several times under these circumstances.

Uses of Lead. More than most metals, the uses to which lead and lead compounds have been put have changed considerably throughout history. One reason is that new opportunities have presented themselves, such as automotive lead-acid batteries, the shielding of dangerous radiation, and anti-knock additives for gasoline—all twentieth century phenomena. Largely, however, this has occurred because people have become increasingly cognizant of the dangers posed by lead's toxicity. While the dangers of exposure to lead have been known since Greek and Roman times, in few cases has this led to regulation of uses. It was not until the 1960's, 1970's, and 1980's that specific controls or regulations were imposed restricting the use of lead in paint pigments, as an additive to gasoline, and in construction. Lead piping is still found in structures built in the 1970's; the use of lead in storage vessels for food or drink has been regulated even more recently. Lead foil was used in capping wine bottles into the early 1990's, and many people are still unaware that storage of wine or other liquids in fine leaded-glass decanters permits leaching of the lead content into the fluid over time.

The post-World War II era has seen the elimination or substantial reduction of the following uses of lead: water pipes, solder in food cans, paint pigments, gasoline additives, and fishing sinkers. The major remaining uses include storage batteries (80 to 85 percent of U.S. lead usage), ammunition, paint pigments (for nonresidential use), glass and ceramics, sheet lead (largely for shielding against radiation), cable coverings, and solder.

Environmental Impacts of Lead Availability. Lead affects the environment in two major ways: through mining and processing, and because many of its uses, particularly in the past, have exposed the general public to its toxicity. Lead mining has environmental impacts similar to those of the mining of any mineral. Surface mining destroys the local ecosystem and disrupts the use of land for other purposes; reclamation rarely prepares the land for as valuable a use as it enjoyed before mining. The majority of lead is mined underground, where surface disruption

Uses of Lead in U.S., 1994

Product	Metric Tons
Metal products:	
Ammunition: shot and bullets	62,400
Bearing metals	5,560
Brass and bronze: billets and ingots	6,320
Cable covering: power and communication	16,000
Caulking lead: building construction	764
Casting metals	18,900
Pipes, traps, other extruded products	3,370
Sheet lead	21,500
Solder	12,400
Storage batteries	1,220,000
Other metal products	5,330
Other oxides	62,700
Miscellaneous uses	12,000
Total lead consumption	**1,450,000**

Source: U.S. Bureau of Mines, *Minerals Yearbook, 1994.* U.S. Government Printing Office, 1996.

is not as great unless subsidence over the mined areas is a problem. In both surface and underground mining, water is generally contaminated, mine wastes must be stored (waste dumps frequently occupy more space than the mine itself), and the transportation of mine products and waste serves as a source of dust, noise, and disruption to the surrounding population. The milling, smelting, and refining of lead pose further problems. First, lead itself escapes and pollutes the atmosphere with toxic substances. Second, most lead is derived from sulfides, which upon heating in the smelting and refining processes form sulfur dioxide. Sulfur dioxide combines with water in the atmosphere to create sulfuric acid, which devastates and denudes the vegetation cover in the immediate vicinity and contributes to acid rain fallout generally.

Humans may come into contact with lead and its toxic effects in the air, dust, and water, and by direct contamination of food, drink, or cosmetics. The effects of lead on human health are diverse and severe, with their greatest impact on children. The effects are exacerbated by the fact that lead accumulates in the body, and damage is often irreversible—especially damage to the brain. Lead damages blood biochemistry, the renal and endocrine system, liver functions, and the central nervous system, and it contributes to osteoporosis, high blood pressure, and reproductive abnormalities. The Environmental Protection Agency and the Occupational Safety and Health Administration set standards of acceptable levels of lead in air, dust, soil, and water; the standards are updated frequently based on new research, and they are quite complex, depending on the duration and nature of exposure.

FURTHER READING: Data on lead production and use are found in annual issues of the U.S. Bureau of Mines' *Minerals Yearbook* (after 1996, published by the U.S. Geological Survey). A review of the state of knowledge and recommendations for federal governmental action are contained in the National Research Council report *Lead in the Human Environment*, 1980, which includes a section by Clair Patterson listing his concerns regading lead pollution. An exhaustive account of early lead mining and its effects, particularly upon the Romans, is *Lead and Lead Poisoning in Antiquity*, by Jerome O. Nriagu, 1983. Dealing with the lead hazard is treated in *Lead: A Guidebook to Hazard Detection, Remediation, and Control*, by Paul N. Cheremisinoff and Nicholas P. Cheremisinoff, 1993. The geology of major lead mines is discussed in *The Geology of Ore Deposits*, by John M. Guilbert and Charles F. Park, Jr., 1986.

Neil E. Salisbury

SEE ALSO: Air pollution and air pollution control; Metals and metallurgy; Mineral resource use, early history of; Recycling; Silver; Zinc.

Leopold, Aldo

BORN: January 11, 1887; Burlington, Iowa
DIED: April 21, 1948; near Baraboo, Wisconsin

In his years of government service and private work, Leopold was active in game management and wildlife preservation. His Sand County Almanac *has been influential with succeeding generations of conservationists.*

ALDO LEOPOLD, BORN in Burlington, Iowa, graduated from the Yale School of Forestry in 1906. After completing his masters degree in 1909 he joined the U.S. Forest Service and fostered the ecological policies of Gifford Pinchot and Theodore Roosevelt. Stationed in the southwestern United States, he advocated game conservation to avoid the erosion of sport hunting. He also helped establish a 500,000-acre roadless wilderness in the Gila National Forest. While pursuing wolf eradication to ensure deer viability, he realized the importance of ecological interactions.

He moved to Wisconsin in 1924, joined the U.S. Forest Products Laboratory, and developed the policy of wildlife management. He published *Game Management*, subsequently retitled *Wildlife Management*, in 1933. In the same year he joined the University of Wisconsin Department of Agricultural Economics at Madison. He assisted Robert Marshall in creating the Wilderness Society in 1935, and in 1939 he established a one-man Department of Wildlife Management.

Leopold advocated integration of local concerns with universities, government agencies, and the private sector to balance farming, forestry, wildlife, and recreation. He escaped on the weekends to his sand farm in Wisconsin, where he wrote prolifically. His *Sand County Almanac*, published posthumously in 1949, represents a lifetime of observations concerning ecology, ethics, and aesthetics and concludes that a policy is right when it tends to preserve the integrity, stability, and beauty of the biotic community; any other policy, according to Leopold, is wrong.

Aaron S. Pollak and Oliver B. Pollak

SEE ALSO: Conservation; Pinchot, Gifford; Roosevelt, Theodore; Wilderness; Wilderness Society.

Lime

WHERE FOUND: Lime is a manufactured product not found in nature. It is usually derived from the common sedimentary rocks limestone, dolomitic limestone, and dolostone, although it can also be produced from other high–calcium materials such as marble, aragonite, chalk, shell, and coral.

PRIMARY USES: An essential industrial chemical, lime is used in the manufacture of steel, pulp and paper, glass and porcelain, and chemicals. It is a component of construction materials such as plaster, mortar, stucco, and whitewash. It is also used in conditioning acidic soils, softening water, and treating wastewater and smokestack emissions.

DESCRIPTION: Lime (also known as quicklime, caustic lime, or calcia) is a common term for the chemical compound calcium oxide (CaO). The name is often applied to several related compounds, including hydrated or slaked lime (calcium hydroxide, $Ca(OH)_2$); dolomitic quicklime ($CaO \cdot MgO$); type N ($Ca(OH)_2 \cdot MgO$) and type S ($Ca(OH)_2 \cdot Mg(OH)_2$) dolomitic hydrates; and refractory lime, also called dead-burned or hard-burned lime. When pure, lime occurs as colorless, cubic crystals or in a white microcrystalline form; often impurities such as iron and oxides of silicon, aluminum, and magnesium are present. Lime has a specific gravity of 3.34, a melting point of 2,570 degrees Celsius, and a boiling point of 2,850 degrees Celsius. A highly reactive compound, it combines with water to produce the more stable hydrated lime. This reaction, known as slaking, produces heat and causes the solid almost to double in volume. At temperatures around 1,650 degrees Celsius, lime recrystallizes into the coarser, denser, and less reactive refractory lime. When heated to approximately 2,500 degrees Celsius, lime is incandescent.

LIME IS A highly reactive manufactured compound that is an essential part of many industrial processes. An alkali, it dissolves in water to produce a caustic, basic solution. Lime is typically obtained from limestone, although other natural substances that are high in calcium are also used as raw materials for lime manufacture. In 1994 total world production of lime was an estimated 118,000,000 metric tons, 17,400,000 metric tons of which were sold or used by producers in the United States (including Puerto Rico). The United States is one of the leading lime-producing countries.

Historical Background. Use of lime in construction dates back at least to the ancient Egyptians, who between 4000 and 2000 B.C.E. employed it as a mortar and plaster. The Greeks, Romans, and Chinese used it in construction, agriculture, textile bleaching, and hide tanning. One of the oldest industries in the United States, lime manufacture began in colonial times. While the use of lime increased with the Industrial Revolution, it remained largely a construction material until the early twentieth century, when it became a crucial resource for the rapidly growing chemical industry.

Obtaining Lime. Lime may be prepared from a variety of naturally occurring materials with a high calcium content. While lime is commonly obtained from limestone, a sedimentary rock composed chiefly of calcite (calcium carbonate, $CaCO_3$), it can also be derived from dolostone, a similar sedimentary rock that is predominantly dolomite ($CaMg(CO_3)_2$), or from rock with an intermediate composition (dolomitic limestone). Lime is also produced from marble, aragonite, chalk, shell, and coral (all mostly calcium carbonate). Because the raw materials for lime manufacture are plentiful and widespread, lime is produced all over the world, with production facilities generally located near the sources for the raw materials.

When calcium carbonate is heated in a masonry furnace to about 1,100 degrees Celsius, it breaks down into lime and carbon dioxide. Heating dolomite in this fashion produces dolomitic quicklime and carbon dioxide. Approximately 100 metric tons of pure limestone yields 56 metric tons of lime. Adding water to stabilize lime or dolomitic quicklime yields the hydrated (slaked) form. Dolomite is typically used to make refractory (dead-burned) lime, which involves heating the materials to temperatures around 1,650 degrees Celsius.

Uses of Lime. A fundamental industrial chemical, lime is used in the manufacture of porcelain and glass, pigments, pulp and paper, varnish, and baking powder. It is employed in the preparation of calcium carbide, calcium cyanamide, calcium carbonate, and other chemicals; in the refining of salt and the purification of sugar; in treating industrial wastewater, sewage, and smokestack effluent; and in softening water. In metallurgy it is used in smelting and in concentrating ores. Lime and other calcium compounds are used in liming, a method for treating acidic soils. The application of lime to soil neutralizes acidity, improves soil texture and stability, and enriches the soil's nitrogen content by increasing the activity of soil microorganisms that secure nitrogen from the air. Lime's incandescing properties are employed in the Drummond Light, or limelight, in which a cylinder of lime is heated with the flame of an oxyhydrogen torch

to produce a brilliant white light. Mixed with sand and water, lime serves as a mortar or plaster. The lime hydrates in combination with water; the mortar hardens quickly as the hydrated lime reacts with carbon dioxide in the air to form calcium carbonate. Dolomitic quicklime is used to produce a hard, strong, and elastic stucco.

Uses of hydrated lime include soil liming, sugar refining, and chemical preparation. In leather tanning, hydrated lime is used to remove hair from hides. In construction, it is used to increase the durability of mortar, plaster, and stucco. Hydrated lime in a very dilute solution is whitewash. Filtering whitewash yields lime water, used in medicine as a burn treatment and as an antacid, and in chemistry as a reagent. Dolomi-

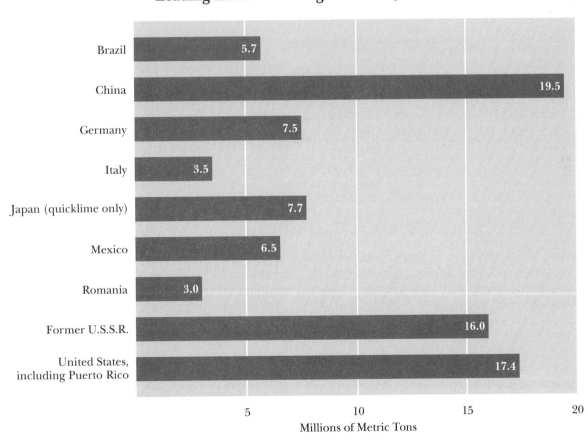

Leading Lime-Producing Countries, 1994

Country	Millions of Metric Tons
Brazil	5.7
China	19.5
Germany	7.5
Italy	3.5
Japan (quicklime only)	7.7
Mexico	6.5
Romania	3.0
Former U.S.S.R.	16.0
United States, including Puerto Rico	17.4

Source: U.S. Bureau of Mines, *Minerals Yearbook, 1994.* U.S. Government Printing Office, 1996.
Note: World total production for 1994 was approximately 118 million metric tons. Figures include quicklime, hydrated lime, and deadburned dolomite; U.S. figure represents lime sold or used by producers.

tic hydrates are used as a flux in the manufacture of glass.

Dead-burned lime is a refractory material, able to withstand contact with often corrosive substances at elevated temperatures. Refractory lime is a component in tar-bonded refractory brick, which is used in the construction of the basic oxygen furnaces employed in steelmaking.

FURTHER READING: A good, thorough source is Robert S. Boynton, *Chemistry and Technology of Lime and Limestone*, 2d ed. 1980, which includes chapters on the properties, manufacture, and uses of lime. Informative articles include M. Michael Miller, "Lime," in the U.S. Bureau of Mines' annual *Minerals Yearbook* (vol. 1, *Metals and Minerals*), 1994; Jean W. Pressler and Lawrence Pelham, "Lime, Calcium, and Calcium Compounds," in the bureau's *Mineral Facts and Problems*, 1985; and Harold A. Hubbard and George E. Ericksen, "Limestone and Dolomite," in Donald A. Brobst and Walden P. Pratt, eds., *United States Mineral Resources*, U.S. Geological Survey Professional Paper 820. An older but still relevant source is O. Bowles, *The Lime Industry*, U.S. Bureau of Mines Circular 7651, 1952.

Karen N. Kähler

SEE ALSO: Calcium compounds; Glass; Limestone; Metals and metallurgy; Oxides.

Limestone

WHERE FOUND: Limestone is a widespread marine sedimentary rock found wherever shallow seas once encroached onto continents. Limestone accounts for 10 to 15 percent of all sedimentary rocks. Some limestones are formed in lakes, around springs, at geysers, and in caves.

PRIMARY USES: Limestone is one of the most widely used rock materials. It is used as road metal, as aggregate for macadam and concrete, and as a building stone. Some limestones that take a good polish are marketed as marble. Limestone is used as a flux in open-hearth iron smelters. It is a basic raw material in the manufacture of portland cement. It is also used as an inert ingredient in pharmaceutical preparations. Limestone is the chief source of chemical and agricultural lime. It is also ground and pressed to make blackboard chalk. Limestone serves as a significant aquifer, and it constitutes about 50 percent of reservoir rocks for oil and gas. Prior to the introduction of electric lighting, carved chunks of limestone were fed into a gas flame to produce a fairly bright light used as stage lighting—hence the term "limelight."

DESCRIPTION: Limestone is a sedimentary rock composed largely of the mineral calcite (calcium carbonate). This relatively soft stone in its pure form is white, but it may be buff, pink, red, gray, or black, depending upon minor materials present. The texture ranges from fine- to coarse-grained and from highly porous to highly compact. Many limestones contain abundant fossils. Dolostone is a closely related rock composed primarily of dolomite (calcium-magnesium carbonate).

THE TERM "LIMESTONE" encompasses many rocks of diverse appearance that have calcite as their essential component. They differ considerably in texture, color, structure, and origin. Although limestones may form by inorganic precipitation of calcite in lakes, springs, or caves, the most widespread limestones are of marine origin. Most limestones are formed by organic processes and consist largely of the shells and shell fragments of marine invertebrates. Because calcite is susceptible to solution and recrystallization, diagenetic processes may completely alter the texture of the original rock.

Coquina is a limestone of comparatively recent formation consisting of loosely cemented shell fragments. Compact rocks with abundant shell material are known as fossiliferous limestone. They may be described more specifically by adding the dominant fossil genera to the rock name. Chalk is a fine-grained, porous, white rock made up of minute tests of foraminifera. Lithographic limestone is a compact, fine-grained rock that is used in the printing process from which it derives its name. Travertine is an inorganic deposit usually formed in caves as coarse, crystalline dripstone. Tufa is a porous, spongy material deposited around springs and geysers. Oolitic limestone is composed of small, spherical bodies of concentrically layered calcite formed in shallow water with moderate agitation. Coarse crystalline limestone forms by recrystallization of primary, fine-grained limestones.

Limestone and other soluble rocks in warm, humid regions are susceptible to solution by meteoric water at the surface and in the subsurface. The resulting landscapes, characterized by abundant sink holes and caverns, are known as karst topography. Because water moves rapidly into the subsurface in karst regions, rapid spreading of contamination in groundwater is of special concern.

René A. De Hon

SEE ALSO: Carbonate minerals; Cement and concrete; Groundwater; Marble; Oil and natural gas reservoirs; Quarrying; Stone and rock.

Lithium

WHERE FOUND: Lithium makes up about 0.006 percent of the earth's crust and is found as a trace element in most rocks. The most important lithium ore is spodumene, with extensive deposits in North Carolina, Quebec, Brazil, Argentina, Spain, and the Congo. Another important commercial source of lithium is lepidolite, found in Canada and Rhodesia.

PRIMARY USES: In combination with other metals, lithium is used as a heat exchanger in nuclear reactors as well as a radiation shield around reactors. Lithium is used as an anode in high-voltage batteries, and lithium compounds are used in the manufacture of rubber products, ceramic products, enamels, dyes, glass, and high-temperature lubricants.

DESCRIPTION: Lithium, symbol Li, is located in Group IA of the periodic table. It has an atomic number of 3 and an atomic weight of 6.941. It is a soft, silvery-white metal and is the lightest known metal. It has a melting point of 180.54 degrees Celsius, a boiling point of 1,347 degrees Celsius, a specific gravity of 0.534, and a specific heat of 0.79 calories per gram per degree Celsius.

LITHIUM WAS DISCOVERED by Swedish industrialist Johan Arfvedson in 1817, and the element was first isolated in 1818 by Sir Humphry Davy through electrolytic reduction of the lithium ion. Lithium quickly becomes covered with a gray oxidation layer when it is exposed to air, and because it combines so easily with other elements, lithium is always found chemically bonded in nature. Although a highly reactive element, lithium is less reactive than the other alkali metals. Like the other alkali metals, lithium easily gives up an electron to form monovalent positive ions.

Lithium chloride is obtained by treating either lithium hydroxide or lithium carbonate with hydrochloric acid. Chemists obtain pure metallic lithium by passing electricity through molten lithium chloride or through solutions of lithium chloride in ethanol or acetone in low-carbon steel cells having graphite anodes.

Lithium is used to make batteries used in electric meters, cameras, and other electronic equipment, and lithium compounds have numerous practical applications. Lithium carbonate and lithium borate are used in the ceramic industry as glaze constituents, while lithium perchlorate is a very powerful oxidizing agent used in solid fuel for rockets. Lithium hydride, a powerful reducing agent, is used in fuel cells, as a shielding material for thermal neutrons emitted from nuclear reactors, and to inflate lifeboats and air balloons. Lithium fluoride is used in infrared spectrometers and as a flux in ceramics, brazing, and welding. Lithium chloride, the most common lithium salt, is used to increase the conductivity of electrolytes in low-temperature dry-cell batteries, as a dehumidifying agent in air conditioners, and in metallurgical applications. Lithium is combined with aluminum and magnesium to produce structural alloys; lithium-magnesium alloys have the highest strength-to-weight ratio of all structural materials. In medicine, lithium amide is important in the synthesis of antihistamines, and lithium carbonate is used as a drug to treat a form of mental illness known as bipolar disorder (or manic-depressive psychosis).

Alvin K. Benson

SEE ALSO: Aluminum; Carbonate minerals; Ceramics; Fuel cells; Glass; Magnesium; Nuclear energy; Rubber.

Lithosphere

The lithosphere ("stone sphere," from the Greek lithos) *consists of the outer, brittle portions of the earth, including the upper mantle and crust. The usable mineral resources of the earth are all within the lithosphere, and knowledge of its properties is particularly important in the search for gas and oil.*

THE INTERIOR OF the earth has a number of layers, or concentric spheres. At the center of the earth is the inner core. Then, moving outward, come the outer core, the lower mantle, the upper mantle, and the earth's crust. Scientists subdivide the upper mantle into the asthenosphere, a partially molten zone, and, above that, the lithosphere. The lithosphere, then, is the rigid (or brittle) outer shell of the earth, which extends to a depth of between 70 and 100 kilometers and rests on the asthenoshere. It includes the earth's crust and part of the upper mantle.

The upper mantle is approximately 700 kilometers thick. The asthenosphere begins at a depth of approximately 70 to 100 kilometers and shows a rapid increase in density and a temperature in excess of 1,000 degrees Celsius. The asthenosphere is partially molten ultramafic material. Because of its partially molten properties, the asthenosphere probably exhibits plastic flow. Above the asthenoshere, the upper brittle portion of the upper mantle that is part of the lithosphere is a dense ultramafic material that directly underlies the earth's crust. The lithosphere comprises seven to ten major lithospheric "plates" that move slowly as they rest on the asthenosphere. Plate tectonics refers to the movement of these plates and the land and ocean forms that are created as a result.

Within the lithosphere, the boundary between the upper mantle and the crust is called the Mohorovičić discontinuity, or Moho, which marks a compositional change in the rock. The earth's crust contains two basic types of crustal material, oceanic and continental, with an average density of 2.9 and 2.6, respectively. Oceanic crust ranges from 5 to 10 kilometers thick and is thinnest over seafloor spreading areas. Oceanic crust is primarily composed of dense basaltic rock with a thin veneer of silt and carbonate precipitates; however, a variety of minerals have been observed at seafloor vents. Continental crust is primarily composed of felsic granitic rock, which is less dense than oceanic crust; however, continental crust also includes sedimentary and metamorphic rock and even uplifted oceanic basalt. A variety of minerals of varying economic importance occur in the continental crust. The conti-

The Mohorovičić Discontinuity (Moho) Between the Crust and Mantle

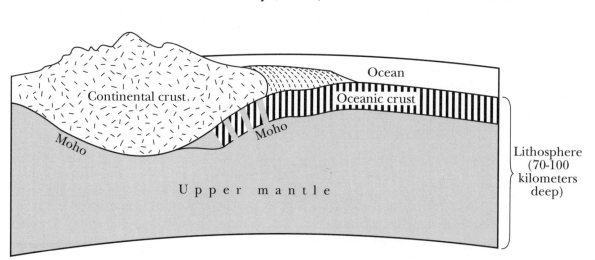

nental crust averages 30 to 40 kilometers in thickness, but it may be more than 70 kilometers thick in some mountain areas.

Oceanic crust is less dense than the parent mantle material. This is probably attributable to partial melting and crystal fractionation. Felsic minerals have a lower melting temperature than mafic minerals, and mafic minerals are the first to crystallize out of a melt. As oceanic crust subducts below continental crust, the subducting plate eventually melts, and its upwelling liquid fraction produces less mafic intermediates.

The lithosphere is highly variable, according to regional studies. In parts of the middle United States and in the Gulf of Mexico region, for example, the crust has thick sedimentary layers. Oil companies were able to measure the seismic wave patterns generated by many controlled explosions and discover petroleum and natural gas within these layers. The later discovery of oil in northern Alaska was prompted by the similarity of the crust there to the crust of these regions. As the study of the characteristics of the lithosphere—including plate tectonics—continues, scientists will increasingly be able to use their knowledge to discover sites of mineral resources.

Ray Roberts

SEE ALSO: Earth's crust; Igneous processes, rocks, and mineral deposits; Magma crystallization; Marine vents; Metamorphic processes, rocks, and mineral deposits; Plate tectonics; Plutonic rocks and mineral deposits; Seafloor spreading; Sedimentary processes, rocks, and mineral deposits; Volcanoes.

Livestock and animal husbandry

Livestock and animal husbandry refers to the management of domesticated animals such as beef or dairy cattle, sheep, goats, pigs, and chickens. Such animals constitute a renewable resource providing humans with food, fiber, fuel, power, implements, and other benefits.

EFFECTIVE ANIMAL HUSBANDRY requires an affinity for the animals being managed, skill in handling them, and knowledge of them and their environment. Respect for animals is important

to good management, as is skill in handling to minimize injuries and stress to both animal and handler. Knowledge is needed of their nutrition, reproduction, and behavior, as well as the physical, biological, cultural, and economic context in which they are managed. While some inputs are beyond the control of the producer (such as aberrant weather and governmental regulations), good management will ensure the most efficient productivity from the available inputs.

Intensive and Extensive Management. These are the two main options for animal husbandry. Intensive management refers to confinement-type operations that provide animals with shelter, food, and water. It has been called "landless" because it requires very little acreage. Examples include beef feed-lots, concentrate-based dairy farms, and confinement swine or poultry operations. In extensive systems, on the other hand, the animals are provided with an area in which they fend for themselves, finding their own food, water, and shelter. Examples are rangeland beef operations, pasture-based dairying, and free-range poultry farms. In practice, animal husbandry often includes both intensive and extensive management.

In the late twentieth century, the U.S. beef industry generally involved extensive operations for at least the first year of life and an intensive phase just prior to market; availability and prices of feed grains may determine the extent to which intensive management is practiced. Dairy operations around the world range from intensive to extensive—from no to exclusive pasture, respectively. Seasonal variation of pasture may dictate when it is available and used. Because dairy cows must be milked two or three times a day, dairy operations are never as extensive as some beef operations, where the producer may have contact with the animals no more than once a year.

Intensive animal management generally requires more management expertise, more capital investment, and more energy utilization. Since the animal is totally under control of the producer, all needs of the animal must be provided. The inevitably greater concentration of animals requires closer attention to their housing and health. The larger capital investment is

Animal husbandry often combines aspects of intensive (confinement-based) and extensive (open range or pasture-based) management. (Ben Klaffke)

attributable to facilities and equipment. More energy utilization is needed to maintain temperature and ventilation as well as to operate equipment. Intensive management also places greater emphasis on maximizing animal performance. Because more capital and energy are used, effort is made to extend animal performance by genetics, nutrition, and other management tools. It also requires more dependence on others for feed. While some intensive livestock producers raise their own feedstuff, many do not. They may depend on crop farmers within the region or half a world away. Contemporary swine operations in Japan and Korea require corn and soybeans from the U.S. Midwest.

Extensive animal management demands more land and more dependence on the animals' abilities. The larger land requirement is a primary feature of this system. The greater dependence on the animals' abilities follows from less direct provision by the producer for their needs. Survival and growth may depend on their locating food, water, and shelter as well as avoiding danger. Reproduction may be left to natural service, easy birthing, and good mothering. Extensive management involves more tolerance for decreased animal performance. When weather conditions do not provide sufficient food, the animals will have less than maximal growth and fertility. Neonatal losses attributed to weather, predators, or terrain are tolerated. Indeed, human intervention may not be a realistic option when animals are widely dispersed. An important parameter is the "stocking rate," the number of animals per land area. Too few animals will not fully use the vegetation, as many grasses are most nutritious at an early stage of development and become less nutritious and coarser if not eaten then. Too many animals will overgraze, impairing regrowth of the vegetation. Optimum "stocking rate" corresponds closely to the ecological concept "carrying capacity," the number of animals that an area can sustain over an extended period of time. Extensive systems can demand substantial management expertise. For instance, pasture-based dairying in New Zealand requires considerable knowledge to optimize pasture growth and utilization.

Biological and Nonbiological Parameters. Any animal management system must take into account numerous biological parameters pertinent to the animal being managed. These include nutritional requirements, biological time lag (time from conception to market), reproduction (gestation length and number of newborn, newborn survival), efficiency of feed conversion, nature of weight gain, genetic selection, and susceptibility to disease. Decisions are made about using natural service or artificial insemination. The extent to which agricultural by-products, crop residues, and/or production enhancers are used depends on their efficacy, availability, and price.

Any animal management system also involves a number of nonbiological parameters. The available climate, water supply, and land are physical attributes that bear upon the husbandry options. Two other facets of the land affecting management are its tenure, whether owned,

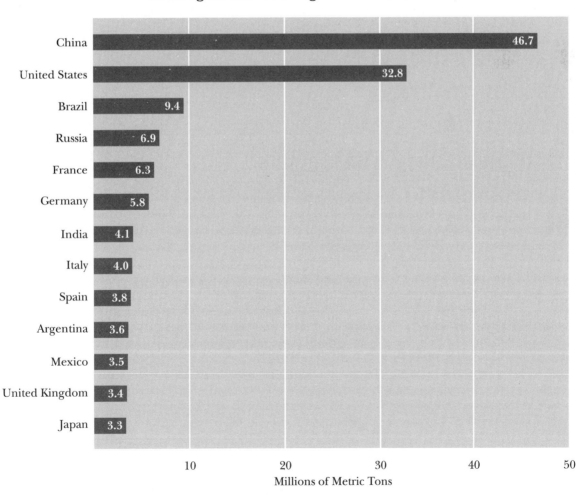

Leading Meat-Producing Countries, 1994

Country	Millions of Metric Tons
China	46.7
United States	32.8
Brazil	9.4
Russia	6.9
France	6.3
Germany	5.8
India	4.1
Italy	4.0
Spain	3.8
Argentina	3.6
Mexico	3.5
United Kingdom	3.4
Japan	3.3

Source: U.S. Department of Commerce, *Statistical Abstract of the United States, 1996*, 1996.
Note: Includes beef, veal, pork, mutton, lamb, horsemeat, and poultry. World total is approximately 195 million metric tons, including countries not shown on graph.

leased, or occupied, and its use, whether restricted or not. Husbandry is also affected by the availability and skill level of labor. Another factor is the infrastructure—the dependability of transportation providing access to markets, postfarm processing, and communication systems. Profitability, the difference between receipts and cost of inputs, as well as any subsidies, determines whether one can engage in any agricultural activity for long. Personal values, including lifestyle and risk management, also impact involvement in animal agriculture. Finally, historical and societal values, particularly those directly touching on the use of animals and natural resources, influence the extent and nature of animal husbandry.

Issues. Three issues of contemporary interest relative to livestock and animal husbandry concern the need for animal agriculture, its sustainability, and its increasing corporate nature. The willingness of people to purchase and consume products of animal origin will always determine the need for animal agriculture. If the price people must pay for such products is too high, demand will decline. At present, as the general affluence of a country increases, the demand for foods of animal origin increases.

The sustainability of contemporary agriculture has been called into question because of its heavy dependence on fossil fuels for energy and its adverse effects on the environment. Properly managed, animals have a role to play in sustainable agriculture. They can help dispose of some agribusiness by-products—crop residues and crops not suitable for human consumption—and generate waste that can be used to fertilize crops.

Animal agriculture is increasingly conducted by corporations rather than by family-owned farms or ranches. Once farming moves away from subsistence farming and generates excess over what the farm family needs, it becomes a business. The pressure for efficiency, as well as for higher and consistent product quality, is driving animal agriculture toward increasingly specialized and integrated enterprises. While this tendency appears to be inevitable, serious concerns arise concerning the oligopolies, if not monopolies, that may control the production of animal products and the management of domes-

tic animals, a valued renewable resource.

FURTHER READING: A good text dealing with contemporary management of livestock animals is R. E. Taylor and T. G. Field's *Scientific Farm Animal Production*, 6th ed. 1997. A comprehensive book on the practical aspects of livestock husbandry is M. E. Ensminger, *The Stockman's Handbook*, 7th ed. 1992. *Impacts of Livestock Production*, by Peter R. Cheeke, 1993, addresses the effects of animal husbandry on society, human health, and the environment. An assessment of the situation in the 1990's and of future prospects and research needs is *Global Agenda for Livestock Research*, edited by P. Gardiner and C. Devendra, 1995.

James L. Robinson

SEE ALSO: Animal breeding; Animal domestication; Animal power as an energy source; Farmland; Rangeland; Overgrazing.

Logging. *See* Clear-cutting; Timber industry; Wood and timber

Los Angeles Aqueduct

Construction of the Los Angeles Aqueduct generated considerable controversy; ultimately the aqueduct enabled Los Angeles to expand by taking water from sources in central California.

DATE: Original aqueduct completed in 1913; extension completed in 1941; second aqueduct completed in 1970

THE LOS ANGELES AQUEDUCT is a 338-mile-long system that transports water from the Owens Valley and Mono Basin east of the Sierra Nevada south to the Los Angeles metropolitan area. The original aqueduct was proposed in the early 1900's as a means of supplying the growing Los Angeles region with an enlarged and reliable water source for the twentieth century. Los Angeles' Department of Water and Power, under the leadership of William Mulholland and with the help of former Los Angeles mayor Fred Eaton, obtained the water rights to the Owens

Legal battles over the right of Los Angeles to pump water from the Owens Valley underscore the crucial importance of water and the complex issues surrounding water rights. (Ben Klaffke)

River by purchasing more than 240,000 acres of land in Inyo County. Much of the population of the prosperous Owens Valley bitterly opposed the aqueduct, but they could not stop the construction once the water rights had been bought by the Department of Water and Power.

The city sold bonds worth over $24 million to fund the construction of the aqueduct down the Owens Valley, across part of the Mojave Desert, and into the Los Angeles basin. Mulholland directed the construction of the mammoth project, which began in 1907 and took five years to complete. The entire 233 miles of the original aqueduct transports water by gravity flow and consists of over 170 miles of open ditch, 12 miles of steel siphons, and 142 tunnels that totaled 53 miles. In addition, the project required the construction of over 500 miles of trails and roads, 120 miles of railroad tracks, and 169 miles of transmission lines. The project was one of the greatest engineering accomplishments of the early twentieth century.

In 1930 Los Angeles approved another $38 million to extend the aqueduct northward into the Mono Basin in order to tap rivers and streams that feed into Mono Lake. The extension was completed in 1941, and waters were diverted into the aqueduct 338 miles north of the city. The diversion of water from Mono Lake eventually caused the lake level to drop 46 feet and the salinity of the lake to rise. Environmental groups went to court to halt the diversion of water, and lengthy litigation ensued. As Los Angeles continued to grow, the city saw the growing need for more water from the eastern Sierra Nevada, and in 1963 it appropriated more money to build another aqueduct from the Owens Valley. This second aqueduct was completed in 1970 and increased the total amount of water that could be transported by about 50 percent to a total average capacity of 666 cubic feet per second. Much of the water for the second aqueduct was to be groundwater pumped from the Owens Valley, but the Department of Water and Power has been restricted in their appropriations by litigation brought by local residents and environmental groups.

Jay R. Yett

SEE ALSO: Irrigation; Water rights; Water supply systems.

Magma crystallization

Magma crystallization is a geologic process in which molten magma in the earth's interior cools and subsequently crystallizes to form an igneous rock. The crystallization process produces many different types of minerals, some of which are valuable natural resources.

MAGMA IS MOLTEN rock material consisting of liquid, gas, and early-formed crystals. It is hot (900 to 1,200 degrees Celsius), mobile, and capable of penetrating into or through the earth's crust from the mantle, deep in the earth's interior. Most magma cools in the earth's crust; in a process similar to ice crystallizing from water as the temperature drops below the freezing point, minerals crystallize from molten magma to form a type of rock called igneous rock. Once completely crystallized, the body of igneous rock is called an intrusion. Some magma, however, works its way to the surface and is extruded as lava from volcanoes.

Mineral Growth. Magma that remains below the surface cools at a slow rate. Ions have time to collect and organize themselves into orderly, crystalline structures to form minerals. These minerals grow larger with time and, if the cooling rate is slow enough, may grow to several centimeters in diameter or larger. Igneous rocks with minerals of this size are said to have a phaneritic texture. Magma that reaches the surface, on the other hand, cools very rapidly and forms rocks that consist of extremely fine-grained minerals or quenched glass. These rocks have an aphanitic or glassy texture. Consequently, it is those minerals which grow beneath the surface that reach sizes large enough to be considered economically feasible resources.

Concentration of Valuable Elements. Minerals do not crystallize from a magma all at once. Instead, they follow a sequence of crystallization as the temperature decreases. In general, silicate minerals (substances with silicon-oxygen compounds) with high contents of calcium, iron, and magnesium crystallize early, followed by silicate minerals with high contents of aluminum, potassium, and sodium. Excess silica crystallizes last as the mineral quartz. Bonding factors such as ionic size and charge prevent some elements from being incorporated into early crystallizing minerals. Thus they are more highly concentrated in the residual magma and become incorporated into the last minerals to crystallize, forming rocks called granites and pegmatites. These rocks may contain minerals such as beryl, spodumene, lepidolite, and uraninite which include important elements such as beryllium, lithium, and uranium. Granites and pegmatites are also important sources for feldspar and sheet mica.

Diamonds and Kimberlites. Perhaps the best-known magmatic minerals are diamonds. Formed deep in the mantle at extremely high temperatures and pressures, diamonds are carried by a certain type of magma as it violently intrudes upward through the crust, sometimes reaching the surface. Upon cooling and crystallizing, this magma forms a pipe-shaped igneous rock known as kimberlite. It is in kimberlites that most diamonds are found. Most kimberlite pipes are less than one square kilometer in horizontal area, and they are often grouped in clusters. In the last half of the twentieth century, most of the known diamond-bearing kimberlite pipes have been found in southern Africa, western Australia, Siberia, and Canada.

Magmatic Sulfide Deposits. Most major metals used in industry (copper, iron, lead, nickel, zinc, and platinum) are found in sulfide minerals, which are substances that contain metal-sulfur compounds. When magma is in the early stages of cooling and crystallizing underground, certain processes can cause droplets of liquid sulfide to form within it. These sulfide droplets attract metallic cations and concentrate them by factors ranging from 100 to 100,000 over their normal levels in the host magma. The droplets eventually cool and solidify to form sulfide minerals such as pyrite ("fool's gold"), galena (lead sulfide), and sphalerite (zinc sulfide). Sulfide minerals such as these become important targets for mining because of their high concentration of metals.

Layered Magmatic Intrusions. Some magmas give rise to layered intrusions in which a specific sequence of minerals is repeated many times from bottom to top in a process called gravity layering (also called rhythmic layering). Dark-colored, heavier minerals such as pyroxene, olivine, and chromite concentrate near the base of each layer, grading to predominantly light-colored minerals such as plagioclase at the top. Each mineral sequence is a separate layer, averaging several meters thick and ranging from less than 2 centimeters to more than 30 meters. It has been suggested that the origin of gravity layering involves multiple injections of fresh magma into a crystallizing magma chamber, effectively replenishing the magma and allowing the same minerals to crystallize repeatedly.

The Bushveld intrusion in South Africa, is one of the largest layered intrusions, contains multiple gravity layers, and is more than 7,000 meters in total thickness. Layered intrusions contain the earth's main reserves for chromium and platinum. In the Bushveld intrusion, chromium occurs in the mineral chromite, and platinum in platinum-iron alloys, braggite, and other platinum-metal compounds. The main source for platinum minerals in the Bushveld intrusion, and the source for approximately half the earth's supply of platinum, is the "Merensky Reef"—a layer of chromite and platinum minerals 1 meter thick and more than 200 kilometers long. Also present in the Bushveld intrusion is the mineral magnetite, which yields important elements used in steel manufacturing such as iron and vanadium. The Bushveld intrusion accounted for approximately 50 percent of the world's production of vanadium in 1996.

FURTHER READING: A general overview of magmatic mineral deposits is given by Anthony Evans in *Ore Geology and Industrial Minerals: An Introduction*, 1993. For a more detailed look at metallic sulfide mineralization and layered magmatic intrusions, see *Magmatic Sulfide Deposits*, by Anthony Naldrett, 1989. A detailed description of the physical properties and occurrence of magmatic minerals can be found in *Simon and Schuster's Guide to Rocks and Minerals*, edited by Martin Prinz, George Harlow, and Joseph Peters, 1979. A description of the origin of diamonds is presented in S. H. Richardson et al., "Origin of Diamonds in Old Enriched Mantle," *Nature* 310 (July 19, 1984). A comprehensive review of granites and pegmatites is given in the Richard Henry Jahns memorial issue of *American Mineralogist* 71, no. 3-4 (April, 1986).

Stephen C. Hildreth, Jr.

SEE ALSO: Earth's crust; Igneous processes, rocks, and mineral deposits; Ophiolites; Pegmatites; Plutonic rocks and mineral deposits; Volcanoes.

Magnesium

WHERE FOUND: Magnesium is a widespread and abundant element. Magnesium chloride and magnesium sulfate are present in dissolved form in seawater and underground brines. Magnesium is found in many minerals, notably magnesite ($MgCO_3$), dolomite ($CaMg(CO_3)_2$), and brucite ($Mg(OH)_2$). Main producers are China, Greece, Austria, Canada, and Mexico.

PRIMARY USES: Magnesium is used principally in alloys, refractory materials, paper, fertilizer, chemicals, and pyrotechnics.

DESCRIPTION: Magnesium (abbreviated Mg), atomic number 12, belongs to Group IIA of the periodic table of the elements (alkaline-earth metals). It has three stable isotopes and an average molecular weight of 24.312. Pure magnesium is a silver-white, ductile metal that is malleable when heated. A chemically active element, magnesium is a potent reducing agent. Its specific gravity is 1.738 at 20 degrees Celsius, its melting point is 651 degrees Celsius, and its boiling point is 1,100 degrees Celsius. Magnesium in the form of powder or ribbons readily ignites when heated, burning with an intense white light and releasing large amounts of heat while forming magnesia (magnesium oxide, MgO). Magnesium reacts with organic halides to produce Grignard reagents, an important class of chemical compounds used in the laboratory.

MAGNESIUM IS AN alkaline-earth metal, a class of hard, heavy metals that are strongly electropositive and chemically reactive. It is the eighth most abundant element; its concentration in the lithosphere is 20,900 grams per metric ton, and the percentage of its ions in seawater is 0.1272.

Magnesium's density (only two-thirds that of aluminum) and the ease with which the element can be machined, cast, forged, and welded contribute to its commercial applications, as do the refractory properties of some of its compounds. In 1994 the United States produced 128,000 metric tons of primary (mined and processed) magnesium, and total world production was 267,000 metric tons. Secondary (recycled) magnesium production figures were 62,100 metric tons for the United States and 88,200 for the world.

Historical Background. Sir Humphry Davy discovered magnesia in 1808. In 1828 A. Bussy isolated pure magnesium by chemical reduction of the chloride, and in 1833 Michael Faraday isolated magnesium electrolytically. The earliest commercial production of the metal may have been in France during the first half of the nineteenth century, where a modification of the Bussy method was employed. At this time, magnesium metal was used primarily in photogra-

phy. Around 1886 Germany developed an improved production process based on an electrolytic cell method devised by Robert Bunsen in 1852. Germany became the world's sole source for elemental magnesium. Magnesium alloys were used in Germany in the early 1900's in aircraft fuselages, engine parts, and wheels. In 1915, when a wartime blockade of Germany by the British interrupted the elemental magnesium trade, magnesium production began in the United States. Large-scale use of dolostone as a refractory material also commenced during World War I. In 1941 Dow Chemical Corporation introduced its process for extracting magnesium from seawater.

Distribution of Magnesium. Magnesium is one of the most common minerals in the earth's crust; its principal commercial source, however, is seawater. Extensive terrestrial deposits of magnesium are also found in the form of magnesite and dolomite. Magnesite, a magnesium carbon-

A magnesite (native magnesium carbonate) mine in Kern County, California. Once used for refractory bricks, magnesite is now important as a source of magnesium oxide. (U.S. Geological Survey)

Leading Magnesium-Producing Countries, 1994

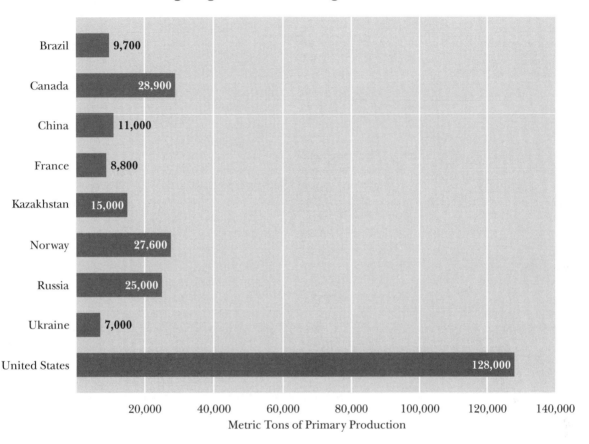

Metric Tons of Primary Production

Source: U.S. Bureau of Mines, *Minerals Yearbook, 1994.* U.S. Government Printing Office, 1996.
Note: World 1994 primary (not from scrap) magnesium production was about 267,000 metric tons.

ate, occurs as a hydrothermal alteration of serpentine ($(Mg,Fe)_3Si_2O_5(OH)_4$), a vein filling and a replacement mineral in carbonate rocks such as dolostone. Dolomite, or calcium magnesium carbonate, is the predominant mineral in dolostone, a widespread sedimentary rock similar to limestone. Most dolomites are thought to have originated from partial replacement of calcium in limestone by magnesium. Major magnesium producers are China, Greece, Austria, Canada, and Mexico.

Environmental Forms of Magnesium. Magnesium occurs in nature as a component of several common minerals. Important ores include magnesite, a white or grayish mineral found in crystalline or porcelainlike masses; dolomite, a white mineral that resembles limestone; and brucite, a pearly foliated or fibrous mineral that resembles talc. Magnesium silicates are found in asbestos, serpentine, and talc. Magnesium chloride and magnesium sulfate occur in dissolved form in sea water and natural underground brines. Magnesium is also a constituent of chlorophyll in green plants.

Obtaining Magnesium. Magnesium is obtained principally from seawater through the Dow seawater process. The water is treated with lime to produce magnesium hydroxide as a precipitate. This precipitate is mixed with hydrochloric acid to form magnesium chloride; the chloride, in turn, is fused and electrolyzed, producing magnesium metal and chlorine gas. From a liter

466 / Magnesium Natural Resources

of seawater, approximately 10 milligrams of magnesium can be extracted. Another common method for obtaining magnesium is the ferrosilicon (Pidgeon) process, which uses dolomite as a raw material. The dolomite is heated to produce magnesia, which is then reduced with an iron-silicon alloy.

Uses of Magnesium. Dead-burned magnesite, produced by heating the mineral in a kiln at 1,500 to 1,750 degrees Celsius until it contains less than 1 percent carbon dioxide, is a refractory material. Able to withstand contact with often corrosive substances at high temperatures, refractory materials are used to line furnaces, kilns, reaction vessels, and ladles used in the cement, glass, steel, and metallurgical industries. Magnesia refractories are materials particularly suited for the basic oxygen furnaces used in steelmaking. Dead-burned dolomite, produced by heating dolostone or dolomitic limestone at about 1,500 degrees Celsius, is also a refractory material used for lining metallurgical furnaces.

In its elemental state, magnesium is soft and weak; its alloys, however, are sturdier and have a variety of uses. Magnesium is used extensively as an alloy metal, particularly in combination with aluminum, zinc, cadmium, and manganese. Magnesium alloys in general are lightweight, fatigue-resistant, free from brittleness, and able to withstand bending stresses; these qualities make magnesium alloys ideal for jet-engine parts, rockets and missiles, luggage frames, cameras, optical instruments, scientific equipment, and portable power tools. Duralumin, a lightweight alloy of aluminum, copper, magnesium, and manganese, is ductile and malleable before its final heat treatment; afterward, its hardness and tensile strength are increased. Its properties make duralumin especially useful to the aircraft industry. Magnalium, an alloy of aluminum and magnesium that is lighter and easier to work than aluminum, is used in metal mirrors and scientific instruments.

Pure magnesium is used in incendiary bombs, signals and flares, thermite fuses, and other pyrotechnic devices. It is an important component of photographic flashbulbs, a deoxidizing agent used in the preparation of some nonferrous metals, a rocket and missile fuel additive, and an agent for chemical synthesis. Magnesium reacts with organic halides to form Grignard reagents, an important class of extremely reactive chemical compounds that are used in synthesizing hydrocarbons, alcohols, carboxylic acids, and other compounds. Magnesium compounds are used in chemicals, ceramics, cosmetics, fertilizer, insulation, paper, leather tanning, and textile processing. Epsom salts (magnesium sulfate heptahydrate), milk of magnesia (magnesium hydroxide), and citrate of magnesium are used in medicines. Caustic-calcined magnesia (magnesite heated to between 700 and 1,000 degrees Celsius to drive off 2 to 10 percent of its carbon dioxide) is mixed with magnesium chloride to create oxychloride (sorel) cement. This cement is used for heavy-duty floorings, stucco, and fireproof building materials. Dolostone, a rock composed chiefly of dolomite, is used as a building stone as well as a refractory material.

Nutritional Aspects of Magnesium. Magnesium is an essential element in all plants and animals. In green plants, it is a component of chlorophyll; in animals, it plays a role in carbohydrate metabolism and is an important trace element for muscle, nerve tissue, and skeletal structure. Serious dietary deficiencies of magnesium can bring on such symptoms as hyperirritability and soft-tissue calcification.

FURTHER READING: For additional information see Deborah A. Kramer's "Magnesium" and "Magnesium Compounds," in the U.S. Bureau of Mines' annual *Minerals Yearbook* (vol. 1, *Metals and Minerals*), 1994, as well as her "Magnesium," in the bureau's *Mineral Facts and Problems*, 1985. Other good overviews are Harold A. Hubbard and George E. Ericksen, "Limestone and Dolomite," and A. J. Bodenlos and T. P. Thayer, "Magnesian Refractories," in Donald A. Brobst and Walden P. Pratt, eds., *United States Mineral Resources*, U.S. Geological Survey Professional Paper 820, 1973. D. A. C. Manning, *Introduction to Industrial Minerals*, 1995, includes a helpful chapter explaining refractory materials. See also Mead L. Jensen and Alan M. Bateman, *Economic Mineral Deposits*, 3d ed. 1979.

Karen N. Kähler

SEE ALSO: Alloys; Limestone; Metals and metallurgy; Steel.

Magnetic materials

Naturally occurring magnetic materials have been known and used for centuries. Today materials that can be temporarily magnetized by an electrical current are widely used in applications ranging from simple electrical appliances and motors to sophisticated computer systems.

SUBSTANCES THAT RESPOND to a magnetic field are called magnetic materials. The most common magnetic materials are iron (Fe), cobalt (Co), nickel (Ni), and their alloys. These three elements belong to Group VIIIB of the periodic table. Four varieties of magnetism are recognized: ferromagnetism, ferrimagnetism, diamagnetism, and paramagnetism. Iron, cobalt, nickel, gadolinium (Gd), and chromium dioxide (CrO_2) are examples of ferromagnetic materials. Ferroferric oxide (Fe_3O_4) is a ferrimagnetic material. Very weak or feeble magnetism is exhibited in certain alloys and elements. A substance that is magnetized in the opposite direction of the external magnetic field is called a diamagnetic material. Some examples are gold, silver, copper, and quartz. A substance that is magnetized in the same direction as the external magnetic field is called a paramagnetic material. Certain types of special alloys are paramagnetic.

Magnets attract materials or objects made of iron (and steel), cobalt, and nickel. A magnet's power is strongest at its two ends, called poles. One is called the north pole and the other the south pole. A compass is, in principle, a magnet pivoted at its center which orients itself in the direction of the earth's magnetic field. A compass has long been one of the most important navigational instruments on board ships and airplanes.

The largest deposits of the mineral magnetite (Fe_3O_4), magnetic iron ore, are found in northern Sweden. Sizable deposits of magnetite are also found in Australia, Italy, Switzerland, Norway, the Ural Mountains, and several other regions. In the United States, magnetite is found in Arkansas, New Jersey, and Utah. The Precambrian rocks of the Adirondacks contain large beds of magnetite.

The ancient Chinese discovered that a freely suspended lodestone (naturally occurring polarized magnetite) would always orient itself in the same geographical direction. This observation led to the development of the compass. In the West, historical records of magnetic materials date back to the ancient Greeks. By 500 B.C.E. the Greeks had discovered that certain rocks were attracted to iron nails on ships and boats. In 1600 C.E. an English doctor, William Gilbert, published *De Magnete*, in which he identified the earth itself as a giant magnet.

A number of fundamental advances in the practical applications of magnetism occurred in the early nineteenth century. In 1820 the Danish scientist Hans Christian Oersted discovered that a magnetic needle could be deflected by a current in a wire. In 1823 English scientist William Sturgeon wound an insulated copper wire around an iron bar and discovered that the iron bar became a strong magnet. Thus the electromagnet was born. In 1821 Michael Faraday demonstrated the first electric motor, the "magnetic rotation of a conductor and magnet." In 1828 Joseph Henry produced silk-covered wires and developed more powerful electromagnets.

Magnetic materials have a tremendous range of uses, from huge industrial electromagnets to the use of "magnetic bubbles" in highly advanced computer systems. Magnetic materials are classified into three major categories: hard, soft, and memory-quality materials. Hard magnetic materials have applications as permanent magnets in small motors, small direct-current generators (dynamos), measuring instruments, and speaker systems. Soft magnetic materials—those that are influenced by external fields—are widely used in transformers, generators, motors, and alternators of all sizes and rating capacities. Almost all appliances used in homes and industry, from shavers to washing machines to relays, contain electromagnets with soft magnetic materials. The materials used most often are iron, silicon-iron combinations, nickel-iron alloys, and ferrites. Memory-quality magnetic materials are used to record and store data, either in analog or digital form. Examples are magnetic tapes, drums, and disks.

Huge electromagnets are used to move automobiles or other metal objects in automobile recycling yards and junkyards. Gigantic electromagnets are essential to nuclear fusion experiments. Magnetic-levitation (maglev) trains are held above the ground by superconducting electromagnets. Superconducting electromagnets are also used in magnetic resonance imaging (MRI) body scanners, devices that produce detailed images of the inside of the body and provide diagnostic data to doctors.

Mysore Narayanan

SEE ALSO: Cobalt; Iron; Nickel; Steel.

Manganese

WHERE FOUND: Although manganese oxides are abundant in nature, large high-grade deposits are relatively rare. Concentrations of the element approximately 250 to 500 times greater than the average crustal abundance are required to produce ore. The major deposits of the world are sedimentary in origin and are located in Russia, Africa, and Brazil.

PRIMARY USES: More than 90 percent of the manganese that is consumed each year is used in the manufacture of steel. Manganese is also used as a component in certain aluminum alloys and in dry cell batteries. Minor amounts are used as a colorant in glass, in fertilizers, and as a gasoline additive.

DESCRIPTION: Manganese (atomic number 25, chemical symbol Mn) is the twelfth most abundant element in the crust of the earth and makes up about 0.1 percent of the crust by weight. In its pure state, which does not occur in nature, it is a hard, brittle metal with a gray color, a melting point of 1,260 degrees Celsius, a boiling point of 1,900 degrees Celsius, and a density of 7.2 grams per cubic centimeter. It resembles iron in many of its properties and has oxidation states of +2, +3, +4, +6, and +7. As is true of iron, the reduced +2 form is quite soluble under near-surface conditions and is carried in solution by stream and groundwater.

MANGANESE IS ONE of the most abundant elements in the crust of the earth and is usually a minor constituent in ordinary rocks. Its chemical and physical properties are quite similar to those of iron, and the two metals often occur together. Although manganese occurs in several oxidation states, the reduced +2 is most common in subsurface waters because of its solubility. Manganese oxide minerals precipitate readily at a boundary between oxidizing and reducing conditions, such as the reducing groundwater percolating into well-oxygenated stream water. As a result, manganese oxide coatings on stream pebbles and rocks are very common. Similar black coatings are also common in arid regions in the form of "desert varnish" and in deep freshwater lakes. In the ocean, large manganese oxide nodules occur. Changes from reducing to oxidizing conditions have been implicated as being important in producing all of these common surface forms of manganese oxide, but it is also likely that manganese oxidizing bacteria play an important role, particularly for desert varnish and stream pebble coatings.

Although manganese is the second most abundant heavy metal in the earth's crust after iron, large ore grade concentrations are unusual. All the major ore deposits are sedimentary in origin and consist of various manganese oxide minerals. More than 20 million metric tons of manganese are produced worldwide each year. Most is used during the manufacture of steel to remove sulfur and oxygen. There are no practical replacements for manganese in this essential role.

Historical Background. Manganese oxide has been known since antiquity, when it was used in glass manufacture, but the metal itself was not isolated until 1770. There was little interest in the metal until 1856, when it was discovered that manganese could be used to remove sulfur and oxygen impurities as a slag from molten steel. All steel up to this time had been very brittle because of the presence of these impurities. An important world market for manganese quickly developed. The world's major deposit of manganese was discovered in the Nikopol Basin in Ukraine in the 1920's. This area has been the world's major producer for most of the time since then. In the nineteenth century, the United States was self-sufficient in manganese, but these deposits are now all exhausted.

World Production and U.S. Imports of Manganese
In Metric Tons

	1990	1991	1992	1993	1994
United States					
Manganese ore:					
Imports for consumption	307,000	234,000	247,000	232,000	331,000
Consumption	497,000	473,000	438,000	389,000	449,000
Ferromanganese:					
Imports for consumption	380,000	320,000	304,000	347,000	336,000
Consumption	413,000	346,000	339,000	341,000	347,000
World					
Production of manganese ore	26,100,000	22,900,000	22,400,000	21,200,000	20,900,000

Source: U.S. Bureau of Mines, *Minerals Yearbook, 1994.* U.S. Government Printing Office, 1996.

Distribution and Sources of Manganese. Because of its great crustal abundance, small amounts of manganese, in the form of dark-colored oxide minerals, are common in most rocks. Manganese in the form of black coatings on stream sediment is so common that it usually goes unnoticed. For commercial production, however, ore bodies averaging at least 35 percent manganese and containing millions of tons of the metal are required. The highest-grade ore contains over 48 percent manganese. Such deposits are not common. All the known major deposits are of sedimentary origin. There are several ore minerals of manganese, but the most important are all oxides: pyrolusite (MnO_2), psilomelane (Mn_2O_3 $2H_2O$), and manganite (Mn_2O_3 H_2O).

In 1994 the five leading manganese-producing countries were China, Ukraine, South Africa, Brazil, and Australia. Together these countries accounted for more than three-quarters of the world's total production. Production in 1994 represented a decline of approximately 20 percent since 1990; however, in the mid-1990's the International Iron and Steel Institute projected a small rate of increase for the near future.

Manganese Deposits. Two types of sedimentary deposits account for most of the world's production. The first type, illustrated by the world's largest deposit at Nikopol in southern Ukraine, consists of manganese in the form of earthy masses and nodules of manganese oxide in beds of sandy clay and limestone. This type of deposit is thought to have originated by a two-step process. First, manganese in its reduced form, derived from the weathering and erosion of continental areas, is carried by streams in solution to the open sea. Second, in the sea, reduced manganese undergoes oxidation, causing it to precipitate as manganese oxide minerals due to the strongly oxidizing conditions in the open ocean. The second important type of deposit has resulted from the weathering of rocks containing small amounts of manganese silicate and carbonate minerals. These minerals are resistant to weathering, so their relative abundance increases as the less resistant minerals are dissolved. Eventually, a large, high-grade deposit of manganese may be produced. Geologists use the term "residual" to refer to any type of mineral deposit in which the valuable material has been concentrated by weathering. Important manganese deposits of this type occur in Brazil and China.

Deep Sea Manganese Oxide Nodules. The Challenger expedition in the 1870's discovered manganese oxide nodules in the deep ocean basin, but their widespread occurrence and abundance did not become known until sampling in the 1960's. These nodules are black and rounded to irregular lumps of pebble and cobble size. They exist in all the world's oceans but are very irregularly distributed. The origin of the nodules has been the subject of much research. Evidence indicates that the nodules are continually growing at a very slow rate by the addition of manganese and other metals from seawater. The absence of sediment to muddy the water increases their rate of precipitation, a fact which explains why most nodules are found only in the deep ocean basins, far removed from sediment being eroded from land masses.

Mining companies became very interested in deep sea manganese nodules in the 1960's and 1970's. The richest area seems to be a portion of the deep Pacific floor extending 3,000 miles eastward from the southern tip of Hawaii. There are places in this region in which the nodules literally cover the seafloor. Interest in the nodules is high because, in addition to averaging 25 percent manganese, they also average about 1.3 percent nickel, 1.0 percent copper, 0.22 percent cobalt, and 0.05 percent molybdenum, all of which could be recovered as by-products. Between 1962 and 1978 several international consortia spent nearly $100 million studying methods for mining the nodules. At least two promising methods were identified, but no commercial mining of the deep seafloor has yet occurred. The present status of these manganese oxide nodules is that they are considered a potential resource for the future.

Manganese and Human Health. Manganese is considered to be one of the least toxic of the trace elements. Several thousand parts per million of manganese in the diet of mammals and birds are usually required to develop symptoms of toxicity. The exact amount that is toxic varies from species to species and is also dependent on the form in which manganese is consumed and the age of the individual. The main symptom reported is a reduced rate of growth due to appetite depression.

While very high levels of manganese are required to produce toxic effects from oral consumption, mammals, including humans, appear to have a considerable lower tolerance to the inhalation of manganese dusts. High levels of such dusts can occur in occupational settings such as steel mills, manganese mines, and certain chemical industries. The lungs apparently act as a sink from which manganese is continually absorbed. The main toxic effect produced is

a serious neurological disease with many symptoms in common with Parkinson's disease. Such manganese-induced neurotoxicity has been the subject of considerable interest because manganese compounds are being used in gasoline as a replacement for lead compounds.

FURTHER READING: A very thorough discussion of all important types of manganese deposits is contained in *Handbook of Strata-Bound and Stratiform Ore Deposits*, vol. 2, edited by K. H. Wolf, 1976. A detailed treatment of the geochemical and geological aspects of manganese is *Geology and Geochemistry of Manganese*, edited by I. M. Varentsov and G. Y. Grasselly, 1976. Deep sea manganese oxide nodules are covered in detail in *Marine Manganese Deposits*, edited by G. P. Glasby, 1977; the health effects of manganese in the environment are discussed in *Trace Elements in the Terrestrial Environment*, by D. C. Adriano, 1986.

Gene D. Robinson

SEE ALSO: Bessemer process; Clean Air Act; Food chain; Iron; Marine mining; Sedimentary processes, rocks, and mineral deposits; Steel.

Manhattan Project

DATE: Manhattan Engineer District created in August, 1942

The Manhattan Engineer District was created to sponsor the Manhattan Project, a top-secret effort to produce the atomic bomb in time to be used during World War II. Its legacy, in addition to the destruction wrought by the two atomic bombs the United States dropped on Japan, includes the proliferation of nuclear weapons and the peacetime development of nuclear power plants.

DURING WORLD WAR II, the United States, Germany, Great Britain, the Soviet Union, France, and Japan all had projects to examine the feasibility of constructing an atomic bomb. Japanese progress was minimal, and French progress halted with the German occupation of France. American efforts were spurred on by the British and by scientists such as Leo Szilard, Eugene Paul Wigner, and Enrico Fermi who fled oppression in Europe. Since the Germans had a considerable head start as well as formidable industrial and scientific resources, there was a driving fear that Adolph Hitler would develop the atomic bomb first.

Enough work had been done prior to the Manhattan Project to convince those involved that the problems of producing a bomb could probably be surmounted if sufficient resources were made available. Because of the war mobilization, the Army Corps of Engineers was managing construction contracts amounting to 600 million dollars a month, and funds for the top-secret Manhattan Project were hidden within that amount. The initial cost estimate for the project was 133 million dollars; the actual cost was about 2 billion dollars.

Before the Manhattan Project, American atomic bomb research was conducted by various scientists at several universities. Progress was intermittent. On September 17, 1942, Colonel (soon to be General) Leslie Richard Groves was ap-

pointed to head the Manhattan Engineer District. Groves was an engineer, and his supervision of the building of the Pentagon had demonstrated a knack for untangling bureaucratic messes. He was regarded as arrogant and abrupt but also as a person who could get the job done right.

Under Groves, the Manhattan Project proceeded at breakneck speed. Factories were built before the machines they would house were fully worked out, and full-scale machines were built before prototypes were fully tested. While this approach did not always work, it worked well enough. At Hanford, Washington, fifty thousand construction workers built three large nuclear reactors to produce plutonium along with three separation plants to remove the plutonium from the used reactor fuel. A huge gaseous diffusion plant and an electromagnet separation plant were built at Oak Ridge, Tennessee, to separate uranium-235 from the more common uranium-238. Because of a copper shortage, more than 12,000 metric tons of silver were borrowed from the federal treasury and made into conductors for the electromagnets. The design and construction of the bombs were done at the Los Alamos weapons laboratory, headed by J. Robert Oppenheimer.

At the project's peak, over 160,000 workers were employed at twenty-five sites. Most of the Manhattan Project workers knew only that they were working on something very important and that it might help end the war. Many of those who knew that they were working on the atomic bomb hoped that it would help end the war and that it might make future wars unthinkable.

Charles W. Rogers

SEE ALSO: Isotopes, radioactive; Nuclear energy; Nuclear waste and its disposal; Plutonium; Uranium.

J. Robert Oppenheimer (left) and Leslie Richard Groves at the Los Alamos, New Mexico, nuclear test site. (Archive Photos/Popperfoto)

Manufacturing, energy use in

Industrial processes consume roughly 40 percent of world energy each year. In the United States, about 80 percent of that energy goes to the basic production industries of iron, steel, aluminum, paper, chemicals, and concrete.

THE SOPHISTICATION OF a society's technology can be judged by what it can make and how efficiently it can make those items. In ancient civilizations, rock and wood yielded to metal, fired pottery, and glass. Bronze and brass weapons swept aside stone. Then iron and steel swept the softer metals aside.

Muscle power was sporadically aided by water power in antiquity, but the intensive use of water power began in Europe in the Middle Ages. Besides grinding flour, water mills supplied power for large-scale weaving, for saw mills, and for blowing air onto hot metal and hammering the finished metals. The gearing required to modify the motion and move it throughout a workshop also applied to wind power, and Dutch mills led manufacturing in the late Middle Ages.

Then a series of inventions led to James Watt's improved steam engine in 1782. The immediate goal was pumping water out of coal mines, but steam engines also allowed factory power to be located anywhere, and steam-powered locomotives allowed materials to be more easily moved to those locations.

Small electric motors at the beginning of the twentieth century allowed a further decentralization of industry: A small shop required only a power cable, the necessary equipment, and a flick of a switch rather than a large engine and the inconvenient (often dangerous) belts used to transfer power to various pieces of equipment.

Energy efficiency and materials efficiency grow as technology evolves. Often, increased efficiency is simply a by-product of increased production or quality. Each doubling of cumulative production tends to drop production costs, including energy costs, by 20 percent. These improvements are connected to control of heat, control of motion, and the development of entirely new processes.

Heat. Heat is the greatest component of manufacturing energy use. Heat (or the removal of heat) involves the same issues that space conditioning of a home does. One can add more fuel or reduce losses through increased efficiency. Efficiency can be increased by having more insulation in the walls, a furnace that burns more completely, a furnace that uses exhaust gases to preheat air coming into it, a stove with a lighter rather than a pilot light, and controls that shut off heat to unused areas.

Manufacturing has the additional option of selling excess heat or buying low-grade heat for cogeneration. Often a manufacturing plant only needs low-grade heat of several hundred degrees for drying or curing materials. This heat production does not fully use the energy of the fuel. An electrical power plant, running at 1,100 degrees Fahrenheit (600 degrees Celsius) can generate electricity and then send its "waste heat" on to the industrial process.

A manufacturing plant is also applying energy to materials, and in these processes there are many choices. Heat may be applied in an oven (large or small); some energy may also be applied directly. For instance, oven curing of paint on car parts has been replaced by infrared ("heat lamp") radiation for quicker production. Some high-performance aerospace alloys are heated by microwave radiation in vacuum chambers.

There are a variety of other energy-saving approaches. Automated process controls are a major energy saver. In chemical industries, separating materials by their different boiling points with distillation columns requires much less steam than other methods. Also, the continuous safety flames at refineries are being replaced by automated lighters.

Another energy-efficient technique is to combine processes. For instance, steelmaking often comprises three separate heating steps: refining ore into blocks of pig iron, refining that into steel, and then forming the steel into products, such as I-beams or wire. An integrated steel mill heats the materials only once to make the finished product. A steel "minimill" tends to be smaller, uses expensive electricity, and goes only a short distance in the production process—from iron scrap to steel. On the other hand, the minimill is recycling a resource, thereby saving both energy and materials. The recycling of paper, plastics, and some metals typically requires half the energy of producing virgin materials. The fraction for aluminum is about a fourth.

Motion. Cutting, grinding, pumping, moving, polishing, compressing, and many other processes control the motion of materials and of heat. They use less energy than heating, but they

The "trim line" at a Nissan automobile plant. The generation of heat and the operation of electric motors in manufacturing consume tremendous amounts of energy. (Photo Network)

often represent the high-grade energy in electricity.

Eighty percent of the electricity used by industry is used for motors. Motors can be made efficient in many ways, including controllers that match power use to the actual load, metal cores that drop and take electric charges more easily, and windings with more turns of wire. Easing the tasks of industrial motors requires many disciplines. For example, fixing nitrogen into ammonia (NH_3) is typically done with streams of nitrogen and hydrogen passing over a catalyst. An improved catalyst pattern increases the reaction rate and thus decreases the hydrogen and nitrogen pumping. Automated controls again can control pumping, using it only where and when it is needed.

Entirely New Processes. The implementation of entirely new processes can reduce energy use. For example, a lower-pressure process for making polyethylene plastic uses a quarter of the energy used in the previous process. Plastics have replaced energy-intensive metals in many commercial products. Silica in fiber-optic cables is replacing copper for communications. Composites, made with plastics and glass, metal, or other plastic fibers, not only require less energy to fabricate than all-metal materials but also have greater capabilities. Composites in railroad cars and airplanes reduce weight and thus energy costs of operation.

Vacuum deposition of metals, ceramics, and even diamond holds the promise of cheaply attained materials that could multiply savings throughout industry. Diamond-edged machine tools could operate significantly faster or longer before replacement. Rubidium-coated heat exchangers could withstand sulfuric acid formed when the exhaust from the burning of high-sulfur coal drops below the boiling point, which would allow both harnessing that lower heat and recovering the sulfur.

Other new processes have been contingent on developments in entirely new, even radical, fields. In *Engines of Creation* (1986), K. Eric Drexler discussed the concept of "nanotechnology," proposing microscopic robots small enough to build or repair objects one molecule at a time. The "nanobytes" could manufacture items with unprecedented strength and lightness. Genetic engineering has been suggested as a way to reduce energy costs in the chemical industry. Parasitic bacteria on legumes (such as peanuts and soy beans) fix atmospheric nitrogen into chemicals the plants can use. Breeding similar bacteria for other crops might largely eliminate the need for ammonia fertilizer (and thereby decrease nitrate runoff). However, there would almost certainly be a decrease in potential yield per acre because the host plant would pay the energy cost.

Economics and Efficiency. Costs are the biggest factor affecting energy efficiency in manufacturing. When the price of natural gas was fixed by law at a low rate, for example, steam lines in some chemical plants had no insulation—it simply was not cost effective to insulate.

Even after prices rise, there is often a long time lag. For example, the use of bigger pipes in a chemical plant means lower pumping costs, but the cost of installing big pipes is not justified when energy costs are low. When energy costs rise, new plants that are being built might use the larger pipes, but old plants might well run for many years before replacement or major refit.

Similarly, highly efficient electrical motors are only about 25 percent more costly than conventional motors and are able to return the extra cost and start generating profit within three years. However, rebuilt conventional motors are available for a third of the price of new motors. Thus the investment in efficient new motors might not pay for itself for several additional years.

Finally, social and political factors affect the adaption of energy efficient technologies. Government policies have often discouraged recycling by granting tax subsidies to raw materials production and establishing requirements for their use rather than recycled materials. Tax policies have not allowed enough depreciation to encourage long-term investments in energy efficiency. Considering that by the 1990's the public and government had generally lost interest in the energy conservation issue, major gains in industrial energy use will probably only come during the next severe energy crisis.

FURTHER READING: Marc H. Ross and Daniel Steinmeyer, "Energy for Industry," *Scientific American* 263, no. 3 (September, 1990), is an excellent summary of methods for decreasing industrial energy use. See also "Beyond the Era of Materials," Eric D. Larson, Marc H. Ross, and Robert H. Williams, *Scientific American* 254, no. 6 (June, 1986). W. F. Kenny provides an exhaustive analysis in *Energy Conservation in the Process Industries*, 1984. *Building on Success: The Age of Energy Efficiency*, Worldwatch Paper 82, March, 1988, argues the case for maximizing energy efficiency. Adam Kahane, "Electricity Use in Manufacturing," *Annual Reviews of Energy* 12, 1987, analyzes many technical issues involving efficiency. K. Eric Drexler, *Engines of Creation: The Coming Era of Nanotechnology*, 1986, introduced this new technology.

Roger V. Carlson

SEE ALSO: Buildings and appliances, energy-efficient; Electrical power; Energy economics; Energy politics; Industrial Revolution and industrialization; Plastics and other petrochemical products; Recycling and recycling technology; Steel.

Marble

WHERE FOUND: Marbles, geologically defined as metamorphically altered calcareous rocks, are found in the core areas of younger mountain chains formed by the collision of tectonic plates and the consequent uplift and distortion of carbonate sedimentary strata. They are also found in the exposed roots of ancient, very eroded mountain chains of continental shield areas. Important marble-producing areas include the Carrara area in the Italian Apennines, and Vermont, Georgia, and Alabama in the United States.

PRIMARY USES: The main uses of marble are in architecture (as both an ornamental and structural stone) and as an artistic medium for three-dimensional art such as sculpture, interior furnishings, and mortuary and historical monuments.

DESCRIPTION: Geologists define marble as a type of rock produced by metamorphic processes acting on either a limestone or dolomite (dolostone), causing recrystallization through heat and pressure to produce a coarser-grained, harder rock. Stonemasons and quarriers have a more generic definition which calls almost any hard rock that accepts a fine polish marble.

As DEFINED GEOLOGICALLY, marble is a type of rock composed primarily of calcite. It can be, like limestone, monomineralic in nature—that is, a rock composed of only one, or nearly only one, mineral. Thus it can be up to 99 percent calcite (calcium carbonate). True marble can be derived from either limestone or dolomite (sometimes called dolostone). Dolomite (calcium magnesium carbonate) is a carbonate rock in which much, if not most, of the original calcium carbonate has been replaced by magnesium. True marbles are formed by two types of metamorphism: regional and contact. Regional

metamorphism is usually tectonic in nature and involves the slow compression and heating of rocks by large-scale crustal movements of the earth over long periods of time. Contact metamorphism is caused by rocks coming into contact, or near contact, with sources of great geologic heat, such as intruding bodies of magma; in these cases change can be effected within a short period of time.

Historical Background. Marble in its various forms has been known and admired since remote antiquity as a stone of choice for many applications. Some of the earliest known works of true architecture that have survived from ancient Mesopotamia, Egypt, and Greece featured marble as either decorative or structural elements. Sculptures, bas-reliefs, dedicatory columns, and triumphal arches have frequently featured various marbles. Thus marble has been in use at least five thousand years, dating back to the first civilizations, and its use continues up to the present. Many sculptors—among them such giants as Michelangelo, working in the fifteenth

Deposit of white marble. (U.S. Geological Survey)

and sixteenth centuries in Italy—through the ages have preferred marble, especially the pure white varieties.

Obtaining and Using Marble. Marble deposits are quarried in large operations that may involve hundreds of workers. In Europe marble is often obtained from quarries that have been worked continuously since antiquity. Until the last century or so, work was laboriously performed with age-old traditional tools and methods, but with the advent of power equipment the methodology and speed of extraction have greatly improved. Some constants have remained, such as the general strategy regarding extraction of large blocks of marble: removing the overburden (overlying sediments and rubble, if any), defining a quarry floor and front by quarrying monolithic blocks of marble parallel to their natural jointing planes, cutting away large blocks on all sides and removing the marble to the quarry floor, trimming, removing the marble from the quarry, and transporting it to the purchaser (often by use of specially built railroad systems).

Marble extraction has never had significant environmental effects, as the true marbles are chemically inert for all practical purposes. The metamorphism they underwent in their natural development stabilized their constituent minerals, including the trace minerals such as iron and magnesium from which colored marbles derive their patterns and hues.

As previously noted, the primary importance of marble is its use in architectural columns, floorings, wall coverings, sculpture, vases and other receptacles, and monuments of all sorts. Since the twentieth century, new minor uses have been found for marble, including electrical outlet baseplates and other electrical insulators, as it is a good natural insulator.

FURTHER READING: A comprehensive and informative discussion of marble in all its forms, including their histories, distributions, and uses, can be found in *Marble: The History of a Culture*, by Luciana and Tiziano Mannoni, 1985. Another good source for understanding marbles as building stones is *Gems, Granites, and Gravels*, by R. V. Dietrich and Brian J. Skinner, 1990. Useful for its in-depth discussions, supported by concrete

examples, of the geologic processes involved in mineral creation and alteration is *Minerals: An Illustrated Exploration of the Dynamic World of Minerals and Their Properties*, by George W. Robinson, 1994. An excellent introduction to the sciences of mineralogy and petrology in general, and to metamorphic rocks such as marble in particular, is *Rocks, Minerals, and Gemstones*, by Walter Schumann, 1993.

Frederick M. Surowiec

SEE ALSO: Calcium compounds; Carbonate minerals; Gypsum; Lime; Limestone; Metamorphic processes, rocks, and mineral deposits; Stone and rock.

Marine mining

The oceans cover 71 percent of the earth's surface, and they represent a vast, largely untapped reservoir of natural resources. The three major classifications of marine mining are the mining of seawater itself, mining along the continental shelves, and mining the ocean floors.

OCEAN MINING REPRESENTS only a small percentage of the total mining done worldwide because land deposits are more easily recognized and obtained than underwater deposits. Until the 1970's, deep ocean deposits could not be mined commercially because precise navigation to survey deposits and guide dredges did not exist. Since then, ocean technologies have improved significantly. Moreover, competing land deposits are being used (or paved over), and expanding economies are increasing demand. Thus the "mines of Neptune" are ripe for use. Marine mining can be divided into three categories: Mining seawater, extending land mining along the continental shelves, and mining the ocean floors.

Mining Seawater. Seawater can be seen as a massive ore body containing mostly water with an assortment of dissolved minerals. If seawater processing were efficient enough, more than sixty elements could be extracted. The major constituents of seawater are water (96.5 percent), sodium chloride (NaCl, 2.3 percent), magnesium chloride ($MgCl_2$, 0.5 percent), sodium sulfate (Na_2SO_4, 0.4 percent), and calcium chloride (0.1 percent).

Sodium chloride, or table salt, has been evaporated from seawater since antiquity, with sunlight and wind supplying the energy for the process. Modern table salt extraction begins with seawater in evaporation ponds that appear somewhat similar to those that have been used for centuries. However, the old single-step pond has been replaced by several ponds. A first pond settles out mud, iron salts, and calcium salts. At a second pond, slaked lime (calcium hydroxide, $Ca(OH)_2$) takes sulfur ions and precipitates out as gypsum plaster (calcium sulfate, $CaSO_4$). The table salt precipitates at a third pond, leaving a brine rich in salts of magnesium and potassium.

Magnesium was first extracted commercially in World War II. One method uses sea shells (calcium carbonate) baked to drive off carbon dioxide. Adding water produces (again) calcium hydroxide, from which the hydroxide combines with magnesium and precipitates out. Later, the precipitate is combined with hydrochloric acid (HCl), making magnesium chloride, which can be separated by electrolysis. Other systems go to magnesium carbonate ($MgCO_3$) or magnesium oxide (MgO). Bromine-rich brine is treated with acid to get elemental bromine. A similar process produces iodine.

Shellfish naturally extract calcium from seawater by growing (accreting) calcium carbonate ($CaCO_3$). This process can be mimicked by electrical accretion, in which a weak electrical charge on a wire screen accretes calcium carbonate, gradually making a sheet of artificial limestone while metal at the opposite electrode dissolves. Calcium carbonate accretion is experimental and expensive. However, it allows one to "grow" structures on site, and it may some day be used to build major oceanic structures.

Water, of course, is the prime constituent of seawater, and desalination (removal of salt from seawater or other salt solutions) has been performed commercially since the 1960's. The water and salts can be separated by distillation (much as evaporation and rain perform distillation in the hydrologic cycle), by low-pressure distillation (in which the water boils at lower temperatures), by refrigeration freezes fresh leaving concentrat by osmotic separation (in which pi tricity pulls water through a memb concentrated brine). Always, howevei, tion is expensive, and natural water sources are cheaper except in desert countries.

Extracting other minerals from seawater is theoretical. Although a cubic mile of seawater contains tons of many elements, those tons can be obtained only by pumping the water through some extraction process. The pumps and extraction process usually cost more than the extracted material is worth. After World War I, renowned German chemist Fritz Haber tried to extract gold from seawater to pay his nation's war debts but met with no success. Likewise, filtering for uranium has failed. Only plants and animals may be able to do such heroic extractions: Certain shellfish and worms in the oceans are able to concentrate minerals hundreds or even thousands of times more than they are concentrated in the surrounding ocean.

Deposits on the Continental Shelf. Where they meet the oceans, the continents generally slope gently for some distance before plunging into deep ocean waters. Worldwide, this shallow continuation (down to roughly 200 meters), called the continental shelf, covers an area equivalent to that of Africa.

Typical land minerals continue outward under the water on the continental shelf. In addition, the continental shelf has water-sorted deposits called placers along continuations of rivers "drowned" by changes in sea level and along beaches. Furthermore, many coastlines are somewhat like a set of stairs with drowned beaches and old beaches above the water line.

Tunnel mines have been extended from shore to obtain particularly desired ores, such as tin off England and coal off Japan. The Japanese have built artificial islands and tunneled from them to the surrounding deposits. Such methods can be extended. However, dredging is now the most common method of mining shallow deposits. A suction dredge (essentially a giant vacuum cleaner) can operate well down to roughly 30 meters. Below that, economics shift toward lines of buckets or other exotic means.

The most commonly dredged materials are sand and gravel, and more than a hundred million tons of these materials are dredged worldwide each year. Shells and coral are also dredged. These are cheap materials per unit, but the vast tonnage makes them important. More valuable ores are dredged in smaller tonnages throughout the world. For instance, gold is dredged off Alaska, and diamonds are dredged off the west coast of South Africa. Tin ore is dredged off Southeast Asia, and iron and titanium ores are mined off Australia.

Deep Ocean Deposits. The deeper waters of the ocean contain potential resources beyond imagining. To take only one example, the phosphorus-containing minerals glauconite and phosphorite, starting at the edge of the continental shelf, can easily be processed for fertilizer.

In tectonically active areas, water seeping down near volcanic rock is heated and eventually expelled back into the ocean. These hydrothermal vents, or marine vents, carry dissolved minerals, usually sulfides of zinc, lead, copper, and silver, along with lesser but still significant amounts of lead, cadmium, cobalt, and gold. Such deposits have been test mined in the Red Sea (where underwater valleys keep rich muds enclosed). In the deep ocean, such deposits make chimneys of metal sulfides that might eventually be mined.

The greatest deposits are in the deep ocean away from land. Rocks, sharks' teeth, and even old spark plugs provide settling points for the accretion of so-called ferromanganese nodules, which are oxides of mostly iron and manganese that also contain potentially profitable small amounts of copper, nickel, and cobalt. These potato-shaped ores cover millions of square kilometers and comprise billions of tons of metal.

Economics, Ecology, and Politics. The difference between potential resources and what are termed mineral "reserves" is what people are willing to do and what it will cost to obtain them. This is particularly true of marine mining. The economics of shallow dredging is cheaper than land mining, but the advantage rapidly disappears as the waters grow deeper and the distance to the processing plant on shore becomes longer. For example, deep ocean mining of fer-romanganese nodules for copper might be much closer to reality if fiber-optics technology had not cut into the applications for copper cables. Finally, mining deep sea ferromanganese nodules might yield the greatest profits from the small amounts of copper and nickel. However, ocean mining could also saturate the markets for cobalt and manganese, with unknown consequences—cobalt might directly replace nickel in stainless steel, making the stainless steel a cheaper competitor of copper.

The ecological factor is that dredging releases tremendous clouds of silt, killing wildlife and causing shallow waters to lose fish production. Dredging in cold deep ocean waters is worse, damaging areas of sparse, slowly reproducing life that require decades to heal. New types of neat dredges may be required if deep ocean deposits are ever to be used commercially.

Politics is an even more powerful part of the picture. A political decision that required coal-burning plants on land to reduce emissions of sulfur oxide and sulfate created a glut of recovered sulfur. That glut largely destroyed offshore sulfur mining. Phosphorite mining off the California coast was cancelled after it was discovered that the area had been used for dumping old bombs and shells. Tax incentives for recycling might delay the need for deep ocean mining by decades, or requirements for electric cars might push ferromanganese nodule mining forward in order to obtain nickel for batteries. Deep sea mining controls from the Law of the Sea Treaty would prevent rival mining dredges from colliding, but the costs of future deep ocean mining would probably include undetermined taxes and subsidies to potential mining rivals.

FURTHER READING: *The Mines of Neptune: Minerals and Metals from the Sea*, by Elisabeth Mann Borgese, 1985, has wide-ranging basic explanations and beautiful illustrations. *Deepsea Mining*, a selection of papers from a series of MIT seminars, edited by Judith Kildow, 1980, has detailed technical descriptions.

Roger V. Carlson

SEE ALSO: Deep drilling projects; Desalination plants and technology; Law of the sea; Manganese; Marine vents; Oceans; Oil and natural gas drilling and wells.

Marine vents

Marine vents are localized areas of the seafloor where cold seawater interacts with magma. The result of this interaction produces spectacular eruptions of hot seawater and enables the precipitation of sulfide minerals of iron, copper, and zinc.

MARINE VENTS, more commonly known as deep-sea hydrothermal vents, are produced along deep fractures in the seafloor. These fractures are associated with the mid-ocean ridges. The mid-ocean ridges are undersea mountain ranges that are sites of active volcanism. Despite being associated with undersea volcanic mountain ranges, all marine vents occur at depths greater than 2 kilometers below the surface. Marine vents are studied primarily by deep submersible vehicles.

Marine vents are formed when fractures in the seafloor develop and cold water flows in from above. As the seawater flows deeper into the fractures, it may encounter rocks heated by close proximity to magma; the rocks heat the seawater. The heated water begins to dissolve minerals from the surrounding rocks, and its chemistry changes from that of common seawater. If a critical temperature is reached, the hot water will rush to the surface. Although their appearance suggests an explosive volcanic eruption on land, marine vents are more like geysers than volcanoes.

As the hot seawater exits the vent, it begins to cool rapidly. Minerals which are in solution begin to precipitate out. This precipitation may give a dark, smoky appearance to the hot water exiting the marine vent. The name "black smoker" is commonly applied to these vents. The minerals which commonly precipitate out in these vents are metal sulfides (combinations of a metal and sulfur). The most common minerals found are sulfides of iron, copper, and zinc. These minerals form crusts around the opening and may precipitate into a tall "chimney" of minerals around the marine vent.

Marine vents are also the site of unique biologic communities. These communities thrive in the total absence of sunlight. The food chain is based on bacteria that derive their energy from chemosynthesis. This process enables the bacteria to derive their energy from chemicals dissolved in the hot water exiting the marine vents. Other animals depend on the bacteria. Some animals associated with the vent communities grow to very large sizes. Tube worms around marine vents may be larger than 3 meters (over 10 feet) in length. Because the communities depend on the vent waters for their source of energy, the animals live closely packed around the vent. When vents become inactive, the communities die. While not a likely source of food for humans, it has been suggested that the vent animals may contain unusual chemicals which may help develop new medicines.

There is a great deal of difficulty and expense involved in reaching deep marine vents. This fact, plus the cost of bringing minerals and animals to the surface and shipping them to shore, must be considered in deciding whether it is feasible to use these valuable resources. Despite the obstacles, marine vents remain the focus of much geologic, biologic, and oceanographic research.

Richard H. Fluegeman, Jr.

SEE ALSO: Biodiversity; Copper; Hydrothermal solutions and mineralization; Iron; Oceanography; Seafloor spreading; Zinc.

Mercury

WHERE FOUND: Mercury is generally found associated with volcanic rocks that have formed near subduction zones. The primary producing areas are in Spain, China, and Algeria.

PRIMARY USES: The primary uses of mercury are in the industrial production of chlorine and caustic soda, in dry cell batteries, in scientific measuring instruments, and in mercury vapor lamps.

DESCRIPTION: Mercury (chemical symbol Hg) is a silvery white metal that belongs to Group IIB (the zinc group) of the periodic table. Mercury has an atomic number of 80 and an atomic weight of 200.5. It has seven stable isotopes and a density of 13.6 grams per cubic centimeter. Also known as quicksilver, mercury has a melting point of −38.87 degrees Celsius, making it the only metal that is liquid at normal room temperature. It boils at a temperature of 356.9 degrees Celsius and has a constant rate of expansion throughout the entire range of temperature of the liquid. Mercury alloys with most metals and is a good conductor of electricity.

MERCURY IS A relatively scarce element on Earth, accounting for only 3 parts per billion in crustal rocks. It is found both as free liquid metal and, more commonly, as the sulfide mineral cinnabar (HgS). It is generally found in areas of past volcanic activity. Mercury compounds are formed from mercury with either a +1 or +2 oxidation state. The most common mercury (I) compound is mercury chloride (Hg_2Cl_2), and the most common mercury (II) compounds are mercury oxide (HgO), mercury bichloride ($HgCl_2$), and mercury sulfide (HgS). (The Roman numerals refer to the valence state of the mercury.)

Mercury forms compounds that are used in agriculture, industry, and medicine. Some organic mercury compounds, such as phenylmercury acetate, are used in agriculture as fungi-cides to control seed rot, for spraying trees, and for controlling weeds. Because of their highly toxic nature, care must be used when applying or using such mercury compounds. Mercuric sulfate and mercuric chloride are used industrially to produce vinyl chloride, vinyl acetate, and acetaldehyde. Pharmacological uses of mercury compounds include mercury bichloride and mercurochrome as skin antiseptics, and mercurous chloride (calomel) as a diuretic.

Historical Background. Mercury has been known since at least as far back as the second century B.C.E. Chinese alchemists used mercury in futile attempts to transform the base metals into gold. Possible earlier records of the use of mercury in Egypt cannot be fully authenticated because of currently incomplete knowledge of ancient writings. Cinnabar, the red ore mineral of mercury, has long been used by aboriginal peoples as an important pigment. By Roman times the distillation of mercury was known, and a mercury trade between Rome and the rich Spanish cinnabar mines was well established. Beginning with the Renaissance and the scientific revolution in the sixteenth and seventeenth centuries, mercury became important for use in measuring devices such as thermometers and ba-

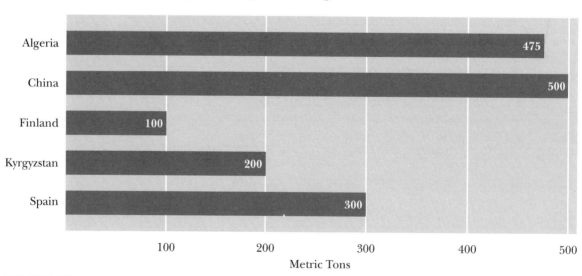

Leading Mercury-Producing Countries, 1994

Country	Metric Tons
Algeria	475
China	500
Finland	100
Kyrgyzstan	200
Spain	300

Source: U.S. Bureau of Mines, *Minerals Yearbook, 1994.* U.S. Government Printing Office, 1996.
Note: Total world 1994 mercury production was about 1,760 metric tons.

rometers. The major modern industrial, medicinal, and agricultural uses of mercury were developed in the nineteenth and twentieth centuries.

The toxicity of mercury compounds has been known since the early poisoning of cinnabar miners. Later, in the early nineteenth century, the mental effects that mercury had on felt makers gave birth to the phrase "mad as a hatter." The tragic effects of mercury poisoning were felt in Japan during the 1950's and Iraq in 1972, when hundreds died from ingesting organic mercury compounds.

Distribution of Mercury. Mercury is a rare crustal element that is both found as liquid elemental mercury and found combined with other elements in over twenty-five minerals. Cinnabar is the primary ore mineral of mercury, and it is generally found in volcanic rocks and occasionally in associated sedimentary rocks. The volcanic rocks were generally formed as volcanic island arc systems near subduction zones. Since the deposits are concentrated in faulted and fractured rocks that were formed at or near the surface, they are very susceptible to erosion. Mercury is a highly volatile element, and it is usually lost to the atmosphere during the erosion of the ore deposits.

Obtaining and Using Mercury. The primary mercury deposits of the world are found in Spain, China, central Europe, and Algeria. Spain is estimated to have the greatest reserves, almost 60 percent of the world's total. World production of mercury in 1994 was approximately 1,760 tons. The United States has very small reserves (about 5,300 tons), and all current U.S. production is now a by-product of gold mining in Nevada, Utah, and California. Mercury is also recovered through the recycling of batteries, dental amalgams, thermostats, fluorescent lamp tubes, and certain industrial sludges and solutions. More than 460 tons of mercury were captured by recycling in the United States in 1994, and this total will increase in the future as more mercury disposal legislation is enacted.

The primary use of mercury in the world is in the industrial production of chlorine and caustic soda. Mercury is used as a traveling anode in the process, and it can be easily recaptured after the chlorine and caustic soda have been formed.

More than 28 percent of all mercury consumption in the United States is for this purpose. Mercury is also used as an electrical conductor in sealed switches and wiring devices. Since mercury expands uniformly over its entire temperature range as a liquid, it is used in thermometers, barometers, and thermostats. Additional major uses of mercury include uses as a fungicide for agricultural purposes and as a medicinal skin antiseptic.

Environmental Impact of Mercury. Mercury is an extremely toxic and volatile element that can be easily released into the environment when mined, processed, or used. Mercury vapors can be inhaled, and mercury compounds can be ingested or absorbed through the skin. Mercury poisoning has been recognized in native peoples who used cinnabar as a face pigment, in gold miners who used mercury in processing gold ore, and in hat makers who used mercury compounds in producing felt.

Inorganic mercury compounds can be converted by bacteria into highly toxic organic mercury compounds such as methyl mercury. These organic mercury compounds become concentrated as they move up the food chain to higher-level organisms such as fish, birds, and humans. Because of this the disposal of inorganic mercury waste can become a major environmental hazard. In Japan the release of mercury waste from an industrial plant into the waters of Minamata Bay resulted in the deaths of forty-three people during the 1950's and early 1960's. In 1972 wheat seed treated with methyl mercury fungicide was used by farmers in rural Iraq. The wheat was enriched in methyl mercury, as was the bread made from the wheat. Animals and plants within the area also accumulated high concentrations of methyl mercury. As a result of this contamination, a total of 460 people died from mercury poisoning during 1972.

FURTHER READING: A general source for the origin of mercury deposits is *Mineral and Energy Resources*, by Douglas Brookings, 1990. An excellent description of the toxic effects of mercury can be found in *Toxics A to Z*, by John Harte et al., 1990. A summary of the effects of mercury poisoning on farmers in Iraq is presented by F. Bakir et al., in "Methyl Mercury Poisoning in

Iraq," *Science* 181 (1973). The current yearly production of mercury in the United States and in the rest of the world is published each year by the U.S. Bureau of Mines (after 1997, by the U.S. Geological Survey) under the title *Annual Review of Mercury*.

Jay R. Yett

SEE ALSO: Food chain; Hazardous waste disposal; Igneous processes, rocks, and mineral deposits; Plate tectonics.

Metals and metallurgy

Enormous amounts of mineral resources are mined each year to supply society's requirements for metals. In addition, large amounts of carbon, oxygen, and electricity are consumed in the various metallurgical processes by which the raw materials are converted for use.

ALTHOUGH THE TERM "metal" is difficult to define absolutely, there are two working definitions that include almost three quarters of the elements of the periodic table classified as metals. Chemically, metals are those elements that usually form positive ions in solutions or in compounds and whose oxides form basic water solutions. Physically, metals contain free electrons that impart properties such as metallic luster and thermal and electrical conductivity. All the elements found in Groups IA and IIA and in the B groups are metals. In addition, Groups IIIA, IVA (except carbon), VA (except nitrogen and phosphorous), and VIA (except oxygen and sulfur) are classified as metals. All the metals are lustrous and, with the exception of mercury, are solids at normal temperatures. Boron (IIIA), silicon and germanium (IVA), arsenic and antimony (VA), selenium and tellurium (VIA), and astatine (VIIA) show metallic behavior in some of their compounds and are known as metalloids.

The bonding in metals explains many of their physical characteristics. The simplest model describes a metal as fixed positive ions (the nucleus and completed inner shells of electrons) in a sea of mobile valence electrons. The ions are held in place by the electrostatic attraction between the positive ions and the negative electrons, which are delocalized over the whole crystal. Because of this electron mobility, metals are good conductors of electricity and thermal energy. This electron sea also shields neighboring layers of positive ions as they move past one another. Therefore most metals are ductile (capable of being drawn into wires) and malleable (capable of being spread into sheets). The absorption of electromagnetic radiation by the mobile valence electrons and its reemission as visible light explains the luster that is characteristic of metals.

Natural Abundance. While all the known metals are found in the earth's crust, the abundance varies widely, from aluminum (over 81,000 parts per million) to such rare metals as osmium and ruthenium (approximately 0.001 parts per million). The metalloid silicon is the second most abundant element in the earth's crust, with an abundance of over 277,000 parts per million. Some of those metals found in low concentrations, such as copper and tin, are commonly used, while many of the more abundant metals, such as titanium and rubidium, are just beginning to find uses. The metal most important to modern industrial society, iron, is abundant and easily reduced to metallic form. The metals that were most important to early civilizations—gold, silver, mercury, lead, iron, copper, tin, and zinc—exist in large, easily recognized deposits and in compounds that are easily reduced to elemental form.

Very few metals occur "free" in nature. The form in which a specific metal is found depends on its reactivity and on the solubility of its compounds. Many metals occur as binary oxides or sulfides in ores that also contain materials such as clay, granite, or silica from which the metal compounds must first be separated. Metals are also found as chlorides, carbonates, sulfates, silicates, and arsenides, as well as complex compounds of great variety such as $LiAlSi_2O_6$, which is a source of lithium.

Metallurgy. Metallurgy is a very large field of science and art that encompasses the separation of metals from their ores, the making of alloys, and the working of metals to give them certain desired characteristics. The art of metallurgy dates from about 4000 B.C.E., when metalsmiths

Metallurgy comprises the variety of processes—including preliminary treatment, reduction to free metal, and refining—that turn ore into refined, usable metals and alloys. (Photo Network)

were able to extract silver and lead from their ores. Tin ores were obtained by 3000 B.C.E., and the production of bronze, an alloy of copper and tin, could begin. By 2700 B.C.E. iron was obtained. There is an obvious relationship between the discovery that metals could be refined and fabricated into objects such as tools and weapons and the rise of human civilizations. Early periods in the history of humankind have long been identified by the metals that became available. Throughout most of human history metallurgy was an art; the development of the science from the art has taken place gradually over the past few centuries.

The production of metals from their ores involves a three-step process: preliminary treatment in which impurities are removed, and possibly chemical treatment used to convert the metallic compound to a more easily reduced form; reduction to the free metal; and refining, in which undesirable impurities are removed and others are added to control the final characteristics of the metal.

The preliminary treatment involves physical as well as chemical treatment. Physical methods include grinding, sorting, froth flotation, magnetic separations, and gravity concentration. Chemical reactions may also be used for concentration. The use of cyanide solution to extract gold from its ores is an example of chemical concentration. Karl Bayer devised a process in 1890 which is based on the fact that aluminum trihydrate dissolves in hot caustic soda but other materials in bauxite do not. The result is almost pure Al_2O_3. Frequently, many metals present in very small percentages are found in ores with more abundant metals. The processes used to concentrate the primary metal also concentrates the minor ones as well and makes their extraction possible. Most ores are mined and processed for more than one metal. Iron is a notable exception.

Large-scale redox reactions are the means by which metals from ores are reduced to free metals. The particular method used depends on the reactivity of the metal. The most active metals, such as aluminum, magnesium, and sodium, are reduced by electrolytic reduction. Metal oxides are usually reduced by heating with carbon or hydrogen. This age-old process produces by far the greatest volume of free metals such as iron, copper, zinc, cadmium, tin, and nickel. Sulfides are usually roasted in air to produce oxides which are then reduced to the free metal. Some sulfides, such as copper sulfide, produce the free metal directly by roasting.

The refining step encompasses an array of processes designed to remove any remaining impurities and to convert the metal to a form demanded by the end user. The major divisions of refining are pyrometallurgy, or fire refining, and electrometallurgy, or electrolysis. There are a few processes that do not fall into either of these major divisions such as the gaseous diffusion of uranium hexafluoride molecules to produce isotopically enriched uranium for the nuclear power industry.

Pyrometallurgy is a general name for a number of processes including, but not limited to, roasting (heating to a temperature where oxidation occurs without melting, usually to eliminate sulfides); calcining (heating in a kiln to drive off an undesirable constituent such as carbon, which goes off as CO_2); and distilling (heating mineral to decomposition above the melting point of the metal, which is collected in a condenser).

Electrolytic refining involves immersing an anode of impure metal and a cathode of pure metal in a solution of ions of the metal and passing an electric current through it. Metal ions from the solution plate out on the cathode and are replaced in the solution by ions from the anode. Impurities either drop to the bottom as sludge or remain in solution. These by-products, often containing gold, silver, and platinum are later recovered by additional processes. Electrolytic refining is expensive in terms of the electricity required and of the often toxic solutions remaining to be safely disposed of.

Metals as Crystals. When a metal solidifies, its atoms assume positions in some well-defined geometric pattern, a crystalline solid. The three most important patterns for metals are the body-centered cubic, the face-centered cubic, and the hexagonal. If atoms of one metal exist in the solid solution of another, the atoms of the minor constituent occupy positions in the crystal pattern of the major constituent. Since atoms of each element have characteristic size, the presence of a "stranger" atom causes distortion of the pattern, and usually strengthening of the crystal. This distortion and strengthening is one of the major reasons that most metals are used as alloys—solid solutions of two or more constituent metals.

Zinc is a hexagonal crystal, while copper atoms occupy the sites of a face-centered cubic lattice. As the larger zinc atoms occupy positions in the copper lattice, they distort the crystal and make it harder to deform. Brass, an alloy of copper and zinc, increases in hardness as the zinc concentration increases up to 36 percent, at which point the crystal changes to a body-centered cubic pattern with very different characteristics. Careful selection of various combinations of elements in differing concentrations can produce alloys with almost any desired characteristics.

The carbon steels are a good example of this. Various amounts of carbon and metals such as molybdenum are introduced into molten iron ore to create desired strength, ductility, or malleability in the finished steel product. Another example is the intentional doping of the semiconductor silicon with boron or phosphorous to create different conduction capabilities.

Metals in Living Systems. "Essential" metals are those whose absence will prevent some particular organism from completing its life cycle, including reproduction. These metals are classified according to the amounts needed as macronutrients or micronutrients. For animals the macronutrients are potassium, sodium, magnesium, and calcium. Sodium and potassium establish concentration differences across cell membranes by means of active transport and set up osmotic and electrochemical gradients. They are structure promoters for nucleic acids and proteins.

Magnesium, calcium, and zinc are enzyme activators and structure promoters. Magnesium is an essential component of chlorophyll, the pigment in plants responsible for photosynthesis. Calcium salts are insoluble and act as structure formers in both plants and animals. In muscles the calcium concentration is controlled to act as neuromuscular triggers.

Among the important micronutrients are chromium and iron. In mammals, chromium is involved in the metabolism of glucose. The oxygen-carrying molecule in mammalian blood is hemoglobin, an iron-porphyrin protein. Many other metals are known to be important in varying amounts but their specific activity is not yet clearly understood. This is and will continue to be an active field of research in biochemistry and molecular biology.

One of the interesting current techniques for studying the activity of metals on a cellular level is fluorescent imaging. Metals such as calcium interact with fluorescent dyes. The dyes have different fluorescent characteristics in presence and absence of its specific metal. Special cameras, called CCDs (charge coupled devices) are mounted on microscopes and feed electrical signals directly to a computer which creates an image and allows its manipulation. Metal concentrations inside and outside cells can be studied in the presence and absence of other nutrients to establish relationships among the various materials that are needed to sustain viable cell activity.

Metals as Toxins. Those materials that have a negative effect on metabolic processes in a specific organism are said to be toxic to that organism. Many metals fall into this category. Today toxic metals are found in the atmosphere and the waters of the earth. Some are present because of natural processes such as erosion, forest fires, or volcanic eruptions, others because of the activities of humankind. The natural toxins are less problematic because many organisms, during the process of evolution, developed tolerances to what might be considered toxic.

Maintaining good air quality is a major problem for industrial nations. Highly toxic metals, whose long-term effects on the health of humans and the environment are of concern, are being released into the atmosphere in large quantities. The atmosphere is the medium of transfer of these toxins from the point of origin to distant ecosystems. Prior to the 1970's attention was focused on gaseous pollutants such as SO_2 and NO_x and on total particulate matter. Since that time improved analytical techniques have provided improved data on trace metals in the atmosphere, making studies on health effects possible.

The largest contributors to trace metal pollution are vehicular traffic, energy generation, and industrial metal production. For some metals, such as selenium, mercury, and manganese, natural emissions on a global scale far exceed those from anthropogenic sources. However, local manganese emissions from human-made sources in Europe far exceed those from natural sources. This illustrates the problem facing humankind. Emission patterns must be studied for local, regional, and global effects. Global emission patterns have been studied and compared with statistical information of the world's use of ores, rocks, and fuels and to the production of various types of goods. These studies allow the major sources of various toxic metals to be identified.

Coal combustion has been identified as the chief emission source of beryllium, cobalt, molybdenum, antimony, and selenium. Nickel and vanadium come mainly from oil firing. Smelters and other noniron refining plants emit most of the arsenic, cadmium, copper, and zinc. Chromium and manganese are released as side products of iron refining and steel production. Finally, gasoline combustion is the main cause of lead pollution. Identification of the main culprits should point the way to the changes needed to reduce emission levels of these metals and to choices with regard to future industrial growth. Installation of scrubbing devices for removal of toxic materials from gaseous emissions and replacement of old boilers will reduce some emissions. New coal technologies such as coal pyrolysis and *in situ* gasification should also reduce the contamination of the environment to some degree. Much more data on regional and local patterns is necessary to restore the health of the atmosphere.

FURTHER READING: The importance of metals in the emergence of early civilization is described in *The Metalsmiths*, by Percy Knauth, 1974. About 1558, Georgius Agricola published *De Re Metallica*, in which he described many metallurgical methods and processes. The work (unexcelled for almost two hundred years) was translated by H. H. Hoover and L. H. Hoover in 1912. John A. Wolfe's *Mineral Resources: A World Review*, 1984, contains a brief overview of specific minerals as well as chapters on exploration, extraction technology, and history of metal use. *Metals in the Service of Man*, by A. Street and W. Alexander, 9th ed. 1989, is a very general work on the field of metallurgy. The important biological role of metals is described by D. A. Phipps in *Metals and Metabolism*, 1976. *Toxic Metals in the Atmosphere*, by J. O. Nriagu and C. I. Davidson, 1986, presents information on the types of metals found in the air and their distribution.

Grace A. Banks

SEE ALSO: Alloys; Earth's crust; Mineral resource use, early history of; Minerals, structure and physical properties of; Strategic resources; articles on specific metals.

Metamictization

Metamictization is the process of rendering crystalline minerals partly or wholly amorphous (glasslike) as a consequence of radioactive decay. Metamict minerals such as zircon are important as gemstones, and metamict minerals that do not lose their radioactive components during the process of metamictization may possibly be used for the disposal of high-level nuclear wastes.

THE TERM "METAMICT" (meaning "mixed otherwise") was proposed in 1893 by W. C. Broegger when he recognized that some minerals, although they show crystal form, are nevertheless structurally very similar to glass. Metamict minerals fracture like glass, are optically isotropic (have the same properties in all directions) to visible and infrared light, and to all appearances are noncrystalline. The discovery that all metamict minerals are at least slightly radioactive and that metamict grains contain uranium and thorium led to the conclusion that the process of metamictization results from radiation damage caused by the decay of uranium and thorium. Although all metamict minerals are radioactive, not all radioactive minerals are metamict. Many metamict minerals have nonmetamict equivalents with the same form and essentially the same composition.

Isotopes of uranium and of thorium decay, through a series of emissions of alpha particles (helium nuclei), into a stable isotope of lead. The alpha particle is emitted from the decaying nucleus with great energy, causing the emitting nucleus to recoil simultaneously in the opposite direction. In the final part of its trajectory, the alpha particle is slowed enough to collide with hundreds of atoms in the mineral, but since the larger recoil nucleus travels a much shorter path, it collides with ten times as many atoms. Consequently, the majority of radiation damage is caused by the recoiling nucleus. The immense amount of heat generated by both particles in a small region of the mineral structure produces damage, but some of the energy also serves to self-repair some of the damage spontaneously. Radioactive minerals that remain crystalline have high rates of self-repair, while metamict minerals do not.

Metamict minerals are not common in nature, and they are generally found in pegmatites associated with granites. Showing little resistance to metamictization, the largest group of metamict minerals includes the thorium-, uranium-, and yttrium-bearing oxides of niobium, tantalum, and titanium. The second-largest group of metamict minerals are silicates, with zircon (a zirconium-silicate mineral) occurring most frequently. The smallest group of metamict minerals are the phosphates, including xenotime (yttrium phosphate), which has the same crystal structure as zircon.

Since metamict gemstones, such as zircon, are isotropic and look clear inside, they are often of greater value than the crystalline varieties, because the anisotropic properties of crystalline gems make them look cloudy inside. In addition, radiation damage often imparts attractive color to the metamict gemstones. Metamict minerals may possibly have another important use in the future: Since some of them retain their radioactive elements over millions of years despite metamictization, they may provide the key for safe disposal of high-level nuclear wastes. Many geochemists believe that synthetic versions of these metamict minerals could be "grown" to produce rocks that would be able to contain hazardous nuclear wastes safely for tens of thousands of years.

Alvin K. Benson

SEE ALSO: Hazardous waste disposal; Igneous processes, rocks, and mineral deposits; Isotopes, radioactive; Niobium; Pegmatites; Silicates; Thorium; Uranium; Zirconium.

Metamorphic processes, rocks, and mineral deposits

The word "metamorphism," based on Greek roots, translates as the "process of changing form." Existing sedimentary or igneous rocks are transformed in the solid state to metamorphic rocks as the temperature and pressure of their environment increase at various depths within the earth. The numerous transformations that occur are collectively termed metamorphic processes.

EVERY METAMORPHIC PROCESS relates either to the formation of new minerals, called neocrystallization, or to the formation of a new texture in the metamorphic rock. The new texture may simply be an increase in size and change in shape of existing minerals (recrystallization). The new texture may also involve the development of a "foliation," in which the elongate and platy minerals assume a parallel orientation. These general processes are further divided depending upon the specific chemical and mechanical changes occurring during the metamorphic transformation. Long periods of erosion can expose metamorphic rocks on the surface of the earth; surface metamorphic rocks are often valuable resources, either because of their new minerals or because of the physical properties that the rocks themselves have as a result of their new textures.

Neocrystallization. New minerals form at the expense of old minerals. As the pressure and temperature increase on an existing igneous or sedimentary rock (called the protolith), the old minerals become unstable and break down into chemical components that recombine to form new minerals. Some of the chemicals, for example, H_2O and CO_2, occur as gases at metamorphic temperatures. These gases mix to form a vapor that exists in the cracks and along the boundaries between the individual grains of the minerals. The gain and loss of gases from the vapor is part of the overall chemical reconstruction that takes place during metamorphism. The vapor inevitably escapes from the rock during the long period of cooling and erosion that exposes such rocks on the earth's surface.

The neocrystallization process is usually expressed as a chemical reaction. The minerals of the protolith (existing rock) are the reactants, shown on the left side of the reaction, and the new metamorphic minerals that form are the products, listed on the right side. The reactions often will generate and/or consume chemicals residing in the vapor. The reactions illustrated in the figures accompanying this article (see next page) are shown in triplicate, first as rock changes, second as mineral changes, and third as chemical recombinations. As an example, refer to the three parts of reaction 1. Reaction (a)

is the conversion of the sedimentary rock (protolith) called dolostone, which commonly contain silica as chert nodules, to the metamorphic rock called marble. Reaction (b) is the same reaction with attention being focused on the transformation of the minerals and the creation of the metamorphic mineral called tremolite, where the beginning vapor was water and the ending vapor is carbon dioxide. Reaction (c) shows how the individual chemical components have recombined, often changing from the mineral to vapor state during the transformation.

As with any chemical reaction, there are specific temperature and pressure conditions that must exist before the reaction can occur. Each metamorphic mineral of interest forms within a specific temperature and pressure region in the earth. The exact temperature and pressure conditions under which a metamorphic mineral or group of minerals will form can by determined by laboratory experiments; geologists then deduce that similar conditions must have existed whenever these minerals are found in the geological environment. The geological environment required for the development of a given metamorphic mineral is usually controlled by plate tectonic movements. Explorations for metamorphic resources are targeted to specific tectonic regions that correspond to the proper temperature-pressure environments for their formation.

There are three tectonic environments with specific pressure and temperature conditions that control the location for the development of metamorphic minerals. Burial metamorphism results from a high-pressure and low-temperature environment that occurs where two plates converge and one plate is being actively subducted. During the recent geological past, the coastline along Oregon and northern California experienced this tectonic environment. Contact metamorphism is a high-temperature, low-pressure environment occurring slightly further inland from the region of burial metamorphism. Contact metamorphism results when magma generated during the subduction of a plate rises into the over-riding plate and solidifies as shallow igneous plutons. Contact metamorphism has occurred along the margins of the Sierra Nevada

Reactions that Form Metamorphic Rocks

1
- a. cherty dolostone + vapor → marble + vapor
- b. 5 dolomite + 8 quartz + water → tremolite + 3 calcite + 7 carbon dioxide
- c. $5CaMg(CO_3)_2 + 8SiO_2 + H_2O → Ca_2Mg_5Si_8O_{22}(OH)_2 + 3CaCO_3 + 7CO_2$

2
- a. peridotite + vapor → verde antique marble
- b. 4 olivine + 4 water + 2 carbon dioxide → serpentine + 2 magnesite
- c. $4Mg_2SiO_4 + 4H_2O + 2CO_2 → Mg_3Si_2O_5(OH)_4 + 2MgCO_3$

3
- a. peridotite + vapor (with dissolved silica) → serpentinite
- b. 3 olivine + 4 water + silica → 2 serpentine
- c. $3Mg_2SiO_4 + 4H_2O + SiO_2 → 2Mg_3Si_2O_5(OH)_4$

4
- a. cherty dolostone + vapor → soapstone + vapor
- b. 3 magnesite + 4 quartz + water → talc + 3 carbon dioxide
- c. $3MgCO_3 + 4SiO_2 + H_2O → Mg_3Si_4O_{10}(OH)_2 + 3CO_2$

5
- a. high-aluminum shales → kyanite schist
- b. kaolinite-clay → 2 kyanite + 2 quartz + 4 water
- c. $Al_4Si_4O_{10}(OH)_8 → 2Al_2SiO_5 + 2SiO_2 + 4H_2O$

6
- a. cherty limestone → marble + vapor
- b. calcite + quartz → wollastonite + carbon dioxide
- c. $CaCO_3 + SiO_2 → CaSiO_3 + CO_2$

7
- a. sodium-rich igneous felsite → blueschist
- b. albite (feldspar) → jadeite + quartz
- c. $NaAlSi_3O_8 → NaAlSi_2O_6 + SiO_2$

8
- a. sedimentary clay-rich shale → corundum-bearing garnet schist
- b. 6 staurolite → 4 garnet + 12 kyanite + 11 corundum + 3 water
- c. $6Fe_2Al_9Si_4O_{23}(OH) → 4Fe_3Al_2Si_3O_{12} + 12Al_2SiO_5 + 11Al_2O_3 + 3H_2O$

batholiths of eastern California. The third tectonic environment is regional metamorphism, often called dynothermal metamorphism, which corresponds to moderately high pressures and temperatures. Regional metamorphism is seen after extensive erosions of a contact metamorphism area has exposed deeper regions within the earth's crust.

Isochemical Processes. Neocrystallization that occurs without any influx of new chemicals (other than the water and carbon dioxide from the vapor) is called isochemical metamorphism. Isochemical metamorphism produces about a dozen minerals that are considered valuable resources. The isochemical-neocrystallization processes responsible for the formation of some of these minerals are described below, with a brief indication of the tectonic environments that favor their formation.

Serpentine. When serpentine $(Mg_3Si_2O_5(OH)_4)$ is the major mineral formed during the low–temperature, low-pressure metamorphism associated with the beginning of regional metamorphism, the resulting metamorphic rock is called a serpentinite. Polished serpentinites are used widely as a facing stone in both interior and exterior applications. When the serpentinites contain some carbonate minerals they are marketed as "verde antique marble." Serpentine can occur in any one of three forms. The form called chrysotile is the most common asbestos mineral. Asbestos veins are common in serpentinites, and in many locations in eastern Canada and northern New England serpentinites are mined for their asbestos.

Serpentine generally forms by metamorphism of ultramafic igneous rocks by one of two reactions. One type of serpentine reaction (see reaction 2) involves a mixed vapor phase of carbon dioxide and water, which produces some carbonate minerals. A second serpentine-forming reaction (see reaction 3) requires that some silica be dissolved in the water vapor.

Talc. Talc ($Mg_3Si_4O_{10}(OH)_2$) can form large masses of randomly oriented interlocking small flakes to make a rock called soapstone, used extensively for carving and as a source of talcum powder for health and beauty applications. The term "steatite" refers to talc-rich rocks that are used because of talc's lack of chemical reactivity or its high heat capacity. Talc forms by regional metamorphism at low to moderate temperatures and low to moderate pressures. When the protolith is a sedimentary limestone or dolostone the reaction for the formation of talc deposits is as shown in reaction 4.

A second common reaction that produces major talc deposits is the continuing metamorphism of a peridotite protolith. Talc forms by this reaction at temperatures slightly above 300 degrees Celsius; however, the temperatures must remain below 700 degrees Celsius to prevent the breakdown of talc.

Graphite. Graphite (a form of carbon, C) is used in a wide variety of applications from lubrication to high-temperature crucibles. Deposits of amorphous graphite form by contact metamorphism of coal beds, whereas deposits of flake graphite form by regional metamorphism of sedimentary rocks with the graphite being disseminated in mica schist and micaceous quartzite. Extensive weathering of these rocks assists in the release of the graphite. The graphite con-

tent of such metamorphic ores is usually 5 to 6 percent.

Clinker is a common term used by English miners for the graphite ore created by the contact metamorphism of coal beds. The reaction involves the breakdown of a wide variety of organic molecules. Continued high-temperature metamorphism of coal beds can transform the graphite into a natural coke, which has been mined in Wyoming and Utah.

Kyanite. Kyanite (Al_2SiO_5) and the related minerals andalusite and sillimanite are used in the production of refractory ceramics, such as those used in spark plugs. Kyanite forms from aluminum-rich clay-shale protoliths during regional metamorphism at moderate to high temperatures (see reaction 5).

Wollastonite. Wollastonite ($CaSiO3$) is used extensively in the manufacturing of tiles. It forms by high-temperature contact metamorphism of silica-bearing limestones. An example may be found in Willsboro, New York, where the wollastonite mine is in a metamorphosed limestone on the margin of the igneous intrusion that forms the Adirondack Mountains. This type of reaction is shown in example 6. This reaction normally occurs at temperatures around 650 degrees Celsius.

Jadeite. The pure form of the mineral jadeite ($NaAlSi_2O_6$) is the best quality of all materials called jade. Jade has been a valued material for sculpture and other art and craft applications for more than twenty-five centuries. It forms during burial metamorphism of alkali-rich igneous rocks that have been subjected to very high pressures and low temperatures. Such conditions are found in the mountains of the Coast Range in California, where jade has been mined (reaction 7).

Corundum. Corundum (Al_2O_3) is used extensively as an abrasive, and its pure colored variants known as ruby and sapphire are valued as gemstones. Corundum forms during regional metamorphism of aluminum-rich shale protoliths. The progressing metamorphism of the shale makes an intermediate mineral called staurolite, which commonly is sold in mineral shops and displayed in museums as "fairy crosses" because of its well-developed cruciform twinning. Corundum forms when the staurolite breaks down at very high temperatures, as shown in reaction 8.

Metasomatism. A special type of metamorphism occurs whenever a major influx of new dissolved chemical components is added to the chemistry of the protolith. A water-rich fluid or vapor is the means of transport for this added chemistry. The process of adding chemistry to the rock through the vapor is called metasomatism. Metasomatism occurs chiefly in regions of contact metamorphism where highly volatile elements such as boron, fluorine, or chlorine are released into a water-rich fluid associated with the igneous pluton.

The igneous-based fluid also carries dissolved silicon, aluminum, iron, magnesium, manganese, minor sodium, potassium, and often some tin, copper, tungsten, lead, and zinc. This saline fluid invades the adjacent limestone and reacts with calcium to form pronounced monomineralic zones at the contact between the pluton and the limestone.

The rocks produced by metasomatism are called skarns or tactites, and they are the coarsest grained of all metamorphic rocks. The garnet zone of a skarn may have individual grains of garnet that are as large as 20 centimeters in diameter. Skarns are mined throughout the world. Scheelite ($CaWO_4$), a major ore of tungsten, is mined from numerous metasomatized contact zones in California, Nevada, Idaho, and British Columbia. Other minerals that are mined from skarns are wollastonite, galena (an ore of lead), sphalerite (an ore of zinc), magnetite (an ore of iron), and chalcopyrite (an ore of copper).

Texture Changes and Recrystallization. During metamorphism changes may occur in the size, shape, and often in the orientation of the mineral grains within the rock. There are at least six different processes related to texture changes; the exact process is dependent upon which of the texture variables are changed and the mechanics of the change.

A change in size and shape of an existing mineral without the formation of any new minerals is a process called recrystallization. Certain sedimentary protoliths may be monomineralic rocks, two common examples are a limestone that is made entirely of the mineral calcite, and a silica-cemented sandstone that is made entirely of the mineral quartz. Such single mineral rocks are unable to promote any form of neocrystallization, and recrystallization is the only result of metamorphism.

Metamorphic Rock Classification Based on Texture and Composition

Texture	Nonfoliated			Foliated			
	Nonlayered			Layered	Nonlayered		
	fine to coarse grained	fine to coarse grained	fine grained	coarse grained	coarse grained	fine grained	very fine grained
Composition	calcite					chlorite	
			mica		mica		
		quartz					
			feldspar				
				amphibole			
				pyroxene			
Name	MARBLE	QUARTZITE	HORNFELS	GNEISS	SCHIST	PHYLLITE	SLATE

Marble. The transformation from a sedimentary limestone to a metamorphic rock called marble often results in more than a thousand-fold increase in the size of the calcite grains. The grains in the limestone protolith are commonly round in shape, whereas the grains in the marble interlock like a jigsaw puzzle to give a mosaic texture.

The interlocking texture in marble imparts a high coherence to the rock, yet its calcite mineralogy gives it a low hardness, allowing marble to be easily cut and polished. Pure white marble is used extensively for sculpting to form statues, as in the Lincoln Memorial, for building stone, as in the Greek Parthenon, and for ornamental carvings. Many marbles may contain an impurity which imparts a striking color pattern allowing their use in architecture as facings, table tops, and flooring. Italy has more marble quarries than any other country. The United States quarries marble from both the Rocky and Appalachian mountain chains, with major quarries in Vermont and Colorado.

Foliation: Slate. A metamorphic rock in which the platy and elongate shaped minerals are parallel in their orientation is said to be foliated. A foliated texture can be seen in the rock by a tendency for the rock to break along parallel planes.

Slate is a foliated metamorphic rock in which the individual mineral flakes are so small that they can be seen only under the highest magnifications of a microscope. The foliation imparts to the slate the ability to break in near perfect plane. Slate is used as flagstones, roofing, floor tile, hearth stones, and table tops, especially billiard tables. A few slates are used not because of their foliation but because of their composition. Very clay-rich slates are ground because the smaller pieces will bloat when heated to form a material used as a lightweight aggregate.

Metamorphic Differentiation: Gneiss. At relatively high temperatures a metamorphic process occurs in which minerals segregate. The light-colored minerals such as quartz and feldspar move into zones parallel to the rock's foliation, leaving behind alternate zones of dark minerals such as biotite and amphibole. Metamorphic differentiations cause a marked dark versus light layering in the rock. Such rock is commonly called gneiss. Gneiss is quarried locally in many places as dimension stone.

Anatexis: Migmatites. At the more extreme temperatures for regional metamorphism, partial melting will begin to occur within the light-colored layers of a gneiss. The process of partially melting a rock is called anatexis, and this process begins the transformation from metamorphic to igneous rocks. Migmatite is the name for such a mixed rock. Migmatites occur in regions that have experienced a great amount of erosion to reveal the highest levels of metamorphism. Migmatites are common in the shield region of the major continents. The shield for the North American continent is exposed in the upper peninsula of Michigan, northern Wisconsin and Minnesota, and throughout most of Canada.

Migmatites are commonly used as monument stone. The contortions of pattern generated by the partial melting make each stone unique and generally quite handsome. Migmatites are quarried in Minnesota, New York, and Michigan and are used as building stone throughout the United States.

Cataclastite. A special texture develops in rocks when the metamorphic pressure involves tectonic forces having a distinctly linear or planar orientation on the rock. Such opposing forces result in shear stress, and they cause mechanical breakage of the mineral grains in the rock. The name "cataclastite" refers to a metamorphic rock that exhibits a sheared texture containing many fragmented and distorted mineral grains that are often cemented together by a calcite matrix. Cataclastites are formed in tectonic regions that are experiencing active crustal movements. Some cataclastites are quarried and polished for use as a decorative "marble." A famous cataclastite, the "Fantastica di Lasa," is quarried from the northern Alps in Italy because of its attractive and unique appearance.

FURTHER READING: A very readable college-level text on metamorphic rocks and processes is *The Study of Igneous, Sedimentary, and Metamorphic Rocks*, by Loren Raymond, 1995. Individual processes are thoroughly treated in *The Encyclopedia of Igneous and Metamorphic Petrology*, edited by D. R. Bowes, 1990. An introductory treatment with an emphasis on the uses of metamorphic rocks is available in *Rocks and Rock Minerals*, by R. V. Dietrich and B. J. Skinner, 1979.

Dion C. Stewart

SEE ALSO: Asbestos; Corundum and emery; Garnet; Gneiss; Graphite; Kyanite; Marble; Mica; Plate tectonics; Slate; Talc.

Methane

Methane is a naturally occurring gas composed of one atom of carbon and four atoms of hydrogen. This stable chemical compound has the formula CH_4 and is classified as a hydrocarbon.

METHANE, A PRODUCT of the decomposition of plant and animal remains, can be found throughout the earth's crust in varying amounts. Where it is found in greater concentrations, methane is the primary constituent in natural gas deposits, which are the target of oil and gas exploration efforts worldwide. Methane is also found in coal deposits as an integral part of the coalification process and can be recovered from wells drilled into the coal in the same manner that oil and gas are obtained.

Methane was considered a waste by-product of oil production in the past, and hundreds of trillions of cubic feet escaped into the atmosphere in worldwide operations. Only since the 1950's has methane-based natural gas been seen as a viable energy source. Several interstate pipelines have been constructed in the United States, primarily to deliver the gas from its origins in the Gulf Coast and Midwest to the metropolitan areas of the Northeast. As late as the 1960's, natural gas had little value in some areas, and wells drilled for oil that discovered natural gas instead were frequently abandoned for lack of markets.

Beginning in the 1980's, methane has been touted by some as the fuel of the future. It is clean burning, relatively inexpensive, and fairly easily transported throughout the United States. Its supply is forecast to continue for hundreds of years. Research is attempting to substitute methane-based natural gas as a motor fuel in cars, trucks, and locomotives, and many vehicles have been converted to use it. Its use as a motor fuel will undoubtedly increase as more facilities are constructed to service existing and future vehicles.

In spite of its advantages, methane has a significant disadvantage: It is explosive if mixed with air in a range of 5 percent to 15 percent by volume, and it has been blamed for several coal mine disasters. As a result, modern coal mining practice removes as much methane from coal deposits as possible in advance of mining and maintains the methane-air mixture in the mining environment below 1 percent by volume. Since methane is not life-sustaining, its accumulation in underground coal mines can also cause a condition known as "firedamp," which may asphyxiate mining personnel if undetected.

The decomposition of landfill materials has resulted in the production of significant amounts of methane, and several landfill sites in the United States have been drilled into as a source. Methane is an excellent fuel for fuel cells. Fuel cells produce electricity directly from the interaction of hydrocarbon and a catalyst. This interaction is not dependent on combustion but is a heat-producer, giving rise to the utilization of waste heat in various ways. It is expected that future fuel cell research, together with advances in the transportation sector, will place a greater demand on methane resources in the future.

Charles D. Haynes

SEE ALSO: Fuel cells; Methanol; Oil and natural gas, chemistry of; Oil and natural gas reservoirs.

Methanol

Methanol is manufactured by the oxidation of natural gas or the reaction of carbon dioxide with hydrogen. It has numerous chemical uses and has potential as a partial replacement for gasoline.

METHANOL (also called methyl alcohol and wood alcohol) is a colorless liquid with very little taste or odor. It boils at 64.51 degrees Celsius and has a melting point (and triple point) of −97.56 degrees Celsius. At 20 degrees Celsius it has a vapor pressure of 97.60 Torricelli units, a density of 0.7913 grams per milliliter, and an index of refraction of 1.32840. Its molar mass is 32.04 grams. Methanol is completely soluble in water and most organic solvents. It has a flash point of only 11 degrees Celsius and is thus highly flammable. Methanol forms numerous binary and ternary azeotropic combinations with a variety of compounds, so it is difficult to purify. Methanol is of considerable importance: It has long been considered a major industrial organic chemical, and it has more recently been identified as a likely automotive fuel source. The world production capacity for methanol is over 25 million tons per year. In the United States in 1993, over 10 billion pounds of methanol was produced.

Primary Uses of Methanol. A major portion of the methanol produced is used for the production of methyl esters such as methyl acrylate, methyl methacrylate, and methyl terephthalate, which are used in the manufacture of high-volume polymers. Methanol has been used to prepare formaldehyde, but now more direct formaldehyde synthetic methods have somewhat reduced that usage. Since formaldehyde is used in enormous quantities for production of synthetic water-based polymers such as the phenolic and urea resins (employed in plywood manufacture, for example), even that reduced formaldehyde production from methanol is still very important. A growing use for methanol is its reaction with isobutene (2-methylpropene) for the synthesis of methyl tertiary-butyl ether, a gasoline additive that is used in winter in many large cities to reduce air pollution. Another group of major uses of methanol is for the chemical synthesis of acetic acid, methyl chloride, vinyl acetate, vinyl chloride, ethylene glycol (antifreeze), and other compounds. Methanol is also used as a solvent and extracting medium. Some methanol is used for the preparation of synthetic protein.

Methanol has an octane number value of 100; therefore, proposed fuel uses for methanol have come forward repeatedly. During the 1970's a number of processes for producing methanol for fuel purposes from wood or other biomass sources were considered, and they may surface again when hydrocarbon fuel shortages develop. Since methanol combustion products (almost entirely carbon dioxide and water) are nonpolluting, and because automobile engines can be easily modified to burn methanol, it is likely to be the object of increasing attention during the twenty-first century. Since methyl tertiary-butyl ether (MTBE) has an even higher octane number than methanol (or ethanol), continued availability of isobutene for the synthesis of the ether could result in MTBE becoming the favored automotive fuel of the future.

Methanol Production Processes. Before 1930 the most common production method was the anaerobic destructive distillation of hardwoods at temperatures below 400 degrees Celsius. However, this method produced low yields (about 6 gallons per ton of wood) of very impure methanol. Small amounts of relatively impure methanol produced in this manner are added to commercial ethanol to "denature" it and prevent the commercial alcohol's use as a beverage. Fermentation processes used to produce other alcohols have not been successful for methanol. Yet since methanol is found in both plants and animals and is utilized by bacteria, fermentation would still appear to be a likely method if appropriate microorganisms could be identified or if genetically engineered bacteria could be developed for that purpose.

The most often used synthetic processes involve reactions of carbon monoxide and hydrogen (called synthesis gas) using catalysts such as copper, zinc, and/or chromium oxides at elevated pressures (above 300 atmospheres) and at temperatures over 300 degrees Celsius. The high-pressure process is sometimes replaced with a lower-pressure one (below 100 atmospheres) at a somewhat lower temperature. The lower-pressure process requires more purified reactants and a more complex catalyst system but allows the reaction to proceed in simpler reactors. The synthesis gas is obtained by treating natural gas (methane) or petroleum fractions with high-pressure steam. Synthesis gas can also be directly obtained from coal, and if carbon dioxide is easily available, it may be more economically desirable to produce the synthesis gas from the prior reaction of the carbon dioxide with hydrogen. More exotic processes for direct oxidation of methane by use of fuming sulfuric acid (sulfur trioxide in sulfuric acid) are being investigated; they have the potential of ending the need for the initial preparation of the synthesis gas.

Toxicity. Methanol even in minute quantities is a powerful poison, acting on many parts of the nervous system, particularly the optic nerves. Blindness, at least temporary, often results from its ingestion. Methanol is oxidized in the body to formaldehyde and formic acid, which are the major direct culprits in methanol poisoning. Coma and death frequently occur as a result of methanol consumption.

FURTHER READING: Good general sources of information on methanol are J. K. Paul's *Methanol Technology and Application in Motor Fuels*, 1978, and W. H. Cheng and H. H. Kung's *Methanol Production and Use*, 1994. Methanol production technology is well described by S. Lee et al. in *Methanol Synthesis Technology*, 1989; E. Supp in *How to Produce Methanol from Coal*, 1996; J. Falbe in *Chemical Feedstocks from Coal*, 1982; and R. A. Sheldon in *Chemicals from Synthesis Gas*, 1983. Possible fuel uses of methanol are also covered by Gordon Press's *Methanol Fuel: A Bibliography*, 1991, and in the Institute of Petroleum's *The Economic Use of Alcohols and Ethers in Transportation Fuels*, 1985.

William J. Wasserman

SEE ALSO: Biotechnology; Energy economics; Ethanol; Methane; Petroleum refining and processing; Plant domestication and breeding; Plastics; Synthetic Fuels Corporation; Wood and charcoal as fuel resources.

Mica

WHERE FOUND: Micas are common rock-forming minerals and are widely distributed throughout the world. They occur in igneous, metamorphic, and sedimentary rocks. They are mined as sheets or flakes and scrap. Sheet mica is primarily found in Brazil, Madagascar, India, and Canada. Muscovite flakes are mined in the United States from igneous pegmatites and metamorphic schists located in North and South Carolina, Connecticut, Georgia, New Mexico, and South Carolina.

PRIMARY USES: Muscovite sheets are used as electrical insulators in the electronic and computer industries. Scrap mica is ground and used primarily as a coating material and in the paint industry.

DESCRIPTION: The mica group of minerals is composed mainly of muscovite, $KAl_2(AlSi_3O_{10})(OH)_2$; biotite, $K(Mg,Fe)_3(AlSi_3O_{10})(OH)_2$; phlogopite $KMg_3(AlSi_3O_{10})(OH)_2$; and lepidolite, $K(Li,Al)_3(AlSi_3O_{10})(OH)_2$; although there are thirty known mica minerals. Micas are hydrous aluminum silicate minerals that have a perfect basal cleavage. Micas have a hardness of 2.5 to 4 and show a vitreous to pearly luster. Muscovite is a type of mica that is colorless and transparent in thin sheets and white to light brown or light yellow in thicker blocks. Phlogopite is yellow to brown with a copper colored reflection off cleavage surfaces. Biotite is primarily black but can appear dark green or brown. Lepidolite has a distinctive lilac to pink color.

MICAS FORM MONOCLINIC CRYSTALS that inevitably show a perfect basal cleavage. Crystals and their cleavage sheets commonly display a hexagonal form. Muscovite and biotite can be found in thick "books" containing layer upon layer of thin cleavage sheets, which can be up to 10 feet across in pegmatites.

Micas are common throughout the world. Muscovite is characteristic of granites and pegmatites. In metamorphic rocks muscovite is the primary constituent of many mica schists. Biotite is found in igneous rocks ranging from granite pegmatites to diorites, gabbros, and peridotites. It also occurs in silica-rich lavas, porphyries, and a wide range of metamorphic rocks. Phlogopite occurs in metamorphosed magnesium limestones, dolomites, and ultrabasic rocks. Lepidolite occurs only in pegmatites.

Mining of mica started as early as 2000 B.C.E. in India, where it was used as medicine, decoration, and paint. Commercial mining of mica in the United States began in 1803. Mica was used in store windows, shades for open light flames, and furnace viewing glass. When electronic vacuum tubes were developed in the early 1900's, mica was used as spacers and insulators in the tubes, thus beginning its use in the electrical industry.

Muscovite and phologopite are still important commercially because they have a low thermal and electrical conductivity and a high dielectrical strength. Sheet mica is used as electrical insulators, retardation plates in neon helium lasers, optical filters, and washers in the computer industry. The isinglass used in furnace and stove doors from the 1800's to the present is sheet muscovite. Lepidolite is the only mica mined and processed for its composition. It is a source of lithium, which is used in the production of heat-resistant glass.

Scrap and flakes of mica are processed into ground mica and used as a coating on rolled roofing, asphalt shingles, and waterproof fabrics. It is also used in wallpaper to give it a shiny luster, as a lubricant when mixed with oils, and as a pigment extender in paint. A magnesium-rich alteration product of biotite, vermiculite, is used as insulation, packing material, and an ingredient in potting soil.

The United States has limited supplies of sheet mica but is the largest producer of scrap mica. Although there are no environmental problems in mining mica, sheet mica is very expensive to mine because of the intense hand labor needed to mine and process the sheets.

Dion C. Stewart

SEE ALSO: Lithium; Metamorphic processes, rocks, and mineral deposits; Pegmatites.

Mineral Leasing Act of 1920

DATE: Took effect February 25, 1920; subsequently amended many times

The purposes of the Mineral Leasing Act were to expand the government's control over public mineral lands, to promote the development of oil and gas deposits on public lands by private enterprise, and to promote the wise use of selected minerals with a reasonable financial return.

NEARLY ONE-THIRD OF the land in the United States is owned by the federal government. These public lands are concentrated in the West and Alaska and are important sites for mineral resources. The Mineral Leasing Act of 1920 was enacted to establish a system for developing energy minerals (coal, oil shale, oil, and gas) and certain soft-rock minerals (phosphate, potassium, sodium, sulfur, and native asphalt) on onshore public lands. The goals of the act were to expand the secretary of the interior's control over specific minerals on public lands, to promote the development of oil and gas deposits on public lands by private companies, and to promote the wise use of natural resources while receiving a reasonable financial return for the public.

The primary system for mineral development on public lands is based on the Mining Act of 1872. This location system cedes government ownership of commercial mineral deposits to private parties who are able to find them; no royalty (share of the revenue) is paid to the government. This system did not work for oil and gas deposits or for a mineral of strategic concern such as coal (essential for the steam-powered navy of the early 1900's). Problems with developing these types of minerals forced several presidents to withdraw sections of public lands from potential mineral development, seeing this as the only alternative to the existing system. The Mineral Leasing Act created a leasing system as the method for developing these types of minerals.

The core of any leasing system is the allocation of leases. With a lease, the government maintains ownership of the mineral deposit but grants the right to exploit the mineral values to a private party for a set period of time. The government receives a royalty on any production that occurs. The government is able to control what properties are developed, who develops them, and what financial return is received. The method for allocating leases and the amount of royalty to be paid varies. Coal, and oil and gas, leases for known deposits are granted under a competitive bidding scheme. The producers must pay at least a 12.5 percent royalty. In addition, sealed bonus bids are made. A bonus bid is an up-front cash payment. The highest bidder receives the lease if the bid is considered adequate. For other properties, a noncompetitive bidding system is used; this may be a lottery or a first-come, first-served system. A royalty still must be paid on production. Typically, this royalty is 12.5 to 16 percent. Sometimes the royalty is much less if the government wishes to encourage production.

Gary A. Campbell

SEE ALSO: Department of the Interior, U.S.; Land-use regulation and control; General Mining Law of 1872; Public lands; Sagebrush Rebellion.

Mineral resource ownership

Individual ownership of minerals, as occurs in the United States, is relatively unusual. In most countries, most or all mineral wealth is controlled by the government. Although the United States government owns vast areas of mineral property, there is also a tremendous amount of privately owned mineral wealth.

THE IDENTIFICATION OF property, which includes both public and privately owned tracts, is made by several methods of land surveying and land notation. The history of an area frequently determines the method of measurement and mapping techniques. In Texas, for example, there is an entirely different method of land identification than there is in Alabama or Ohio. As far as mineral ownership is concerned, a number of additional complications are involved that do not exist regarding surface ownership.

Surface Versus Mineral Ownership. Much of the individually owned minerals in the United States have resulted from original U.S. government patents and land grants to institutions and private entities. Originally, most land ownership concerned land in its entirety; this type of ownership was called "fee ownership" and implied both surface ownership and mineral ownership all the way down to the center of the earth. Subsequent land transactions have subdivided fee ownership into smaller tracts as well as separating ("severing") surface ownership from mineral ownership. It is also common to find private surface ownership overlying government-owned mineral ownership. The reverse is rare. Sometimes the government-owned minerals in areas of extensive mining activity have been inadver-

tently extracted because of confusion as to the rightful owner.

Mineral ownership can be nebulous and is not as closely defined and monitored in some situations as is surface ownership. As a result, even basic property tax obligations may be ignored through misunderstandings so that mineral property is often "orphaned" by rightful owners and can be secured by more knowledgeable individuals by paying the taxes due or otherwise convincing the local property assessor that they are in possession of the mineral ownership. The folklore of mineral property ownership is filled with stories of the incidental property transfer that leads to vast wealth for the acquirer through subsequent mineral extraction. Although surface property has been known to escalate to hundreds or even thousands of times its initial value, mineral ownership can result in a million or more times its original value through proceeds from minerals extraction. Yet the management of mineral ownership is often not of primary importance to the individual because its value is frequently misunderstood.

The separation of surface from mineral ownership often creates a unique set of problems. If mineral owners have the opportunity to have their minerals extracted, the consequence to the surface owner must be considered. In some states, the mineral owner has "primacy" such that reasonable access to the minerals must be provided; the surface owner must be compensated for damages resulting from mineral-extraction activities. In some areas where mineral extraction is not feasible from surface operations, such as in urban or environmentally sensitive sites, the fate of mineral ownership may be determined in courts of law.

Mineral ownership in many remote areas across the United States has minimal value because no identifiable commercial minerals are evident, or, if they are present, they are too far from markets to have value. In areas of extensive mineral extraction, such as traditional mining provinces or in oil and gas fields, mineral ownership is closely protected and its subdivision complicated. In these areas, the severance of mineral types, depths, and locations is common. For example, if multiple coal deposits exist from the surface to depth, the individual deposits may be identified as to ownership. In southern Illinois, for example the many shallow coal deposits are exclusively reserved for mining, while deeper coal deposits are used for coalbed methane extraction through drilled wells. In oil and gas areas, producing formations are identified and may be separated as to ownership. Frequently, a shallow oil and gas zone may be included in a lease along with deeper zones. A time limit is imposed on the development of the shallow zone such that it reverts to the mineral owner if not exploited. Oil and gas developers may be surprised to learn that they cannot exploit the shallow zone even after committing funds to it. Individual minerals may be separated as well, with coal, oil, natural gas, sulfur, metallic minerals, and industrial minerals being identified as individual entities.

Transactions and Appraisals. Mineral ownership can be exchanged through like-kind trades or exchanges for virtually anything of value. The appraisal of mineral ownership is a frequent activity but involves specialized training. Since many estates contain mineral ownership, the payment of estate taxes depends on an appraisal of the mineral ownership. As compared with surface ownership, which may often be appraised through comparable sales, mineral transactions may be so rare in some areas as to have no standard of comparison. This fact places an additional burden on the appraiser in arriving at an accurate evaluation.

Mineral ownership may be appraised by calculating a discounted present value of future revenues from mineral exploitation. If active mineral extraction operations are under way on a tract, projection of these activities into the future may be relatively accurate. If assumptions of minerals pricing and operating expenses are accurate, the appraisal of mineral ownership may well depend on discounted present value calculations.

Determination of Ownership. The determination of mineral ownership is similar to determination of surface ownership. Title searches are made by professionals who execute a study of the ownership history of a tract of mineral ownership. A chain of title is made to determine if any "clouds" on the title are indicated and to recom-

mend remedies to these deficiencies. A title search may be very simple if the ownership is created from the original United States patent. It can be extremely complicated if the mineral ownership has been involved in numerous transactions, its ownership subdivided, and its minerals severed. No mineral extraction operation, such as mining or oil and gas drilling, is begun without a reasonable title opinion. Otherwise, the mineral exploitation is at-risk as to the payment of proceeds to the rightful owner as well as lawsuits from maligned mineral owners.

Disputes involving mineral property ownership are common, and include boundary disagreements, geological misinterpretations, and depth disputes. Even the classification of minerals sometimes involves litigation. Mineral disputes can also be settled by mediation or arbitration in lieu of court appearances. The nature of dispute settlement may depend on the language agreed upon by parties in earlier transactions.

Wealth is created by mineral ownership transactions as discussed above, where trades may increase the value of the ownership. The greatest amount of wealth enhancement, however, usually results when a royalty from minerals extraction is negotiated. If the mineral deposit is large and valuable, the mineral owner can realize millions of dollars in royalties from mineral extraction. As an example, a coal deposit 6 feet in thickness contains about 10,000 tons per acre. If royalty is negotiated to be $3 per ton, the proceeds to the mineral owner are $30,000 per acre. Only in developed suburban areas will surface property values be greater. Even greater wealth can be generated in areas where solid minerals as well as oil and gas can be exploited. This frequently occurs in the Appalachian Basin in the eastern United States as well as in the Rocky Mountains.

Mineral Leasing. If mineral leasing is desired, there are guidelines that govern most lease transactions. Mineral leases involve a mineral owner, called the lessor, and a mineral operator or intermediary called the lessee. A mineral lease usually contains a primary term, bonus, and royalty rate. The term is the time extent of the lease agreement, and can vary from one year to as much as ten years. Multiple-year leases may also involve delay rentals, or annual rental fees to retain the lease. Others are paid up at the outset of leasing, meaning that no delay rentals are due for the primary term of the lease. Some leases also have extensions past the primary term. Oil and gas leases usually specify that a lease can be held past the expiration of the primary term if commercial production has been established and is sustained with no cessation over a term, usually ninety days. Stone and coal mining leases do not usually have a held-by-production clause, but rather provide for protection of future mining activity by using extensions to the primary term that can be unilaterally requested by the lessee with suitable advance notice to the lessor.

Lease bonuses are defined as the amount of consideration due to the lessor at the time of lease execution. This amount varies with the value of the lease, and it may be as little as zero or as much as thousands of dollars per acre. In places where an oil and gas "play" is under way, lease bonuses can be in the thousands of dollars for land parcels no larger than town lots. On the other hand, tracts intended for pure exploration drilling ("wildcats") may secure lease bonuses of only one to ten dollars per acre, if anything. Governmental agencies, such as the Bureau of Land Management in the U.S. Department of the Interior, often demand larger than average bonuses because they may control the fate of mineral development.

The most important part of a mineral lease is the royalty. This is the income accruing to the mineral owner over the productive life of the lease. Royalty arrangements can be as varied as there are minerals and areas of the United States, but these arrangements often involve a percentage of the minerals produced. In times past, the royalty was paid "in-kind," meaning that the royalty owner was issued the proportionate share of the mineral in the same form as the operator and could market or keep it for domestic use as desired. Modern operating practice, which usually includes long-term contracts for the marketing of minerals, provides the royalty owner with a percentage of the selling price. Royalty percentages vary from 2 percent of the selling price in the rock and stone industry to as high as 25 percent or even 30 percent in off-

shore oil and gas operations. Coal mining has royalty rates in the 5 percent to 10 percent range. In most cases, there has been a tendency for royalty percentages to increase over the past several decades. Another trend in mineral leases is for the royalty interest to bear certain expenses of operation, particularly if a very large development cost is necessary to jump-start the mineral exploitation. These are usually fees involved in refining or marketing the product.

Measurement of the bulk mineral or even the basis for its pricing are often the cause of litigation where the royalties are based on selling price. For example, if the mineral commodity is sold to an affiliate, a "sweetheart price" lower than fair-market value may result. Endless disputes over property boundaries and language in mineral conveyance documents, leases, and deeds have given rise to a legal specialty in mineral law and even to subspecialties such as oil and gas law.

Certain clauses in leases protect the lessor from a mineral operator making a half-hearted effort to develop the lease. One such clause requires timely development of the leased tract either through continuity of production or, in the case of oil and gas development, the steady drilling of new wells to prevent forfeiture of the lease.

Development Priorities. The question of mineral development priority frequently arises in areas having multiple mineral resources. Interference is minimized if the minerals in question can be recovered simultaneously. However, there are situations where the exploitation of a particular mineral commodity must wait until another is fully exploited. Examples of this include the extraction of near-surface minerals or the recovery of deep minerals where the exploitation of one would compromise the exploitation of the other.

Even relatively simple situations can result in expensive and time-consuming litigation. Some mineral ownership assignment documents specify the "superiority" of certain mineral commodities and place priorities on their extraction. If the purchase of mineral ownership is contemplated, the title search should reveal whether exploitation priorities are specified. As mentioned above, disputes involving mineral ownership and minerals development have been and still are quite common for a number of practical reasons. Inaccuracies in land surveying, the evolution of geologic nomenclature, the shifting of streambeds, and dishonest transactions all create discord. Attorneys and experts in mineral development team to convince regulatory agencies, courts of law, and mediators that the evidence supports their client's claims. Sometimes, the evidence is clear-cut. Most often, however, a judgment decision is necessary where the evidence is far from perfect.

Measurements and Disputes. A classic type of dispute in oil and gas development involves the drilling of wells to drain underneath an adjacent tract. In the past, innumerable disputes concerned this "hot oil" problem. Modern drilling technology, with its downhole drilling motors, permits drilling a vertical well and then directing it to the horizontal in a prescribed radius of curvature, such that a well could be 5,000 feet in depth and its bottom could be 2,000 feet laterally from its surface location. These wells are "surveyed" by using dip and azimuth tools in the drillhole to pinpoint the location of the bottom of the hole at any time, thus preventing a dispute over whether adjacent property rights are being violated.

Downhole depth surveys also ensure that the oil or gas well has not penetrated a lower zone that is severed from upper zones in a multiple-pay area. Instruments can be used to determine whether an oil or gas zone is being produced from any zone downhole.

Both the potential inaccuracy of measuring devices and the possibility of dishonest measurement of bulk commodities typify the problems associated with being a mineral owner seeking a royalty payment. The production of solid bulk minerals such as coal is determined by weighing a truck or railroad car on a large drive-through scale, then loading it and subtracting its "tare" weight to determine the amount of solid material being transported. Liquid commodities such as oil are measured by flow meters or storage tank measurements. Gaseous commodities such as natural gas are measured by rotating meters or orifice plates. All these measurement systems contain inherent inaccuracies such that the sys-

tems must be "proved," or calibrated against a measurement standard at regular intervals.

The measurement of solid or liquid minerals in floating vessels such as barges is made by displacement of the barge in water. This is done by scaling its draft in water in an unloaded and loaded condition. The draft per weight of cargo is then converted into tonnage.

Timber Rights and Water Rights. Other types of property rights may be seen in certain parts of the United States. Examples of these rights are timber ownership and the right to use surface or underground water resources. The ownership of water resources is particularly important in the more arid areas of the southwest, and legal battles are frequently fought over access to potable and irrigation water.

Timber ownership is frequently bought and sold in the southeast and northwest areas of the United States. In areas where tree harvesting is a recurring endeavor, the right to grow timber is valuable and is often at odds with the extractive industries.

FURTHER READING: Good sources for in-depth analyses include Richard V. Hughes, *Oil Property Valuation*, 1978; Robert S. Thompson and John D. Wright, *Oil Property Evaluation*, 1985; *Energy Law and Transactions*, vols. 1-5, published by Matthew Bender, 1990; and John S. Lowe, *Oil and Gas Law*, 1984.

Charles D. Haynes

SEE ALSO: Mineral Leasing Act of 1920; Oil and natural gas drilling and wells; Oil industry; Takings law and eminent domain; Timber industry; Water rights.

Mineral resource use, early history of

Beginning with the Stone Age, people have used minerals both to forge the material part of civilization and to express their artistic natures.

THERE WERE GENIUSES in the family tree of humankind many thousands of years before recorded history began. One of them was the first to use a stone as a tool, an important step in the ascent of humankind, for it gave people greater control over their world and their lives. Someone was the first to make a clay pot, the first to find a use for tar, the first to beat native copper into a useful shape. Somewhere in Mesopotamia in the seventh millennium B.C.E., another genius invented the kiln. A kiln is a furnace that retains and focuses a fire's heat and allows the air flow to be controlled. The kiln technology of the eastern Mediterranean, Mesopotamia, and Egypt was unsurpassed, and it was there that production techniques for pottery, bricks, cement, glass, copper, and iron were first mastered.

Stone Tools. The oldest stone tools were crude and were made from whatever rocks were at hand. Later tools were made from stones chosen because they could be shaped by chipping and retain a sharp edge. Flints, cherts, and jaspers were among the most common stones used. Obsidian is more brittle than flint, but its edge can be made very sharp. When it was available and there was someone skilled enough to work it, obsidian was preferred for cutting tools.

To shape a stone by chipping, a second stone may be used to strike glancing blows along the edge of the first stone. Common stone tools include hand axes, scrapers, flint knives, and awls (used to make holes in hides). Stone points were fastened to spears and arrows. Sickles to cut grain were made by setting sharp stone chips into wooden handles. A hollow can be formed in a stone by pecking with a hard sharp rock. Stone bowls, lamps, and traylike grindstones were made with this procedure from limestone, sandstone, granite, and basalt. (Grain was ground by placing it in the grindstone and then rubbing it with a smaller hand-held stone.)

Building with Stone. Because of the relative ease with which they can be shaped, limestone and sandstone are often used in buildings. Granite is more durable but is harder to shape. Granite is formed from an underground mass of molten rock that cools very slowly. Limestone and sandstone are sedimentary rocks. Sediments turn to rock as the pressure of overlying layers squeezes water from between the sediment particles. As the water is driven out, compounds dissolved in the water come out of solution and cement the sediment particles together. Calcite (calcium carbonate), silica (silicon dioxide) and hematite (iron oxide) are typical cementing agents.

Limestone is mostly calcium carbonate. It occasionally is precipitated as a shallow sea evaporates, but more often it is built up from shells of dead sea organisms. A limestone-like sediment containing a large fraction of calcium magnesium carbonate is called dolomite and is a little harder than limestone. Limestone and dolomite subjected to sufficient heat and pressure become marble.

With the passage of time, people became proficient at quarrying, shaping, and moving stone. The great pyramid of Khufu was constructed about 2600 B.C.E. It is 50 percent taller than the Statue of Liberty and is estimated to contain 2,300,000 stone blocks weighing an average of 2.5 tons each. The core is made from huge yellowish limestone blocks from a nearby quarry, while the outer face and the inner passageways are of a finer limestone brought from farther away. Khufu's burial chamber lies deep within the pyramid and is built of granite from Aswan.

The leaning tower of Pisa, another fine example of early stone construction, was begun in 1174 C.E., more than three thousand years after the construction of the great pyramid. The tower is constructed of white marble and has colored marble inlays on the exterior. Its walls are nearly 4 meters thick at the base and taper to about half that at the top, 56 meters above the ground. In spite of its pronounced tilt, it is a beautiful structure of arches and columns.

Cement. Gypsum is a soft rock that forms as a precipitate when a restricted body of seawater evaporates. Chemically, it is hydrous calcium sulfate. ("Hydrous" means that water molecules are incorporated into the mineral's crystal structure.) If powdered and heated to drive off its water content, gypsum becomes the basic ingredient of mortar. The Egyptians used gypsum mortar in building the pyramids. When limestone is heated in a kiln, carbon dioxide is driven off, leaving quicklime (calcium oxide). If clayey limestone is used, the quicklime will contain large amounts of silica and alumina. This mix is called hydraulic lime. Adding water to hydraulic lime produces a cement that will set and harden even underwater by forming calcium silicates and aluminates. The Romans produced a hydraulic lime mortar called pozzolana

In the first century C.E., *Romans used stone and pozzolana, a cement made of quicklime, sand, and volcanic tuff, to build the Colosseum.* (Archive Photos)

by combining quicklime with sand and powdered volcanic tuff mined near the Italian town of Pozzuli. Pozzolana was used in the construction of the Colosseum at Rome.

Building with Brick. Construction stone is rare in the fertile land beside the Euphrates, so the ancient Mesopotamians built with bricks. Ruins at Ur of the Chaldees have yielded both burned and unburned bricks that are five thousand years old. Clay suitable for making bricks is found throughout the world. Clay particles are very fine and consist primarily of various forms of hydrous aluminum silicates along with organic material and other minerals. Bricks are usually shaped in a mold and then left in the sun to dry. Dried bricks may then be placed in a kiln for a process called "burning," in which they are heated enough to cause the clay particles to fuse.

The ancient city of Babylon, which reached its zenith under Nebuchadnezzar in the sixth century B.C.E., was built with bricks. Its massive outer wall was built with a core of sun-dried brick and faced with burned brick. The famous Ishtar gate stood 12 meters high and featured 575 glazed brick mosaics in which golden dragons and young bulls stood out in relief against a blue-green background. One hundred twenty golden lions on blue-green backgrounds lined the walls of the street that led from the Ishtar gate to the temple of Marduk.

Pottery and Porcelain. Pottery making is probably as old as civilization itself. To be durable, a clay pot must be fired in a kiln so that clay particles fuse and the glaze (if present) melts to form a glasslike surface. In the Near East, pottery dating back to the seventh millennium B.C.E. has been discovered. Painted pottery was already common in northern Mesopotamia before 5000 B.C.E., and the high-speed potter's wheel was being used in ancient Susa by 4000 B.C.E. About that same time, the Egyptians began working with colorful and lustrous glazes that may have led them to the development of glass.

Porcelain is a type of ceramic made from kaolin (a special white clay with very few impurities), feldspar (aluminum silicates), and quartz (silica). Porcelain paste is stiff and harder to shape than normal clay paste, but it retains its shape well at high temperatures. Because of this, porcelain pieces with very thin walls can be made. The Chinese became experts at crafting porcelain pieces and in using colorful enamels and glazes to decorate them. Vases made during the Ming dynasty (1368-1644 C.E.) have become legendary.

Glass. Some of the oldest glass objects known are beads found in an Egyptian tomb dated at 2500 B.C.E. About a thousand years later, the first glass vessels appear in Egypt. These vessels were made by winding a string of glass around a clay mold held on the end of a rod. The technique of glassblowing was in use by the first century B.C.E., although some tomb murals may show it being used much earlier.

The Romans were the first to use glass windows, and there are glass windows in the public baths of Pompeii, the city destroyed by an eruption of Mount Vesuvius in 79 C.E. As with pottery, some artists created glass vessels of exquisite beauty. Other artists turned their talents to stained glass windows such as those of the Sainte-Chapelle in Paris (consecrated in 1248 C.E.). Its stained glass windows depicting biblical scenes completely dominate the walls and soar upward in a kaleidoscope of red, blue, green, yellow, and white.

The chief constituent of glass is white sand (silica), but melting pure silica requires a temperature above 1,700 degrees Celsius. If soda ash (sodium carbonate) is added as a flux, the melting point is reduced to 850 degrees Celsius, a temperature more easily achieved. The resulting glass is water soluble, but adding limestone (calcium carbonate) to the melt results in insoluble glass. A typical mixture is 75 percent silica, 10 percent lime, and 15 percent soda. Soda ash can be obtained by leaching wood or seaweed ash or by mining natron, another salt deposited as an entrapped sea evaporates.

The Seven Metals of Antiquity. As far back as 8000 B.C.E., Stone Age people gathered shining bits of gold to use as ornaments and decorations. Seams of gold in solid rock such as granite are called lode deposits. They are mined by tunneling into the rock. As gold-bearing rock weathers away, gold dust and gold nuggets wash into streambeds to form placer deposits. Placer deposits may be mined by scooping up sand and gravel in a pan and then carefully washing away everything but the dense grains of gold. The story of Jason and the Golden Fleece probably refers to the ancient practice of placing a fleece in running water where it could collect gold dust as placer deposit sand was washed over it. The golden death mask of Tutankhamen (1352 B.C.E.) is an excellent example of the artistry with which gold was worked in ancient times.

Copper was discovered about the same time as gold, since it can also be found naturally as a metal. Copper pins dating from 7000 B.C.E. have been found in Turkey. Malachite is a green-colored copper ore often found near a seam of copper metal. Copper metal may be produced from malachite by mixing it with charcoal and heating the mixture in a kiln. The earliest tools cast from molten copper appear in Mesopotamia around 4000 B.C.E.

Lead may have been the next metal discovered, since lead beads dated to 6500 B.C.E. have been found in Turkey. Lead does not occur as a free metal in nature, but the lead ore called galena (lead sulfide) does have a metallic look. If galena is combined with charcoal and heated to only 327 degrees Celsius, metallic lead is produced. Since lead is soft and ductile, the Romans found it well suited for making pipes. Lead often contains traces of silver. Silver artifacts date back to about 4000 B.C.E. Metallic silver is rarely found in nature, but it does occur. Pure silver is harder than gold but softer than copper. As with gold, silver was first used to make ornaments and jewelry.

By 2500 B.C.E. the Sumerians discovered that mixing different types of ore produced a metal that melted at a lower temperature and was harder than copper. They had produced a copper-tin alloy now called bronze. Bronze was widely used to make tools and weapons. Tin was not produced as a separate metal until five hundred years later. Tin ore is stannic oxide, a hard material that remains after softer surrounding rock weathers away. Mercury can be obtained by heating cinnabar (mercury sulfide) in the presence of oxygen. Mercury has been found in tombs dating from 1500 B.C.E. It is a liquid at room temperature and can dissolve silver and gold to form an amalgam, a process that is sometimes used in mining.

Smelted iron did not become common until around 1500 B.C.E., although it was first produced a thousand years earlier, and meteoric iron was used even before that. Metallic iron may be produced by heating a mixture of hematite (iron oxide) and charcoal in a kiln. Only the rich could afford bronze, but when iron became cheaper than bronze, iron tools and weapons were made in large numbers. Being more broadly distributed through society than bronze, iron greatly changed farming and warfare.

Salt. Salt (sodium chloride) is essential for human health. It is generally accepted that a diet consisting mostly of raw or roasted meat requires no added salt, but if the meat is boiled or if the diet consists primarily of grains, some salt is essential. Salt has also been used as a preservative for fish and meat since ancient times.

People collected salt at brine springs or from dried tidal pools at the seashore. Later, ocean water was let into artificial pools that were then sealed and allowed to dry. In colder climates salt water was boiled down in ceramic trays and later in metal trays. Many areas of the world have underground salt beds formed as ancient seas dried up. Rock salt has been mined from such deposits beginning in Roman times, if not earlier.

Petroleum Products and Natural Gas. The use of petroleum goes back to the Stone Age, when bitumen was used to cement stones to wooden handles. ("Bitumen," loosely used, refers to various tars and asphalt.) The Sumerians of 3000 B.C.E., and later the Assyrians and the Babylonians, used a mortar of bitumen, sand, and reeds for their great brick structures. They also made asphalt roads, used tar as an adhesive for tiles, and caulked ships with tar. Dioscorides, a surgeon in Nero's army, said that the Sicilians burned petroleum oil in their lamps in place of olive oil. Eventually, petroleum grease was used as a lubricant, paraffin wax was used for candles, and naphtha (a highly volatile oil) found use as an incendiary agent in warfare.

At first, bitumen was taken from natural tar pits and oil and gas seeps. Three of the most famous are the La Brea Tar Pits of California, the Pitch Lake of Trinidad, and the Perpetual Fires of Baku, a large gas seep area in Azerbaijan. Later, oil was taken from tunnels and pits dug near oil seeps. By the sixth century B.C.E. the Chinese could drill wells 100 meters deep. While drilling for fresh water or salt water, Chinese miners occasionally found oil or natural gas instead. This is exactly what happened to the Chinese while drilling for salt water in Szechwan about 250 C.E. Being opportunists, the workers at some salt works burned the gas to provide heat to evaporate the brine. With the passage of time, the production and use of petroleum increased, but it did not become a major resource until kerosene became cheaper than whale oil in the mid-nineteenth century.

Coal. Coal is the fossilized remains of plants that lived hundreds of millions of years ago. A coal bed begins as a thick layer of peat in a swamp that is later invaded by the advancing sea. Layers of sediment compress the peat, which dries, hardens, and eventually turns into coal. Coal consists primarily of carbon but also contains smaller amounts of water, light oil, tar, sulfur, and phosphorus.

The Chinese are said to have used coal in the first century B.C.E., and in the thirteenth century C.E. Marco Polo described a black stone that the Chinese dug from the mountains and burned for fuel. Polo seems to have been unaware that coal was already being used in Europe and England. In fact, Theophrastus described various Mediterranean locations where coal was used as fuel in the fourth century B.C.E. Long before Polo's time, "sea coal" was gathered regularly from some of England's beaches, where it washed ashore, and coal was mined from shallow pits in other regions. However, Europeans used coal only on a small scale until the fifteenth century C.E., when it became widely used in kilns.

FURTHER READING: The classic work on Renaissance mining and metals is *De Re Metallica*, by Georgius Agricola, 1556. Skimming the text and studying the drawings of wooden machinery is fascinating. *Gold: An Illustrated History*, by Vincent Buranelli, 1979, has some marvelous pictures of ancient artifacts. *The Coming of the Age of Iron*, edited by Theodore Wertime and James Muhly, 1980, is an excellent but somewhat demanding treatment. *The Illustrated Encyclopedia of the Mineral Kingdom*, Alan Wooley, consulting editor, 1978, is a nicely illustrated reference on native elements, ores, and minerals. *Neptune's Gift: A History of Common Salt*, by Robert Multhauf, 1978, is a sound and comprehensive treatment. *Ceramics of the World from 4000 B.C. to the Present*, edited by Lorenzo Camusso and Sandro Bortone, 1992, is full of magnificent pictures and authoritative text. *The Atlas of Early Man*, by Jacquetta Hawkes, 1976, is a well-illustrated and easily read historical overview of innovations.

Charles W. Rogers

SEE ALSO: Brick; Bronze; Ceramics; Clays; Coal; Copper; Glass; Gold; Iron; Lead; Mercury; Metals and metallurgy; Native elements; Oil and natural gas drilling and wells; Silver; Tin; Zinc.

Minerals, structure and physical properties of

Minerals—naturally occurring inorganic solids with definite chemical composition and definite crystal structure—are the primary constituents of rocks; they are also found in soil. The variety of minerals is huge, and their myriad uses range from use as gemstones and precious metals to applications in building materials, electronics, food, and pharmaceuticals.

MINERALS ARE THE building blocks of rocks, and they have many economic uses. Minerals such as diamond, ruby, emerald, and sapphire are precious gems. Other minerals are valuable metals (gold, silver, platinum, copper) or metal ores, such as hematite (iron), sphalerite (zinc), ga-lena (lead), and bauxite (aluminum). Other minerals are used as salt (halite), lubricants (graphite), abrasives (corundum), and fertilizer (apatite), as well as in pharmaceuticals (sulfur), steel making (fluorite), plaster (gypsum and anhydrite), lime, and portland cement (calcite and dolomite).

A mineral is defined as a naturally occurring, inorganic solid with a definite chemical composition (or range of compositions within certain limits) that can be expressed by a chemical formula, and an orderly internal crystalline structure (its atoms are arranged in a definite pattern which is reflected in the shape of its crystals and in its cleavage). Only substances that meet these precise requirements are considered minerals. As a result, synthetic gems, which may be physi-

Physical Properties of Minerals

Property	Explanation
Chemical composition	Chemical formula that defines the mineral
Cleavage	Tendency to break in smooth, flat planes along zones of weak bonding; depends on structure
Color	Depends on presence of major elements in the chemical composition; may be altered by trace elements or defects in structure; often not definitive
Crystal shape	Outward expression of the atomic crystal structure
Crystal structure	Three-dimensional ordering of the atoms that form the mineral
Density	Mass per unit volume (grams per cubic centimeter)
Electrical properties	Properties having to do with electric charge; quartz, for example, is piezoelectric (emits charge when squeezed)
Fracture	Tendency for irregular breakage (not along zones of weak bonding)
Hardness	Resistance of mineral to scratching or abrasion; measured on a scale of 1-10 (Mohs hardness scale)
Luminescence	Emission of electromagnetic waves from mineral; some minerals are fluorescent, some thermoluminescent
Luster	Reflectivity of the surface; may be either metallic or nonmetallic
Magnetism	Degree to which mineral is attracted to a magnet
Radioactivity	Instability of mineral; radioactive minerals are always isotopes
Specific gravity	Relative density: ratio of weight of substance to weight of equal volume of water at 4 degrees Celsius
Streak	Color of powdered form; more definitive than color
Taste	Salty, bitter, etc.; applies only to some minerals
Tenacity	Resistance to bending, breakage, crushing, tearing: termed as brittle, malleable, ductile, sectile, flexible, or elastic

cally and chemically identical to natural gemstones, are not considered minerals.

Minerals have specific physical properties that result from their chemical composition and crystal structure, and many minerals can be identified by these properties. Physical properties include hardness, color, luster, streak, cleavage, density or specific gravity, and crystal form. Some minerals also have additional diagnostic physical properties, including tenacity, taste, magnetism, electrical properties, luminescence, reaction to hydrochloric acid, and radioactivity.

Hardness. Hardness is a mineral's resistance to scratching or abrasion. Hardness is a result of crystal structure or atomic arrangement. The stronger the chemical bonds between the atoms, the harder the mineral. For example, two minerals may have an identical chemical composition but different crystal structures, such as diamond and graphite, which are both carbon. Diamond is the hardest known mineral, but graphite is so soft that it rubs off on the fingers or a piece of paper (it is used as pencil "lead"). The differences in crystal structure produce the vastly different hardnesses of these two minerals.

Ten minerals have been arranged in order of increasing hardness and are referred to as the Mohs hardness scale, devised in 1822 by a German mineralogist, Friedrich Mohs. The minerals of the Mohs hardness scale, in order from softest to hardest, are: (1) talc, (2) gypsum, (3) calcite, (4) fluorite, (5) apatite, (6) potassium feldspar (orthoclase), (7) quartz, (8) topaz, (9) corundum, and (10) diamond. Minerals can scratch other minerals of the same or lesser hardness. The hardness of minerals can be tested using common materials, including the fingernail (a little over 2), copper (about 3), a steel nail or pocket knife (a little over 5), a piece of glass (about 5.5), and a steel file (6.5).

Color. Although a prominent feature of minerals, color is not a reliable indicator for identifying minerals. The color of some minerals is the result of major elements in their chemical formula, such as the blue color of azurite and the green color of malachite (copper), the pink color of rhodonite and rhodochrosite (manganese), and the yellow color of sulfur. Many minerals come in a variety of colors. Quartz is color-

less and transparent when pure, but it may also be white (milky quartz), pink (rose quartz), purple (amethyst), yellow (citrine), brown (smoky quartz), or other colors. Similarly, feldspar and fluorite come in many hues. Color may be caused by impurities, such as iron (pink, green, or greenish yellow), titanium (pink or blue), chromium (red or green), vanadium (green), and nickel (yellow). Milky quartz is white because it contains tiny fluid inclusions. Coloration can be the result of defects in the crystal structure; for example, the purple of amethyst and fluorite, and the brown of smoky quartz. Unusual colors may also be induced in minerals by exposing them to radiation, which damages the crystal structure (such as black quartz).

Luster. Luster refers to the "shine," or quality of reflectivity of light from the mineral's surface. Minerals can be divided into two luster groups: metallic luster and nonmetallic luster. Metallic minerals include economically valuable metals such as gold, silver, and native copper, and some metal sulfides such as pyrite (FeS_2 or iron sulfide) and galena (PbS or lead sulfide). Nonmetallic minerals include those with vitreous or glassy luster (quartz), earthy or dull luster (kaolinite and other clays), pearly (talc), silky (fibrous minerals such as gypsum, malachite, and chrysotile asbestos), greasy (nepheline), resinous (resembling resin or amber, such as sulfur), and adamantine or brilliant (diamond).

Streak. Streak refers to the color of the mineral in powdered form, viewed after the mineral is rubbed on an unglazed porcelain tile or streak plate. Streak color is more diagnostic than mineral color because it is constant for a particular mineral. A mineral may come in several colors, but its streak is the same color for all. Streak color is not always what one might predict from examining the mineral; a sparkling silver-colored mineral, specular hematite, has a red-brown streak, and pyrite, a golden metallic mineral, has a dark gray streak. Not all minerals have a streak. The streak plate has a hardness of about 7 on the Mohs hardness scale. Minerals harder than this will not leave a streak, but their powdered colors can be studied by crushing a small piece.

Cleavage. Cleavage is one of the most diagnostic physical properties of minerals. Cleavage re-

Feldspar is one of the two most abundant mineral types in the earth's crust (quartz is the other). Here feldspar's typical two-directional, 90-degree cleavage can be seen. (U.S. Geological Survey)

fers to the tendency of some minerals to break along smooth, flat planes which are related to zones of weak bonding between atoms in the crystal structure. Some minerals, however, have no planes of weakness in their crystal structure and therefore lack cleavage. Cleavage is discussed by referring to the number of different sets of planes of breakage and the angles between them. Minerals that have a prominent flat, sheetlike cleavage (such as the micas, muscovite and biotite) have one direction of cleavage, or perfect basal cleavage. This sheetlike cleavage makes muscovite economically valuable; it was once used in window-making material and is still used in some stove windows and in electrical insulation.

Feldspar and pyroxene have two directions of cleavage at right angles to each other, and the amphiboles (hornblende and others) have two directions of cleavage at approximately 60 degrees and 120 degrees to each other. Other minerals have three directions of cleavage. Halite (table salt) and galena have cubic cleavage (three directions of cleavage at right angles to one another) and break into cubes. Calcite has rhombohedral cleavage (three directions of cleavage not at right angles; the angle is about 74 degrees) and breaks into rhombohedrons. Fluorite has four directions of cleavage and breaks into octahedrons with triangular faces. Sphalerite has six directions of cleavage.

Fracture. Irregular breakage in minerals without planes of weak bonding is fracture. There are several types of fracture. Many minerals have uneven or irregular fracture. Conchoidal fracture is characterized by smooth, curved breakage surfaces, commonly marked by fine parallel lines resembling the surface of a shell (seen in quartz, obsidian, and glass). Rocks and minerals with conchoidal fracture were used by American Indians for arrowheads. Hackly fracture is jagged with sharp edges and is characteristic of metals such as copper. Fibrous or splintery fracture occurs in asbestos and sometimes gypsum. Earthy fracture occurs in clay minerals such as kaolinite.

Density and Specific Gravity. Density is defined as mass per unit volume, or how heavy a material is for its size. Specific gravity (or relative density) is commonly used when referring to minerals. Specific gravity expresses the ratio between the weight of a mineral and the weight of an equal volume of water at 4 degrees Celsius. The terms density and specific gravity are sometimes used interchangeably, but density requires the inclusion of units of measure, whereas specific gravity is unitless. Quartz has a specific gravity of 2.65. Barite has a specific gravity of 4.5 (heavy for a nonmetallic mineral), which makes it economically valuable for use in oil and gas well drilling. Metals have higher specific gravity than nonmetals, for example, galena (7.4 to 7.6), and gold (15.0 to 19.3). The high specific gravity of gold allows it to be separated from less dense minerals by panning.

Tenacity, Taste, and Magnetism. Tenacity is the resistance of a mineral to bending, breaking, crushing, or tearing. Minerals may be brittle (break or powder easily), malleable (can be hammered into thin sheets), ductile (can be drawn into a thin wire), sectile (can be cut into thin slivers with a knife), elastic (bend but return to their original form), or flexible (bend and stay bent). Metallic minerals are commonly malleable and ductile (gold, copper). Copper is used for electrical wire because of its ductility.

Some minerals can be identified by taste. Taste is a property of halite (NaCl), used as table salt. Sylvite (KCl, or potassium chloride) has a bitter salty taste and is used as a salt substitute for people with high blood pressure because it does not contain sodium.

Magnetism is a property that causes certain minerals to be attracted to a magnet. Magnetite (Fe_3O_4) and pyrrhotite ($Fe_{1-x}S$) are the only common magnetic minerals. Lodestone, a variety of magnetite, acts as a natural magnet. In the presence of a powerful magnetic field, some other iron-bearing minerals become magnetic (garnet, biotite, and tourmaline), whereas other minerals are repelled by the magnet (gypsum, halite, and quartz). Electromagnetic separators are used to separate minerals with different magnetic susceptibilities.

Electrical Properties. Some minerals have electrical properties. Piezoelectricity occurs when pressure is exerted in a particular direction in a mineral (along its polar axis), causing a flow of electrons or electrical current. Piezoelectricity was first detected in quartz in 1881, and it has since been used in a number of applications ranging from submarine detection to keeping time (in quartz watches). When subjected to an alternating electrical current, quartz is mechanically deformed and vibrates; radio frequencies are controlled by the frequency of vibration of the quartz.

Pyroelectricity is caused when temperature changes in a mineral create uneven thermal expansion and deformation. Tourmaline and quartz are pyroelectric.

Luminescence. Luminescence is emission of light from a mineral. Minerals that luminesce or glow during exposure to ultraviolet light, X rays, or cathode rays are fluorescent. If the luminescence continues after the radiation source is turned off, the mineral is phosphorescent. The glow results from impurities in the mineral absorbing invisible, short-wavelength radiation and then reemitting radiation at longer wavelengths (visible light). Minerals vary in their ability to absorb different wavelengths of ultraviolet (UV) light. Some fluoresce only in short wavelength UV, some fluoresce only in long wavelength UV, and some fluoresce in both types. Fluorescence is unpredictable; not all minerals of a given type fluoresce. Minerals that commonly fluoresce include fluorite, calcite, diamond, scheelite, willemite, hyalite, autunite, and scapolite. Fluorescence has some practical applications in prospecting and mining. Synthetic phosphorescent materials have also been developed for commercial uses.

Some minerals emit light when heated. This property is called thermoluminescence. Thermoluminescent minerals include fluorite, calcite, apatite, scapolite, lepidolite, and feldspar. Minerals that luminesce when crushed, scratched, or rubbed are triboluminescent. This is a property of fluorite, sphalerite, and lepidolite, and less commonly of pectolite, amblygonite, feldspar, and calcite.

Reaction to Hydrochloric Acid. Calcite ($CaCO_3$) and other carbonate minerals effervesce or fizz in hydrochloric acid, but some will not react unless the acid is heated or the mineral is powdered. Bubbles of carbon dioxide (CO_2) gas are released, and the reaction proceeds as follows:

$$CaCO_3 + 2 \ HCl \rightarrow CaCl_2 + H_2O + CO_2 \ (gas)$$

Radioactivity. Radioactive minerals contain unstable elements that alter spontaneously to other kinds of elements, releasing subatomic particles and energy. Radioactivity can be detected using Geiger-Müller counters, ionization chambers, scintillometers, and similar instruments. Some elements have several different isotopes, differing by the number of neutrons in the nucleus. Radioactive isotopes include uranium-235 (^{235}U), uranium-238 (^{238}U), and thorium-232 (^{232}Th). Uranium-235 is the primary fuel for nuclear power plants. Radioactive minerals include uraninite (pitchblende), carnotite, uranophane, and thorianite. Radioactive minerals occur in granites and granite pegmatites, in sandstones, and in black organic-rich shales, and are used for nuclear energy, atomic bombs, coloring glass and porcelain, in photography, and as a chemical reagent. Radioactivity is also used in radiometric dating to determine the ages of rocks and minerals.

Classification of Minerals. Minerals have been classified or grouped in several ways, but classification based on chemical composition is the most widely used. Minerals are grouped into the following twelve categories on the basis of their chemical formulas: native elements, oxides and hydroxides, sulfides, sulfosalts, sulfates, halides, carbonates, nitrates, borates, phosphates, tungstates, and silicates.

Native Elements. Native elements are minerals composed of a single element that is not combined with other elements. About twenty native elements occur (not including atmospheric gases), and they are divided into metals, semimetals, and nonmetals. The native metals include gold (Au), silver (Ag), copper (Cu), iron (Fe), platinum (Pt), and others. They share the physical properties of malleability, hackly fracture, and high specific gravity, along with metallic luster. Their atoms are held together by weak metallic bonds. They are excellent conductors of heat and electricity and have fairly low melting points. The native semimetals include arsenic (As), bismuth (Bi), antimony (Sb), tellurium (Te), and selenium (Se). They are brittle and much poorer conductors of heat. These properties result from bonding intermediate between true metallic and covalent. The native nonmetals include sulfur (S) and two forms of carbon (C), diamond and graphite. These minerals have little in common, but they are distinctive and easily identified. Diamond and graphite are polymorphs, a term meaning "many forms." Their chemical composition is identical, but they have different crystal structures. Diamond has a tight, strongly bonded structure, whereas graphite has a loose, open structure consisting of sheets of atoms.

Oxides and Hydroxides. Chemically, the oxide and hydroxide minerals consist of metal ions (of either one or two types of metals) combined with oxygen in various ratios, such as Al_2O_3 (corundum) or $MgAl_2O_4$ (spinel), or metals combined with oxygen and hydrogen, such as $Mg(OH)_2$ (brucite) or $HFeO_2$ (goethite). The oxides and hydroxides are a diverse group with few properties in common. Several minerals of great economic importance occur in this group, including the chief ores of iron (magnetite, Fe_3O_4, and hematite, Fe_2O_3), chromium (chromite), manganese (pyrolusite, manganite, psilomelane), tin (cassiterite), and aluminum (bauxite). Some minerals in this group form from molten rock or hydrothermal (hot water) solutions, but others form on or near the surface of the earth as a result of weathering and may contain water.

Sulfides. Chemically, the sulfides consist of a metal ion combined with sulfur. They are an economically important class of minerals that includes numerous ore minerals. Many of the sulfides are metallic, with high specific gravity, and most are fairly soft. They tend to be brittle, and they have distinctive streak colors. Many sulfides have ionic bonding, but others have metallic bonding, at least in part. Sphalerite has covalent bonding.

Among the sulfides are ores of lead (galena, PbS), zinc (sphalerite, ZnS), copper (chalcocite, Cu_2S; bornite, Cu_5FeS_4; and chalcopyrite, $CuFeS_2$), silver (argentite, Ag_2S), mercury (cinnabar, HgS), and molybdenum (molybdenite, MoS_2), as well as pyrite (FeS_2), used to manufacture sulfuric acid.

Sulfosalts. The sulfosalts are a type of unoxidized sulfur mineral. They consist of a metal and a semimetal combined with sulfur. There are nearly a hundred sulfosalts, including arsenopyrite (FeAsS), tetrahedrite ($Cu_{12}Sb_4S_{13}$), and pyrargyrite (Ag_3SbS_2). Some are useful as ore minerals.

Sulfates. The sulfates consist of metal plus a sulfate (SO_4) group. The sulfates are typically soft, and some are translucent or transparent. They include both anhydrous (without water) and hydrous (water-bearing) sulfate minerals. Anhydrous sulfates include barite ($BaSO_4$), anhydrite ($CaSO_4$), celestite ($SrSO_4$), and anglesite ($PbSO_4$). The hydrous sulfates include gypsum ($CaSO_4 \bullet 2H_2O$) and epsomite ($MgSO_4 \bullet 7 H_2O$). The structure of gypsum consists of sheets or layers of calcium and sulfate ions separated by water molecules. Loss of water molecules causes the structure of the mineral to collapse into anhydrite, with a decrease in volume and loss of cleavage. The most common sulfate, gypsum is used in the production of plaster of paris, drywall, soil conditioner, and portland cement.

Halides. The halides contain negatively charged halogen ions (chlorine, fluorine, bromine, and iodine), ionically bonded to positively charged ions (such as sodium, potassium, calcium, mercury, and silver). Many have symmetrical crystal structures resulting in cubic cleavage (halite, NaCl, and sylvite, KCl) or octahedral cleavage (fluorite, CaF_2). Many of the halides are water-soluble salts (such as halite and sylvite), and may form from the evaporation of water. Many are transparent or translucent. All are fairly soft and are light in color when fresh. Some of the silver and mercury halides will darken in color on exposure to light, hence their use in photography.

Carbonates. Carbonate minerals contain the carbonate ion, CO_3^{2-}. Carbonate minerals are readily identified by their effervescence in hy-drochloric acid, although for some carbonates, the acid must be hot or the mineral must be powdered to obtain the reaction. Some carbonates (such as cerussite, $PbCO_3$) react to nitric acid. Carbonates include calcite and aragonite ($CaCO_3$), dolomite ($CaMg(CO_3)_2$), magnesite ($MgCO_3$), and siderite ($FeCO_3$). The colorful malachite (green), azurite (blue), and rhodochrosite (pink) are also carbonates. Most carbonates are fairly soft, and rhombohedral cleavage is common.

Nitrates. The nitrate minerals contain the nitrate ion, NO_3^-. Most nitrates are water soluble and are fairly soft. They are light in color, and some are transparent. The nitrates include soda niter ($NaNO_3$), which is found in desert regions and used in explosives and fertilizer, and niter or saltpeter (KNO_3), which forms as a coating on the walls of caves and is used as a fertilizer.

Borates. The borates contain boron bonded to oxygen and associated with sodium or calcium, with or without water. Some borates form in igneous deposits, but most are found in dry lake beds in arid areas. Among the borates are borax, kernite, and ulexite. Borax is used for washing, as an antiseptic and preservative, in medicine, and in industrial and laboratory applications.

Phosphates. The phosphate minerals contain the PO_4^{3-} group, bonded to positively charged ions such as calcium, lithium, iron, manganese, lead, and iron, with or without water. Apatite ($Ca_5(F,Cl,OH)(PO_4)_3$) is the most important and abundant phosphate mineral. It is the primary constituent of bone and is used for fertilizer. Turquoise is a phosphate mineral.

Tungstates. The tungstates contain tungsten (chemical symbol W). Tungstates form a small group of minerals that include wolframite and scheelite (which is fluorescent); both are ores of tungsten.

Silicates. The silicates are the largest group of minerals, and they include the major rock-forming minerals of the earth's crust, feldspar and quartz, as well as olivine, pyroxene, amphibole, and the micas. Most are fairly hard, with glassy luster, low to moderate specific gravity, and crush to a light colored powder. Silicates consist of silicon and oxygen, generally accompanied by other ions such as aluminum, potassium, calcium, sodium, iron, and magnesium. Silicate structure is based on the silicate tetrahedron, which consists of four oxygen atoms arranged around one silicon atom. These tetrahedra are arranged in several characteristic patterns which allow the silicates to be classified into a number of groups, including isolated tetrahedra (neosilicates), pairs of tetrahedra (sorosilicates), rings of tetrahedra (cyclosilicates), single and double chains of tetrahedra (inosilicates), sheets of tetrahedra (phyllosilicates), and three dimensional frameworks of silicate tetrahedra (tectosilicates).

Neosilicates tend to be compact and hard, with fairly high specific gravity. Olivine, garnet, zircon, topaz, staurolite, and kyanite are neosilicates. Sorosilicates (or "sister" silicates) include the minerals epidote, prehnite, and hemimorphite. Cyclosilicates are characterized by prismatic, trigonal, tetrahedral, or hexagonal habits. Beryl has rings of six silicate tetrahedra, reflected in its hexagonal (six-sided) crystals. Tourmaline and chrysocolla are also in this group.

Inosilicates (single-chain and double-chain silicates) tend to be fibrous or elongated, with two directions of cleavage parallel to the elongation. They include pyroxenes (including hypersthene, augite, and diopside), pyroxenoids (including wollastonite), and amphiboles (hornblende, tremolite, actinolite, and others).

Phyllosilicates, or sheet silicates, have one prominent direction of cleavage and tend to have a platey or flaky appearance. They are generally soft, have low specific gravity, and may have flexible or elastic sheets. The micas (muscovite, biotite, lepidolite, and phlogopite), and the clay minerals (kaolinite, illite) belong to this group, as do talc, serpentine, chlorite, and others.

The earth's crust is dominated by tectosilicates, or framework silicates. This is the group that contains feldspar and quartz, the two most abundant minerals in the earth's crust. Quartz is chemically the simplest silicate, with the chemical formula SiO_2. Feldspar is a group of minerals, including orthoclase and microcline (two different crystal structures with the formula $KAlSi_3O_8$) and plagioclase (a solid solution series which ranges in composition from $NaAlSi_3O_8$ to $CaAl_2Si_2O_8$). Tectosilicates tend to be of low density and compact habit. Feldspathoids (including nepheline and sodalite) and zeolites (analcime and others) are also in this group.

FURTHER READING: Thorough coverage of minerals is found in *Manual of Mineralogy*, by C. Klein and C. S. Hurlbut, 21st ed. 1993. Other information on minerals can be found in *A Field Guide to Rocks and Minerals*, by Frederick H. Pough, in the Peterson Field Guide series, 1960; in *Simon and Schuster's Guide to Rocks and Minerals*, edited by Martin Prinz, George Harlow, and Joseph Peters, 1978; and in the National Audubon Society's *Field Guide to North American Rocks and Minerals*, by C. W. Chesterman and K. E. Lowe, 1995. More general information can be found in *Rocks and Minerals*, by Herbert S. Zim and Paul R. Shaffer, 1957.

Pamela J. W. Gore

SEE ALSO: Crystals; Gems; Isotopes, radioactive; Mohs hardness scale; Native elements; Silicates; Silicon; individual mineral resource articles.

Minerals Management Service

DATE ESTABLISHED: 1982

The Minerals Management Service is the agency within the U.S. Department of the Interior that collects, accounts for, and distributes revenues from mineral production on federal and Indian lands. It also manages the mineral resources and the natural gas and oil leasing programs for federal lands that exist below sea level on the continental shelf.

THE MINERALS MANAGEMENT SERVICE (MMS) was established in 1982 on the recommendation of the Independent Commission on Fiscal Accountability. The MMS formed the Royalty Management Program to account for revenues related to mineral production on all federal lands and Indian reservations and the Offshore Minerals Management Program to account for revenues generated on the outer continental shelf. The outer continental shelf includes submerged lands that lie between individual states' seaward jurisdiction and the seaward extent of federal jurisdiction. The MMS also seeks to ensure that exploration and production of the United States' offshore natural gas, oil, and mineral resources is done in an environmentally safe manner.

The day-to-day management of oil and gas development and leasing programs on the federal outer continental shelf is supervised by three regional offices located in New Orleans, Louisiana; Camarillo, California; and Anchorage, Alaska. The MMS headquarters, located in Washington, D.C., is responsible for providing national policy guidelines and regulations for offshore leasing programs, conducting resource and environmental safety assessments, and directing international marine minerals programs.

The establishment of the MMS increased government efficiency in minerals management. The Royalty Management Program designed a centralized automated fiscal and production accounting system that increased timely revenue disbursement from 92 percent to 99 percent. The Offshore Minerals Management Program has increased the number of leases, the number of acres leased, and the volume of gas and oil production that it oversees. It has also increased the number of pipeline miles available to the producers. The MMS has conducted studies on the continental shelf of the United States to support risk assessment analysis regarding oil spills and to provide safer transport of potential pollutants on the ocean. Ocean circulation studies have been conducted in order to plan safer routes and reduce oil spills. The MMS has also significantly reduced the rate of oil spills since its inception.

The MMS has performed air quality studies in the northern Gulf of Mexico to assess the effect of emissions on air pollutants generated on the outer continental shelf as a result of offshore natural gas and oil development activities near the states of Texas and Louisiana. Research is also being done on the long-term, chronic, sublethal impacts to marine life from offshore gas and oil discharges. The MMS monitors the distribution, behavior, habitats, and migrations of bowhead whales and other marine mammals and sea turtles to ensure that they are not being adversely affected by the oil and gas industry. The MMS studies the effects on the environment and the social and economic benefits and costs

to communities before making decisions regarding leasing arrangements, pipeline routings, and landfalls.

Dion C. Stewart

SEE ALSO: Coastal Zone Management Act; Council of Energy Resource Tribes; Department of the Interior, U.S.; Exclusive economic zone; Law of the sea; Marine mining; Oil spills; Public lands.

Mining. *See* Open-pit mining; Quarrying; Strip mining; Underground mining

Mining safety and health issues

Mining is an inherently hazardous industry. Significant reforms and improvements have been made in the twentieth century to address the health and safety hazards faced by miners, often in response to major disasters that heightened public awareness of these problems.

MINING IS ONE of the most hazardous of major industries. Miners, particularly in underground operations, face a wide range of safety and health hazards, from immediate threats such as fire or explosion to the risk of developing lung disease or other illnesses from years of exposure to adverse conditions. Most of the effort to address mining safety and health has come in the twentieth century, with labor organizations, mining management, and government working (both separately and collectively) toward reform. Increased worker and management awareness as well as the efforts of regulatory agencies have led to a decrease in industry-related injury and illness. However, while the industrialized nations have made considerable progress in mining safety and health, technological and labor standards vary greatly throughout the world.

Safety Hazards. One of the greatest safety hazards facing underground miners is that of fire and explosion. Workers can be trapped underground and asphyxiated, or crushed as mine structures collapse. Many gases found in mines have explosive properties. Firedamp, a highly

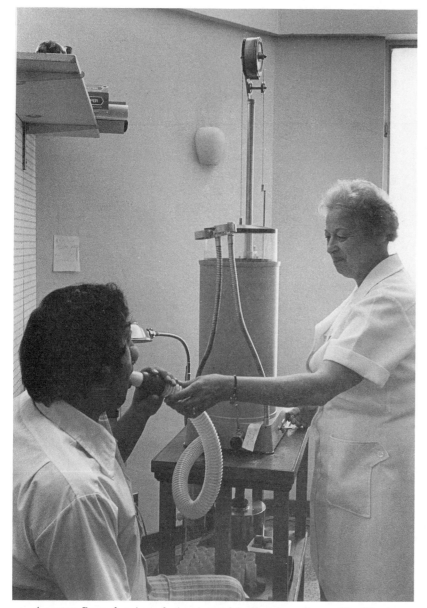

A western Pennsylvania coal miner is tested for black lung disease. (Jim West)

ignition sources, such as electrical equipment that could spark or heat excessively, is another way to reduce the risk of fire and explosion.

Airborne dust is also capable of igniting and exploding. Drilling, cutting, and breaking rock with compressed-air equipment generates airborne rock dust. Drills and other equipment with an internal water feed that sprays rock surfaces during operation help to reduce dust concentrations. Exhaust ventilation and dust collection systems also reduce the dust-ignition hazard.

Other safety hazards that miners face include cave-ins, flooding, falling rocks and other objects, slipping and falling, handling of explosives, and working with and around heavy machinery and vehicles. While some accidents and injuries are inevitable, many can be reduced or eliminated through worker training and safe work practices.

Health Hazards. As noted above, mining equipment generates airborne dust. Dust particles measuring 0.5 to 5 micrometers in diameter are especially dangerous, as they can settle in the lungs. Prolonged inhalation of metallic or mineral dusts can lead to a lung disease called pneumoconiosis. Black-lung disease is a well-publicized form of pneumoconiosis brought on by coal dust. The effects of asbestos exposure are also widely known: inhaling particles of this fibrous mineral can cause asbestosis, a chronic lung inflammation, and lung cancer. Workers in quarries and limestone mines can develop silico-

flammable gaseous mixture composed mainly of methane, is common in coal and lignite mines and is sometimes found in potassium mines and bituminous shales. It is explosive in concentrations of 5 to 15 percent in air. In some coal mines, huge amounts of carbon dioxide may be released from the exposed coal with explosive force. Increasing ventilation or the draining off of flammable and explosive gases can dilute their concentrations to safe levels. Controlling outside sis, a fibrous lung disease caused by inhaling silica dust. Dust control measures and respiratory protection equipment are crucial to miner health.

Gases and vapors pose another inhalation hazard for miners. Certain ores—notably those of arsenic, manganese, mercury, and sulfur—can emit toxic fumes. Hydrogen sulfide, a gas produced by the decomposition of pyrites by water, is poisonous and kills quickly. Radium and uranium disintegrate to form radon gas, which when inhaled can cause lung cancer. Other gases, such as methane, can cause asphyxiation. Ventilation systems, air monitoring, and respiratory protective equipment all contribute to worker safety where inhalation hazards are present.

Another common problem in mines is extreme heat, the result of the increase of temperature with depth (the geothermal gradient) coupled with the heat generated by mining equipment. Many mines are also naturally damp, a problem compounded by water sprays used for dust suppression. High humidity interferes with the evaporation of sweat and hence with the body's natural cooling ability. The warm, damp environment not only leads to heat-related illnesses such as heat stroke but also is conducive to parasite infestation. Overly hot conditions can be eased through good ventilation systems, climate control, clothing cooled by dry ice, and limited work times.

Historical Overview. The importance of the physical well-being of miners has been recognized for centuries. Georgius Agricola, the sixteenth century German scientist known as the father of mineralogy, writes of the hazardous conditions in mines of his day. In addition to the health and safety hazards noted above, early miners (particularly prospectors in the American West during the 1800's) contended with food shortages, vermin, cold, epidemics, and general poor health brought on by poor sanitation and a lack of proper medical attention for injuries and illnesses.

Early safety measures employed at mining operations included the drilling of ventilation tunnels to provide fresh air at depth; the use of canaries or dogs to test for carbon monoxide; the introduction of the Davy safety lamp for use in coal mines in 1815; and the introduction of ventilation blowers in 1865.

The first officially recorded mining disaster in the United States was an explosion at the Black Heath Coal Mine near Richmond, Virginia, in 1839, in which 52 men died. In 1869 there were two major coal-mine disasters: a fire at the Yellowjacket Mine that claimed 49 miners' lives, and another at the Avondale Mine in Plymouth, Pennsylvania, in which 179 miners died. Subsequent legislation was passed that required two exits at every mine and prohibited the placement of ore-breaking equipment over the shaft.

There were several large coal-mining disasters in the United States in the early twentieth century. In 1900 an explosion at the Scofield Mine in Scofield, Utah, killed 200 miners. Another 361 died in 1907 in an explosion and fire at Monongah, West Virginia, the worst mining disaster in the history of the United States. Two weeks later 239 miners were killed at Jacobs Creek, Pennsylvania. In 1908 at Marianna, Pennsylvania, 154 miners were killed. Another 259 died in 1909 in a fire at Cherry, Illinois.

This series of disasters led Congress to pass the Organic Act of 1910, which established the U.S. Bureau of Mines (USBM) under the Department of the Interior. The idea of such a bureau, which would oversee the collection, evaluation, and dissemination of scientific, technical, and economic data of value to the mineral industries, had been under consideration for a number of years. The early USBM focused on reducing the mortality rate of miners; to this end, it investigated mine explosions, promoted miner safety and accident prevention through training, and strove toward improvement of working conditions for miners. However, the Organic Act did not permit the USBM to inspect mines, and adoption of its technical recommendations was entirely voluntary. In 1915 Congress passed an act that authorized the establishment of seven mine-safety stations.

While the USBM's early research helped to reduce the rate of mining-related fatalities, disasters continued to claim miners' lives. From about 1910 until about 1940, miners died in work-related accidents at an average rate of 2,000 per year. The death of 276 miners in a 1940 coal mine disaster led to passage of the Coal Mine Inspection and Investigation Act of 1941, which authorized the USBM to enter and inspect mines and recommend corrective action.

Coal mine explosions killed 111 miners at the Centralia Number 5 Mine in southern Illinois in 1947 and 119 miners at the Orient Number 2 Mine of the Chicago, Wilmington, and Franklin Coal Company in West Frankfort, Illinois, in 1951. These disasters led to passage of the Federal Coal Mine Safety Act of 1952, in which federal mine inspectors were given limited enforcement power to prevent major disasters. Hearings led to the closure of 518 unsafe mines.

The 1960's to the 1990's. The Federal Metal and Nonmetallic Mine Safety Act of 1966, which applied to operations at mines other than those producing coal and lignite, provided for the establishment of mandatory standards addressing conditions or practices that could cause death or serious physical harm. Inspectors were empowered to stop operations that were deemed health- or life-threatening.

In 1968 a series of explosions at Consolidation Coal's Number 9 Mine in West Virginia killed 78 miners. In response, Congress passed the Federal Coal Mine Health and Safety Act of 1969. It established procedures for developing mandatory standards for the coal mining industry and called for expanded health and safety research to eliminate or reduce the risk of health impairment, injury, or death. Inspectors were given authority to withdraw miners from dangerous areas. It also provided benefits for miners disabled by black-lung disease. (A 1965 survey had found more than 100,000 active or retired coal miners in the United States suffering from black-lung disease.)

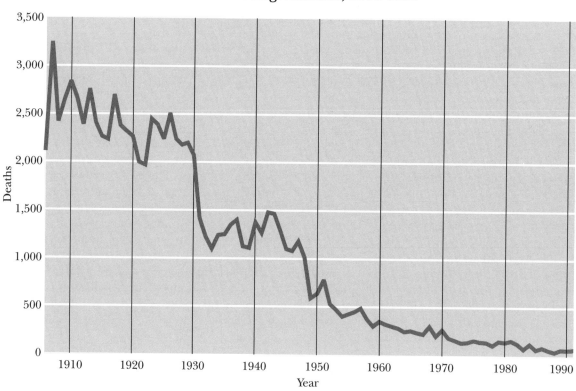

U.S. Coal-Mining Fatalities, 1906-1991

Source: U.S. Bureau of Mines, *Minerals Yearbook, 1994.* U.S. Government Printing Office, 1996.
Note: The highest figure is 3,250 deaths in 1907; the lowest is 38 deaths in 1988.

Injuries and Fatalities in Mineral Industries, 1994

Item	Coal Mining	Quarrying and Related Industries	Metal/ Nonmetal Mining	Sand and Gravel Mining
Total number of injuries	11,353	5,369	4,498	1,863
Fatal injuries	44	22	13	5
Rate per million work-hours:				
Fatal	0.04	0.03	0.02	0.02
Nonfatal	7.24	4.70	3.35	4.05
Fatalities per 1,000 employees	0.33	0.26	0.18	0.15

Source: U.S. Department of Commerce, *Statistical Abstract of the United States, 1996,* 1996. Primary source, U.S. Mine Safety and Health Administration.

In 1973 the secretary of the interior separated the USBM's regulatory function from its mining research function by establishing the Mining Enforcement and Safety Administration (MESA). MESA was responsible for administering the 1966 and 1969 mine safety acts, which included enforcing mining health and safety regulations, assessing penalties for violating those regulations, prioritizing education and training in mining health and safety, and developing mandatory health and safety standards.

The Federal Coal Mine Safety and Health Amendments Act of 1977 provided the first single piece of comprehensive legislation for all types of mining operations and extended the research directives of previous legislation to all segments of the mining industry. Under this act, MESA became the Mine Safety and Health Administration (MSHA) of the Department of Labor. With the closure of the U.S. Bureau of Mines in 1996, the Department of Energy assumed responsibility for conducting mine safety and health research.

FURTHER READING: For additional information see William S. Kirk, "The History of the U.S. Bureau of Mines," in the bureau's *Minerals Yearbook, 1994* (vol. 1, *Metals and Minerals*), 1996; Kristina Lindbergh and Barry Provorse, *Coal: A Contemporary Energy Story,* 1977; "Health and Safety," in Ivan A. Given, ed., *SME Mining Engineering Handbook,* vol. 1, 1973; and Howard N.

Sloane and Lucille L. Sloane, *A Pictorial History of American Mining,* 1970.

Karen N. Kähler

SEE ALSO: Asbestos; Bureau of Mines, U.S.; Coal; Department of the Interior, U.S.; Health, resource exploitation and; Methane; Strip mining; Underground mining.

Mining wastes and mine reclamation

Mining and related operations generate waste materials that mar the landscape and pose a threat to human health and the environment. Reclamation and pollution-control efforts minimize the impact of mining on its surroundings and make the land fit for nonmining use.

HUMANKIND IS DEPENDENT on mineral resources extracted from the earth. These resources cannot be obtained without impacting the environment. Mining involves not only the mine itself—either a large, open excavation or a small surface opening leading to extensive subsurface workings—but also access roads, utilities such as water and power, processing facilities, and other support buildings and equipment. These all take a toll on their surroundings, as do the solid, liquid, and gaseous wastes produced during mining, milling, and smelting. Unconstrained mining operations and wastes can alter and litter the landscape, pollute surface water and groundwater, foul the air, harm plant and animal life, threaten human health and safety, and render land useless for subsequent purposes.

As the world's human population grows and the overall standard of living continues to rise in both developed and undeveloped countries, the demand for mineral resources increases. Likewise, there are increasing and often conflicting demands upon the land where those resources are found. Wise management of mining wastes and reclamation efforts after mining makes it possible to use land for timber, crops, grazing, recreation, or other nonmining purposes once mineral wealth has been extracted from it.

Mining Wastes and Their Impact. During mining operations, rock that does not contain economically significant concentrations of an ore must be removed. This waste material is known as spoil. In the case of surface mining, extensive areas are disrupted and laid bare as the vegetation, topsoil, and rock overlying the desired ore are stripped away. During ore processing, additional solid waste is generated in the form of tailings, the portions of washed or milled ores that are too poor to merit further processing. Surface-mined areas and piles of spoil and tailings generally cannot support vegetation without first undergoing treatment; as a result, they are vulnerable to erosion and flooding. Silt from these unvegetated slopes finds its way into streams and other surface waters, where it impacts aquatic life. The barren waste materials remain unstable, increasing the likelihood of landslide. Substantial piles of spoil or tailings can also be a physical obstruction to continued mineral exploration in the area.

At mines where pyrite (iron sulfide) is associated with the ore body and water is present, acid mine drainage can result. Exposed pyrite breaks down in the presence of oxygen to form iron sulfate and sulfur dioxide. The decay of pyrite is self-perpetuating; as the mineral breaks down and crumbles away, new surfaces are exposed to the air. Water, which is found in most mines in the form of direct precipitation, surface runoff, seeping groundwater, or atmospheric moisture, completes the reaction: Added to pyrite's breakdown products, it creates sulfuric acid. As the

acidified water flows, it dissolves and transports minerals from the surrounding rock, further degrading the quality of the water. This acid mine drainage affects streams, ponds, lakes, and the fish and other life they support. Neglected piles of spoil and tailings can also be a source of acid runoff.

Mining and related activities generate air pollution in the form of airborne dust and gaseous processing effluent. Drilling, excavating, blasting, and similar operations cause dust particles to become airborne. Fine metallic and mineral dusts can have particularly deleterious effects on mine workers and other persons inhaling them. Smelting produces gaseous effluents that, if not treated, are not only a nuisance, obscuring visibility and spreading noxious odors, but also a serious threat to animal and plant life. Gaseous smelter waste can contain such toxic metals as arsenic, lead, and mercury.

Inappropriate handling of mining wastes can change the contours of a landscape, leaving an area vulnerable to landslide and flood; can disrupt an ecosystem's food chain, especially in the waste's effects on land plants and aquatic organisms; can introduce toxic materials into the air and water; and can degrade the economy and overall quality of life in mined areas.

Reclamation and Pollution Control. Basic reclamation involves correcting undesirable conditions brought on by mining and related operations. Reclamation can proceed beyond this level to include the rehabilitation of restored land and water resources for agriculture, forestry, rangeland, recreation, industry, residences, or other productive use.

Modern mining efforts have incorporated reclamation into their preplanning and operational phases. Before mining commences, most industrialized countries require mine operators to prepare an environmental impact statement that addresses the potential impact of operations on surface water, groundwater, soil, local topography, plant and animal life, and other mineral reserves. Mine operators must plan in advance the reclamation and pollution-control measures that will minimize environmental damage.

In the case of surface coal mining, reclamation usually begins as soon as the resource has been removed. After the coal has been dug from a strip of land, overburden from an adjacent strip is backfilled into the newly excavated strip and molded with heavy equipment to a shape resembling premining topography. Topsoil is emplaced over the fill material and seeded, mulched, and irrigated. Topsoil and vegetation covers are also used to stabilize mounds of spoils and tailings at underground mining sites. An alternative method for handling these solid wastes is to mix them with the grout or slurry used to fill inactive underground mines. Properly filling the mines keeps the overlying land from subsiding, thereby preventing any resulting disruption of local surface-water and groundwater systems and damage to overlying structures. In the case of underground coal mines, filling also seals them to prevent the outbreak of mine fires.

The best way to control acid mine drainage and runoff is to prevent their formation. If exposed pyrite, oxygen, or water is not present to sustain the chemical reaction, acid cannot form. To inhibit the reaction, water is diverted from mines, tailings, and spoil piles. Solid wastes are crushed and compacted to minimize oxidation and water infiltration. Inactive mines are sealed with grout or slurry to isolate pyrite from the other reactants; mixing the solid mining wastes with the fill material isolates them as well. Where the formation of acid drainage and runoff cannot be averted, the effluent is contained and treated. Treatment typically involves neutralizing the acid with lime or other alkaline materials, and retaining the effluent in a treatment pond to allow impurities to settle out.

To suppress airborne dusts, water sprays are typically employed. Gaseous emissions from smelters are filtered and otherwise treated before being released to the atmosphere.

Historical Overview. Before the twentieth century, mining's focus was on short-term economic gain. Deposits of the greatest accessibility and grade were mined as cheaply as possible. Particularly in the United States, where land and resources appeared limitless, mining interests extracted the richest ores and exploited other natural resources as they saw fit, confident that they were putting the land to its highest and best economic use. Spoils and tailings were left to

litter the landscape. Roads were cut indiscriminately through wilderness and across waterways. Surface waters were dammed or channeled into ditches, and drinking-water sources became tainted with heavy metals. Forests were denuded to provide wood for support operations or merely to clear the area for mineral exploration. Valleys grew clouded with toxic, acidic smelter smoke that killed vegetation and animals and eroded the health of human populations. As technology improved and made possible such techniques as hydraulic mining, dredging, strip mining, and open-pit mining, the potential for greater environmental damage arose.

In the late nineteenth and early twentieth centuries, mining companies experimented with reclamation and reworked spoils and tailings to extract low-grade ores. While driven by profit, these practices were more environmentally sound than what went before. Similarly, early regulations in the United States that controlled mining wastes and the use of water in mining defended downstream mining operations from conditions that would impede their efforts; they were not intended as environmental protection legislation, regardless of whatever positive effect they may have had on environmental quality.

In 1939 West Virginia enacted the first state legislation to control surface mining. Over the next few decades other coal-producing states followed suit. Reclamation increased significantly after these laws were enacted; however, lack of funding and other factors influenced the states' ability to enforce the laws. The 1960's saw a profusion of environmental laws that affected the mining industry, including the Appalachian Regional Development Act of 1965 (Public Law 89-4), under which the United States Bureau of Mines studied the effects of surface coal mining in the United States and made recommendations regarding a national program for reclamation and rehabilitation. This study led to the Surface Mining Control and Reclamation Act of 1977, or SMCRA (Public Law 95-87), which regulates surface coal-mining operations within the United States and provides for the reclamation of contaminated surface coal-mining sites. Federal clean air and clean water legislation regulates other environmental aspects of mining.

FURTHER READING: For additional information see the section on acid mine drainage in J. Richard Lucas and Lawrence Adler, "Ground Water and Ground-Water Control," in Ivan A. Given, ed., *SME Mining Engineering Handbook*, vol. 2, 1973. Also in the handbook is Eugene P. Pfleider, "Planning and Designing for Mining Conservation," which includes a section on reclamation. Duane A. Smith, *Mining America: The Industry and the Environment, 1800-1980*, 1987, follows the evolution of the mining industry's attitudes toward conservation and environmental protection. See also Kristina Lindbergh and Barry Provorse, *Coal: A Contemporary Energy Story*, 1977; and the U.S. Department of the Interior's *Surface Mining and Our Environment*, 1967.

Karen N. Kähler

SEE ALSO: Environmental degradation, resource exploitation and; Mining safety and health issues; Open-pit mining; Strip mining; Surface Mining Control and Reclamation Act of 1977; Underground mining; Water pollution and water pollution control.

Mohs hardness scale

The Mohs hardness scale, proposed in 1822, provides a method of ranking minerals according to their relative hardness and thus is a way to help identify them.

THE RESISTANCE OF minerals to abrasion or scratch is a valuable diagnostic physical property used in mineral identification. In 1822 Friedrich Mohs, an Austrian mineralogist, developed a relative scale of mineral hardness. This scale consisted of ten common minerals that were ranked from one (softest) to ten (hardest). The values assigned to each member of the scale indicate the relative hardness of the minerals. Intervals between minerals in the scale are approximately equal, except between nine and ten.

The resistance of a mineral to scratch is tested by sliding a pointed corner of one mineral across the smooth surface of another mineral. If the mineral with the point is harder, it will cut or scratch the other mineral. The scratch should be as short as possible, not more than five or six

millimeters. If the pointed mineral is softer, a smear or powdered residue is left on the flat surface of the other mineral. This residue could be mistaken for a scratch; however, the smear can be easily rubbed off. A mineral from the high end of the scale will usually produce a significant "bite" on the softer mineral. Two minerals that have the same hardness will scratch each other equally well. Common objects are sometimes used as aids in hardness determination.

Mohs Hardness Scale

	Reference Mineral		Common Objects
1	Talc		
2	Gypsum		
		Up to 2.5	Fingernail
3	Calcite	Up to 3	Copper coin
4	Fluorite		
5	Apatite		
		Up to 5.5	Knife blade
6	Feldspar	About 5.5	Window glass
7	Quartz	6 to 7	Steel file
8	Topaz or beryl		
9	Corundum		
10	Diamond		

Brass rods set with conical-shaped fragments of test minerals on the ends are sometimes used to determine the hardness of small specimens and gemstones; these rods are known as hardness pencils. Most gems, with the exception of pearls, have a hardness of six or above. In testing rough and uncut gems, some jewelers use these pencils to determine the specific hardness of the stones. Other minerals, such as chrysoberyl, epidote, olivine, and zircon, are included with the set of instruments. Six test pencils are sometimes conveniently arranged in a hardness wheel.

With the advent of extremely hard manufactured abrasives in the second half of the twentieth century, a new sequence of index minerals was proposed for the upper part of the Mohs scale. This modified Mohs scale has found some use in industry. In this scale, quartz was elevated to eight, garnet was introduced as ten, and corundum was elevated to twelve. Diamond, the hardest naturally occurring substance derived from the earth, topped the scale at fifteen. The artificial abrasives silicon carbide and boron carbide were designated as thirteen and fourteen, respectively. Silicon carbide is produced by heating a mixture of carbon and sand in a specially designed electric furnace. Boron carbide, the hardest known substance next to diamond, is manufactured in an electric furnace from coke and dehydrated boric acid.

Donald F. Reaser

SEE ALSO: Abrasives; Corundum and emery; Diamond; Feldspars; Fluorite; Gems; Gypsum; Minerals, structure and physical properties of; Quartz; Talc.

Molybdenum

WHERE FOUND: Molybdenum has been found associated with thirteen minerals, but it is relatively uncommon in bulk ore. The United States' Colorado deposit of molybdenum disulfide (molybdenite) is the biggest producer, but Chile, Mexico, Peru, and Norway are also commercial sources. Significant molybdenum is also extracted from the by-products of tungsten and copper smelting. Trace molybdenum is found in most soils and is critical to plant health.

PRIMARY USES: The primary use of molybdenum is as a hardening agent and corrosion inhibitor for steel and other metals and alloys, but it is also used for high-temperature components such as electrodes, filaments, resistive heaters, electrical contacts, and mesh, and as a mount for tungsten filaments in light bulbs. Molybdenum compounds are used as pigments, catalysts, fertilizer supplements, lubricants, semiconductors, and coatings.

DESCRIPTION: Molybdenum (abbreviated Mo), atomic number 42 and atomic weight 95.94,

belongs, with chromium and tungsten, to Group VIB of the periodic table of the elements. It is a hard, corrosion-resistant, silvery-white metal. Its melting and boiling points are, respectively, 2,610 and 5,560 degrees Celsius. Its density is 10.22 grams per cubic centimeter at 20 degrees Celsius.

MOLYBDENUM'S PRIMARY ORE, molybdenite (MoS_2), was once confused with graphite and galena. Carl Scheele of Sweden identified it as an ore of a new element in 1778, and the metal was produced by Peter Jacob Hjelm, also from Sweden, in 1782. Hjelm called the new element "molybdos," Greek for "lead." Molybdenum did not see significant application until there arose a need for stronger steels in the automotive industry. Most molybdenum is still alloyed with steel to improve its hardness, wear resistance, corrosion resistance, and high-temperature strength.

Molybdenum is not found naturally in the metallic state but as ores with sulfur and oxygen. It has an abundance of 1.2 part per milium in the earth's crust and 0.01 part per milium in seawater. Other sources include wulfenite ($PbMoO_4$), molybdite ($Fe_2O_3 \bullet 3MoO_3 \bullet 7H_2O$), powellite ($Ca[Mo_{1-x}W_x]O_4$), and copper and tungsten smelting by-products.

The product of ore smelting is molybdenum trioxide, MoO_3. Metal powder is formed by high-temperature reduction of MoO_3 or ammonium molybdate ((NH_4)$_2 MoO_4$) with reducing agents such as hydrogen; subsequent powder metallurgy or arc-casting techniques form the bulk metal. Molybdenum alloys with up to 50 percent iron ("ferromolybdenum") can be produced from the oxide by electrical furnace or thermite processes.

Molybdenum dissolves in hot, concentrated acids such as nitric, sulfuric, and hydrochloric acid, aqua regia, and molten oxidizers such as sodium peroxide, potassium nitrate, and potassium chlorate. Heating in air oxidizes the surface to molybdenum oxides. Its heats of fusion and vaporization are, respectively, 6.7 and 117.4 kilocalories per mole. Natural molybdenum consists of seven isotopes with the following approximate distribution by mass number: 92 (16 percent), 94 (10 percent), 95 (15 percent) 96 (16 percent), 97 (10 percent), 98 (23 percent), and

10° (10 percent). It exhibits common chemical valences of +2, +3, +4, +5, and +6 and is monovalent in hexacarbonyl molybdenum ($Mo(CO)_6$). Other rare valences include the −2 state in $[Mo(CO)_5]^{-2}$ and the +1 state in $[Mo(C_6H_6)_2]^{+1}$.

Metallurgical Applications. The largest application of molybdenum is in metallurgy. It has one of the highest melting points of all metals. It is sufficiently ductile and malleable that foils as thin as 0.001 inch, wires as fine as 0.004 inch, and other shapes can be produced for specialized applications such as electrodes, filaments, resistive heaters, arc-resistant electrical contacts, and screens. Although rarely used as a light bulb filament because of its greater volatility than tungsten, it is often used to support the tungsten filament.

Molybdenum is not hardened by heat treatment alone; it also requires working. Rolled molybdenum has a tensile strength of 260,000 pounds per square inch (psi) with a Brinell hardness of 160 to 185, while unalloyed molyb-denum has a tensile strength of 97,000 psi. Its high thermal conductivity (twice that of iron), low thermal expansion coefficient, low volatility, and excellent corrosion resistance allow molybdenum to be used for high strength/high temperature parts in jet engines, missiles, turbines, and nuclear reactors.

Molybdenum is hardened by alloying agents. Adding titanium at 0.5 percent yields a tensile strength of 132,000 psi that decreases only to 88,000 psi at 1,600 degrees Fahrenheit. Zirconium may also be added to increase strength further. Such alloys are used for parts such as tubing that maintain rigidity up to the melting point. Other common molybdenum alloys include Hastelloy (with nickel), molybdenum-chromium (roughly 70 percent molybdenum, 29 percent chromium, and 1 percent iron), and molybdenum-tungsten (70 percent molybdenum and 30 percent tungsten).

Molybdenum finds application as a flame-resistant, wear-resistant, and corrosion-resistant

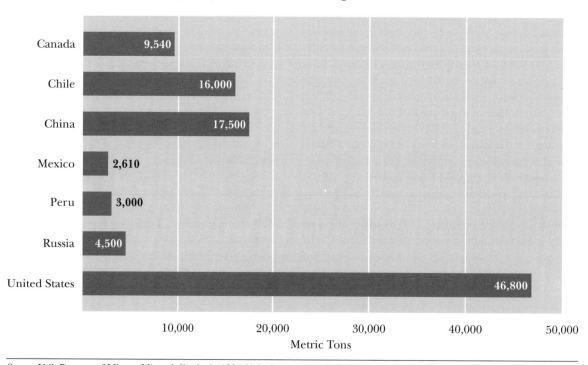

Leading Molybdenum-Producing Countries, 1994

Canada — 9,540
Chile — 16,000
China — 17,500
Mexico — 2,610
Peru — 3,000
Russia — 4,500
United States — 46,800

Metric Tons

Source: U.S. Bureau of Mines, *Minerals Yearbook, 1994.* U.S. Government Printing Office, 1996.
Note: Total world 1994 molybdenum mine production was about 104,000 tons.

coating. It may be arc-deposited, but better coatings are produced by hydrogen chloride reduction of molybdenum pentachloride ($MoCl_5$) at 850 degrees Celsius. Its adherence to steel, iron, and aluminum is good. This strong bonding is utilized as molybdenum serves as a substrate for deposition of other coatings, such as semiconductor layers in solar cells.

Molybdenum is among the most successful elements in steel for increasing strength, rigidity, and hardness. It improves other metals' corrosion resistance, increases elastic limit, and reduces grain size. It reacts with carbon to form hard molybdenum carbides within steel. Molybdenum steels have from 0.1 to 1 percent molybdenum. Higher percentages are used in molybdenum-containing stainless steels containing iron, chromium, and/or nickel.

Biological Involvement. Molybdenum plays a role in the biochemistry of plants and animals. Although not normally considered hazardous, excess molybdenum can be toxic—for example, to livestock grazing on forage grown in molybdenum-rich soils. Excess molybdenum induces a copper deficiency because of competition between molybdenum and copper for active sites in biochemicals such as enzymes. Symptoms include hair loss and gastrointestinal difficulties. The problem is corrected by adding copper to the diet or by directly injecting copper into the animal. Cattle are highly sensitive, while swine and horses are relatively insensitive; severe symptoms in cattle are given the name "teart" disease. There is evidence that molybdenum decreases tooth decay but there has been little study of the effect of chronic excesses of molybdenum in people, although molybdenum deficiencies exist and molybdenum is sometimes found as a trace mineral in vitamin and mineral supplements.

Molybdenum is critical to plants, especially in their utilization of nitrogen-bearing compounds such as nitrates. Bacteria and fungi participating in nitrogen utilization require molybdenum for the enzyme nitrate reductase. Vegetables such as lettuce, spinach, cauliflower, radish, beets, and tomatoes are susceptible. As nitrate accumulates in leaves due to insufficient molybdenum, leaves yellow and die. "Whiptail" in cauliflower results in leaf malformation and eventual death.

Such problems are corrected by adding trace molybdenum (usually as ammonium molybdate) to the soil or by increasing soil pH. In acidic soils, molybdenum exists primarily as insoluble molybdenum trioxide and may not be absorbed by plants. Increasing pH with limestone may increase availability of molybdenum as the molybdenum oxide is converted to soluble molybdates.

Chemistry and Applications. Molybdenum exhibits interesting chemistry because of its many valence states; molybdenum forms MoO_2, Mo_2O_3, Mo_2O_5, and MoO_3. Molybdenum trioxide (MoO_3) is insoluble in weak acids but dissolves in basic/alkaline aqueous solutions to form molybdate ions, MoO_4^{-2}. Molybdenum also forms halide compounds (MoX_3, MoX_4, MoX_5, MoX_6) with X representing F, Cl, and Br. It is highly reactive with fluorine, even at room temperature, but very nonreactive with iodine. The halides are unstable in water and convert to oxyhalides such as $MoOCl_2$ or $MoOF_4$.

Molybdenum disulfide, MoS_2, is a light-sensitive semiconductor used in conversion of light to electrical energy in photovoltaic/photoelectrochemical cells, as high-temperature solid lubricants, and in organic catalysis, as for hydrogenation-dehydrogenation reactions. Molybdenum also forms MoS_3. The red tetrathiomolybate ion, MoS_4^{-2}, is formed by saturating $(NH_4)_2 MoO_4$-bearing solutions with H_2S. Acidification causes MoS_3 to precipitate. Heating coverts it to MoS_2 or MoO_3, depending upon temperature and atmosphere. Mo_2S_3 also exists, as does molybdenum selenides and tellurides such as semiconducting $MoSe_2$ and $MoTe_2$.

At high pH's, the simple molybdate ion, MoO_4^{-2}, exists, but in neutral to weakly acidic solutions, more complex species, such as $(NH_4)_6 Mo_7O_{24} \cdot 4H_2O$ form in addition to colloidal MoO_3. With elements such as phosphorus or silicon, heteropolyacids such as molybdophosphates and molybdosilicates form and contain large macrostructures with twelve molybdenum and many oxygen atoms. Other large molecular compounds include "molybdenum blue," a complex, colloidal molybdenum oxide.

Molybdenum forms organic compounds such as hexacarbonyl molybdenum $Mo(CO)_6$, molybdenum alkoxides, and acetonates that are precursors for other molybdenum species or films. Molybdenum also forms complexes with cyanide, CN^{-1}, and ions such as $Mo(CN)_8^{-2}$ and $Mo(CN)_6^{-3}$.

MoO_3 is used as a catalyst in organic chemistry, in electroplating, and for analysis for elements such as phosphorus or lead. Related compounds are used as pigments because of their brilliant coloration; for example, the orange molybdate/chromate, blue molybdenum blue, and white zinc molybdate pigments. They also find use as corrosion inhibitors, abrasives, ceramic constituents, and optical coatings. Molybdenum halides such as $MoCl_5$ are also used as catalysts and precursors for molybdenum and its compounds and alloys, especially as thin films or coatings.

FURTHER READING: For additional information, consult the *Chemical Rubber Company Handbook of Chemistry and Physics,* edited by David R. Lide, 71st ed. 1990-1991. Other good sources include *The Chemical Elements and Their Compounds,* vol. 2, by N. V. Sidgwick, 1950; *The New Encyclopedia Britannica,* vol. 8, 1992; *Materials Handbook,* by George S. Brady, 19th ed. 1971; *Materials in Industry,* by W. J. Patton, 2d ed. 1976; *Plant Mineral Nutrition,* by E. J. Hewitt and T. A. Smith, 1975; and *Trace Elements in Plants,* by Walter Stiles, 1961.

Robert D. Engelken

SEE ALSO: Alloys; Chromium; Fertilizers; Metals and metallurgy; Solar energy; Tungsten.

Monoculture agriculture

Monoculture agriculture involves repetitively planting a single plant species rather than growing a variety of types of plants. There has been considerable debate regarding the advantages and disadvantages of this type of plant production.

MONOCULTURE AGRICULTURE IS a plant production system in which a single plant species, typically one producing grain (such as corn, wheat, or rice), forage (such as alfalfa or clover), or fiber (such as cotton), is grown in the same field on a repetitive basis to the exclusion of all other species. In its most extreme version, a single variety of a plant species is grown—in this case all plants are virtually identical clones of one

another. Monoculture can be contrasted with other agricultural production practices such as multiple cropping (in which sequential monoculture crops are grown in the same year) or intercropping (in which two or more different crops are grown at the same time and place). Monoculture can also apply to perennial produce systems such as fruiting trees, citrus crops, and tea, coffee, and rubber plantations.

Monocultures are unnatural ecological occurrences. They are maintained through the use of other resources such as labor, energy, and capital (fertilizers, chemicals, and so on). Left to itself, a monoculture crop will quickly revert to being a mixed plant community. However, monoculture agriculture has several inherent advantages that caused its widespread adoption from the moment agriculture began. Monocultures allow agriculturalists to focus their energy on producing a single crop best adapted to a particular environment or to a particular market. For example, a premium is paid for white corn, used in making snack foods. Monoculture is an appropriate agricultural strategy to optimize crop yield per unit of land when either temperature (in temperate regions) or water (in arid and semiarid regions) limits the growing season. Monoculture agriculture also lends itself to mechanization, which is an important consideration when labor is expensive relative to energy costs. Consequently, monoculture agriculture in the United States has developed in concert with the resources required to support it—markets, credit, chemicals, seed, and machinery—and with the social conditions that have caused the United States to change from a largely rural to a largely urban and suburban population.

The disadvantages of monoculture agriculture are numerous. There are apparent limits to the increase in crop yields brought about by new hybrid seed, fertilization, and pesticides, and yield increases in monoculture agriculture have diminished since the 1980's. There is an economy of scale at which farm size becomes too small to permit effective mechanization or for which insufficient markets exist for reliance on a single crop. The focus on production of a single crop may lead to unbalanced diets and nutritional deficiencies in agricultural communities where no external supplies of produce are available. More important, monoculture crops are biologically unstable, and considerable effort must be made to keep other plants and pests out. Since every plant is the same, or nearly the same, these systems are inherently susceptible to adverse natural events (storms, drought, and wind damage) and to biological invasions by insects and plant pathogens. The classic example of over-reliance on monoculture was the Irish Potato Famine in the early 1800's. The famine was instigated by natural climatic conditions that allowed the plant pathogen *Phytophthora infestans* to destroy successive potato crops in a population too impoverished to afford other food staples that were available.

Mark S. Coyne

SEE ALSO: Agriculture industry; Agronomy; Biological invasions; Farmland; Fertilizers; Green Revolution; Slash-and-burn agriculture; Soil; Soil testing and analysis.

Montreal Protocol

DATE: Signed September 16, 1987; took effect January 1, 1989; amended 1990

The Montreal Protocol was intended to help preserve the earth's ozone layer by severely limiting the production and use of chlorofluorocarbons (CFCs) and other halogenated compounds.

THE MONTREAL PROTOCOL on Substances That Deplete the Ozone Layer was signed in 1987 by forty-six nations, including the United States. It entered into force on January 1, 1989. The Montreal Protocol was designed to control the production and consumption of chlorofluorocarbons (CFCs) and other halogenated compounds that were suspected of causing destruction of the ozone layer. Industrialized countries, such as the United States, were committed to freezing consumption of certain CFCs at 1986 levels by mid-1989 and to reducing 1986 consumption levels by 20 percent by mid-1993. By mid-1988, a 50 percent reduction in 1986 consumption levels was required. Halons (such as CF_2BrCl, CF_3Br, and $C_2F_4Br_2$) were to be frozen at 1986 consumption levels in 1992.

As amended in 1990, the Montreal Protocol called for a total phasing out of specified CFCs, halons, and carbon tetrachlorides by the year 2000 and methyl chloroform by 1995. It also accelerated the rate at which the phasing out would be conducted for CFCs, calling for a 50 percent reduction by 1995, an 85 percent reduction by 1997, and a 100 percent reduction by 2000.

The Montreal Protocol was directed at protecting the ozone layer, a global natural resource 10 to 20 kilometers above the earth's surface that screens out most of the ultraviolet radiation emitted by the sun. Ultraviolet light can lead to mutations and cancer in living things. Participating nations were motivated to act by four major scientific events: First, in 1974 the mechanism by which CFCs deplete ozone was demonstrated, which led the United States to ban CFCs in aerosols unilaterally in 1978. Second, a hole in the ozone layer was discovered over Antarctica in the early 1980's. Third, evidence linking the ozone hole to CFCs was provided in 1985; fourth, CFC substitutes were developed by important CFC producers such as DuPont.

The major innovation of the Montreal Protocol was that it called for a gradual reduction in CFC production and allowed for adjustments in the members' activities based on updated scientific information. Thus the amended protocol in 1990 accelerated reduction levels because new data suggested that the extent of ozone destruction was greater than anticipated. An immediate total ban of CFCs would have been unworkable, since CFCs were crucial in important cooling and air-conditioning applications: Without reasonably inexpensive alternatives, the distribution of temperature-sensitive medical supplies such as blood, 75 percent of food shipments, and the habitability of many workplaces dependent on air conditioning would have been affected.

There was, and is, considerable disagreement on the extent and effect of ozone depletion. There were substantial arguments among the signers of the Montreal Protocol regarding the level of production cuts required to amend the problem. There were also disagreements regarding the level of support that developing nations were entitled to in their efforts to do without CFCs. For them, compliance meant forgoing the benefits of CFCs (particularly for refrigeration) that industrialized countries had enjoyed at crucial phases in their economic growth. Eventually compensation of at least $350 million was set aside by industrialized countries to induce developing nations to eliminate their CFC production.

FURTHER READING: *International Environmental Law*, edited by Michael R. Molitor, 1991, provides the full text of the Montreal Protocol. Joseph P. Glas gives an industrial perspective in *Technology and Environment*, 1989. Lawrence Susskind, *Environmental Diplomacy*, 1994, discusses the Montreal Protocol as an example of successful international negotiation.

Mark S. Coyne

SEE ALSO: Developing countries, resource use by; Earth Summit in Rio de Janeiro; Greenhouse gases and global climate change; Ozone layer and ozone hole debate.

Muir, John

BORN: April 21, 1838; Dunbar, Scotland
DIED: December 24, 1914; Los Angeles, California

Muir is best known as an American naturalist who worked diligently to gain popular and federal support for forest conservation. His efforts influenced Congress to pass the Yosemite National Park Bill in 1890, which established both Yosemite and Sequoia National Parks.

JOHN MUIR TRAVELED throughout the United States, Alaska, Europe, Asia, Africa, and the Arctic in an effort to draw attention to the need to conserve land, water, and forests. He spent six years in California's Yosemite Valley studying its forests and glacial rock formations, and he was the first to explain the valley's glacial origin. In 1879 Muir discovered a glacier in Alaska that is now known as Muir Glacier. The Sierra Club, which has become a leading conservation organization, was founded by Muir in 1892. In 1908 a redwood forest near San Francisco was named Muir Woods, and President Theodore Roosevelt established the Muir Woods National Monument in Marin County, California, in honor of Muir's accomplishments. Muir helped persuade Roosevelt to set aside 148 acres of forest reserves in the United States.

Also a noted author, Muir wrote a number of books about his travels, including *The Mountains of California* (1894), *Our National Parks* (1901), *The Yosemite* (1912), and *Steep Trails*, which was published in 1918 after Muir's death. His books did much to arouse public interest in conservation issues in the United States.

Alvin K. Benson

SEE ALSO: Conservation; Conservation biology; Forest Service, U.S.; Forests; National Park Service and national parks; Natural Resources Conservation Service; Roosevelt, Theodore; Sierra Club.

Multiple use approach

The multiple use approach is a management practice that is teamed with sustained yield. It began as a working policy, generally associated with forestry, and was enacted as law in 1960.

MULTIPLE USE PERTAINS to a concept of resource use in which land supports several concurrent managed uses rather than single uses over time and space. As a concept of land use management it has most often been applied to questions related to the use of forest lands. Historically, multiple use has been frequently linked with another concept, that of sustained yield. This combination was codified into law with the passage of the Multiple Use-Sustained Yield Act of 1960.

Historical Background. The history of the intertwined multiple use-sustained yield approach to land management in the United States dates from the late 1800's. Prior to that time, land management practices often focused on one land use at a time. Forest lands were used for timber production, rangeland for grazing, park lands for recreation, and so on. Little attention was given to the interrelated aspects of land use. By the late 1800's, however, some resource managers began to see land resources as something to be managed in a more complex, integrated fashion which would lead to multiple use. This awakening to more complex management ideas grew out of the need for sustained yield, especially in the forest sector of the resource economy.

Sustained Yield. Since the beginning of European settlement of North America, forest resources had been seen both as a nearly inexhaustible source of timber and as something to be cleared to make way for agriculture. This policy of removal and replacement led to serious concern by the late 1800's about the future of the nation's forests. In 1891 power had been granted to President William Harrison to set aside protected forest areas. Both he and President Grover Cleveland took action to establish forest reserves. These reserves, however, needed overall direction in their management. To secure this management, Gifford Pinchot was appointed chief forester. Pinchot was trained in European methods of forestry, well traveled, and experienced. Moreover, Pinchot managed his re-

sources, as noted by Stewart Udall in *The Quiet Crisis* (1963), "on a sustained yield basis." The sustained yield basis for forest management was thus established, and with its establishment came an interest in not only yield from the land but also multiple use of the land. Essentially, the sustained yield philosophy restricts the harvesting of trees to no more than the ultimate timber growth during the same period.

Multiple Use. Forest lands have the obvious capability of supplying timber for a variety of structural and aesthetic needs. Properly managed, these lands can meet such needs on an ongoing, renewable basis. However, land in forest cover is more than a source of timber. Watersheds in such an area can be protected from

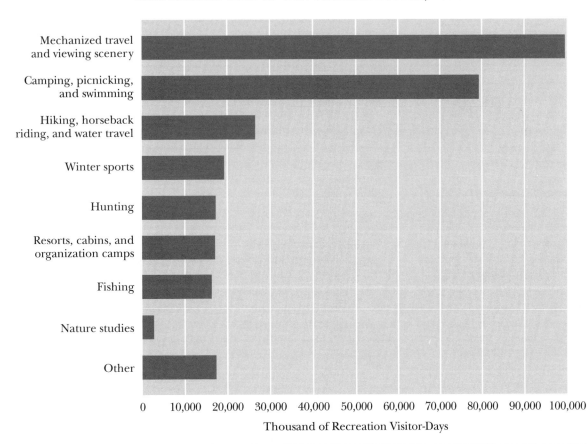

Recreational Uses of U.S. National Forests, 1993

Source: U.S. Department of Commerce, *Statistical Abstract of the United States, 1996,* 1996.
Note: One "recreation visitor-day" is the recreation use of national forest land or water that aggregates 12 visitor-hours. This may entail 1 person for 12 hours, 12 persons for 1 hour, or any equivalent combination of individual or group use.

excessive runoff and sedimentation through forest management if watershed protection is kept in mind. Forest areas are also potential areas of wildlife habitat and outdoor recreation. The combination of forest management for renewable resource production and for complex, interrelated land uses provided the basis for the development of multiple use-sustained yield as a long-term forest management strategy.

Multiple Use-Sustained Yield. The merging of these two concepts took shape over a period of many years beginning in the early twentieth century. The establishment of national forests by Presidents Harrison and Cleveland provided a base for their expansion under President Theodore Roosevelt in the early 1900's. With the active management of Pinchot and the enthusiastic support of President Roosevelt, the national forests began to be managed on a long-term multi-

ple use-sustained yield basis. The desirability of this kind of a management approach eventually led to its formalization by law: On June 12, 1960, Congress passed the Multiple Use-Sustained Yield Act. To some, this act was the legal embodiment of practices already in force. However, the act provides a clear statement of congressional policy and relates it to the original act of 1897 that had established the national forests. Thus, historical reference and continuity are provided.

The 1960 act also specifies that "the national forests are established and shall be administered for outdoor recreation, range, timber, watershed, and wildlife and fish purposes." The act goes on to state in section 2 that "[t]he Secretary of Agriculture is authorized and directed to develop and administer the renewable resources of the national forests for multiple use and sustained yield of the several products and services obtained therefrom." From a management standpoint, this act is brief and to the point. However, it gives no specifics, providing a great deal of freedom in choosing ways to meet its provisions. It also refrains from providing guidelines for management. In practice, the achievement of a high level of land management under the act has called for advocating a conservation ethic, soliciting citizen participation, providing technical and financial assistance to public and private forest owners, developing international exchanges on these management principles, and providing and extending management knowledge.

FURTHER READING: The general subject of multiple use-sustained yield is contained in many conservation texts. Particularly good treatments are in *Exploitation, Conservation, Preservation: A Geographical Perspective on Natural Resource Use*, by Susan Cutter, Hilary Renwick, and William Renwick, 1991, and *Resource Conservation and Management*, by G. Tyler Miller, Jr., 1990. Good historical material is in *The Quiet Crisis*, by Stewart Udall, 1963, and *Perspectives on Conservation*, edited by Henry Jarrett, 1969. Primary material can be found in the Multiple Use-Sustained Yield Act itself, Public Law 86-517, June 12, 1960.

Jerry E. Green

SEE ALSO: Forest management; Forest Service, U.S.; Land management; Pinchot, Gifford; Roosevelt, Theodore.

The U.S. Forest Service's "Land of Many Uses" slogan states its mandate to follow the principles of the 1960 Multiple Use-Sustained Yield Act. (McCrea Adams)

National Audubon Society

DATE ESTABLISHED: January 5, 1905

The National Audubon Society seeks to preserve wild-life and habitats through education and active protective measures.

THE NATIONAL AUDUBON SOCIETY (NAS) grew out of concern over the widespread use of bird plumes in women's fashions in the late nineteenth century. Taking their name from famed painter John James Audubon, whose art depicted more than a thousand bird species, several state and local Audubon societies were founded, beginning in the late 1880's. By 1903 societies existed in thirty-seven states. Viewing wildlife as part of the country's heritage, the societies united and founded a national office in 1905. The organization instituted a policy of educating the public and promoting awareness of the depletion of birds and other wildlife. Its successes include helping to preserve whooping cranes, flamingos, and bald eagles.

During the mid-twentieth century, the organization expanded its policy to promote awareness and protection of all natural resources, including wildlife habitats. Through educational endeavors, the NAS expanded into creating nature centers and reserves that conferred renewed importance on their conservation cause. By the late twentieth century, the NAS was supporting more than 250,000 acres of wildlife sanctuaries.

Aware of the importance of grassroots environmental efforts (like those from which it had come), the NAS adopted a new motto in the late 1970's, calling on citizens to "Think Globally, Act Locally." The idea spread, and the phrase became a rallying cry for conservation groups across the country.

Jennifer Davis

SEE ALSO: Conservation; Endangered Species Act; Fish and Wildlife Service, U.S.; Greenpeace; National Wildlife Federation; Sierra Club; Wildlife.

National Biological Service

DATE ESTABLISHED: 1993

A part of the U.S. Department of the Interior, the National Biological Service (NBS) provides scientific and research support for the ongoing process of managing and conserving the countries biological resources.

THE NATIONAL BIOLOGICAL Service was formed in 1993 through the transfer of certain operations from a number of other bureaus to the new agency. Functions from the U.S. Fish and Wildlife Service, the National Park Service, the Bureau of Land Management, the Minerals Management Service, the Office of Surface Mining Reclamation and Enforcement, the U.S. Geological Survey, and the Bureau of Reclamation were transferred to the National Biological Service. The headquarters is in Washington, D.C. There are also two regional offices, one in Seattle and one in Leetown, West Virginia, and cooperative research units located at fifty-four college and university campuses.

The service seeks to provide the scientific understanding and technical assistance needed to support management and conservation of U.S. biological resources. Among the service's activities in this regard are research, inventorying and monitoring, and sharing information. It works in partnership with state and local agencies as well as with other federal agencies, museums and universities, and private organizations.

Vincent M. D. Lopez

SEE ALSO: Biodiversity; Bureau of Land Management, U.S.; Department of the Interior, U.S.; Fish and Wildlife Service, U.S.; Minerals Management Service; National Park Service and national parks; U.S. Geological Survey; Wildlife.

National Environmental Policy Act

DATE: Passed by Congress in 1969; signed into law January 1, 1970

The first major law enacted in the modern environmental period, the National Environmental Policy Act (NEPA) provided a foundation on which a series of more specific laws have been passed to protect the environment of the United States.

THE NATIONAL ENVIRONMENTAL POLICY ACT was an important step toward creating federal law that could effectively protect the environment and resources of the United States. Before its enactment, the few ambiguous laws that had been passed offered no real solutions. When he signed the act into law, President Richard Nixon declared the 1970's to be the "environmental decade." NEPA made it U.S. policy that the federal government was to "use all practical means and measures, including financial and technical assistance, to create and maintain conditions in which man and nature can exist in productive harmony."

The most important section of the law is a requirement that all federal agencies perform an environmental assessment (EA) and publish an environmental impact statement (EIS) before taking any final action on legislation or projects that would significantly affect the environment. The purpose of the EIS is to identify the short- and long-term environmental consequences of land-use decisions. The EISs are also used to support governmental decisions. Risk assessment began to be employed as a tool for environmental assessments as defined by NEPA.

NEPA has had an impact on the management of public lands by the Bureau of Land Management and the U.S. Forest Service. Requiring EISs for all new actions affecting public lands or new uses of those lands, NEPA was an attempt to legislate environmentally safe uses of the land. Federal agencies, however, have found ways to circumvent the law. One is to use an "environmental record" to reach a finding of no significant impact (FONSI). Another is to declare an action to be an "everyday action," thereby exempting it from the EIS requirement.

As a regulatory law, NEPA is considered a piecemeal approach rather than a comprehensive one. Although there has been litigation based on NEPA, the impreciseness of the law has made it difficult to enforce. Generally NEPA has not been upheld in federal court suits. One reason is that its original grant to the public of an inalienable right to a healthful environment was lessened by changes in the law during the early 1970's. The use of EISs by federal agencies has diminished over the years.

NEPA also created the President's Council on Environmental Quality (CEQ). It role is to ad-

vise the president, publish annual reports for the president and Congress, and oversee compliance with NEPA. However, NEPA gave the CEQ only limited power of surveillance, and the council must work within the policy coordination process of the executive branch. Under the Bill Clinton administration, the CEQ staff was reduced and its future became doubtful.

NEPA was intended to assist the federal government in comprehensive environmental decision making and to have an effect on all related policy areas. Although it is often difficult to interpret and apply as law, NEPA provided the first real basis for defining the nation's environmental priorities, for evaluating what activities are environmentally acceptable, and for determining what role law can play.

Colleen M. Driscoll

SEE ALSO: Bureau of Land Management, U.S.; Environmental impact statement; Environmental law; Environmental Protection Agency; Forest Service, U.S.; Public lands.

National Mining Association

DATE ESTABLISHED: 1995

The National Mining Association promotes American mining products in national and international markets and represents the mining industry before the U.S. Congress, federal agencies, state governments, and international agencies.

THE NATIONAL MINING ASSOCIATION (NMA) was formed by the merger of the National Coal Association and the American Mining Congress. The National Coal Association was formed in 1917 and the American Mining Congress in 1897. The merger of these two strong groups enabled a single voice to represent all the businesses affiliated with the U.S. mining industry. Groups belonging to the NMA include mining companies (in the areas of coal, metals, hard rock, and minerals), mining equipment manufacturers, mineral processors, bulk transporters, and financial and engineering firms and other support services companies.

The purpose of the NMA is to promote mineral resources developed from U.S. mines. It fosters both domestic use and exports to international markets. It maintains a strong political presence in Washington, D.C., and represents U.S. mining interests in international deliberations. The NMA has two political action committees, COALPAC and MinePAC. The NMA provides legal counsel and representation in judicial, administrative, and regulatory proceedings that involve the U.S. mining industry. Finally, the National Mining Association conducts public education programs, informing people of their dependency on minerals that are used in producing common items such as carpeting, telephones, automobiles, and even doorknobs.

Dion C. Stewart

SEE ALSO: American Mining Congress; Mining safety and health issues; Mining wastes and mine reclamation; Reclamation Act; Surface Mining Control and Reclamation Act of 1977.

National Oceanic and Atmospheric Administration

DATE ESTABLISHED: October 3, 1970

The National Oceanic and Atmospheric Administration has a wide range of responsibilities relating to resources and the environment. It is charged with exploring the ocean and conserving ocean resources, with monitoring and predicting weather and atmospheric conditions, and, since the disbanding of the U.S. Coast and Geodetic Survey, with providing precise geodetic surveys.

THE NATIONAL OCEANIC and Atmospheric Administration (NOAA), part of the Department of Commerce, was founded in 1970 to study and predict changes in the ocean and atmosphere and to help conserve U.S. coasts and marine resources. It is a descendent of an army weather warning service and a fishing commission begun a hundred years earlier. Its earliest predecessor was a coastal survey that took place in 1807. The NOAA both performs scientific research—some of it concerned with long-term environmental and resource issues—and helps formulate government policy in such areas as ocean mining

and energy. Subdivisions of the NOAA include the National Weather Service, the National Marine Fisheries Service, the National Environmental Satellite Data and Information Service, the National Ocean Service, and the Office of Oceanic and Atmospheric Research.

Preserving coastlines is a priority of the NOAA because more than half the U.S. population lives near the coasts. In recent decades uncontrolled pollution, overfishing, and coastal development have begun to make even the eternal ocean appear fragile at times. To combat deterioration of the oceans, the NOAA works with the Environmental Protection Agency (EPA), also founded in 1970. The NOAA monitors activities that affect the environment, and the EPA, working with the Justice Department, enforces measures to protect it. Together these two agencies help enforce several acts Congress passed between 1972 and 1980, notably the Marine Mammal Protection Act; the Marine Protection, Research, and Sanctuaries Act; the Coastal Zone Management Act; the Endangered Species Act; the Magnuson Fisheries Conservation and Management Act; and the Deep Seabed Hard Minerals Resources Act.

NOAA scientists study how the ocean and atmosphere influence each other. For example, the Gulf Stream current moves with the force of 750 Mississippi Rivers as it brings the warm waters of the Caribbean up the Atlantic Coast and moves them eastward to England. For such studies the NOAA works with other agencies, such as the National Aeronautics and Space Administration (NASA), whose TOPEX/POSEIDON satellite charts ocean currents in a joint project with France. NASA instruments aboard Japan's Advanced Earth Observing System can detect levels of ozone in the atmosphere as well as wind speed and direction; this latter capability will greatly help scientists forecast seasonal and annual climate changes, because winds are an essential key to predicting changes in the weather.

The NOAA has a number of other functions. It is dedicated to building sustainable fisheries and helping endangered marine life to recover. When overfishing cuts fish populations such as cod and salmon, it also shrinks their gene pool, making them more susceptible to disease. Part of the solution is to identify key species and their habitat requirements.

The NOAA gives advance warnings of hazardous weather. Each year in the United States hundreds of lives and billions of dollars are lost to severe storms, floods, and other natural disturbances. To minimize these losses, NOAA is involved in modernizing the National Weather Service by refining the computer models it uses to predict impending disasters and upgrading the means of disseminating warnings.

The NOAA also promotes safe navigation. Since the 1940's the size of ships has doubled, and maritime commerce has tripled, leading to more than eight hundred groundings or collisions of oil tankers between 1980 and 1988. The NOAA plans to use satellite-based locating systems as well as new electronic navigation systems to address this problem.

Charles V. Cordaro

SEE ALSO: Coast and Geodetic Survey, U.S.; Coastal engineering; Environmental Protection Agency; Fisheries; Landsat satellites and satellite technology; Oceans; U.S. Geological Survey; Weather and resources.

National Park Service and national parks

DATE ESTABLISHED: August 25, 1916

The U.S. Congress established the National Park Service to manage and promote the use of federal parks, monuments, and reservations. Its purpose was to ensure that the scenery, natural and historic objects, and wildlife in the parks could be enjoyed by the public and at the same time left unimpaired for future generations.

THIRTY-SEVEN NATIONAL PARKS were already in existence when Congress formed the National Park Service. The creation of Yellowstone, the first national park in the United States (and the world), like that of later parks, was beset by struggles between those who wanted to preserve federal lands (preservationists) and those who wanted to use them (utilitarians). In general, Congress encouraged the economic development of federal lands. Yet many different groups, each with its own particular intrests (preservationists, local businessmen, the railroads, scientists), were able to convince Congress to pass the Yellowstone Act in 1872, thereby preserving more than two million acres. Despite the law, Yellowstone's pristine status was soon under attack. Conflicts continue to the present; in the late twentieth century, for example, attempts to establish a gold mine outside the park and to prevent the reestablishment of wolves inside the park were defeated.

Congress used the Yellowstone Act as the basis for establishing other early parks. For most of these, preservation was more theoretical than practical. For example, in Yosemite National Park, established in 1890, preservationists, including John Muir, lost a long battle to utilitarians, including Gifford Pinchot, over the flooding of the Hetch Hetchy valley to provide San Francisco with water in 1913. This loss would later be used by preservationists as a rallying cry against future attempts to impinge on the national parks.

The Antiquities Act. In 1906 Congress passed the Antiquities Act to protect federal lands of historical, scientific, and cultural interest. Congressman John Lacey of Iowa had recognized that scenic wonders were not the only lands worthy of preservation. Lacey's original objective was to protect Indian ruins and artifacts of the Southwest from looters, vandals, and other criminals. The wording of the act, however, has allowed presidents to have considerable latitude in setting aside sites as national monuments. Some national parks, including Mesa Verde and Grand Canyon, were first made into national monuments. Their conversion into national parks involved compromise, including permitting railroad rights of way, farming by Native Americans, and the recognition of valid land claims and mining rights within park boundaries.

Establishment of the National Park Service. With no one central federal office coordinating national parks, many problems developed. The parks competed with one another for federal appropriations. No government agency had the authority to determine national park criteria, thus allowing local interests to convince Congress of the value of protecting natural wonders in places few people had seen. Protection of

National Park System Statistics

	1985	1990	1994
Expenditures: millions of dollars	848.1	986.1	1,404.0
Revenue from operations: millions of dollars	50.6	78.6	97.0
Recreational visitors: millions of visits	263.4	258.7	267.6
Overnight stays: millions of stays	15.8	17.6	18.3
Park system lands: millions of acres	75.7	76.4	74.9

Source: U.S. Department of Commerce, *Statistical Abstract of the United States, 1996,* 1996.
Note: Includes visitor data for national parks, monuments, recreation areas, seashores, and miscellaneous other areas.

resources from economic exploitation in all parks was difficult. Congress was not interested in adding to the federal bureaucracy and establishing a new government agency to administer the parks.

The Forest Service, in the Department of Agriculture, wanted to maintain its role as a major federal landholding agency. It and the Reclamation Service, in the Department of the Interior, opposed new national parks in general, since, from their viewpoint, parks overemphasized preservation of federal lands and did not allow sufficient economic use. Years of campaigning by such men as secretaries of the interior Richard Ballinger, Walter Fisher, and Franklin Lane, J. Horace McFarland (president of the American Civic Association), Representative William Kent, Senator Reed Smoot, and Frederick Law Olmsted, Jr. (son of Frederick Law Olmsted, and a renowned landscape architect in his own right), helped to convince Congress of the value of a new agency. After much controversy, Congress in 1916 passed the National Parks Act, establishing a central authority within the Department of the Interior and stating its responsibilities.

Impact of the Park Service. The law that established

the National Park Service, the Organic Act of 1916, has been interpreted in many ways, not always emphasizing conservation and preservation. The first director of the National Park Service, Stephen Mather, tried to enforce his preservationist beliefs but was not always successful. Mather worked hard to make the service a professional organization and an influential part of the Washington bureaucracy.

He also recognized that, in order to make the national park system truly national, some parks needed to be established in the East. All existing parks were in the West, but the majority of the

The Yellowstone River gorge in Yellowstone National Park. Established in 1872, Yellowstone was the first national park in the world. (McCrea Adams)

country's population and wealth were in the East. Although the scenery of the East was not considered as spectacular as that of the West, local groups worked with state and local governments as well as with residents to establish Shenandoah, Great Smoky Mountains, Acadia, and Mammoth Cave National Parks in the 1920's and 1930's.

New Resource Responsibilities. In 1933 the federal government expanded the role of the National Park Service to include federal lands that had been under the control of the Departments of War and Agriculture, including monuments, historic sites and buildings, and national military parks. By preserving and managing important historical sites along with natural ones, the Park Service enlarged its role and more completely fulfilled its mission of 1916.

Today there are more than three hundred national park units. Their popularity with Americans and foreigners continues to grow, frequently resulting in damage to the very resources that the visitors come to enjoy. In recent years federal funds have not kept pace, and the National Park Service has been forced to close sections of parks and to depend more on volunteers. Yet the national parks remain unique national treasures, and the National Park Service continues to manage the parks by balancing use and preservation.

FURTHER READING: John Ise, *Our National Park Policy: A Critical History*, 1961, presents a detailed history of the national parks. Alfred Runte, *National Parks: The American Experience*, 3d ed. 1997, is another examination of the history of the national parks. *International Handbook of National Parks and Nature Reserves*, edited by Craig W. Allin, 1990, provides several essays about national parks around the world, including "United States: National Parks," by M. Frome, R. W. Waver, and P. Pritchard. James Ridenour, *The National Parks Compromised: Pork Barrel Politics and America's Treasures*, 1994, discusses politics and the national parks.

Margaret F. Boorstein

SEE ALSO: Department of the Interior, U.S.; Forest Service, U.S.; Pinchot, Gifford; Muir, John; National Parks Act of 1930; Roosevelt, Theodore.

National Parks Act of 1930

DATE: May 30, 1930

The Canadian National Parks Act removed the parks from authority of the Dominion Forest Reserves and Parks Act and stated that they should be used but left unimpaired for the enjoyment of future generations.

THE 1930 NATIONAL PARKS ACT changed the purpose of Canada's existing national parks from serving as areas of resource exploitation to becoming places to be preserved for future generations. J. B. Harkin, the commissioner of national parks, was the primary force behind its passage, which involved many compromises among national ministries as well as the provinces. It was passed concurrently with other acts that transferred natural resources within the boundaries of their respective provinces from the Dominion to the provinces themselves. New national park boundaries were also drawn. The resources inside the parks remained attractive, and conflict continued for decades about whether they should be preserved or exploited.

The act permitted, under government regulation, the granting of leases in town sites for lots for residence and trade, and it provided for public works and utilities. The national parks therefore were to be places where plants and animals were protected, but they were also to contain permanent homes and places of business for human beings.

The act remains in force today, with some modifications. The first "parks policy" was developed in 1964 to change the parks from serving primarily as areas of recreation to areas of natural conservation and to deal with the great increase of visitors over the 1950's and early 1960's. This modification was developed under the administration of John I. Nicol, director of the National and Historic Parks Branch. Federal expropriation of Indian lands was ended. The National Parks branch became part of Environment Canada, Parks, contained in the Department of the Environment.

In the 1970's Canada identified thirty-nine natural regions within its borders to be represented by its national parks. With more than

A backpacker in Canada's Banff National Park. The 1930 National Parks Act steered the purpose of the country's parks away from resource exploitation and toward conservation, preservation, and recreation. (Jim West)

one-half included by the mid-1990's, the government continued to aim for total representation. The 1979 Parks Canada Policy called for both protection of natural ecological processes with little human interference and provision of quality visitor services and recreational opportunities. In 1988 amendments to the National Parks Act of Canada emphasized the overall importance of preserving natural ecological processes.

Conflicts remain. Although the parks are protected from development, many parks contain towns and the concomitant human activities and natural disruptions. Highways running through parks bring visitors while serving as vital components of major transportation routes. In the newly established northern parks, indigenous peoples are permitted to use resources as part of their traditional ways of life. In outside areas adjacent to the parks, activities such as logging and mining affect wildlife and contribute to air and water pollution within and around the parks.

In 1994 Parliament replaced the Parks Canada Policy of 1979 with new Guiding Principles and Operational Policies, placing more emphasis on protecting natural and historic heritage areas. It called for ecosystem management while meeting social and economic needs, including tourism. The document emphasized the importance of cooperation with the public and with adherence to international conventions such as the world heritage convention and the convention on biological diversity.

Margaret F. Boorstein

SEE ALSO: Biodiversity; Canadian Environmental Protection Act; National Park Service and national parks; Public lands.

National Wildlife Federation

DATE ESTABLISHED: 1936

The National Wildlife Federation is a conservation education organization that works to promote the wise use of natural resources.

THE NATIONAL WILDLIFE FEDERATION (NWF) is an organization of approximately six million private citizens interested in influencing state and national conservation policies. Its programs are based on the organization's beliefs that wildlife, an important indicator of environmental quality, can be protected through awareness, understanding, and action. The NWF believes that clean air, pure water, rich soil, and abundant plant and animal life should be seen as gifts to be used wisely, and it views the welfare of wildlife as inseparable from that of humans.

The NWF sponsors the Institute for Wildlife Research, which focuses on studies of species of special interest, and the National Biotechnology Policy Center, which addresses the environmental implications of biotechnology. Each year it sponsors National Wildlife Week, which reaches millions of students annually to promote awareness about the needs of wildlife. The NWF has developed science and social studies supplements for middle schools and runs Wildlife Camp for children.

Among the many publications of the National Wildlife Federation are *Ranger Rick*, a monthly magazine for elementary schoolchildren, *NatureScope*, a curriculum supplement of science and nature activities, and *National Wildlife.*

The NWF has helped defend the Clean Air Act and Clean Water Act, worked to prevent most oil and gas leasing in national wildlife refuges, fought to help endangered species such as the red squirrel and the bald eagle, and initiated a nationwide campaign to amend the U.S. Constitution with an Environmental Quality Amendment.

Grace A. Banks

SEE ALSO: Biotechnology; Conservation; Mineral Leasing Act of 1920; Wilderness; Wildlife; Wildlife biology.

Native elements

Twenty-four elements are found in their "native" state (uncombined with other elements in nature), but only eight of these native elements are important ores. These eight significant native elements are divided into metals (gold, silver, copper, and platinum), semimetals (antimony), and nonmetals (sulfur, graphite, and diamond).

ONLY GOLD AND PLATINUM are important ores of the native metals. The main ores of silver and copper are derived from silver and copper sulfides. Gold comes from South Africa, Commonwealth of Independent States, China, and the United States. Native silver occurs in Germany, Canada, and the United States. Native copper occurs in the United States and Bolivia. Native platinum occurs in South Africa, Colombia, and Russia. Native sulfur is a major ore, and it occurs in Texas and Louisiana, and Sicily. Most diamonds are found in Africa, Australia, or Russia. The main producers of graphite are India, Mexico, China, Commonwealth of Independent States, and Korea.

The native elements have a number of important uses. Gold is used as a world monetary standard and is used in jewelry, dental fillings, and various scientific applications. Silver is used in photographic film, silverware, and electronic equipment. Copper is used for wire, brass, and bronze. Platinum is used as a catalyst to control automobile emissions and in jewelry and dentistry. Sulfur is used for the manufacture of sulfuric acid, insecticides, hydrogen sulfide, and rubber. Diamond is used as a gemstone, for cutting glass, and as a fine powder for polishing gemstones. Graphite is used as a lubricant in oil, as a writing tool (it is mixed with clay in pencils), and in paints, batteries, and refractory crucibles.

Gold (abbreviated Au; atomic number 79; atomic weight 196.97) is chemically inert and is in the same column on the periodic table as the transition elements copper and silver. Native gold is gold to yellow in color and has a high density (19 grams per milliliter). Silver (Ag; atomic number 47; atomic weight 107.87) is chemically more reactive than gold. Native silver is white on a fresh surface, but it is quickly tarnished; it has a density of 10.5 grams per milliliter. Native copper (Cu; atomic number 29; atomic weight 63.5) has a red color, but it is stained green on weathered surfaces. Native copper has a density of 8.8 grams per milliliter. Sulfur (S; atomic number 16; atomic weight 32.064) is in Group 6 of the periodic table. Native sulfur is a pale to deep yellow color, and it has a density of only 2.1 grams per milliliter. Graphite and diamond are both composed of carbon (C). Carbon (atomic number 6; atomic weight 12.011) is in Group 4 of the periodic table with chemical properties similar to silicon. Graphite is submetallic, lead gray, and has a density of 2.1 grams per milliliter, whereas diamond can be almost any color and has a density of 3.5 grams per milliliter.

The metallic native elements have metallic chemical bonds with delocalized outer electrons; this situation results in their metallic luster and their high conductivity of heat and electricity. The native nonmetals have localized bonding electrons because they share electrons between atoms; this results in nonmetallic luster and low electrical and heat conduction. The native semimetals have properties intermediate between the metals and nonmetals.

The native metals in some deposits are formed by hot, ascending water vapor called hydrothermal deposits, and they are associated with a wide variety of minerals. Native gold may be weathered out of the hydrothermal deposit without alteration and may be concentrated in streams. Native silver may also be concentrated in the oxidized zone by weathering of the original hydrothermal deposits. The most abundant sulfur deposits are formed in the cap rock of salt domes in the southern United States. Diamond is found mostly in igneous rocks called kimberlites and lamproites. Diamond may also be weathered out of the original igneous rocks and be concentrated in streams. Graphite is formed in metamorphic rocks by heating the original organic material in sediments to the high temperatures of metamorphism (more than 200 degrees Celsius and more than 2 kilobars of pressure).

Robert L. Cullers

SEE ALSO: Antimony; Copper; Diamond; Gold; Graphite; Hydrothermal solutions and mineralization; Platinum and platinum group metals; Salt domes; Silver; Sulfur.

Natural gas. *See* Oil and natural gas entries; Propane

Natural Resources Conservation Service

DATE ESTABLISHED: 1933, as temporary Soil Erosion Service; became Soil Conservation Service in 1935; renamed Natural Resources Conservation Service in 1994

The Natural Resources Conservation Service (NRCS), part of the U.S. Department of Agriculture, works with farmers, ranchers, and local government agencies in conserving and protecting resources. The NRCS's areas of activity include soil and resource conservation, plant materials, flood protection, and wetlands preservation.

THE SOIL CONSERVATION SERVICE was established as a response to the devastation being wrought by winds and erosion in the Dust Bowl of the 1930's. It was at first briefly called the Soil Erosion Service, a temporary agency established by the 1933 National Industrial Recovery Act. The NIRA was one of the cornerstones of President Franklin D. Roosevelt's New Deal, intended to help pull the country out of the Great Depression. In 1935, under the Soil Conservation Act, the agency was given permanent status and moved from the Department of the Interior to the Department of Agriculture.

Soil Conservation Service. Hugh H. Bennett, considered the father of modern soil conservation, was the first head of the Soil Erosion Service and then the Soil Conservation Service. The Civilian Conservation Corps, another New Deal program, provided considerable manpower for the SCS's early erosion-prevention efforts. Farmers signed five-year agreements with the SCS; in return for putting the SCS's recommendations into practice, they could receive equipment, seeds and seedlings, lime, fertilizer, and in many cases labor from the Civilian Conservation Corps or Works Project Administration. Conservation approaches (such as strip-cropping under longer rotation) were designed for individual farms.

In 1937 the country was divided into soil conservation districts; the plan was intended to foster local participation in conservation operations. District boundaries were based on such factors as local watersheds and county lines. Districts elected local supervisors and signed agreements with the U.S. Department of Agriculture. The Department of Agriculture employed trained soil conservationists to work with the local districts. The activities of the Soil Conservation Service had considerable impact in stabilizing the United States' landscape, most notably farmland and rangeland.

Natural Resources Conservation Service. The agency's name was changed to the Natural Resources Conservation Service in 1994, reflecting the agency's expanding focus in the late twentieth century. The NRCS has the responsibility of helping the country's farmers, ranchers, and other private landowners conserve and protect natural resources. Through a wide variety of programs, the NRCS is active in soil conservation, flood protection, watershed protection, resource conservation, and wetlands preservation.

The Conservation Technical Assistance program is the central or foundational program of the Natural Resources Conservation Service. More than a million landowners receive its services annually, as do local government entities; services are channeled through nearly three thousand conservation districts in the United States. It provides assistance in sustaining agricultural productivity and enhancing the natural resource base. Assistance includes comprehensive approaches to reducing soil erosion, improving soil and water quality (and quantity), conserving wetlands, enhancing fish and wildlife habitat, improving air quality, improving pasture and range conditions, reducing flooding, and improving woodlands.

The National Cooperative Soil Survey provides information on the uses and capabilities of local soils throughout the country. Published soil surveys include maps, soil classifications, and scientific interpretations that can aid landowners in farm planning and other land-use decisions as well as help guide federal, state, and local governments in policy decisions. Millions of acres are mapped each year; well over a billion acres have been mapped. The Natural Resources Inventory, issued every five years, reports on the nation's progress in sustaining resources on nonfederal land. It provides extensive and comprehensive data on land use and predicts how trends will affect the future of resources.

A number of programs are concerned with water—both with water use and conservation and with river management and flood control. The Snow Survey and Water Supply Forecasting Program collects snowpack data and forecasts seasonal water supplies for areas most affected by snowmelt. The River Basin Surveys and Investigation program works with state and local agencies in such areas as flood hazard analysis, floodplain management, and water conservation and quality. The Small Watersheds program helps local groups plan and install watershed protection projects on private lands; the Emergency Watershed Protection Program provides emergency assistance to safeguard lives and property from natural disasters that impair watersheds. The Public Law 78-534 Flood Prevention Program applies specifically to eleven flood prevention projects that cover about 35 million acres in eleven states.

The Plant Materials Program tests and selects new or improved plants for their usefulness in conservation efforts such as erosion reduction, wetland restoration, water quality improvement, streambank protection, coastal dune stabilization, and biomass production. It has twenty-six plant materials centers across the country. The program works with conservation districts, other government agencies, commercial entities, and seed and nursery associations. Two NRCS programs are directed specifically toward wetlands conservation: the Wetlands Reserve Program and the Water Bank Program.

The intent of the Great Plains Conservation Program is to find long-term solutions to resource problems in the country's ten Great Plains states. It aims to provide conservation treatment for ranches and farms. The program has been effective in addressing the needs of low-income farms and ranches, including many under American Indian ownership. Other programs of the NRCS include the Resources Conservation and Development Program, the Rural Abandoned Mine Program, the Forestry Incentives Program, and the Farms for the Future program.

Vincent M. D. Lopez

SEE ALSO: Civilian Conservation Corps; Department of Agriculture, U.S.; Dust Bowl of the 1930's; Erosion and erosion control; Farmland; Land management; Soil; Soil management; Soil testing and analysis.

Natural Resources Defense Council

DATE ESTABLISHED: 1970

The Natural Resources Defense Council seeks wise management of natural resources through education, research, and governmental policies. Its concerns include land use, air and water pollution, and wildlife protection.

THIS NONGOVERNMENT ORGANIZATION was begun by two groups of lawyers, recent graduates of Yale and Harvard Universities and well-established lawyers from New York. They sought to protect the environment and public health. The staff has grown to include not only lawyers but also scientists, planners, and public health specialists. The council works to increase public education for the protection of natural resources, monitors federal resource agencies, and seeks protection in the courts to preserve natural resources.

The council is supported by more than one hundred foundations, employs about 150 persons, and has an annual budget of $16 million. Its 150,000 members receive *Amicus Journal*, a quarterly that covers national and international environmental policy, books, and reports. The threat of global warming is one of the organization's priorities. A specialized Coastal Program

studies the possible effects of a rise in sea level caused by global warming and the resulting melting of polar ice packs.

Albert C. Jensen

SEE ALSO: Air pollution and air pollution control; Greenhouse gases and global climate change; Land-use planning; Water pollution and water pollution and control; Wildlife.

Nature Conservancy

DATE ESTABLISHED: 1951

The Nature Conservancy is a private, nonprofit organization devoted to the preservation of plants, animals, and natural communities by direct acquisition of ecologically significant lands and other means.

THE NATURE CONSERVANCY has its headquarters in Arlington, Virginia, and offices (local chapters) in all fifty states. It also operates in Canada, fourteen Latin American countries, and the Pacific region. It operates the world's largest system of privately owned nature preserves.

Ecologically significant properties are obtained by direct purchase, gifts, and bequests. The Nature Conservancy also arranges conservation easements and other arrangements in which landowners agree not to develop ecologically important lands. Many of the Nature Conservancy's conservation projects are conducted in cooperation or partnership with other private or government organizations. Some properties are sold to state or national government conservation agencies, but many—over fourteen hundred as of 1996—are managed by the Nature Conservancy staff and volunteers. From its inception through 1996, the Nature Conservancy has been responsible for the protection of over 9 million acres of prime wildlife habitat in the United States and Canada.

The Nature Conservancy's first acquisition, in 1955, was 60 acres of New York's Mianus River Gorge. A 1995 acquisition in southwestern New Mexico was Gray Ranch, a 321,000-acre property including mountain ranges and vast grasslands. Most holdings are between 100 and 1,000 acres of carefully selected wildlife habitat, with special

The Nature Conservancy has helped to preserve millions of acres of wildlife habitat either by buying the land or by making special arrangements with landowners. (Jim West)

emphasis placed on rare and endangered species of plants and animals. Beyond purely protective activities, the Nature Conservancy staff participates in research on ecosystems and conducts educational field trips and programs for members and the general public.

Robert E. Carver

SEE ALSO: Conservation; Ecosystems; Wilderness; Wilderness Society; Wildlife.

Nickel

WHERE FOUND: Sudbury, Ontario, Canada, has the largest exploited nickel ore deposit in the world. Other major ore deposits include those in Norway, Australia, the Dominican Republic, northwestern Siberia, and the Kola peninsula.

PRIMARY USES: Nickel is widely used in stainless steel and other alloys as well as in plating, catalytic processes, and batteries. Stainless steel is commonly about 8 percent nickel. Nickel alloys are also used in marine hardware, magnets, coinage, and tableware. The consumption of primary nickel in the United States was about 107,000 metric tons in 1994, while world production was about 700,000 metric tons.

DESCRIPTION: Nickel (symbol Ni) is a shiny metal with a density of 8.9 grams per cubic centimeter (slightly greater than that of iron). Nickel melts at 1,455 degrees Celsius and boils at 2,920 degrees Celsius. Along with iron and cobalt, it constitutes the iron group triad in the periodic table—traditionally Group VIII, now Group 10. Nickel (atomic number 28) has five stable isotopes and an atomic weight of 58.71. It is malleable and ductile, and it resists corrosion in air.

THE EUROPEAN HISTORY of nickel began with Saxon miners who encountered an ore of nickel they thought contained copper and derisively named *kupfernickel,* or "devil's copper." Axel Frederik Cronstedt investigated a sample of ore from a mine in Helsingland, Sweden, and in 1751 he concluded that it contained a new element, which he obtained in impure form. In 1754 he named the element. Torbern Bergman obtained a sample of the pure metal in 1775. The first nickel smelter began operating in Sweden in 1838 and was followed by others in Norway and elsewhere in Europe. One early motivation for nickel production was the desire to produce nickel-silver alloy from local resources instead of importing it from China. The nickel reserves in New Caledonia were noted by Jules Garnier, who helped establish a French nickel industry and later served as a consultant in Ontario, Canada, after the Sudbury nickel deposits started to be exploited in 1888. The founder of the nickel industry in the United States was Joseph Wharton, whose smelter in Camden, New Jersey, at one time in the nineteenth century produced one-sixth of the world's nickel.

In Britain the nickel carbonyl process was developed in the late nineteenth century by Ludwig Mond and soon became commercially important. Only nickel—not copper or the other metals in nickel ores—reacts with carbon monoxide, yielding volatile tetracarbonyl nickel. This substance, after being separated by distillation, yields pure nickel upon heating to 180 degrees Celsius.

Uses of Nickel. Nickel finds its most important uses in stainless steel and other alloys, in plating, and in catalysts. Valued for its resistance to rusting, stainless steel exists in a multitude of types and compositions, but it is most typically 18 percent chromium, 8 percent nickel, and the rest iron. Nickel-copper alloys such as Monel (68 percent nickel) possess corrosion resistance toward chlorine compounds and salt and are used in

marine hardware. Nichrome (60 percent nickel, 40 percent chromium) is used for heating elements in resistance heaters, while nickel silver (composed of nickel, copper, and zinc) is used for coinage, jewelry, and tableware. Powerful permanent magnets make use of a steel alloy called alnico (*al*uminum, *ni*ckel, *co*balt). Nickel plating is important for protecting steel from corrosion and for steel's appearance. Rechargeable batteries for portable equipment such as radios, cordless telephones, and flashlights are often nickel cadmium cells, while nickel hydride cells are being used in computers and electric vehicles. Thomas Edison developed a battery using hydrated nickel oxide as an electrode coating, and recently a nickel chloride-sodium battery has been developed.

Nickel in finely divided form accelerates the reactions of hydrogen gas with various substrates. Thus nickel catalysts are used in the hydrogenation of vegetable oils and in "methanation"—the conversion of carbon monoxide to hydrocarbons. Nickel carbonyl derivatives and cyclooctadiene-nickel complexes are homogeneous catalysts for oligomerization of dienes and acetylenes. Small amounts of nickel oxide are used to impart a green color to glass. Because nickel alloys are vital in aircraft engines and armor plate, nickel is considered a strategic resource and is stockpiled by the U.S. government.

Distribution and Environmental Aspects. Nickel occurs in detectable amounts in the earth's crust, the atmosphere, and the seas. The earth's core is thought to contain nickel and iron, and some meteorites do. The average crustal concentration is about 100 micrograms per gram, which ranks twenty-second among the elements. Rural air may contain as much as 10 nanograms per cubic meter, and urban air ten times as much. Average nickel content in seawater is 0.1-0.6 microgram per liter, and there are about 4 micrograms per liter in groundwater.

Elemental nickel occurs in meteorites, marine nodules, and the metallic core of the earth. Ores of nickel include oxides, sulfides, arsenides, and silicates, which often also contain copper. The largest commercially exploited nickel ore deposit is in Sudbury, Ontario, Canada. The ore there is a complex sulfide called pentlandite, which contains in addition to nickel a number of other metals, including iron and platinum group elements. Approximately 25 percent of the world's known reserves of nickel are in Sudbury. Major ore deposits also occur in the western Siberian arctic and the Kola peninsula in the Commonwealth of Independent States (former U.S.S.R.). Silicate ores such as garnierite (a nickel-magnesium silicate) are mined in Australia, Cuba, Indonesia, and New Caledonia. Twenty-three different countries mine nickel ore to some extent, major produc-

ers being Canada, Norway, Australia, and the Dominican Republic. The U.S. imports about 60 percent of its nickel, although some is produced in Oregon. A large body of ore has been discovered in Labrador, making it likely that Canada will continue to be a major producer for many years.

Elemental nickel moves through the environment via water-soluble compounds such as nickel chloride or sulfate, through particulate matter, and possibly through the formation of volatile tetracarbonyl nickel. In the biosphere,

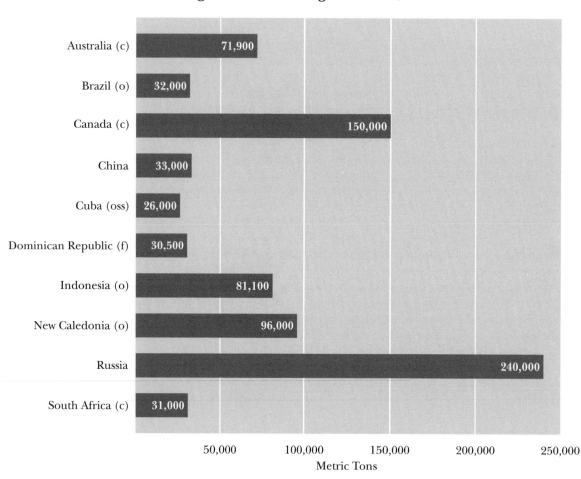

Leading Nickel-Producing Countries, 1994

Australia (c) — 71,900
Brazil (o) — 32,000
Canada (c) — 150,000
China — 33,000
Cuba (oss) — 26,000
Dominican Republic (f) — 30,500
Indonesia (o) — 81,100
New Caledonia (o) — 96,000
Russia — 240,000
South Africa (c) — 31,000

Metric Tons

Source: U.S. Bureau of Mines, *Minerals Yearbook, 1994.* U.S. Government Printing Office, 1996.
Note: Where there are no parenthetical notes by countries, figure denotes recoverable mine production. World 1994 nickel production was about 895,000 metric tons. (c) = content of concentrate; (o) = content of ore; (oss) = content of oxide, sinter, sulfide; (f) = content of ferronickel.

nickel is found to a greater extent in plants than in animals. Many plants are harmed by absorbing nickel from the soil, but some 150 species have been found to hyperaccumulate, resulting in nickel contents up to 25 percent of dry weight. Mosses and sponges are among the organisms that accumulate nickel.

Biological Effects. Four types of nickel-containing enzymes have been identified: urease, hydrogenase, methyl coenzyme M methylreductase (abbreviated MCR), and carbon monoxide dehydrogenase (also called acetyl coenzyme A synthase). Urease, which catalyzes the breakdown of urea into ammonia, is found in plants, bacteria, algae, lichens, fungi, and certain invertebrates. Urease from the jack bean (*Canavalia ensiformis*) was the first enzyme to be obtained in crystalline form (by J. B. Sumner in 1926) but was not known to contain nickel until 1975. The other nickel enzymes are found mainly in bacteria. For example, MCR occurs in methanogenic bacteria that flourish in the bodies of termites. These insects release enormous amounts of methane (a greenhouse gas) as a result of the bacteria. Bacterial carbon monoxide dehydrogenase catalyzes the conversion of carbon monoxide to carbon dioxide and is responsible for removing about 10^8 tons per year of carbon monoxide from the atmosphere.

There is evidence from animal studies that nickel may be an essential trace element in rats and pigs, which fail to show normal weight gain if nickel is rigorously excluded from the diet. Similarly, many plants suffer a distortion of their nitrogen metabolism if deprived of nickel. On the other hand, toxic and even carcinogenic effects can result from particular types and levels of nickel exposure. In rats the LD_{50} (lethal dose for 50 percent of the test subjects) for orally administered nickel (II) acetate is 350 milligrams per kilogram.

The average 70-kilogram human being carries a burden of 0.5 milligrams of nickel, which is concentrated in the hair and nails. Dietary intake is 100-200 micrograms per day, with elimination largely through the urine and perspiration. Oils and fats, meat, seafood, and cereals all contain traces of nickel. Individuals who suffer myocardial infarction, stroke, or extensive thermal burns of the skin exhibit elevated levels of nickel in the blood. Skin contact with nickel or nickel compounds can produce dermatitis; the immune system becomes involved, and once sensitized, a person reacts to very small exposures. There is also a long and melancholy history of lung lesions and cancer in miners who breathed dust containing nickel sulfide. Nickel-containing dust and smoke badly polluted the area around Sudbury, Ontario, at one time, causing widespread blighting of all types of vegetation.

FURTHER READING: Robert P. Hausinger, *Biochemistry of Nickel*, 1993, reviews what is known about the four nickel-containing enzymes and the metabolism of nickel in microbes, plants, and animals. F. B. Howard-White, *Nickel: An Historical Review*, 1963, traces the development of the nickel industry in various countries and has many illustrations. A. F. Kolodziej, "The Chemistry of Nickel-Containing Enzymes," *Progress in Inorganic Chemistry* 41, no. 493 (1994), includes discussion of the physical evidence for the structure of the active sites in nickel enzymes. S. Lippard and J. M. Berg, *Principles of Bioinorganic Chemistry*, 1994, is a textbook that provides a general background in bioinorganic chemistry. The U.S. Bureau of Mines' (after 1996, the U.S. Geological Survey's) annual *Minerals Yearbook* (vol. 1, *Metals and Minerals*) has statistics on the import, export, production, price, and uses of nickel.

John R. Phillips

SEE ALSO: Alloys; Cobalt; Iron; Magnetic materials; Mining safety and health issues; Steel; Strategic resources.

Niobium

WHERE FOUND: Niobium is most often found as niobium pentoxide in the mineral niobite (also called columbite or tantalite), which in the United States is found in Colorado, Connecticut, Maine, North Carolina, South Dakota, and Virginia. This mineral is also found in Australia, Brazil, Madagascar, South Africa, Congo (formerly Zaire), Nigeria, Norway, and Russia.

PRIMARY USES: Niobium is used to toughen and harden steel and to make low- and high-temperature superconductors.

DESCRIPTION: Niobium (symbol Nb), or columbium (symbol Cb), has an atomic number of 41, an atomic weight of 92.9064, and sixteen isotopes. It is a hard, lustrous metal, gray or silver-white in color, malleable (capable of being bent or flattened), and ductile (capable of being stretched). It has a melting point of 2,468 degrees Celsius, a boiling point of 4,742 degrees Celsius, and a specific gravity of 8.4.

NIOBIUM IS NAMED for Niobe, the mythical daughter of the Greek god Tantalus. The designation niobium was officially adopted by the International Union of Pure and Applied Chemistry in 1949. However, an alternative name, columbium, is still used by many metallurgists in the United States and, to a lesser degree, England.

Niobium was discovered by the English chemist Charles Hatchett in 1801, and it was first prepared in 1864 when Christian Wilhelm Blomstrand of Sweden isolated it from niobium chloride by reduction in a stream of hydrogen. Niobium is easily welded and resists tarnish. It exhibits a variable valency of +2, +3, +5, and possibly +4. At high temperatures, it reacts with oxygen, carbon, nitrogen, sulfur, chlorine, fluorine, bromine, iodine, and other nonmetals.

Niobite forms in pegmatite (exceptionally coarse-grained igneous rocks typically made of granite), often with tin and tungsten minerals. Ores of niobium are also sometimes found in placer deposits. Niobium is rarely found without a similar element called tantalum. Seventy-two percent of all niobium reserves are located in Brazil, and 18 percent are in Russia. The element niobium is extracted from niobite by reducing the complex alkali fluoride with sodium, or the oxide with calcium, aluminum, or hydrogen.

Because niobium has excellent gas-absorbing qualities and a high melting point, it is used in the manufacture of vacuum tubes. Niobium is used as an alloying agent in carbon and alloy steels. In the preparation of stainless steel, it is used to prevent corrosion at high temperatures and to permit fabrication without added heat treatment. Niobium adds strength, toughness, and ductility to chrome steel. Niobium alloys are used in jet and rocket engines. In the form of a carbide, niobium is used in making cutting tools. Combined with selenium and hydrogen, it forms a low-temperature superconductor (a material that can conduct electricity without any resistance), which is used in the construction of superconducting magnets. Applications include monorail trains, where the tracks are made of superconductor material and the trains are magnetized and glide along without any resistance. It is also combined with other elements to form high-temperature superconductors. Since niobium allows neutrons to pass through it without interference, it is used in nuclear reactors, particularly in the walls of experimental fusion reactors.

Alvin K. Benson

SEE ALSO: Alloys; Igneous processes, rocks, and mineral deposits; Minerals, structure and physical properties; Nuclear energy; Pegmatites; Placer deposits; Steel; Tantalum.

Nitrogen and ammonia

WHERE FOUND: Nitrogen (N_2) gas constitutes 78 percent of the earth's atmosphere. There are deposits of potassium nitrate in India and of sodium nitrate in Chile, but nitrogen only ranks thirty-third among the elements in crustal abundance with an average concentration of 0.03 percent by weight. Natural gas, petroleum, and coal contain nitrogen, and all plants and animals contain nitrogen in the form of proteins. The human body is about 3 percent nitrogen by weight. Ammonia occurs as ammonium chloride salt in volcanic ejecta, but industrially produced ammonia is the predominant form used. Ammonia from sewage, agricultural run-off, and industrial activities can be a water pollutant.

PRIMARY USES: The largest use of nitrogen compounds (ammonia, nitrates, and urea) is in fertilizer for crops such as wheat, corn, and soybeans. Nitrogen gas is used as a protective gas in the food, electronics, and metals industries. Although fertilizer uses are predominant, ammonia is also used as a refrigerant and as a chemical intermediate in the manufacture of nitric acid and nitrogen-containing plastics and fibers (polyamides, polyacrylonitrile, and polyurethane).

DESCRIPTION: Nitrogen (symbol N), atomic number 7, belongs to Group V of the periodic table of the elements. There are two naturally occurring isotopes, and the element has an atomic weight of 14.007. Nitrogen occurs as a colorless, odorless gas weighing 1.25 grams per liter (0.0 degrees Celsius and 1 atmosphere pressure). Liquid nitrogen is a colorless liquid boiling at −195.8 degrees Celsius and freezing to a colorless solid at −210 degrees Celsius. Gaseous, liquid, and solid nitrogen all consist of diatomic (N_2) "dinitrogen" molecules. Ammonia (NH_3) is a pungent, toxic gas, weighing 0.76 grams per liter (0.0 degrees Celsius and 1 atmosphere pressure). Liquid ammonia boils at −33.4 degrees Celsius and freezes at −78 degrees Celsius. Ammonia is soluble in water to the extent of 28 percent by weight, and it forms explosive mixtures with air.

NITROGEN (N_2) RESOURCES in the atmosphere amount to 4×10^{21} grams, a virtually inexhaustible supply. Nitrogen ranked second among all chemicals produced in the United States in 1995, with 31 million metric tons produced. Ammonia ranked sixth, with 16 million metric tons. Nitrogen from the atmosphere must undergo "fixation" (conversion to ammonia or oxy compounds) before it is available for plant nutrition. Fixation of nitrogen occurs in the atmosphere during fires or thunderstorms, when temperatures rise enough to make nitrogen and oxygen react. In the soil, nitrogen fixation occurs with the mediation of an enzyme, nitrogenase, present in Rhizobium bacteria that live in the root nodules of peas, clover, and alfalfa. Industrial production of ammonia by the high-pressure, catalyzed reaction of hydrogen and nitrogen (the Haber-Bosch process) probably accounts for less than half of all nitrogen fixation. Fixed nitrogen ultimately returns to the atmosphere through decay of plants and animals and the action of denitrifying bacteria. (This process in called the nitrogen cycle.)

The world's growing population of both humans and cattle creates increasing demand for the fixed nitrogen that goes into fertilizer and animal feed. Ammonia plants are being built worldwide to meet this need. Over 111 million metric tons per year of ammonia are produced, with seventy-five countries contributing to the total.

Nitrogen was isolated about 1770 by Daniel Rutherford, Carl Wilhelm Scheele, and Henry Cavendish. Ammonia was isolated by Joseph Priestley in 1774. He prepared the gas by heating ammonium chloride with lime, and he used a pneumatic trough filled with mercury to collect the gas. Justus von Liebig suggested in 1862 that nitrogen is essential for plant nutrition and theorized that plants obtain it from the atmosphere; however, the details of microbial nitrogen fixation were not clear until much later.

Obtaining Nitrogen and Ammonia. The commercial production of nitrogen became possible after the development of the Lindé process for liquefaction of air in 1895. Nitrogen is separated from the other elements in liquid air by fractional distillation, selective adsorption on zeolites, or by membrane technology.

Large-scale production of ammonia from hydrogen and nitrogen (the Haber-Bosch process) began in Germany in 1913. Fritz Haber had developed the ammonia synthesis on a small scale, and he demonstrated it to management at I. G. Farben, the giant German chemical company. Carl Bosch led the team that designed the first ammonia plant, inventing the technology of high-pressure hydrogen reactions in the process. The Nobel Prize in Chemistry was awarded to both Haber (1918) and Bosch (1931) for their achievements.

Nitrogen and hydrogen react at 400-550 degrees Celsius and 100-1,000 atmospheres pressure in the presence of an iron catalyst. The hydrogen is obtained by reacting steam with natural gas over a nickel catalyst ("steam reforming"), and energy requirements are about 25 million British thermal units (Btus) per ton of ammonia. The gaseous reactants used must be

Leading Ammonia-Producing Countries, 1994

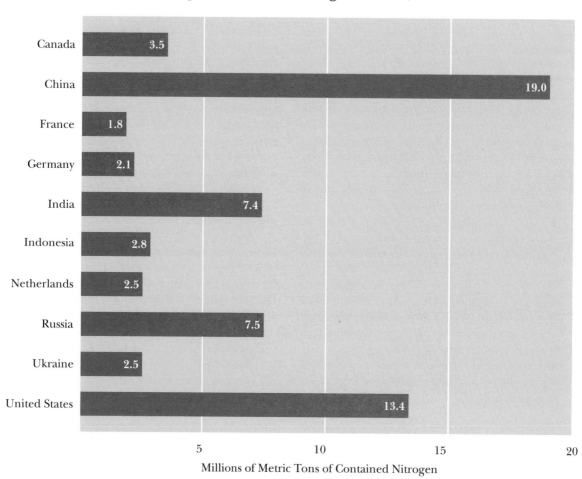

Canada — 3.5
China — 19.0
France — 1.8
Germany — 2.1
India — 7.4
Indonesia — 2.8
Netherlands — 2.5
Russia — 7.5
Ukraine — 2.5
United States — 13.4

Millions of Metric Tons of Contained Nitrogen

Source: U.S. Bureau of Mines, *Minerals Yearbook, 1994.* U.S. Government Printing Office, 1996.
Note: World total production for 1994 was approximately 91.6 million metric tons.

purified to free them of substances that might interfere with the action of the catalyst.

The cost of feedstock is over half the cost of producing ammonia. Ammonia prices usually range around $200 (U.S. dollars) per ton and are sensitive to the cost of energy and of natural gas. There is a futures market in liquid ammonia that helps users hedge against possible price increases. Minor amounts of ammonia are recovered from coke-oven gases, usually being directly converted to ammonium sulfate by reaction with sulfuric acid.

Uses of Nitrogen. As previously mentioned, nitrogen gas, because of its low chemical reactivity, is used to protect foods, pharmaceuticals, electronic parts, and hot metal surfaces from damage by oxygen or other reactive gases. Liquid nitrogen is used to freeze biological samples (such as blood and semen) and foods, and to solidify rubbery materials that need to be pulverized or ground up. Nitrogen gas also inflates the air-bags in automobiles, being evolved from sodium azide in a rapid exothermic reaction triggered by a collision.

Although most ammonia is used in fertilizers, some is used as a chemical intermediate to make other nitrogen compounds. Mixtures of ammonia and air, passed over a platinum/rhodium catalyst at around 500 degrees Celsius, produce oxides of nitrogen that combine with water to produce nitric acid. Mixtures of ammonia and methane can be catalytically oxidized to make hydrogen cyanide, and with propene in place of methane, acrylonitrile can be produced. Explosives such as gunpowder, nitroglycerin, and TNT require nitric acid for their manufacture. Hydrogen cyanide is used in making sodium cyanide for the mining industry and methyl methacrylate, the precursor of plexiglas, while acrylonitrile is used to make polyacrylonitrile synthetic fibers for clothing and carpets.

A host of other synthetic compounds, including many dyes and pharmaceuticals, derive their nitrogen content from nitric acid or ammonia. Two examples are synthetic indigo, used to dye blue jeans, and acetaminophen, an over-the-counter headache remedy.

Environmental Impacts of Nitrogen Compounds. Nitrogen oxides ("NOx" compounds) produced when fuels burn in air are toxic and contribute to acid rain, since they react with water to produce nitric acid. Nitrates and nitrites from agricultural run-off fertilize the growth of algae in lakes and streams (causing eutrophication), and drinking water containing nitrate interferes with red blood cells, causing methemoglobinemia in infants. Federal drinking water standards require there be less than 10 milligrams of nitrate per liter of water.

Nitrogen oxides in the atmosphere contribute to photochemical smog and catalyze the destruction of stratospheric ozone. Photochemical smog is associated with automobile exhaust: the unburned hydrocarbons and nitrogen oxides are acted on by sunlight. A particularly irritating substance called peroxyacetyl nitrate (PAN) can form. The federal clean air amendments contain a limit on the allowable concentration of nitrogen oxides of only 0.05 parts per million, annual arithmetic mean. It is estimated that more than 20 million tons of nitrogen oxides enter the atmosphere each year from the burning of fuels.

Nitrogen oxides that reach the stratosphere can cause destruction of ozone by a catalytic process. Supersonic aircraft flying in the stratosphere would emit nitrogen oxides, and reduce the concentration of ozone. This in turn might result in a harmful increase in the flux of ultraviolet radiation at the surface of the earth, since it is the ozone that absorbs ultraviolet light and exerts a protective effect. Atmospheric chemistry is very complex, and there are many other gases that interact with ozone.

Another nitrogen oxide, nitrous oxide, or dinitrogen oxide (N_2O), is emitted by certain industrial processes. Although it is less toxic than other oxides of nitrogen and is odorless, it does absorb infrared radiation and may contribute to global warming (the "greenhouse effect"). Nitrous oxide also enters the atmosphere as the result of microbial action in the soil.

Ammonia is toxic, with a maximum allowable concentration in the workplace of 50 parts per million in air. Air pollution by ammonia is rare except in cases of accidental release. Because ammonia is extensively transported by truck and pipeline, there are occasional releases, necessitating evacuation of the surrounding area. Since it is less dense than air and is soluble in water, ammonia tends to dissipate rapidly after a spill.

Nutritional Aspects of Nitrogen. Humans obtain most of their nitrogen from the proteins in meat, milk, or legumes. The recommended daily allowance of protein for an adult male is 70 grams, and protein deficiency results in a debilitating condition called kwashiorkor, suffered mainly by children in underdeveloped countries in Africa.

FURTHER READING: An extensive discussion of nitrogen and its utilization is given by Raymond L. Cantrell in the 1993 edition of the U.S. Bureau of Mines' annual *Minerals Yearbook* (vol. 1, *Metals and Minerals*). A primary resource is the article on nitrogen by K. Jones in Pergamon Press's 5-volume *Comprehensive Inorganic Chemistry*, 1973. The Haber-Bosch process is covered in *Industrial Inorganic Chemistry*, by W. Buchner et al., 1989. Material on nitrogenase is found in *Biochemistry*, by G. Zubay, 1993. *Automobiles and Pollution*, by Paul Degobert, 1995, is an authoritative study including information on pollution by nitrogen oxides.

John R. Phillips

SEE ALSO: Agriculture industry; Atmosphere; Eutrophication; Fertilizers; Guano; Haber-Bosch process; Nitrogen cycle.

Nitrogen cycle

Nitrogen (N) is one of the most dynamic elements in the earth's biosphere; it undergoes transformations that constantly convert it between organic, inorganic, gaseous, and mineral forms.

NITROGEN IS AN essential element in all living things, where it is a crucial component of organic molecules such as proteins and nucleic acids. Consequently, nitrogen is in high demand in biological systems. Unfortunately, most nitrogen is not readily available to plants and animals. Although the biosphere contains 300,000 terrograms (a terrogram is a billion kilograms) of nitrogen, that amount is 100 times less nitrogen than is in the hydrosphere (23 million terrograms) and 10,000 times less nitrogen than is in the atmosphere (about four billion terrograms). Atmospheric nitrogen is almost all in the form of nitrogen gas (N_2), which composes 78 percent of the atmosphere by volume. The greatest reservoir of nitrogen on Earth is the lithosphere (164 billion terrograms). Here the nitrogen is bound up in rocks, minerals, and deep ocean sediments.

Even though living things exist in a "sea" of nitrogen gas, it does them little good. The bond between the nitrogen atoms is so strong that nitrogen gas is relatively inert. For living things to use nitrogen gas, it must first be converted to an organic or inorganic form. The nitrogen cycle is the collection of processes, most of them driven by microbial activity, that converts nitrogen gas into these usable forms and later returns nitrogen gas back to the atmosphere. It is considered a cycle because every nitrogen atom can ultimately be converted by each process, though that conversion may take a long time. It is estimated, for example, that the average nitrogen molecule spends 625 years in the biosphere before returning to the atmosphere to complete the cycle.

Nitrogen Fixation. The first step in the nitrogen cycle is nitrogen fixation. Nitrogen fixation is the conversion, by bacteria, of nitrogen gas into ammonium (NH_4^+) and then organic nitrogen (proteins, nucleic acids, and other nitrogen–containing compounds). It is estimated that biological nitrogen fixation adds about 160 billion kilograms of nitrogen to the biosphere each year. This represents about half of the nitrogen taken up by plants and animals. The microorganisms that carry out nitrogen fixation are highly specialized. Each one carries a special enzyme complex, called nitrogenase, that allows it to carry out fixation at temperatures and pressures capable of permitting life something industrial nitrogen fixation does not allow.

Nitrogen-fixing microbes may either be free-living or grow in association with higher organisms such as legumes (in which case the process is called symbiotic nitrogen fixation). Symbiotic nitrogen fixation is a very important process and is one reason legumes are so highly valued as a natural resource. Because they are able to form these symbiotic associations with nitrogen-fixing bacteria, legumes can produce seeds and leaves with more nitrogen than other plants. When

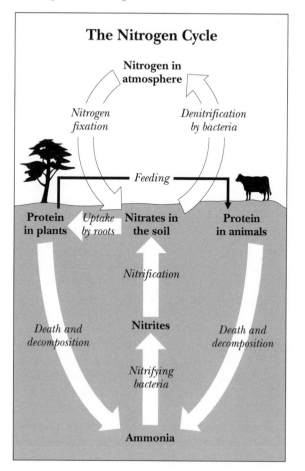

The Nitrogen Cycle

Nitrogen in atmosphere

Nitrogen fixation

Denitrification by bacteria

Feeding

Protein in plants

Uptake by roots

Nitrates in the soil

Protein in animals

Nitrification

Death and decomposition

Nitrites

Death and decomposition

Nitrifying bacteria

Ammonia

they die, they return much of that nitrogen to soil, enriching it for future growth.

Mineralization and Nitrification. When plants and animals die they undergo a process called mineralization (also called ammonification). In this stage of the nitrogen cycle, the organic nitrogen in decomposing tissue is converted back into ammonium. Some of the ammonium is taken up by plants as they grow. This process is called assimilation or uptake. Some of the ammonium is taken up by microbes in the soil. In this case the nitrogen is not available for plant growth. If this happens, it is said that the nitrogen is immobilized. Some nitrogen is also incorporated into the clay minerals of soil. In this case it is said that the nitrogen is fixed—it is not immediately available for plant and microbial growth, but it may become available at a later date.

Ammonium has another potential fate and this step in the nitrogen cycle is nitrification. In nitrification the ammonium in soil is oxidized by bacteria (and some fungi) to nitrate (NO_3^-) in a two-step process. First, ammonium is oxidized to nitrite. Next, nitrite is rapidly oxidized to nitrate. Nitrification requires oxygen, so it only occurs in well-aerated environments. The nitrate that forms during nitrification can also be taken up by plants and microbes. However, unlike ammonium, which is a cation and readily adsorbed by soil, nitrate is an anion and readily leaches or runs off of soil. Hence, nitrate is a serious water contaminant in areas where excessive fertilization or manure application occurs.

Denitrification. Obviously some process is responsible for returning nitrogen to the atmosphere; otherwise organic and inorganic nitrogen forms would accumulate in the environment. The process that completes the nitrogen cycle and replenishes the nitrogen gas is denitrification. Denitrification is a bacterial process that occurs in anaerobic or oxygen-limited environments (waterlogged soil or sediment, for example). Nitrate and nitrite are reduced by denitrifying bacteria which can use these nitrogen oxides in place of oxygen for their metabolism. Wetlands are particularly important in this process because at least half of the denitrification that occurs in the biosphere occurs in wetlands.

The major product of denitrification is nitrogen gas, which returns to the atmosphere and approximately balances the amount of nitrogen gas that is biologically fixed each year. In some cases, however, an intermediate gas, nitrous oxide (N_2O), accumulates. Nitrous oxide has serious environmental consequences. Like carbon dioxide, it absorbs infrared radiation, so it contributes to global warming. More important, when nitrous oxide rises to the stratosphere, it contributes to the catalytic destruction of the ozone layer. Besides the potential for fertilizer nitrogen to contribute to nitrate contamination of groundwater, there is the concern that some of it can be denitrified and contribute to ozone destruction.

The nitrogen cycle is a global cycle involving land, sea, and air. It circulates nitrogen through various forms that contribute to life on Earth. When the cycle is disturbed—as when an area is deforested and nitrogen uptake into trees is stopped, or when excessive fertilization is used—nitrogen can become an environmental problem.

FURTHER READING: William Schlesinger, *Biogeochemistry: An Analysis of Global Change*, 1991, does a good job of introducing global nitrogen cycling. Janet Sprent takes a more biological view of nitrogen in *The Ecology of the Nitrogen Cycle*, 1988. Advanced readers can find a large amount of information about nitrogen in the environment by reading the articles in *Nitrogen in Agricultural Soils*, edited by Frank Stevenson, 1984.

Mark S. Coyne

SEE ALSO: Atmosphere; Deforestation; Eutrophication; Haber-Bosch process; Nitrogen and ammonia; Soil; Soil testing and analysis; Wetlands.

Nuclear energy

FIRST DEVELOPED OR USED: The first nuclear plant began operation in 1951; significant expansion occurred in the late 1950's and early 1960's

Nuclear power, an outgrowth of the development of the atomic bomb during World War II, once seemed to hold the promise of abundant, clean energy, but nuclear

power has become tremendously controversial and is more expensive than had been predicted.

THE FISSION REACTION that occurs in a nuclear reactor releases tremendous amounts of energy in the form of heat. This heat can be used to produce steam, and the steam can be used to drive an electric generator. It appears that uranium, the fuel for nuclear reactors, will far outlast oil and coal as a source of energy. However, concerns about the safety of nuclear reactors and about the disposal of used fuel and other wastes have dramatically slowed the pace of reactor development.

Scientific Principles. Naturally occurring uranium consists of 99.3 percent uranium-238 and 0.7 percent uranium-235. The nuclei of both of these isotopes contain 92 protons. Uranium-238 nuclei also contain 146 neutrons, while uranium-235 nuclei contain 143 neutrons. When a neutron strikes the nucleus of a uranium-235 atom, the nucleus splits roughly in half. Several neutrons and considerable heat are released. This process is called fission. The neutrons that are released can cause the fission of other uranium-235 nuclei, so the process continues in a chain reaction. The smaller nuclei that result from fission are called fission products. They are highly radioactive, and this radioactivity is accompanied by significant heat generation. When one gram of uranium fissions, it releases the same amount of heat as burning about 3 tons of coal or more than 12 barrels of oil.

Historical Background. In 1934 Enrico Fermi, working in Rome, was bombarding uranium atoms with neutrons. He expected the neutrons to be absorbed and new, heavier atoms to result. However, the chemical properties of the atoms he produced were not what he expected. Lise Meitner, Irène Joliot-Curie (the daughter of Nobel Prize-winner Marie Curie), and Otto Hahn reproduced Fermi's experiments. They too were baffled by the results. Finally Hahn realized what was happening: Instead of being absorbed into the uranium-235 nucleus, the neutrons were causing that nucleus to split roughly in half. The result was two lighter atoms rather than one heavier one. Because these researchers were working with very small quantities of uranium,

they did not produce a chain reaction, and they did not detect the heat being released.

In 1939 William Laurence, a science reporter for *The New York Times*, asked Fermi and Niels Bohr, another famous physicist, whether a small quantity of uranium-235 could be used as a bomb as powerful as several thousand tons of TNT. Fermi simply said, "We must not jump to hasty conclusions," but apparently Fermi and Bohr had already considered this possibility. On May 5, 1940, *The New York Times* carried a front-page story by Laurence under the headline "Vast Power Source in Atomic Energy Opened by Science."

Fermi apparently approached the U.S. Navy with his information, but they were not interested. Finally, in 1941, Albert Einstein signed a letter informing President Franklin Roosevelt of the possibilities of nuclear power, and the government finally took notice. Under Fermi's direction the first nuclear reactor was built in an abandoned squash court under Stagg Field at the University of Chicago. This reactor consisted of tubes of naturally occurring uranium embedded in large blocks of graphite. On December 2, 1942, this reactor "went critical" for the first time. A reactor is said to be "critical" when the number of fissions in one second is the same as the number in each second that follows.

Although Fermi's reactor used naturally occurring uranium, bombs could not be built that way. There were two possible ways to build an atomic bomb: Either the uranium-235 could be separated from the uranium-238, or uranium-238 could be bombarded with neutrons and transformed into plutonium-239. Both uranium-235 and plutonium-239 fission easily when struck by neutrons. In these early days it was very difficult to separate uranium-235 from uranium-238, but it could be done. Transforming uranium-238 into plutonium-239 appeared to be the easier route. Large plutonium production reactors were build along the Columbia River near Richland, Washington, and by 1945 enough plutonium had been produced to build the bomb that destroyed Nagasaki, Japan. Ultimately the separation of the two types of uranium proved to be somewhat easier than expected, and the Hiroshima bomb was built of uranium-235.

During the operation of the plutonium production reactors it became obvious that large amounts of heat were produced by the fission reaction, and people began to think of ways to use this heat. This led to the idea of using reactors to generate steam to drive electric generators.

Nuclear Reactor Design. The electric generators and the steam turbines at a nuclear plant are very similar to those at a coal-, oil-, or natural gas-fired plant. The difference lies in how the steam that drives the turbine is produced. Nuclear reactor fuel consists of uranium or plutonium oxide pellets contained inside zirconium tubes called fuel rods. These rods are arranged in a grid pattern with space between them for coolant to flow. This part of a nuclear reactor is called the core. Movable control rods of neutron absorbing material such as cadmium are used to regulate the fission rate in the reactor. The reactor core is housed in a strong steel container called the pressure vessel. Coolant flows into the pressure vessel, from which it flows through the core and absorbs the heat produced by fission. Then the heated coolant flows out of the pressure vessel and into other parts of the system. This heat is used to

A nuclear reactor generating electricity near Toledo, Ohio. (Jim West)

make steam. The cooling fluid can be a gas such as air or carbon dioxide, a liquid such as water, or a molten metal such as sodium. Nearly all reactors in the United States that are associated with the generation of electricity are water cooled. There are two basic designs: pressurized water reactors and boiling water reactors.

In a pressurized water reactor, water at very high pressure passes through the reactor core, the place where the uranium fuel is located. This water, which is called the primary water, absorbs the heat released by fission but does not boil because it is under such high pressure. After this very

hot water leaves the reactor, it passes through a heat exchanger called a steam generator. In the steam generator, heat is transferred from the primary water to water at lower pressure. This lower-pressure water, which is called secondary water, boils as it absorbs heat from the primary water. The steam produced when the secondary water boils is used to spin the turbines that drive the electric generators, while the primary water returns to the reactor to pick up more heat. Both the reactor and the steam generator are housed inside a large, strong concrete structure called a containment building. The primary water, which becomes radioactive as it passes through the reactor core, never leaves the containment building; the secondary water, which does leave the containment building, is not radioactive. In 1987 there were sixty-nine operating nuclear power plants with pressurized water reactors.

In a boiling water reactor, about 10 percent of the water passing through the core is turned directly into steam. This steam leaves the reactor and goes directly to the turbines. No steam generator is required in this system, because steam is generated directly in the reactor. Since steam absorbs heat more slowly than liquid water, care must be taken to avoid the formation of too much steam in the reactor. This could lead to overheating of the uranium and damage to the core. As a result, a boiling water reactor generates less power than a pressurized water reactor of the same core size. Many of the problems with pressurized water reactor plants have been caused by the steam generators. Since boiling water reactors do not have separate steam generators, these problems are eliminated. On the other hand, the steam from a boiling water reactor is mildly radioactive, so the turbines and other equipment must be treated as radioactive material. This is not the case with a pressurized water reactor. In 1987 there were thirty-eight power stations using boiling water reactors.

Gas-cooled reactors have not been used much in the United States, but Great Britain has used them extensively. Commonly, carbon dioxide under high pressure is passed through the reactor core. Leaving the core, the carbon dioxide passes through a steam generator, where it heats and boils water to produce steam. This steam is used to drive the turbines. In a sense a gas-cooled reactor is similar to a pressurized water reactor; however, the steam generators are quite different because the primary fluid is a gas rather than a liquid.

Some reactors are cooled by molten metals such as sodium. Since sodium melts at about 98 degrees Celsius, it is a liquid at the temperatures found in a reactor system. Sodium conducts heat far more rapidly than water does, so a sodium-cooled reactor can generate heat at a higher rate than a water cooled one. On the other hand, sodium becomes highly radioactive as it passes through the reactor core, while water becomes only mildly radioactive. Also, sodium reacts violently with water, so great care must be taken to prevent leaks between the sodium reactor coolant and the steam being produced in the steam generator. Typical sodium-cooled reactors have three coolant loops. The primary sodium that flows through the reactor core transfers its heat to a secondary sodium loop in an intermediate heat exchanger. All this takes place inside the containment building. The secondary sodium flows to a steam generator that is outside the containment building. Here steam is produced to drive the turbines.

Molten metal-cooled reactors are also called fast reactors, a name which refers to the fact that the neutrons, which emerge from fission at very high speed, are not slowed down before they cause another fission. In water-cooled reactors the neutrons are slowed down a great deal; these reactors are called thermal reactors. Although fast reactors are potentially more efficient and economical than thermal reactors, it appears that thermal reactors are safer. As a result, thermal reactors dominate the electric power generation business.

Another advantage of a fast reactor is that it can act as a breeder reactor. In a breeder reactor some of the neutrons produced by fission go on to produce other fissions, but some of the neutrons react with uranium-238 and transform it into plutonium-239. Plutonium can be used to build bombs, but it can also be used in place of uranium-235 as reactor fuel. It is actually possible in a breeder reactor for the amount of plutonium produced to exceed the amount of uranium consumed. Therefore the nuclear industry is not limited to using the 0.3 percent of natural uranium that is uranium-235; it can also use the uranium-238 after converting it into plutonium.

Reactor Safety. One of the major factors limiting the development of nuclear power is concern about reactor safety. On March 28, 1979, there was a major accident in reactor number 2 at the Three Mile Island facility near Harrisburg, Pennsylvania. The accident began when one of the turbines stopped because of a minor malfunction. Although the fission reaction was stopped by the insertion of control rods very early in the accident, the uranium fuel continued to generate considerable heat becuse of the radioactive decay of the atoms produced when the uranium nuclei split. Water must continue to flow over the fuel rods long after fission stops in order to remove this heat. Through a series of errors by operating personnel at Three Mile Island, this flow of water was not maintained, and later part of the core was not even submerged in water. As a result much of the core overheated and melted. Although a core meltdown is a very serious event, in this case the exposure of people outside the reactor complex to radioactivity was negligible. Despite widespread concern over the Three Mile Island accident, it could be argued that it demonstrated that pressurized water reactors are actually quite safe. Such was not the public perception, however, and there were no new commercial reactor contracts signed between 1979 and 1996.

On April 26, 1986, there was a much more serious reactor accident at the Chernobyl nuclear power station in Ukraine. As a result of serious errors by operating personnel, the reactor went out of control. More and more fissions occurred every second, and the water could not carry away all the heat. Steam pressure built up until the reactor burst, and much radioactive material was expelled into the atmosphere. This radioactive material was detected as far away as Sweden. About 135,000 people were evacuated from the area around the reactor. Two people died immediately as a result of the bursting of the reactor. Another twenty-nine died of acute radiation poisoning within a short time. It is estimated that cancer deaths worldwide will increase by seventeen thousand over the fifty years following this accident as a result of the radioactive material released into the atmosphere. The design of the Chernobyl reactor is very different from the pressurized and boiling water reactors used in the United States. This accident seems to demonstrate that the type of reactor used at Chernobyl is not safe enough. In the United States, several government-owned reactors of a similar design were permanently shut down after the Chernobyl accident. These were plutonium production reactors rather than commercial electric power generation reactors.

Reactor safety is an important and a complicated issue. Unfortunately it is an issue that is difficult for nontechnical people to understand. Politicians who may or may not fully understand reactor safety have used the issue for their own purposes. Undeniably, nuclear reactors involve some risk, but so do other forms of power generation (as do driving a car or flying in an airplane). Deciding what level of risk is acceptable is a difficult issue. Many people envision a reactor accident with large loss of life and conclude that the risk is unacceptable. Such an accident has not occurred with the types of reactors in use in the United States, but it cannot be completely ruled out.

Nuclear Waste. Because the new nuclei that form during fission are highly radioactive, the spent fuel that is periodically removed from the reactor must be handled with great care. The radioactivity is accompanied by considerable heat generation, and provision must be made to remove this heat from the used fuel. It takes thousands of years for the radioactivity to diminish to safe levels, so used fuel must be stored in places that are expected to remain unaffected by earthquakes, hurricanes, and other natural disasters for a very long time.

At present reactor plants are required to provide storage facilities for their own used fuel, but this is not a permanent solution. Although the government has been making plans for permanent, long-term storage of used fuel, technical and political problems have delayed the opening of such facilities. In addition to the used fuel, radioactive waste is created during the mining, refining, and processing of reactor fuel. Although this waste is generally less hazardous than used fuel, provision must be made for disposing of it safely.

Finally, the reactors themselves have a useful life of about forty years. Once a reactor is retired, provision must be made to seal it permanently, because many parts of the reactor will remain radioactive for a long time.

Fusion. Fusion is an entirely different process from fission. Fission is the splitting apart of the nucleus of a uranium or plutonium atom. Fusion is the joining of two light atoms to form a heavier one. For instance, two hydrogen atoms can fuse to form a helium atom. The fusion reaction is also accompanied by the release of large amounts of heat. In fact it is the fusion reaction that generates the tremendous heat that stars give off. The potential of fusion to drive nuclear reactors is being explored, but there are significant problems involved.

An ordinary hydrogen atom has a nucleus composed of a lone proton, but there are two other forms of hydrogen. Different forms of the same element are called isotopes, and the isotopes of hydrogen are called deuterium and tritium. A deuterium nucleus contains a proton and a neutron, while a tritium nucleus contains a proton and two neutrons. Deuterium occurs naturally. Some of the hydrogen atoms in natural water molecules are actually deuterium. The deuterium in a cup of coffee could produce enough energy through fusion to drive a car for about a week of normal driving.

Fusion, like fission, was first used in weapons of war. In a hydrogen bomb one deuterium nucleus and one tritium nucleus fuse to make a helium nucleus, which is composed of two protons and two neutrons, plus a free neutron. Unlike deuterium, tritium is radioactive and does not occur in nature. It is commonly made in fission reactors by bombarding lithium atoms with neutrons. The deuterium-tritium reaction is one of the most promising for power-producing fusion reactors.

The most difficult aspect of fusion is that the fuel atoms must be heated to temperatures in the range of 100 million degrees Celsius in order to make the reaction occur at all. In 1989 there were newspaper reports of "cold" fusion—that is, fusion occurring at or near room temperature. Unfortunately these claims have not stood up under closer inspection. Although scientists have been able to produce the extremely high temperatures required for fusion, they have only been able to maintain them for very short times.

The biggest problem is how to contain the fuel at these temperatures. Certainly no material known could remain a solid at these temperatures. Instead, researchers have explored the use of magnetic fields or powerful laser light pulses to contain the fusion fuel. The magnetic confinement method uses a doughnut-shaped vacuum chamber with a very intense magnetic field inside it. The fuel is heated by passing an electric current through it until the required temperature is reached. Experimental fusion reactors that use magnetic containment are called tokamak reactors. The Tokamak Fusion Test Reactor at Princeton University in Princeton, New Jersey, is an example of this type.

Laser containment involves placing the fusion fuel in a pellet and illuminating the pellet with extremely powerful laser light. Details of pellet construction are highly classified. It is known that the laser light compresses the inner layers of the pellet while burning off the outer layers. As the inner layers are compressed they heat up, and fusion begins. Each pellet reacts for only a small fraction of a second, so it is not clear how a sustained fusion reaction could be maintained in this way. The NOVA laser fusion facility at the Lawrence Livermore National Laboratory uses the laser containment approach.

As of the late 1990's fusion was still in the experimental stages. In the 1950's researchers predicted that commercial fusion reactors were twenty years away. In the mid-1990's commercial exploitation still seemed to be about twenty years away. There are experts who believe that commercial fusion will not be achieved in the foreseeable future. The attraction of fusion is that fusion products are not radioactive. If fusion can be harnessed for the generation of electricity, the significant waste-disposal problems posed by fission can be eliminated.

FURTHER READING: Sheldon Novick provides much useful information in *The Careless Atom*, 1969, which takes a negative view of nuclear power. Richard Wolfson, *Nuclear Choices*, 1991, is a more recent and more balanced view of the subject. It covers fusion and the accidents at Three Mile Island and Chernobyl. *Atomic Energy in Cosmic and Human Life*, by George Gamow, 1947, contains beautifully clear explanations of the basic physics of nuclear fission. *Introduction to Nuclear Power*, by John Collier and Geoffrey Hewitt, 1987, is rather technical in some chapters but contains excellent drawings of reactors and detailed descriptions of major accidents. *Atoms to Electricity*, Department of Energy Report DOE/NE-0085, 1987, provides a somewhat simplistic view but contains good drawings and photographs of reactors. *Nuclear Reactors Built, Being Built, or Planned: 1990,* Department of Energy Report DOE/OSTI-8200-R54, 1990, provides statistics on every reactor in the United States. *Nuclear Power and the Environment,* 1973, published by the American Nuclear Society, 1973, addresses a wide range of issues in a question-and-answer format. T. A. Heppenheimer, *Man-Made Sun,* 1984, is an excellent overview of nuclear fusion written in a very readable style.

Edwin G. Wiggins

SEE ALSO: Electrical power; Manhattan Project; Nuclear Regulatory Commission; Nuclear waste and its disposal; Plutonium; Steam and steam turbines; Uranium.

Nuclear Energy Institute

DATE ESTABLISHED: 1994

The Nuclear Energy Institute is the nuclear industry's private, nonprofit, Washington-based trade association, representing about four hundred companies and organizations worldwide. It is an advocate for the nuclear energy industry regarding public information, legislation, and the implementation of regulatory policies and procedures.

THE FUNCTIONS PREVIOUSLY performed by four Washington-based nuclear energy industry organizations were incorporated into a single organization called the Nuclear Energy Institute (NEI) in March of 1994. The first of the four organizations was the American Nuclear Energy Council, which was responsible for government affairs. The second organization was the Nuclear Management and Resources Council, which managed regulatory and technical issues. Third was the U.S. Council for Energy Awareness, which maintained a national nuclear energy communications program. The fourth organization, the Edison Electric Institute, continues to exist, although its nuclear activities and programs in nuclear waste and nuclear fuel supply have been turned over to the NEI.

The NEI promotes the use of nuclear energy and supports the nuclear energy industry. The institute's stated purpose is "to foster and encourage the safe use and development of nuclear energy." The types of companies and organizations belonging to the NEI include utilities that own and operate nuclear power plants, nuclear plant equipment suppliers, construction and engineering firms, nuclear fuel cycle companies, producers of radionuclides and radiopharmaceuticals, law firms, consulting firms, and labor unions.

Dion C. Stewart

SEE ALSO: Atomic Energy Acts of 1946 and 1954; Edison Electric Institute; Nuclear energy; Nuclear Regulatory Commission; Nuclear waste and its disposal.

Nuclear Regulatory Commission

DATE ESTABLISHED: 1975

The Nuclear Regulatory Commission is the independent U.S. government agency that regulates civilian use of nuclear technology. Its most important duty is the regulation of nuclear power plants and fuels.

THE NUCLEAR REGULATORY Commission (NRC) was established in 1975 under the Energy Reorganization Act of 1974. The NRC's parent agency, the Atomic Energy Commission (AEC), was responsible for promoting and regulating civilian uses of nuclear energy following the development of nuclear weapons technology during World War II. At the time, public policy regarded nuclear energy as a resource with unlimited potential, promising inexpensive electricity and benign environmental impact.

Soon after the AEC was established, critics saw a conflict between promoting nuclear energy and strictly regulating its safety, because the latter would lead to slower adoption of the technology. Their concerns eventually were answered with the reorganization of 1974, which left the NRC with a mandate to protect public health and safety but no promotional responsibility. The NRC's commissioners are appointed by the president and confirmed by the Senate, serving staggered five-year terms. The agency has broad authority to regulate nuclear technology.

NRC decisions have a major effect on the economy's ability to replace conventional fuels with nuclear energy. If all safety measures proposed by environmental groups and nuclear critics were imposed, the money costs of nuclear power frequently are calculated to be greater than those of alternative energy sources. Including only the safety measures considered necessary by the industry, money costs of nuclear power generally are less than those of alternatives. The NRC has regulatory responsibility for the disposal of nuclear power plant wastes, some of which remain significantly radioactive for thousands of years.

The NRC's safety decisions are complicated by the nature of nuclear risk: A major accident at a nuclear facility is estimated to be highly unlikely but to have potentially catastrophic consequences. As long as the accident is possible, additional safety spending may be justified to further lower the probability or lessen the consequences. However, at lower probabilities, further reductions in accident danger become more and more costly. The NRC's legislative mandate calls for it to assure public health and safety but provides no specific guidance on how far the mandate must be pursued.

NRC safety decisions have been criticized both by the nuclear industry and by environmental interests. The industry contends that NRC regulations have sometimes been unnecessary, counterproductive, and overly prescriptive in techniques for achieving safety. Environmental interests have asserted that the NRC has compromised safety to ensure the economic viability of nuclear projects.

Safety concerns reached a peak when a reactor accident occurred at the Three Mile Island nuclear plant in Pennsylvania in 1979. In response to investigations of the accident, the NRC reformed its licensing and regulatory processes. However, no new plants of that type were begun, and a number of nuclear projects then in progress were canceled.

William C. Wood

SEE ALSO: Atomic Energy Acts of 1946 and 1954; Atomic Energy Commission; Energy economics; Nuclear energy; Nuclear waste and its disposal; Three Mile Island nuclear accident.

Nuclear waste and its disposal

The question of what to do with high-level radioactive waste is one of the most significant problems of the nuclear power industry; various methods of burying and destroying the material have been proposed.

UNWANTED RADIOACTIVE MATERIALS are usually classified as either low-level or high-level nuclear waste, depending on the concentration of radioactivity. Low-level waste (LLW), such as syringes contaminated by radioactive pharmaceuticals, is much less dangerous than the high-level waste (HLW) generated in nuclear reactors. According to the 1980 Low-Level Radioactive Waste Policy Act, individual states are responsible for the development of low-level waste disposal sites in conformity with licensing rules established by the U.S. Nuclear Regulatory Commission. Disposal of high-level waste, however, must be accomplished on the national level, as specified by the Nuclear Waste Policy Act of 1982. Most of that waste comes from nuclear plants producing electricity.

Most electricity is still produced by burning fossil fuels, predominantly coal. This process is associated with the emission of carbon dioxide (CO_2), the unavoidable by-product of combustion. The rising concentration of CO_2 in the atmosphere is a factor in global warming. The energy-related emission of that gas is expected to increase by at least 30 percent between 1992 and 2010. The only demonstrated alternatives to fossil fuel plants—that is, sources that can produce power on a comparable scale—are nuclear plants, in which energy is released through fission of uranium. Such plants do not produce CO_2, but their operation is associated with the accumulation of large amounts of high-level waste. In 1995 about 24 percent of the world's electricity was generated in 340 nuclear power plants.

The fuel for a typical reactor is a rare isotope of uranium, uranium-235, which is mixed with common uranium (uranium-238); the enrichment ratio is 1 to 30. The fuel is consumed through a nuclear reaction, called fission, a process in which atoms of uranium are broken into radioactive fragments. The energy released in fission becomes heat, part of which is converted into electricity. Once or twice a year a reactor must be shut down for refueling. The removed waste is usually stored in a local isolated area for several years, because it is highly radioactive and its presence in the biosphere would be a great danger to all living organisms. But this type of procedure is not sufficient: Tens of thousands of years are necessary to reduce the radioactivity in spent fuel to a nonthreatening level.

Burying Spent Fuel. The nuclear industry faces the critical challenge of isolating radioactive components of spent fuel from the human habitat. One possibility is to bury spent fuel deep in geologically stable formations. A site tentatively selected for that purpose is Nevada's Yucca Mountain; the U.S. government has spent millions of dollars developing the site. According to the plan, high-level waste would be stored in corrosion-resisting containers and monitored for fifty years. The depository would be sealed to prevent human interference. The project, however, is controversial. Some scientists think that an unacceptable number of radioactive atoms would leak into the biosphere with slowly percolating water or steam generated by radioactive heat. Others fear the possibility of future volcanic activities and earthquakes.

Not everyone agrees that spent fuel should be buried without preliminary processing. In France, for example, where 75 percent of electricity is nuclear, the proposed solution is to process spent fuel before burying it. Chemical processing is already used to extract valuable by-products, such as plutonium, from spent fuel. One isotope of plutonium that is as fissionable as uranium-235 has already been used to manufacture new fuel. The Yucca Mountain tunnels are sufficiently large to hold the radioactive waste already accumulated in the United States, where only 20 percent of electricity is produced by nuclear power. New sites, however, will be needed to store the high-level waste that will be produced in the twenty-first cen-

tury and beyond. Proliferation of such sites is not desirable.

Destroying Radioactive Waste. Proposals are being developed to "incinerate" spent fuel. Nuclear incineration refers not to chemical burning but to nuclear reactions by which long-lived radioactive atoms are transmuted into short-lived or nonradioactive atoms. For example, consider technetium-99, a metallic by-product of fission that remains radioactive for hundreds of thousands of years. By absorbing a neutron, that isotope becomes technetium-100, which rapidly decays into a nonradioactive isotope, ruthenium-100. Another example is highly radioactive

Canisters of low-level nuclear waste from the Three-Mile Island accident being dumped at the Hanford Nuclear Reservation near Hanford, Washington, in 1979. (AP/Wide World Photos)

strontium-90. The half-life of that fission product is twenty-nine years. But by absorbing a neutron, that isotope becomes strontium-91, which decays into radioactive yttrium-91 and then into nonradioactive zirconium-91. The decay of strontium-91 into zirconium-91 is more rapid than the decay of the original strontium-90 into zirconium-90. Nuclear reactions in which atoms of one kind are turned into atoms of another kind through particle bombardment have been routinely used to fabricate radioactive isotopes for medical and industrial applications in microgram and milligram quantities, but the idea of transmuting hundreds of kilograms of long-lived waste materials is unprecedented. The spent fuel generated by a commercial nuclear reactor in one year, after ten years of preliminary storage, typically contains 120 kilograms of various fission products, 285 kilograms of plutonium, and 35 kilograms of other actinides (mostly neptunium, americium, and curium).

In a nuclear incinerator high-level waste would be progressively destroyed by a flux of neutrons of an intensity several orders of magnitude higher than occurs in an ordinary reactor. The flux would be produced in a reactor whose central region is bombarded by an intense beam of high-energy protons delivered by an accelerator of charged particles—for example, by a cyclotron. On the average each proton would produce many neutrons, the number depending on its initial energy. These neutrons would participate in a chain reaction producing heat and secondary neutrons. Heat would be used to generate electricity while the destruction of waste by secondary neutrons is in progress. An anticipated accelerator-reactor combination for the transmutation of high-level waste is called a nuclear hybrid system. The reactor of such a system is often referred to as a blanket reactor because it surrounds the material bombarded by protons. The blanket reactor will be designed as a so-called subcritical device: Its chain reaction could not be sustained without protons. That feature would make the incinerating reactors considerably safer than those now used to produce electricity.

Several hybrid systems have been developed. One of them has a blanket that contains graphite and molten salt. Materials to be transmuted are mixed with the fuel, dissolved in the salt, and pumped with it through a network of pipes. That network passes through the high neutron flux region (where nuclear reactions take place), through a heat exchanger, and through a fully automated chemical plant. The composition of circulating material is monitored and adjusted to optimize the overall performance without stopping the reactor. An alternative solution is to separate the hybrid system from the chemical plant. This can be accomplished in a sealed blanket loaded with fuel rods surrounded by small containers of waste material. The fuel and waste are immersed in molten lead. The lead circulates by convection and delivers energy to a heat exchanger situated in the upper part of the vessel. The arrangement resembles a traditional power plant cooled by water but is designed to operate without a pump. The blanket would have to be opened for refueling once every four or five years. It has been estimated that the cost of electricity generated by a network of nuclear incinerators would be lower than the cost of a network of contemporary power plants. Three teams of scientists have been actively pursuing incineration projects since 1993 at the Los Alamos National Laboratory, the International Center of Nuclear Research in Switzerland, and Japan's Atomic Energy Research Institute.

The by-products of nuclear incineration are highly radioactive. Their radioactivity, however, is expected to decrease more rapidly than the radioactivity of unprocessed spent fuel. According to detailed calculations, the time for reducing the radioactivity of secondary waste to a safe level is approximately five hundred years. (This can be contrasted with approximately fifty thousand years for unprocessed spent fuel.) Nuclear incineration would not eliminate the necessity of isolating radioactive materials from the biosphere, but it would shorten the isolation time considerably. Predictions of what might happen in several hundred years are likely to be considerably more reliable than predictions involving much longer time intervals. It has been suggested that containers of secondary waste be kept near the earth's surface in protected areas—for example, in a desert—so they could be monitored, repaired, and moved if necessary.

FURTHER READING: Raymond L. Murray, *Understanding Radioactive Wastes*, 1989, provides good background on generation and disposal of radioactive waste. Issues associated with geological depositories of high-level waste are described in an article by Chris G. Whipple, "Can Nuclear Waste Be Stored Safely at Yucca Mountain?" *Scientific American* (June, 1996), and in D. Savage's book *The Scientific and Regulatory Basis for the Geological Disposal of Radioactive Wastes*, 1995.

Ludwik Kowalski

SEE ALSO: Air pollution and air pollution control; Biosphere; Department of Energy, U.S.; Electrical power; Energy economics; Nuclear energy; Plutonium; Three Mile Island nuclear accident; Uranium; Water pollution and water pollution control.

Ocean current energy

The use of ocean currents as an energy source carries great potential, but development has proceeded slowly because the cost is not competitive with that of other energy sources.

JUST AS WINDS flow through the earth's atmosphere, currents flow throughout the world's oceans. These currents are a potential power source as great as wind, although winds harnessed for power have greater speed than the currents. The energy available in a fluid flow varies both with velocity (by the square) and with density:

$$\text{Kinetic Energy} = (\text{Density}) \times (\text{Velocity})^2$$

Because water is nearly 800 times denser than air (1,000 and 1.27 kilograms per cubic meter, respectively), a current of 1 mile per hour (1.6 kilometers per hour) has as much energy as a wind of 28 miles per hour (45 kilometers per hour), which is considered an excellent average speed for wind energy. Furthermore, currents are more dependable than winds and flow in a constant direction.

Ocean Temperature and Salinity. Ocean currents are caused by differences in temperature and salinity. For example, as water near the poles is cooled, its density increases, and much of this cooler water sinks toward the ocean floor. From there it flows toward the equator, displacing warmer water as it goes. Meanwhile, water near the equator is warmed, becoming less dense. It tends to flow along the surface toward the higher latitudes to replace the sinking denser water.

The Gulf Stream is such a current. It starts from an area of warm water in the equatorial Atlantic and in the Gulf of Mexico. This warm water flows generally northward parallel to the coast of North America and bends gradually to the right due to the rotation of the earth. This tendency to curve (right in the Northern Hemisphere, left in the Southern Hemisphere) is called the Coriolis effect, and it bends the flow northeast as the West Wind Drift, bringing warm, moist air to western Europe. It continues south as the Canaries Current (carrying cooler water) past western North Africa. Finally, the bending turns back west toward North America as the North Equatorial Current.

Similar circular patterns, or gyres, occur in all the world's oceans, with many locations having great potential for electrical power generation. For instance, the Gulf Stream has more energy than all the world's rivers combined. The area off Florida might yield 10,000 megawatts (10 billion watts) without observable change in the heat flow to Europe.

Salinity differences also cause major flows. The most easily tapped salinity currents are those between a sea with high evaporation and the open ocean. High-salinity water flows along the bottom from the Mediterranean Sea, for instance, while less saline Atlantic water flows in to replace it. (German submarines used these currents during World War II for drifting silently past the major British base at Gibraltar.) Two lesser potential sources of current power are tidal currents and the currents at the mouths of rivers.

Methods for Harnessing Ocean Currents. Electrical power generation from currents requires three things: mooring power stations to the ocean floor, generating power, and transmitting power to customers on shore.

Mooring and transmitting power are related economic constraints on ocean current power. Although an underwater cable from a mid-Atlantic power station could technically supply power, deeper mooring lines and longer cables eventually cost more than the power delivered. Thus, ocean current stations, if built, will tend to be near shore on the continental shelf and slope before investors attempt to moor a plant to the depths of the ocean floor.

Using currents in deeper and more distant waters will require some means of energy storage. This issue has been considered in design studies for ocean thermal energy conversion (OTEC) power stations, which would harness the temperature difference between warm tropical waters and the colder deep waters. Electricity could be used for some energy-intensive process (such as refining aluminum) or for electrolyzing hydrogen from water. Hydrogen could be used to synthesize chemical products, such as ammonia or methanol. Once the potential of current power is proven, investors may consider the second set of risks inherent in such mid-ocean ventures.

Among various proposals, two methods have been studied in detail: turbines and sets of parachutes on cables. Turbines were first proposed by William Mouton, who was part of a study team led by Peter Lissaman of Aerovironment Inc. Their design is called Coriolis. In the study design, one 83-megawatt Coriolis station has two huge counter-rotating fan blades (so it does not pull to one side), roughly a football field in diameter. The blades move slowly enough for fish to swim through them.

With blades so large, neither rigid blades nor the central hub could be made strong enough without being too heavy and expensive. However, a catenary (free-hanging, like the cables of the Golden Gate Bridge), flexible blade can be held in the proper shape by the current while the generators are in a rim around the blades. The rim also acts as a funnel to increase current speed past the blades and as an air reservoir for raising the station when necessary.

A more revolutionary concept, parachutes on cables, was proposed by Gary Steelman. His water low-velocity energy converter (WLVEC) design is an endless loop cable between two pulleys, much like a ski lift cable. Parachutes along the cable are opened by the current when going downstream and closed when coming back upstream. The WLVEC is cheaper than Coriolis, but there is a question of how well any fabric could withstand sustained underwater use.

Ocean currents are sufficiently powerful and predictable to supply electricity effectively. However, costs of competing fossil fuels must rise significantly before investors will overcome their timidity about constructing offshore power plants.

FURTHER READING: *Oceans of Energy: Reservoirs of Power for the Future*, by Augusta Goldin, 1980, provides an engrossing description of ocean energy sources, including waves, currents, tides, temperature differences, and salinity differences. "Tapping the Oceans' Vast Energy with Undersea Turbines," P. B. S. Lissaman, *Popular Science* (September, 1980), summarizes the proposed Coriolis Project. *Offshore and Underground Power Plants*, edited by Robert Noyes, 1977, summarizes work on ocean current energy and most other ocean energy possibilities.

Roger V. Carlson

SEE ALSO: Energy storage; Ocean thermal energy conversion; Ocean wave energy; Tidal energy.

Ocean thermal energy conversion

FIRST DEVELOPED OR USED: First experimental ocean thermal energy plant operated in 1926; feasibility was demonstrated in the 1980's

In some tropical regions of the earth there is virtually limitless energy in the ocean for possible conversion to electric power. The efficiency of the conversion is very low, however, and the engineering problems are challenging. Development of ocean thermal energy conversion (OTEC) has been slow.

IN TROPICAL OCEANS, the temperatures of warm and cold layers of water may differ significantly even though the layers are less than a thousand meters apart. This phenomenon results from global circulation currents caused by the sun. Solar energy warms water near the surface, and colder, more dense water moves to lower depths. At the same time, the rotation of the earth causes the cold water to flow from the poles toward the tropics. As it is warmed, this cool water then rises toward the surface as its density decreases, causing the warm surface water to flow toward the polar regions, where it is cooled.

Differences of 20 to 25 degrees Celsius over a distance of 500 to 1,000 meters are found in the Caribbean Sea and the Pacific Ocean near the Hawaiian Islands. In accordance with the second law of thermodynamics, thermal energy from the warm layer can be used as a "fuel" for a heat engine that exhausts energy to the cool layer. Typically, the warm layer has a temperature between 27 and 29 degrees Celsius, and the cool layer is between 4 and 7 degrees. The second law of thermodynamics indicates that the maximum efficiency of the conversion from thermal energy to mechanical energy will be very low. For example, if the warm layer is at 25 degrees Celsius and the cold layer is at 5 degrees, the maximum efficiency will be less than 7 percent; even this figure is between two and three times the actual efficiency that can be achieved in an energy conversion plant.

History. The concept of OTEC was first suggested in 1882 by the French physicist Arsene D'Arsonval, but it was not until 1926 that the French scientist Georges Claude made an attempt to implement the idea at Matanzas Bay, Cuba. The facility in Cuba was a small, land-based plant which was so inefficient that it required more power to operate than it produced. It ran for only a few weeks. Since the 1960's improvements in design and materials have led to considerable research. Feasibility as a practical method of power generation was first demonstrated in the 1980's.

Advances in OTEC have depended very much on governmental support. In the mid-1970's only the U.S. and Japanese governments were supporting research and development. The French government later became interested, and sponsorship has followed in the Netherlands, the United Kingdom, and Sweden.

Basic Designs. Broadly speaking, designs are either open cycle (OC) or closed cycle (CC). In the OC method, the incoming warm seawater is continuously sent into an evaporator operating at low pressure, where a small portion of the water "flashes" into steam. The steam in turn passes through a turbine connected to an electric power generator. The low-pressure steam leaving the turbine is then cooled and condensed in a heat exchanger by the cold seawater stream. The condensed water is fresh water, the salt of the ocean having been left behind in the evaporator. Hence, this water can be used for drinking and other household uses.

In the CC process, heat from the warm stream is transferred in a heat exchanger to a "working fluid" such as propane or ammonia. This fluid is vaporized and passed through a turbine-generator in the same fashion as in the OC process. The vapor leaving the turbine is then condensed in a second heat exchanger. The condensate is recycled to the first exchanger, where it is again vaporized. Thus, the working fluid is never in direct contact with the seawater. Some hybrid plants have been designed which are combinations of OC and CC technology.

Though the first plant was a land-based unit, some plant designs involve plants located offshore, possibly floating or submerged. One of the key elements in the process is the water pipe which carries the cold water to the plant. This pipe is typically between 1 and 2 kilometers long. Originally, Claude used a corrugated steel pipe, 1.6 meters in diameter, which was fragile and not corrosion-resistant. Steel has been replaced by fiberglass-reinforced plastic or high-density polyethylene. Diameters larger than this have been considered in some studies but are not very feasible owing to a lack of flexibility.

Engineering Problems. Designs for OTEC plants with power capacities on the order of 10 megawatts or more have been made, but actual plants have been much smaller, with outputs on the order of tens of kilowatts. In spite of these relatively small outputs, the equipment and the engineering problems are challenging. Both cold and warm water flow rates are large because the efficiency of the conversion process is so low. The seawater carries considerable dissolved gases, notably nitrogen and oxygen, and these gases must be vented if flash evaporation is used. The presence of noncondensable gases poses difficult problems in both the evaporator which precedes the power turbine and in the condenser which follows it. These gases not only increase the sizes of the units but also, because they are below atmospheric pressure, must be pumped out to maintain the vacuum levels in the process.

The CC method can avoid some of these problems. The operating pressures in the cycle using propane are relatively high, so a turbine of reasonable size can be used. Moreover, because the pressures are greater than atmospheric, vacuum and deaeration problems are eliminated. The CC process introduces additional problems, however, owing to the heat-transfer steps between the working medium and the hot and cold water.

Advantages. In view of the very low efficiency of OTEC, it may seem hard to imagine how the process can be profitable. However, the "fuel" is free and virtually unlimited. In addition, the OC process can produce sizable quantities of fresh water, which is often valuable in places where OTEC plants are located. Indeed, some OC plants may even be profitable on the basis of their fresh water production alone. Nevertheless, OTEC, even in the best of circumstances, poses both engineering and economic challenges that will continue to plague its development for many years.

FURTHER READING: Some technical background and an example of a design are presented in the textbook *Energy Conversion Systems*, by Harry A. Sorensen, 1983. A number of papers on OTEC can be found in *Ocean Energy Recovery*, the proceedings of the International Conference on Ocean Energy Recovery, held in Honolulu, Hawaii, in 1989; it was edited by Hans-Jurgen Krock and published by the American Society of Civil Engineers, 1990. An overview is given by Dylan Tanner in his paper "Ocean Thermal Energy Conversion: Current Overview and Future Outlook," *Renewable Resources* 6, no. 3 (1995).

Thomas W. Weber

SEE ALSO: Electrical power; Ocean current energy; Ocean wave energy; Oceans; Tidal energy.

Ocean wave energy

A number of designs for harnessing wave energy have been proposed, and some are used on a small scale, but the vast potential of this power source has not been tapped because of the uncertainties and expense involved.

WAVES CRASHING AGAINST a beach are a vast, almost mystical, display of mechanical power. For centuries people have sought ways of tapping it. In 1699 a father and son named Girard applied to the French government for a patent on a wave power device. They noted that waves easily lifted even mighty ships. Hence, a lever from a ship to shore could power all manner of mills. (There are records of Girard mills on rivers, but the wave machine was probably never built.) Hundreds of patents later, wave power is still largely dream, although a dream that is becoming closer to reality.

The Nature of Waves. Waves are the product of wind blowing on the ocean surface. The energy available comes from the wind speed and the distance (or "fetch") that the wind blows: A breeze blowing on a small bay produces ripples, whereas a hurricane blowing across several hundred miles builds hill-sized waves. Waves hitting a beach can be the result of a storm on the opposite side of an ocean. From that standpoint, waves are a collecting and concentrating mechanism for wind power. However, there is some loss of wave energy over great distances, so the best places to take advantage of wave potential are along high-wind coasts of the temperate and subpolar latitudes.

Water waves mostly consist of a circular motion of the water molecules as the wave energy continues until it meets a barrier, such as a shore line. Then the energy hurls water and pieces of the shore until gravity pulls them back. Ultimately, the energy is transformed into heat, hardly noticed in the water. Along the way, the energy is vast. The North Pacific is estimated to have a flux of 5 to 50 megawatts of mechanical energy per kilometer. The British coasts may have more, and a serious proposal was made to generate the bulk of British electrical power with waves.

One limitation of wave energy is that timing and power are variable (although not as much as with winds). The crests and troughs of one storm may be out of phase with another, in which case they largely cancel each other out. Winds may be low, or they may be directly against waves approaching the power plant. Any of these factors can limit power production at unpredictable times. Conversely, waves from two or more storms may be in phase and stack, creating monster waves that have been observed as high as 112 feet (34 meters) in the open ocean. Extraordinary waves have been the death of countless ships and of more than one wave power station. They are probably the greatest obstacle to widespread use of wave energy.

Methods for Harnessing Ocean Waves. Electrical power generation from waves requires three things: mooring the power stations to the ocean floor or building along the coast, generating power, and transmitting the power to customers inland. As with wind energy, a useful fourth item would be storage to deal with low-wave days.

Building and power transmission are straight-forward operations, because most wave-harvesting designs are on or near shore. Even though these installations must be reinforced against especially strong waves, they do not have the cost and complexity of deepwater structures.

Proposed energy-harvesting techniques have great variation because many researchers have been attempting to harness wave potential. The researchers face three major problems. First, generators face the previously mentioned fluctuations in awesome power. Second, wave power is large but moves at a slow pace, and the machinery to obtain high speed (needed for an electric

This ocean wave power plant at Toftestallen, on the west coast of Norway, began operation in 1985. Two violent storms, three days apart, destroyed the plant in December, 1988. (Kværner Brug)

generator) is expensive. Third, complex hinges, pistons, and other moving parts need frequent replacement in the salty ocean environment.

The simplest approach is a ramp and dam facility that traps water splashing above sea level. Water draining back down goes down a pipe (penstock) to turbines, just as in a hydroelectric dam. The "Russel rectifier" is sort of a dam with chambers and flaps so that both rising and falling waves cause water in a turbine to flow continuously in the same direction. The various dam schemes are familiar and can be built on land. The disadvantage is that power dams must be large and capable of surviving the surf; thus they are expensive.

The "dam atoll" is an open-ocean variant of the ramp. A half-submerged dome in the ocean bends waves around it so that waves come in from all sides, just as with coral atolls. The water sloshes to a central drain at the top and drains back through a penstock. The central collection increases efficiency, and being a floating structure allows submerging below the waves during major storms. However, increased distance from shore increases power transmission costs.

Air pressure can translate slow wave motion into a fast spin. In many schemes, waves rise and fall either in a series of open rooms at the bottom of a floating structure or in cylinders at the end of funnel-shaped passages facing the waves. In both cases, the waves alternately push air out and suck it in. Both processes run turbines at high speed. Extensive work on air-pressure designs has been done by the British, the Norwegians, and the Japanese, who have the Kamai, an 80-meter ship with a number of chambers for testing various turbine designs.

Directly harnessing wave motion has some advantages to offset the slow motion and exposure of moving parts. The necessary equipment can be much smaller (thus cheaper) per unit of electricity generated than the other schemes. For many years, Japanese buoys have used pendulums and pulling units to power lights and horns. Scaling these units to larger sizes is difficult and expensive. Experimental units have used hinges between rafts (Cockerell's design), "nodding duck" cam-shaped floats to activate rotary hydraulic pumps to turn a generator (Salter's design), paddles on rollers, and many other techniques.

Once produced in quantity, ocean wave power may have economics similar to hydroelectric plants—expensive to build but inexpensive overall because of low operating costs. However, development will continue to be slow as long as energy from other sources remains cheap.

FURTHER READING: Augusta Goldin, *Oceans of Energy: Reservoirs of Power for the Future*, 1980, includes a good discussion of wave energy. *Energy from the Waves*, by David Ross, 1979, details how wave power systems would have to work and discusses British development initiatives in the 1970's. T.A. Nobbe, "Converting Wave Action to Electricity," *Machine Design* (June 25, 1987), describes two Norwegian experimental wave power devices (one of which was subsequently smashed by wave action). A. Conway, "Set for a Surge in Ocean Power," *Modern Power Systems* (February, 1990), summarizes approaches to wave power development being considered at that time.

Roger V. Carlson

SEE ALSO: Energy storage; Ocean current energy; Ocean thermal energy conversion; Tidal energy.

Oceanography

Oceanography includes physical and biological studies of the world's oceans. It comprises both applied and theoretical science disciplines concerned with understanding the functioning of the oceans and obtaining ocean resources.

OCEANOGRAPHY IS DEFINED as the exploration and scientific study of the oceans. The word is derived from two ancient Greek words, *Oceanus*, a mythological god of the seas, and *graphon*, writings.

Physical oceanographers study the transmission of energy through the water. Waves, tides, and currents involve great amounts of energy—energy derived from the wind and the earth's rotation. At first the energy was primarily of interest to mariners as it affected their vessels. Later research sought to harness the ocean's energy. The world's first operational tidal power

station was built in France at the mouth of the Rance River. The rise and fall of the tides drives generators to produce electricity. During the 1930's, a cooperative United States-Canada project was proposed to harness the energy of the 15-meter tides in Passamaquoddy Bay in eastern Canada, but the project was abandoned because of economic and political problems.

Biological oceanographers study the living resources of the oceans, from microscopic plankton to the great whales. The animal resources of the oceans have long been a major source of human food. Chemical oceanographers treat the world's oceans as a vast reservoir of more than fifty chemical elements and about six gases dissolved in water. Sodium chloride (common salt) accounts for 86 percent of the chemicals in seawater. Other chemical resources obtained from seawater include magnesium and bromine. Dissolved gases include carbon dioxide, nitrogen, and oxygen. The oceans are considered a major sink for carbon dioxide from atmospheric pollution.

The geology of the ocean basins was largely unknown for centuries until the development of SONAR ("sound navigation and ranging") in the mid-twentieth century. The SONAR devices revealed features as varied as those found in terrestrial landscapes, except on a greater scale. The development of submersible vessels made it possible for oceanographers to view the underwater geology directly and to see it with the help of television and photography. The great depths involved make it difficult to economically "mine" the seafloor. Erosion of the continents has deposited large amounts of sand and gravel on the near-coastal continental shelves. Annual world production of approximately 112 billion tons of sand and gravel for buildings, road beds, and landfills is taken from the seafloor. Ninety percent of the mineral value produced from the seafloor is petroleum and natural gas.

Oceanography helps provide a better understanding of the history of the earth and, especially, of global weather and climate. Oceanography can also lead to increased productivity and efficient utilization of both food and mineral resources and energy production.

Albert C. Jensen

SEE ALSO: Bromine; Fisheries; Magnesium; Marine mining; Oceans; Oil and natural gas reservoirs; Salt; Sand and gravel; Tidal energy.

Oceans

Oceans cover 71 percent of planet Earth. The seafloor beneath them holds an abundance of minerals; there are also minerals dissolved in seawater. Oceans contain 97.2 percent of Earth's water (317 million cubic miles, or 510 million cubic kilometers). In addition, the preponderance of life on Earth is ocean life, and present fishing operations represent only the wasteful beginnings of what will be produced in the future. The oceans provide avenues of commerce, serve as a (now overworked) sink for wastes, and, most important, regulate Earth's climates.

WATER IS AN excellent solvent, so seawater contains more than sixty dissolved elements or their salts. The major constituent percentages of seawater are water (H_2O), 96.5 percent; table salt, or sodium chloride (NaCl), 2.3 percent; magnesium chloride ($MgCl_2$), 0.5 percent; sodium sulfate (Na_2SO_4), 0.4 percent; and calcium chloride ($CaCl_2$), 0.1 percent. This slightly alkaline broth was probably the first home to life on Earth. Chemically, human blood is essentially seawater contained in the body for carrying nutrients to, and wastes away from, individual cells.

Table salt has been evaporated from seawater since antiquity, with sunlight and wind supplying the energy. In the twentieth century, additional processes began producing magnesium, bromine, and iodine. Extracting other minerals from seawater is generally not profitable at present because the vast potential resource is highly dilute, requiring more pumping and processing cost to refine than the return. Some plants and animals are able to do such extractions, and eventually genetic engineering may harness such organic processes. Water is the prime constituent of seawater, and desalination (removal of salt from seawater or other salt solutions) has been done commercially since the 1960's. Desalination is expensive, however, and competing natural sources of fresh water are cheaper except in desert regions.

Water and the Cycles of Climate. Nature desalinates on a global scale through the hydrologic cycle of evaporation and resulting moisture. This cycle not only waters land plants but also affects climate in two ways. First, evaporation transfers heat from the oceans to places where the moisture condenses. Second, water flow off the land carries minerals containing a large percentage of calcium oxides that are part of the carbon cycle. Seawater has a smaller percentage of calcium ions than the runoff water because various sea plants and animals extract calcium from seawater and fix carbon dioxide from the air to grow (accrete) calcium carbonate ($CaCO_3$) shells. Much of the calcium carbonate goes to the seafloor. This process helps balance the other half of the carbon cycle, carbon dioxide entering the air from animal respiration and the burning of fossil fuels. Because atmospheric carbon dioxide is an insulator for Earth (the greenhouse effect), more oceanic life absorbing more carbon dioxide from the air could decrease Earth's temperatures. It has been suggested that airborne dust from the Himalayan highlands may have fertilized blooms of sea plants, triggering ice ages.

Currents, Climate, and Energy Sources. The ocean waters themselves redistribute heat from sunlight. The flows of this heat engine control the climate of Earth, and they hold the potential for energy production many times that used by humankind.

Water near the poles loses heat through evaporation, conduction, and radiation. As it cools, its density increases, and it sinks toward the ocean floor. From there it flows toward the equator, displacing warmer water as it goes. Meanwhile, water near the equator is warmed, becoming less dense. It tends to flow along the surface toward the higher latitudes to replace the sinking denser water.

The Gulf Stream is such a current. Warm water from the equatorial Atlantic and the Gulf of Mexico flows generally northward, parallel to the coast of North America, and bends gradually to the right (northeast) due to the rotation of Earth. This tendency to curve (right in the Northern Hemisphere, left in the Southern Hemisphere) is called the Coriolis effect, and it eventually bends the flow northeast past western Europe, warming and moistening air that, in turn, moderates the climate in western Europe. The cooled water bends south and west back to the start.

Similar circular patterns (gyres) occur in all the world's oceans. The gyre in the North Pacific warms East Asia and cools California. Along the way, the gyres help determine fertile areas in the oceans. Sinking water off Antarctica pushes other nutrient-rich water to the surface; currents flowing south past California cause upwelling, and flow from two gyres meeting and turning west leaves a gap that causes upwelling off Peru. Changes in the gyres, as probably happened in the ice ages, would shift fertile ocean areas as they influence climate changes. A weaker Gulf Stream might chill Europe to a climate like that of Siberia. Conversely, a warmer Gulf Stream might completely melt the ice in the Arctic Ocean. Greatly increased evaporation would increase the snowfall of lands around the Arctic, which currently have relatively little snowfall. Glaciers in Canada and Russia could grow in a matter of decades. Sunlight also indirectly causes salinity currents. Areas of high evaporation, such as the Mediterranean Sea, have dense saline water that flows out along the bottom to the open ocean as less saline water flows in along the surface.

Theoretically at least, turbines could harness these currents. For instance, the Gulf Stream has more energy than all the world's rivers combined. The area off Florida might yield 10,000 megawatts (10 billion watts) without observable change in the heat flow to Europe.

One nonsolar energy input is the tides, bulges of water pulled along by gravitational attraction of the moon and (to a lesser extent) the sun. These bulges, which are only a few feet in the open ocean, are funneled by some geographic features into much larger rises. For instance, the Bay of Fundy in Nova Scotia, Canada, has tides as great as 56 feet (17 meters). Sites with such high tides are limited.

Another potential energy source is the difference between warm tropical surface waters and near-freezing deep waters. Proposed ocean thermal energy conversion (OTEC) power plants would send a gas through a turbine either by boiling a low-boiling-point fluid, such as ammonia, or by boiling water in a partial vacuum. A large insulated pipe would bring up cold water to chill the working gas back to a liquid. The heat difference is small, however, so efficiency is low and capital cost per kilowatt is high. Thus, it may be some time before these vast resources are competitive with power stations on land. Nonetheless, the energy potential is great, and the raised waters would also be high in nutrients, so they could be used to fertilize surrounding waters.

Continental Shelves and Slopes. The continents are essentially blocks of lighter rock, such as granite, floating on heavier rock, such as basalt. The oceans fill the low spots between and lap at the edges of continents. These edges, the conti-

The continental shelves generally support the richest marine life. In many places—as here, in the Gulf of Mexico—they also contain mineral and petroleum deposits. (Photo Network)

nental shelves, usually slope gently for some distance before the continental slopes plunge into oceanic depths. Globally, the continental shelves, which extend down to roughly 650 feet (200 meters) represent an area equivalent to that of Africa. They include areas such as most of the Baltic Sea, wide areas off eastern North America, and narrower areas off western North America. Being close to land nutrients, the shelves usually have the richest marine life, but they are also most vulnerable to pollution from land.

Land minerals continue out onto the continental shelves. Shelf areas in the South China Sea and the Gulf of Mexico have major petroleum deposits. In addition, water-sorted deposits called placers extend along ancient beaches now covered below sea level. (Sea levels have been several hundred feet higher and lower in different geologic times.)

Some minerals are obtained through tunnel mining. Tunnel mines extend from shore to reach particularly desired ores. Dredging, however, is the most common method of mining shallow ocean deposits. More than a hundred million tons of sand, gravel, and shells are dredged yearly worldwide. Smaller tonnages are mined of more valuable minerals, such as gold, diamonds, and tin.

The continental slopes are a comparatively small area, with a correspondingly small mineral or fishing potential. However, they are awe-inspiring: Their edges plunge to the average 2-mile (2.8-kilometer) depths of the abyssal seafloor, often via submarine canyons, some with depths comparable to the Grand Canyon. Such changes in marine elevation (or depth) are dangerous for sea-bottom facilities, such as cables or drilling platforms, because landslides on the slopes carry mud, sand, and pebbles in turbidity currents. A 1929 earthquake on the Grand Banks east of Canada caused turbidity currents that moved at nearly 50 miles per hour (83 kilometers per hour) and carried roughly 24 cubic miles (100 cubic kilometers) of material over an area of 39,000 square miles (100,000 square kilometers). The speed was clocked by the snapping of transatlantic cables one by one.

The Abyssal Zone. The abyssal zone represents more than three quarters of the ocean floor. It is an area with water consistently just above freezing. It starts at a depth of 0.6 to 1.8 miles (1 to 3 kilometers) and extends to roughly 3.6 miles (6 kilometers). Because the abyssal zone has no light and depends on scraps falling from above, the biomass per unit volume can be a hundredth or even a thousandth that of surface waters. The lifeforms are some of the most alien on the planet—usually small, often luminescent. Animals may have jaws capable of swallowing something twice their size. Abyssal topography is often low rolling hills. However, areas with heavy sediment inflow, such as much of the Atlantic, have underlying topography buried under abyssal plains composed of fine ooze; these slope less than 1 part in 1,000.

These differences have mining implications. Some abyssal plains have sediments several miles deep. Under pressure and heat, organic material in these sediments decomposes into hydrocarbons, particularly methane (CH_4) and other hydrocarbons that make up petroleum. Meanwhile, the ocean bottom is only slightly above freezing and is under high pressure. With those conditions, a combination of methane and water called methane hydrate freezes, forming a layer that holds methane and acts as a cap rock to block the escape of other hydrocarbons. Therefore, it is possible that much of the sedimented ocean floor may be underlain by oil and gas deposits, perhaps many times those found to date.

Abyssal Mineral Resources. The waters without heavy land sediments, such as much of the Pacific, have other major potential resources. In tectonically active areas, water seeping down into the seafloor containing magma is heated and eventually expelled back into the ocean. The hydrothermal (water plus heat) vents, or marine vents, that exist where this occurs carry dissolved minerals, especially sulfides of zinc, lead, copper, and silver, along with lesser but still significant amounts of lead, cadmium, cobalt, and gold. Such deposits have been test mined in the Red Sea, where underwater valleys keep rich muds enclosed. In the deep ocean, such deposits make chimneys of metal sulfides that might eventually be mined.

Other, more soluble minerals may be carried hundreds or even thousands of miles before precipitating as potato-shaped ferromanganese nodules on the ocean floor. These nodules—commonly called simply manganese nodules—contain mostly oxides of iron and manganese, plus potentially profitable small amounts of copper, nickel, and cobalt. They cover millions of square kilometers and contain billions of tons of metal. The nodules accrete slowly and could be easily buried by land sediments (as exist in the Atlantic), so they are more commonly observed in the deep Pacific far from land.

Mining of ferromanganese nodules has been considered but not done for several reasons. (A ship that was once thought to be involved in a serious mining venture, the *Glomar Explorer*, was actually on a spy operation salvaging a wrecked Soviet submarine.) First, raising material from the ocean floor and processing at sea would be expensive compared with land mining. Second, deep sea mining controls according to the proposed 1982 Law of the Sea Treaty include undetermined taxes and subsidies to potential mining rivals. Finally, lifeforms in the cold deep waters might be slow to recover from silt pollution from mining operations. Eventually however, as offshore oil and gas drilling has demonstrated, effective technologies will evolve as the prices of competing land deposits increase.

Oceanic Ridges and Trenches. Another feature of the deep ocean—and perhaps the largest geographic feature on Earth—is the Mid-Oceanic Ridge (also called the Mid–Atlantic Ridge). This 35,000-mile (56,000-kilometer) mountain range is the area where new seafloor is spreading the ocean apart. It extends from the Arctic Ocean, through the Norwegian Sea, through the North and South Atlantic; it continues around South Africa through the Indian, Antarctic, and South Pacific Oceans. This is an area of intense hydro-thermal activity, and it contains hydrothermal deposits similar to those in the Red Sea.

Areas of seafloor spreading are balanced by other areas where tectonic plates are being driven under other plates. This process leads either to rising mountains on land (such as the Himalayas and Andes) or trenches at sea, such as the Marianas Trench, often with an arc of volcanic islands beside the trenches. At 6.8 miles (11 kilometers), the Marianas Trench contains the deepest known spot on Earth.

Suggestions have been made that toxic chemicals and radioactive wastes be placed into sediments in deep sea trenches for disposal. The suggestion is based on the idea that trenches are areas where plates are being submerged into Earth's mantle, so the wastes would be entombed. However, an unexpected volcano tens of thousands of years in the future might punch through that heated layer of diving sediments and belch toxic material into the stratosphere, and hence around the globe. Also, costs of placing material into deep sea trenches would be considerable.

Commerce. From Carthaginian traders through clipper ships to steam and container ships, ocean commerce has become ever more important in the world economy. Since the onset of steam power in the nineteenth century, power

The oceans help regulate the global climate and provide essential food sources; they also serve as avenues of commerce. (Photo Network)

plants and ship structures have steadily improved.

However, until the 1960's, even slower freighters spent a majority of time in port loading and unloading. Containerization—the use of standard-sized large cargo containers—allows one crane to do in an hour what a crew of laborers might need a day to do. Furthermore, the containers can be placed on rail cars or trucks for quick movement without tedious hand operations. This advance allows factories on opposite sides of the planet to compete directly, increasing world competition and decreasing wages in developed countries. There are dangers to this ex-

panded commerce. Giant (and underpowered) supertankers have had spectacular oil spills. Those involving the *Torrey Canyon* and the *Exxon Valdez* are among the most famous, but they were not the largest.

Sea Life and Food from the Sea. During most of the time since life on Earth began, the majority of life has existed in the ocean. A majority of living tonnage is still there—perhaps as much as a hundred billion tons. That oceanic life supports high-protein food production that approached ninety million tons during the 1990's. Eventually that figure will be much larger. The oceans, covering an area three-and-one-half

Commercial Fisheries Catch of Major Producers, 1992

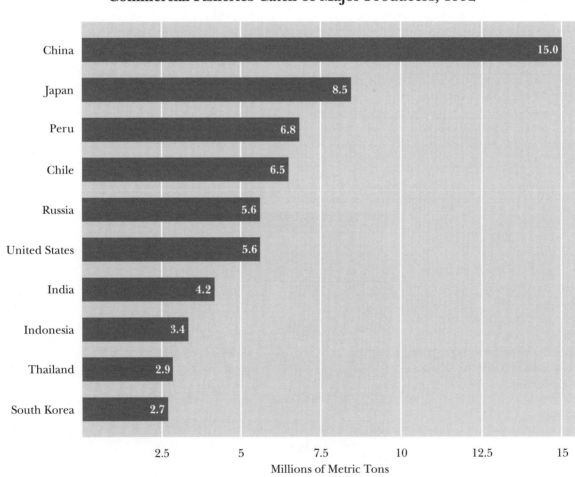

Millions of Metric Tons

China: 15.0
Japan: 8.5
Peru: 6.8
Chile: 6.5
Russia: 5.6
United States: 5.6
India: 4.2
Indonesia: 3.4
Thailand: 2.9
South Korea: 2.7

Source: U.S. Department of Commerce, *Statistical Abstract of the United States, 1996*, 1996.
Note: Weights are live weight in thousands of metric tons. Figures include fish, crustaceans, and mollusks.

Small fish such as these are in the middle of the oceanic food chain, feeding on plants or the smallest fish and in turn being eaten by larger predators. (Photo Network)

times larger than all the land and never limited by lack of water, have the potential to produce many times the amount of food produced on land when they are used for carefully planned sustainable production.

However, it has been predicted that before that happens the existing fishing industry will collapse. This dire prospect is based on significant differences between food production from the sea and agriculture on land. Except for nearshore plants, such as eel grass and kelp, oceanic plants are drifting algae, most barely large enough to see without magnification. These phytoplankton support most of the animal life in the oceans and live in the top few hundred feet, where sunlight penetrates. All oceanic photosynthesis (that is, the use of light and nutrients to make food) occurs in this euphotic (lit) zone, and most life depends directly or indirectly on this zone.

The tiny plants of the phytoplankton are eaten by tiny animals (zooplankton), which are

food for small shoaling fish such as sardines and anchovy. These fish are in turn eaten by higher predators in the food chain, such as mackerel, jack, tuna, sharks, and porpoises. Each stage on the way from phytoplankton to the "top predators" loses about 90 percent of the food content.

This situation leads to the first great failing of contemporary fishing: It focuses on those top predators, which is the equivalent of hunting lions and eagles. Harvesting zooplankton yields one tenth the food of phytoplankton, sardines give one hundredth, and tuna yields one thousandth. Land agriculture, in contrast, delivers vegetable matter directly to people (or, with a seven-eighths loss, to cattle, then people).

Second, fishing is essentially a high-technology hunting operation that does virtually nothing to improve the environment or nurture the young of fished species. Fishers who hold back in catching fish to save fish for breeding stock simply lose out to other boats. Third, fishing excesses were overmatched by the size of the oceans until the twentieth century, when power boats, synthetic netting materials, and efficient transport of fish to world markets multiplied fishing yields, leading to an ongoing string of fishery collapses. Miles-long seine nets swept large areas of the open ocean clean. The more powerful boats and "rock-hoppers" (able to drag rough bottom areas with less danger of snagging nets) have allowed trawlers to work intensively down nearly to abyssal depths. The habitat for the young of many species and food for many others is being compacted, silted, and ground down to wasteland.

Fourth, the areas closest to land, in which countries can exercise limits on overfishing, are often poisoned by pollutants. The Chesapeake Bay produces only a fraction of what the region's early settlers found. The Black Sea, naturally darkened by anaerobic decomposition (material rotting without oxygen), is blacker because of fertilizer runoff and toxic contaminants. In 1991 three thousand people in Peru died from cholera linked to sewage-contaminated seafood.

These problems have caused a series of "crashes" in production from formerly rich fishing grounds. John Steinbeck's 1945 novel *Cannery Row* describes the shoreside support for a fishery off California that no longer exists. In the early 1970's, yearly anchovy production off Peru collapsed and has never fully recovered. In the 1990's, the Grand Banks (east of Canada) began collapsing. Yet production is being maintained by various subsidies for bigger and more sophisticated boats going farther and deeper to catch dwindling fish stocks.

On the brighter side, as fisheries decline, cultured production is expanding. There is already mariculture of fish on land, which includes the growing of shrimp and other sea creatures. (Unregulated production in poorer countries often has grave environmental costs in pollution and lost mangrove swamps.) Production in existing fisheries must be strictly controlled. Finally, artificial fertilization in the deep ocean away from land might conceivably transform "blue-water desert" into fertile green zones.

Politics. Hugo Grotius defined "freedom of the seas" for the Dutch in 1608 when they had a powerful fleet to defend their boats fishing in

waters near Great Britain. The British did not share the Dutch view, however, and drove the Dutch boats away in a bloody war. Later the British fleet became the most powerful in the world, and Britain embraced freedom of the seas.

The concept held that territorial waters extended about 3 nautical miles (5.6 kilometers) from shore, which was the farthest range of cannons. Beyond territorial waters were international waters where a ship could fish or dump anything. In the twentieth century many countries proclaimed territorial waters out 12 nautical miles (22.2 kilometers) and often farther where the continental shelf was wide.

In 1982 negotiations concluded on the International Law of the Sea Treaty. It includes the concept of a 200-nautical-mile (370-kilometer) exclusive economic zone (EEZ) within which the coastal country has exclusive control of all resources. The United States and many other countries adopted the EEZ but not the treaty itself. Following the doctrine of the exclusive economic zone, ownership of the tiniest spit of land confers control of a wide circle of ocean. Where circles overlap, claims conflict and are resolved in various ways. European countries have carefully negotiated boundaries in the North Sea. In the South China Sea, the Chinese and Vietnamese have negotiated with naval gunfire. The Philippines, Indonesia, and Malaysia also have claims.

FURTHER READING: *Oceans of Energy: Reservoirs of Power for the Future*, by Augusta Goldin, 1980, provides an entertaining description of ocean energy sources including waves, currents, tides, temperature differences, and salinity differences. P. B. S. Lissman, "Tapping the Oceans' Vast Energy with Undersea Turbines," *Popular Science* (September, 1980), summarizes the proposed Coriolis Project for the Gulf Stream. *Offshore and Underground Power Plants*, edited by Robert Noyes, 1977, summarizes work on ocean current energy and most other ocean energy possibilities. Two excellent introductions to marine life and mariculture are *The Sea Around Us*, by Rachel Carson, 1950, and *The Challenge of the Sea*, by Arthur C. Clarke, 1960. *Sea Change: A Message of the Oceans*, by Sylvia Earl, 1995, updates the earlier works and includes the more somber environmental worries that had become evident by the mid 1990's. *The Millennial Project: Colonizing the Galaxy in Eight Easy Steps,* by Marshall T. Savage, 1992, discusses mariculture and ocean energy in an entertaining manner. *Fire Under the Sea,* by Joseph Cone, 1991, describes hydrothermal vents. See also *Into the Hidden Environment: The Oceans,* by Keith Critchlow, 1972, which is nicely illustrated and provides an excellent introduction to the ocean, and *Explorations: My Quest for Adventure and Discovery Under the Sea,* by Robert D. Ballard, 1995.

Roger V. Carlson and Robert J. Wells
SEE ALSO: Carbon cycle; Desalination plants and technology; Fisheries; Greenhouse gases and global climate change; Hydrothermal solutions and mineralization; Law of the sea; Marine vents; Mineral resource ownership; Ocean current energy; Ocean thermal energy conversion; Ocean wave energy; Oceanography; Oil and natural gas, worldwide distribution of; Plate tectonics; Salt domes; Seafloor spreading.

Oil and natural gas, chemistry of

The dominant chemical components of crude oil, or petroleum, are carbon and hydrogen; it also contains smaller quantities of nitrogen, oxygen, and sulfur. Oils consist of hundreds of individual chemical compounds. The dominant component of natural gas is methane, with smaller quantities of ethane, propane, and butane. Some natural gas deposits contain inorganic impurities, such as carbon dioxide, nitrogen, or hydrogen sulfide.

OIL (PETROLEUM) AND natural gas are two of the most important sources of energy in the world. They can be classed as hydrocarbon fuels, since the dominant chemical compounds in each contain only hydrogen and carbon. They are also classed as fossil fuels, since they derive from once-living organisms. Crude oil, or petroleum, is a liquid of variable characteristics, usually having color ranging from light amber to black, of moderate to high viscosity, and less dense than water. Natural gas is a colorless gas, usually odorless unless contaminated with sulfur compounds.

Kerogen Formation. Most oil and natural gas deposits derive ultimately from plankton and algae. When these aquatic organisms die, their remains can be kept from complete decomposition if they accumulate in an anaerobic environment (an environment without oxygen). For example, they may accumulate on the bottom of a lake or lagoon and be covered by silt or mud. The remains are partially degraded by anaerobic bacteria, which rapidly decompose proteins and less slowly attack fats and oils (lipids). Other components of the organisms may resist bacterial attack. The partially altered remains of these organisms collect and are compacted into materials called kerogens. The principal kerogen precursors to oil and natural gas are algal (type I) kerogen, which are derived primarily from algae, and liptinitic (type II) kerogen, which are derived from plankton and algae. These kerogens consist primarily of carbon and hydrogen, with small amounts of oxygen, nitrogen, and sulfur. The conversion of remains of organisms to kerogens is called diagenesis, or the biochemical phase of fuel formation.

When the kerogen is buried more deeply in the earth, its temperature may rise to a point at which thermal reactions begin to take place. These reactions involve the heat-induced breakdown of the kerogen; as they proceed, the large, complex hydrocarbon molecules of the kerogen eventually reach a point at which some of the molecules appear as a liquid. This process represents the onset of oil generation. The process of actual formation of oil and gas from kerogen is called catagenesis, maturation, or the geochemical phase.

Catagenesis. Early in catagenesis, some of the oxygen-containing molecules, such as alcohols, fats and oils, and organic acids, may be partially broken down to form carbon dioxide or water. The carbon dioxide and water escape, thereby reducing the oxygen content of the organic material remaining behind. As molecules are broken apart, their fragments are stabilized by hydrogen atoms that are picked up from other molecules in the system. This internal transfer of hydrogen generates a family of compounds that are generally hydrogen-rich and that dominate the composition of the products as well as a second family of compounds that are low in hydrogen. The hydrogen-rich compounds are the paraffins (or alkanes) and naphthenes (cycloalkanes), while the hydrogen-poor compounds are olefins (alkenes) and aromatic compounds. At this stage of maturation, many of the sulfur-containing compounds have not yet broken down. The oils formed in the early stages of maturation could therefore contain dissolved aromatic compounds and potentially have a high sulfur content. Because the paraffin molecules are still fairly large, the oils may be waxy and of high viscosity.

As maturation continues, the size of paraffin molecules continues to decrease. The viscosity of the oil drops. The sulfur compounds may begin to break apart, though the hydrogen sulfide that forms from the breakdown of sulfur compounds might remain dissolved in the oil. The continuing stabilization of molecular fragments requires more and more internal shuttling of hydrogen, and as a result larger molecules of aromatic compounds form. A point may be reached at which these big aromatic molecules are no longer soluble in the oil, and they precipitate as a separate material. The precipitated materials are called asphaltenes or asphaltites, and may be solids or highly viscous semi-solid materials.

Further breakdown of paraffin molecules may reach a point at which some of the molecules are small enough to be in a vapor phase. Depending on the temperature, these molecules might contain up to about eight carbon atoms (those with eight carbon atoms are "octane" molecules). The formation of the vapor phase represents the onset of gas formation. As maturation continues, the relative proportions of gas and oil change, favoring gas. At high temperatures or extensive maturation, only gas will form. At these conditions, the gas contains very small paraffin molecules: methane, ethane, propane, and butane. The gas may also contain various inorganic components, including carbon dioxide, water vapor, nitrogen, helium, and hydrogen sulfide. Very extensive catagenesis could produce a gas that is almost pure methane.

Classification Systems. Several classification systems are used for oils. One is based on the three major classes of hydrocarbon components, par-

affins, naphthenes, and aromatics. Depending on the proportions of each, oils are classified as paraffinic, paraffinic-naphthenic, naphthenic, aromatic-intermediate, aromatic-naphthenic, or aromatic-asphaltic. Paraffinic crudes are usually the most desirable for refinery feedstocks, and aromatic-asphaltic are the least desirable. Oils are also classified in terms of their geological age and depth of burial of the kerogen. Young-shallow oils have had little time to mature and have not been exposed to high temperatures. These oils can be viscous and contain relatively high contents of aromatics and sulfur. Old-deep oils have seen high temperatures and had long burial times; thus they have experienced the greatest extent of maturation. Old-deep crudes are likely to be paraffinic, rich in relatively low-boiling compounds, and very low in sulfur content. They are ideal refinery feeds. Young-deep and old-shallow crudes are intermediate classifications. Some of the best quality old-deep oils in the United States were first found in Pennsylvania. These oils are low-viscosity, low-sulfur, paraffinic oils. The term "Pennsylvania crude" is used as a classification term for oils of such quality.

Nitrogen, sulfur, and oxygen compounds in oils are sometimes lumped together and abbreviated NSOs. The major concern regarding NSOs is their impact on the environment if they are not removed from the oil during refining. Combustion of nitrogen- and sulfur-containing compounds produces the oxides of these elements, which, if emitted to the air, can result in serious air pollution. Oils that are high in NSOs will require more extensive refining for the products to comply with environmental regulations. Oils that contain sulfur compounds or dissolved hydrogen sulfide are said to be "sour." In contrast, low-sulfur oils are "sweet."

Depending on the temperature at which gas is confined underground, it may contain vapors of some compounds that would be liquids at ordinary temperatures (these compounds include pentane, hexane, heptane, and octane). When the gas is brought to the surface, where temperatures are lower, these vapors condense to a product called natural gasoline. In addition, the gas may contain appreciable amounts of butane and propane, which are relatively easy to condense if the gas is cooled further. Butane and propane may be separated and sold as separate fuel gases or combined as liquefied petroleum gas (LPG); they may also be sold as chemical feedstocks. A gas that contains more than 0.04 liters of condensable products per cubic meter of gas is said to be "wet." If the condensable liquids are less than 0.013 liters/cubic meter, the gas is "dry." Gases that contain hydrogen sulfide are sour, whereas sweet gases do not have this component. A sour gas is undesirable for several reasons: Hydrogen sulfide has a dreadful odor, it is a mild acid and can be corrosive to fuel handling systems, and it produces sulfur oxides when the gas is burned. Unless a company can derive benefit from selling natural gasoline or LPG, the ideal gas would be a sweet, dry gas.

FURTHER READING: An excellent resource is *The Chemistry and Technology of Petroleum*, by James Speight, 1991. Useful references concerning oil and gas formation include *Petroleum Geochemistry and Geology*, by John Hunt, 1996; the classic *Geology of Petroleum*, by A. I. Levorsen, 1954; *Petroleum Geology*, by F. K. North, 1985; and *Elements of Petroleum Geology*, by Richard Selley, 1985. An excellent general treatise is *Organic Geochemistry*, by Michael Engel and Stephen Macko, 1993.

Harold H. Schobert

SEE ALSO: Gasoline and other petroleum fuels; Methane; Oil and natural gas, worldwide distribution of; Oil and natural gas drilling and wells; Oil and natural gas exploration; Oil and natural gas formation; Oil industry; Propane.

Oil and natural gas, worldwide distribution of

The majority of the world's reserves of crude oil and natural gas are concentrated in a few regions. About two-thirds of the world's reserves are in Middle East nations. Saudi Arabia has larger oil reserves than any other country at about 250 billion barrels, and Iraq, the United Arab Emirates, Kuwait, and Iran each have reserves of about 100 billion barrels. The United States has only about 2 percent of the world's reserves.

PETROLEUM (CRUDE OIL and natural gas) is a mixture of many kinds of hydrocarbon com-

pounds—organic molecules made largely of hydrogen and carbon. Crude oil is refined to produce a variety of fluid fuels which, with natural gas, provide most of the energy that powers the world's industrialized societies. Petroleum also provides raw materials for the manufacture of plastics, synthetic fabrics, many medicines, fertilizers, insecticides, road pavement, floor coverings, roofing materials, and hundreds of other products.

History of Production. Large-volume production of petroleum began in the United States, and until 1974 the United States was the world's leading petroleum producer. The United States, however, was endowed with only about 11 percent of the world's original producible oil, so it is easy to understand why the United States was soon ahead of the rest of the world in depletion of petroleum resources.

In 1974 the Soviet Union replaced the United States as the world's leading oil-producing country, but oil production declined precipitously in the former Soviet Union from 1988 to 1995. Saudi Arabia then became the leading oil producer. As of 1996, the former Soviet Union was second, and the United States was third in its rate of oil production. Neither the former Soviet Union nor the United States, however, has very large reserves of oil in comparison with several other nations.

Distribution of Reserves. Reserves of a natural resource are the economically producible deposits that have been discovered but not yet consumed. About two-thirds of the world's approximately 1,000 billion barrels of oil reserves are in the Middle East nations near the Persian Gulf. Saudi Arabia has larger oil reserves than any other country in the world. About 250 billion barrels of oil, a quarter of the entire world's oil reserves, are in Saudi Arabia. Iraq, the United Arab Emirates, Kuwait, and Iran each have reserves of about 100 billion barrels of oil.

Most of the remaining one-third of the global reserves are in Venezuela, the countries of the former Soviet Union, and Mexico, which have 50 billion to 60 billion barrels each, and in the United States, China, Libya, and Nigeria, which have 18 billion to 25 billion barrels each. The United States, which has produced more oil than any other nation in the world and is the world's leading oil consumer, has oil reserves of only about 22 billion barrels, which is approximately 2 percent of the global total.

The world has about 4,500 trillion cubic feet of natural gas reserves, about two-thirds of which is in the former Soviet Union and the Middle East. The leading producers of natural gas are the former Soviet Union and the United States. The United States, in 1995, with only 3.5 percent of the global reserves of natural gas, produced approximately a fourth of the global natural gas output. Nevertheless, the United States natural gas consumption rate is great enough that its natural gas production cannot satisfy domestic

demand. For this reason, the United States imported, mostly from Canada, more than 10 percent of the natural gas that it consumed in 1995.

United States reserves of natural gas reached their maximum of 293 trillion cubic feet in 1968 and had diminished to 160 trillion cubic feet by 1995. This 45-percent decline reflects increasing consumption rates as well as progressively less success in domestic exploration for natural gas. The amount of natural gas discovered per million feet of exploratory drilling in the United States has been decreasing for more than fifty years. The United States, being more advanced than the rest of the world in its oil and natural gas production, provides an instructive case his-

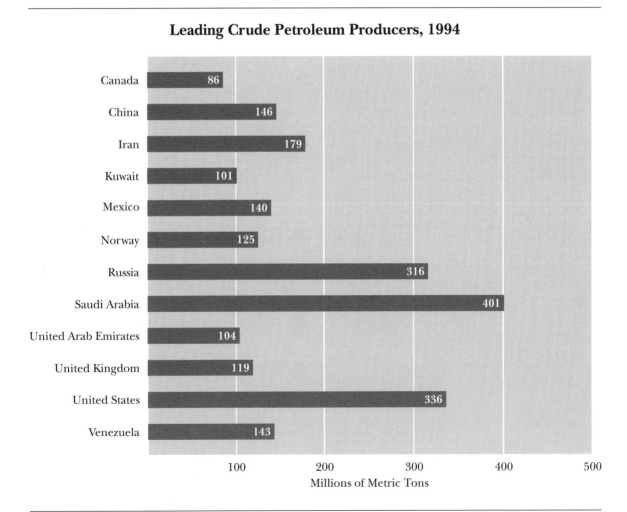

Leading Crude Petroleum Producers, 1994

Country	Millions of Metric Tons
Canada	86
China	146
Iran	179
Kuwait	101
Mexico	140
Norway	125
Russia	316
Saudi Arabia	401
United Arab Emirates	104
United Kingdom	119
United States	336
Venezuela	143

Source: U.S. Department of Commerce, *Statistical Abstract of the United States, 1996*, 1996.
Note: World total for 1994 was approximately 3 billion metric tons.

tory in depletion of these resources.

Future Production and Consumption. Global consumption of natural gas was approximately 80 trillion cubic feet in 1995. At this consumption rate, the 4,500 trillion cubic foot global reserve of natural gas would provide about fifty-six years of supply. The average estimate of undiscovered producible natural gas is about 5,000 trillion cubic feet, or an additional sixty-three years of supply. Thus, gas reserves plus the mean estimate of undiscovered producible gas sum to more than a hundred years of supply at the 1995 consumption rate. But the natural gas consumption rate, like that of oil, does not remain constant. Rather, it has grown historically.

From 1985 through 1995, annual world consumption of natural gas increased approximately 25 percent. A century of supply at current consumption rate is only fifty-five years of supply if consumption rate grows 2 percent per year. It is only forty-six years of supply if consumption rate grows 3 percent per year.

Moreover, consumption rate cannot continue to increase until the resource is depleted. Rather, the unrestricted production rate of a finite natural resource reaches its maximum and begins to decline when about half of the total producible resource has been consumed. This is why the United States' oil production rate has been declining since 1970 in spite of improved exploration and drilling technology and in spite of record high rates of exploration for oil during the early 1980's. The United States is now dependent on foreign sources for more than half of the oil it consumes.

Since the drilling of the first commercial oil well in 1858, the world oil production rate has grown tremendously. From 1858 until 1973, global oil consumption grew at an average rate of about 7 percent per year, with a consequent doubling of oil consumption rate every decade. As a result, the world consumed more oil from 1960 to 1973 than it had consumed throughout its entire pre-1960 history.

Since 1973, this rate of growth has diminished considerably. For example, from 1985 though 1995, world oil consumption rate increased about 16 percent. Nevertheless, the world has consumed more than twice as much oil since 1973 as throughout its entire pre-1973 history. As is the case for natural gas, oil consumption rate cannot continue to grow indefinitely. The 1,000 billion barrels of global oil reserves added to the 550 billion barrel average estimate of producible oil yet to be discovered plus the 800 billion barrels of oil already consumed as of 1996 sum to 2,350 billion barrels of ultimate oil consumption. At the 1995 global oil consumption rate of 25 billion barrels per year, the world will have consumed half of all the producible oil it ever had by the year 2011. World oil production rate will reach its maximum and begin its permanent decline within a decade of that year. This is a serious prospect for governments to contemplate, because the industrialized world's history of unprecedented economic growth during the twentieth century has been based largely on increasing availability of cheap petroleum.

Oil-producing nations will not all pass their peaks in oil production rate at the same time. The United States, as stated, passed this point in 1970 and has since seen its crude oil production drop from a record high of 9.6 million barrels per day in 1970 to about 6.5 million barrels per day for 1995. The former Soviet Union also has passed its maximum in oil production rate. Several other oil-producing countries will experience the beginning of permanent decline in their oil production rates before the year 2005.

As oil production in the rest of the world declines, only the Middle East nations will have the excess oil production capacity necessary to compensate with increasing production rates. But the Middle East countries as a whole will reach the mid-point of their ultimate oil production well before the year 2020. As they pass their maximum oil production rate, they will not be able to delay the beginning of permanent decline in world oil production beyond the second decade of the twenty-first century. The economic and social implications of this coming event demand serious planning by the world's governments.

FURTHER READING: Brief summaries of the distributions of oil, natural gas, and other fuel resources are provided in chapter 23 of *Physical Geology*, by John Renton, 1994, and in chapter 13 of *Energy*, by Gordon Aubrecht, 1989. *The Golden*

Century of Oil, 1950-2050, by C. J. Campbell, 1991, offers a more complete presentation of global distributions of petroleum reserves. Cumulative production, production rates, reserves, and estimates of undiscovered producible resources are presented for both crude oil and natural gas for each of the world's oil-producing countries and for the world as a whole in C. D. Masters et al., "Resource Constraints in Petroleum Production Potential," *Science* 253 (July 12, 1991).

Craig Bond Hatfield
SEE ALSO: Energy politics; Oil and natural gas, chemistry of; Oil and natural gas drilling and wells; Oil and natural gas exploration; Oil and natural gas formation; Oil industry; Organization of Petroleum Exporting Countries.

Oil and natural gas drilling and wells

Wells drilled to produce oil and natural gas are designed to pump oil as long as the source is economically viable; they often provide many years of service. Drilling procedures are rigorous and exacting and are intended to avoid hazards such as blowouts.

OIL AND NATURAL GAS are recovered through drilled wells that are designed and constructed to ensure many years of service. These wells may vary from a few hundred feet to over 20,000 feet in depth. They must recover oil and gas from their reservoirs in the subsurface. The location of the well is determined by an exploration team, which produces maps of the subsurface showing possible accumulation of oil and gas. A team of land agents investigates the ownership of the drill location and provides information so that the right to produce the oil and gas can be secured from the landowner—be it an individual, a state, the federal government, or a foreign nation. After the right to drill is secured, the drilling plan is converted into action.

Drilling Procedures. A suitable drilling rig is selected through the solicitation of information from drilling companies. After selection and transportation to the drilling site, the rig is positioned over the marked location, which has been accurately determined by surveying instru-

Working on a drilling rig. (Ben Klaffke)

ments. A drill bit is connected to drill pipe and drill collars. Drill collars are thick-walled cylinders about 30 feet in length used immediately above the drill bit to prevent the bit from wandering as it cuts through rock formations of varying strength and inclination. The drill pipe and collars are rotated by a rotary table at the surface, causing the drill bit to rotate. The weight of the drill string, as the downhole assembly is called, along with its rotation, causes the rock underneath the bit to be crushed. This crushed rock is circulated to the surface by drilling fluid. This fluid, called "mud," is a mix of chemicals suited to the downhole environment. It is pumped down the well through the drill string, through the bit nozzles, and then back up to the surface in the annular space between the drill string and the wall of the drilled hole.

The drill bit eventually becomes dull and must be replaced. When this happens, the drill string must be unscrewed so that the bit can be brought to the surface. This process is called "tripping the bit." The drilled hole must be lined with steel casing to prevent slumping of the borehole wall and unwanted migration and mixing of subsurface fluids. Casing is very similar to the steel pipe seen in pipelines on the surface, but it is designed for the pressures and temperatures encountered in the subsurface. Casing setting depths are either predetermined or selected while drilling to control a hazardous condition such as a blowout or lost circulation.

After the first casing "string" is run, it is secured in the borehole by circulating a thin cement slurry downward through the casing, then up the annular space between the casing wall and the borehole wall. Two casing strings are necessary in the simplest well, while several strings may be necessary for deep wells. As additional casing strings are run, each succeeding string must be smaller in diameter than its predecessor. In this way, an oil and gas well becomes smaller in diameter as its depth increases. For example, it is common to begin at the surface with a drill bit one-third meter in diameter, while the final well diameter at total depth may be as small as one-tenth meter. This concept is simple to understand by noting that as each casing string is secured in the wellbore, the succeeding bit size must be reduced in order to enter the newly secured casing.

When the borehole penetrates the rock formation containing oil and gas, the depths of interest are evaluated using electrical, acoustic, and radioactive techniques to determine the presence of oil and gas. If the evaluation indicates that oil and gas are there in commercial quantities, "completion" of the well is begun. Completion involves installing the final casing string, perforating the casing wall adjacent to the rock formation containing oil and gas by using gas jets or mechanical cutters, and installing production equipment. Depending on the initial success of the completion procedure, additional measures may be necessary to increase the rate of oil and gas produced. These measures include using reactive chemicals to dissolve the rock formation near the wellbore or using hydraulic pressure to fracture the rock forma-

tion. After the completion procedure, the well is tested to determine the rate of oil and gas being produced. Depending on the rate of production, a small string of pipe called tubing is placed inside the casing to provide a flow conduit for the produced fluids.

Most oil and gas wells are drilled as near vertical as possible. The reason is that most regulatory agencies closely monitor the surface and bottomhole locations of wells in order to protect mineral property rights. In many situations, however, it is impossible to locate the drilling rig over the desired bottomhole location. A river, lake, or building, for example, on the surface may necessitate the drilling of a well directionally to the desired bottomhole location. The progress of drilling is monitored by noting the azimuth (deviation from true north) and dip (deviation from vertical) of the well on a continual basis. Specialized directional drilling consultants oversee this complicated task. Sometimes wells are started vertically at the surface, then forced to dip all the way to the horizontal, then kept horizontal in the subsurface. Horizontal wells are much more expensive to drill than vertical wells, but good ones yield production rates far in excess of vertical wells.

A unique situation for well deviation exists offshore. A series of wells is drilled from an offshore location. The pattern of these wells, called a template, includes the deviation of all but the well immediately underlying the platform or floating rig. The proper locating of many wells from the same surface location ensures the broadest distribution of bottomhole locations and involves highly specialized technical knowledge.

Hazards. While the well is being drilled, there are always potential hazards that must be recognized by the drilling personnel. These include, among others, blowouts and lost circulation. A blowout is the uncontrolled escape of subsurface fluids to the surface. These spectacular events have been identified with the oil and gas industry since its beginnings, and they remain as one of its most newsworthy subjects. A properly drilled well should not encounter a blowout if adequate diagnosis and detection are made. The weight of the drilling fluid may be increased to control abnormal pressures in the subsurface.

Blowout preventers, a type of valving used with the drilling rig, are designed to protect against blowouts until the well can be controlled and drilling resumed without spoiling the surface area adjacent to the well.

Lost circulation involves drilling fluid that is lost because it seeps into the pore space or fractures in the subsurface rock formations. If enough drilling fluid escapes downhole, well control can be lost and a blowout can occur. Lost circulation is controlled by decreasing the weight of the drilling fluid or using plugging agents circulated into the subsurface leak zones.

Oil and Gas Pumping and Production. When the well has been completed and production is assured, a wellhead is installed to replace the blowout preventers. The wellhead, nicknamed the "Christmas tree," is a series of valves designed to seal the casing, its annular space, and the tubing to prevent leaks.

Crude oil is processed at the site only to remove unwanted foreign matter. Surface equipment used to process oil and gas includes dehydrators to remove water and water vapor, and separators to remove foreign matter, including rock particles, paraffin, and other debris prohibited by the buyer of the oil and gas. Large tanks are used to store oil prior to delivery.

Oil is transported by pipeline, truck, and train to the refinery for further breakdown into gasolines, motor oils, and other products and chemicals. Natural gas is odorized by placing a distinctive odorant in it, and its pressure is elevated by compression for delivery to the customer through a series of pipelines.

An ideal oil and gas well will flow to the surface using its internal energy. Oil wells eventually reach the point where their flowing energy is depleted and they must be pumped in order to continue producing. A variety of pumps have been used in the oil and gas industry; among them is the familiar beam pump, sometimes called a "horse's head" or "nodding donkey," that is seen in oil producing areas around the world.

Depletion and Economic Limit. When a well's energy is depleted, an enhanced oil recovery (EOR) project may be started. EOR techniques are used to produce additional oil from an oil and gas formation that has depleted its primary

energy source. Various fluids ranging from fresh water to exotic liquids, gases, and even steam are injected into oil-producing rocks to force more oil from them. Very often EOR projects can produce an amount of oil equivalent to that recovered during the well's primary operating life.

All oil and gas wells eventually reach their "economic limit," at which point economic production ceases. The economic limit is an arbitrary production rate that depends on the expenses associated with producing the well, the percentage of ownership of the well's operator, and the price of the oil and gas. This limit may be reached in a very short period after production begins for poorly performing wells, or it may exceed fifty years. Once the production rate falls below the economic limit, the well is either plugged and abandoned (cement plugs are used

The beam pump (nicknamed the "horse's head" and "nodding donkey"), a familiar sight in oil-producing regions throughout the world. (Ben Klaffke)

to seal the wellbore) or converted into a liquid disposal or EOR injection well. After the well's operators have plugged the wellbore to the satisfaction of regulatory authorities, the surface location in the vicinity of the well is restored in an environmentally acceptable manner. Little or no trace of the well itself should be left.

FURTHER READING: Good sources for more detailed information on drilling and wells include Preston L. Moore, *Drilling Practices Manual*, 1986; Michael Economides et al., *Petroleum Production Systems*, 1993; T. E. W. Nind, *Principles of Oil Well Production*, 1964; and H. Dale Beggs, *Gas Production Operations*, 1984. The University of Texas Petroleum Extension Division has a comprehensive set of booklets describing all phases of oil well drilling and the petroleum industry in general.

Charles D. Haynes

SEE ALSO: Gasoline and other petroleum fuels; Oil and natural gas, worldwide distribution of; Oil and natural gas exploration; Oil industry; Propane.

Oil and natural gas exploration

Drilling for oil is not the first, but the last, step in oil exploration. Surface mapping, the use of seismic technology to study sedimentary rock sequences, and other geological and geophysical studies all precede drilling.

PETROLEUM (CRUDE OIL and natural gas) is a mixture of hydrocarbons, which are organic compounds made largely of hydrogen and carbon. Exploration for petroleum accelerated during the early 1900's as demand for fluid fuels increased following the development of the internal combustion engine.

Origin of Petroleum. The search for petroleum requires an understanding of its origin. Oil and natural gas are formed, during immense spans of time, from microscopic floating marine organisms that live by the billions in the world's oceans. As these die and sink to the seafloor, they may be buried in areas where there is rapid influx of sediment from erosion of adjacent land. When buried by mud and thus removed from contact with oxygen dissolved in seawater, the organic matter cannot completely decom-

pose to gases, as it otherwise would.

If sediment continues to accumulate, the high confining pressure and high temperature at depth can change the organic matter to liquid or gaseous hydrocarbons—crude oil or natural gas. As compaction changes the sediment to rock, the fluid hydrocarbons are squeezed out of the sediment originally containing them and move upward through the compacting sedimentary accumulation. The petroleum may migrate upward into a coarser sediment, such as sand. Sand can be very permeable to fluid migration because of the large interconnected pore spaces between adjacent sand grains. The petroleum continues to rise through such a sand layer, because most of the pore space in marine sediments and sedimentary rocks is filled with water, and petroleum is less dense than water. If the petroleum, during this upward migration, encounters a fine-grained sedimentary layer that will not permit fluids to move through it, then the petroleum can be restricted to a particular porous zone, such as a sandstone layer beneath the fine-grained barrier.

In some regions, the petroleum-bearing sedimentary rocks may be folded or otherwise deformed so that they are no longer a sequence of horizontal layers. In this way, the petroleum can be concentrated in commercial quantities. Commonly, petroleum is concentrated in the highest parts of the deformed or folded layer containing it, because all the pore space beneath is filled with seawater. Thus, exploration for oil and natural gas requires study of sedimentary rock sequences that extend hundreds of meters or even several kilometers into the subsurface. The settings in which these sequences accumulated and the geographic distributions and thickness variations of the sedimentary layers must be understood.

Searching for Petroleum. Most sedimentary rocks were not deposited in settings where large quantities of organic matter were preserved. Even if the sedimentary rocks are rich in petroleum-forming hydrocarbons, subsequent deformation of the rocks most commonly has not produced a potential trap to concentrate the petroleum in commercial quantities. Thus, the search for petroleum does not begin with exploratory well

In 1982 the American drilling ship Discoverer Seven Seas *drilled a record-setting 1,714-meter well off the coast of Marseilles, France. The venture involved French and American scientists and technology.* (Exxon Corp.)

drilling. Deep drilling is very expensive, and most wells do not find commercial concentrations of petroleum. In order to know where to locate exploratory wells, various kinds of geological studies must precede drilling.

For example, the search for petroleum includes the study of sedimentary rocks at depth using geophysical techniques such as seismic studies. Seismic studies generate, commonly via explosions, sound waves that are reflected and refracted (bent) by the sedimentary layers in the subsurface. The sound returning to the surface is recorded by sensitive receivers, and reflections from layers of particular rock types can be recognized. The time required for the sound to travel to a particular sedimentary rock layer and be reflected from it back to the surface is used to determine the depth of the sedimentary layer. The velocity of sound through a given layer is a function of the rock density, which in turn is an indication of rock type. After surface mapping, seismic examination of the subsurface, and other geological and geophysical studies have revealed sufficient information, it is possible to place exploratory wells in locations where there is higher probability of petroleum discovery.

Petroleum Supply Problems. In spite of improving technology, the search for petroleum has become progressively less successful since the 1960's and 1970's, especially in the United States. Petroleum exploration and large-scale petroleum production began in the United States earlier than in any other country, and for many decades prior to 1974 the United States was the world's leading oil producer. Partly for these reasons, the United States' petroleum resources are being depleted earlier than those of the rest of the world.

The oil fields closest to the earth's surface were the easiest to find and therefore were the first to be discovered. As exploration and exploitation of petroleum resources continued and grew, oil fields became increasingly difficult to find. In the United States, where exploration for petroleum began, oil companies have nearly run out of places to look for large new oil fields. Even for the world as a whole, petroleum has become progressively more difficult to find, so that the search for it has extended into far offshore areas of the deep sea and into hostile climatic environments.

In the history of any oil-producing region, the oil discovery rate reaches its maximum several years before the maximum in oil production rate. For example, in the United States (exclusive of Alaska), the oil discovery rate reached its peak in the late 1950's and has since diminished greatly. The United States oil production rate, however, reached its maximum in 1970 and has declined since. The global oil discovery rate was at its maximum in the 1960's and has since diminished in spite of record high rates of exploration in the early 1980's. The global oil production rate, however, as of 1996, had not yet reached its maximum.

Global Oil Reserves. The reserves of a natural resource are that amount which has been discovered but not yet consumed. The 1996 global reserves of oil were enough to last about forty years at the 1996 global oil consumption rate. The consumption rate, however, does not remain constant. Rather, it has grown historically. In 1996 the world oil consumption rate was growing more than 2 percent annually. A forty-year supply at the 1996 consumption rate becomes a thirty-year supply with a 2 percent growth in consumption per year. It is not known how much producible oil remains to be discovered, but various published estimates average about 550 billion barrels, which, if discovered, would increase by roughly 50 percent the oil remaining to be consumed. Global natural gas reserves plus estimates of undiscovered producible gas resources are a few decades larger than those for oil as measured in terms of remaining consumption time.

Discovery of new oil from 1985 to 1995 averaged less than 9 billion barrels annually, while consumption rates averaged more than 23 bil-

lion barrels annually. In other words, most of the oil burned during this interval had been discovered during earlier decades. If global oil consumption continues to grow at the rate of the decade ending in 1996, and if oil discovery rates continue to decline, global reserves of oil will dwindle, which will lead to declining production rates—possibly within the first decade of the twenty-first century.

FURTHER READING: A good book for nongeologists on the exploration for oil and natural gas is *Introduction to Petroleum Exploration for Non-geologists*, by Robert Stoneley, 1995. A more complete presentation for geologists or university students majoring in geology is *Petroleum Geochemistry and Geology*, by John Hunt, 1995. A brief overview of petroleum exploration and refining is included in *Facts About Oil*, a short account prepared by the American Petroleum Institute and updated periodically. It is available from the American Petroleum Institute in Washington, D.C. Future petroleum production potential is covered in C.D. Master et al., "Resource Constraints in Petroleum Production," *Science* 253 (1991).

Craig Bond Hatfield

SEE ALSO: Landsat satellites and satellite technologies; Oil and natural gas, chemistry of; Oil and natural gas, worldwide distribution of; Oil and natural gas drilling and wells; Oil and natural gas formation; Oil industry; Seismographic technology and resource exploration.

Oil and natural gas formation

The formation of usable oil and gas deposits involves the deposition, transformation, and migration of various types of organic material; these processes take place over huge expanses of time.

OIL, OR PETROLEUM, is not a single chemical compound but a variety of liquid hydrocarbon compounds—that is, compounds made up of different proportions of the elements carbon and hydrogen. There are also gaseous hydrocarbons—natural gas—of which the compound methane (CH_4) is the most common. The relative amount of oil and gas produced from any source rock depends principally on the ratio of hydrogen to carbon. The formation of any fossil fuel requires a large initial accumulation of biomass rich in carbon and hydrogen. Another requirement is that the organic debris be buried quickly to protect it from the air so that decay by biological means or reaction to oxygen will not destroy it.

Deposition and Transformation. Microscopic plant and animal life is abundant in much of the oceans. When these organisms die, their remains usually settle to the sea floor. When this takes place in near-shore marine environments, such as on continental shelves, or where large rivers form marine deltas, sediments derived from continental erosion accumulate rapidly. In such a setting, the initial requirements for the formation of oil are satisfied: An abundance of organic matter is rapidly buried by sediment so that it is free from aerobic and biological contamination. The majority of oil and natural gas deposits are believed to have been formed by such accumulated marine organisms. Oil fields reflect the presence of prehistoric marine environments that now exist below the surface as marine deposited sedimentary rocks.

As sedimentary deposition continues to bury the organic matter, it begins to change into a solid organic material called kerogen. At relatively low temperatures and shallow burial depths, kerogen is chemically inert. Kerogen consists primarily of hydrocarbons that are in the solid state and that are insoluble not only in water but also in a variety of organic solvents. Kerogen from the lower plants and animals, with a high lipid content and a relatively high hydrogen ratio, will produce oil. Kerogen from the higher vascular plants is lower in hydrogen content and will produce only gas.

As pressures increase from the weight of continued deposition of overlying sediment, the sediments are gradually transformed into lithified rock. Temperatures increase with depth below the earth's surface; slowly, over long periods of time, chemical reactions take place. These reactions break down the large, complex organic molecules into simpler, smaller hydrocarbon molecules. The nature of the hydrocarbon changes with time and continued heat and pressure. In the early stages of petroleum formation, the deposit may consist mainly of larger hydrocarbon molecules, which have the thick, nearly solid consistency of asphalt. These are referred to as low-gravity crudes. As the petroleum matures, and as the breakdown of large molecules continues, successively lighter hydrocarbons are produced. Thick liquids give way to thinner ones, from which are derived lubricating oils, heating oils, and gasoline. In the final stages, most or all of the petroleum is further broken down into very simple, light, gaseous molecules—natural gas. Most of the maturation process occurs in the temperature range of 50 to 100 degrees Celsius (120 to 210 degrees Fahrenheit). Above these temperatures, the remaining hydrocarbon is almost wholly methane; with further temperature increases, methane can be broken down and destroyed in turn. A given oil field yields crude oil containing a distinctive mix of hydrocarbon compounds, depending on the burial history of the material. The commercial petroleum refining process separates the different types of hydrocarbons for different uses through the application of heat. Some of the heavier hydrocarbons are broken up during heat refining into smaller, lighter molecules through a process called cracking. Cracking is an artificial method of maturing the hydrocarbons and allows lighter compounds such as gasoline to be produced as needed from the heavier components of crude oil.

Migration of Deposits. Once the solid organic matter is converted to liquids and gases, hydrocarbons can migrate from the rocks in which they formed. Such migration is necessary if the oil or gas is to be collected into an economically valuable and practically usable deposit. The majority of petroleum source rocks are fine-grained clastic sedimentary rocks of low permeability. Despite the low permeabilities, oil and gas are able to migrate from their source rocks and move through more permeable rocks over long spans of geologic time. The amount of time required for oil and gas to mature is not known precisely. Since virtually no petroleum is found in rocks younger than one to two million years old, geologists infer that the process is comparatively slow.

Though many properties of sedimentary rocks influence the generation, migration, and accumulation of oil and gas, none has more direct control on hydrocarbon movement and entrapment than do the amount and distribution of pore space. Interstitial pores must be present in the source rocks and enclosing rock layers in order for fluids containing oil and gas to be expelled into the migration system. Migration itself requires an interconnected system of pores in order for these fluids to move from the source to impermeable trapping rocks. The pores, holes, and cracks in rocks in which fluids can be trapped are commonly full of water. Most oil and all natural gases are less dense than water, so they tend to rise as well as to migrate laterally through water-filled pores of permeable rock. Unless stopped by impermeable rocks, oil and gas may keep rising right up to the earth's surface, escaping into the air or the oceans or flowing out onto the ground. The La Brea Tar Pits of California are an example of such a seep.

FURTHER READING: General overviews of oil and gas formation can be found in *Environmental Geology*, by Carla Montgomery, 1995, and in *Environmental Geology*, by Edward Keller, 1996. More in-depth and specific information can be gained from *Oil and Gas: The Production Story*, by Ron Baker, 1983, and *The Story of Petroleum*, by Shell Oil Company Office of Public Affairs, 1982.

Randall L. Milstein

SEE ALSO: Oil and natural gas, chemistry of; Oil and natural gas, worldwide distribution of; Oil and natural gas reservoirs; Petroleum refining and processing.

Oil and natural gas reservoirs

By the 1870's the hydrocarbon industry had accepted the concept that a subsurface rock volume with sufficient porosity, permeability, and capping element effectively trapped localized concentrations of crude oil and natural gas. Such a concentration was termed a hydrocarbon (oil and/or natural gas) reservoir. This concept greatly increased early successes in finding hydrocarbon, and it remains a fundamental tool in worldwide exploration for oil and natural gas.

WITH THE ADVENT of the petroleum age in the United States, initiated by the drilling of the first oil well in Pennsylvania in 1859, the search began for scientific methods useful in the direct or indirect indication of the presence of accumulations of subsurface oil and gas. Early methodologies included river bottom locations ("creekology"), geographic projection of discoveries ("ruler geology"), and the presence of surface hydrocarbon seeps ("seepology") or surface mounds ("topography"). While of varying success in establishing new reserves, none of these methods adequately explained the concentration of oil and natural gas in subsurface rocks of the earth.

Subsequently, publications by John F. Carll of the Pennsylvania Geological Survey explained that hydrocarbon concentrations were not present in subsurface caverns, pools, or lakes, but rather were contained in the natural pore space common to the sedimentary class of rock. By the end of the nineteenth century, consensus suggested that economic hydrocarbon accumulations were associated with: subsurface rock of porosity adequate to contain significant volumes of hydrocarbon, sufficient permeability to allow transfer of the contained hydrocarbon to the surface by way of a borehole, and the presence of a cap or roof rock which effectively holds the oil and gas in place until released through the borehole. This combination of rock porosity, rock permeability, and cap rock defines an oil and natural gas reservoir.

Reservoir Rock Type. Throughout the world, hydrocarbon reservoirs are commonly composed of sandstone or carbonate rock, the latter being either limestone (calcium carbonate) or dolomite (calcium and magnesium carbonate). Studies indicate that approximately 57 percent of all reservoirs are composed of varying types of sandstone, with conglomerate, greywacke, orthoquartzite, and siltstone being common types. About 40 percent of reservoirs are composed of carbonate rock. The remaining 3 percent of reservoirs are composed of shale, chert, and varieties of igneous and metamorphic rock.

Rock Porosity and Permeability. Rock porosity refers to the percentage of rock volume that is occupied by interstices or voids, whether connected or isolated. Under normal conditions, subsurface rock porosity is filled with water varying in chemistry from fresh to very saline. In rock provinces favorable to the formation of hydrocarbon, long-term geologic processes cause migrating microvolumes of dissipated oil and natural gas to concentrate into reservoir accumulations by replacing water-filled pore space with hydrocarbon-filled pore space. Sandstone reservoir porosities normally range from a low of 10 percent to a high of 35 percent. Carbonate rock reservoir porosity is generally lower than sandstone porosity.

Rock permeability is the measure of ease with which contained gas or liquid under pressure can move freely through interconnected pore space. Reservoir permeability is expressed in terms of millidarcy units, named for Darcy's law. Sandstone and carbonate reservoir permeabilities generally vary from a low of 5 to more than 4,500 millidarcies.

Porosity and permeability are very important physical characteristics of the reservoir, as they determine, respectively, the amount of oil and gas the reservoir contains and the potential volumetric production rate of the reservoir over time. Under normal conditions porosity and permeability are primary characteristics—in other words, characteristics that were created at the time of the rock's formation. Secondary porosity and permeability can be created through post-deposition weathering or fracturing of reservoir rocks. Oil and natural gas reservoirs possessing high porosities and permeabilities, whether primary or secondary in origin, are greatly valued.

Reservoir Cap Rock. While porosity and permeability are essential elements of any reservoir, a relative lack of permeability in the rock forming the reservoir cap is equally essential. The reservoir cap, or roof rock, is an impermeable rock unit that keeps the oil and natural gas in place until that time when reservoir integrity is altered by a borehole. The presence of oil and natural gas seeps throughout the world is indicative of reservoirs that have lost their integrity, allowing the contained hydrocarbon slowly to leak out of the reservoir and rise to the surface of the earth.

Reservoir Trap. While a combination of poros-

ity, permeability, and cap rock is common in subsurface rock, these reservoir characteristics must be contained within rock geometry of a nature such that oil and natural gas can by concentrated into economic volumes. The overall combination of porosity, permeability, cap rock, and rock geometry is termed the reservoir trap. Reservoir traps are formed under varying conditions of rock attitude (general disposition and relative position of rock masses) and rock lithology (physical characteristics). Two common types of reservoir traps are recognized: structural and stratigraphic.

A basic premise of geology states that sedimentary rock—that class which forms all but a minor percentage of reservoir rock—was deposited originally in a horizontal or near-horizontal state. Any subsequent deviation from the horizontal is caused by compressive or earthquake forces acting within the crust of the earth. One of the most common and sought after structural traps is the anticline, a convex upward flexing of rock strata. In an anticline, the inner core of arched rock, if porous and permeable, allows the concentration of migrating microvolumes of hydrocarbon. Such concentration is achieved because oil and gas have a lower density than saline or fresh water, the normal fluids found within the pore space of sedimentary rock. Without a proper reservoir cap rock forming the outer surface of the anticlinal flexure, usually an impermeable shale, hydrocarbon concentrations will slowly leak to the surface. An anticline, composed of an inner porous/permeable rock core and outer impermeable cap rock, forms the ideal structural reservoir trap. Of the 250 largest oil fields in the world, approximately 90 percent are classified as anticlinal reservoir traps.

In contrast to the structural trap, the stratigraphic trap is dependent upon lateral variability of porosity and permeability within a rock layer as caused by changes in grain size, shape, cementation, compaction, and degree of weathering. For example, in a sequence of tilted sedimentary rock, an upward decline in permeability would block the surface migration of oil or gas as effectively as would a structural reservoir trap. Such a loss of permeability may be caused by a combination of a reduction in grain size, an

Examples of Structural and Stratigraphic Hydrocarbon Traps

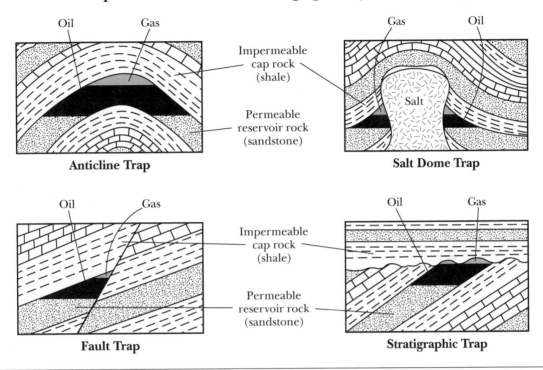

increase in the degree of cementation filling in the space between individual rock grains, or an increase in compaction resulting from rock burial. Approximately 10 percent of all reservoir traps are stratigraphic in classification.

Examples of Oil and Gas Reservoir Traps. Throughout the Middle East (notably Iran, Iraq, Kuwait, and Saudi Arabia), which contains approximately 49 percent of the recoverable oil and at least 27 percent of the total natural gas of the world, the anticline reservoir trap is ubiquitous. The Ghawar oil field, in northeast Saudi Arabia, is formed by the merging of several elongate anticlines, creating a gigantic anticlinal arch extending more than 233 kilometers in length by 21 kilometers in width. The reservoir rock is limestone, which is overlain by an anhydrite (calcium sulphate) cap rock. Variable porosity and permeability, ranging from 9 to 14 percent and from 10 to 20 millidarcies respectively, is responsible for the average well in this field having a very high potential production that is in excess of 10,000 barrels of oil per day.

In contrast to the Ghawar field, the Santa Fe Springs oil and gas field southeast of Los Angeles, California, is formed of an anticline approximately 3 kilometers in length by 1 kilometer in width. Hydrocarbon production here is enhanced by eight vertically superimposed oil reservoirs overlain by a natural gas reservoir. Each reservoir is composed of sandstone, capped by an impermeable shale.

The Hugoton gas field of southwestern Kansas is an excellent example of a reservoir formed by changes in stratigraphy (physical character). The reservoir is formed of porous and permeable carbonate rock, both dolomite and limestone in composition. In a westward direction, the carbonate rock gradually alters to shale, resulting in a decrease in porosity to the point where commercial quantities of gas cannot be obtained. Further north in southern Alberta, Pembina, one of great oil fields of Canada, contains similar stratigraphic changes. In this case, four separate oil-producing sandstone reservoir rocks gradually change to shale, the latter acting as the cap rock.

The Chapman oil field of Texas is an excellent example of hydrocarbon production from igneous rocks, normally void of porosity and permeability. Originally formed as lava flows, with minimal porosity associated with gas vesicles, these rocks were subsequently altered and weathered, resulting in an increase in permeability. Overlying shales act as cap strata for the contained oil.

FURTHER READING: A fundamental introduction to reservoirs and reservoir traps is presented in *Petroleum Formation and Occurrence*, by Bernard Tissot and D. H. Welte, 1984, and in *Elements of Petroleum Geology*, by R. C. Selley, 1985. A worldwide survey of significant oil and gas fields is presented in *Classic Petroleum Provinces*, edited by J. Brooks, 1990. Introductory facts regarding oil and gas formation, distribution, and reserves are given in chapter 4, "Energy from Fossil Fuels," in *Resources of the Earth*, by James Craig, David Vaughan, and Brian Skinner, 1988.

Albert B. Dickas

SEE ALSO: Oil and natural gas, chemistry of; Oil and natural gas, worldwide distribution of; Oil and natural gas drilling and wells; Oil and natural gas exploration; Oil and natural gas formation; Oil industry.

Oil embargo and energy crises of 1973 and 1979

DATES: October, 1973, to March, 1974, and January through September, 1979

The energy crises of 1973 and 1979 produced new energy consciousness, high unemployment and inflation, negative economic growth, and foreign policy shifts within the oil-importing countries of the industrialized world.

THE 1973 AND 1979 energy crises differed importantly in timing and gravity. The 1973 crisis emerged in a matter of days; the 1979 crisis unfolded over eight months. The 1973 crisis involved the availability and affordability of the petroleum essential to the industrialized countries of the northern hemisphere. Oil's availability was never in doubt in 1979; only the ability of

the oil importers to pay for it was. At their most basic levels, however, the two crises had much in common. Both resulted from sudden, largely unforeseen events in the Middle East. Both generated periods of global stagflation. And both dramatized the extent to which, by the 1970's, the lifestyle of developed states had come to depend upon an energy source which they did not control.

The 1973 Oil Crisis. The immediate causes of the 1973 crisis were the October, 1973, war between Israel and Egypt, Jordan, and Syria (the Yom Kippur War), and the United States' decision to resupply Israel during the war. On October 17, 1973, the Organization of Arab Petroleum Exporting Countries (OAPEC) responded by agreeing to end or reduce oil shipments to countries supporting Israel. OAPEC's decision set petroleum-importing states bidding against one another for the oil upon which their economies depended. Oil's spot market price soared from under $3 a barrel to over $20 a barrel, and the Organization of Petroleum Exporting Countries (OPEC) successfully exploited the situation to wrest control over the international petroleum market from the cartel of private oil companies which had controlled it for half a century.

The Yom Kippur War was probably less responsible for causing the first oil crisis than influencing its timing. By 1973 oil supply and demand trends had combined with political events to make oil-importing states dependent on Arab producers and to render that dependency vulnerable. Following World War II industrialized states began doubling their energy use approximately every dozen years. To meet energy needs, Japan and the countries of Europe used ever larger quantities of imported petroleum—the cheapest and most efficient energy source available. Meanwhile, they allowed their indigenous coal industries to decay. Thus, whereas coal had accounted for nearly 78 percent of the energy being used in Western Europe and over 60 percent of Japan's energy in 1950, by 1970 coal was producing less than 25 percent of their energy needs. Conversely, by 1970 imported oil accounted for over 55 percent of Western Europe's energy use and nearly 70 percent of Japan's. Even in the United States, with its large domestic petroleum industry, imported oil became the postwar way of sustaining the good life. On the eve of the Yom Kippur War Americans were importing nearly a third of their petroleum and a sixth of their total energy needs.

These shifting demand-supply patterns would have been less significant were it not for the political changes that occurred between 1950 and 1970. The primary source of supply of the oil-importing world shifted to the Middle East, where many of the oil-exporting states were shedding pro-Western governments in favor of more radical regimes. These states were at once more likely to cooperate with one another in using the oil weapon against Israel and less willing to accept the prices being paid to them by the seven western oil companies who as late as 1950 still controlled nearly 90 percent of all production outside of the United States and the Soviet Union. By 1971, this cartel had already lost its ability to fix the price of oil on the world market.

Against this backdrop, the 1973 oil crisis unfolded as a culmination of events. The higher oil prices produced a major shift of wealth toward OPEC states (whose combined $10-12 billion surplus on their combined current account in 1973 jumped to a $65 billion surplus in 1974) and ended the 1968-1973 economic boom in the Western industrialized world. The crisis also produced significant diplomatic ruptures within the Western alliance, as Japan and most of America's allies in Europe were forced to break ranks with the United States on Mideast policy in order to avoid having their oil shipments curtailed.

The 1979 Crisis. The 1973 crisis also had the effect of making energy a major policy issue as importing states began to consider the lifestyle changes necessary to reduce their levels of dependency on OPEC oil. The choices were inevitably unpleasant, and by the mid-1970's the United States in particular preferred to regard the 1973 crisis as an aberration. It was a convenient fiction which made it unnecessary to re-

The most visible sign of the 1979 energy crisis: lines of motorists waiting to buy gasoline. (AP/Wide World Photos)

think America's love affair with large cars, suburban dwelling patterns, and generally profligate lifestyle of energy use. The 1979 crisis exploded this myth.

Chronologically, the second oil crisis unfolded between two political events: The fall of the shah of Iran in January and the outbreak of war between Iraq and Iran in September of 1979. The first event plunged Iran into disarray, effectively shutting down its oil industry and depriving an already tight international petroleum market of Iran's 3 to 4 million barrels per day of oil exports. The price of oil rose almost daily with Iran's continuing political turmoil. Then, in late summer, the turbulence in Iran tempted Iraq into invading the country. The resultant war removed Iraq's more than 3 million barrels of oil per day from the market as well. The cost of oil skyrocketed. By late September, OPEC oil, which had been selling for $16 a barrel in January cost over $36 a barrel.

The $20-per-barrel increase in the price of oil had a devastating impact on the global economy. Western oil importers hastily employed harsh monetary policies to combat the new inflationary pressure. As their economies sharply contracted (U.S. economic growth, for example, was −5.5 percent in 1980), unemployment rates unseen since the Great Depression ensued. By 1980, Japan's unemployment rate, which had averaged 1.0 percent during the 1960-1978 period, was 13.5 percent; for France and the United States, the 1980 figure was 15 percent; for the United Kingdom, 23 percent. Fifteen years later, double-digit unemployment dating from the second oil crisis still lingered in much of Western Europe.

Aftermath: The 1980's and 1990's. Deteriorating economic conditions in the oil-importing world produced a burst of political activity. Oil crises could no longer be treated as aberrations. The United States enacted the National Energy Security Act of 1980, whose centerpiece was the quasi-private Synthetic Fuels Corporation (SFC), charged with fostering the development of an oil- and gas-from-coal industry to reduce oil imports. Initially capitalized at $88 billion, the corporation became a political casualty of Ronald Reagan's election in November, 1980. President

Reagan preferred to leave energy matters to the private sector, and by the mid-1980's the SFC had been dismantled without a commercial-scale coal liquefaction demonstration plant ever being built.

Abroad, most countries responded to the 1979 oil crisis by following some variation of the "Co-Co-Nuk" policy adopted by Margaret Thatcher's government in Britain—that is, by stressing various mixes of increased conservation, greater coal use, and the development of more nuclear energy for electrical needs. In practice, few states succeeded in significantly lowering their levels of dependency on imported oil.

On the other hand, during the mid-1980's the international energy market began to correct itself in an effective if traumatic fashion. High oil prices encouraged oil importers to seek oil outside of OPEC (in the North Sea, in Alaska) and led the Soviet Union to sell some of its oil on the world market to obtain hard currency. As a result, the availability of non-OPEC oil increased at the same time that the demand for petroleum was declining due to the global economic stagflation caused by the post-1979 price of OPEC oil. By the mid-1980's, the demand for OPEC exports was only 60 percent of the demand that had existed for its oil when the shah fell in early 1979. Yet by then many OPEC members needed to earn more rather than less income to pay for the costly development plans they had launched on the anticipation of ever higher oil prices and profits. Led by Nigeria, they began to sell below OPEC's posted price in order to enlarge their market share and increase their income. Gluts resulted, and the price of oil plummeted—from over $38 a barrel in the early 1980's to $7 a barrel—before rebounding to approximately $25 a barrel by the time Iraq invaded Kuwait in the late summer of 1990.

The collapse of oil prices, in turn, caused many countries and private corporations to abandon their search for additional high-cost oil and costly petroleum substitutes. Exploratory drilling in the North Sea virtually ended; synthetic fuel projects were abandoned by countries (Britain, Germany, Japan, and Australia) and by corporate giants (Exxon and British Petroleum). By the time Iraq occupied Kuwait, the relatively low cost of imported oil had fueled a new round of economic growth in the developed world, but one based on a new round of increased oil imports from the Middle East.

Iraq's invasion of Kuwait grimly reminded oil importers of their continuing state of energy dependency. As the price of oil began to rise in response to this new crisis in the oil-exporting world, that dependency eased President George Bush's task in assembling an allied army to protect the Saudi Arabian oilfields, to evict Iraqi troops from oil—rich and pro-Western Kuwait, and to place postwar controls on Iraq's ability to mount future threats against its oil-exporting neighbors.

FURTHER READING: For still serviceable guides to OPEC and OAPEC, see Ian Skeet, *OPEC: Twenty-Five Years of Prices and Politics*, 1988, and Mary Ann Tetreault, *The Organization of Arab Petroleum Exporting Countries: History, Policies, and Prospects*, 1981. The best set of articles on the first energy crisis remains *Daedalus* 104 (Fall, 1975), a special issue entitled "The Oil Crisis in Perspective," edited by Raymond Vernon. For an account of Western reaction, see *The Arab Oil Embargo: Ten Years Later*, edited by Bettina Silber, 1984.

Joseph R. Rudolph, Jr.

SEE ALSO: Coal gasification and liquefaction; Energy economics; Energy politics; Oil industry; Organization of Arab Petroleum Exporting Countries; Organization of Petroleum Exporting Countries; Synthetic Fuels Corporation.

Oil industry

One of the world's largest industries, the petroleum industry made the twentieth century the "petroleum age," developed numerous third world countries, and helped the United States become a military and economic superpower.

THE OIL INDUSTRY's story is preeminently one of enormous wealth. American oil companies have persistently represented eight to ten of the country's largest twenty-five industrial companies. Collectively, the eight largest oil companies accounted for $400 billion in sales in 1990, virtually tying with the automotive sector as the United States' largest industry. Moreover, American-based multinational oil corporations such as Exxon, Gulf, Mobil, Texaco, and Chevron have consistently ranked among the major multinational corporations, with Exxon (number three) and Mobil (number eight) controlling more money than 80 percent of the world's countries.

The United States. In the United States as abroad, the industry's story is also one of towering individuals such as John D. Rockefeller, who founded the huge Standard Oil monopoly, and J. Paul Getty, who found great wealth under the sands near Kuwait. It is also the tale of the famous who walked on lesser stages, such as T. Boone Pickens, often cited as the inspiration for the J. R. Ewing character on television's *Dallas.* Above all, however, the industry's development is the story of people largely unknown to the broader public—such as Robert O. Anderson, one of America's great wildcatters and the man responsible for discovering oil in Alaska in 1969.

With wealth came economic and political power as well as success in gaining such benefits from the political system as quota protection against foreign petroleum imports, substantial tax advantages, and the right to purchase government-built pipeline systems at a bargain price. Initially, however, the tremendous monopolistic economic power of Rockefeller's Standard Oil Company drew unwelcome government attention to the oil industry.

At the beginning of the twentieth century, Standard Oil controlled 87 percent of production, 82 percent of refining, and 85 percent of all petroleum marketing operations in the United States. In 1911 the Sherman Antitrust Act was used to break the cartel into its regional components. Yet so large was the whole that many of its parts—Standard Oil of New Jersey (now Exxon), Standard Oil of New York (Mobil), Standard Oil of Indiana (Amoco), and Standard Oil of California (Chevron)—soon established themselves among the United States' leading industries.

On the eve of the 1973 oil crisis, the American petroleum industry was generating 30 percent of all domestic investment and 40 percent of all American investment in the developing

U.S. Oil and Gas Extraction Industry Statistics, 1992

| | *Businesses* | | *All Employees* | | *Production Workers* | | *Shipments and Expenditures* | |
| | | | | | | | *Value of Shipments and Receipts (in millions of dollars)* | *Capital Expenditures (in millions of dollars)* |
	Total	*With 20 or More Employees*	*Number (in 1,000s)*	*Payroll (in millions of dollars)*	*Number (in 1,000s)*	*Wages (in millions of dollars)*		
Totals	**20,877**	**2,686**	**344**	**13,526**	**187**	**5,992**	**111,518**	**11,423**
Crude petroleum and natural gas	9,388	1,017	174	8,409	64	2,601	72,298	9,850
Natural gas liquids	591	197	13	532	9	360	27,206	619
Oil and gas field services	10,898	1,472	157	4,585	114	3,031	12,014	955
Drilling wells	2,129	450	48	1,371	38	982	3,584	289
Exploration	1,489	85	14	462	8	238	980	182
Other field services	7,280	937	96	2,753	68	1,811	7,451	484

Source: U.S. Department of Commerce, *Statistical Abstract of the United States, 1996*, 1996.

world. In the aftermath of the 1973 oil crisis, the oil industry became the principal owner of the country's coal and uranium resources. Meanwhile, between the days of Rockefeller and those of the 1973 oil crisis, the industry provided the United States with the fuel source needed to become an economic and military power, and physically and psychologically remolded America—cheap domestic petroleum fueling other industries and enabling a lifestyle of personal mobility built around the automobile.

During the same period the industry also rebuilt its relationship with the government. Uncontrolled competition in the oil market led to overproduction, oil gluts, falling prices, reduced exploration, and periodic oil shortages and high prices. The pattern was undesirable for a country with a growing industrial economy, and it was unacceptable for one that was increasingly powering its military with oil. Beginning with World War I, the petroleum industry was thus able to inaugurate a new relationship with government. Intra-industry cooperation in price management was subsequently tolerated by Washington; indeed, government facilitated it with state pro-rationing schemes and federal legislation supporting them. The desire for a secure supply of oil

also prompted the federal government to redesign its tax laws to encourage more domestic oil companies to venture abroad after World War II.

The International Oil Industry. The world into which these corporations ventured was largely controlled by a cartel of the seven major multinational oil companies who had already developed major fields in Latin America, North Africa, and the Persian Gulf area by the 1930's. Known as the Seven Sisters (Exxon, Royal Dutch Shell, Mobil, Texaco, Gulf, Standard Oil of California, and British Petroleum), these companies in 1950 controlled 90 percent of all world production outside the United States and the Soviet Union, 80 percent of all refining operations, and 70 percent of all marketing operations. Their arrangements with the oil producing countries varied, evolving from a concession system to profit sharing arrangements to partnerships. Their rule of operations, however, was inevitably the same. The host government sold to its Sister, or it did not sell its oil.

The post-World War II search for petroleum by smaller American firms and other oil-importing countries gradually weakened the Sisters' hold on the market. By 1970 they accounted only for approximately 70 percent of the production and 50 percent of the marketing activities involving imported oil. More important, as the postwar industrialized world began to import ever greater amounts of oil, the presence of these smaller companies further increased the bargaining position of the oil-producing states vis-à-vis the Sisters. The 1973 Arab oil embargo on countries friendly to Israel allowed the Organization of Petroleum Exporting Countries (OPEC) to capitalize on these developments and replace the Seven Sisters cartel in setting the price of international oil.

The international oil industry's subsequent fortunes have in part fluctuated with OPEC's. Though the firms now serve producer states as salaried employees, their operations remain enormously profitable. Moreover, although they have had to retrench in periods of declining prices, the wealth and importance of the major firms remains secure. The developed world continues to run on petroleum, and they produce, refine, and market a considerable share of that oil. More important, obtaining increasingly hard-to-reach oil in the future will inevitably re-quire the knowledge, technology, and experience of the corporations that have been finding and extracting oil abroad throughout most of the twentieth century.

FURTHER READING: For an outstanding general discussion, read Daniel Yergin, *The Prize: The Epic Quest for Oil, Money, and Power*, 1991. Good treatments of the history of oil in American politics and oil's influence on the United States can be found in David Howard Davis, *Energy Politics*, 1993, and Carl Solberg, *Oil Power: The Rise and Imminent Fall of an American Empire*, 1976. For accounts of the international oil industry, see Anthony Sampson, *The Seven Sisters: The Great Oil Companies and the World They Shaped*, 1980, and *The International Oil Industry: An Interdisciplinary Perspective*, edited by Judith Rees and Peter Odell, 1988.

Joseph R. Rudolph, Jr.

SEE ALSO: Energy politics; Getty, J. Paul; Oil and natural gas exploration; Oil embargo and energy crises of 1973 and 1979; Organization of Petroleum Exporting Countries; Rockefeller, John D.; United States government, energy policy of.

The sprawling Mobil oil refinery complex southeast of Los Angeles. (McCrea Adams)

Oil shale and tar sands

WHERE FOUND: Tar sands are most abundant in sandstone and limestone. Most large deposits occur near sedimentary basin margins in deltaic, estuarine, or freshwater rocks. Oil shale occurs in lacustrine (lake) sediments, associated with coal, or in marine shale.

PRIMARY USES: Oil shale and tar sand are sources of oil and gas fuel, lubricants, and chemical feedstock.

DESCRIPTION: Tar sands are rocks with pore spaces filled by solid or semisolid bitumen. Oil shale is any fine-grained sedimentary rock containing kerogen and yielding petroleum when heated in the absence of oxygen.

KEROGEN IS A waxy, insoluble organic compound with a very large molecular structure. Almost all sedimentary rocks contain some kerogen; those that both contain kerogen and yield a few gallons of oil per ton are considered oil shale. Ten gallons per ton generally is the minimum figure used for calculating reserves. Twenty to thirty gallons are required for development. Some shales contain as much as fifty gallons per ton. Worldwide shale oil resources have been estimated at 3.1 trillion barrels, of which the United States has two trillion.

Origin of Oil Shale. Oil shale forms in oxygen-deficient environments where organic debris accumulates more rapidly than it is destroyed by oxidation, scavengers, or decay. Deep, confined ocean basins with stagnant water or restricted water circulation may preserve organic debris. Baltic and Manchurian oil shales are of this origin. Swamp lakes, with slow circulation and rapid accumulation of plant debris, also may produce oil shale. Oil shale accompanying coal in Scotland and North America are examples. Lakes with noncirculating water at the bottom also may accumulate oil shale. The gigantic Green River oil shale deposit of Wyoming and Colorado is of this type.

Producing Oil Shale. Very great amounts of shale are needed for economically significant petroleum production. Open-pit mining is much more economic than underground mining, although there are some large underground mines. Pits 1,000 feet deep and 2 miles across equal costs of underground mining in the Green River deposit. Further expansion reduces expense, making gigantic pits the most economical mining option. Heating shale in the absence of oxygen (retorting) converts kerogen (solid organic material that is insoluble in petroleum solvents) to liquids. The liquid then requires hydrogenation to make petroleum.

Retorted shale is saline and/or alkalic powder. Open pits are ready disposal sites for waste material, and underground mines may be backfilled. The remaining 10 percent or more of retort waste, however, requires disposal elsewhere. Finally, the waste must be isolated from surface water and groundwater to prevent contamination. *In situ* processing solves some disposal problems. In this method large blocks of oil shale are undermined and collapsed, creating an underground porous rubble. Gas introduced to the top of the rubble is ignited, after which the shale burns on its own. Gas and oil "cooked" from the rock are withdrawn from the base of the rubble, leaving the spent shale underground.

History of Oil Shale Use. Shale oil for medicinal purposes was produced in 1350 at Seefeld, Austria. The manufacture of illuminating oil and lubricants from oil shale began in France around 1830 and quickly spread through Europe and North America. Petroleum almost entirely supplanted shale oil during the late nineteenth century. Since then shale oil production has been largely limited to periods of oil shortage or of military or economic blockade. Flammable oil shale, rich in kerogen, has been burned to generate steam in Latvia. Scotland, the former Soviet Union, Manchuria, Sweden, France, Germany, South Africa, the United States, Brazil, and Australia all have produced shale oil, but total world production through 1961 was only about 400 million barrels.

Tar Sand Occurrence. Tar sand bitumens are larger, heavier, and more complex hydrocarbon compounds than those in liquid petroleum, and they include substantial nitrogen and sulfur. ("Bitumen" is a term for a very thick, natural semisolid material such as asphalt or tar.) Deposits are most abundant in sandstone or limestone.

Most large deposits are in deltaic, estuarine, or freshwater sandstone. The largest occur at depths of less than 3,000 feet on sedimentary basin margins where inclined layers of petroliferous rocks approach the surface. Here, upward migrating petroleum could lose volatiles and, with oxygenation and biodegradation, leave asphalt-impregnated rock. Some solid bitumens may be hydrocarbons not yet sufficiently altered to form liquids rather than residues of once liquid material.

United States reserves of 20 to 30 billion barrels of tar sand oil are insignificant compared to the 710 billion barrels and 200 billion barrels in Canada and Venezuela respectively. Additional deposits of more than 15 million barrels each are known in Albania, Siberia, Madagascar, Azerbaijan, the Philippines, and Bulgaria. In 1987 world reserves were estimated at about 1,577 billion barrels.

Tar Sand History. Tar sands have been used since ancient times for surfacing roads, laying masonry, and waterproofing. The Athabasca tar sand deposit of northern Alberta, Canada, was discovered in 1778 when Peter Pond, a fur trader, waterproofed his canoes with tar. Geologic exploration began in the 1890's, and by 1915 tar sand was being shipped to Edmonton, Alberta, to pave streets. Pilot plant extraction of oil began in 1927. Since then exploitation has continued with provincial and federal subsidies and support. By the 1990's operations apparently were self-supporting.

Tar Sand Exploitation. Canadian tar sand is mined in large open pits and transported to processing plants. There steam treatment produces bitumen froth and sand slurry. Naphtha steam removes the remaining sand, leaving viscous bitumen. Raw bitumen then is "cracked," a chemical process by which the large organic molecules in the bitumen are broken into smaller, more liquid molecules, gas, and coke. Finally, cracked oil is hydrogenated to produce synthetic crude oil. Sulfur is a salable by-product. Sand ultimately is returned to the pit, overburden is replaced, and the site reforested.

Open-pit production, however, is feasible only at the shallow periphery of the deposit, so *in situ* extraction will be required for about 90 percent of the Canadian deposit. In one system, wells drilled into the deposit are injected with steam to liquify the bitumen. Bitumen then is pumped until flow ceases, after which the well is again steamed. In another system wells sunk into the tar sand are ignited. Heat then cracks the bitumen, producing liquid and gas that flow to production wells.

FURTHER READING: *Oil Shales of the World*, by Paul L. Russell, 1990, comprehensively describes oil shale deposits. *The Elusive Bonanza: The Story of Oil Shale, America's Richest and Most Neglected Natural Resource*, by C. Welles, 1970, chronicles American oil shale development to that time. *Exploration for Heavy Crude Oil and Natural Bitumen*, edited by Richard F. Mayer, 1987, presents oil sand geology. *The Tar (Extra Heavy Oil) Sands and Oil Shales*, by Walter Ruhle, 1982, describes the variety of tar sands and oil shales.

Ralph L. Langenheim, Jr.

SEE ALSO: Energy economics; Mining wastes and mine reclamation; Oil and natural gas formation; Open-pit mining; Strip mining.

Oil spills

Major oil spills can be environmentally devastating. Not all spills are catastrophic, however, and a number of techniques have been developed to contain and clean up the oil; a spill's location is the single most important factor in the amount of damage it causes.

THE WORLD'S OIL RESERVES are developed by drilling, a process that brings oil to the surface, where it can be temporarily stored in tanks until transportation by pipeline or oil tanker. The oil is then transported: Pipelines move oil long distances across land, while tankers carry oil across the oceans. Transported oil is delivered to refineries, where it is separated into various useful components, including gasoline, jet fuel, home heating oil, diesel fuel, and lubricants. These refined products are shipped to storage facilities where they await delivery.

The drilling, storage, and transportation of oil sometimes result in the accidental release of oil into the natural environment. Even with improvements in technology and safety, accidental spills are inevitable because of the unpredictable natures of human error, faulty equipment, and weather. During the drilling of a well, oil can surge upward to the surface and spill out into the environment, an event referred to as a "blowout." Oil storage tanks can leak oil through a faulty valve or through a valve accidentally left open. Oil transported by pipeline can escape into the environment if the pipeline is accidentally ruptured. Oil tankers can spill oil into the ocean after grounding during severe weather.

The Fate of Spilled Oil. Oil spilled onto the ground generally soaks into the soil and does not spread far from the source of the spill. Large populations of soil bacteria eventually degrade most of the oil. Oil spilled into water, however, spreads over the surface into a thin film. After spreading, the oil covers a large area far away from the source of the spill.

Once on the water's surface, oil is subjected to a sequence of weathering processes. Volatile components in the oil are rapidly lost to the atmosphere. Ultraviolet radiation in sunlight breaks down some oil components in a process called photooxidation. Water-soluble components of oil dissolve into the water. Oil remaining on the surface begins to break up into small droplets that enter the water, a process aided by high winds and waves. Water turbulence at the surface can mix oil and water together into a mixture called a mousse. In the water, oil collects suspended particles, and this mixture eventually sinks to the bottom. Bottom oil is rolled along by water currents while collecting more oil and particles. Eventually bottom oil is buried or washed ashore.

Oil that remains for any length of time in the natural environment is subjected to the natural process of biodegradation. The bacteria that carry out this process are widespread in the environment. These organisms use the oil as a nutrient source to grow. In the process, they degrade the chemical components of the oil into harmless end products. This process, if given sufficient time, can remove the majority of spilled oil from the natural environment.

Oil Cleanup Techniques. Oil spilled on the ground can be soaked up with straw or commercially available oil sorbents. The oil-soaked mate-

rials can then be disposed of by burning or burial. Oil spilled into water presents a far greater challenge to clean up, since it can quickly spread over a large area. Since spilled oil spreads quickly, a rapid response is essential. The flow of oil into the environment must be stopped, and the spread of spilled oil must be minimized. Oil containment booms are often used to stop the spread of oil across water. Booms are placed around the source of the spill in an effort to restrict oil to a small area where it can be picked up by skimmers. Skimmers dip a belt into the water to pick up oil from the surface and then scrape the belt across a roller to remove the oil. The oil scraped off the belt falls into a storage tank.

Oil that has escaped to cover large areas of water surface can be removed by the use of chemical dispersants. Dispersants break up the oil into tiny droplets that readily mix into the water. Oil that has been mixed into the water is less likely to strand along the shoreline.

Oil that strands on the shoreline can be difficult to remove. Shoreline cleanup of sandy beaches is often labor intensive and employs rakes, shovels, and sorbents to remove oil. Rocky shorelines can sometimes be safely cleaned by low-pressure water spraying, but high-pressure spraying can be harmful. Certain shoreline types, like marshes, are particularly sensitive to disturbance and should be left alone.

One of the more effective tools to emerge for the cleanup of oiled shorelines is bioremediation. This method relies on the natural ability of bacteria in the environment to break down oil. In bioremediation, natural breakdown is stimulated by the addition of a fertilizer to the shoreline, because the natural process is often limited by a lack of nutrients. With the addition of nutrients to the fertilizer, oil biodegradation occurs at a much accelerated rate. This technique was used successfully on the shorelines of Prince William Sound after the *Exxon Valdez* oil spill.

Environmental Effects of Oil Spills. Pictures of dead and dying animals are often used to depict the biological damage that oil spills can cause. The effects of major spills are indeed devastating. The effects of smaller spills—or of spills in the open ocean—are significantly less severe.

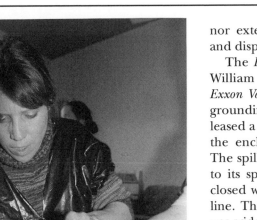

In March, 1989, the Exxon Valdez *ran aground off the coast of Alaska, causing the worst oil spill in U.S. history. Here Dr. Jessica Porter attempts to save a sea bird that was covered with the oil.* (Reuters/Mike Blake/Archive Photos)

The degree of damage varies with a number of factors, including the type of oil spilled, the amount of oil spilled, and the location of the spill. Spill location is perhaps the single most important factor. Spills that occur in open water areas, such as coastal seas, typically have less biological impact than those that occur in enclosed water areas, such as bays and sounds. A comparison of the biological damage after the 1969 Santa Barbara oil spill and the 1989 *Exxon Valdez* oil spill will illustrate this point.

The Santa Barbara oil spill occurred in the Santa Barbara Channel off the coast of California. A total of three million gallons of oil was released as a result of a well blowout. The oil spread over a large area of coastal seas and weathered for a period of seven days before portions began to strand on shorelines. Only a fraction of the spilled oil eventually came ashore along beaches and rocky shores. The oil caused the death of shore animals, seabirds, and marine mammals, but mortality was neither widespread

nor extensive because of the prior weathering and dispersal of the oil.

The *Exxon Valdez* oil spill occurred in Prince William Sound, Alaska, in 1989. The tanker *Exxon Valdez* ruptured its oil storage tanks after grounding on Bligh Reef. Ruptured tanks released a total of eleven million gallons of oil into the enclosed waters of Prince William Sound. The spilled oil did not weather or disperse prior to its spread across 10,000 square miles of enclosed water and 1,200 miles of adjacent shoreline. Therefore, the death of shoreline animals was widespread and extensive, as was the death of seabirds and marine mammals. An estimated 300,000 to 645,000 seabirds died as a result of the spill, in addition to an estimated 4,000 to 6,000 marine mammals. Oil was still found buried beneath the surface of some shorelines four years after the spill.

FURTHER READING: Basic oil-spill cleanup techniques are described in the American Petroleum Institute's *Oil Spill Cleanup: A Primer*, 1982. Bioremediation as a cleanup tool is described in Ronald Atlas and Carl Cerniglia, "Bioremediation of Petroleum Pollutants," *Bioscience* 45, no. 5 (1995). The aftermath of the Santa Barbara oil spill is discussed in Robert Easton, *Black Tide: The Santa Barbara Oil Spill and Its Consequences*, 1972. The aftermath of the *Exxon Valdez* oil spill in Prince William Sound is described in Bryan Hodgson, "Alaska's Big Spill: Can the Wilderness Heal?" *National Geographic* 177, no. 1 (1990), and Rick Steiner, "Probing an Oil-Stained Legacy," *National Wildlife* 31, no. 3 (1993).

Steve K. Alexander

SEE ALSO: Alaska pipeline; American Petroleum Institute; Biotechnology; Environmental biotechnology; Oil and natural gas drilling and wells; Oil industry; Petroleum refining and processing; Water pollution and water pollution control.

Olivine

WHERE FOUND: Olivine is common in the earth's crust; fine-quality peridot, the gemstone variety of olivine, is found in Arizona and on the Red Sea island of Zebirget.

PRIMARY USES: The main use of olivine is the use of peridot as a gemstone.

DESCRIPTION: Olivine generally appears in a variety of yellowish-green and yellowish-brown colors, depending on its specific chemical composition. It has a hardness of 6.5 to 7 on the Mohs scale.

OLIVINE IS THE group name for a series of minerals that have the end members forsterite and fayalite. The olivine group of minerals is one of the more important rock-forming minerals that make up the earth's crust. It is a high–temperature mineral group that is often associated with the volcanic rock basalt. It is a very common mineral in the rocks that constitute the earth's lower crust and upper mantle. Olivine is also one of the essential minerals found in the stony variety of meteorites.

The name olivine refers to a series of high-temperature minerals that have the end members forsterite (Mg_2SiO_4) and fayalite (Fe_2SiO_4). When the two are chemically combined they form the magnesium iron silicate that is commonly called olivine. The higher-temperature member, forsterite, is rich in the element magnesium. It was named after Johann R. Forster, an eighteenth century German naturalist who sailed with the English explorer Captain James Cook. Fayalite, the lower-temperature end member of the series, is rich in iron. It was named after the island Fayal in the Azores, where it is abundant.

Olivine often occurs as attractive crystals. In color, olivine can appear with differing shades of yellowish-green. Depending upon its specific chemical composition, olivine can also appear in shades of yellowish-brown to an almost reddish color.

Since olivine is a high-temperature mineral, it is usually absent from the earth's surface. Large deposits of olivine are often associated with certain volcanoes. An unusually explosive volcano can rapidly transport olivine up from great depths and then expel it as it erupts. Lavas produced by such volcanoes often have numerous individual olivine crystals scattered throughout; the crystals may also clump together and form as nodules. In both cases these crystals were forming within the magma at depth and were then transported upward with the rising magma. When the magma eventually flowed out of the volcano as lava, it contained the olivine that originally formed at great depth. Associated with these eruptions are other rocks called xenoliths, which also formed at depth; they contain olivine as one of their principal minerals. This kind of rock is called periodite.

Peridot is the variety of olivine that is used as a gemstone. It is somewhat transparent and ranges in color from a yellowish-green to olive green. The dark yellow-green stones are considered to be the most valuable. Flawless peridot is common, and it can be faceted in many different ways. Fine-quality peridot comes from the San Carlos Indian Reservation in Arizona. The most sought-after stones come from the island of Zebirget in the Red Sea. Peridot is the birthstone for the month of August.

Paul P. Sipiera

SEE ALSO: Gems; Igneous processes, rocks, and mineral deposits; Iron; Magma crystallization; Magnesium; Minerals, structure and physical properties of; Mohs hardness scale; Silicates; Silicon; Volcanoes.

Open-pit mining

Open-pit mining refers to the removal of mineral resources from the earth without the use of either tunnels or wells. A gravel pit represents the simplest example of an open-pit mine. Although some mining engineers distinguish between strip mining and open-pit mining, the methods employed in both are similar. The major difference is that strip mines are generally shallow, while a pit may eventually descend to hundreds of feet below the original surface of the earth.

OPEN-PIT MINING IS the method mine owners prefer to use when the mineral body lies close enough to the surface of the earth to allow the removal of the ore in continuous layers. It is both the safest and most economical method of extracting mineral resources from a site. It has been estimated that worldwide 70 percent of all minerals mined are obtained through open-pit mining processes. There is a strong economic incentive for mine operators to use the open-pit method. Mining by the open-pit method allows the mining company to extract 100 percent of the ore-bearing rock. In underground mines using tunnels and shafting, the recovery rate of ore-bearing rock is generally 60 percent or less. Open-pit mining is also considerably safer than underground mining, as the ore is removed with power shovels and large trucks. Although underground mining also uses mechanized equipment, the workers are still exposed to risks such as cave-ins and explosions not present in open pits.

Methods. A few minerals are soft enough to be mined without the use of explosives. More commonly, mining proceeds through a series of drilling holes, placing explosive charges in the holes and blasting, and then removing the shattered rock with extremely large power shovels and trucks. Most equipment used in open-pit mining is gargantuan in size. Power shovels, excavators, and draglines are custom-assembled at the mine since they are too large to transport other than in pieces. In the past when a mine closed, this equipment was abandoned at the site. Today it is more likely to be salvaged as scrap metal. In a few former mining districts, specialized equip-

ment has been left in place and preserved as part of historic landmarks.

In some cases the ore body lies close enough to the surface that mining begins directly. More often, a layer of waste material known as the overburden must be removed before the ore itself is exposed. The overburden consists of the topsoil and underlying dirt and rock that contains no extractable ore. When mining begins, the layer of topsoil will be removed carefully and piled separately from other waste material as the topsoil will be needed for use in the restoration process when the mine site is exhausted.

Depending on the mine site, the type of ore being mined, and other factors, the mining may proceed in parallel strips or may be done in a circular pattern that gradually expands in diameter. Coal is often mined in strips, as the mineral frequently occurs in layers that can cover a wide area but are only a few feet in thickness. The mine operator removes the overburden from a strip of coal, excavates the coal, and then repeats the process in a strip running next to the first strip. When the ore body is exhausted, the overburden will be backfilled into the stripped

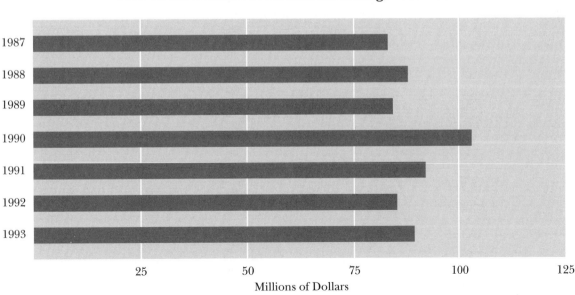

U.S. Gross Domestic Product in Mining, 1987-1993

Source: U.S. Department of Commerce, *Statistical Abstract of the United States, 1996,* 1996.
Note: Figures are in current dollars, not constant dollars.

area as part of the restoration process. In the past, before legislation required mine operators to practice restoration, a strip mined area often consisted of a devastated landscape dominated by alternating trenches and ridges, with the land left unusable for either agriculture or wildlife habitat. Since the passage of environmental regulations in the 1960's, in the United States strip mined areas are backfilled, leveled, and seeded with grass and trees.

Metals such as iron are generally mined in pits that become both deeper and wider over time. The mining operation will commence as close as possible to the known center of the site and expand both out and down as ore is removed. As time passes, the pit may become surrounded by large piles of tailings, or waste rock. The final depth of the pit will be determined by factors such as the thickness of the ore body and the stability of the surrounding walls of the pit. A pit developed to excavate material such as gravel often has walls composed of soft materials, such as a mixture of sand and gravel, and at risk of collapsing in to the pit. Gravel pits therefore are generally quite shallow. Even a pit mine for hard minerals, such as copper or iron, where the mineral is found in rock, may eventually reach a depth where the height of the walls makes it unsafe to dig the pit any deeper. If the ore is sufficiently valuable, mining of the remaining ore body may continue using shaft mining.

In the past, large open-pit mines often operated next to or within communities, such as Butte, Montana, and Bisbee, Arizona, both of which had enormous copper mines. At one time the Anaconda operation at Butte was reputed to be the largest open-pit mine in the world. As the mines expanded, homes and businesses were forced to relocate to accommodate the mine's operation. By the 1990's, however, the general public had grown less tolerant of mining. Property owners have sued mining companies over quality of life issues such as noise pollution and dust. Developers now generally try to avoid opening new open-pit mines close to towns or suburbs.

The mammoth Kennecott open-pit copper mine in Utah is the world's largest. (Photo Network)

Environmental Issues. Open-pit mining raises a number of obvious environmental protection questions. Even at its most innocuous, the mining process tends to be both noisy and dusty. Truck or rail traffic to and from the mine can create a nuisance as well as a safety hazard for area residents. As the pit is deepened, it may affect the local water table. Water can seep into the pit, lowering the water table for the surrounding area, and can then present a hazard to local streams as it is pumped out loaded with sediment. Strip mining on hillsides can lead to erosion and contamination by mine spillage of the local streams.

Depending on the ore being mined, the open-pit mine may present potentially life-threatening problems in addition to dust and noise. The mine itself may be relatively harmless, but processing plants built next to the mine to remove the ore from waste rock may involve the use of dangerous chemicals and produce toxic by-products. Precious-metals mining can be particularly hazardous. In gold mining, for example, the ore often occurs in such small amounts within the ore body that remarkably large amounts of ore must be processed to obtain the precious metal using a method that employs cyanide and mercury. If these substances leak into the environment, they can poison streams and kill wildlife miles away from the mine itself. Iron ore mining can release sulfides into the environment, as can mining coal. Although not as toxic as cyanide and mercury, sulfides raise the acidity of water and can make lakes and streams uninhabitable by aquatic life.

In the United States, Canada, and many other nations, mine owners are now required by law to restore an open-pit mining site as closely as possible to its original condition. Toxic wastes must be removed or neutralized and the pit filled in. Restoration efforts at strip mining sites in eastern states that enjoy a relatively wet climate, such as Tennessee and Ohio, have been very successful. Phosphate mining areas in Tennessee, for example, have been restored for use in agriculture. Gravel pits and limestone quarries may be used as small wetlands. Water has always been prone to build up in abandoned pit mines; by the 1990's engineering consulting firms existed that specialized in preparing abandoned pits to become wetlands and ponds. These firms cleaned up the site, sloped the walls to make the pit safer, removed any potentially dangerous mining debris, and planted the species of vegetation most beneficial to wildlife native to the region. Restoration efforts in arid climates have been less successful. Lack of rain makes it difficult to restore native vegetation and, even if tailings dumps and mine pits are bulldozed to less artificial contours, the scars from mining will be visible for centuries.

FURTHER READING: See Eugene N. Cameron, *At the Crossroads: The Mineral Problems of the United States,* 1986; *Mining for the Future: Trends and Expectations,* edited by the Chinese Organizing Committee of the Fourteenth World Mining Congress, 1990; the Institution of Mining and Metallurgy's *Surface Mining and Quarrying: Papers Presented at the Second International Surface Mining and Quarrying Symposium,* 1983; and Duane A. Smith, *Mining America: The Industry and the Environment, 1800-1980,* 1987.

Nancy Farm Mannikko

SEE ALSO: Mining wastes and mine reclamation; Quarrying; Strip mining; Underground mining.

Ophiolites

Ophiolites are pieces of oceanic crust and upper mantle that have been thrust up on continental crust; they contain a wide range of minerals.

THE PROCESS THAT forms ophiolites occurs where continental crust is bent down and slips under oceanic crust, generally in a subduction zone. Ophiolites consist of a vertical sequence of (from bottom to top) mantle rocks, gabbro, sheeted dykes, and pillowed lavas. Ophiolites are remnants of ancient ocean basins, demonstrating that an ocean basin once existed in the area and that plate convergence has destroyed the ocean basin. Ophiolites generally define and decorate suture zones, places where once-separated continental blocks have collided. Ophiolites host a wide range of minerals, including chromite, platinum-group elements, and gold. Ophiolites are also important from a natural resources perspective because the tectonic forces that have put them in place often also form sedimentary basins that can contain fossil fuel deposits (oil, gas, and coal).

The term "ophiolite" comes from the Greek word *ophis*, meaning snake or serpent; the term's origin is similar to that of the rock called "serpentinite." Both terms refer to the mottled green (reptilelike) appearance of these rocks. Ophiolites are sequences of oceanic crust and upper mantle that have been emplaced on continental crust by a process known as "obduction" Obduction often faults, folds, and otherwise disrupts the original sequence of rocks. Ophiolites nevertheless provide the best known example of the structure of oceanic crust.

The typical ophiolite sequence is on the order of 5 kilometers (3 miles) thick, and it records the products of seafloor spreading. The top kilometer is composed of pillowed basalt. (Basalt is a dense black lava containing about 50 percent by weight silicon dioxide formed as a result of melting of the mantle.) A sequence of these basalts looks like a huge pile of black to green pillows. Pillows form when basalt lava erupts and is quenched underwater, perhaps two miles or more beneath the surface. These basalt flows are fed from a system of vertical magma channels known as a sheeted dyke complex (about 1 kilometer thick). The dykes are supplied magma from an underlying magma chamber, which upon cooling forms gabbro (about 3 kilometers thick). Gabbro is the base of the crustal section and is underlain by mantle rocks called peridotite.

Although there is wide agreement that ophiolites form by seafloor spreading, scientists do not agree on precisely where these form. Early ideas, that ophiolites formed at true mid-ocean ridges such as the East Pacific Rise or Mid-Atlantic Ridge, have been superseded by the idea that they form at convergent margins undergoing extension. A more recent idea, that ophiolites for the most part represent back-arc basin crust, is being challenged by the hypothesis that ophiolites form in forearc environments during the initiation of subduction zones.

Ophiolites prove that processes of seafloor spreading and plate tectonics operated at the time the ophiolites formed. Therefore, the record of ophiolites can be interpreted as a record of when plate tectonics occurred on Earth. Ophiolites are common in rock sequences of the following time ages: 1,800 million years ago, 800 to 400 million years ago, and younger than 180 million years ago.

Robert J. Stern

SEE ALSO: Earth's crust; Lithosphere; Plate tectonics; Seafloor spreading.

Organisation for Economic Co-operation and Development

DATE ESTABLISHED: Establishing treaty signed December 14, 1960; took effect September 30, 1961

With a 1997 membership of twenty-five of the world's industrialized countries, the OECD is a forum for intergovernmental policy discussions and policy coordination as well as a "think tank" that researches and publishes information on a variety of economic problems and resource issues.

THE ORGANISATION FOR Economic Co-operation and Development (OECD) was created as a successor to the Organisation for European Economic Co-operation (OEEC), which had been established in 1948 to coordinate the use of Marshall Plan aid following World War II.

The OECD conducts extensive research and publishes on a broad range of economic-related issues. It has worked with developing nations to help them enter the world free-market system. In 1994 Mexico became the first new member of the OECD in twenty years. The organization has been working closely with Russia and with potential members Poland, Hungary, the Czech Republic, Slovakia, and South Korea.

A number of OECD committees work on resource issues. The Industry and Energy Committee has been studying alternate sources of energy in order to lessen reliance on oil and encourage the development of multiple energy sources. Among the Agricultural Committee's concerns are fisheries issues, including conservation of stocks.

The Organisation for Economic Co-operation and Development is also involved in water quality studies, especially concerning ecosystem deterioration in lakes. In January, 1991, it reported that oxygen content in surface waters has improved in its member states. However, it found algae growth, resulting from nonpoint pollution sources and agricultural runoff, to be a major problem and saw no significant decrease in heavy metal content.

Colleen M. Driscoll

SEE ALSO: Developing countries, resource use by; Energy economics; Energy politics; Fisheries; Lakes; United Nations Environment programme; Water pollution and water pollution control.

Organization of Arab Petroleum Exporting Countries

DATE ESTABLISHED: 1968

OAPEC profoundly affected international economics and politics in 1973 when it curtailed oil shipments to countries supporting Israel.

KUWAIT, LIBYA, AND Saudi Arabia founded the Organization of Arab Petroleum Exporting Countries (OAPEC) in 1968 to advance the political as well as the economic interests of Arab oil-exporting states. Unlike the non-Arab members of the Organization of Petroleum Exporting Countries (OPEC), OAPEC founders shared a Mideast political agenda: the use of oil as a weapon in the Arab-Israeli conflict. Most of the Persian Gulf's oil-exporting states eventually joined OAPEC.

On October 17, 1973, OAPEC ministers responded to a U.S. decision to resupply Israel during the ongoing Yom Kippur War by agreeing to reduce oil shipments to countries supporting Israel. OAPEC's action set petroleum-importing states bidding against one another for the oil upon which their economies depended. The price of oil soared, and OPEC was able to wrest control over the international petroleum market from the cartel of private oil companies which had controlled it for much of the twentieth century.

It took the oil-importing world nearly three years to adjust their economies to the resultant fourfold increase in the price of oil. The political fallout from OAPEC's embargo was equally substantial. Japan and most European allies were forced to break with the United States on Mideast policy in order to avoid having their oil shipments curtailed. Energy became a major policy issue everywhere in the developed industrial world.

Joseph R. Rudolph, Jr.

SEE ALSO: Energy economics; Energy politics; Oil embargo and energy crises of 1973 and 1979; Oil industry; Organization of Petroleum Exporting Countries.

Organization of Petroleum Exporting Countries

DATE ESTABLISHED: September 14, 1960

Largely ignored for twelve years, the Organization of Petroleum Exporting Countries achieved control over the international oil market in 1973.

VENEZUELA, IRAN, IRAQ, Kuwait, and Saudi Arabia established the Organization of Petroleum Exporting Countries (OPEC) in September, 1960, in order to acquire as much control as possible over the international oil market. Subsequent joiners included the United Arab Emirates, Qatar, Libya, Algeria, Indonesia, Nigeria, Gabon, and Ecuador.

Prior to 1973 OPEC was essentially a bureaucratic entity providing members with oil market information. Between 1960 and 1973, however, the growing demand for imported oil had created a seller's market. In October, 1973, a crisis ensued when the Organization of Arab Petroleum Exporting Countries declared an oil embargo against states friendly to Israel. OPEC exploited the situation, taking over the pricing of oil.

OPEC failed the first real test of its ability to control the oil market. During a second oil crisis in 1979, OPEC increased the price of oil from $16 a barrel to $36 a barrel. A global recession followed, drastically reducing the demand for oil

OPEC president Erwin Arrieta of Venezuela (left) and secretary general Rilwanu Lukman of Nigeria at a 1995 OPEC meeting. (Reuters/Peter Bader/Archive Photos)

at a moment when producers needed revenue to pay their development bills. OPEC's members began underselling OPEC's posted price to expand their individual shares of the market. The price of oil dropped, eventually to less than $7 a barrel.

Subsequently, the most important influence on oil's cost has been the fact that most imported oil comes from the volatile Middle East, where political events have periodically threatened new energy crises and affected the price of oil.

Joseph R. Rudolph, Jr.

SEE ALSO: Energy politics; Oil and natural gas, worldwide distribution of; Oil embargo and energy crises of 1973 and 1979; Oil industry; Organization of Arab Petroleum Exporting Countries.

Orthosilicate minerals

Orthosilicates are silicate minerals (minerals containing silicon and oxygen) in which the silicate groups are not linked to one another. Found worldwide, they are often used as abrasives, and some are used as gemstones.

ORTHOSILICATES, ALSO KNOWN as nesosilicates, are distinguished from other silicates by the fact that their silicate groups (one silicon atom bonded to four oxygen atoms) are not linked to one another. The properties of the different orthosilicates are determined by the type of metal atoms that are bound to the silicate groups. Orthosilicates are usually hard minerals with a glassy luster in a variety of colors. Orthosilicates are found worldwide, usually within igneous and metamorphic rocks. The most common ortho-silicates are the olivines, which make up about 3 percent of the earth's crust by weight.

Because of their hardness, orthosilicates are often used as abrasives. Many orthosilicates are used as gemstones because of their varied colors and glassy luster. Some orthosilicates are used to line the interior of furnaces. A few orthosilicates are used as sources for certain elements.

Orthosilicates, unlike other silicates, have silicate groups that are not linked to neighboring silicate groups. These silicate groups may be bound to atoms of magnesium, iron, aluminum, oxygen, fluorine, manganese, calcium, chromium, zirconium, or titanium. They may also be bound to hydroxyl groups (one oxygen atom bonded to one hydrogen atom).

The most common orthosilicates are the olivines, which contain magnesium or iron. Olivines are green, glassy minerals. Transparent olivines, known as peridots, are used as gemstones. Garnets are a group of orthosilicates with various chemical compositions, usually containing aluminum atoms in combination with other metallic atoms. In some garnets another metal takes the place of aluminum. Garnets are hard, glassy minerals in a variety of colors including red, yellow, green, and brown. Garnets are often used as abrasives and gemstones.

Orthosilicates in which the silicate groups are bound only to aluminum atoms exist in three forms: andalusite (usually pink or red), sillimanite (usually white), and kyanite (usually light blue). All three varieties are often used to line the inside of furnaces because they resist high temperatures. Kyanite's unusual color has led to its use as a gemstone.

Topaz is an orthosilicate containing aluminum and fluorine atoms along with hydroxyl groups. It is a very hard, glassy mineral which is used as a gemstone. Topaz may be colorless, resembling diamond, or may be yellow, blue, brown, or green. Red topaz is rare. Yellow topaz turns pink when subjected to heat, and some colors of topaz fade when exposed to light.

Zircon, which contains zirconium, is a hard, brown, glassy mineral used as a gemstone or as a source of zirconium. Sphene, which contains calcium and titanium, is a moderately hard, brown,

shiny mineral used as a source of titanium. Staurolite, which contains iron, aluminum, oxygen, and hydroxyl groups, is a hard, brown, glassy mineral which often occurs as intersecting crystals that form natural crosses used as decorations.

Rose Secrest

SEE ALSO: Abrasives; Garnet; Gems; Olivine; Silicates; Silicon.

Overgrazing

The effects of overgrazing occur where there are more grazing animals than the land and vegetation can support. Overgrazing has negatively affected regions of the United States, primarily in the Southwest. Areas that have been severely damaged by overgrazing typically show declining or endangered plant and animal species.

HERBIVORES ARE ANIMALS that feed on plant material, and grazers are herbivores that feed specifically on grass. Common examples are horses, cows, antelope, rabbits, and grasshoppers. Overgrazing occurs when grazer populations exceed the carrying capacity of a specified area. (Carrying capacity is the number of individual organisms the resources of a given area can support.) In overgrazing conditions, there is insufficient food to support the animal population in question. Depending on the grazer's strategy, emigration or starvation will follow. It must be noted that grasslands can handle normal grazing; only overgrazing adversely affects them.

Grasses' Defenses Against Grazing. Grasslands and grazers coevolved, so grasses can withstand grazing within the ecosystem's carrying capacity. All plants have a site of new cell growth called the meristem, where growth in height and girth occur. Most plants have the meristem at the very top of the plant (the apical meristem). If a plant's meristem is removed, the plant dies. If grasses had an apical meristem, grazers—and lawn mowers—would kill grasses. Grasses survive mowing and grazing because they do not have an apical meristem. On grasses the meristem is located at the junction of the shoot and root, close to the ground. With the exception of sheep, grazers in North America do not disturb the meristem, and sheep do so only during overgrazing conditions. At proper levels of grazing, grazing actually stimulates grass to grow in height in an attempt to produce a flowering head for reproduction. Grazing also stimulates grass growth by removing older plant tissue at the top that is functioning at a lower photosynthetic rate.

Grazers. Mammalian grazers have high, crowned teeth with a great area for grinding to facilitate opening of plants' cell walls in an attempt to release nutrients. The cell wall is composed of cellulose, which is very difficult for grazers to digest. Two major digestive system grazing strategies have evolved. Ruminants, such as cows and sheep, evolved stomachs with four chambers to allow regurgitation in order to chew food twice to maximize cellulose breakdown. In addition, intestinal bacteria digest the cellulose, releasing fatty acids that nourish the ruminants. Other grazers, such as rabbits and horses, house bacteria in the cecum, a pouch at the junction of the small and large intestines. These bacteria ferment the plant material ingested. The fermented products of the bacteria nourish these grazers.

Impacts in the Southwest. As previously mentioned, in the United States the negative effects of overgrazing are most intense in the Southwest. Some ecologists believe that one significant factor was the pattern of early European colonization of the area. Missions were abundant in the Southwest, and the missions owned cattle that were rarely slaughtered except on big feast days. Since Catholic priests received some financial support from their religious orders in Europe, mission cattle were not restrained as strictly as were those owned by cattlemen whose sole livelihood came from raising and selling cattle. Mission cattle roamed greater distances and began the pattern of overgrazing in the Southwest. The impact of overgrazing was particularly intense because much of the Southwest has desertlike conditions. Extreme environmental conditions result in particularly fragile ecosystems. Hence the southwest was, and is, vulnerable to the effects of overgrazing.

Another possible—though disputed—contribution to overgrazing may stem from the fact that much of the land in the Southwest is public land under jurisdiction of the Bureau of Land Management. This federal agency leases out land to private concerns for the purpose of grazing cattle or sheep. Some observers feel that the bureau has a conflict of interest in that its primary source of income is money obtained from leasing public land under its jurisdiction. They suspect that the bureau has granted, and fear that it may continue to grant, grazing leases in regions threatened with or suffering from overgrazing.

Effects of Overgrazing. Overgrazing can lead to a number of basic ecological problems. Overgrazed regions can experience desertification, for example. Other possible results are the endangering of some species of grass and the creation of monocultures in regions where certain species have been removed. Desertification is the intensification and expansion of deserts at the expense of neighboring grasslands. When overgrazing occurs along desert perimeters, the plant removal leads to decreased shading. This decreased shading increases the local air temperature. When the temperature increases, the air may no longer be able to cool down enough to release moisture in the form of dew. Dew is the primary source of precipitation in deserts, so without it desert conditions intensify. Even a slight decrease in desert precipitation is serious. The result is hotter and drier conditions which lead to further plant loss and potentially to monocultures.

The overgrazing of grasslands, combined with the existence of non-native species in an ecosystem, can result in the endangerment of species of native grasses. At one time, cattle in the Southwest fed exclusively on native grasses. Then non-native grass species arrived in the New World in the guts of cows shipped from Europe. They began to compete with the native grasses. European grass species have seeds with prickles and burs; southwestern native grasses do not, making them softer and more desirable to the cattle. Hence European grasses experienced little, if any, grazing, while the much more palatable southwestern native grasses experienced cattle grazing to the point of overgrazing. The

result was drastic decline or loss of native grassland species. Animals dependent on native grassland species must then emigrate or risk extinction. For example, many ecologists conjecture
that the Coachella Valley kit fox in California is
threatened because of the loss of grassland habitat upon which it is dependent.

Solutions. Desertification may be irreversible,
but the elimination of grazing along desert perimeters can at least help to prevent further desertification. One method being tried to reestablish native grass species involves controlled burn
programs. Non-native grassland species do not
appear to be as fire resistant as native grass species. Controlled burn programs are therefore
being used in some overgrazed grassland areas
in an attempt to reestablish native grass species
and eliminate non-natives. If successful, such
programs will increase the biodiversity of the
area and therefore will improve the health of the
ecosystem.

FURTHER READING: Basic relevant ecological
principles, including fire ecology and carrying
capacity, are explained in *A Primer of Ecological
Principles*, by Richard J. Vogl, 1995. The importance of natural disturbances in maintaining an
ecosystem's health is discussed in Wayne P.
Sousa, "The Role of Disturbance in Natural
Communities," *Annual Review Ecological Systems*
15 (1984). A good introduction to controlled
burns in California can be found in Richard J.
Vogl, "Some Basic Principles of Grassland Fire
Management," *Environmental Management* 3, no. 1
(1979). An example of grazing research and the
many interrelated issues involved is Heather
McBrien et al., "A Case of Insect Grazing Affecting Plant Succession," *Ecology* 64, no. 5 (1983).

Jessica O. Ellison

SEE ALSO: Biodiversity; Fires; Land management; Sagebrush Rebellion; Species loss; Taylor
Grazing Act.

Oxides

*Oxygen is an abundant element that is also reactive;
that is, it easily forms compounds with other elements.
Oxides are combinations of oxygen and metals. Oxides*
*are ores of a number of minerals and may themselves be
used as abrasives.*

A SIMPLE OXIDE contains only one metal,
whereas a multiple oxide contains two metals.
Examples of simple oxides are tin oxides, manganese oxides, and iron oxides. When one tin
atom is combined with two oxygen atoms, tin
dioxide (SnO_2) is formed. Tin dioxide is also
called cassiterite, which is derived from the
Greek word for tin, *kassiteros*. Cassiterite can be
found in high-temperature hydrothermal veins.
When one manganese atom is combined with
two oxygen atoms, manganese dioxide (MnO_2,
or pyrolusite) is formed. Pyrolusite can be found
in bog, lake, or shallow marine deposits.

If two iron atoms are combined with three
oxygen atoms, hematite (Fe_2O_3) is formed. If
three iron atoms are combined with four oxygen
atoms, magnetite (Fe_3O_4) is formed. Examples
of multiple oxides are magnesium-aluminum-
oxide (spinel, $MgAl_2O_4$), beryllium-aluminum-
oxide (chrysoberyl, $BeAl_2O_4$), and iron-titanium-
oxide (ilmenite, $FeTiO_3$). Spinel can be found
in basic igneous rocks, the original rocks of the
earth, formed directly from molten mineral matter billions of years ago. Chrysoberyl can be
found in granite pegmatites, which are coarse-
grained rocks formed after the bulk of the igneous rocks had been produced. Ilmenite can be
found in both igneous rocks and pegmatite.
When hydrogen is provided, hydroxides such as
$MnO(OH)$ (manganite), $Al(OH)_3$ (gibbsite),
and $Mg(OH)_2$ (brucite) may be formed.

According to their chemical compositions,
there are seven types of oxides: A_2O, AO, A_2O_3,
ABO_3, AB_2O_4, AO_2, and $A_mB_nO_{2(m+n)}$; where A
and B are metals and m and n are integers.
Cuprite (CuO_2), an important ore of copper,
belongs to type A_2O. Both periclase (MgO) and
tenorite (CuO) belong to type AO. Corundum
(Al_2O_3), hematite, and ilmenite belong to type
A_2O_3. Corundum can be utilized as an abrasive
and a gemstone. Hematite is an important ore of
iron. Ilmenite is an ore of titanium. Perovskite
($CaTiO_3$) belongs to type ABO_3. Spinel, chrysoberyl, and gahnite ($ZnAl_2O_4$) belong to type
AB_2O_4. Pyrolusite, cassiterite, and rutile (TiO_2)
belong to type AO_2. Pyrolusite is an ore of

Percentages of Oxides in Crustal Rocks

Oxide	Unmelted Peridotite in the Mantle	Basalt Formed at Oceanic Ridges or Rises	Andesite Formed at Subduction Zones	Granitic Rock Along Continental Subduction Zones	Continental Rift Basalt	Shale	Sandstone Near the Source	Sandstone Far from the Source	Limestone
SiO_2 (silicon oxide)	45.0	49.0	59.0	65.0	50.0	58.0	67.0	95.0	5.0
TiO_2 (titanium oxide)	0.4	1.8	0.7	0.6	3.0	0.7	0.6	0.2	0.1
Al_2O_3 (aluminum oxide)	8.7	15.0	17.0	16.0	14.0	16.0	14.0	1.0	0.8
Fe_2O_3 (ferric iron oxide)	1.4	2.4	3.0	1.3	2.0	4.0	1.5	0.4	0.2
FeO (ferrous iron oxide)	7.5	8.0	3.3	3.0	11.0	2.5	3.5	0.2	0.3
MnO (manganese oxide)	0.15	0.15	0.13	0.1	0.2	0.1	0.1	—	0.05
MgO (magnesium oxide)	28.0	8.0	3.5	2.0	6.0	2.5	2.0	0.1	8.0
CaO (calcium oxide)	7.0	11.0	6.4	4.0	9.0	3.0	2.5	1.5	43.0
Na_2O (sodium oxide)	0.8	2.6	3.7	3.5	2.8	1.0	2.9	0.1	0.05
K_2O (potassium oxide)	0.04	0.2	1.9	2.3	1.0	3.5	2.0	0.2	0.3

Note: Compositions are given as weight percentages of the oxide in the entire rock.

manganese. Cassiterite is an important source of tin. Rutile is an ore of titanium. Columbite-tantalite $\{4[(Fe,Mn)(Nb,Ta)_2O_6]\}$ belongs to type $A_mB_nO_{2(m+n)}$.

Besides chemical compositions, the structural, optical, and physical properties of oxides are studied. Structural information can be revealed by X-ray diffraction. Optical properties include color appearance, reflection, and transmission. Physical properties include density, mechanical strength, and thermal capacitance.

Some of the oxides are distributed throughout the world, while others are limited to a few regions. For example, magnetite can be found in the United States; hematite can be found in the United States, Venezuela, Brazil, Canada, and Australia; and cassiterite can be found in Malaysia, Bolivia, and other countries.

Xingwu Wang

SEE ALSO: Aluminum; Beryllium; Copper; Igneous processes, rocks, and mineral deposits; Iron; Manganese; Oxygen; Pegmatites; Quartz; Sand and gravel; Silicon; Tin; Titanium.

Oxygen

WHERE FOUND: Oxygen is the most abundant element in the earth's crust (46.6 percent by weight), occurring mainly as oxides and silicates of metals. The earth's waters are 85.8 percent by weight oxygen, and the atmosphere is 23.0 percent oxygen. The combined weight of oxygen in the crust, hydrosphere, and atmosphere is about 50 percent.

PRIMARY USES: In addition to its importance in the combustion of food for energy by living organisms, oxygen has many commercial applications. It is used in the iron and steel industry, in rocket propulsion, in chemical synthesis, and to hasten the aerobic digestion of sewage solids.

DESCRIPTION: Oxygen (abbreviated O), atomic number 8, belongs to Group VI of the periodic table of the elements. Its chemical properties are somewhat similar to those of sulfur. It has an average molecular weight of 15.9994 and six naturally occurring isotopes, three of which are radioactive with half-lives on the order of seconds and minutes. At ordinary temperatures, oxygen is a colorless, odorless gas. Its liquid form is pale blue. Oxygen melts at −218 degrees Celsius and boils at −183 degrees Celsius. Oxygen can form compounds with all other elements except the low-atomic-weight elements of the helium family.

MOST CHEMISTS AGREE that the discovery of oxygen was made independently by Carl Scheele in Sweden and Joseph Priestley in England at about the same time. In 1774 Priestley heated mercuric oxide and collected the liberated gas over water. He showed that the "dephlogisticated air" (oxygen) was capable of supporting burning and was respirable. Scheele prepared oxygen in 1771-1772 by heating various carbonates and oxides. Although his experiments were performed earlier than those of Priestley, the latter published his results first. The great French chemist Antoine-Laurent Lavoisier was the first to recognize that oxygen is an element, and he was able to explain the combustion process correctly. This explanation revolutionized the field of chemistry and provided the stimulus for the discovery of many new elements.

The Distribution of Oxygen. The total content of oxygen in the earth's air, crust, and oceans is approximately 50 percent by weight. In chemically combined form, it is found in water and in the clays and minerals of the lithosphere. Despite the fact that it is an active element, forming oxides easily by the process of combustion, elemental oxygen makes up about 23 percent of the atmosphere. Dissolved gaseous oxygen is found in the waters of the earth, where it provides for the respiration of most marine animals

and for the gradual oxidation of waste materials in lakes and rivers.

Elemental oxygen is found in three allotropic forms: the ordinary diatomic molecule found in the atmosphere (O_2), ozone (O_3), and the unstable, nonmagnetic, and rare pale blue O_4 form, which decomposes easily to O_2. Unstable atomic oxygen is a short-lived species that results from the absorption of ultraviolet radiation by ozone in the upper atmosphere or from electrical discharges.

Obtaining Oxygen. For many years the only means of obtaining oxygen was by the fractional distillation of liquid air. A variation of this basic process is still used when high-purity oxygen is needed. In 1971 an ambient temperature process was introduced by the Linde Division of Union Carbide Corporation. The process uses a pressure cycle in which "molecular sieves" are used to selectively absorb nitrogen from the air. The resulting product contains about 95 percent oxygen and about 5 percent argon and is economically preferable in situations where the argon will not interfere.

Uses of Oxygen. The greatest consumers of oxygen are the steel, chemical, and missile industries. The oldest use of oxygen is in the welding of steel by means of a hot acetylene-oxygen torch. Thicknesses of steel of up to 2 feet can be cut by a high-pressure oxygen stream after heating with an acetylene torch. An oxygen stream passed through molten iron can remove carbon impurities by means of combustion to carbon dioxide.

In the chemical industry oxygen is used for the production of hydrogen from natural gas or "synthesis gas":

$$CH_4 + 0.5\ O2\ \rightarrow\ CO + H_2$$

Other important industrial processes are the manufacture of hydrogen peroxide, sodium peroxide, ethylene oxide, and acetylene.

Large rockets are propelled from their launch pads by the combustion of a kerosenelike fuel. The fuel and oxygen are kept in liquid form in separate tanks until ignition. (In some rockets the second stage is propelled by the combustion of hydrogen.)

Oxygen has limited but important uses in the health-care industry in the treatment of pneumonia, emphysema, and some heart problems. Hyperbaric chambers provide high-pressure, oxygen-rich atmospheres for the treatment of both carbon monoxide poisoning and decompression sickness ("the bends").

Oxygen in Water. The solvent properties of water are attributable to the great difference in the strength of attraction for the bonding electrons between hydrogen and oxygen, which makes the resulting molecule very polar. The H_2O molecules are attracted to both cations and anions, surrounding them by the attraction of the negative oxygen or the positive hydrogen, respectively. Water also dissociates slightly into H+ and OH− ions. These processes allow water to form hydrates with, and to react with, many compounds.

FURTHER READING: A good introduction to oxygen is found in *Oxygen: Elementary Forms and Hydrogen Peroxide*, by Michael Ardon, 1965. A treatment of atmospheric oxygen is in *Atmospheric Oxygen and Antioxidants*, by Gerald Scott, 1965. B. Lewis and G. von Elbe discuss the important combustion reactions of oxygen in *Combustion, Flames and Explosions of Gases*, 1961. The important biological reactions of oxygen are discussed in *Molecular Oxygen in Biology*, edited by O. Hayaishi, 1974, and in *Oxygen and Living Processes*, edited by D. Gilbert, 1981. Mary Elvira Weeks describes the discovery of oxygen in the chapter "Three Important Gases," in her *Discovery of the Elements*, 1956.

Grace A. Banks

SEE ALSO: Atmosphere; Fuel cells; Minerals, structure and physical properties of; Oxides; Ozone layer and ozone hole debate; Water.

Ozone layer and ozone hole debate

Ozone, a form of the element oxygen, forms naturally in the stratosphere and provides the earth with a filter from ultraviolet radiation. Some human activities cause a decrease in the amount of ozone present, an effect which has been described as a hole in the ozone layer.

OZONE IS A highly reactive form of oxygen. It is composed of three oxygen atoms in a molecule (O_3) rather than the more usual two atoms, (O_2). Ozone is formed from diatomic oxygen where high energy is present. Near the earth, ozone forms in high-temperature combustion processes, such as in automobile engines, and in electrical sparks. In the stratosphere it forms because of high-energy ultraviolet radiation. Once formed, ozone is quick to react with other molecules. Near the earth there are many molecules with which to react, and the ozone concentration remains low. In the stratosphere there are few molecules present, so the ozone concentration builds up and forms what is termed the ozone layer. Ozone also disappears naturally by decomposing to ordinary oxygen, so there is a natural limit to the concentration that accumulates, and a steady state occurs. The ozone layer is actually quite diffuse and the ozone concentration is never very high.

Changes in the Ozone Layer. Since the mid-1950's, measurements of ozone concentrations in the atmosphere have been made regularly. In the early 1970's, analysis of the measurements suggested that something new was causing a reduction in the concentration of ozone in the stratosphere, particularly in the region over the south pole. Continued measurements established a similar lowering over the north pole and a spreading of the effect over a larger area. Laboratory experiments show that molecular fragments containing unpaired electrons are very effective in speeding the decomposition of ozone. This catalytic effect is particularly strong in the presence of small ice crystals, as are present in the stratosphere in the polar regions in winter.

Chlorofluorocarbons (CFCs) are a class of chemicals that have found wide use as propellants in aerosol cans, cleaning solvents for electronic circuit boards, and working fluids in air conditioning and refrigeration. The stability of these molecules is a prime factor in their utility, but this property also allows the molecules to drift into the stratosphere when they are released. Most other escaping molecules react or are washed out by precipitation before they gain much height in the atmosphere. In the stratosphere CFCs decompose by irradiation and form molecular fragments to which ozone is sensitive. CFCs are not the only artificial cause of ozone depletion, but they have been recognized as a major contributor. Much of what is known about the way that the ozone layer forms and decomposes comes from the work of Paul Crutzen, Mario J. Molina, and F. Sherwood Rowland, who received the 1995 Nobel Prize in Chemistry for their work on this subject.

The Importance of Ozone. Ozone is decomposed when the energy available in part of the ultraviolet region of the spectrum is absorbed by the molecule. When the energy is used in such a fashion it is no longer present in the sunlight that comes through the stratosphere to the earth. This type of energy, if it does make it to the earth, is capable of causing the reaction of other molecules, including those of biological importance. The evidence is overwhelming that the primary cause of nonmelanoma skin cancers is chronic long-term exposure to ultraviolet light. Australia has the highest incidence of skin cancer in the world. Other human interactions may lead to melanoma skin cancers and cataracts. Increased ultraviolet levels also cause cellu-

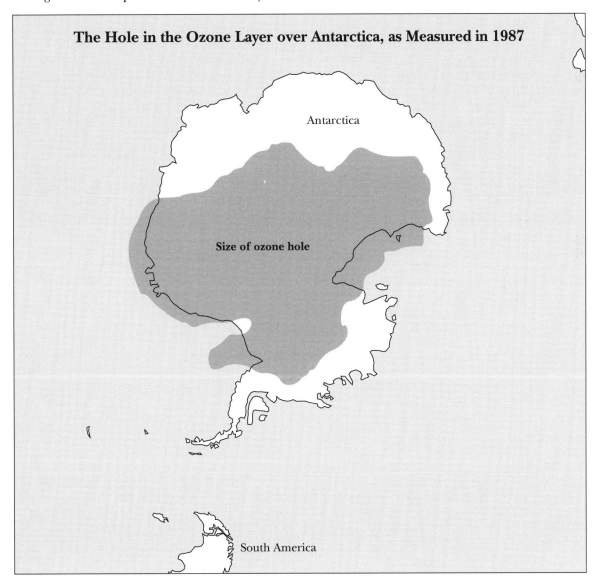

The Hole in the Ozone Layer over Antarctica, as Measured in 1987

Antarctica

Size of ozone hole

South America

lar modifications in plants, including food crops, which may lead to their death. Of particular concern is the inhibition of photosynthesis in the phytoplankton which forms the base of the ocean food chain.

The ozone layer acts as a filter to limit the earth's exposure to high-energy light. With a diminishing level of filtering, one would expect that there would be a global increase in the effects of overexposure to ultraviolet radiation.

The Ozone Debate. Some scientists contend that ozone depletion is a part of a natural cycle related to sunspot activity. Knowledge of what has happened in the distant past is circumstantial and not easy to interpret, but most scientists agree that human activities play a significant role in the current decrease in the ozone layer. In terms of the human contribution, CFCs have received the major attention, and their production was severely limited by international agreement in the 1987 Montreal Protocol and later revisions. CFCs are no longer used for propellants, and their role as cleaners is all but over. However, their use as refrigerant fluids continues while economically viable, safe substitutes are being sought. The people in developed countries have become extremely dependent on air conditioning (nearly all large buildings are designed to be air conditioned rather than open to the outside). The search for substitutes has proved difficult, with economic, safety, and environmental concerns all placing limits on what is acceptable.

Part of the controversy concerning banning CFCs is based on ethical considerations. The developed countries utilized CFCs to gain their positions; should they then prohibit the use of CFCs in developing countries? Should these countries not be allowed to reap the same advantages as others even if there is an environmental price to be paid? There are no easy, satisfactory answers to such questions.

FURTHER READING: Good coverage of the early days of the controversy is found in *Ozone Crisis: The Fifteen-Year Evolution of a Sudden Global Emergency*, by Sharon Roan, 1989. Three good sources for general readers are *What's Happening to the Ozone Layer*, by Isaac Asimov, 1993; *The Ozone Layer*, by Jane Duden, 1990; and *The Ozone Layer*, by Tony Hare, 1993. Health aspects of ozone depletion are discussed by M. Roach in "Sun Struck," *Health* 6, no. 3 (1992). William Brune presents the evidence of the chlorofluorocarbon-ozone depletion link in "There's Safety in Numbers," *Nature* 379, no. 6565 (1996), and Michael Prather, Pauline Midgley et al. present a sound argument in "The Ozone Layer: The Road Not Taken," *Nature* 381, no. 6583 (1996).

Kenneth H. Brown

SEE ALSO: Atmosphere; Chemical Manufacturers Association; Environmental ethics; Montreal Protocol; Oxygen.

Paper

RESOURCES USED: Forests (timber), water, coal, and chemicals including sodium sulfide, sodium hydroxide, and sulfurous acid

The pulp and paper industry produces a number of different primary products, including newsprint, printing and writing papers, packaging and industrial papers, corrugated containers, gray and bleached boxboards, bags, dissolving pulps, and wood pulp. All pulping processes involve tremendous amounts of water—the pulp and paper industry is the largest industrial user of water in the United States—and most also require large amounts of timber.

THE CHINESE ARE credited with the invention of paper around 105 C.E. Historians note that this date has been chosen somewhat subjectively, as early experiments in the process of papermaking probably stretched over a long period of time before the process was perfected. There are no records to indicate how the Chinese first made paper, but it is believed that this early paper was made by pouring fibrous pulp onto flat cloth-covered molds—essentially the same way paper is produced today. The first major improvement in papermaking was dipping the molds directly into the fibrous pulp (the exact date of this improvement is unknown); dipping the molds allowed artisans to produce a greater quantity of higher quality paper.

Paper was made by hand until the early nineteenth century, when Nicholas-Louis Robert invented the first papermaking machine in France. Robert received a patent for his breakthrough from the French government in 1799. Lacking funds to promote his design, Robert sold the rights to his invention to Henry and Sealey Fourdrinier in England, who produced the first papermaking machine. The principle of Robert's machine was to construct the paper on an endless woven-wire cloth which retained the matted fibers while allowing the excess water to drain through—this same principle holds with all modern papermaking machines. The first successful use of papermaking machines in the United States was by the Thomas Gilpin Mills in Brandywine Creek, Delaware, in August of 1817.

Economic History. The U.S. Census Bureau reports that in 1967 there were 792 plants manufacturing pulp and paper in the United States; by 1987 the number had decreased to 526 plants. Pulp and paper plants can be separated into three types: market pulp plants, which only produce pulp; non-integrated plants, which only produce paper from pulp; and integrated plants, which produce both pulp and paper products. The geographic distribution of pulp and paper plants varies according to the type of plant. Pulp mills tend to be located in regions which are heavily forested with pulp trees (softwood trees, such as conifers and spruces); therefore, about 94 percent of pulp mills are located in only eleven states (Alaska, Alabama, California, Florida, Georgia, Maine, Mississippi, North Carolina, Tennessee, Washington, and Wisconsin), while most of the remaining 6 percent are located in Kentucky and Michigan. On the other hand, paper plants tend to be more widely distributed, as they may be located near pulp mills or converting sector markets; 81 percent of all paper plants are located in twelve states; California, Louisiana, Maine, Massachusetts, Michigan, Minnesota, New Hampshire, New York, Ohio, Pennsylvania, Washington, and Wisconsin.

The pulp and paper industry's production was $26.2 billion in 1967 and $46.8 billion in 1987 (adjusting for inflation), representing an average growth of approximately 4 percent per year. During the same time frame, the pulp and paper industry went from using 35.4 million to 60.5 million tons of timber (approximately 30 percent and 28 percent of all timber produced, respectively), an average annual growth of 3.5 percent. During the 1960's the percentage of timber used in the production of wood pulp rose from 23 percent to 34 percent, and it peaked at 35 percent in 1974. By 1979 the amount of timber used to produce pulp had fallen to roughly 28 percent. In other words, since 1974, the demand for timber by the pulp and paper industry has not grown relative to the other usages of timber such as lumber, plywood, and veneer. However, the absolute amount of timber used by the pulp and paper industry did rise by an average of 3.6 percent per year between 1979 and 1987.

The pulp and paper industry is highly capital intensive, involving large facilities. For example, a typical kraft mill (which uses sodium sulfate to break down wood into pulp) producing 1,000 tons of unbleached pulp per day costs $359 million to build (in 1984 dollars); a facility to produce bleached pulp costs $415 million. Likewise, a typical paper mill producing 1,000 tons per day of newsprint costs $254 million. Over time, the industry has tended to become even more capital intensive, as the number of employees has declined from 222,000 in 1967 to 195,000 in 1987, while the capital stock has grown from $28 billion to $51 billion, more than doubling the capital-labor ratio between 1967 and 1987; during the same period the capital-labor ratio for the rest of manufacturing grew by only 74 percent.

Production of Pulp and Paper. The manufacturing of paper and paperboard involves the production and conversion of pulp from some fibrous furnish. "Furnish" is any blend of fibrous materials (such as timber, wood chips, or recycled paper) used to produce pulp. According to the *1990 National Census of Pulp, Paper, and Paperboard Manufacturing Facilities*, wood is the most commonly used furnish—roughly 95 percent of all pulp and paper manufacturers use wood in some form. The second most widely used form of furnish is secondary fibers from either mill waste or post-consumer fibers, such as newsprint and corrugated boxes. The usage of secondary fibers grows as consumer demand increases for products made from recycled paper.

Pulp Production. The production of pulp involves the breaking down of homogeneous furnish feedstock into its fibers, possibly bleaching to increase its whiteness, and mixing with water to produce a slurry. There are four types of pulping processes: chemical, semichemical, mechanical, and secondary fiber pulping. Chemical pulping includes the kraft (sulfate) process, soda pulping, sulfite pulping, and neutral sulfite chemical pulping. Mechanical pulping includes chemi-mechanical, thermo-mechanical, chemi-thermo-mechanical, refiner mechanical pulping, and stone groundwood pulping. The type of pulping process affects the durability, appearance, and intended use of the resulting paper

product. Regardless of the pulping method employed, pulping is "dirty." During the pulping stage of production, nuisance odors may be released into the air, and dioxins from kraft chemical bleaching may be released into wastewater. Thus the pulping process is a major concern to the Environmental Protection Agency (EPA).

Chemical pulping liberates the fibers from the furnish by dissolving the lignin bonds holding the cellulose fibers together by cooking wood chips in liquid chemical solutions at extremely high temperatures and pressures. Kraft pulping is by far the dominant form of chemical (and nonchemical) pulping due to its early development in the 1800's, its ability to use nearly every species of wood as furnish, and the fact that its resulting pulps are markedly stronger than those of other chemical processes. Chemical pulp yields are roughly 45 to 50 percent. In other words, roughly 50 percent of the furnish is converted into pulp.

Semichemical pulping produces very stiff pulp and is used mainly for corrugated containers. The semichemical process consists of the partial digesting of hardwood furnish in a diluted chemical solution before it is mechanically refined to separate the fibers from the weakened furnish. Pulp yields range between 55 percent and 90 percent, depending on the process employed.

Mechanical pulping processes, involving the reduction of furnish to fiber by either beating or grinding, are the oldest known methods of releasing the cellulose fibers from wood furnish. The pulp yields are high, up to 95 percent, especially when compared with chemical pulping yields of 45 to 50 percent. However, the mechanically produced pulp is of low strength and quality. Thus, mechanical pulp is often combined with chemical pulp to increase both its strength and quality.

Finally, secondary fiber pulping relies on recovered (recycled) papers as furnish. Typically, secondary fibers are presorted and preprocessed before they are sold to a pulp and paper mill. If the recovered papers have not been processed, before pulping can begin, they must first be treated to remove common contaminants, such as adhesives, coatings, inks, and dense plastic

Pulp Processes

Pulp Process	% of Mills*	Description/Principal Products
Dissolving kraft	1	Highly bleached and purified kraft process wood pulp, suitable for conversion into products such as rayon, viscose, acetate, and cellophane.
Bleached paper-grade kraft and soda	24	Bleached or unbleached kraft process wood pulp, usually converted into paperboard, coarse papers, tissue papers, and fine papers such as business, writing, and printing papers.
Unbleached kraft	10	
Dissolving sulfite	1	Highly bleached and purified sulfite process wood pulp, suitable for conversion into products such as rayon, viscose, acetate, and cellophane.
Paper-grade sulfite	3	Sulfite process wood pulp with or without bleaching, used for products such as tissue papers, fine papers, and newsprint.
Semi-chemical	6	Pulp processed by chemical pressure and mechanical (sometimes) forces with or without bleaching, used for corrugating medium (for cardboard), paper, and paperboard.
Mechanical pulp	12	Pulp manufacture by stone groundwood, mechanical refiner, thermochemical, chemi-mechanical, or chemi-thermomechanical means for newsprint, coarse papers, tissue, molded fiber products, and fine papers.
Nonwood chemical pulp	2	Production of pulp from textiles (e.g. rags), cotton linters, flax, hemp, tobacco, and abaca to make cigarette wrap papers and other specialty products.
Secondary fiber deink	8	Pulps from waste papers or paperboard using a chemical or solvent process to remove contaminants (such as inks, coatings, and pigments), used to produce fine, tissue, and newsprint papers.
Secondary fiber non-deink	61	Pulp production from waste papers or paperboard without deinking processes to produce tissue, paperboard, molded products, and construction papers.
Fine and lightweight papers from purchased pulp	44	Paper production from purchased market pulp or secondary fibers to make clay coated printing, uncoated free sheet, cotton fiber writing, and lightweight electrical papers.
Tissue, filter, nonwoven, and paperboard from purchased pulp	NA	Paper production from purchased market pulp to make paperboard, tissue papers, filter papers, nonwoven items, and any other products other than fine and lightweight papers.

Source: U.S. Environmental Protection Agency. *Development Document for Proposed Effluent Limitations Guidelines and Standards for the Pulp, Paper, and Paperboard Point Source Category,* October, 1993.
* Percentages are not additive, since plants use multiple pulping techniques.

U.S. Paper and Paperboard Production
In Thousands of Short Tons

	1990	*1991*	*1992*	*1993*
Total paper	39,361	39,084	40,973	41,745
Total paperboard	39,423	40,416	41,985	43,213
Unbleached kraft	20,357	20,950	21,658	21,447
Semichemical	5,640	5,552	5,762	5,672
Bleached kraft	4,399	4,572	4,503	4,583
Recycled	9,026	9,332	10,063	11,510

Source: U.S. Department of Commerce, *Statistical Abstract of the United States, 1996,* 1996. Primary source, American Forest and Paper Association, *Monthly Statistical Summary of Paper, Paperboard, and Woodpulp.*

Note: A short ton is 2,000 pounds, or 0.907 metric ton.

chips. The most common technique of secondary fiber pulping involves mixing the recycled furnish in a large container of water, which is sometimes heated. Pulping chemicals may be added to induce the dissolution of paper or paperboard. The mix is then stirred by a rotor to produce the pulp.

Pulping processes involve tremendous amounts of water, and most require large amounts of timber. The Environmental Protection Agency reports that, in 1988, an average pulp mill used 16,000 to 17,000 gallons of water per ton of pulp produced, which translates into a discharge of nearly 16 million cubic feet of wastewater per day. The papermaking process generates large amounts of air and water pollutants, especially during the pulping stage. Total timber used by the industry in 1988, according to the U.S. Forest Service (USFS), was 62 million tons, nearly 28 percent of all timber produced in the United States.

The Manufacturing of Paper. There are two general steps in the process of making paper and paperboard: wet-end operations and dry-end operations. During the wet-end operation, processed pulp is transformed into a paper product via a paper machine, the most common of which is the Fourdrinier (the name comes from the Fourdrinier brothers) paper machine. Pulp slurry (more than 90 percent water at the start) is deposited on a rapidly moving wire mesh for removal of the water by gravity, vacuum chambers, and vacuum rolls. After vacuum rolling, a continuous sheet is left, which is then pressed between a progression of rollers to extract any additional water and to compress the fibers. The sheet is now ready for dry-end operations. During this stage, the sheet enters a drying area,

U.S. and Canadian Production and Shipments of Newsprint
In Thousands of Metric Tons

	1970	*1980*	*1985*	*1987*	*1988*	*1989*	*1990*	*1991*	*1992*
Canada									
Production	7,808	8,625	8,890	9,630	9,840	9,640	9,068	8,977	8,931
Shipments from mills	7,795	8,622	8,899	9,718	9,740	9,606	9,074	8,728	9,143
United States									
Production	3,142	4,239	4,924	5,300	5,427	5,523	5,997	6,206	6,424
Shipments from mills	3,136	4,234	4,927	5,310	5,415	5,515	6,007	6,152	6,464

Source: U.S. Department of Commerce, *Statistical Abstract of the United States, 1996,* 1996.

After the pulping process, two further general steps—wet-end and dry-end operations—are needed to produce paper. (Photo Network)

where the paper fibers start to bond as they are compressed by steam-heated rollers. The sheets are then pressed between massive rollers to reduce paper thickness and to produce a smooth surface. After a smooth thin sheet of paper is produced, coatings may be applied to improve the color, luster, printing detail, and brilliance. Finally, the paper product is spooled for storage.

Pollution control measures have represented a significant cost to the industry. The U.S. Census Bureau estimates the cost of pollution control for U.S. manufacturing based on its Pollution Abatement Costs and Expenditures (PACE) survey. The PACE survey asks plants to report the costs associated with purchasing new capital equipment and other operating costs for pollution abatement. According to the survey, the pulp and paper industry spends billions of dollars every year on pollution abatement. For example, in 1992, the industry spent nearly $2 billion to reduce pollution—approximately 10 percent of the total spent by all manufacturing

industries. (Actual costs are probably higher, as environmental regulations often tend to reduce productivity as well as require expenditures.)

A relatively small, but significant and growing, amount of the pulp and paper products manufactured by the United States is exported to other countries. In 1967 exports amounted to just over $500 million, representing 3 percent of the industry's total output, but by 1992 exports amounted to over $10 billion, approximately 7 percent of the total value of shipments for the industry. Major export markets include Canada, Mexico, and Japan.

FURTHER READING: Good histories of papermaking can be found in *Papermaking: The History and Technique of an Ancient Craft*, by Dard Hunter, 1942, and *History of Papermaking in the United States (1691-1969)*, by David C. Smith, 1971. An excellent introduction to the economic and environmental concerns of the pulp and paper industry can be found in the *EPA Office of Compliance Sector Notebook Project: Profile of the Pulp and*

Paper Industry, available from the U.S. Government Printing Office, 1995. Detailed information regarding pulp and paper technology can be found in *Forest Products: Advanced Technologies and Economic Analysis*, edited by David A. Tillman, 1985. A solid treatment of the effects of government regulation on U.S. manufacturing productivity can be found in *Productivity Versus OSHA and EPA Regulations*, by Wayne B. Gray, 1986.

Ronald John Shadbegian

SEE ALSO: Coal; Environmental Protection Agency; Forests; Rain forests; Timber industry; Wood and timber.

Paper, alternative sources of

The paper industry depends on the vegetable kingdom for its raw materials. Ninety-five percent of the world's fiber in paper manufacture comes from forests, and the rest comes from alternative sources such as bagasse (sugar cane residue), bamboo, cereal stalks, leaves, and other fibrous annual plants.

MOST PAPER IS made from wood, although wood is not technically suitable for producing many types of paper. Moreover, wood shortages periodically occur, and wood pulp prices are steadily increasing (they more than doubled between 1990 and 1996). Typical pulp in the paper industry comes from mixed hardwoods and mixed softwoods. Southern yellow pine, a softwood, makes up the bulk of pulpwood in the United States. Increased demand for pulp products could cause future wood supplies to be inadequate, leading to further increases in the price of paper. Recycled paper can make up part of the deficit, but with continued use, recycled paper begins to degrade and its quality decreases. Consequently, there has been growing interest in alternative sources of paper.

Historical Sources of Paper. The first materials used as paper were not made from wood. Papyrus, for example, was used to make paper in ancient Egypt. Papyrus was made from aquatic plants of the sedge family, which includes the paper reed (*Cyperus papyrus*) and paper rush (*Papyrus antiquorum*). Bamboo is the principal

papermaking raw material in India. The bark of the paper mulberry (*Broussonetia papyrifera*) has traditionally been used to make paper in China and Japan. Old rags and linen were used to make paper in Europe.

Alternative Paper Sources. Many nonwood fiber and pulp sources are used to make specialties such as fine writing paper as well as industrial paper, currency, cigarette paper, paper for wrapping electrical wiring, and fiber paper. The dominant sources include flax (*Linum usitatissimum*), sisal (*Agave sisalana*), abaca (*Musa textilis*), and esparto (*Stipa tenacissima*). Among other suggested sources of paper are sunn hemp (*Crotoloaria juncea*), sesban (*Sesbania sonorae*), kenaf (*Hibiscus cannabinus*), okra (*Hibiscus esculentus*), China jute (*Abutilon theophrasti*), and sorghum (*Sorghum vulgare*). "True" hemp (*Cannabis sativa*) shows considerable promise as a source of paper pulp from a technical standpoint, but its production is rigidly controlled in the United States to prevent its use as an illegal drug.

Fiber from the bamboo plant has been widely used for making paper in India. (McCrea Adams)

Periodic shortages in paper pulp and fiber have prompted screening programs to identify alternative vegetable fibers that could be used to make paper. For example, milkweeds (*Asclepias incarnata* and *Ascelpias tuberosa*) were considered for use in spinning during World War II. In the 1950's, because no annual plants were being grown solely to make paper, the U.S. Department of Agriculture (USDA) started a screening program to identify annual plants that would be suitable for paper pulp production. Almost four hundred species in forty-four plant families were studied, and the mallow, grass, and legume families were found to be most useful. Annual plants have a lower lignin content and higher hemicellulose content than wood does, which means that they are more easily treated chemically and respond rapidly to refining. The cellulose fibers in alternative paper sources are comparable in length to those in hardwoods (0.5 to 1.0 millimeters in length) but one-half to one-third as long as fibers from softwoods (3 millimeters). So the paper made from alternative sources is about midway in quality between that made from hardwoods (the least desirable pulp source) and softwoods (the most desirable). One significant drawback to using annual plants as a source of raw pulp is that materials for paper production have to be available throughout the year, and this is difficult with annuals. Therefore, storage and handling become expensive.

Kenaf as an Alternative Paper Source. Kenaf (*Hibiscus cannabinus* L.), a plant native to Africa, was the one plant among hundreds in the USDA screening programs with the greatest potential as an alternative paper source. Kenaf is the Persian name for this annual, nonwoody plant, which was first domesticated in Sudan and East Central Africa as long ago as 4000 B.C.E. Fibers from both its outer bark and inner core are used. Ninety percent of Kenaf is produced in Asia, where it is usually used for sacking material rather than paper. China produces most of the world's supply.

The yearly yield of kenaf is three to five times greater per hectare than that of trees, because it is an annual with rapid growth. Kenaf yields 11,000 to 20,000 kilograms per hectare, compared with an average yield of pine pulpwood of about 2,500 kilograms per hectare. Kenaf grows 2 to 6 meters in height and flowers in 100 to 150 days. In pilot project studies carried out in the 1950's at the USDA Northern Regional Research Center in Peoria, Illinois, kenaf pulp was found to be superior to hardwood pulp. The quality of kenaf paper's burst, tear, and fold characteristics (measures of paper strength) was better than those of hardwood paper and almost as good as softwood paper. Furthermore, less energy and fewer chemicals are used in turning kenaf into paper than in traditional paper-making processes.

The Future of Kenaf as an Alternative Paper Source. The economic potential of kenaf ultimately rests with the pulp and paper industry. No country yet produces the volume of kenaf (or any other alternative paper source) required for commercial paper production. A problem with kenaf is that it is susceptible to various parasitic worms known as nematodes. This problem, combined with other handling and storage costs, makes turning kenaf into paper more expensive than using wood pulp in spite of the energy savings. As of 1996 U.S. pulp producers had not been convinced to develop and market kenaf pulp, and there was no significant market for it. Japan is a growing market, however, and supporters of kenaf production are optimistic that this fact will stimulate further interest in kenaf paper.

FURTHER READING: The best source for monitoring up-to-date information on alternative paper sources is *TAPPI: The Journal of the Technical Association of the Pulp and Paper Industry.* For information about papermaking as a craft, read Dard Hunter's *Papermaking: The History and Techniques of an Ancient Craft*, 1947. To learn about the paper industry, see the textbook *Pulp and Paper Manufacture*, 1969.

Mark S. Coyne

SEE ALSO: Paper; Plant Domestication; Plant Fibers; Wood and timber.

Peat

FIRST DEVELOPED OR USED: Burned for heating and cooking or used as soil for agriculture since the New Stone Age, at least 5,500 years before the present

Leading Peat-Producing Countries, 1994

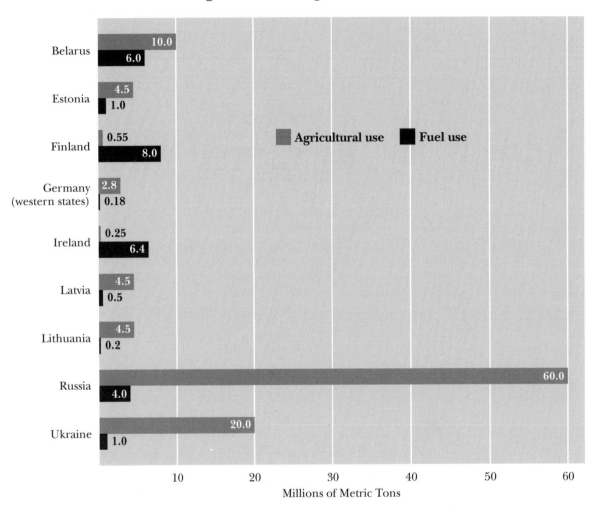

Belarus — Agricultural use 10.0, Fuel use 6.0
Estonia — Agricultural use 4.5, Fuel use 1.0
Finland — Agricultural use 0.55, Fuel use 8.0
Germany (western states) — Agricultural use 2.8, Fuel use 0.18
Ireland — Agricultural use 0.25, Fuel use 6.4
Latvia — Agricultural use 4.5, Fuel use 0.5
Lithuania — Agricultural use 4.5, Fuel use 0.2
Russia — Agricultural use 60.0, Fuel use 4.0
Ukraine — Agricultural use 20.0, Fuel use 1.0

Agricultural use   Fuel use

Millions of Metric Tons

Source: U.S. Bureau of Mines, *Minerals Yearbook, 1994.* U.S. Government Printing Office, 1996.
Note: Venezuela and the eastern German states are also major peat producers, but output is not reported, so no reliable estimates can be made concerning production. Reported world 1994 peat production was about 139 million metric tons.

Peat has many uses in agriculture, industry, and energy generation because of its organic chemical content and combustion properties; although abundant in the middle latitudes of the northern hemisphere, it has been exploited as fuel primarily in northwestern Europe.

LIKE CRUDE OIL and coal, peat is composed of the remains of dead organisms compressed underground, and it can be burned in home stoves and fireplaces or in factories and public power plants. Because peat is lightly compressed plant matter, it also works well as soil for agriculture and horticulture. Worldwide, reserves of peat are comparable to those of other fossil fuels. For example, according to some estimates, resources in the United States surpass the combined potential energy yield of the nation's petroleum and natural gas.

Peat forms in bogs, fens, sedge meadows, and some swamps as the debris of peat mosses (sphagnum), grasses, and sedges falls to the wet earth and becomes water-soaked. In the absence of oxygen underwater, the plant matter and microorganisms compact without completely decomposing, forming soft, usually fibrous soils that are tan to black in color. The organic component, which includes cellulose, lignin, and some humus, is always greater than 20 percent, and in most peat soils plant fragments are visible; the ash content is less than 50 percent, usually as low as 10 percent. Although the rate varies widely, in general a peat field increases in depth about three centimeters yearly. The bottoms of large peat fields are typically about ten thousand years old and can be as much as 50 meters below the surface, although 3-meter to 6-meter fields are common.

Geographical Distribution. Most deposits lie between 40 and 65 degrees latitude of the northern hemisphere. World reserves of exploitable peat exceed 200 billion tons, of which more than half is in Russia. Canada, the United States, the United Kingdom, Ireland, Finland, Norway, Sweden, Germany, Iceland, France, and Poland also have substantial peat fields. In the United States, Alaska contains more than half the reserves, but peat is also abundant in Minnesota, Washington, Michigan, Wisconsin, Maine, New York, North Carolina, Florida, and Louisiana. Some countries well below the fortieth meridian have exploitable peat reserves, especially Indonesia, Cuba, and Israel.

Energy Potential and Uses. In northern Europe, peat has fueled fires since the New Stone Age. It provides one-half to two-thirds as much energy as coal, or about 3.8 megajoules per dry kilogram, yet gives off far fewer pollutants, such as sulfur and ash. It can be converted into coke, charcoal, or a synthetic natural gas.

Only in Ireland, Russia, Finland, and the United Kingdom is peat employed primarily as a fuel, where in fact it is a traditional domestic resource. Dried and pressed into briquettes, peat burns easily in fireplaces, stoves, and braziers. During the twentieth century the four countries have burned increasing amounts of peat to generate electricity. Because it has very limited wood and fossil fuel resources, Ireland has consumed about three times as much peat for power generation as for domestic heating, whereas the other countries primarily rely on coal for that purpose.

Agricultural and Horticultural Uses. The United States and Canada, as well as some European countries, process most of their peat as potting soil, lawn dressing, and soil conditioners. Because they are much lighter and fluffier than mineral soils, peat preparations let water and oxygen penetrate easily and increase water retention, and so can be soil supplements or mulch. Throughout the United States commercial nurseries and homeowners apply such products to gardens and tree beds. Farmers have raised grasses, clover, wild rice, cranberries, blueberries, strawberries, Christmas trees, and root and leafy vegetables on peat fields, and ranchers have used them for hay and grazing. However, peat fields are difficult to drain and clear, often remain wet, promoting rot and disease, and can be low in nutrients.

Other Uses. During the energy crisis of the 1970's researchers investigated peat as an alternative to petroleum for many organic substances, although few of the efforts resulted in commercial products because oil again became cheaper than peat for industrial chemicals in the 1980's. Peat yields such mineral and organic sub-

An important fuel resource in some parts of the world, peat is also used in potting soil and soil conditioners. (Yasmine Cordoba)

stances as dyes, paraffin, naphtha, ammonium sulfate, acetic acid, ethyl and methyl alcohol, waxes, and phenols. Combined with clay, it forms lightweight blocks for construction. It can remove heavy metals from industrial waste and can be turned into coke for iron processing or into charcoal for purifying water. With its mildly antibiotic properties, peat served as a lightweight surgical dressing during World War I. Another of peat's well-known functions—and one of its oldest—is giving the smoky flavor to Scotch and Irish whiskeys as their malts slowly dry over open peat fires.

Because peat fields, once harvested, regenerate only after thousands of years, peat is not a renewable resource in any practical sense. Accordingly, intensive peat "mining" has caused concern among environmentalists. They worry that the rapid exploitation of peat fields, especially in Ireland and the United Kingdom, may permanently destroy bogs and fens and thereby threaten the many animals and birds dependent upon the wetland habitats.

FURTHER READING: Howard Crum's *A Focus on Peatlands and Peat Mosses*, 1988, surveys the types, ecology, and uses of peat in detail with many maps, drawings, and photographs. Color photographs accompany the descriptions of sphagnum species in *Field Guide to the Peat Mosses of Boreal North America*, by Cyrus B. McQueen, 1990. P. D. Moore and D. J. Bellamy examine the biochemistry, ecology, stratification, and resource availability of peat worldwide in *Peatlands*, 1974, and Harry Godwin does much the same in *The Archives of the Peat Bogs*, 1981, although he also discusses the importance of peat to Stone Age cultures. Charles H. Fuchsman explains the chemicals contained in peat that have commercial value in *Peat, Industrial Chemistry, and Technology*, 1980.

Roger Smith
SEE ALSO: Coal; Fertilizers; Soil; Wetlands.

Pegmatites

A pegmatite is an irregular igneous rock structure that is associated with a batholith or volcanic stock. Large crystals and gem-quality minerals are often present within pegmatites.

THE MOST COMMON form of pegmatite is associated with a granite magma body such as a batholith or other plutonic structure. Most pegmatites appear as veins, dikes, or sheets that extend outward from the larger granitic structure. When exposed by a road cut or on the side of a mountain, pegmatites appear as lighter colored narrow features that cut through the surrounding rock. Upon closer examination, large crystals of quartz, feldspar, and mica can be easily seen. When contact metamorphism occurs, minerals like garnet can form within the contact zone.

The most common form of pegmatite has a chemical composition that is similar to that of granite, although pegmatites are usually richer in their silica and water content than the average granite is. The higher water content contains large amounts of dissolved metallic elements, various gases, and other rarer elements such as lithium and beryllium. The essential minerals that define a granite pegmatite include quartz, various feldspars, and muscovite mica, with biotite mica and hornblende as the dark minerals present. Depending upon the specific chemistry of the pegmatite, other minerals include apatite, topaz, tourmaline, beryl (emerald), corundum, and zircon. Because of the presence of large quantities of dissolved elements, the minerals within a pegmatite can grow to very large size. Pegmatites of rocks such as diorite, gabbro, or peridotite do not have any special minerals present.

A typical granite pegmatite results from the rapid crystallization of minerals from residual fluids and gases that are escaping from a larger magma body. As the large body cools and thickens, the less dense components tend to concentrate at the top of the structure. This concentration creates an intense pressure against the existing rock and fractures it. The lower-density silica-rich and water-rich magma quickly fills these cracks and rapidly crystallizes, thus filling the fissures with minerals.

Pegmatites are the source of many minerals of economic importance. Feldspar, which is one of the principal mineral phases, is used to make ceramic and glass products. Mica, which is also abundant, is used as an insulating material in the electronics industry. Two less common minerals, spodumene and lepidolite, are both sources of lithium. Lithium is used in the manufacture of special high-temperature alloys and in the nuclear energy industry. The mineral beryl, in its common form, is used as a hardening material for copper alloys and in the manufacture of refractory materials. Various other minerals present such as topaz, tourmaline, kunzite, and beryl (the emerald variety) occur in gem quality. Occasionally pegmatites are also good sources of gold, as gold is associated with quartz, pyrite, and other sulfur-bearing minerals.

In the United States the most important pegmatites can be found in South Dakota, North Carolina, Virginia, and the New England states. These locations historically have been good sources for many economic minerals.

Paul P. Sipiera

SEE ALSO: Beryllium; Crystals; Gems; Granite; Lithium; Magma crystallization; Mica; Plutonic rocks and mineral deposits; Rare-earth elements; Silicates; Silicon.

Perlite

WHERE FOUND: Perlite is primarily found in the western United States, especially in New Mexico, Nevada, California, Arizona, Colorado, Idaho, and Utah. It is also found in Hungary, Greece, and the former Soviet Union.

PRIMARY USES: Perlite is mostly used in construction, where it is mixed with substances such as cement or gypsum to form concrete or plaster. Perlite is also used in insulation, ceramics, filters, and fillers.

DESCRIPTION: Perlite, also known as pearlstone, is a naturally occurring glass of volcanic origin that contains numerous curved fractures. These fractures allow perlite to be broken into small, pearl-like objects. Perlite has a waxy or pearly luster and may be gray, green, brown, blue, or red. The term "perlite" is also more loosely used to mean any natural glass that expands into a light, frothy material when heated.

PERLITE IS A form of natural glass. Natural glasses form when molten lava from volcanoes is cooled rapidly. The lava hardens too quickly to allow crystals to grow, resulting in a substance with a glassy rather than a stony texture. Perlite is distinguished from other forms of natural glass in that it contains many tiny curved fractures structured like the layers of an onion. These fractures may be microscopic or may be visible to the naked eye. Because of these fractures, perlite breaks apart into small, round particles.

Like other volcanic glasses, perlite consists mostly of silicon dioxide, which makes up about 70 percent of its chemical content. About 10 to 15 percent is aluminum oxide. Perlite also contains small amounts of various other oxides, along with about 3 to 5 percent water. The water content of perlite causes it to expand up to twenty times its normal volume when heated, resulting in a light, foamy material. Other volcanic glasses that do not contain perlite's distinctive fracture pattern are often called "perlite" if they contain enough water to expand in a similar fashion.

Most of the world's perlite is found in the western half of the United States. New Mexico supplies about three-quarters of the nation's perlite. Because underground deposits of natural glass slowly crystallize into stony substances over time, perlite is almost always found at or near the earth's surface.

Because it is found near the surface, perlite is mined using the open-pit method. It is then crushed to the desired particle size and transported to a processing center, where it is heated to expand it. The expanded perlite is used as an aggregate; that is, it is mixed with other substances such as gypsum to form plaster or cement to form concrete. Although perlite is not as strong or inexpensive as other aggregates such as sand or gravel, it has the advantages of being light, fire-resistant, and a good insulator of heat and sound. Perlite is also used as insulation or filler and in ceramics and filters.

Rose Secrest

SEE ALSO: Cement and concrete; Glass; Gypsum; Igneous processes, rocks, and mineral deposits; Magma crystallization; Open-pit mining; Pumice; Volcanoes.

Pesticides and pest control

Pesticides are agents used to kill or otherwise control organisms that are harmful to humans or crops. In addition to chemical agents, alternative pest-control methods are available.

AN ANIMAL OR PLANT is regarded as a pest if it causes nuisance or harm to humans or crops or otherwise negatively impacts human health, well-being, or quality of life. Pests such as silverfish consume paper and fabrics. Termites cause serious damage to houses and other wooden structures. Weeds, aphids, and snails play havoc with flower gardens. Beetles and fungi attack shade trees, timber, crops, orchards, and stored foods. Mosquitos, ticks, mites, and rodents transmit viruses and other disease organisms to humans.

Pest control is the ongoing process of managing insects, rodents, weeds, fungi, and other pest organisms where their lives intersect human lives. The twentieth century saw a rapid escalation in the use of chemical pesticides, which have become a mainstay of pest control. These chemicals have suppressed pest populations, increased crop yields, protected property, and kept disease in check. However, indiscriminate use of chemical pesticides has damaged the environment, which has led to governmental regulation of pesticides, outright bans on some substances, and increased interest in alternative pest-control methods.

Types of Chemical Pesticides. Chemical pesticides are often classed based on the organisms that they target. Avicides kill or repel bird pests. Rodenticides are for use against rats and mice. Acaracides and miticides target ticks and mites. Insecticides, the largest category of pesticide, are used against insects. Nematicides are used to kill nematodes, soil- and water-dwelling roundworms that are often parasitic on plants and animals. Fungicides are used to treat crops and other plants for fungal (and sometimes bacterial) conditions such as root rot, smut, gall, rust, and blight. Herbicides target the weeds and other unwanted vegetation that encroach on lawns, gardens, crops, and paths. Defoliants are a class of herbicide that induces leaf fall from trees and other plants.

Pesticides can also be categorized on the basis of chemical composition. Mineral pesticides such as arsenic, borax, copper, lead, and zinc were among the first pesticides employed by humans; these minerals have mostly been replaced by more efficient chemical compounds. Botanical pesticides are insecticidal substances derived from plants or are synthetic analogs to such substances. These include pyrethrins, chrysanthemum-derived insecticides which are not highly toxic to humans. Chlorinated hydrocarbons, which include chlorine, hydrogen, and oxygen in their chemical makeup, are highly effective poisons that do not readily degrade in the environment. Compounds such as aldrin, endrin, dieldrin, chlordane, and dichloro-diphenyl-trichloroethane (DDT) were widely employed before the environmental implications of their persistence were fully understood. Organophosphate pesticides are organic phosphate compounds that break down in the environment more easily than the chlorinated hydrocarbons, particularly in the presence of water. Examples include malathion, naled, dichlorvos, methyl and ethyl parathion, and diazinon. Carbamates, characterized by carbamic acid, include carbaryl, carbofuran, and methylcarbamate; these compounds degrade more quickly than organophosphates.

Pesticides may be categorized further as selective or nonselective. A selective pesticide targets a particular pest, while a nonselective pesticide (also called a broad-spectrum or general-usage pesticide) is toxic to a wide range of organisms and does not confine its effects to the target species once it is released into the environment. Selectively toxic chemicals minimize the pesticide's impact on the environment. Chemical pesticides are applied in various forms, including wet sprays, dusts, atomizable fluids, low-pressure aerosols, smokes, gases, and seed treatments.

History of Use. The "first generation" of chemical pesticides was the minerals and botanicals. In 1867 farmers in the United States began using Paris green, a then-common pigment containing arsenic and copper, to control outbreaks of the Colorado potato beetle. Lead arsenate was introduced as an insecticide in 1892. By the 1920's pesticide use in the United States had become

Pesticide being applied to a Florida bean crop. (Photo Network)

commonplace, and concerns over arsenical residues in foods had begun to arise.

In 1939 the next generation of chemical pesticides was ushered in with the discovery of DDT's insecticidal properties. The compound was first disseminated on a large scale during the Naples typhus epidemic of 1943-1944, and it found widespread use during the remainder of World War II. DDT and other potent broad-spectrum poisons were popular pesticides from the early 1940's through the 1960's. However, as concerns mounted over the environmental impact of these chemicals—watersheds being contaminated; beneficial species being killed off while pests became pesticide-resistant; pesticides accumulating in the bodies of higher animals, including humans; and food chains being poisoned—use of chlorinated hydrocarbons fell into disfavor. Use of DDT and similar chemicals has been banned or restricted in many countries, including the United States.

The disadvantages of chemical pesticides have led to an increased interest in alternative pest-control methods. Biological control agents include microorganisms that are harmful to pests but not to other life; natural predators and parasites; and the release of large numbers of laboratory-sterilized insects, which then mate with normal insects without producing offspring. While biological control agents usually involve no environmental pollutants and are often highly selective, the many complex factors that affect their action sometimes hinder their effectiveness.

U.S. Regulation of Chemical Pesticides. The Insecticide Act of 1910 prohibited adulteration of insecticides and fungicides. In 1947 the Federal Insecticide, Fungicide, and Rodenticide Act (FIFRA) authorized the Department of Agriculture (USDA) to oversee registration of pesticides and to determine their safety and effectiveness. In December, 1970, the newly formed U.S. Environmental Protection Agency (EPA) assumed statutory authority from the USDA over pesticide regulations. Under the Federal Environmental Pesticide Control Act of 1972, an amendment to FIFRA, manufacturers must register all marketed pesticides with the EPA before the product is released. Before registration, the chemicals must undergo exhaustive trials to assess their potential impact on the environment and human health. The EPA's decision to grant registration is based on the determination that unreasonable adverse effects on human health or the environment are not anticipated within the constraints of approved usage. Since October, 1977, the EPA has classified all pesticides to which it has granted registration as either a restricted-usage (to be applied only by certified pest control operators) or unclassified (general-usage) pesticide.

FURTHER READING: Rachel Carson, *Silent Spring*, 1962, brought the dangers of indiscriminate use of DDT and other pesticides to the public's attention when it was first published; it remains worthwhile reading. James Whorton, *Before Silent Spring*, 1974, examines the early evolution of pesticide use in America. See also George W. Ware, *Fundamentals of Pesticides*, 1986; and R. J. Cremlyn, *Agrochemicals*, 1991.

Karen N. Kähler

SEE ALSO: Agriculture industry; Carson, Rachel; Environmental Protection Agency; Food chain; Herbicides; Monoculture agriculture.

Petrochemical products

Petrochemicals are organic chemicals derived from petroleum or natural gas. They are of extreme importance in contemporary life, accounting for the production of about 95 percent of plastics, other synthetic materials, and organic chemicals. Although an enormous variety of organic chemicals can be (and are) made from petroleum or natural gas, usually the term "petrochemicals" is restricted to those substances produced in very large amounts.

THE ORIGIN OF the petrochemical industry may be traced to the first production of isopropyl alcohol from propylene in 1920. This effort was originated by the Standard Oil Company in New Jersey. The industry grew slowly but steadily during the 1920's and 1930's and then received an enormous boost from World War II, with its tremendous demand for synthetic materials. By about 1950 the industry was firmly established in the United States.

Ethylene and Polyethylene. The most important petrochemical is ethylene. It is manufactured in greater quantity than any other organic chemical. Various raw materials can be used to manufacture ethylene, including ethane, propane, and petroleum distillates such as naphtha. Regardless of the raw material, the ethylene production process involves thermally driven reactions (so-called cracking) in a temperature range between 750 and 900 degrees Celsius. Steam is used to dilute the feed to the ethylene production furnace. The amount of steam used varies, depending on the specific material being used to make the ethylene. The annual production of ethylene in the United States is about 47 billion pounds; worldwide production is about 120 billion pounds.

About half of the ethylene produced is converted to polyethylene. The two major types of polyethylene are known as low-density polyethylene (often abbreviated as LDPE) and high-density polyethylene (HDPE). One of the most important applications of LDPE is in clear plastic wrapping film. HDPE has a wider range of uses by virtue of its superior mechanical properties. Familiar applications of HDPE include bottles, such as those used for laundry detergents, and housewares, such as storage crates and home cleaning accessories such as buckets, pans, and pails.

Vinyl Chloride and Ethylene Glycol. A second major use of ethylene is its conversion to vinyl chloride. This conversion is effected by a process called oxychlorination: reaction of ethylene with hydrogen chloride and oxygen. Vinyl chloride is used in the manufacture of polyvinyl chloride, or poly, most commonly known as PVC. Depending on how the PVC is produced (specifically, through the addition of "plasticizers" that alter its physical or mechanical properties), it can have a range of hardness and flexibility. Consequently, PVC is a very versatile material with many common uses that include floor tile, garden hose, artificial leather, house siding, plastic films, pipe, and toys. In the days when music was recorded on phonograph records, they were usually made of PVC—hence the slang term "vinyl."

The oxidation of ethylene produces ethylene oxide, a chemical that easily reacts with water to form ethylene glycol, a useful component of antifreeze. Ethylene glycol is also used in the manufacture of polyethylene terephthalate, commonly known as PET. This polymer is an example of the largest class of synthetic textile fibers, the polyesters. PET is also used for both audio and video magnetic recording tapes, in soft drink bottles, and in "microwave-in-a-pouch" food containers.

Propylene, Polypropylene, and Propylene glycol. Propylene is the second most important of the petrochemicals. Although ethylene has now superseded it in importance (in terms of tonnage production), propylene was the first significant petrochemical. In the 1920's and 1930's propylene was a by-product of gasoline manufacture. To increase the yield of gasoline from a refinery,

Injection molding machinery used for manufacturing plastic products. Some 95 percent of plastics are produced from petrochemicals. (Photo Network)

other petroleum products of lower value were subjected to intense heating (thermal cracking), which broke the molecules into new, smaller compounds, many of which could be used in gasoline. In addition, however, thermal cracking led to some by-products of molecular size even smaller than gasoline, propylene being an example. The beginning of the petrochemical industry was the use of this by-product propylene for producing isopropyl alcohol. Most people encounter isopropyl alcohol primarily as the active ingredient in "rubbing alcohol," but it has more important uses as an industrial solvent and as raw material for making acetone, another useful solvent.

Today the propylene situation is greatly changed. The thermal cracking process for gasoline is obsolete, so there is no by-product propylene. Instead, propylene is made in much the same way as ethylene, using either propane or naphtha as the raw material. The raw material, mixed with steam, is cracked at temperatures of 800 to 900 degrees Celsius. The annual production of propylene in the United States is about 40 billion pounds. The dominant use of propylene is in the production of polypropylene.

The properties of polypropylene—and consequently its uses—depend heavily on the way the propylene molecules are connected. Special catalysts to control the outcome of the polymerization of polypropylene were discovered by Karl Ziegler and Giulio Natta, for which achievement they were awarded the 1963 Nobel Prize in Chemistry. A common application for high-quality polypropylene is in microwave-safe dishes and food containers. Some of the lower-strength grades of polypropylene are useful as flexible, clear plastic films—for example, as food wrap and as the plastic coverings on disposable diapers. Polypropylene and "copolymers" of polypropylene and polyethylene are widely used as materials in automobiles. Examples of automotive applications include bumper covers, air ducts, body trim panels, interior trim and seat covers, and battery casings.

Propylene can also be converted to propylene oxide and then to propylene glycol. This material is used directly in antifreeze, brake fluid, and hydraulic fluid. It is also used as a moisturizer in pet foods and tobacco products. Propylene glycol is converted to a special family of compounds called urethanes, the basic materials for the production for polyurethane products. Many kinds of urethanes can be made from propylene glycol, depending on the chemicals chosen for the process. Consequently, the eventual polyurethanes have, as a family, a wide range of properties. Common applications of polyurethanes include sound and heat insulation, furniture cushions, automobile bumpers, and plastic flooring and roofing.

Acrylics, Polyacrylates, and Polyacrylonitrile. A more severe oxidation of propylene leads to acrylic acid, the starting material for acrylic paints. Sodium or ammonium salts of acrylic acid polymerize to the polyacrylates. When polyacrylates are mixed with small amounts of other copolymers, they form polyacrylate "super-absorbing" polymers that have an exceptional capacity for absorbing water or water solutions. The major use of these remarkable materials, amounting to about a billion pounds per year, is in the lining of disposable diapers.

The reaction of propylene with ammonia in the presence of oxygen ("ammoxidation") forms acrylonitrile. This is the starting material for polyacrylonitrile, or PAN. Acrylic textiles, such as Acrilan and Orlon, amount to about 20 percent of all synthetic fibers produced. PAN is also used to make carbon fibers. Initially, PAN-based carbon fibers were very expensive (about $45 per pound), so they were limited to military and aerospace applications. As an example,

At the 1940 National Chemical Exposition in Chicago, representatives of Dow Chemical Company display new products made from petrochemicals. The tubing is polystyrene. (Post Street Archives)

about 10 percent of the weight of an F-18 fighter aircraft is PAN-based materials. Other applications include use in the space shuttle's cargo bay doors and in nozzles in the shuttle's rockets. Improved manufacturing know-how reduced the cost of carbon fibers significantly, and carbon- or graphite-fiber items are increasingly available to consumers; among them are graphite tennis rackets and golf clubs.

The BTX Compounds and Styrene. Catalytic reforming of petroleum, a process used to enhance the octane number of gasoline, produces as by-products the family of compounds benzene, toluene, and xylene, sometimes lumped together and called BTX. They are high-tonnage materials but not as important as ethylene and propylene. For example, annual production of benzene in the United States is about 10 billion pounds.

Benzene and ethylene react to produce ethylbenzene, which is converted to styrene. Styrene is the raw material for making polystyrene. Polystyrene is another example of the petrochemical products that seem ubiquitous in modern life. Applications of polystyrene include Styrofoam food cartons (such as those used for eggs in supermarkets), cups and food packaging at fast food restaurants, plastic utensils, toys, and the foam "peanuts" used as packaging material. Polystyrene and other uses of benzene are so important that the major use of toluene is conversion to benzene. Xylenes are used as solvents. One particular xylene, para-xylene, is converted to terephthalic acid. This compound, reacted with ethylene glycol (described above), produces PET.

The petrochemical industry has an immense economic impact, both in the United States and worldwide. In the United States, twenty-nine of the top fifty industrial chemicals are organic (though not all are petrochemicals) and account for annual production of over 260 billion pounds. The annual sales of the world's top thirty chemical companies (though again, not all are petrochemical companies) are about a third of a trillion dollars.

FURTHER READING: An excellent introductory book that covers petrochemicals and other important industrial chemicals is *The Top Five Industrial Chemicals*, by Raymond Chang and Wayne Tikkanen, 1988. Other useful books, though they generally assume that the reader has a good background in organic chemistry, include *Industrial Organic Chemicals*, by Harold Wittcoff and Bryan Reuben, 1996; *Petrochemicals*, by P. Wiseman, 1986; *Organic Building Blocks of the Chemical Industry*, by Harry Szmant, 1989; and *Petrochemical Processes*, by A. Chauvel and G. Lefebvre, 1989.

Harold H. Schobert

SEE ALSO: Gasoline and other petroleum fuels; Oil and gas, chemistry of; Petroleum refining and processing.

Petroleum. *See* Gasoline and other petroleum fuels; Oil and natural gas; Petroleum refining and processing

---

Petroleum refining and processing

Petroleum is separated into a variety of fuels—gasoline, kerosene, and diesel fuel—and into feedstocks for the chemical industry. Petroleum is first distilled, then each of the "cuts" is further treated or blended to provide the various marketed products. A significant effort is devoted to gasoline production, in order to obtain the quantities needed and the desired engine performance.

PETROLEUM, OR CRUDE OIL, is found in many parts of the world. It is not a chemically pure substance of uniform properties. Rather, petroleum is a complex mixture of hundreds of individual chemical compounds that occur in various proportions, depending on the source and geological history of the particular sample. As a result, various kinds of petroleum range in properties and appearance from lightly colored, free-flowing liquids to black, tarry, odiferous materials. It would be impractical to design furnaces or engines capable of efficient, reliable operation on a fuel whose characteristics varied so widely. Therefore, to provide products of predictable quality to the users, petroleum is separated into specific products that, through treating, blending, and purification, go on the market as the familiar gasoline, kerosene, and diesel and heating oils. Some petroleum supplies also contain impurities, most notably sulfur compounds, that must be removed for environmental reasons. The sequence of separation, blending, treating, and purification operations all make up the processes of petroleum refining.

Distillation. The first major step in refining petroleum is distillation, the separation of components based on boiling point. In principle, it would be possible to separate petroleum into each of its component compounds, one by one, producing many hundreds of individual pure compounds. Doing so would be so laborious that the products would be too expensive for widespread use as fuels or synthetic chemicals. Instead, petroleum is separated into boiling ranges, or "cuts," such that even though a particular distillation cut will still be composed of a large number of compounds, its physical properties and combustion behavior will be reasonably constant and predictable.

Many crude oils contain dissolved gases, such as propane and butane. These are driven off during distillation and can be captured for sale as liquefied petroleum gas (LPG). The first distillation cut (that is, the one with the lowest boiling temperature) that is a liquid is gasoline. Products obtained in higher boiling ranges include, in order of increasing boiling range, naphtha, kerosene, diesel oil, and some heating oils or furnace oils. Some fraction of the crude oil will not distill; this is the residuum, usually informally called the resid. The resid can be treated to separate lubricating oils and waxes. If the amount of resid is large, it can be distilled further at reduced pressure (vacuum distillation) to increase the yield of the higher-boiling-range products and a so-called vacuum resid.

Catalytic Cracking. The product that usually dominates refinery production is gasoline. Gasoline produced directly by distillation, called straight-run gasoline, is not sufficient in quantity or in engine performance to meet today's market demand. Substantial effort is devoted to enhancing the yield and quality of gasoline. The yield of straight-run gasoline from very good quality petroleum is not more than 20 percent; from poorer quality crudes, it may be less than

Crude oil is separated into various materials in fractional distillation towers. Oil is heated to the boiling point, and as the vapor rises in the tower it condenses into gasoline, kerosene, diesel oil, heating oil, and other materials. (Ben Klaffke)

10 percent. About 50 percent of a barrel of petroleum needs to be converted to gasoline to satisfy current needs. Gasoline engine performance is measured by octane number, which indicates the tendency of the gasoline to "knock" (to detonate prematurely in the engine cylinder). Knocking causes poor engine efficiency and can lead to mechanical problems. Most regular grade gasolines nowadays have octane numbers of 87; straight-run gasolines may have octane numbers below 50.

Increasing the yield of gasoline requires producing more molecules that boil in the gasoline range. Generally the boiling range of molecules relates to their size; reducing the boiling range is effected by reducing their size, or "cracking" the molecules. Octane number is determined by molecular shape. The common components of most crude oils are the paraffins, or normal alkanes, characterized by straight chains of carbon atoms. These paraffins have very low octane numbers; heptane, for example, has an octane number of 0. A related family of compounds, isoparaffins, have chains of carbon atoms with one or more side branches; these have very high octane numbers. The compound familiarly referred to as iso-octane (2,2,4-trimethylpentane) has an octane number of 100. Increasing the yield and engine performance of gasoline requires both cracking and rearranging the molecular structures.

Both of these processes can be performed in a single step, using catalysts such as zeolites. For this reason, the overall process is known as catalytic cracking. The feedstock to a catalytic cracking unit is a high-boiling cut material of low value. Different refineries may choose to use different feeds, but a typical choice would be a vacuum gas oil, which is produced in the vacuum distillation step. Much effort has gone into the development of catalysts and into evaluating appropriate choices of temperature, pressure, and reaction time. Catalytic cracking is second only to distillation in importance in most refineries. It can produce gasolines with octane numbers over 90 and increases the yield of gasoline in a refinery to about 45 percent.

Catalytic Reforming. Straight-run gasoline and naphthas have acceptable boiling ranges but suffer in octane number. Treating these streams does not require cracking, only altering the shapes of molecules—re-forming them—to en-

Separation and Uses of Petroleum

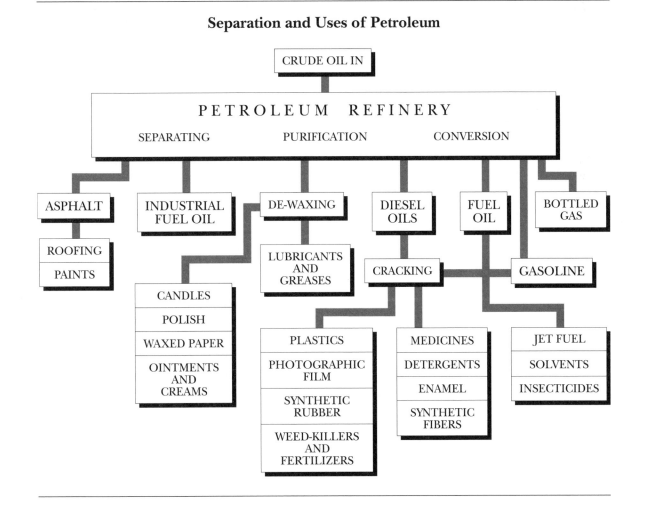

hance octane number. This process also relies on catalysts, though of different type than those used in catalytic cracking. Reforming catalysts usually include a metal, such as nickel or platinum. Catalytic reforming can produce gasolines with octane numbers close to 100.

Hydrotreating. Other distillation cuts, such as kerosene and diesel fuel, require less refining. Two processes of increasing importance, for environmental reasons, are the removal of sulfur and removal of aromatic compounds. Since both involve the use of hydrogen, they are referred to as hydrotreating.

Sulfur removal—hydrodesulfurization—is done to reduce the amount of sulfur oxide emissions that would have been produced when the fuel is burned. Additionally, sulfur compounds are corrosive and can have noxious odors. Hydrodesulfurization is performed by treating the feedstock, such as kerosene, with hydrogen using catalysts containing cobalt or nickel and molybdenum. As environmental regulations become more stringent, hydrodesulfurization will become increasingly important.

Aromatic compounds also have several undesirable characteristics. Some compounds, such as benzene, are suspect carcinogens. Larger aromatic molecules, that might be found in kerosene or diesel oil, contribute to the formation of smoke and soot when these fuels are burned. Soot formation is unpleasant in its own right, but in addition, some soot components are also carcinogens. Aromatic compounds are reacted with hydrogen to form new compounds—naphthenes or cycloalkanes—of more desirable properties.

Resid Treating. Resids can be treated with solvents to extract lubricating oils (these oils can also be made during the vacuum distillation of resid), waxes, and asphalts. Although lubricating oils are produced only in low yield (about 2 percent of a barrel of crude may wind up as lubricating oil), they are commercially very valuable products. Asphalts are of great importance for road paving. Resid is also converted by heating into petroleum coke, a solid material very high in carbon content. High-quality petroleum cokes are used to manufacture synthetic graphite, which has a range of uses, the most impor-

tant being for electrodes for the metallurgical industry. Poorer quality petroleum cokes can be used as solid fuels.

Petrochemicals. Petroleum is the source not only of our liquid fuels but also of most of our synthetic chemicals and polymers. Some products having low value as fuels, such as naphtha or even waxes, can be decomposed to produce ethylene, the most important feedstock for the chemical industry. Ethylene is converted to polyethylene, polyvinyl chloride, polyvinyl acetate, and polystyrene, which together make up a large share of the total market for plastics. Another petroleum product of great use in the chemical industry is propylene, the starting material for making polypropylene and polyacrylonitrile.

FURTHER READING: A variety of useful books is available, most of which presume some familiarity with chemistry and engineering principles. These include *The Chemistry and Technology of Petroleum*, by James Speight, 1991, which is the most useful single source. Other good sources include *Elements of Petroleum Processing*, by D. S. L. Jones, 1995; *The Petroleum Handbook*, by Royal Dutch Shell, 1983; *Handbook of Petroleum Refining Processes*, by Robert Meyers, 1986; *Petroleum Refining*, by James Gary and Glenn Handwerk, 3d ed. 1994; and *Modern Petroleum: A Basic Primer of the Industry*, by Bill Berger and Kenneth Anderson, 1992. Readers interested in petrochemicals will find an excellent treatment in *Organic Building Blocks of the Chemical Industry*, by Harry Szmant, 1989.

Harold H. Schobert

SEE ALSO: Gasoline and other petroleum fuels; Oil and natural gas, chemistry of; Oil industry; Plastics and other petrochemical products; Propane.

Phosphate

WHERE FOUND: The most widespread, continuous deposits of phosphate rock in the United States occur in the Phosphoria formation of Utah, Wyoming, Idaho, Montana, and Nevada. Other rich fields occur in Florida, Tennessee, and North Carolina. By far the most important phosphate localities worldwide are in North Africa and Russia.

PRIMARY USES: The major use of phosphate rock is to provide phosphorus for agricultural fertilizers. It is also used in many industrial processes, including the manufacture of phosphoric acids and other chemicals used in the fields of metallurgy, photography, medicine, sugar refining, soft drinks, preserved foods, ceramics, textiles, matches, and both military and commercial pyrotechnics (munitions and fireworks).

DESCRIPTION: Phosphate rock is the ore of the element phosphorus (P). It occurs mostly as marine (saltwater) sedimentary deposits in which the predominant phosphorus-bearing mineral is apatite, a hydrated calcium phosphate.

PHOSPHATE ROCK IS a general term for any earth material from which phosphorus can be extracted at a profit. The principal phosphorus-bearing mineral in these deposits is a hydrated calcium phosphate called apatite ($Ca_5(PO_4)_3(OH)$). Apatite can also accommodate variable amounts of fluorine (F) and carbonate ion (CO_3) and contains from 18.0 to 18.7 percent phosphorus. In its organic form apatite occurs as the main component of bones and teeth, and it makes up the shells of some marine invertebrates. Some phosphate deposits, particularly those in Florida, also contain certain aluminum phosphate minerals. Commercial phosphate deposits occur in two major forms: (1) marine sedimentary deposits in which phosphate-rich beds are associated with carbonate rocks (limestones, dolostones) and mudstones or shales deposited on the floor of an ocean or shallow sea, and (2) igneous deposits in which apatite has crystallized from formerly molten plutons (molten magma that solidifies below ground).

The sedimentary deposits are by far the most important phosphate producers. In the United States these areas are located in the eastern states of Florida, Tennessee, and North Carolina, and the western states (the "western field") of Wyoming, Montana, Idaho, Utah, and Nevada. Production started in the United States in 1867, with mining of the extensive Florida deposits beginning in 1888. Elsewhere in the world, significant deposits are found in North Africa, specifically Algeria, Tunisia, Morocco, and Egypt. The principal igneous deposits occur in Russia (the Kola Peninsula) and in Ontario, Canada.

Research studies show that marine phosphate deposits form under special environmental conditions. Elemental phosphorus originates in volcanic and other igneous rocks which weather to release phosphorus for use by biological organisms. Biological decay and animal metabolism release phosphorus that is then transported to the sea as phosphoric acid. In shallow near-shore waters, marine organisms use phosphorus in protein-rich tissue and hard parts. Subsequent deposition of phosphorus in sediments occurs as these organisms die, settling down to the bottom where they form phosphorus-rich deposits with as much as 50 percent phosphorite (phosphate-rich minerals). Preservation of these phosphorus-rich sediments depends upon oxygen starved and somewhat acidic water. Such zones generally only occur parallel to coastal areas. Thus both the east and west coasts of the United States are considered rich areas of currently deposited phosphate rock.

John L. Berkley

SEE ALSO: Eutrophication; Fertilizers; Mohs hardness scale; Phosphorus cycle; Sedimentary processes, rocks, and mineral deposits.

Phosphorus cycle

The phosphorus cycle describes the continuous movement of organic and inorganic phosphorus from the earth's crust and living organisms to water bodies and the atmosphere. Phosphorus stimulates rapid growth of algae in water and is the main cause of eutrophication. Fertilizers, detergents, and animal waste are major sources of phosphorus.

THE ELEMENT PHOSPHORUS (abbreviated P) primarily exists in its highest oxidized state—that is, the phosphate ion (PO_4). Phosphorus can be found in a variety of inorganic and organic compounds. Geochemical phosphorus occurs mainly as calcium phosphate (apatite), Ca₃(PO₄)₂, and as hydroxyapatite, Ca₅(PO₄)₃(OH), and is relatively insoluble. Even when phosphorus is leached into solution through weathering, it readily reacts with other elements to form calcium, aluminum, manganese and iron phosphates or binds to clay minerals, resulting in other insoluble phases. Phosphorus has no stable gaseous compounds. Therefore, phosphorus is transported mainly in particulate form by means of overland and riverine runoff and to a lesser extent by atmospheric precipitation.

Phosphorus is essential to all life processes. Along with carbon and nitrogen, phosphorus is a very important nutrient of freshwater bodies. Carbon and nitrogen are more readily available than phosphorus, and the short supply of phosphorus can control the growth of aquatic vegetation and other microorganisms. Thus, phosphorus can act as a limiting factor. An abundance of phosphorus can lead to excessive growth of filamentous algae, which can create odor and taste problems and can cause biofouling of the filters, pipes, and instrumentation that are crucial parts of water supply systems.

Much phosphorus input is anthropogenic—in other words, human activities contribute to phosphorus input at a much greater rate than natural processes do. Human waste and detergents in domestic and industrial sewage, along with leaching and runoff of fertilizers and animal waste from agricultural lands, are the major sources of phosphorus.

Inorganic phosphorus is taken up by living cells and becomes a major constituent of nucleic acids, phospholipids, and different phosphorylated compounds. In nature, organic phosphorus is derived from dead and living cells through excretion and decomposition respectively.

Generally, both inorganic and organic phosphates are transformed into dissolved inorganic orthophosphate. The orthophosphate either precipitates or is consumed or released by phytoplankton or bacteria. Through these lower forms of life, phosphorus is first assimilated by zooplankton and subsequently by higher order organisms. Precipitated phosphorus is utilized by aquatic plants and is diffused into the ambient water or is buried in deep sediments. In eutro-

phic (nutrient-rich, particularly phosphorus-rich) lakes the amount of phosphorus precipitated from the atmosphere is relatively insignificant in comparison to the amount present in water and sediments. On the other hand, atmospheric phosphorus may be a significant source of phosphorus for oligotrophic (oxygen-rich) lakes.

In stratified lakes during spring season under well-mixed oxidized conditions phosphorus may bound to the bottom sediments. However, in winter, under anoxic (oxygen-deficient) conditions, phosphorus is released from the sediments into the water column. Therefore, phosphorus-laden sediments can serve as internal sources of phosphorus and can continue to promote eutrophication long after the external sources have ceased to exist.

Panagiotis D. Scarlatos

SEE ALSO: Agriculture industry; Clean Water Act; Environmental engineering; Eutrophication; Fertilizers; Food chain; Lakes; Phosphate; Soil; Water pollution and water pollution control.

Pinchot, Gifford

BORN: August 11, 1865; Simsbury, Connecticut
DIED: October 4, 1946; New York, New York

A leading figure in the conservation movement of the late nineteenth century, Pinchot advocated the scientific management of the nation's forests to assure a continuing supply of wood for future growth.

GIFFORD PINCHOT GRADUATED from the Yale College School of Forestry, which his father had helped to found, in 1889 and then studied forestry in Europe, the first American to do so. When a federal Bureau of Forestry was established, Pinchot was appointed as its head. The bureau became the United States Forest Service in 1905, and Pinchot continued as its leader until 1910, at which time he became president of the National Conservation Committee. He also taught forestry at Yale University from 1903 to 1906.

Pinchot established the basic principles of American forest policy. In contrast to later environmentalists, Pinchot viewed wooded lands principally in terms of their economic value and

Gifford Pinchot, the first head of the U.S. Forest Service, was a conservationist but not a preservationist. (Archive Photos)

was concerned with optimizing the yield per acre of wooded land. He built a strong Forest Service, financed in part by the sale of mature timber. He actively opposed the institution of national parks to be used for recreation, considering them a waste of natural resources. After leaving the Forest Service, Pinchot became active in the Progressive Party, founded by supporters of Theodore Roosevelt. Pinchot became chief forester of Pennsylvania in 1920, and he campaigned for and won election as governor of Pennsylvania in 1923 and again in 1931.

Donald R. Franceschetti

SEE ALSO: Conservation; Forest management; Forest Service, U.S.; Leopold, Aldo; Roosevelt, Theodore.

Placer deposits

Placer deposits are mechanical concentrations of debris weathered out of rocks. Commonly, economically impor-

tant minerals have higher densities, so they are concentrated as the lighter-density minerals are winnowed out by the action of water or wind. Placer deposits are found throughout the world wherever the mechanisms of concentration have been active and the resulting concentrates have not been redispersed by later processes. The most well-known types of placers occur in river channels and in beach sediments.

THE WEATHERING AND EROSION of rocks release particles of varying size, shape, and density. Soluble materials are dissolved and removed in surface water or groundwater. Some minerals, such as feldspars, are hydrated and converted into clay minerals, which, being soft, small, and of low density, are relatively readily removed in suspension. Quartz (SiO_2), common in many kinds of rocks, generally weathers out as roughly equant grains that, because of their hardness and insolubility, wash into streams and rivers, where they are moved by rolling, bouncing, and pushing along toward the oceans. The abundance of quartz and its resistance to mechanical and chemical weathering results in its being the most abundant placer mineral and the principal constituent of temperate and cold climate beaches throughout the world.

During the weathering and erosional processes, other minor or trace minerals, which are resistant to breakdown, are also transported along with the quartz grains and pebbles in river channels to the ocean margins. If the mineral particles possess high densities, they may be selectively concentrated as the transporting agent (usually water) more readily removes the lighter density minerals. Thus, gold nuggets, with densities of 15-19 grams per cubic centimeter, are commonly concentrated in residual materials as the quartz grains, with a density of about 2.65 grams per cubic centimeter, are removed. The densities of several other valuable and resistant minerals are sufficiently higher than quartz to allow them to also be concentrated in placer deposits as well (examples include ilmenite, $FeTiO_3$, 4.8; rutile, TiO_2, 4.25; zircon, $ZrSiO_4$, 4.7; cassiterite, SnO_2, 7.0; and diamond, C, 3.5).

Economically Important Placer Minerals. Many types of minerals and rock materials can occur in placer deposits; among the most important are gold, titanium minerals, zircon, tin oxide, diamonds, platinum, and sand and gravel. Throughout history, gold has no doubt been the most important placer mineral. Gold is soft and malleable but is otherwise nearly inert in the weathering realm. Hence, once gold is weathered out of the lode deposits where it initially formed, the grains may survive transport in streams and rivers over long distances. It was the discovery of such gold grains that led to nearly all of the world's major gold rushes, including the California Gold Rush in 1849. Gold placers have formed throughout geologic time; the world's largest gold reserves in South Africa occur in placers formed 2 billion years ago.

The titanium minerals, ilmenite and rutile, occur in minor amounts as small grains in many types of igneous and metamorphic rocks. These minerals are very resistant to weathering and hence are liberated intact from their host rocks. Although their densities are less than twice that of quartz, they are quite effectively concentrated by flowing water in rivers and by the agitation of waves along beaches as the lower density quartz grains are winnowed out. The zirconium silicate zircon is a common accessory mineral in alkaline igneous rocks. It weathers out as the titanium minerals do and is generally found with those minerals in river and beach deposits.

The tin oxide cassiterite, like the titanium minerals, is heavy, hard, and very resistant to weathering. Consequently, where there are cassiterite-bearing lode deposits, the cassiterite weathers out and may be concentrated into economic placers. The hardness of diamonds and their resistance to normal weathering agents has allowed them to wash down rivers that drain from the areas of exposed diamond pipes and to occur in placer river and beach deposits. Because the density of the diamonds is only about one third greater than that of quartz, the diamonds are not as well selectively concentrated in these placers as are the heavier minerals noted above. Platinum, like gold, is chemically inert and has a very high density, 15-19 grams per cubic centimeter. Platinum lode deposits are much more restricted geologically than are gold deposits; hence, placer platinum deposits oc-

A nineteenth century magazine depiction of a miner using a "cradle" to mine a placer deposit in 1880's California. (Library of Congress)

cur in only a few places in the world.

The sand and gravel deposits found in rivers and lakes and on beaches constitute the largest placer deposits in that they represent mechanically concentrated residual materials. Although they have a much lower per unit value than many other placer materials, the very large volumes of sand and gravel mined from these deposits actually make them economically the most important placer deposits.

Types of Placer Deposits. Placer deposits have been classified into several different types on the basis of location of formation. The major types include residual placers, eluvial placers, stream or river placers, riverbank and flood placers, eolian placers, and beach placers. Residual placers are occurrences of minerals at or near their point of release from the original source rocks. There has been some degree of enrichment of the placer minerals as the result of the removal of other portions of the host rocks by weathering. Eluvial placers are transitional placers in which concentrations of placer minerals occur downslope from the source rocks but where the valued minerals have not yet washed into streams and rivers that would transport them for long distances.

Stream or river placers are the most well-known placers and are the types responsible for most famous gold discoveries. The movement of the running water, especially where there is turbulence, is effective in sorting rock fragments and mineral grains according to size and density. Because of their higher densities, gold grains and several other placer minerals settle out. They are readily trapped in crevices and irregularities on the stream bed or among larger boulders, as the lower density materials are more easily washed away. This type of placer sometimes grades into deltaic beds where a river drains into a lake or the ocean.

Riverbank and flood placers are deposits adjacent to streams and rivers that have been left as the rivers meander, cut downward, or overflow their banks in flood conditions. During the natural development of rivers, they commonly shift laterally across their floodplains, eroding banks one side while depositing materials on the other side. In some areas, changes in base levels result in rivers cutting downward though the sediments they had previously deposited in their floodplains. In both these circumstances, valuable placer deposits may be left in the riverbank sediments that are adjacent to the present rivers. Flood placers also occur in the sediments adjacent to rivers. They form during episodic flooding when water flow is sufficiently rapid and turbulent to transport gold or other valued placer mineral grains up and out of the channels onto the adjacent flood plains. As the water spreads laterally and its velocity decreases, the gold grains are left as placer deposits along the adjacent floodplains.

Eolian placers are wind-formed placers that occur locally in desert regions where high winds have removed lighter mineral grains, thereby enriching the heavy minerals in the residuum. Beach placers are generally formed by the combined effects of river transport of weathered materials to coastal margins and the action of tides and storm waves along beaches. The ebb and flow of the waves and the generation of longshore currents, especially under storm conditions, can effectively winnow and sort beach materials such that certain areas are highly enriched in heavy minerals. Gold-bearing beach placers are known in many localities, but the most famous are probably those at Nome, Alaska, where the beaches were actively mined for many years. Diamond-bearing beach placers have been extensively mined along the west coast of central and southern Africa, where rivers draining the interior have transported diamonds into the beach sands. Beach placers containing ilmenite, rutile, and zircon are the world's major sources of these minerals.

Mining of Placer Deposits. Gold panning is probably the best-known method of exploiting placer deposits. A circular motion of water in a pan containing gold along with other sediments effectively separates the minerals on the basis of their densities. The same general principal is used in sluices, channel-like boxes with barriers to create turbulence in the water so that sorting can take place. On a large scale, modern placers are mined by the scooping up of the unconsolidated materials and the use of either spiral classifiers or heavy media to separate the heavy materials from the light materials. The differences in the densities of the minerals allows for very effective separation.

FURTHER READING: *The Geology of Ore Deposits*, by J. M. Guilbert and C. F. Park, 1986, and the *Atlas of Economic Mineral Deposits*, by C. J. Dixon, 1979, provide good reviews of many types of ore deposits, including placers. *Placer Examination*, by J. H. Wells, 1989, provides a good overview of types of placers and their evaluation.

James R. Craig

SEE ALSO: Diamond; Gold; Marine mining; Residual mineral deposits; Sand and gravel; Tin; Titanium; Weathering; Zirconium.

Plant domestication and breeding

Plant domestication and breeding refers to the process by which wild plants are intentionally bred and grown to meet human food, fiber, shelter, medicinal, or aesthetic needs.

PERHAPS ANY NATION'S greatest resource is its ability to sustain an agricultural system with the capacity to feed, shelter, and clothe its population. The development of an agricultural system depends on an ability not only to cultivate wild plants but also to selectively breed plants to increase or improve the production of products that are useful for food, clothing, shelter, medicines, or aesthetic purposes.

No one knows exactly when the first crop was cultivated, but most authorities believe that it occurred at some time between eight and ten thousand years ago. For centuries prior to that time, humans had known that some wild plants and plant parts (such as fruits, leaves, and roots) were edible. These plants appeared periodically (usually annually) and randomly throughout a given region. Eventually humans discovered not only that these wild plants grew from seed but also that the seed from certain wild plants could be collected, planted, and later gathered for food. This most likely occurred at about the same time in both the Sumerian region between the Tigris and Euphrates Rivers in the Old World and in Mexico and the Central American region of the New World. While the earliest attempts at domesticating plants were primarily to supplement the food supply provided by hunting and gathering, people soon improved their ability to domesticate and breed plants to the point that they could depend on an annual supply of food. This food supply allowed the development of permanent settlements and decreased reliance on hunting and gathering.

Early Crop Domestication. By six thousand years ago, agriculture was firmly established in Asia, India, Mesopotamia, Egypt, Mexico, Central America, and South America. Even before recorded history, these areas had domesticated some of the world's most important food (corn or maize, rice, and wheat) and fiber (cotton, flax, and hemp) crops. The place of origin of wheat is unknown, but many authorities believe that it may have grown wild in the Tigris and Euphrates Valleys and spread from there to the rest of the Old World. Wheat was grown by Stone Age Europeans and was reportedly produced in China as far back as 2700 B.C.E. Wheat is now the major staple for about 35 percent of the people of the world. The earliest traces of the human utilization of corn (or maize, as it is also called), dates back to about 5200 B.C.E. It was probably first cultivated in the high plateau region of central or southern Mexico and represented the basic food plant of all pre-Columbian advanced cultures and civilizations, including the Inca of South America and the Maya of Central America.

Botanists believe that rice originated in southeast Asia. Rice was being cultivated in India as early as 3000 B.C.E. and spread from there throughout Asia and Malaysia. Today rice is one of the world's most important cereal grains and is the principal food crop of almost half of the world's people. Hemp, most likely the first plant cultivated for its fiber, was cultivated for the purpose of making cloth in China as early as the twenty-eighth century B.C.E. It was used as the cordage or rope on almost all ancient sailing vessels. Linen made from flax is one of the oldest fabrics. Traces of flax plants have been identified in archaeological sites dating back to the Stone Age, and flax was definitely being cultivated in Mesopotamia and Egypt five thousand years ago. Cotton has been known and highly valued by people throughout the world for more than three thousand years. From India, where a vigorous cotton industry was present as early as 1500 B.C.E., the cultivation of cotton spread to Egypt and then to Spain and Italy. In the West Indies and South America in the New World, a different species of cotton was being grown long before the Europeans arrived. Other important plants that have been under domestic cultivation since antiquity include dates, figs, olives, onions, grapes, bananas, lemons, cucumbers, lentils, garlic, lettuce, mint, radishes, and various melons.

Modern Plant Breeding. Genetic variability is prevalent in all sexually reproducing organisms, and like all other sexually reproducing organisms, plants produce spontaneous mutants. Throughout most of history, plant domestication and breeding were primarily based on the propagation of these mutants. When a grower observed a plant with a potentially desirable mutation (such as a change that produced a characteristic such as bigger fruit, brighter flowers, or increased insect resistance), the grower would collect seed or take cuttings (if the plant could be propagated vegetatively) and produce additional plants with the desirable characteristic.

Grapes, along with the cereal grains and several other plants such as figs, olives, onions, lettuce, and lemons, have been domesticated since antiquity. (Ben Klaffke)

Advances in the understanding of genetics in the early part of the twentieth century made it possible to breed some of the desirable characteristics resulting from mutation into plants that previously had lacked the characteristic. The obvious advantages of producing plants with improved characteristics such as higher yield made plant breeding very desirable. As populations continued to grow, there was a need to select and produce higher-yielding crops. The development and widespread successful use of new high-yield varieties of crop plants in the 1960's is often referred to as the Green Revolution. Basic information supplied by biological scientists allowed plant breeders to fuse a variety of characteristics from different plants to produce new, higher-yielding varieties of numerous crops—

particularly the seed grains that supply most of the calories necessary for maintenance of the world's population.

When a plant characteristic is identified as desirable, it is studied both morphologically and biochemically to determine the mechanism of inheritance. If it is determined that the mechanism is transferable, attempts are made to incorporate the trait into the target plant. If the plants are closely related, traditional breeding techniques are used to crossbreed the plant with the desirable trait with the plant that lacks the characteristic. Although this process is often tedious, is sometimes difficult to accomplish, and requires considerable patience and hard work, it is based on a fairly simple concept. Basically, pollen from one of the plant types is used to fertilize the other plant type. This process often requires specialized handling techniques to ensure that only the pollen from the plant with the desired characteristic is allowed to fertilize the eggs of the recipient plant.

Sometimes this process involves the use of bags or other materials to isolate the recipient flowers, which are then pollinated by hand. Another technique involves the introduction of a gene for male sterility into the recipient plant. In these cases, only pollen from another plant can be used to fertilize the egg. Once plants with the desirable characteristics are developed, the lines are often inbred to maintain large numbers of progeny with the desired traits. In many cases, inbred lines will lose vigor after several generations. When this occurs, two inbred lines are often crossed to produce hybrids. A majority of the hybrid offspring will still contain the desired characteristics but will be more vigorous.

Until relatively recently, the use of traditional breeding techniques between two very closely related species was the only means of transferring heritable characteristics from one plant to another. The advent of recombinant deoxyribonucleic acid (DNA) technology, however, made it possible to transfer genetic characteristics from any plant (or, in actuality, from any organism) to any other plant. The simplest method for accomplishing this transfer involves the use of a vector, usually a piece of circular DNA called a plasmid. The plasmid is removed from a micro-

organism such as bacteria and cut open by an enzyme called a restriction endonuclease or restriction enzyme. A section of DNA from the plant donor cell that contains the gene for a previously identified desirable trait is cut from the donor cell DNA by the same restriction endonuclease. The section of plant donor cell DNA with the gene for the characteristic of interest is then combined with the open plasmid DNA, and the plasmid closes with the new gene as part of its structure. The recombinant plasmid (DNA from two sources) is placed back into the bacteria where it will replicate and code for protein just as it did in the donor cell. The bacteria is then used as a vector to transfer the gene to another plant, where it will also be transcribed and translated.

FURTHER READING: An authoritative presentation of numerous topics in food science, including the harvesting, preservation, and marketing of a variety of horticultural food crops, can be found in *Principles of Food Science*, by O. R. Fennema, 1976. *Horticulture Science*, by Jules Janick, 1986, contains sections on crop production and breeding. An authoritative presentation of numerous topics in crop science, including the harvesting, preservation, and marketing of numerous field crops, can be found in *Field Crops*, by H. C. Rather and C. M. Harrison, 1951. An old but authoritative treatise on the cultivation and products of grain, fiber, forage, and cash crops is *Production of Field Crops*, by T. K. Wolf and M. S. Kipps, 5th ed. 1959. One of the most valuable sources available on the practical aspects of crop production is *Crop Production: Principles and Practices*, by D. S. Metcalfe and D. M. Elkins, 4th ed. 1980.

D. R. Gossett

SEE ALSO: Agricultural products; Agriculture industry; Biotechnology; Corn; Green Revolution; Horticulture; Monoculture agriculture; Plant fibers; Rice; Wheat.

Plant fibers

Fiber crops provide a natural source of the raw materials used to produce textiles, ropes, twine, and similar materials. The major fiber plants are cotton, flax, and hemp, although less important crops such as ramie, jute, and sisal are produced in small amounts.

WITH A TOTAL annual production of over 13 million tons, cotton is by far the most important fiber crop in the world. Since humans heavily rely on cotton for clothing and other textiles, it enters the daily life of more of the world's people than any other product except salt.

Cotton (Gossypium spp.). Cotton fiber has been known and highly valued by people throughout the world for more than three thousand years. As is true of most crop plants that have been in cultivation for long periods of time, the early history of cotton is obscure. A vigorous cotton industry was present in India as early as 1500 B.C.E.

From India, the cultivation of cotton spread to Egypt and then to Spain and Italy. In the New World, a different species of cotton was being grown in the West Indies and South America long before the Europeans arrived. In the United States, cotton is currently grown from the East Coast to the West Coast in the nineteen southernmost states.

Botanically, cotton is in the mallow family, which includes such plants as okra, hollyhock, hibiscus, and althea. The plant has a taproot and branching stems. Flowers form at the tips of fruiting branches, and the ovary within each flower develops into a boll which contains the seed, fiber, and fuzz. The fiber, most commonly referred to as lint, develops from epidermal cells in the seed coat of the cottonseed. The fiber

The production of cotton fiber, valued for thousands of years, is labor-intensive and relatively expensive. The cotton plant is native to the tropics. (Ben Klaffke)

reaches maximum length in twenty to twenty-five days, and an additional twenty-five days are required for the fiber to thicken. Fiber length from 2.0 to 2.4 centimeters is referred to as short-staple cotton, and fiber length from 2.4 to 3.8 centimeters is called long-staple cotton. The boll normally opens forty-five to sixty-five days after flowering. Cotton is native to tropical regions but has adapted to the humid, subtropical climate where there are warm days (30 degrees Celsius), relatively warm nights, and a frost-free season of at least 200 to 210 days. There are eight species of cotton in the genus *Gossypium,* but only three species are of commercial importance. *Gossypium hirsutum,* also known as upland cotton, has a variable staple length and is produced primarily in North and Central America. *Gossypium barbadense,* a long-staple cotton, is primarily produced in South America and Africa. *Gossypium herbaceum* is a shorter-staple cotton native to India and eastern Asia.

Cotton is one of the more labor-intensive and expensive crops to produce. The most opportune time to plant cotton is at least two weeks after the last killing-frost date of the region. Prior to seeding, the field is prepared by plowing to a depth of 2.5 centimeters. Fertilizer, which is applied before seeding or at the same time the seeds are planted, is placed to the side and below the cotton seed. Once the seeds germinate and emerge from the soil, they often have to be thinned, and shortly afterwards, the producer begins to apply irrigation water as needed. After the plants have developed a stand, weed control becomes crucial. Weeds are controlled both by cultivation and chemical herbicides. Cotton plants are subject to invasion by a variety of insect pests such as the boll worm and boll weevil; therefore considerable attention is given to insect control, typically using a number of different insecticides. When the bolls ripen with mature fiber, the leaves of the plant are removed by the application of a chemical defoliant, and the cotton fiber is harvested. Harvesting was once done almost entirely by hand, but today mechanical pickers harvest almost all the cotton produced in the United States. The picked cotton is ginned to remove the seed and compressed into bales. The bales are transported to the cotton mill where the cotton is cleaned and spun into yarn, which is then woven into fabric. One pound of fiber is sufficient to produce up to six square yards of the fabric used for shirts and simple dresses.

Flax (Linum usitatissimum). Flax is the natural fiber used to make linen. While some flax is still produced for the purpose of producing this fabric, much of the flax, particularly that grown in the United States, is used to produce the flaxseed from which linseed can be extracted. Linen made from flax is one of the oldest fabrics. Flax was definitely being cultivated in Mesopotamia and Egypt five thousand years ago, and traces of flax plants have been identified in archaeological sites dating back to the Stone Age. Flax was one of the first crops brought to America by the early settlers. Today, most of the flax produced in the United States is grown in the north central states.

Flax, an annual plant, grows to a height of 60 to 100 centimeters and bears five-celled bolls or capsules with ten seeds each at the ends of fertile branches. Since the flax fiber is found in the stems from the ground to the lowest branches, varieties that are long-stemmed with little branching are grown for fiber production. Selection of quality, disease-free seed is essential in flax production. Flax fields are usually prepared in the fall to allow the soil to settle before planting. Flax is usually sown in early spring two to three weeks prior to the date of the last killing frost of the region. Considerable attention is given to controlling weeds in a flax field. When the crop is harvested for fiber, the plants are pulled from the soil, the seeds are removed, and the flax straw is "retted" to separate the fiber from the woody part of the stem. When the straw is completely retted, it is dried and then broken apart to remove the fifty centimeter fibers which can be woven into fabrics.

Hemp (Cannabis sativa). Hemp, a term used to identify the plant and the fiber it produces, is used to make the strongest and most durable commercial fibers available. Hemp was most likely the first plant cultivated for its fiber. It was cultivated for the purpose of making cloth in China as early as the twenty-eighth century B.C.E. It was also used as a drug by the ancient Persians as early as 1400 B.C.E. It was used as the cordage or rope on almost all ancient sailing vessels. Today hemp is commercially produced for heavy textiles in numerous countries, but less than a thousand acres is devoted to commercial hemp production in the United States. Hemp production is problematic in the United States because it is illegal to grow *Cannabis sativa*, as it is the source of marijuana.

Hemp is an annual plant in the mulberry family. The plant is dioecious, meaning that it has staminate or "male" flowers and pistillate or "female" flowers. It has a rigid stalk which can reach a thickness of more than 2.5 centimeters in diameter and a height of 5 meters. The plant has a hollow stem, and the bark or "bast" located outside the woody shell is used to make the bast fiber, which is then used to make hemp twine, ropes, and other textiles where strength and durability are desired. Humid climates with moderate temperatures and a period of at least 120 frost-free days are necessary for hemp production. Unlike flax, hemp requires that the soil be plowed and thoroughly disked or harrowed prior to planting. The entire above-ground portion of the plant is harvested when the male plants are in full flower. After two to three days the plants are tied in bundles and set in shocks. Hemp fiber is retted and prepared for the mills in a manner very similar to that described for flax except that heavier machines are used to handle the stronger hemp stalks.

Minor Crops. As for the minor fiber crops, ramie (*Boehmeria nivea*) is produced primarily in Asia and is used to make strong cloth such as Chinese linen. Jute (*Corchorus capsularis*) is grown primarily in India and Pakistan and is used to manufacture burlap for bags and sacks. Sisal (*Agave sisalana*) is produced in East Africa and the West Indies and is used to make different types of cordage, such as baler twine.

FURTHER READING: *The Production of Field Crops*, by M. S. Kipps, 6th ed. 1970, has excellent discussions of the importance and production of cotton, hemp, and flax. One of the most valuable sources available on the practical aspects of cotton production can be found in *Crop Production: Principles and Practices*, by D. S. Metcalfe and D. M. Elkins, 4th ed. 1980. An authoritative pres-

entation of numerous topics in crop science, including the harvesting, preservation, and marketing of fiber crops, can be found in *Field Crops*, by H. C. Rather and C. M. Harrison, 1951. *Cotton Physiology*, edited by J. R. Mauney and J. M. Stewart, 1986, contains excellent discussions of the physiology of the cotton plant. Two old but very useful U.S. Department of Agriculture publications on hemp and flax production are D. H. Lester, "Hemp," in the 1913 U.S. Department of Agriculture *Yearbook*, and A. C. Dillman, "Flaxseed Production," in the 1935 U.S. Department of Agriculture *Farmer's Bulletin Number 1747*.

D. R. Gossett

SEE ALSO: Agricultural products; Agriculture industry; Horticulture; Monoculture agriculture; Plant domestication and breeding; Textiles and fabrics.

Plants as a medical resource

Because plants are so biochemically diverse, they produce thousands of natural products commonly referred to as secondary metabolites, and many of these secondary metabolites have medicinal properties that have proven to be very beneficial to humankind.

THE USE OF PLANTS for medicinal purposes predates the recorded history of humankind. Primitive people's use of trial and error in the constant search for edible plants inevitably led them to the discovery of plants that contained substances that caused appetite suppression, stimulation, hallucination, or other side effects. Written records show that drugs such as opium have been in use for over five thousand years. From antiquity until fairly recent times, most practicing physicians were also botanists or at least herbalists. Today medicinal plants are perhaps one of the most overlooked natural resources. Because modern commercial medicines are obtained in neat packages in the form of pills, capsules, or bottled liquids, most people do not realize that many of these drugs were first extracted from plants. In some cases, chemists have learned how to duplicate synthetically the natural product that was initially identified in a plant, but in many cases, a plant may still be the only economically feasible source of the drug.

Plant-Derived Medicines. There are numerous ways to categorize medicinal compounds from plants. For this discussion, medicinal drugs will be categorized as antibacterial substances, anti-inflammatory agents, drugs affecting the reproductive system, drugs affecting the heart and circulation, drugs affecting the central nervous system, anti-asthma drugs, drugs affecting the gastrointestinal tract, antiparasitic agents, and anticancer agents. The first effective antibacterial substance was carbolic acid, but the first truly plant-derived antibacterial drug was penicillin, which was extracted from a very primitive plant, the fungus *Penicillium,* in 1928. The work with penicillin led to the discovery of other fungal and bacterial compounds that have antibacterial activity. The most notable of these are cephalosporin and griseofulvin.

Inflammation can be caused by mechanical or chemical damage, radiation, or foreign organisms. For centuries poultices of leaves from coriander (*Coriandrum sativum*), thornapple (*Datura stramonium*), wintergreen (*Gaultheria procumbens*), witchhazel (*Hamamelis virginiana*), and willow (*Salix niger*) were used to treat localized inflammation. In the seventeenth and eighteenth centuries cinchona bark was used as a source of quinine, which could be taken internally. In 1876 salicylic acid was obtained from the salicin produced by the willow leaves. Today, salicylic acid, also known as aspirin and derivatives such as ibuprofen, is the most widely used anti-inflammatory drug in the world. The most effective home remedy for preventing pregnancy was a tea made from the leaves of the Mexican plant zoapatle (*Montana tomentosa*). The drug zoapatanol and its derivatives were extracted from this plant to produce the first effective birth control substance—which has not been used in human trials, however, because of potential harmful side effects. Other plant compounds that affect the reproductive system include diosgenin, extracted from *Dioscorea* species and used as a precursor for the progesterone used in birth control pills, gossypol from cotton (*Gossypium spp.*), which has been shown to be an effective birth control agent for males, ergometrine, extracted from the ergot fungus (*Claviceps spp*) and

used to control post-partum bleeding, and yohimbine from the African tree (*Corynanthe yohimbe*), which apparently has some effect as an aphrodisiac.

Through the ages, dogbane (*Apocynum cannabinum*) and milkweeds (*Asclepias spp*) have been prized for their effects on the circulatory system because of the presence of a group of compounds called cardiac glycosides, but foxglove (*Digitalis spp*) has produced the most useful cardiac glycosides, digitalis and digoxin. Opiate alkaloids such as opium extracted from the poppy (*Papaver sonniferum*) and its derivatives such as morphine, as well as cocaine from *Erythroxylum coca* and *Erythroxylum truxillense*, have long been know for their analgesic (pain-relieving) properties through their effects on the central nervous system. Both these drugs can also produce harmful side effects, however, and both have addictive properties. The major anti-asthma drugs come from ephedrine, extracted from the Ma Huang plant (*Ephedra sinaica*), and its structural derivatives. Plant-derived drugs that affect the gastrointestinal track include castor oil, senna, and aloes as laxatives, opiate alkaloids as antidiarrhoeals, and ipecac from *Cephaelis acuminata* as an emetic. The most useful plant-derived antiparasitic agent is quinine, derived from the bark of the chincona plant (*Chincona succirubra*). Quinine has been used to control malaria, a disease that has plagued humankind for centuries. The primary plant-derived anticancer agents are vincristine and vinblastine, extracted from *Catheranthus roseus*, maytansinoids from *Maytentus serrata*, ellipticine and related compounds from *Ochrosia elliptica*, and taxol from the yew tree (*Taxus baccata*).

The Future. Many as-yet-unknown plant-derived medicinal drugs await discovery, particularly in the tropical rain forests. Also, modern biotechnology has provided the methods by which plants can be bioengineered to produce new and novel pharmaceuticals. Progress toward the production of specific proteins in transgenic plants provides opportunities to produce large quantities of complex pharmaceuticals and other valuable products in traditional farm environments rather than in laboratories. These novel strategies open up routes for production of a broad array of natural or nature-based products, ranging from foodstuffs with enhanced nutritive value to the production of biopharmaceuticals.

FURTHER READING: One of the most complete treatises on the production of drugs from plants can be found in *Pharmacognosy*, by G. E. Trease and W. C. Evans, 11th ed. 1978. *Murder, Magic, and Medicine*, by J. Mann, 1994, is a most interesting and readable book on the use of natural plant products for medicinal purposes. A very good study of plants and the medicines they produce can be found in *Medical Botany*, by M. P. F. Elvin-Lewis and W. H. Lewis, 1977. *The Evolution of Modern Medicines*, by W. Sneader, 1986, provides excellent coverage of how plants contributed to the development of many of today's pharmaceuticals. An excellent discussion of natural plant products can be found in *Nature's Pharmacy*, by C. Stockwell, 1989.

D. R. Gossett

SEE ALSO: Agricultural products; Agriculture industry; Animals as a medical resource; Biotechnology.

Plate tectonics

The theory of plate tectonics provides an explanation for the present-day structure of the outer part of the earth. It provides a framework for understanding the global distribution of mountain building, earthquake activity, and volcanism; the geology of ocean basins; various associations of igneous, metamorphic, and sedimentary rocks; and the formation and location of mineral resources.

PLATE TECTONIC THEORY is based on a concept of the earth in which a rigid, outer shell, the lithosphere, lies above a hotter, weaker, partially molten part of the mantle known as the asthenosphere. The thickness of the lithosphere varies between 50 and 150 kilometers, and it consists of crust and the underlying upper mantle. The asthenosphere extends from the base of the lithosphere to a depth of about 700 kilometers. The brittle lithosphere is broken into a pattern of internally rigid plates that move horizontally across the earth's surface relative to each other.

Seven major plates and a number of smaller ones have been distinguished, and they grind and scrape against one another as they move independently, similar to chunks of ice on water. Most of the earth's dynamic activity, including earthquakes and volcanism, occurs along plate boundaries, and the global distribution of these tectonic phenomena delineate the boundaries of the plates.

Plate Boundaries and Motion. Geophysical data, geological observations, and theoretical deductions support the existence of three basic types of plate boundaries: divergent boundaries, where adjacent plates move apart (diverge) from each other; convergent boundaries, where adjacent plates move toward each other; and transform boundaries, where plates slip past one another in a direction parallel to their common boundary. The velocity with which plates move varies from plate to plate and within portions of the same plate, ranging from two to twenty centimeters per year. This rate is determined from radioactive dating estimates of the age of the seafloor as a function of distance from mid-oceanic ridge crests (seafloor spreading ridges).

Divergent Plate Boundaries. At mid-oceanic ridges, or divergent plate boundaries, new seafloor is created from molten basalt (magma) rising from the asthenosphere. A great deal of volcanic activity thus occurs at divergent boundaries. Because of the pulling apart (rifting) of the plates of lithosphere, earthquake activity will also occur along divergent boundaries, and since the rift is caused by magma rising from the mantle, the earthquakes will be frequent, shallow, and mild.

An example of continental rifting (divergence) in its embryonic stage is seen in the Red Sea, where the Arabian plate has separated from the African plate, creating a new oceanic ridge. Another modern-day example is the East African Rift system, which is the site of active rifting. If it continues, it will eventually fragment Africa, and an ocean will separate the resulting pieces. Through divergence, or rifting, large plates are broken up into smaller ones.

Convergent Plate Boundaries. Because the earth is neither expanding nor contracting, the increase in lithosphere created along divergent

Major Tectonic Plates and Mid-Ocean Ridges

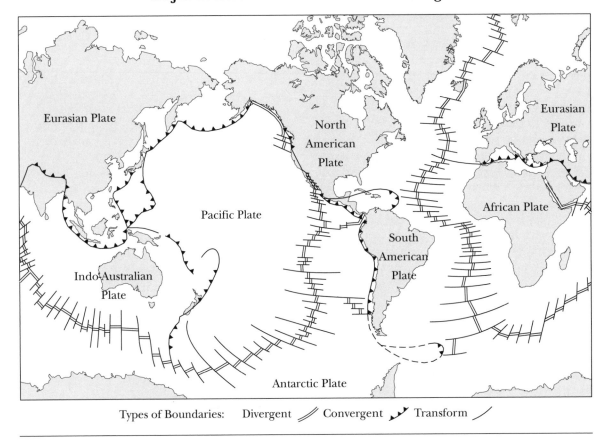

Types of Boundaries: Divergent // Convergent ⪤ Transform /

boundaries must be compensated for by the destruction of lithosphere elsewhere. Otherwise the radius of the earth would change. At convergent plate boundaries, plates are moving together, and three scenarios are possible depending on whether the crust of the lithosphere is oceanic or continental.

If both converging plates are made of oceanic crust, one will inevitably be older, and thus cooler and denser than the other plate. The denser plate will plunge (subduct) below the less-dense plate and descend down into the asthenosphere. This type of plate boundary is called a subduction zone, and the boundary along the two interacting plates forms a trench. The subducted plate is heated by the hot asthenosphere and, in time, becomes hot enough to melt. Some of the melted material rises buoyantly through fissures and cracks to form volca-

noes on the overlying plate, whereas other parts of the melted material will eventually migrate to and rise again at a divergent boundary (spreading ridge). Thus the oceanic lithosphere is constantly being recycled. The volcanoes along the overriding plate may form a string of islands called island arcs. Japan, the Aleutians, and the Mariannas are good examples of island arcs resulting from subduction of two plates consisting of oceanic lithosphere.

If the leading edge of one of the two convergent plates is oceanic crust but the other leading edge is continental crust, the subduction differs from the case above. Since continental crust is less dense than oceanic, the oceanic plate is always the one subducted. A classical example of this case is the western boundary of South America. On the oceanic side of the boundary, a trench is formed, where the oceanic plate plunges underneath the continental plate. On the continental side, a fold mountain belt (the Andes) is formed as the oceanic lithosphere pushes against the continental lithosphere. As the oceanic plate descends into the mantle, some of the material melts and works its way up through the fold mountain belt to form quite violent volcanoes. The boundary between the plates is a region of earthquake activity, with the earthquakes ranging from shallow to relatively deep, and some are quite severe.

The last type of convergent plate boundary involves the collision of two continental masses of lithosphere. When the plates collide, neither is dense enough to be forced into the asthenosphere. Thus the collision compresses and thickens the continental edges, twisting and deforming the rocks and uplifting the land to form unusually high fold mountain belts. The prototype example is the collision of India with Asia that resulted in the formation of the Himalayas. In this case the earthquakes are typically shallow, but frequent and severe.

Transform Plate Boundaries. The actual structure of a seafloor spreading ridge is more complex than a single straight crack. Rather, ridges consist of many short segments slightly offset from one another. The offsets are a special kind of fault, or break in the lithosphere, known as a transform fault, and their function is to connect segments of a spreading ridge. The opposite sides of a transform fault belong to two different plates, and these are moving apart in opposite directions. The transform faults are just boundaries along which the plates move past one another. The classic transform boundary is the San Andreas fault that slices off a sliver of western California that rides on the Pacific plate from the rest of the state, which is on the North American plate. As the two plates scrape past each other, stress builds up and is released in earthquakes.

Why Do Plates Move? One mechanism that creates energy to move the huge plates is convection currents that are driven by heat from radioactive decay in the mantle. These convection currents in the earth's mantle carry magma up from the asthenosphere. Some of this magma escapes to form new lithosphere, but the rest

spreads out sideways beneath the lithosphere, slowly cooling in the process. As it flows outward, it drags the overlying lithosphere outward with it, thus continuing to open the ridges. When it cools, the flowing material becomes dense enough to sink back deeper into the mantle at convergent boundaries. A second plate-driving mechanism is the pull of the dense, cold, downward-moving slab of lithosphere in a subduction zone on the rest of the trailing plate, opening up the spreading ridges so magma can move upward.

Mineral Deposits. The theory of plate tectonics has greatly enhanced understanding of why many mineral deposits form where they do and has thus made mineral exploration more efficient. During the evolution of new oceanic plates and mountain belts by plate tectonics, a large number of mineral deposits form, particularly in association with the plate boundaries.

Hot fluids (hydrothermal fluids) circulate at spreading ridges (divergent boundaries) and deposit minerals. For example, niobium deposits are found in the intrusions in the East African Rift zone, and iron and manganese are found in the sediments of the Red Sea. Hydrothermal fluids also flow through the cracks and pores in rock along convergent boundaries and deposit metals along these boundaries as they cool. Good examples are the copper ore deposits associated with the collisional boundary of the Himalayas and tin ores in southwestern England. A general sequence of minerals found when passing inland from a trench associated with subduction are iron, gold, copper, molybdenum, gold, lead, zinc, tin, tungsten, antimony, and mercury.

FURTHER READING: A comprehensive treatment of the theory of plate tectonics is found in *Plate Tectonics*, by Allan Cox and Robert Brian Hart, 1986. A basic discussion of plate tectonics with good illustrations is presented by W. Kenneth Hamblin in *The Earth's Dynamic Systems*, 5th ed. 1989. Plate tectonic theory is outlined and connected with mineral deposits in *Fundamentals of Geology*, by Carla W. Montgomery, 2d ed. 1993. The role that plate tectonics plays in shaping the earth is explained by Edward A. Keller and Nicolas Pinter in *Active Tectonics*, 1996. Rifting and seafloor spreading are discussed in Enrico

Bonatti, "The Rifting of Continents," *Scientific American* (March, 1987). The possible forces driving plate tectonics are detailed by Geoff Brown and Alan Mussett in *The Inaccessible Earth,* 2d ed. 1993.

Alvin K. Benson

SEE ALSO: Earthquakes; Earth's crust; Geology; Hydrothermal solutions and mineralization; Lithosphere; Seafloor spreading; Volcanoes.

Platinum and the platinum group metals

WHERE FOUND: The platinum metals are extremely rare in the earth's crust. All occur together, with platinum and palladium predominating. The mineral sperrylite (platinum arsenide) is a major source in Canada. Significant deposits are also located in South Africa and the former Soviet Union. Smaller deposits have been found in Columbia, South America, Australia, and the United States, chiefly in Alaska and Montana.

PRIMARY USES: The most common application of the platinum metals is as catalysts for various industrial chemical reactions. They are also used to make a variety of alloys and are frequently used in jewelry.

DESCRIPTION: Chemists generally refer to the block of six transition metals—ruthenium (Ru), rhodium (Rh), palladium (Pd), osmium (Os), iridium (Ir), and platinum (Pt)—as the platinum metals. Their atomic numbers are, respectively, 44, 45, 46, 76, 77, and 78. Using the recommended group designations of the International Union of Pure and Applied Chemistry, ruthenium and osmium belong to Group 8, rhodium and iridium to Group 9, and palladium and platinum to Group 10. In the older system of group numbering, the platinum metals were placed in Group VIII. Ruthenium has seven naturally occurring isotopes with an average atomic mass of 101.07. It has another thirteen artificial (radioactive) isotopes. Pure ruthenium is a hard metal and has a gray-white appearance. Rhodium has only one natural isotope,

with an atomic mass of 102.906. More than thirty artificial isotopes are known. Rhodium has a silvery white metallic luster. Palladium has six natural isotopes with an average atomic mass of 106.42. It has eighteen artificial isotopes. Palladium is a steel-white metal that does not tarnish in air. Osmium has seven natural isotopes and an average atomic mass of 190.2. It has nearly thirty artificial isotopes. The metal has a slight bluish color due to a thin surface film of the oxide. Iridium has only two natural isotopes, with an average atomic mass of 192.2. It has nearly forty artificial isotopes. The metal has a white appearance with a slight yellowish tinge and is very hard and brittle. Platinum has six natural isotopes and an average atomic mass of 195.08. It has thirty artificial isotopes. It is a silvery-white metal with a lustrous appearance. Ruthenium, rhodium, and palladium all have densities of about 12 grams per cubic centimeter (12.45, 12.41, and 12.02, respectively), while osmium, iridium, and platinum are about twice as dense (22.61, 22.65, and 21.45 grams per cubic centimeter, respectively). The melting points increase in the order: palladium, platinum, rhodium, ruthenium, iridium, and osmium—1,554, 1,772, 1,966, 2,310, 2,410, and 3,054 degrees Celsius, respectively. The boiling points increase in the order: palladium, rhodium, platinum, ruthenium, iridium, and osmium—3,140, 3,727, 3,827, 3,900, 4,130, and 5,027 degrees Celsius, respectively.

THE PLATINUM METALS are among the rarest of all nonradioactive elements in the earth's crust. As a group, they are strong siderophiles (they tend to be concentrated in the earth's metallic core). Consequently, they are generally found in areas rich in other transition metals such as nickel and copper. In these concentrated regions, the abundance of the platinum metals can be more than a million times that of the crustal average. Most of the world's platinum resources come from sulfide ores of magmatic origin found in large stratiform bodies of basaltic rocks. The annual world production of all the platinum metals totals only about 300 tons. By contrast, millions of tons of copper are produced worldwide annually. Since the quantity of platinum metals mined is comparatively small, the environmental impact of these metals is minimal. None of the six metals has any significant biological role in the plant or animal kingdoms.

Historical Background. Hundreds of years before Europeans explored the Americas, the Indians of Colombia and Ecuador used platinum-gold alloys to make small artifacts by heating and hammering the alloy. Because of platinum's high melting point, it was not possible for these people to melt and work pure platinum. In their relentless search for gold in the late seventeenth century, the invading Spanish conquistadores discovered the Indians' platinum. Being a white-colored metal it was called *platina*, derived from the Spanish word for silver. Initially it was considered a rather annoying contaminant rather than a precious metal. By the mid-eighteenth century samples of platinum had reached Europe. In 1803 William Wollaston produced the first pure samples of the metal after dissolving crude platinum in aqua regia (a mixture of hydrochloric and nitric acids).

In the same year, Wollaston's studies with platinum ores led to his discovery of two new

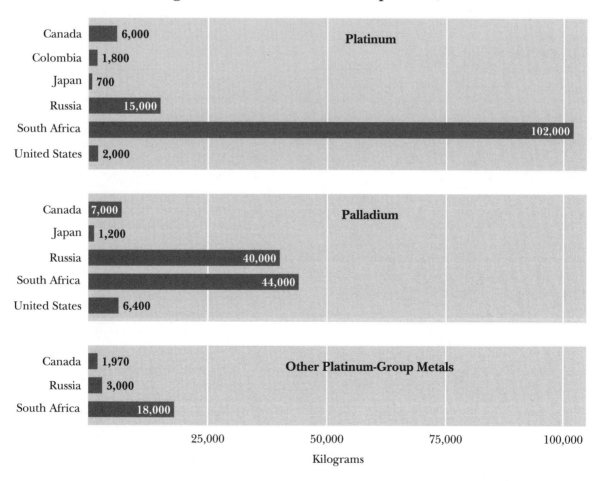

Leading Producers of Platinum-Group Metals, 1994

Source: U.S. Bureau of Mines, *Minerals Yearbook, 1994*. U.S. Government Printing Office, 1996.
Note: Total world 1994 platinum-group metals production was about 250,000 kilograms.

metals, palladium and rhodium, in the samples of crude platinum. After dissolving the ore in aqua regia and neutralizing it with sodium hydroxide, he added ammonium chloride to remove the platinum as ammonium chloroplatinate. By then adding mercuric cyanide, he removed the palladium as palladium cyanide. Metallic palladium was recovered by reduction of the palladium cyanide compound. After the palladium cyanide was extracted, the residue was washed and dried; it yielded a red compound of rhodium, which was reduced to the metal itself. Because many of the rhodium compounds Wollaston prepared were pink to red in color, he named the new metal from the Greek word *rhodon*, meaning rose. Palladium was named after the recently discovered asteroid Pallas.

Both osmium and iridium were also discovered in 1803. In London, Smithson Tennant showed that the black metallic substance remaining after reacting platinum ores with aqua regia was actually a mixture of two new metals. He named one iridium (from the Latin *iris*, meaning rainbow) because it formed many colored compounds. The other new metal he called osmium (from the Latin *osme*, meaning odor) because of its unpleasant smell.

Ruthenium was the last platinum metal to be discovered. In 1808 the Polish chemist Jedrzej Sniadecki claimed to have discovered and extracted a new metal from platinum ores. Since others were unable to reproduce Sniadecki's work, his discovery was soon dismissed. In the mid-1820's extensive alluvial deposits of platinum were discovered in the Russian Ural Mountains. Soon after, platinum coins were minted

Platinum mining operation in the Stillwater River Valley, Montana. (U.S. Geological Survey)

and issued by the Russian government. As a result of the new mining industry, scientists began to examine the insoluble residues that were produced from the platinum refining. In 1828 Gottfried Osann claimed to have discovered three new metals in these residues. But it was not until 1844, when Karl Klaus showed that there was only one new metal in the residues, that ruthenium was actually isolated and shown to be a new element. Its name was taken from *Ruthenia*, the Latin name for Russia.

Distribution of the Platinum Metals. As a group, the platinum metals have the lowest abundances of nearly all nonradioactive elements in the earth's crust; only gold, rhenium, and bismuth are metals with comparable low abundances. Values range from 0.0001 parts per million (ppm) for ruthenium to about 0.015 parts per million for palladium. In regions where the platinum metals are concentrated (Canada, South Africa, and the former Soviet Union), levels of platinum reach 0.5 to 20 parts per million. Fortunately the platinum metals frequently occur in ores that contain large quantities of other metals, such as nickel, making recovery of the platinum metals commercially feasible. The low crustal abundances of the platinum metals and the fact that their minerals usually occur as small inclusions (less than 1 millimeter) in other minerals hindered the development of platinum metals mineralogy. With the development of the electron microprobe in the 1960's and its ability to analyze mineral particles as small as 10 micrometers, the mineralogy of the platinum metals was greatly enhanced. More than eighty clearly defined minerals containing the platinum metals have been identified, most being minerals containing palladium and platinum. These minerals are generally compounds with other elements such as sulfur, selenium, tellurium, arsenic, and antimony, or alloys with metals such as tin, lead, and bismuth. Several hundred less clearly defined minerals have also been detected.

In the Canadian deposits, platinum occurs in copper-nickel sulfide ores that are associated with the igneous rock norite. The South African ores are predominantly pyroene as well as chromite and sulfides of iron, copper, and nickel.

Platinum is also found in native metallic form alloyed with iron or in mineral form as the sulfide or arsenide. Iridium, osmium, ruthenium, and rhodium generally occur uncombined in nature; they can also be considered by-products of the transition metals mining industry. Osmium and iridium occur alloyed as iridosmine (also known as osmiridium). This alloy also contains varying amounts of platinum, ruthenium, and rhodium, depending on the location.

Obtaining the Platinum Metals. Because of their low natural abundances and the difficulty in extracting them, commercial production of the platinum metals is often viewed as a by-product of the mining of other metals such as nickel, copper, and silver. For example, if it were not for the huge tonnage of nickel ore processed annually, it is likely that the extraction of the rarer platinum metals would not be economically feasible. In general, the platinum metals are obtained by subjecting the ores to a series of complicated and costly chemical reactions. Not surprisingly, the platinum metals are among the most expensive of all elements to manufacture. Prices can fluctuate enormously depending on economic and environmental conditions. For instance, during the three-year period between 1990 and 1993, the price of rhodium (in U.S. dollars per troy ounce) varied from $850 to $7,000. The high cost and rarity of the platinum metals is also responsible for their extensive recycling.

Platinum is obtained from crude ores by a process which eliminates other impurities: Magnetic metals such as iron and nickel are removed with powerful electromagnets; less dense impurities are removed by flotation methods in aqueous solution; volatile impurities are baked off at high temperatures; various acids dissolve away other metals. Pure platinum is obtained through additional chemical processes. The method for separating palladium from platinum is often determined by the type of ore being refined, but in general also involves a series of chemical processes to obtain the metal. Like platinum, iridium is separated by treating the other accompanying platinum metals as impurities and removing them stepwise. Treatment with molten lead, followed by aqua regia, and then baking at

2,000 degrees Celsius concentrates iridium. Ruthenium and osmium are converted into highly volatile (and toxic) tetroxide compounds that can easily be collected by distillation. Reaction with base converts them to safer substances, such as sodium osmate, which are then reduced to the metal. Rhodium is obtained from the residue remaining after the removal of platinum, and the total world production of this rare metal is only a few tons annually.

Uses of the Platinum Metals. Of the six platinum metals, palladium and platinum have the greatest economic importance. Both are fairly soft metals having a brilliant silvery appearance and are therefore widely used in the jewelry trade. When alloyed with palladium, gold takes on a silvery appearance (white gold) but will not tarnish as jewelry made from pure silver does. Palladium is also used in dentistry, surgical instruments, and electrical contacts. The mainsprings of many older wristwatches were fashioned from palladium. Powdered palladium is a good catalyst and is used for hydrogenation and dehydrogenation reactions. Platinum is used to make wires and vessels for laboratory use and as a coating on missile nose cones and jets, which are subject to very high temperatures. It is also used to make medical and dental alloys and electrical contacts. Finely divided platinum powder is an excellent catalyst that is used in the production of sulfuric acid and in petroleum refining.

The uses of the other four platinum metals are very limited. Their major use is in alloys, and most have some catalytic activity. All are fairly brittle metals and therefore difficult to machine into shapes when pure. Ruthenium, rhodium, and iridium are all used as hardening agents for softer platinum and palladium. Osmium is used to strengthen alloys where frictional wear must be minimized as in electrical switch contacts, ballpoint pen tips, phonographic needles and instrument pivots. Rhodium lends itself readily to electroplating and has been used to protect silver objects from tarnishing, on optical instruments, and on high-grade reflectors for searchlights. Because of its resistance, iridium has been used for spark-plug electrodes in aircraft engines. When alloyed with other metals, such as titanium, the presence of platinum metals can enhance corrosion resistance. Literally thousands of chemical compounds which contain the platinum metals have been prepared, and many play important roles as industrial catalysts. Considerable research has revealed that some platinum compounds can inhibit the growth of certain tumors and therefore have applications in chemotherapy.

Unique Properties. Palladium is the most reactive of the platinum metals, and it readily dissolves in acids. At room temperature it has the unusual property of absorbing up to nine hundred times its own volume of hydrogen. Palladium is highly malleable and can be beaten into sheets as thin as 0.000002 centimeter thick. Iridium has the greatest resistance to corrosion of any metal. It was used to make the old standard meter bar in Paris, which was an alloy of platinum (90 percent) and iridium (10 percent). Iridium levels in certain regions have been related to meteor impacts on Earth and have been used to study geological and biological processes such as extinction. Levels of iridium in meteors are generally higher than levels found on Earth. High terrestrial iridium levels in rocks from the Cretaceous-Tertiary boundary have provided evidence that extensive meteor impacts could have played a role in the earth's geologic history.

FURTHER READING: The *Handbook of Chemistry and Physics,* published by the Chemical Rubber Company, contains a summary of the properties of the platinum metals in its section on the elements, and it is updated regularly in frequent new editions. Considerable information on each metal is to be found in the *Encyclopedia of the Chemical Elements,* edited by Clifford A. Hampel, 1968. Likewise, *Exploring the Chemical Elements and Their Compounds,* by David. L. Heiserman, 1992, is devoted to describing the unique properties of the elements. Mary Week's *Discovery of the Elements,* 1968, has long been a popular reference for anyone interested in the history of the discovery of the elements. A treatment of the platinum metals is found in *A History of Platinum and Its Allied Metals,* by D. McDonald and L. B. Hunt, 1992.

Nicholas C. Thomas

SEE ALSO: Alloys; Metals and metallurgy; Native elements; Nickel.